Stories of Herself
When Young

Stories of Herself When Young

AUTOBIOGRAPHIES OF CHILDHOOD
BY AUSTRALIAN WOMEN

J O Y   H O O T O N

OXFORD
UNIVERSITY PRESS

Melbourne
Oxford   Auckland   New York

OXFORD UNIVERSITY PRESS AUSTRALIA

Oxford   New York   Toronto
Delhi   Bombay   Calcutta   Madras   Karachi
Petaling Jaya   Singapore   Hong Kong   Tokyo
Nairobi   Dar es Salaam   Cape Town
Melbourne   Auckland
and associated companies in
Berlin   Ibadan

OXFORD is a trade mark of Oxford University Press

National Library of Australia
Cataloguing-in-Publication data:

Hooton, Joy W. (Joy Wendy), 1935–
   Stories of herself when young: autobiographies of
   childhood by Australian women.

   Bibliography.
   Includes index.
   ISBN 0 19 554853 1.

   1. Australian literature—Women authors—History and
   criticism.   2. Women authors, Australian—Biography—
   Youth—History and criticism.   3. Women—Australia—
   Biography—History and criticism.   4. Autobiography—
   Women authors.   I. Title.

A820.9492

Edited by Christine Connor
Designed by Steven Randles
Typeset by Best-set Typesetter Ltd Hong Kong
Printed by Condor Production Ltd
Published by Oxford University Press,
253 Normanby Road, South Melbourne, Australia

For Sheridan, Zoe, Alexander and Alice

Contents

Acknowledgements

The research for this book was partly made possible by a grant in 1987 from the then Australian Research Grants Committee for part-time research assistance in locating both male and female autobiographies. Kay Walsh's endeavours at the National Library of Australia resulted in a listing of over 3000 narratives, some of which are the subject of this book, and my greatest debt is to Kay, both for her help in 1987 and for her continued interest in the project after the money ran out. From 1985, when this project first took shape as an idea, the pursuit of published and unpublished autobiographies led me to most of the capital cities. Librarians were invariably helpful but I would particularly like to thank the staff of the Battye Library in Perth, the Fryer Library in Queensland, the Tasmaniana Library in Hobart and the library of the Royal Historical Society of Victoria. Tony Marshall proved a mine of information at the La Trobe Library and I am especially grateful for his arrangements with the library at University College which made it possible to study several unpublished autobiographies in Canberra. My debt to the staff of the Petherick Room at the National Library and their unflagging efforts to track down elusive texts is immense. Jean James's help, in particular, is much appreciated. Of the individuals who have filled in some of the gaps in my knowledge of women's life writing or autobiography in general, my greatest debt is to Debra Adelaide, whose bibliographic searches at the Mitchell Library greatly supplemented my own, but I am also indebted to Patricia Clarke, Susan McKernan, Paul Eggert, Katie Holmes, Margaret King and Jeffrey Doyle. Harry Heseltine's general support and co-operation during the project were also invaluable. The technical side of production was greatly enhanced by Margaret McNally who not only sorted out what was originally an inexpertly typed manuscript but resolved several situations when the Macintosh was not in a user-friendly mood. I am also very grateful to Loes Slattery, who compiled the index, and to the book's copy editor, Christine Connor.

My family and friends will be greatly relieved that this book is finally finished and as always I am grateful to them for their tolerance and encouragement; my daughters' feminist interests in particular were often challenging and to some extent I see this book as a dialogue with them. I am also grateful for the encouragement of our friends, Jill and Michael, and Susie and Trevor. Writing a book is probably as much a threat to a marriage as completing a PhD, but when a spouse uses long-service leave to complete the project, the relationship might be expected to be particularly strained. My greatest good fortune, however, was that my husband, Viv, was as enthusiastic about the project as I was and showed amazing patience as a reader of successive drafts. Indeed, for a long time he was my only reader, thus performing the dual but inconsistent role, he maintained, of resident guinea pig and male chauvinist pig.

For permission to publish brief extracts from Australian autobiographies, I am grateful to the following: Collins Dove: Josie Arnold, *Mother Superior Woman Inferior*, 1985; Century Hutchinson: Hilda Abbot, *Among the Hills*, 1948; Kangaroo Press: Barbara Corbett, *A Fistful of Buttercups*, 1983; Curtis Brown Group Ltd: Nene Gare, *A House With a Verandah*, 1963; Curtis Brown Group Ltd: Katharine Susannah Prichard, *Child of the Hurricane*, 1963; Curtis Brown Group Ltd: Katharine Susannah Prichard, *The Wild Oats of Han*, 1928; Martin Secker & Warburg: Christina Stead, *The Man Who Loved Children*, 1940; Fremantle Arts Centre Press: Connie Miller, *After Summer Merrily*, 1980; Fremantle Arts Centre Press: Connie Miller, *Season of Learning*, 1983; Fremantle Arts Centre Press: Eve Hogan, 'The Hessian Walls', *Selected Lives*, 1983; Fremantle Arts Centre Press: Sally Morgan, *My Place*, 1987; Virago Press: *The Writings of Anna Wickham*, 1984; Longman Cheshire: Nancy Adams, *Family Fresco*, 1966; Collins/Angus & Robertson: Mary Gilmore, *Old Days, Old Ways*, 1934; Collins/Angus & Robertson: Mary Gilmore, *More Recollections*, 1934; Collins/Angus & Robertson: Miles Franklin, *Childhood at Brindabella*, 1963; Collins/Angus & Robertson: Miles Franklin, *My Brilliant Career*, 1901; Collins/Angus & Robertson: Christina Stead, *For Love Alone*, 1944; Collins/Angus & Robertson: Glenda Adams, *Dancing on Coral*, 1987; Collins/Angus & Robertson: Jane Lindsay, *Portrait of Pa*, 1973; Collins/Angus & Robertson: Eve Langley, *The Pea Pickers*, 1942; Collins/Angus & Robertson: Henry Handel Richardson, *The Adventures of Cuffy Mahony and Other Stories*, 1979; Patsy Adam Smith, *Hear the Train Blow*, 1964; Thomas Nelson: Mary Rose Liverani, *The Winter Sparrows*, 1975. Part of the sections on *The Man Who Loved Children* and *Childhood at Brindabella* first appeared in *Maridian* and *Meanjin* respectively and I am grateful to the publishers and editors for permission to reprint the material.

Every effort has been made to trace the original source of material contained in this book. Where the attempt has been unsuccessful the publishers would be pleased to hear from the author/publisher to rectify any omission.

Introduction

'A true life story appeals to the human mind in a far greater degree than the most vividly written fiction.' Katherine McKell's words in *Old Days and Gold Days in Victoria* appear to express a common reaction amongst contemporary readers, given the general popularity of autobiography in Australia and, in particular, the extraordinary reception accorded such books as Sally Morgan's *My Place* and Albert Facey's *A Fortunate Life*. It is not only their uniquely mixed freight of cultural and personal meaning that makes these books strongly attractive, it is the unique reading experience that they offer. More of a collaboration than any other form of writing, autobiography creates a special intimacy between reader and writer, and a special creative partnership. Responding to the story of another's life, the reader is also curiously close to becoming a story-teller too, granted at least the potential of experiencing the life as story. In the words of Christina Stead, 'the story has a magic necessary to our happiness', for it is the hope of recognizing and having our experience explained that makes narrative in all its forms so entrancing. And of all stories, the story of childhood is often the most intriguing; retrieving the beginning, reliving the deceptive permanence of childhood before clock-time became the time of one's life, seems to be a very common human preoccupation.

It is surprising, therefore, that critical study of autobiography in Australia is both sparse and highly selective. Privileging a few so-called 'literary' texts, the critical tradition has consistently ignored a mass of writing by lesser-known individuals of both centuries. Not only have autobiographies been largely ignored by literary scholars, bibliographers, cultural commentators and even historians, but autobiography as a genre has not found a home in library classifications. Many of the narratives considered here have been discovered masquerading as regional or local histories, biographies or even juvenile fiction. Meanwhile, in the literary arena, New Criticism has narrowed attention to the genres of poetry, fiction and drama, excluding what was perceived as non-fictive from the dominant definition of 'Literature'. We are now much more appreciative of the way that all writing produces meaning through forms and conventions and more willing to accept that no writing is unproblematically factual. Autobiography, moreover, is now accepted as a highly artful mode, incurably problematic, vulnerable to all the devices of fictional narration and bound by few of the restrictions as to accuracy, impartiality and inclusiveness that bind, at least provisionally, other forms of historical literature. Above all, simultaneously subject to the filterings of memory and the quicksilver changes of the mind's present, the autobiographer is committed to making a fiction of the life, to telling a story which can be no more than a tantalizing approximation or version of the truth. Some writers, of course, like Richardson and Franklin, attempt to resolve this universal predicament by writing a series of life stories, just as Rembrandt attempted to seize the identity in a series of self-portraits. There are obvious rhetorical differences between autobiography and fiction, as well as different costs and advantages for the writer, but the differences are more of degree than of kind and for this reason both fictional and historical autobiographies are considered here.

Since both male and female autobiographical writings have suffered neglect, the selection of women's life stories as a subject of study might be questioned. There are several reasons for this bias. First, it is generally admitted that women have been omitted from Australian historiography, an omission that the so-called new history seeks to rectify with a grass-roots approach to past experience which relies heavily on oral memories. Like the oral history interview, autobiography is a powerful reflector of the quality and variety of the past lives of Australian women, while it is more likely than the interview to be a revealing record of how these women have imagined themselves and how they have been led to imagine themselves. Autobiographies of childhood are, of course, particularly keen reflectors of this second meaning, for a retrospective contemplation of the growing self inevitably implies a degree of explanation. Although the narratives considered here cannot be considered comprehensively representative, they are sufficiently voluminous and substantial to make some pertinently representative comments. Women have also been historically omitted or slighted in Australian literary criticism, an omission that is currently being vigorously addressed; this study seeks to be part of this attempt to disinter the female writer from oblivion, although the liveliness and variety of women's autobiography have no need of special pleading. Secondly, what there is of an autobiographical canon in Australia is largely male in emphasis. Texts such as *My Brilliant Career*, *The Getting of Wisdom* and *The Man Who Loved Children* have recently received some interesting treatment from feminist writers, but the general critical preoccupation with the national or cultural meaning of autobiography has led to a bias towards male versions of the self. Less obviously self-conscious and preoccupied with the fictive, female authors have also largely failed to qualify as sophisticated, post-modernist writers of the self, dear to the fashionable critic of autobiography. Thirdly, autobiographical theory as developed in America and Europe has been dependent on male models, as I argue in Chapter 4; although this study is too culturally confined to be a general poetics of women's autobiography, it attempts to make some conclusions about the differences in male and female versions of the self within the rhetorical options offered by nineteenth and twentieth century Australia. Lastly, women autobiographers in the nineteenth century are far more frank and inward than their male counterparts, given the pioneering ethos of the country and the cult of the documentary. Some male autobiographies of this century are deservedly valued as complex explorations, but the middle range of writing has some broad reaches of contrived impersonal dullness.

This study focuses on prose narratives, both published and unpublished, which are consecutively structured and independently shaped. Some short stories are included, but only when they form a series or cycle. The episodic form of the diary or the letter and the collaborative form of the oral history interview are omitted, although one form of collaboration, unique to female writing, the dual-authored text, usually narrated by mother and daughter, is included. It should also be emphasized that the study concentrates on accounts of formative experience, that is on autobiographies of childhood and adolescence. Autobiographies of adult life have been included where these concentrate on the childhood at some length, and in any event 'maturity' has been interpreted broadly as equating with the sense of having grown up. The bibliography reveals the range of autobiographies considered, but perhaps it is worth emphasizing that this book does not confine itself to so-called literary autobiography. Franklin, Richardson and Stead are undoubtedly the most complex of these autobiographers of childhood, but numerous texts, some written by unknown or disregarded authors or by authors who wrote nothing but an autobiography, are both lively and artful. They are also cumulatively valuable, casting fresh light on female writing as a whole and the acknowledged great texts in particular. The limitations of space meant that not all the narratives listed in the bibliography receive a mention, although many are implicit in my general conclusions; some were reluctantly excluded as it became obvious that certain interesting perspectives would have to be abandoned; some are too slight for the specific purposes of this study; some are likely to be more interesting to the historian than to the reader with literary interests. They are nevertheless listed in the expectation that future studies of women's writing will find them useful and since the general absence of bibliographical guides and finding aids makes the location of autobiographies extremely difficult. This study would not have been possible without a grant for research assistance from the Australian Research Grants Committee; even so, it is likely that many unpublished narratives and perhaps some published ones have eluded the author and it is hoped that interested readers will fill in some of the gaps.

1

Invisible Lives? Childhoods to 1920

It has become a truism of recent cultural studies that women did not appear in Australian historiography in any important way until 1970. Publicly relegated to a lesser, ahistorical sphere by their male contemporaries, and usually by themselves, women were doubly penalized by the prejudices of twentieth century historians in favour of history as the arena of public events. The 1970s appeared to open up exciting opportunities, but these have proved more slow to realize themselves than anticipated and the 'new history' which would include women without depositing them yet again in the margins of an alternative, different experience is as yet more of a challenge than a realized goal. Writing in 1977 in the introduction to one of the most substantial building blocks of recent feminist research, the bibliography *Women in Australia*, Kay Daniels emphasized the compilers' commitment to:

writing the history of women not as a separate study but in the context of social history; if women are to be put into a history from which they have been excluded it will be into a history of society and a history that is radically different because of the inclusion of women in it ... We have not thought that women's invisibility in historical writing is because they have in some way 'fallen through' the fabric of society into its 'cracks and crevices' but that historical writing has been deficient in the examination of that fabric and has consequently left unrevealed the basic processes and relationships of society and the integral role of women in them.[1]

Five years later, the same writer underlined the major irony of contemporary feminist reinterpretations, that they have 'at so many points been constrained and reabsorbed ... reinterpreted as conventional and ... remoulded in the tradition of the old'. The first major women's histories of the mid-1970s, for instance, Anne Summers's *Damned Whores and God's Police* and Miriam Dixson's *My Wife, My Daughter and Poor Mary Ann*, took the form of 'a different reading of known material rather than an investigation of unused sources

or the development of a new methodology'. Both Dixson and Summers presented important alternative interpretations but they were
interpretations of documents from the public world of public men,
traditionally visited by conventional historians and resistant to the
sorts of questions that the new historian should pose. 'What is
needed', comments Daniels, 'is a new social history: a reconstruction
of life from below in the context of an analysis of basic social
relationships'.[2]

More recently several studies, drawing on letters and diaries,
government and court records, newspapers and magazines, have
attempted this reconstruction of women's social history 'from below'.
Books such as *Double Time: Women in Victoria–150 Years* (1985),
Exploring Women's Past (1983), *Families in Colonial Australia*
(1985), *In Her Own Name* (1986) and *Nothing Seemed Impossible*
(1985) have gone some way to filling in the gaps. Meanwhile the new
boom in oral history, producing such texts as Morag Loh's *With
Courage in Their Cases* (1980) and Jan Carter's *Nothing to Spare*
(1981), has helped to illuminate the daily texture of both women's
and men's experience and incidentally to feed the increasingly eager
public appetite for individual memories of places and periods. The
current rash of suitably illustrated colonial diaries, journals and
collections of letters is a shrewd publishing response to the same
appetite, along with the more clichéd, coffee-table compilations of
Australiana.

Included in this rediscovery of the historical and even recent past
is a growing number of autobiographies, both male and female,
'fictional' and 'factual'. The 'literary' distance between, say, Albert
Facey's *A Fortunate Life* and Patrick White's *Flaws in the Glass*, and
the chronological one between Jennifer Dabbs's *Beyond Redemption*
and Mary Brennan's *Better than Dancing* indicate something of the
scope and variety of these texts of the 1980s. The popular response to
these narratives has been uninhibitedly welcoming; the academic
response has been more constrained. Apart from Facey's book,
which seems to have struck a universal sympathetic chord, literary
criticism has confined itself to what is perceived as literary autobiography and to the tracing of a (mainly male and mainly twentieth-
century) tradition. Nor have new historians and cultural commentators been quick to draw on the resources of autobiography, although
the diary and the oral history interview are widely used. Autobiography, however, is in many ways a more interesting and complex
literary form than the diary and more revealing historically than
the oral history interview. What the diary gains in immediacy and accuracy, it loses via its necessarily episodic form. Far more challenging
than the diary, which easily degenerates into a record of trivial
events, the autobiography involves the author in the active
remembering of the texture and shape of experience. Texture is

particularly important for autobiographers of childhood who are frequently more interested than diarists in recalling the daily pulse of the personal past, the distinctive sights and sounds of the childhood landscape, the pains and pleasures of the seasonal cycle, or the significant interior geography of the childhood home.

Some diaries, of course, which are retrospectively shaped, are really autobiographies in disguise; *Annabella Boswell's Journal* (1965), originally published in a more extensive form in 1908 as *Early Recollections and Gleanings, from an Old Journal* and reshaped as its title suggests from the jottings of an old journal, is more autobiography than diary. If autobiography lacks the immediacy of the diary, the former's distinctive subjectivity may, on the other hand, be an advantage, both from the literary critic's and the historian's point of view, for the most naïve of writers is inevitably implicated in finding story or meaning, notwithstanding meaning's notorious resistance to authorial control. Story, however defective or even denied as in *My Brilliant Career*, is intrinsic to autobiography, and record and assessment go hand in hand. Story, of course, also implies experience, and usually the most interesting accounts are those written in old age, when the power of remembering seems to be at full tide. As Wilhelmina McKerron comments in her autobiography, *The Wheel of Destiny*:

These are the years I dreaded secretly but suddenly find it is a lovely age, and that I was blind to beauty that must follow when the ears are more attuned to listening, and the eyes have learned at last to see detail and not always go hurrying past to newness.[3]

Story also implies some account of the self, which in the case of women's autobiographies is often more of an inward than a public account, tentative and open. Writing from the microcosm of the family and on the sidelines of political and economic power, women have produced narratives which are nevertheless profoundly revealing of their societies; as Jane Miller comments: 'What women can tell us about a society comes from their ambiguous relation to the sources of power'.[4] Autobiography is also often more satisfactory than the oral history interview. The one-to-one interview is not always particularly productive, or it may produce information that responds more to the predilections of the interviewer than the interviewee. More often it produces a mass of socio-historical data which, lacking the imaginatively interpreted context of autobiography, has all the bald appeal of a catalogue. Collaboration is often necessary for the production of autobiography, but usually the relationship between collaborators is one of intimacy or family as in the mother/daughter narratives *A Bunyip Close Behind Me* and *Ladies Didn't*, and in the form of a mutually satisfying dialogue.

Two other prose genres have appealed to women as capable of

expressing the life-history—the novel and the children's novel. The twentieth century has provided some major achievements in fictional autobiography (*My Brilliant Career*, *The Man Who Loved Children*, *The Getting of Wisdom* and *Monkey Grip*) but the nineteenth century novel was a less satisfactory form. Confined to the stock feminine plot of love and marriage, the Victorian novel imposed stereotypical impersonations on authors. Undoubtedly, certain skilful novelists were able to find oblique ways of writing the self and even of subverting the stock ingredients of the female novel, but the autobiography, even in the form of the pioneering memoir, could be a more capacious genre. Necessarily more inward and closer to the self's needs, the memoir was less restrictive in the audience expectations it aroused. Occupying more neutral, extra-literary territory, it also acquired a certain ready-made respectability as the supportive record of pioneering derring-do.

The other alternative autobiographical genre for women, children's fiction, was no doubt extensively used, and in fact several of the narratives considered here figure in histories of children's literature. To some extent the children's novel was more liberating than the adult novel and less oppressed by the genteel; often providing scope for celebration of the childhood self as a little bush-maid, it also had the advantage of spontaneity and natural expression. The limitations of the genre as an exploration of adult consciousness, however, are obvious.

Although numerous pioneering memoirs were published in the nineteenth century, they have rarely appeared in female histories to date. Those life-writings which are used are invariably the tried and true, such as *The Letters of Rachel Henning*, the texts which have become almost as integral to the national culture as *Such is Life* and *For the Term of his Natural Life*; occasionally a little-known narrative, usually by a wife or daughter, may be found lurking at the close of an entry in the *Australian Dictionary of Biography* or surviving in a general history as an enigmatic footnote documenting some social practice, but such appearances are rare. Some observations indicate a general ignorance of existing texts: a reviewer of a female autobiography of the 1970s, for instance, hopefully sees it as the beginning of 'a veritable flood . . . of women's life experiences', or a commentator on Australian childhood remarks that 'the evidence is overwhelmingly the evidence of the literate, the important and the socially advantaged'.[5] Literary criticism, meanwhile, appears largely ignorant of or indifferent to the large body of published autobiographies of both centuries. Texts such as Kathleen Fitzpatrick's *Solid Bluestone Foundations* or Nancy Adams's *Family Fresco*, have received sympathetic reviews but have strangely avoided extended critical attention, presumably because their authors are not recognized as mainstream writers. Earlier significant narratives such as Jane Watts's *Memories of Early Days in South Australia*, Agnes Gosse Hay's *After-Glow Memories*, or Sarah Conigrave's *My Reminiscences* have been totally ignored by the literary community. The result has been that such culturally significant books as *My Brilliant Career* and *The Getting of Wisdom* appear to exist in a literary and cultural vacuum.

Undoubtedly one of the reasons for the literary community's neglect of autobiographical narrative has been the gradual narrowing of 'literature' to equate with the three distinctive genres of poetry, fiction and drama. It is after all only recently that autobiography has acquired academic respectability, partly in response to post-modernist, reader-oriented critical theories, while other forms of prose discourse (such as biography, history and travel narratives) are still disregarded or are read only in terms of content. We seem to have lost the capacity to appreciate certain discourses, unlike our ancestors of the previous century who relished Macaulay as much as Scott and Dickens. As one critic has put it: 'Historically the boundary of *literature* has shrunk: in eighteenth century England *literature* comprehended almost all printed and many oral works; in the nineteenth century it narrowed to *belles lettres*'. With the advent of New Criticism and the enshrining of 'a group of texts which the principles of intrinsic criticism separated from non-literary matter', this narrowing intensified.[6]

The results of this critical impairment are also reflected in the bibliographical *lacunae*. There are no bibliographies or even finding aids to autobiography in Australia, unlike Britain and America, nor is autobiography recognized as a genre by library catalogues or periodical indexes. Bibliographies such William Matthews's *British Autobiographies* and Louis Kaplan's and Russell Brignano's similar listings for America, which have provided material for the major international critical studies, are non-existent in Australia. Unpublished narratives are even more elusive, given the incomplete state of archival documentation.

Although these difficulties afflict both male and female life-writing, the heavy bias of male narratives towards occupational titles makes them easier to retrieve. Titles such as *Experiences of a Victorian Manufacturer, Australian Ambassador* or *Adventures of a Mounted Trooper* are typical of the style of male self-portrayal. Occasionally the same tendency affects female narratives (*Indiscretions of a Headmistress, New Guinea Nurse* or even *Ambassador's Wife*) but generally women are more inventive. Reflective of women's different approach to self-writing, titles are chosen to express something of the quality of the remembered experience (*A Fistful of Buttercups, After-Glow Memories, The Winter Sparrows* or *Joy and Sorrow Interwoven*) or more often of the remembered place. In fact, so heavily invested with a sense of place are many titles, that numerous female narratives masquerade in catalogues as local histories (*Belta-na—Six Miles*, *No Stranger in Paradise*, *The Golden South*, *Far-North Memories* and *Wild Wood Days at Panton Hill*). Others present themselves as memoirs of parents (*The Little Byron*, *Portrait of Pa* and *Ma and Pa*), or even of an employer (Marjorie Butler's *Time Isn't Long Enough*), or as histories of families (*Family Fresco* and *An Australian Story*).

Another striking difference between the two genders is their relative profusion. Male narratives greatly outnumber female until recently and much of the current volume of publishing of female autobiographies is swelled by texts which were written decades previously. Of the nineteenth century narratives of childhood discussed here, it is perhaps not surprising that only a handful was published pre-1900, given the normal tendency to write the self's story in old age. But the relative scarcity of texts in the first sixty years of this century compared with their profusion in the last twenty is itself some indication of the extent of past neglect. Many, as I hope this study shows, are still neglected. Some scrutiny of the publishing process is also revealing. Until recently publishers have been reluctant to publish female histories and authors have been dependent on their own resources, or on those of local history or genealogical societies. Some, such as Agnes Stokes's *A Girl at Government House* and *Annabella Boswell's Journal* have been discovered in the obscurity of early British editions by enthusiastic historians or feminists and restored to readers, or revitalized by publishers with an eye on the market for colonial Australiana, or reprinted in facsimile form by history-conscious Library Boards. Several, such as Emily Churchward's *In Paths Directed*, have depended on the piety of descendants, while others, such as Laura Todd's *A Place Like Home* and Mary Brennan's *Better than Dancing*, have waited for the services of an editor or translator. Since the 1970s these combined activities have retrieved enough narratives to produce a substantial group.

Reading the accounts of pre-1920 childhoods as a group—that is, as a loosely unified historical group and initially ignoring publication dates—is an extraordinary experience. Probably the first impression is of diversity, followed by the paradoxical impression of sameness. The diversities of region, distinctions of class and wealth and differences in family and personal circumstances, not to mention the temperamental differences of authors, have produced a rich mixture of individual stories. It is obvious, for instance, that regional differences and historical disparities of settlement in nineteenth century Australia refute the notion of a uniform rate of progress, but reading the experiences of those involved makes the historical fact real with a new kind of vividness. The distance between Rose Scott Cowen's experiences in Western Queensland in the 1880s, for example, and

Mary Stawell's in 1840s Victoria seems as vast as the distance between Surrey and Siberia. Where Stawell's measured prose and
well-chosen phrases reflect her impressions of a charming pastoral
mildness, enhanced by colourful flora and fauna, Cowen's breathless
and even exuberant catalogue of disasters and near-disasters reflects
the pressures of living in an environment where both landscape and
people can be unpredictably and actively hostile. In Cowen's world
survival means unremitting feats of superhuman resource and endurance; Stawell's world is a rather more exotic, isolated version of the
English Victorian lady's. Yet both these women belonged to families
which were wealthy and well-connected. Differences of class and
wealth could have equally discriminating effects. At a time when
Margaret Gifford's father was entertaining his guests on a vastly
opulent scale, on one occasion leading a procession of automobiles
from one holiday mansion to another by means of a trail of rice ('The
story had a sad sequel. Small birds gorged themselves on the rice and
the next day the road was strewn with corpses', *I Can Hear the
Horses*, p. 15), Laura Todd in the same city was incarcerated in a
children's home of Dickensian grimness (*A Place like Home*). And at
roughly the same time in Melbourne, Agnes McEwin, after a career
as an unpaid 'mother's help' from the age of ten, was enjoying the
peak of her career as a nursery-maid with the privilege of dusting her
employers' drawing-room ornaments ('The Girlhood Reminscences
of Agnes McEwin').

Diversity of circumstance is matched by diversity of personality
and hence of selected perceptions, structure and narrative voice.
Inevitably counteracting or moderating the impression of authenticity
to a greater or lesser degree, is the impression of a subjectivity, an
implicated and distinctive 'I', for in autobiography there are multiple
alternatives in the choice of reality that authors wish to understand,
and multiple alternatives in the mode of expressing that reality. Thus
the 1840s Sydney of the interesting if paranoid Eliza Davies differs
strikingly from the city of Kathleen Lambert's almost synchronical
perceptions, and Janet Mitchell's impressions of her family and circumstances in *Spoils of Opportunity* vary widely from those of her
elder sister Nancy in *Family Fresco*. In fact, to read a number of these
narratives is to savour a range of unexpected refracted ironies.
Breaker Morant's skill in breaking some of her father's horses in-
clines Rose Scott Cowen in *Crossing Dry Creeks* to a sympathetic
view of his character; Elyne Mitchell in *Chauvel Country* presents
some intriguing intimate glimpses into Ethel Anderson's personality;
Mary Stawell, who dances with 'Rolf Boldrewood' in *My Recollections*, is the mother of Dick Stawell of Maie Casey's *An Australian
Story*; Professor Edgeworth David appears as a loved father in his
daughter's *Passages of Time*, as a valued friend in Dulcie Deamer's
'The Golden Decade' and as an unscrupulous rival in Georgiana

King's 'Autobiography'; Mrs Parker in 'Early Days at Lake Innes' writes of Port Macquarie and the McInnes family, is taught by Mrs McInnes and later meets Annabella Boswell; Joice Loch in *A Fringe of Blue* has memories of Vida Goldstein and of Ellis Rowan, who is also described at length by her niece Maie Casey in *An Australian Story*. Emily Churchward in *In Paths Directed* acts as a companion to the Jane Watts of *Memories of Early Days in South Australia*, giving an external picture of that accomplished woman and incidentally providing concrete evidence of the existence of a female autobiographical tradition. Frances McGuire in *Bright Morning* describes a lively encounter with the elderly Catherine Spence, and Mary Helpman in *The Helpman Family Story* gives an account of her family's relations with Adam Lindsay Gordon. Melba is almost ubiquitous, enlivening the days of Lady Stanley with gossip of past loves while irritating Lord Stanley with her contrived charms, briefly encouraging Janet Mitchell in a musical career, whisking Margaret Gifford off for an impromptu holiday in Hawaii, or vying with Ellen Terry in admiration of Frederick McCubbin's paintings during an unexpected visit to the painter's home.[7] Joseph Furphy appears in more than one narrative, although the most delightful account is Katherine McKell's in *Old Days and Gold Days in Victoria 1851–1873*. By the time Furphy steps into her life Katherine McKell has lost her mother and is heavily weighed down by her domestic responsibilities and by the loneliness and cultural poverty of her life in outback Victoria. Furphy's gift of a collection of Scott's verse turns out to be a priceless one, so enlivening the tedium of her days that even butter-churning has a new rhythmic attraction.

Children and servants are notoriously acute observers of their elders and betters and many of the great who appear in these narratives might be less than pleased with the sharp impressions they evoked in these apparently impassive observers. Jane Watts's impressions of some of the leaders of South Australian colonial society are particularly acute. She describes the Colonial Secretary (George Milner Stephen, afterwards Acting-Governor) as:

a good-looking, dapper little man, with light curly hair and whiskers, extremely fond of dress, and *small* in every way; he wore ladies' number fours in boots . . . and possessed various showy accomplishments. He danced well, sang soft sentimental ditties, such as 'Love's Ritornella', 'Come Away Love', and other songs of that class, to the accompaniment of a guitar, adorned with blue ribbon, and was in fact what usually goes by the term of a 'lady's man', with an abundance of small talk considered suitable to the feminine capacity! (*Family Life in South Australia*, p. 37)

Less controlled but equally acid are Eliza Davies's astonishing accounts in *The Story of an Earnest Life* of the Sturts in various degrees of domestic or external crisis, while Agnes Stokes's employers are stripped of all pretensions and judged solely in terms of their humanity.

Counteracting the impression of diversity in this group of narratives is the paradoxical one of sameness. However diverse the circumstances of these women's early lives, there is a broad similarity in their concerns. Briefly, these might be described as a concern with relationships, both personal and other; with family roots and places of origin; with daily rituals and the domestic solidities of everyday life; with social and family activities, customs and conventions; and with recalling the distinctive personality of the childhood home. Against, or rather within, this dense recreation of a communal past, the female narrator of this period traces her own story. If the mirror is an archetypal metaphor in autobiography, female mirrors are usually crowded with other faces. As Alexandra Hasluck expresses it, looking into the autobiographical mirror is to see it as 'crowded with other figures and a coloured blur of great events. Not only does my own face look back at me, but also the faces of ancestors and contemporaries, all wanting to get into the picture; and I cannot keep them out' (*Portrait in a Mirror*, p. 1).

Unlike male autobiographies of this period, in female autobiographies great or public events are invariably a 'coloured blur' and only rarely does the narrator bother even to reconstruct the political or historical background. Stella Bowen, for instance, both concedes and retains her ignorance: 'I must be wrong. There must have been more in it than ever met my eye. My poor small eye was placed very close to the ground, and my view was doubtless a worm's eye view. But it was the only view I had' (*Drawn from Life*, p. 11). Male autobiographies of the same period, on the other hand, are usually committed to the public duty of recording the facts of early settlement and the narrator's role in its establishment. Writing in a well-established pioneering tradition, which evoked certain clear-cut reader expectations of style and content, men apparently felt constrained to subscribe to the ends of Empire, or, if self-consciously Irish, at least to the ends of white settlement. Accuracy, impersonality, and public spirit seem to have been the requirements of this genre and the result has often been a humdrum guide-book flavour. Where childhood experiences are included, they are presented as the site of extraordinary hardships or as the foundation of the future career. Generally committed to a public usable past, which comprises a catalogue of British achievement and dominance (Agincourt, the defeat of the Spanish Armada, Trafalgar, Waterloo, and later Gallipoli, Messines Ridge and Passchendaele), male narratives inevitably immerse the personal in the public or functional role. Fictional versions of the self were another matter, of course, as *Quintus Servinton* illustrates. As far as factual autobiographies were concerned, women were initially luckier in that they were allotted the more trival genre of the supportive memoir, the record of pioneering life from the periphery. Time performs strange revolutions, however, and for the contemporary reader periphery and centre have exchanged places; the private world has acquired a new interest, while the public has become as dated as its imperial frame. For the 'new historian' these narratives should prove a valuable resource, illuminating, in Patricia Grimshaw's words, 'life-styles on a selection rather than land legislation, the rituals of Sunday school picnics and church bazaars rather than churches and bishops, the experience of surviving as an aborigine rather than government aboriginal policy'.[8] For if women have tended to be less interested in external events and their causes, less aware of the epochal dimensions of experience and less sensitive to the interconnections between public and private events, they have often been keener registers of the personal impact of those events. This is particulary true of stories of childhood, which frequently convey something of the immediacy of the struggle to survive in the foreshortened, vivid way of actual experience. Less constrained by the need to project a courageous self-image, women have been able to recreate the personal stress of living with the unpredictable, to recall the memory of feeling vulnerable. In the numerous instances of accounts written in old age, this immediacy is often heightened by the narrator's retrospective awareness of the ironies of fate and life's Pyrrhic victories. Less certain of progress and even meaning, womens' narratives are often as sad as they are spontaneous.

To return to the experience of reading these accounts as a group, the dominant topic is undoubtedly family relationships. The family as an extended, mutually supportive group, with well-defined systems of obligations and rights, is as often as not presented as a central character, and this continues to be the case however retrospective the narrative. One of Miles Franklin's most revolutionary aspects, in fact, lies in her protagonist's abandonment of family and country at the end of *My Career Goes Bung* to seek more adequate scope overseas. There are numerous inadequate or even disastrous families in accounts of nineteenth century experience but the pattern of casting off the clog of relatives is not visible until well into the next century.

For the first settlers, of course, the family ensured survival and many stories describe the unusual roles and activities that members assumed for the maintenance of the common life. In Jane Watts's case, for instance, when her family settled on Kangaroo Island in the 1830s, she was obliged to turn baker and nursemaid, while her sister became dressmaker. 'Poor Myra', reflects her sister, was well educated and accomplished; her hands were more accustomed to piano, harp and pencil than to the tools of a tailor's craft but 'all the more refined and congenial occupations of her English life were cheerfully

surrendered from love to those dear to her and the call of duty'
(*Family Life in South Australia*, p. 24). Jane herself, though still a
child, battled with that 'perverse, *iron-hearted*' culinary utensil the
camp-oven, turning out bread in the form of 'masses of sodden
dough' or blackened cinders, and suffering her family's good-natured
ridicule in consequence. These incidents, the narrator observes, are
described so that younger members of the family may realize the
difficulties their elders endured:

For six months Mr A's only couch was a mattress on the bare boards of their
little sitting room, one of the daughters occupying a similar resting place in
the sleeping chamber adjoining. But they 'slept the sleep of the just' on most
occasions, hard as their couches were, for all were too tired with the labours
of the day to lie awake long. (pp. 25–6)

This pattern of family solidarity, in which children were respon-
sibly and heavily involved from an early age, clearly persisted in the
case of poorer or outback families well into the twentieth century.
Both Sarah Conigrave and Jane Watts, for instance, seem to have
enjoyed a good measure of leisure in later youth; Mary Brennan, on
the other hand, in the backwoods of Gippsland and then in the
Wimmera in the 1900s spent her own childhood looking after her
twelve siblings ('I guess I managed. I just took it as my job. When
you're young you don't worry that you're being put upon or, at least,
you know better than to complain', *Better Than Dancing*, p. 73). It
was only when she discovered at the age of sixteen that her mother
was expecting another baby that she decided to leave home. 'Leaving
home', however, merely meant moving to an uncle's neighbouring
property where she worked from daylight to dark at 'the hardest
work I ever did'. Even so she had to endure strictures from her other
relatives on her 'selfishness' in leaving her mother 'with all those
children'.

Few writers dwell at length on their childhood labours, but incidental impressions of the vital role played by children in the work of the
family proliferate in these narratives; Frances Purcell in 1870s Sydney
became a milk-girl at the age of ten when her 'widowed' mother was
compelled to take on a dairy farm, intrepidly delivering her wares
through the hazardous alleys of Surry Hills before rushing to school
(*A Surry Hills Childhood, 1870*); Sarah Musgrave became so pro-
ficient in all the outside work of running a station that on marriage
her husband had to teach her how to cook (*The Wayback*); Agnes
Prince's pioneer mother used the individual members of her family as
efficiently as the head of a large business enterprise (*Esther Mary, My
Pioneer Mother*). In fact, the family frequently emerges as a mini-
business in its organization and self-sufficiency. The more extended
the family, the more it could cushion disasters or expand into new
areas. When Annabella Boswell's father died her uncle provided a

home for her mother and sisters (*Early Recollections*), Mary Mc-
Manus's uncle and his dependents stayed for a year with her family
before settling on a property selected for them by Mary's father
(*Reminiscences of the Early Settlement of the Maranoa District*) and
Joice Loch's relations frequently intervened to rescue her mother
from her father's disastrous experiments in farming (*A Fringe of
Blue*). Meanwhile there are countless accounts of more mundane
forms of support such as child-minding, and medical or educational
help during times of crisis. Children seemed to move frequently
between members of a family, often staying for long periods with
grandparents or aunts. Miles Franklin's experience in *My Brilliant
Career* is representative and Mary Brennan describes how one of her
sisters was 'given' to the grandparents with sad consequences for her
future.

Instances of inter-family networks also abound. Christiane Hiller's
brief autobiography describes the interdependence of German settlers in South Australia in the 1840s ('Autobiography of Frau Pastor
Christiane Hiller'), while Anna Ey's narrative relates the support
provided by another German sect to poor emigrants of their own
faith (*Memoirs*). In Rosa Praed's *My Australian Girlhood*, which
illustrates life in Northern Queensland in the 1850s and 1860s,
families are presented as depending heavily on each other in the
unequal daily struggle to survive in a harsh environment, becoming
even more closely welded during the frequent periods of Aboriginal
unrest. And in the records of bushfires and floods, which nearly all of
the rural narratives contain, there are invariably accounts of heroic
feats of rescue by neighbours and friends. At a more rarified level,
the inter-relationships of wealthy or influential families are perceptible in such autobiographies as Maie Casey's *An Australian Story*,
Margaret Gifford's *I Can Hear the Horses*, Nancy Adams's *Family
Fresco* and Elyne Mitchell's *Chauvel Country*; the Chauvels are
friendly with the Boyds, Maie Casey's family is intimate with the
Mitchells and Maie is another of that small schoolroom of future
writers described in *Family Fresco* and *Spoils of Opportunity*. Some
accounts, such as Fairlie Taylor's *Bid Time Return*, Laura Todd's
A Place Like Home and Eugénie McNeil's *Ladies Didn't*, provide
insights into the personal significance of economic depressions, while
others, such as Nancy Adams's *Family Fresco*, Kate Rodd's
'Lisdillon' and Miles Franklin's *My Brilliant Career*, confront the
gradual and mysterious decay of great families.

The clannishness of the family, which was noted by Jessie Ackermann on her visits to Australia between 1891 and 1912 ('The individual is not the unit. The family is the unit. Each member seems to
be included in every action, whether it is one of duty or pleasure.
Thought for the others obtains in every relation in life'[9]), and
described in Mary Gilmore's *Old Days, Old Ways*, is one of the most

characteristic features of these narratives. Those autobiographies which describe its breakdown do so in tones of grief. Thus Laura Todd's story of her years of deprivation in the 'School of Industry' from 1915 to 1922 is also the story of a general breakdown in normal family relations. Her maternal grandmother was deeply concerned about the girls but, given ill-health, poverty and other heavy responsibilities, was powerless; her paternal grandmother was an unstable, malicious alcoholic; and both her parents, though well-intentioned, failed the children in one way or another. Within the 'home', nevertheless, the sisters formed a tight defensive group that perhaps may have even ensured their survival. Lecky Payne's story is an account of her attempt to retrieve the home that was taken from her at her mother's death ('[The] slipping away of people and things dear to me had recurred in bursts all my life', *Beltana—Six Miles*, p. 171), and to understand the sequence of betrayals she had suffered on the part of her father, grandmother and aunt. Bessie Lee's suffering at the hands of her alcoholic aunt and uncle following the death of her mother leaves this normally loquacious woman lost for words ('That one year of my childhood stands out as a great black blot on the white page of memory', *One of Australia's Daughters*, p. 13). As for the occupational hazards of governessing, one of the greatest seems to have been an emotional one caused by distance from relations and the potential status of alien within the employer's family. Even if one were lucky and the family turned out to be congenial, there was still the difficulty of establishing oneself within it. Kathleen Lambert describes the experience: 'One of the greatest trials of my life had been the inevitable feeling of utter loneliness when first entering a family as a stranger, where they were all so familiar, so bound up together by the ties of home affection' (*The Golden South*, p. 173).

On the reverse side of the coin, numerous narrators recall with delight the enjoyment derived from family activities and entertainments. Florence Alsop's autobiography of the 1880s, 'The Wheel is Turning', indulges in extensive descriptions of the dances, theatrical performances and musical entertainments that her family frequently combined to produce, Sarah Conigrave describes the extraordinary gymnastic competitions and organized pranks of her brothers and sisters on Hindmarsh Island in the 1850s, while Kathleen Lambert nostalgically recalls an interlude of living with her brothers and sisters: 'It was a very happy home, three girls and the head of the house not thirty years of age. All our friends were young . . . Life for a time was like one long summer day' (*The Golden South*, pp. 52–3). Several accounts, such as Ellen Campbell's *An Australian Childhood*, dwell lovingly on the self-contained, communal life of stations, which were also foci in the wider community, supporting long- and short-term visitors and providing children with unusual freedoms and eccentric social contacts. Others, such as Annabella Boswell's *Early*

Recollections and Mary Stawell's *My Recollections*, recreate the daily diversions of life in the great houses, uniquely combining elegance, liberality and outside adventure.

Liberality was not confined to the great families, however; Josephine McDonald (Liardet), for instance, writing of the 1840s, recalls the endless bounty of her father, who established the first hotel at Port Phillip. Her description of his fishing parties illustrates his gregarious, colourful nature:

When my father was going to take out a large fishing net called a seine he would go out with his guitar and play a piece called the 'March round the Village' and that was a call for all our neighbours on moonlight nights to come and see the big net drawn in, and which contained a good sized cart load of fish . . . then my father used to invite his friends to come in our boats for a row in the bay . . . we used to row or sail about the bay for two or three hours with music and song. When we were just landing my brother Jack would sound his cornopeon loudly and the darky cook would hear it and by the time we got to the house a fine fish supper was ready. ('Old Time Reminiscences of the Early Dawn of Melbourne', p. 12)

In this case, however, liberality proved the 'greatest misfortune and greatest curse . . . for this reason that [the hotel] was not a place for making money, but a house open to everyone'. Since Mr Liardet had no idea of business and his wife no idea of housekeeping, 'everyone was hospitably entertained. No books kept, and I do not think that at this time that ever a bill was handed to anyone' (p. 9). On a smaller scale, Rose Lindsay in *Ma and Pa* recalls the generosity of neighbours and tradesmen during her father's frequent absences.

Underlying these accounts of family and neighbourly solidarity are memories of hardships which sometimes imposed intolerable strains on people. Mary Gilmore's *Old Days, Old Ways* describes the general effects of settlers substituting the labour of themselves and their families for the animals and tools they could not afford: 'everywhere families paid the price of land in premature ageing through overwork after birth, and through parental overwork before they were born' (p. 22). And several of these narratives dwell on the physical and emtional strains of life in a new country. 'Any trouble out there was big trouble because it was so remote; help was hours away', comments Mary Brennan of the backwoods of Gippsland, and with her usual gift of terse summary: 'everything was brought in by pack-horse, whether it was a child or a coffin' (*Better than Dancing*, p. 64). Christiane Hiller, for example, describes her family's extraordinary trek in 1852 from South Australia to Portland in company with seven other families who had been unable to reconcile their religious differences within the small community, which itself had only recently been set up at enormous human cost. The elder children walked the entire distance which took four weeks, averaging twenty miles (thirty-two kilometres) a day, and were sustained only by black tea, and the bread which the mothers baked each night. Anna Ey in her *Memoirs* gives a poignant account of her mother's extreme poverty after losing her husband on the voyage to South Australia in 1847. The effort to maintain her family's gentility eventually caused a lengthy interlude of insanity, which appears to have been misunderstood by both her son and her pastor. Left alone to cope with her mother's trouble, the sixteen-year-old Anna almost gave way to despair: 'I felt very lonely and forsaken, so that I often felt tempted to give way to lamentations. But then I would remember wonderful comforting hymns, which I would sing and then again feel uplifted and light of heart' (p. 45). Mrs Henry Parker, writing of the 1850s, describes her genteel widowed mother's efforts to support her family of six children by dairy farming, 'myself the eldest not quite sixteen years of age, a cousin aged twenty-three years and a hired man being the only help' ('Early Days at Lake Innes', p. 24). Katherine McKell gives a moving account of the emotional and physical isolation of her life in outback Victoria following her mother's death:

My mind and memory seem dull when I try to recall that sorrowful time. Grace took charge of the household; the next two sisters were at school at Kyneton. Bella and I were called from our play and flower-gathering to help in the manifold home duties ... Our ages were that Christmas month, respectively Bella thirteen, I eleven. I was small for my age but lightfooted, quick of hand and eye, and was called upon to perform many tasks. (*Old Days and Gold Days in Victoria*, pp. 82–3).

Deaths of parents are major catastrophes; deaths of children are more frequent but often more poignant experiences. Jane Watts, for instance, describes the death of a younger brother due to an ignorant doctor's carelessness ('Not a week had elapsed since, full of health, activity and merriment, he was the prime mover in all their sports; and now, without a farewell to her, or anyone else, little S. was gone—the first to create a blank in the hitherto unbroken family circle' (*Family Life in South Australia*, p. 64). If the family was lucky enough to escape the major catastrophes, the minor difficulties and hazards of life in the bush were almost as character-forming. Every narrative has its ration of snake stories and accounts of riding accidents, and accidents with farm machinery or severe illnesses are almost as frequent. Many children refer with pride to their mothers' nursing achievements, for wives frequently appear to have performed the function of doctor, even to the extent of setting bones and sewing up wounds, while midwifery was a profession often awaiting the woman who went into the outback.

Loneliness was a common enemy. Running as a threnody through all the accounts of early settlement are nostalgic memories of the family at 'home', or, if the narrator is young or Australian-born, a sympathetic awareness of the parents' longings. Rose Lindsay witnesses her mother's homesickness and acquires an extended, absent family via the stories of her aunts' and uncles' childhoods; Sarah Musgrave in *The Wayback* expresses great admiration for her mother who once lived for three years without seeing another woman; and Josephine McDonald describes her mother's great joy, weeping and running down to the ship, when another woman arrived in the colony. Rural life at a much later date could also include great loneliness: Laura Pfitzner gives a mainly oblique account of her loneliness in a strict German family of the 1900s; forced to leave school to work on the farm, she was also unable to respond to her sense of a religious vocation ('for a farmer's daughter these careers were simply unheard of and out of the question. And besides, 1914 was the year of the worst drought in South Australia this century . . .'). From the age of fourteen she was her mother's household and farm help: 'Of social life I had nothing in my early teens. On a few occasions when I was invited to a party my parents did not permit me to go' ('Reflections at Eventide', p. 20). Elyne Mitchell, writing from a very different background, stoically describes in *Chauvel Country* her loneliness in the midst of a family of masculine values and achievements. Divided from her younger sister by age difference, and from her much-loved brothers by distance, she responded with enormous enthusiasm and energy to the holidays which the latter spent in Australia.

One curious publication of 1897, written in the form of a novella, but professing to be 'on real, true life', takes up cudgels on behalf of rural women with a vehemence which implies autobiographical content. This is Alice Paterson's *Life's Clouds, with Sunshine Intermingled*. In her Preface the author declares her intention 'to show the hard lives which the Australian farmers had to endure in the early days of the colony', but the writer's sympathies are clearly with the wives and daughters of farmers. Condemned to work for sixteen hours a day and deprived of any intellectual and social life, these women evoke the author's pity. A visit to a neighbouring farm during a stay in the country excites her scorn for the men who engross the fire and the privilege of after-dinner conversation while their women do the washing up ('Each man smoked a pipe and expectorated into the fire, and sometimes perchance the fender. They talked pigs, red rust, horses, wheat etc., which lasted until tea-time, the only interruption being when one of the men called out for a piece of wood . . .' (p. 10). These women, the narrator declares pityingly, are worse off than destitute people and lunatics who 'have concerts and picnics arranged for them as a real necessary of life' (p. 12).

But these experiences of loneliness and insensitivity pale into insignificance compared with the accounts of cruelty which intersect these stories. Constance Mackness, for instance, in her unpublished autobiography, 'Pioneering Gold-Diggers from Ballarat', recalls both the severities of her parents' youth and her own experiences of a primitive violent environment. The narrator lived in a protected world, not even attending the local school, but she was nevertheless aware of the betrayals, desertions, beatings, sexual humiliations and alcoholic tempests that raged outside. On at least one occasion the cruelty was invasive when a neighbour killed their dog by feeding it with eggs filled with crushed glass. Mrs Henry Parker recalls the way her widowed mother was duped into paying a large sum for a man's 'entire herd' of cattle, only to find that it consisted of one cow. Laura Todd describes the insensitivity of her grandmother who brought toys to the 'School of Industry' only for her preferred grandaughter. Lecky Payne's account of grandmotherly cruelty is almost too painful to read. Rose Lindsay's father had committed some terrible crime against the mother in the past:

There was always a dark hint of something that Pa had done in the past. It seemed to whisper through the years as we grew up. Pa would be heard pleading with her to forget, a tear on his cheek would soften her; but that skeleton was never brought out . . . (*Ma and Pa*, p. 66)

The skeleton that does come to light is grim almost beyond belief. On one occasion, a baby had arrived without the help of a midwife, when 'Pa was away on the drink'. Returning home just as the baby died, he lay in an alcoholic stupor all night, coming round to see 'Ma white-faced and silent holding the dead baby'. Overcome with shame, he did the chores, placed some milk near the bed, locked the children in the mother's room for safety and took the only three pounds in the house for the undertaker. He did not in fact return until late the next day after another drinking spree, and after having spent the money for the burial. 'Ma had lain there with the dead baby, feeding the toddlers from the jug of goat's milk and taking sips herself' (p. 67).

If this is on a par with the horror of Barbara Baynton' stories, Rose Scott Cowen's *Crossing Dry Creeks* surpasses it. Even though this narrative is embued with ideas of mateship and the bush myth, it is crowded with violent events from drunken fights to murders. One concerns a stabbing incident when a shearer wounded another with shears, deliberately closing them in his enemy's belly; immediately trussed up by a rope on a beam by the foreman, the would-be murderer was very lucky to escape death. Another describes the terrible death of an Aboriginal woman pressed to death in a wool bale. Several texts have stories of cruelty to Aborigines, while a few express sympathy for the witnessed sufferings of convicts. Many register the destructive influence of alcohol, the effects of bigotry, ignorance and prejudice, and the cruel treatment of animals. An ubiquitous phenomenon is the account, either hearsay or firsthand, of the male predator, whether in the bush or the city. The editors' comment in *The Penguin Book of*

Australian Autobiography that the 'picture that emerges from Australian autobiography is of a strongly authoritarian society, intolerant of human differences'[10], should perhaps be qualified with the phrase 'and capable of extreme cruelty'.

Notwithstanding these impressions of suffering and passivity, it is hard to find consistent evidence for Miriam Dixson's contentions about the impact of pioneer life on women:

During the formative times of all States, except South Australia, women were widely treated with contempt, in its many variations, and often with brutality. We have never outgrown the former attitude, and our women are still deeply if unconsciously impoverished by this dominant cultural characteristic.[11]

'Things are exceptional in Australia', comments Mary Stawell's mother, 'we have brought our manners, our education and our individuality with us but left conventionality behind' (*My Recollections*, p. 79), and it is a sentiment that is frequently endorsed by the authors of many of these autobiographies. If life in a new country brought certain limitations, it also presented women with new challenges and there are countless accounts of the equality of women's efforts and of their pride in their achievements. On arrival at Port Phillip in the 1840s, Mrs Liardet was left alone with the children in an isolated area while her husband went into New South Wales; the skills of Mrs Hughes's mother are presented as vital for the family's survival in a remote area of South Australia in the 1850s ('she could do anything after [she] had once tried', *My Childhood in Australia*, p. 9). The father of this account had to work hard, but the mother was busier, often carrying out all the work of the house herself; contending with snakes, wild bulls and the dangerous pets and pranks of her children, she still had time for play and for gardening, moving huge limestones with a crowbar for the sake of a flower garden:

The huge stones piled up outside the garden long remained a memorial of mother's strength, energy and devotion to her purpose. I admire her pluck when I think of it; I am sure she had a superabundance of energy and strength as well, for whatever she did she did it thoroughly. (p. 98)

Margaret Mickle, writing of rural Tasmania in the 1830s, describes her mother's fearlessness and compassion towards the convicts who were employed on their farm, intervening in a murderous exchange on one occasion and instantaneously winning the men's respect ('Her Diary', p. 9). Sarah Conigrave feels as proud as a soldier with a V.C. when she recalls her bravery at the age of twelve, in diverting a herd of belligerent cattle from the family's encampment (*My Reminiscences of the Early Days*, pp. 10–11); and Sarah Musgrave confides her pride in her achievements on her uncle's station: 'I look back on that twelve months of work well done' (*The Wayback*, p. 48). This narrator is also very anxious that the work of the pioneering women should not be forgotten and devotes her last chapter to listing the outstanding women she had known ('The men of these high qualities had to look to their wives to be equally endowed with the pioneering spirit, and that the man found the woman so endowed is proved by the record of their lives' p. 92). Agnes Prince's autobiography is mainly an account of her mother's extraordinary enterprise and resource in outback Western Australia with only the help of her young children; Fairlie Taylor describes her achievement in running her father's business at the age of eleven. Accounts of riding feats, overland treks, and skilfully resolved encounters with the hazards of the bush are legion. And later urban-bound, wealthier women display the same confidence and sense of challenge; Janet Mitchell and Nancy Adams are inspired by strong female models, while Maie Casey's mother is presented as equal both to the challenge of running the finances of her mother's wealthy family and extinguishing a bush fire. Numerous narratives describe the successful efforts of women to sustain the family in the face of a husband's or a father's failure or inadequacy.

'In the first place, or so they tell me, I came into the world under my own steam', declares Mary Brennan at the beginning of her autobiography. 'I arrived before the nurse; no wonder I'm independent!' (*Better than Dancing*, p. 1) If few of the authors of these narratives have 'arrived' in quite the same way, most would agree with the confidence of the sentiment.

2

Early Conventions and Traditions

'[T]his story is all about myself—for no other purpose do I write it', declares Miles Franklin's Sybylla at the beginning of *My Brilliant Career* (1901), boldly challenging autobiography's previous stratagems of indirection and its dual, gendered rhetoric. Given the obliquity of women's autobiography to this time, Franklin's challenge is almost as bold as Rousseau's 'I am commencing an undertaking hitherto without precedent' for the narrative structures inherited by Australian women ostensibly offered meagre scope for self-expression. The first autobiographer to question the partriarchal system with any thoroughness, Franklin is also the first to declare unequivocally her interest in the self, even though she cloaks her intentions by using a fictional form. Not that self-absorption is unknown before Franklin; it is the frankness of the confession that is unusual. Eliza Davies's *The Story of an Earnest Life* (1881) is just as self-engrossed as *My Brilliant Career* but Davies makes some show of a religious motive and may well be writing in a different American tradition; Kathleen Lambert's *The Golden South* (1890) is almost as preoccupied with the meaning of bush experience but, written in old age, her narrative is also more other-directed. Franklin's feminist challenge was also an innovation; there is some explicit feminist anger in earlier narratives, but on the whole the impact of men's power, decisions and mistakes on women's lives is accepted fatalistically. I emphasize here that 'earlier' indicates date of writing; many narratives remained unpublished for lengthy periods after writing while actual dates of writing are in many cases obscure so that the chronological record is almost impossible to determine in any final way.

Revolutionary as her approach was, Franklin was nevertheless writing within a tradition in more ways than one; in her second autobiography, *My Career Goes Bung*[1], she describes the genesis of *My Brilliant Career* as an alternative to traditional rhetorical forms.

The second Sybylla describes herself as the author of 'a new style of autobiography'. Inspired by the potential of the genre for 'disseminating personal facts straight from the horse's mouth', she had nevertheless been intensely irritated by the patent dissimulation of conventional autobiographies: 'Every one of those productions, whether the fiction that passes for reality or the decorated reality that is termed fiction, was marred by the same thing—the false pose of the autobiographer'. She determined, therefore, to write an 'imitation autobiography that would wade in without apology or fear, biffing convention on the nose'. Setting out 'to do the equivalent of taking two photographs on the one plate', she intended to 'burlesque autobiography and create the girl of my admiration, and fill in with a lot of lifelike people as a protest against over-virtuous lay figures'. (*My Career Goes Bung*, pp. 28, 30, 37). Both Sybyllas are vehement in their defence of the frankness of their 'egoism', but both are also acutely conscious of an audience and indeed *My Career Goes Bung* is largely a history of the author's relationship with the readership of the first book. And notwithstanding her defiant solipsism, the Sybylla of *My Brilliant Career* frequently addresses her fellow Australians of the bush and wryly identifies herself with her female readers. Like her predecessors and successors, she is implicitly concerned with the common experience of women and speaks not just for herself, but for her mother, sisters, aunts and friends. In fact, one of the curious side-effects of the publication of *My Brilliant Career* was the overwhelming response from girls who, somewhat to the author's chagrin, felt that the book was telling *their* story.

The absence of feminist protest before Franklin is no doubt inevitable in a literature of early settlement; survival takes precedence over all other circumstances in these conditions. As the struggle to survive began to be assessed retrospectively, women's writing found a ready-made niche in the form of the pioneering memoir which fairly rapidly modulated into its close associate, the memoir of place. The pioneering memoir was a prescribed rhetorical structure, which privileged the public, achieving self, if one was male, and the representative, supportive self, if one was female. Barrett Mandel has described the autobiographer as 'an ego—a subject, a perceiver—floating in a sea of things. His yelp of self-assertion is, on one level, an affirmation that among the bric-à-brac of the world, he at least is alive and no thing'.[2] Colonial women faced a social as well as an existential challenge; consigned to the bric-à-brac of nation-building, they had unusual difficulty in retrieving the self from the 'sea of things', so that it is not surprising that Franklin's cry of self-assertion received a ready response.

The main qualification for female authorship of the pioneering memoir was the role of witness to the experience of early settlement. Frequently, of course, women were regarded as natural recorders of the local human history of specific regions, and were often encouraged to set down their memories of births, deaths and marriages and the chronology of settlement. Many in fact open with self-deprecating statements, affirming some external initiative or expressing a suitably modest reluctance to foreground the self. Ostensibly, at least, women's colonial autobiography presented itself within a rhetoric that was inherently male; women were able to circumvent the rhetoric to a large degree, but some superficial recognition of the conventions was *de rigeur*.

Women's life-writing has not only been *written* in a sexist manner, it has also been *read* in the same way; first as demonstrating the strength of women's supportive role in the pioneering context and secondly as itself supportive, documenting the domestic, local details on the historical map which pioneering men were presumed to have charted. When Jane Watts's fine narrative of the 1830s, *Family Life in South Australia*, was reprinted in facsimile form in 1979, for example, it received scant attention from reviewers, who generally considered it with a group of reprinted male accounts. Described as 'gossipy' and concerned 'mostly with family doings or social occasions' or as a useful source of local history, it was firmly consigned to the miscellaneous basket.[3]

The pioneering memoir was not the sole sub-genre open to colonial women, but was rapidly supplemented by other forms as the century progressed. Briefly, I have been able to distinguish at least seven other forms or sub-genres which took root in the nineteenth century and largely persisted into the twentieth century and which I shall refer to as memoirs of place, of family, of parents, collaborative texts, 'children's' texts, career autobiographies, and autobiographical novels. I should emphasize that the groupings outlined above are empirical rather than prescriptive and result from a search for order in a wide range of material. These groupings emerge as distinctive in that they entail different reader expectations and have varying rhetorical options. (Some narratives which commemorate families, places or parents are, of course, not at all autobiographical and are not considered here.)

The most closely allied to the pioneering memoir is the memoir of place and this form in fact has provided by far the most scope. From Margaret Mickle's 'Her Diary' (1892) to Laura Todd's *A Place Like Home* (1987) the memoir of place has been a flexible form for women writers of the self. In the twentieth century Barbara Hanrahan's *The Scent of Eucalyptus* (1973) and Nancy Phelan's *A Kingdom by the Sea* (1969) belong in the same tradition. A less popular category for the recording of nineteenth century experience but one which has produced some significant narratives is the memoir of family, a genre which includes such texts as Agnes Gosse Hay's *After-Glow Memories* (1905) and Maie Casey's *An Australian Story* (1962).

Smaller still is a group of narratives, all published before 1900, which are ostensibly written for children but which have an adult autobiographical scope. Two closely related groups have produced a narrow range of texts but some of the most interesting: the collaborative autobiographies, which are usually mother/daughter collaborations, and the memoirs of parents. In both cases part of the attraction of these texts is the impression of dialogue between generations. Unlike male autobiographies, which are frequently records of careers or exploits, there are few female narratives which focus on a career, although religious careers are a different matter and several interesting nineteenth century texts exist as records of individual vocations. Finally there is a small group of autobiographical novels. *My Brilliant Career* is not the first autobiographical female novel in Australian literature, but it is the first which is concerned with the development of the creative self and comes closest to the traditional *Bildungsroman*; succeeded by such novels as *The Getting of Wisdom* and *The Man Who Loved Children*, it could be seen as the first Australian female text in an international tradition which includes both male and female narratives, although it has more probably a complicated root, drawing on both the native and English autobiographical traditions and overseas fictional models.

Several texts, of course, straddle two or more categories and several further provisos are in order. These groupings omit autobiographies which are almost solely concerned with adult experience in Australia, such as Ada Cambridge's *Thirty Years in Australia*, while the narratives which are the subject of this chapter are either wholly or in part concerned with youthful experience before 1920. That year has been chosen as a convenient cut-off point since there is a marked change in the national consciousness after the First World War. Obviously, an author writing in the 1950s and recalling the 1890s enjoys greater freedom of expression and reflects different attitudes than her predecessor of, say, 1900, who is writing of the same period. Personal age at time of writing also obviously affects a narrative in multiple ways, although temperamental differences mean it is impossible to make general conclusions. These factors, aggravated by the indeterminacy of dating already referred to, mean that women's autobiographical narratives refuse to fit into a tidy chronological structure. Nevertheless, the shared experience of a specific historical period, combined with the persistence of women's rhetorical conventions, make it possible to consider accounts of pre-1920 childhoods as a reasonably unified group. This chapter will discuss only five of the above-mentioned groups: memoirs of pioneering, place, and family, collaborative texts and 'children's' texts. Career autobiographies, memoirs of parents and autobiographical novels are discussed at relevant junctures in the text. It is not possible to consider every narrative of this period, but reference to the bibliography will illustrate the extent of the above groupings while several of the most significant are discussed separately in Chapter 3.

Pioneering Memoirs

Of all the rhetorical structures available to the first female autobiographers in Australia, the pioneering memoir was the least congenial and the most conscious of a male audience. Sidonie Smith in her study of American and English texts, concludes that all nineteenth century autobiographies by women were written primarily for men: 'the autobiographer, at least until the twentieth century, approaches her "fictive" reader as if "he" were the representative of the dominant order, the arbiter of the ideology of gender and its stories of selfhood'. Submissive to the silent claim of power made by the male reader, the colonial female autobiographer, according to Smith, was condemned to an uneasy 'double-voicedness'.[4] Certainly, there are numerous Australian narratives that self-consciously circumnavigate male expectations of content and voice, but there are also some extraordinarily open texts, such as Katherine McKell's *Old Days and Gold Days in Victoria*, Jane Watts's *Family Life in South Australia* (see Chapter 3) and Clara Ellen Campell's *Memoirs* (see Chapter 10), which are clearly written with female readers in mind. The implied female reader is even more apparent in the memoir of place or of family and indeed many of these texts give the impression of being a literate extension of an oral tradition of story-telling.

A narrative which is rigidly bound by the rhetorical prescriptions of the pioneering memoir is Mrs Dominic Daly's account of the settlement at Port Darwin, *Digging, Squatting, and Pioneering Life in the Northern Territory of South Australia* (1887).[5] This writer, the daughter of Captain Bloomfield Douglas who was appointed Government Resident of the Northern Territory in 1870, is clearly conscious of her responsibilities in describing her experiences of 'a settlement hourly attaining more importance', a subject which has never been 'brought before the world in the form of a book' (pp. 1–2). Accompanied by a map, appendices and a brief history of the attempts to colonize the Northern Territory up to 1870, it is also dependent in the latter part on 'official reports' made available to the author and on her own research in contemporary newspapers. The description of the first three years of the settlement from 1870 to 1873, however, is written 'entirely from memory, unaided by notes, journals, or letters'. A competent writer with a gift for dramatic narrative, Mrs Daly gives graphic and sometimes colourful descriptions of the settlers' experiences. The sharp current along the eastern coast is compared to 'the proverbial cat in a London boarding-house [which] is blamed for every accident that cannot be accounted for in any other way' (p. 18), or relationships among the Larrakiah tribe are described as 'complicated as those of an ancient Irish family' (p. 66).

This narrative is one of the least inward, but the narrator emerges as a confident, lively girl who takes the greatest delight in overseeing their vessel's navigation of the reef, surreptitiously interviewing the helmsman or ostentatiously deploying nautical terms. On one occasion she takes pride in recording her refusal to remain battened down in the saloon, preferring to make her way 'against orders' to the deck, 'fierce though the elements undoubtedly were' (p. 16). Some personal comment on her own or her sisters' chagrin at leaving the gay social life of Brisbane, on the fact that they leave 'heart-whole', or on the family's anxiety for her little brother, sharpened by their loss of an earlier child, intersect the narrative, but the narrator's eye is firmly on her public audience and the intimate is largely excised in favour of general descriptions of life in the territory. On one occasion, however, the personal thrusts to the surface in her account of her psychic anticipation of the return of the Roper party. Apart from this, her sensitivity to the changing moods of the little settlement as they wait for a ship and news of the outside world, or as they absorb the death of one of their number, enlivens the narrative. Representative in her interest in the domestic minutiae of pioneering life, her sympathy for other women and her response to a paradisal but 'lonely and desolate' landscape (p. 43), Mrs Daly becomes quite unrepresentative in the imperial sentiments which intrude into the latter part of her account.

Some of the same problems afflict Mary MacLeod Banks's *Memories of Pioneer Days in Queensland* (1931).[6] Another well-written account, but more inward than Mrs Daly's, it is almost quenched by the patronizing foreword by Lord Lamington, who had not had 'the pleasure of reading the transcript of the volume' but was 'sure that Mrs Banks, as a member of the well-known and highly respected McConnel family, will do justice to the claim of being a worthy daughter of Sunny Queensland' (p. 8). Notwithstanding her claim that these impressions are those 'as received on the mind of a child, without attempting to recast them in the light of later knowledge' (p. 9), this narrator feels it incumbent on her to include chapters on the external economy of this south-east Queensland station in the 1860s. Once she turns to the 'Realm of the Mistress' and her more specific memories of childhood, though, her account becomes far more spontaneous and includes some delightful descriptions of the games and pranks of children. Quite early in the narrative, fortunately, there is a clear instance of memory's quickening as the narrator describes a near-drowning incident and the child's shock at her mother's indecorous appearance:

We watched, awe-inspired, from the knoll; it seemed as if the end of all things had come when my mother, the ruler of the house, the upholder of seemliness and order, was seen making her way through the river, a wide wake following her, her shady garden hat still on her head, her crinoline only half submerged and moving up or down with each step forward. Consternation held us breathless for some time after her triumphant return to dry land. (p. 31)

One chapter is devoted to pets while an incident between a bishop and a tenacious sloth is related with some comic spirit. But it is the descriptions of the child's response to the bush that are the most vivid, with one whole chapter devoted to 'Teachers, Logs and Fancies'. The power of logs over the bush-child's imagination proves to be a particularly fertile topic, anticipating Hanrahan's and Fullerton's sensitive recordings of childhood landscapes. This narrator also recalls the Jesuitical processes of the child's mind, which result in unfortunate literal interpretations of religious doctrine, and some of childhood's quarrels and cruelties. And like other narrators of early bush childhoods, she is ambivalent about the changes pioneering brings to the landscape; on one hand she praises Australia's 'capitalist settlers who built up the herds on which her material life depended' and on the other laments the passing of trees and flowers and the erosion of the tribal way of life. On the whole a controlled narrative, manipulated to meet male expectations, *Memories of Pioneer Days in Queensland* compromises with its audience to some extent but finds several crevices for the self.

Mary A. McManus's *Reminiscences of the Early Settlement of the Maranoa District in the Late Fifties and Early Sixties*[7], written between 1899 and 1900 and first published in 1913, is an interesting example of the pioneering memoir which becomes subject to the subversions of personal memory. Beginning with a characteristic disavowal of egoism, which is immediately undercut by her pride in being one of the first two white women in the Maranoa district[8], two-thirds of McManus's account is a record of the names of new settlers, dates and locations of their settlements, general descriptions of conditions and a catalogue of 'firsts'. A resilient, confident girl, who was exceptional in the outdoors life she led, McManus includes treatment of female subjects ('those little trivialities which ladies love to read about in books') purely as an indulgence of her weaker sisters. She is exceptional in her pride in Queensland's progress, clearly associating herself with the colony's achievements. Then, two-thirds of the way through, her narrative suddenly becomes more complicated and inward. Turning her attention to a journey with her parents out west in 1864, she recalls several disturbing incidents. None of these are of any moment, except that they still seem to tantalize the recording mind, and are extraordinary outcrops in an otherwise external narrative. On one occasion, riding ahead of the group, she comes upon the camp of some men; the mutual surprise of the encounter—the men too stunned to reach for their guns, the girl 'for once ... at a loss for an explanation'—still thrills the memory.

On another, she encounters a woman herding some sheep and lambs 'toiling through the heat and sandy soil covered with dust and tormented with flies and mosquitoes, to say nothing of the sandflies'. Carrying a heavy child in her arms, she is hampered by two more children clinging to her skirts and by her advanced pregnancy. The encounter is still a moving one for this narrator, retrospectively conscious of her own free and confident girlhood.

An interesting unpublished autobiography, Eliza Chomley's 'My Memoirs', dated 1920[9], recalls the family's arrival in Melbourne in 1850 when the narrator was eight. The daughter of Thomas Turner à Beckett and sister of Sir Thomas à Beckett, Eliza married H. B. Chomley in 1863. Prompted to write her own memoirs by the examples of her father and brother, she gives delightful insights into the personalities of both men. Her descriptions of the dullness of home life, presided over by her severely conservative father, are devastating. T. T. à Beckett, described by the *Australian Dictionary of Biography* as a 'cultured man of many interests, an upright, God-fearing citizen, conservative in thought and often rigid and severe towards those with whom he disagreed'[10], seems to have been completely devoid of any empathy with the young. Doomed to moulder in the family home where there are 'absolutely no young visitors' and which is 'infested' with clergy, Eliza responds like a parched plant to water when her lively brother returns from England. Accepted as 'an adequate chaperon for all but very special occasions', he immediately transforms her life. A witty writer, Eliza also describes her difficulties with her stepmother, the turbulent period following her mother's death, the games, pranks and pets of childhood, and her rigorous experiences at school. Subject to severe discipline, which extends to a taboo on any socializing during the daily crocodile walks, the girls nevertheless have their means of communication: 'eyes were often more expressive than a bow could be, and were not under control'. After such repressions, it is not surprising that Eliza on her honeymoon responded with rebellion to her mother-in-law's call for total mourning following the death in Ireland of an unfamiliar half-sister of her husband.

Spirited though it is, this autobiography is not without more troubled currents. The death of her mother, which at the time is less disturbing than the earlier death of a sister, is retrospectively a source of grief; commenting on the effects of the child's death, which instigated the mother's own fatal illness, the narrator reflects on her undoubted loneliness and anxiety in a strange country. Later, the death of one of her own children reinforces her bonds with her mother's experience. Apart from her memoirs, Eliza Chomley never ventured into print, so it is interesting to discover that she was not only the grandmother of Martin Boyd but also the mother of the novelist C. H. Chomley (friend of Norman Lindsay, editor of *Arena*, proprietor of the *British Australasian* and supporter of women's suffrage.)

Another Victorian autobiography which contrastingly records the experience of a lower, rural class is K. McK.'s (Katherine McKell's) *Old Days and Gold Days in Victoria (1851–1873) being Memories of a Pioneer Family* (1924).[11] One of a family of eleven children, Katherine McKell was born in 1851; her father, who had emigrated from Scotland in 1841, managed a station in Victoria before buying his own land in heavily timbered country near Daylesford. Leaving the narrator's first childhood home was typical of those inner migrations of colonial life, repetitions of the first migration which could be almost as disturbing. In this case it was the Scots pride of the father that compelled the family to move on, even though the father himself, 'of a delicate, slender physique', was unsuited to manual labour. A simple, plangent account of a rural childhood, this narrative is written in a stripped-down style that has moments of transparent clarity. McKell's recreation of a child's consciousness is remarkably sensitive, encouraged no doubt by the habits of silent observation in a household of exceptional severity ('My sister Bella and I, looking on at the passing scenes but not allowed to make remarks in the presence of our elders, became very observant and discerning, reading people with the child's instinctive clearness' p. 78). At the same time, an adult awareness of the extraordinary aspects of her experience inserts implicit criticisms:

We children, having no shop-made toys, played with cattle-horns, bleached sheep-skulls and such things. In the long hot days, hours were spent in the shade of big gum-trees, scraping the horns with bits of broken glass, and polishing them. (p. 16)

As the story progresses these criticisms become more severe and cluster mainly around the father. A man of 'unflinching sternness' with little taste for the community life which would have been a stimulus for the children ('I can see now that he did not give a moment's thought to our needs' p. 71), his limitations become far more of a liability after the mother's death:

In those sad years, Father, as had been his custom always, walked afar off in stern coldness, irritable, unapproachable. Never did he, in our memories, stop and take the least interest in the childish play and occupations. The sorrowful little hearts, asking with silent, appealing faces for the bread of love, received a stone. (p. 83)

Memories of the dead mother, meanwhile, reverberate in the narrative. Remembered in certain archetypal visual scenes, as busily engaged in domestic tasks or taking a few moments' rest, she is the narrator's female ideal, described also as the Biblical ideal, 'keepers at home' and 'looking well to the ways of [the] household' (p. 104).

A more buoyant autobiography by a remarkably resourceful pioneer is Sarah Musgrave's *The Wayback*, first published in 1926[12] when the author was ninety-six and revised four years later. Centring on her memories of station life in New South Wales near Young from the mid-1830s, her narrative is packed with accounts of relations with the Aborigines, outback lawlessness and climatic disasters. Although this account is enlivened by the author's sense of drama and her expressive style, the moments of inwardness are few, restricted to indirect indications of pride in her own resource and that of other women, or sympathy with the sufferings of animals. Conscious of her role as recorder, Musgrave allows herself few moments to expand on her own feelings, and even the sequence of her life has to be indirectly pieced together. Apparently separated from her mother at an early age, she appears to have lived mainly with her much-loved uncle. Recalling a period of severe drought, however, she indulges 'a little truth about herself', which includes her pride in work well done. The motive for her effort, she realizes now, was 'love': 'It was love for [my uncle] that kept up my strength and my spirits'. Inspired by the noble example of this man, she and her sister manned the windlass 'keeping the water flowing for ten hours a day for all that long, dry year'. Her joy during this time expressed itself in singing and, with her sisters she 'sang and talked all day', not once getting angry: 'What love I showed my uncle then, as also when I shepherded his sheep, he truly deserved , and deserved it tenfold; for what I was at that time, a happy, healthy girl, I owed to him' (pp. 48–9). Externally directed as this narrative is, it is the personal that is valued: the remembered conversations, the fellowship of work, the charisma of a domineering Aboriginal leader, the poignancy of a man's rescue of his fiancée at the expense of his own life and even the strange excitement of a personal psychic experience that led to the capture of a murderer. Often referring to herself as 'talking', Musgrave clearly sees herself as recording the local folklore, although the impression of an independent mind and of a pair of sharply observant eyes is unmistakable. Her account of being bailed up by bushrangers at the age of four and of responding to their gifts of 'bulls-eye lollies' by immediately ceasing to cry is virtually a metaphor of her resilient philosophy: 'One thing I do not grizzle and mourn over lost youth', she concludes, 'I have had a long and good run for my money' (p. 95).

Less well known than *The Wayback* is Anna Ey's *Memoirs*.[13] Written mainly in 1900, with additions made in 1904 and 1907, this narrative was not published until 1986, although it deals with life only a decade later than *The Wayback*, and would probably even now be inaccessible were it not for the author's granddaughter, Dorothea Freund, who translated the manuscript. Born in 1839 in France, Anna Ey migrated with her family from Germany to South Australia in 1847; her father, a Lutheran pastor and missionary, died at sea and the family joined a congregation settled at Lobenthal. Like *The Wayback*, this narrative extends into adulthood, although an extensive section is devoted to the childhood years. The narrator is as spirited and independent as Sarah Musgrave, but there the resemblance ends. Whereas *The Wayback* recalls an open life, reminiscent of Furphy's *Such is Life* in its variety, this autobiography is written from within the confines of a Lutheran sect, which is as isolated and self-contained as the Puritan community of *The Scarlet Letter*. Like Christiane Hiller's briefer, unpublished account[14], it reveals the force of the Lutheran beliefs, the ferocity of doctrinal divisions and the intensity of personal religious feeling. Apart from the congregation's dependence on the weather, it might as well be located within Europe, so strongly does it guard the common language, customs and faith; indeed, perhaps the most telling indication of its total self-sufficiency is that this narrator never sees fit to remark on it. Profoundly pious, and turned further inward by the family's misfortunes and extreme poverty, Anna Ey is remarkably sensitive to her inner life. Writing in a fairly disconnected way according to the slenderest of chronologies, she allows incidents, personalities, disputes, conversations and the events of her religious life to mingle with memories of intense feeling. Whether it is the helpless pity of her response to her mother's period of insanity or her joy at receiving a rare present (a dress length and a box of texts) or her anger at an unjust punishment at school, these recollections are invariably spontaneous. One of the most unselfconscious of narrators, Ey records the struggles and emotional deserts of her experience with an attractive integrity. Particularly striking is her response to the power of Biblical language; reflecting the power of her religious feeling, it is otherwise similar to Mary Fullerton's delight in Shelley and Katherine McKell's in Scott and illustrates the consoling power of the written word which is a familiar theme in women's autobiography:

The box of texts became my life's companion. The texts and verses, which impressed themselves on my memory long ago, gave me wonderful strength and comfort in the hours of anguish and sorrow, which I experienced in later life. They disciplined and admonished me when I deserved it, but they also refreshed and comforted me when I needed it. (p. 29)

Not unexpectedly, this autobiographer has a keen eye for the vivid, emotionally representative detail, the picture of her 'lanky' brother in search of an umbrella after their arrival in Adelaide or the vision of her severe teacher, tears streaming down his face, as he farewells his students. In common with other autobiographies of this period, there is little attempt to draw a lesson from her experience other than the general religious one that life is a severe testing ground, alleviated only by the comforts of religion; the humour of her response to her brother's admonishment to be patient during her mother's illness, for instance, ('there certainly was plenty of opportunity to practice it') is clearly unconscious (pp. 44–5). Indirectly, however, the narrative is packed with insights into the poverty and loneliness of fatherless women, even within a tight-knit community, and into their distinctive freedoms and constraints within one form of authoritarian Protestantism.

Memoirs of Place

If the pioneering memoir provided women with some scope for writing the self, what I have termed the memoir of place proved much more liberating. Records of place, inherently quietist rather than activist, implying being as against the doing of pioneering, have allowed women substantial freedom to inscribe their past selves; not so unequivocally patriarchal as the pioneering record, this form of discourse has been chosen by the vast majority of autobiographers of both centuries and includes several major achievements. Some of these appear in the discussion of other topics or in Chapter 3 and there is space here to consider only a few.

One of the earliest of this group in terms of period is Annabella Boswell's *Early Recollections and Gleanings from an Old Journal* (1908). Born near Bathurst in 1826, Annabella Boswell lived there and in Sydney and at Port Macquarie and Newcastle until 1864, when she went with her husband to Scotland, where they remained. From 1843 to 1848 she lived with her sister and mother at her uncle's home at Lake Innes, Port Macquarie. *Early Recollections*, based on a diary begun when the author was a young girl, was one of several books published in Scotland before her death in 1916. It was retrieved by Morton Herman, who edited a new edition published in 1965.[15] As an historian of colonial architecture, the editor was most interested in Boswell's account of Lake Innes, and rearranged her narrative, reassembling 'Parts of the original opening pages relating to Annabella's ancestors, and her earliest childhood memories, which, though interesting in themselves, impeded the flow of the narrative' (p. xiv) and omitting some other sections. Most importantly, he also omitted the note which Boswell appended to the beginning of her narrative, explaining her identification with Australia ('I am so thoroughly Australian in heart as well as by birth that my mind often wanders from present scenes') and her reason for writing, that is, to change the 'strange indifference of her children to the land of their birth'.[16]

Although Boswell retains the diary form for parts of her narrative, especially and appropriately for the period dealing with her years at Lake Innes, several sections are in the form of a straightforward narrative; by far the largest of these (almost half the text and about one-third in the 1965 edition) is the section dealing with her earliest

years. Far from 'impeding the narrative', these early recollections set
the author in context. Characteristic in their interest in family origins,
these pages also establish the relationship between the narrator and
her mother, her fascination with the ancient female custom of recreating the past ('I have often listened with delight to my mother's
descriptions of her early days'), and her assorted memories of the
significant trivia of childhood. A deceptively artless and spontaneous
flow, this whole early section is a significant self-conscious exploration of the past and the strange experience of remembering. 'From
my fifth birthday I am certain of my own identity' (p. 8), writes the
older narrator, and, sensitive to the interdependence of writing and
identity, by the age of nine she has already acquired her own written
record. Boswell's attractive and even unconventional persona is
particularly sensitive to the subtle effects of time, including its
deceptions. The last paragraphs of her vivid recreation of life in a
wealthy, hospitable family, for example, are particularly sensitive;
just when time appears to have slowed to the point of stagnation, it is
about to work a major revolution:

The green door (entrance from the garden to the back verandah and back
door) no longer swung merrily on its hinges, giving notice to us in the
schoolroom that Bachelor's Hall was occupied, and as day after day passed
we used to wonder if our lives would be always so uneventful. Sometimes as
we four girls sat on the hill by the flagstaff and looked out over the wide
Pacific, we built castles in the air, and wove romances for the future . . . A
change came all too soon, and although nothing startling ever happened,
things were never the same to any of us again. (p. 147)

   This narrative is also interesting as an early example of the importance of houses and domestic interiors in female autobiographies; the
geography of the great house at Lake Innes is an emotional geography, diverse in the moods and attractions of its various features,
but unified as the place of remembered community; for the narrator,
whose early childhood had been marked by constant migrations,
unpleasant school experiences and the loss of a much-loved father,
Lake Innes is the symbol of stability, family feeling, hospitality and
culture in both senses of the word. It is the self's home, the ideal
remembered nucleus, and hence the use of the diary at this point to
record the ebb and flow of its social life. Both metaphor and actual
place, constructed of both emotion and stone, Lake Innes cannot be
separated from the life of the narrator. As an account of the days of
gracious living, Boswell's journal is deservedly well known; as an
autobiography, however, it deserves further attention.

   Kathleen Lambert's *The Golden South: Memories of Australian
Home Life from 1843 to 1888* (1890), published under the pseudonym
'Lyth'[17], is one of the most inwardly probing of these early autobio-
graphies of place. After emigrating with her parents in 1843, the

author worked as a governess for various squatters in New South Wales. Her account is loosely chronological, ending shortly after her marriage, and reads more as a personal meditation than a record of events. As her title indicates, Lambert's 'plot' is the typical female one, concerning changes in relationships in family, community and place. Men's life-stories of this period, obsessed with 'becoming', are concerned to categorize and order, to produce an individual sequence that 'makes sense' in terms of the perceived national sequence, and to create hierarchies, even if they are only hierarchies of significance. Women are generally content to leave matters unresolved, to express the mixed and even puzzling quality of experience, meanwhile suspending judgement on its meaning.

Although Lambert declares that she intends to reconcile differences between the old country and the new, she is basically unresolved in her primary allegiance. Writing in 'a small village in Hampshire, with a bitter north-easterly wind blowing' (p. 20), she often engages in a debate with supposedly English detractors of the colony, but occasionally admits her own ambivalent loyalties. If England is 'hallowed by youthful associations', her Australian youth acquires in retrospect the golden colour of her title. Intensely sensitive to the beauty of the bush and the relative freedom and equality of colonial life, she recalls the happiest period of her youth when she was housekeeper for her brother on his property near Wellington. Like other female narrators, Lambert deliberately ignores political events, even registering a dislike of the 'needy self-seeking politician' (p. 30) and the brashness of the public world which allows 'Impudence, assurance, egotism', to push their way to the front (p. 26). She is also unusually self-conscious about her intentions: after the usual self-deprecating gesture to the effect that she writes because asked, she declares her determination to describe 'the real homes [and] lives' of the people, in response to the external impressions of such men as Froude, Trollope and Forbes (p. 2).

The Golden South is also a particularly good example of the openness to the small but telling personal event, which is characteristic of women's writing. Often sensitive to what might only be called the symbolic suggestions of the trivial, women frequently record the drama of their response to a face, a gesture, a stray encounter, a conversation. Thus Lambert recalls the emotional content of a chance meeting with convicts, a meeting she will 'never forget':

As all were agreeable, we soon entered the quarries; but what to see! A gang of men chained together, with armed warders on either side guarding them. I stood aghast! To my companions such sights were but too familiar; to me, for many a day, it cast a shadow over all that once had appeared beautiful. The face of one of the prisoners remained in my memory for years—a weak, though handsome face. We shrank back as he raised his dark eyes, and for a second when they met ours, the blush of shame could be seen through his tanned skin. Who and what was he? (pp. 33–4)

And for this narrator the horror of the wreck of the *Dunbar* is vividly expressed in its pathetic flotsam: 'needlework half-finished, with needles and crochet hooks stuck in reels of cotton, most likely in use a few hours previously; combs from some loved one's hair; writing from another's hand' (p. 99).

Like Jane Watts in her consciousness of life's reversals and the effects of time, Lambert frequently digresses to reflect on the contrast between then and now. 'Where are those many dancers?' she asks herself after describing the bush dances of her youth, 'Strange to say, though the oldest amongst us was under thirty, not half a dozen are living; most of them died in the prime of life' (pp. 66–7). Similarly, her memories of happy social occasions are sharpened by other memories of loneliness, the result of her 'wandering' life as a governess. If entering a new family is a lonely experience, leaving a congenial one can be as heart-rending: 'I felt more lonely than ever, after being nearly a year with such a family, the mother like an elder sister, the children so companionable' (p. 87).

Darkening the tone of this text is a half-submerged personal sadness, which seems to focus on the narrator's immediate family. Identifying with the loneliness of her mother who never became reconciled to 1840s Sydney and who suffered other nameless griefs[18], the narrator hints at troubles in the family home: 'Circumstances at this period made me decide upon leaving home' (p. 35) and 'leaving home was entirely my own act, as my mother felt I was too young for such responsibility'; characteristically 'leaving home' is less dramatic than it appears and the narrator is careful to emphasize her continued care for her mother. Afterwards the mother 'acknowledged the wisdom of the step, as it took me away from cares that might have crushed my spirit' (p. 38). As with other autobiographies, the silences speak volumes.

Place is also strongly integrated with self in an unpublished autobiography dealing with life at Port Fairy from the late 1840s. The 'Memoirs of Margaret Emily Brown (Youngman). A Recording of 58 Years of Life Mainly in Port Fairy' was written in 1907.[19] Born at Leamington, England, the narrator emigrated with her mother to Australia in 1848, her father having arrived a year earlier. A curious narrative, which combines passages of precise, concentrated prose with some slack writing, it sometimes reveals surprising depths.

For this narrator, the relationship with the mother is of the first importance; identifying strongly with her mother's early loneliness as an orphan, which was compounded by her experience as an emigrant in 1840s Port Fairy, the narrator feels convinced that she is her mother's favourite child; 'the first thing that I ever had of my own', in the mother's words. Several passages meanwhile dwell on the mother's noble qualities. Faced with the father's failure as proprietor of a newspaper, the mother becomes involved in a struggle to keep the family solvent, a struggle which the daughter shares; both of them are described as doing work only fit for men and of toiling to produce every necessity of life: 'Our food was poor and coarse, so little could be had, for months no butter, never any fruit, a hard and toilsome road was ours' (p. 32). When the father finally faces ruin, the mother makes sure that all debts are paid—'at what cost to her, she and I alone could have told' (p. 38). Other women are also perceived as facing lives of hardship and there are expressions of sympathy for their unrecognized and unrecorded efforts, as there are for the Port Fairy tribe of Aborigines, doomed to rapid extinction. Meanwhile, merging with this sad story are extensive, vivid descriptions of Port Fairy during the author's childhood:

We found great orchises there, deep crimson some and some green with red lines, while the little lilac ones were in myriads. Great white daisies also and little dainty lilac ones, tiny wild violets like pansies, blue flax, pink and purple vetches, splendid buttercups, bindweed, flat golden flowers set in the midst of silvery leaves and a lovely marsh violet springing from a clump of bronze arrow pointed leaves, the same plant bearing on long graceful stems large blossoms, some dark, others light, a most lovely flower. (pp. 30–31)

This is a 'playground' which the children exclusively own ('I never remember seeing a single person even passing in those days'). It is also a place of disinheritance and forgetfulness; the numerous Aboriginal middens, 'relics of a vanished race', have disappeared for ever and the numerous wrecks, once remembered by the 'old sailors of early years' are now completely forgotten. The personal past too is threatened by the erosions of time and the frailty of memory, and in an extensive, emotionally heightened passage the narrator asserts her power to recall her 'ain countree' of childhood. The comparison is not explicit, but the links between the shifting sands of Port Fairy and those of time and memory are obvious. In a highly coloured passage, however, the narrator celebrates those features of place which have survived time (the flagstaff, the 'cruel reef', the 'broad flower grown paddocks'), just as she celebrates her own power to remember; and in the latter instance she values the honing power of bitter memories as much as the pleasures of the sweet ('I love them too, Lord keep my memory green!' p. 42). Thus for this narrator, who is preoccupied with thoughts of disinheritance, place, memory and identity are perceived as interdependent possessions. Uneven or unfinished as this narrative is, it has some deep reaches.

Another interesting unpublished autobiography, written at a much later date but not strikingly more frank than the previously discussed colonial narratives, is Kate Rodd's 'Lisdillon: The Story of John

Mitchell MHA, JP 1812–1880 & his Family'.[20] Born in 1896, Kate
Rodd was the granddaughter of John Mitchell who emigrated to
Tasmania in 1837. A member of the first Tasmanian House of
Assembly, Mitchell was better known as the founder of a model
community at Lisdillon. Encouraging young couples from his native
Cornwall to emigrate under the current government scheme, he
developed a self-supporting community at this idyllic spot on the
Derwent River. Provided with a post office and a church, the settlement 'became a reproduction of the English self-supporting farm of
the last century' (p. 3), including buildings for smoking and salting
meat and fish, a coach house, stables, blacksmith's shop and walled
gardens. By the time of the narrator's childhood, however, the
settlement was already in a state of advanced decay. Kate Rodd's
maternal family also had the same talent for productive order, and
memories of her grandmother's ménage are a small raft of stability in
this account of disorder and neglect. After describing her grandmother's house in detail, the narrator concludes: 'The garden, the
freedom, and yet the firm authority, I fully appreciated . . . to me
here was kindness and stability, and Grandmother was a wonderful
old lady' (p. 9).

But it is Lisdillon that tantalizes the imagination; 'To me, a child of
nine, it was all so quiet and neglected—I was not afraid, but puzzled
by it all' (p. 24). Combining exceptional natural beauty, traces of a
history of communal activity and family associations, the decaying
Lisdillon represents frustrated potential and neglect. The reasons for
the settlement's decay are never probed but are as much a 'puzzle' or
a 'sad muddle' as the author's own early experiences. For the
narrator shares this sense of neglect and undeveloped potential.
After her father dies when she is twelve months old, the family of
mother and five children move to Hobart, where they seem to live in
a haphazard way; absorbed in her own activities, the mother appears
to leave them to the care of servants. For a while a formidable
woman, who is sexually attracted to the mother, dominates and even
exploits the small household, but she is superseded before long by an
even more forceful man. The impressions of neglect in this section of
the narrative are rarely explicit, emerging more in the descriptions
of the children's meagre school lunches or of a visit from the
grandmother, who is appalled by their unkempt condition. This
narrative is remarkable for an impressionistic, artless style which
recreates the child's vulnerable openness; superficially episodic, it
allows events and people to impinge on the narrator's consciousness
with little retrospective explanation or even anticipation.

If the family as a whole is neglected, this particular child is almost
totally ignored. Suffering from dyslexia, she is unable to read and as
the youngest in a group of talented, active siblings, she appears to be
thrust to the margins of the family's life. A few key incidents, such

as accompanying her brother on an afternoon's expedition into the countryside or listening to stories told by a servant during an illness, are oases in a desert of loneliness. Time and again she laments that no one would help her to read. In love with stories, she is cut off from books; sensitive to the power of music, she cannot sing in tune. Meanwhile, as absorptive observer, she records the declining destinies of both her immediate family and Lisdillon. The malign influence in both is the man who has formed a relationship with her mother; appointed as manager of Lisdillon, he introduces new methods which mean dismissing the last tenants of her grandfather's cottages. One incident in particular illuminates the link between place and self. Accompanying her mother and the manager on one errand of dismissal, she is inadvertently bitten badly by a horse, and then comforted by the grandmother of the cottage household, who reminds her that both her father and grandfather were good men who would never have evicted their tenants. Riding home she is conscious of both her painful arm and a 'feeling of great sadness that these people, who had known the father I never knew, were all gone' (p. 21).

The manager's impact on the other members of the family is also destructive. Refusing to marry the mother, literally on the steps of the church, he pursues the narrator's older sister, intervening in this girl's other relationships with lifetime effects. So strong, in fact, is the narrator's hatred of him that on one occasion she even contemplates shooting him. Eventually Lisdillon has to be sold and the final scenes of packing up are among the most grief-stricken of the narrative. Describing the sale as a 'tragedy', she feels most sympathy for her brother Tom, the rightful heir of Lisdillon but now assigned to dumping the more 'hopeless' relics of family life in the river.

The final abandonment of Lisdillon, however, has been preceded by a specific personal abandonment that crystallizes the narrator's sense of her own predicament. Usually described as ignoring or barely tolerating the child, the mother on one occasion is more actively wounding when she cruelly rebuffs her daughter's expressions of love: 'I love somebody much more than I love you, and someday you will love somebody much more than you could love me' (p. 17). Severely distressed, the child takes refuge in her hideaway in the garden until her sorrow is eased by a natural incident which has the role of a personal epiphany and which occurs more than once: 'A lark flew up, up, until I could not see it, singing all the time—it was beautiful, and the sky and the colour of everything was beautiful' (p. 17). The personal metaphoric force of the bird's empyrean freedom and self-expression are obvious. Given her early disappointments, it is reassuring to discover that in young adulthood she experienced a measure of this self-expression. Reminiscent of Albert Facey's *A Fortunate Life* in its artlessly limpid form and stoic philosophy, this narrative also illustrates the inevitable shaping that is involved in writing the self.

'Children's' Texts

Without doubt some women's life-writing in the nineteenth century was deflected into adult fiction; both Catherine Spence's *Clara Morison* (1854) and Catherine Martin's *An Australian Girl* (1890) show traces of autobiographical content, while Marion Knowles's *Barbara Halliday* (1896) draws strongly on the author's Gippsland childhood. But such texts as these are deflected from concentration on the self either by the demands of a particular audience or by an objective didactic impulse which shapes the material in a certain direction. Catherine Martin has certain religious irons in the fire and Marion Knowles is committed to notions of female purity which slant her presentation of a bush childhood in a propagandist direction. Thus the self becomes less a subject for exploration and more a sounding board for ideas. Adult fiction of the nineteenth century was also burdened with the conventions of a love plot; however close to the writer's self, the heroine must be taken through the vicissitudes of courtship and disappointed love to the proper culmination of her brief autonomous career, the wedding ceremony. Yet one of the extraordinary features of women's autobiographical writing is its neglect of this theme; finding a mate is far more often an incidental event than a central one. It is true that the question of love is central to some significant texts, such as Christina Stead's *For Love Alone* and Eve Langley's *The Pea Pickers*, but it is the unconventionality or subversiveness of these authors' approaches that is striking. Yet another handicap facing the colonial female novel in terms of audience appeal was that it had to please both the British and Australian publics. The female terrain of domestic realism was already well served by British writers while the terrain of bush romance was firmly occupied by men. One of the advantages of the pioneering memoir was that it fell into both camps.

Children's fiction provided room for more spontaneous treatment of the young self, but was beset by even more stringent limitations. Apart from the obvious restrictions of writing for an immature audience, the genre has objective implications which make it unsuitable as autobiography. Thus Ethel Turner's *Three Little Maids* (1900), which is the most autobiographical of her output, is committed to a well-rounded story which allows only intermittent glimpses of the past self's inner experience, and Ellen Campbell's *Twin Pickles* (1898), a fictional reworking of her *An Australian Childhood* (1892)[21] focuses as much on her brother's experiences as her own. As children's fiction, *Twin Pickles* is a more shaped work and obviously more successful than its predecessor; as autobiography, *An Australian Childhood* is a more interesting and open text.

An Australian Childhood is in fact one of a thinly mined vein that produced some delightful writing. Not exactly children's literature, these books are written in the form of a talk to children or grandchildren but have a distinct adult appeal. They are predated by the quaint narrative, apparently by Charlotte Barton, *A Mother's Offering to her Children* (1841). The invisible author of this text, distinguished by not so much as a pseudonym, has been severally identified, although the latest findings have established that Barton is responsible. Autobiographical only in the addiction to truthful personal observation, this narrative is too self-consciously bent on instruction to allow scope for the individual self. Nevertheless it shares several features with later autobiographies: a sense of wonder at the strange and hazardous bush, detailed knowledge of the natural environment, respect for the pioneering achievement, pride in the role of women, and a keen awareness of the brevity of 'life's uncertain space'.

The most striking of this group are *An Australian Childhood* and Mrs F. Hughes's *My Childhood in Australia* (1890?).[22] One of the attractions of the Campbell and Hughes texts is that neither attempts to instruct. The main impulse is to recreate the spontaneous and exotic world of the child. Written for the author's English grandchildren, Ellen Campbell's *An Australian Childhood* returns to her childhood home of the 1850s, a station in outback New South Wales which, as in numerous other bush childhoods, is perceived as a sheltered and isolated Eden. The impulse to recreate a unique time and place, irretrievably changed in the author's lifetime, is a common characteristic of nineteenth-century autobiography and is perpetuated in the next century's interest in the isolated, self-contained location.

One of the incidental delights of this narrative is the impression of the child's closeness to nature, whether she is disputing the honey of the bignonia with the bees 'that could walk right down the deep throat of the flowers', or conserving a stick of tobacco from an intelligent but villainous-looking magpie, or acting as ineffective parent to some mischievous possums. A remarkably resourceful, confident child, she lives in a challenging world which has few gendered restrictions; it is also a highly comic world, which becomes more comic in retrospect. If the child is equipped with a resilient sense of humour, the older narrator enjoys puncturing some of the pretensions of the younger self. Comedy is a well-mined shaft in Australian female autobiography, and it is satisfying to find it worked so early. This child, for instance, will have no truck with the moralisms of conventional children's fiction; if a dunking ensues as a result of her attempt to appropriate eggs or young birds:

The water was not very deep, and a fall, unlike the fate of naughty children in the story-books, never ended with repentance or an untimely grave, but with a wetting of frocks and stockings, and a firm determination to try again on the first convenient opportunity. (p. 10)

Both older and younger selves have a keen sense of the dramatic: the younger self derives enormous enjoyment from the central role in the misadventures she generates; the older self recaptures that enjoyment by means of dramatic interchanges and finely paced narration.

Three or four simple stories form the bones of the narrative and in all of them the narrator is either an instigator or firmly in the foreground. One concerns her purchase of *Martin Chuzzlewit* from a passing pedlar. Dickens is immensely popular with the family but money is a scarce commodity for both mother and child and the price of fifteen shillings is initially impossible. The book meanwhile has potently inserted itself into her destiny:

There, in a neat dark-green binding with gilt lettering, lay a copy of the very book I so wished to possess. I took it up and fingered it longingly. I tried to peep into the contents, but the uncut pages baffled me. (p. 15)

When the book is replaced on the pedlar's cart she is in 'despair' but quickly consoles herself with plans for earning money and with picturing self-congratulatory scenes in which she gives the book to her mother on her birthday. As the most obvious childish means of acquiring funds (such as reciting 'John Gilpin' straight through to her father) are soon exhausted, she is delighted to stumble on the unexpected resource of gathering leeches for the local doctor. Acquiring leeches is literally an exercise in self-sacrifice as she submits her leg to the creatures' attentions. Self-consciously aware of her affinity with the Spartan boy who did his lessons with a fox gnawing at his vitals, she endures the torture for another hour. 'Sport was good' and she acquires about twenty of the creatures. That night, however, there is more trouble, as her existing leeches escape from the bedroom cupboard and attack her sisters in a scene whose comic potential is fully exploited. About twelve of the precious creatures are swept up and disposed of by her father; half-angry and half-amused, he quickly uncovers the culprit, who is left to reflect on the unhappy twists of fate. Next day, however, she comes across a potential tool in her schemes, the mentally retarded son of one of the working men. With the charm that she later works successfully on the Aborigines, the cook and even her 'passionate' uncle, she persuades the boy to catch the leeches for her, which he does by using a horse as bait. Eventually the pile of shillings is complete ('Shall I ever forget the huge satisfaction' p. 46) and her plans come to fulfilment, all except the 'pretty speech', which is forgotten at the critical moment.

Another account of her purchase of some possums from an

Aborigine in exchange for a stick of tobacco which she wheedles from the station-manager ('I went closer up to his broad shoulder and slipped my hand round his neck. He softened at once.' p. 51), has the same elements of confident adventure and comic mishap. Obedience only becomes real in the case of certain serious cautions from the mother; otherwise adult prohibitions exist to be defied. Forbidden to frequent the Aborigines' camp, she makes sure her visits are surreptitious; aware of her governess's sensitive nose for mischief, she takes care to hide her tobacco in the barn. If nemesis descends, childhood's emotions fortunately are elastic, and even a terrifying interview with the uncle whose bald pate has been scarred by her possums, recedes after 'a good meal from the friendly hands of the cook'. By the end of the evening, 'I could look without a shudder on Jock's handiwork as it stood out in deep red seams on my uncle's head' (p. 71).

The world of *An Australian Childhood* is undoubtedly a male-dominated one; men have total command of existing resources and their word, theoretically, is law. They are also effectively served by their juniors, the male cousins or the brother who give the narrator scant sympathy in her self-imposed sufferings. They are perceived as benign deities, nevertheless, and if they cannot be opposed, they can be circumvented; intelligent resource, feminine charm and patience are potent weapons, and the narrator has her share of power in an environment which is generally enabling. Like the lively possums or the confident magpie, she is endowed with a sturdy adventurous sense of self. Not all adventures are equally harmless, however, and as a counter to her early optimism the author includes an account of an adopted Aboriginal boy who becomes devoted to her brother and dies when he catches measles from him. *Twin Pickles* ends on a similar note of sadness, recording the distance which developed in the previously close brother/sister relationship after the former went to school.

Similarly confident and exuberant is Mrs F. Hughes's *My Child-hood in Australia. A Story for My Children* (1890?). This 1850s childhood was spent in a remote part of South Australia on the banks of the Murray and is crammed with extraordinary incidents. Living in close quarters with the Aborigines, the children imitate their activities, crafts and eating habits, hatching tortoises, plundering birds' nests or paddling in their canoes down the Murray. Retrospectively impressed by her range of activities, the narrator gives a vivid picture of her past tomboy self. As eldest child and therefore 'chief climber', since the younger children are not able to fight against the hawks and eagles, she suffers numerous falls:

Of course the top branches would not bear my weight, but I ventured, and was frequently picked up stunned and stupefied by falls. When I fell clear,

I generally came down a good 'whop', I can tell you; but more often I got hung up by my skirts, and dangled in the air till I righted myself, or something gave way or someone unhooked me. A travelling missionary did so one day as he was passing, and I remember he laughed a good deal. What holes I made in my clothes! I often came home with slits all over them, and with only the crown of my hat, having left the rim up in a tree. (pp. 84–5)

Her freedom from the restrictions of gender, meanwhile, is indirectly apparent in her prominent role in combating the various hazards such as bushfire, her familiarity with fire-arms and her family name, 'Jack'. Men are not so omnipotent in this less structured, challenging environment, and the mother's efforts are presented as even more crucial to the family's survival than the father's.

Quite apart from its interest as autobiography, this narrative deserves to be better known as illustrating the exotic experience of some bush children. What novelist, for example, would dare to include an incident where a child becomes literally stuck by the mouth to a wattle-gum for an hour, to be threatened by first one wild bull and then a herd of cattle and saved only by the courage of the unarmed mother? As dramatic and expressive as Campbell's, this text is also more adult and inward. One extensive section, for instance, is devoted to the author's 'midnight adventures', when she leaves her bed to experience the landscape's different moods. Introduced by a particularly vivid description of corroborees, it celebrates her sense of dreaming oneness with nature. These experiences are private and secret and take place in her favourite place under a great she-oak; they can also be dramatic and anticipate the metaphysical experiences which occasionally occur in later autobiographies:

I have been there, too, when there was no moon and no stars, when the night was black, so dark and so black that I could only grope my way there, and have stood trembling, listening to nothing. That was the awful part of it—nothing, nothing to see, nothing to hear but my own heart beating and my own breath coming quicker and quicker . . . (p. 25)

An unpublished narrative in the same genre is Jane Caverhill's 'Reminiscences 1840s–1850s'.[23] Dated 1881, this autobiography is also addressed to the author's children, although these children are clearly adults and the narrative is intended to provide them with the same delight that the narrator would have enjoyed had her own mother seen fit to record her story. The author also has her grandchildren in mind, cautioning them to show kindness to a woman who had earlier helped the family and comparing their clothes and activities to hers as a child. More poignant than the published narratives, this account dwells on the family's hardships as they undertake and fail at various projects, dairy-farming at Colac or inn-keeping at Geelong; on the death of siblings; and on the sufferings of the much-loved mother. This narrator also shares with other writers a great indifference to clergymen. Recalling the weariness of their summer journeys to church to listen to a dull sermon, she crystallizes her resentment of the clerical breed in the memory of a mishap to a much prized ornament; it is another of those trivial but symbolic incidents which are so characteristic of these life-writings:

To my great sorrow one day he lifted from the mantelpiece a brilliant blown glass bird of mine and it fell off its stand and broke. Great was my grief and also my anger when he put 2/- in my hand thinking money would compensate for the loss of my precious bird. (p. 20)

Although these are the texts which are the most obviously directed towards children, numerous other accounts are written with the author's children in mind; thus Annabella Boswell writes to inform her children of the land of their birth, Mary Stawell's *My Recollections* (1911) is written in response to frequent requests from her daughter, and Jane Watts has the younger members of the Giles family firmly in mind. But the recreation of childhood is not the primary aim of these writers, whereas Hughes and Campbell and, to a lesser extent, Caverhill are self-consciously interested in re-appropriating an extraordinary, primal state of being. Given the spontaneity of this form of discourse, it is unfortunate that it has not been more extensively employed.

Collaborative Texts

Closely related to the autobiography written for children is the collaborative text, written to a greater or lesser degree in the form of dialogue between women. The relationship is usually that of mother and daughter as in *A Bunyip Close Behind Me* (1972) and *Ladies Didn't* (1984) by Eugénie McNeil and Eugénie Crawford or Meg Steward's *Autobiography of My Mother* (1985), but it may be a relationship between great-aunt and niece as in Elaine McKenna's collaboration with Mary Brennan in *Better Than Dancing* (1987), or between friends, as in the 1970s text *Puberty Blues*. Numerous autobiographies have been published, edited or translated by daughters or other female relations who may well have played a collaborative role, but in the absence of clear evidence they must be regarded as one-author texts. Numerous others are written in the informal style of conversation and give the impression of retelling an oft-told tale.

The collaborative text appears to be the most prominent outcrop of an oral tradition of women's autobiography, which it is impossible to overestimate. Time and again women's stories imply a female listening audience; intimate, informal and frankly domestic, they insinuate solidarity of feeling, interests and attitude, if not experience. To dismiss them as 'gossipy' is to miss the point; in the words of Jean

Bedford in a recent collaboration, an anthology of short stories, women are constantly 'colouring in' their lives.[24]

If autobiographies are any evidence, women also 'colour in' the past in the same collaborative way. The stories of maternal and paternal grandparents and great grandparents, handed down from mother to daughter, which open the majority of autobiographies are obviously satisfying expressions of continuity; they also often provide the grounds for personal myth. These accounts of the author's for-bears are frequently inseparable from family legend and have the effect of humanizing the past for both speaker and listener. Mythic in the cultural sense, they may also be mythic in a literal one. Their truth or falsity hardly matters, however, since they might as well be true, so central are they to the collaborative recreation of the past. Annabella Boswell's great grandmother is not just Mrs Campbell, wife of the commandant of Fort William, she is the young wife who is almost as fond of her doll as of her baby, once dropping the former out of the bedroom window to the consternation of her husband, and Nancy Phelan's childhood is already peopled by her legendary writing aunts long before they return from Europe, so powerful are her mother's stories of the Macks. Many narrators record their depen-dence on this mythical past in creating their own personal myth; thus, Maie Casey carefully circumnavigates the question of her own identity via the very different histories of her paternal and maternai families, and Nancy Adams intertwines her own history with memories and acquired knowledge of her grandfather. Conversely, several autobiographies, such as Sally Morgan's *My Place* (1987) and Ivy Arney's *Twenties Child* (1987), record the acute sense of loss when the family past is somehow jettisoned.

Paul Eakin in his study of autobiography has suggested that the autobiographical act is 'a mode of self-invention that is always practised first in living and only eventually—sometimes—formalized in writing'.[25] Narrative or storytelling plays a major role in every life for, as Barbara Hardy puts it: 'we dream in narrative, daydream in narrative, remember, anticipate, hope, . . . hate, and love by narra-tive. In order really to live, we make up stories about ourselves'.[26] Women in particular appear to have extended this inalienable human habit to the traditional collaborative ritual of telling stories of self and family, so that it is not surprising to find 'telling' a more ubiquitous term in their autobiographies than 'writing'. Even an account of a public career may take this form of 'telling', so that Nellie Stewart's reminiscences are explicitly presented as a tale:

So I offer you myself pretty much as I am. I shall talk of things as they come to me. It will probably be found that in the telling of the tale I often drop into a style casual and informal, even a bit disorderly. I want it to be a quiet talk at evening. I don't want to bore or weary you with any trivialities. I want to recall the most vivid impressions of my life, the things that have meant most to me, the things most productive of happiness and content, and the things laden with pain only as they are essential to the honest story. (*My Life's Story*, p. 2)

It is also, above all, a tale for women:

It is a great joy and consolation to me to feel that the people I have given so much of my life to entertain and amuse and enliven still think so sweetly of me. It is the greater joy to me because so many of them have been women . . . Times beyond count I have been helped over rough places by the unobtrusive sympathy of women. (p. 3)

Eakin has also suggested, drawing on Derrida, that 'psychologically speaking, reflexive consciousness—the self's sense of itself as a self—is liveliest and most immediate in the moment of speech'[27]; this may perhaps account for the fact that the narrative voice of so many women's autobiographies is primarily a speaking voice. In the collaborative text 'speaking' modulates into 'talking' with its implication of 'listening'.

Of the collaborative texts which concentrate on childhood experience of the previous century, *A Bunyip Close Behind Me* and *Ladies Didn't* are the most interesting. Often described as 'charming period pieces', these are significant comic texts in the history of Australian women's autobiography. A recent collaboration which has benefited from the women's movement in that its cynical tone and values would not have been much appreciated before 1970, is Mary Brennan's *Better Than Dancing* (1987).[28] Born in 1889 into a mainly Irish farming family in a remote part of Gippsland, Brennan moved with her family to the Wimmera when she was five and later worked in Western Australia. She was a munitions worker in London during the First World War, an event she remembers with great bitterness. Narrated in Brennan's words in the form of informal conversation, the account is a sequence of loosely chronological memories each headed by a quintessential pronouncement: 'I disliked Grandfather right from the start', 'All that time there was trouble', 'Mother was young and skittish' or 'Cot Lot'. Conscious of her implicit younger audience, the narrator frequently inserts explanatory asides ('You weren't allowed to air your opinion in those days' p. 60) or retrospective opinions ('Everything was wonderful with the British in those days. In the time of Queen Victoria they ruled the seas. But, they were false friends as it turned out' p. 13).

To relate this extraordinary account of hardship, isolation and emotional neglect, the narrator resorts to an idiom that is effectively salty but off-hand. Like her conclusion—'As long you don't expect much it's okay. I didn't expect much and didn't get it. Lots of hard work keeps you from feeling sorry for yourself' (p. 229)—it amounts to a verbal shrug of the shoulders, a surface display of cynicism that barely conceals the awareness of an exceptionally harsh lot. Not without humour, the comic moments are nevertheless more dour than light-hearted: 'in our family there was no in-between drinking—it seemed to be all, or none at all, right down the line' (p. 106) or, reflecting on a lover who was too keen on gambling: 'Someone said to me, "It could be he'd like drink; or he'd like horses; or he'd like other women." Not much of a choice is it?' (p. 221).

In common with other writers, Brennan is conscious of the family's past, in this case an Irish past of poverty and even famine, illness, early death and emotional separation; in a more muted form the same patterns repeat themselves in her life, for the abrupt, laconic narration is a catalogue of deprivations, cruelties and accidents, in which the narrator's personal hardship is merely a casual incident. If Brennan herself as a child is forced into a round of toil that would have daunted an adult, one of her sisters suffers a worse fate when she is 'given' to the grandparents and one of her aunts is allotted the role of lifetime drudge according to the unfair practice of families in those days ('One would get educated and another would stay at home' p. 50). Nor are men immune: two of the most striking incidents are her recollection of a wounded young man ('It stuck in my mind, seeing him there, with the blood running down his face, down his shirt and everywhere. He'd broken his teeth and his jaw' p. 17) and of her father's stoic response to an accident with a chaff cutter in which his hand was 'sliced'.

Emerging from the interstices of this account is a resentful anger, notwithstanding the display of fatalism. It is implicit in the negatives, in the criticism of the absence of help with homework, of the unstated sexism that freed boys from household drudgery while also consigning girls to outside chores and the perverse assumption that daughters are born to help shoulder the mother's burden. Anger, for instance, fuels the account of her mother's action when she catches fire; 'Mother flung the baby from her knee and beat out the flames. I s'pose she didn't want her little helper burnt' (p. 35). And an imperfectly displaced grief underlies the account of the family's emotional life: 'We were brought up without a scrap of love shown to us—not a bit—but it didn't affect us because we had each other' (p. 40).

Countering this, however, are frequent expressions of pride at her capacity and resilience, her farming skills and precocious knowledge of child care. Looking back at her past self the narrator is amazed at her endurance, resource and acceptance ('I must have been pretty tired, but I never fretted or dreamt of working less' p. 85). Oscillating between pride in her past self and grief at her waste, she opts for a wry ambivalence. Thus, reflecting on her years on her uncle's farm which were highlighted only by her love for a splendid horse, she characteristically undercuts her own affirmations: 'That was the toughest job I ever had, but I didn't mind. Those two years gave me self-confidence, and a feeling that I could paddle my own canoe. But when I think back to that time, the only thing I regret is the horse' (p. 93).

Memoirs of Family

'Telling' and 'colouring in' are also characteristic of the memoir of family. The earliest of these, Mary Stawell's *My Recollections* (1911)[29], dealing mainly with Melbourne of the 1840s and 1850s, and Agnes Gosse Hay's *After-Glow Memories* (1905), set mainly in Adelaide from 1850 to 1870, are really accounts of the establishment of influential families. Both are written for children and grand-children but with different effects. Agnes Gosse Hay's narrative is the more remarkable as autobiography and is considered in Chapter 5. A later narrative in the same tradition, Maie Casey's *An Australian Story* (1962), is discussed in Chapter 3.

Family piety is the outstanding characteristic of Mary Stawell's autobiography, which is partly a collage of family letters, the reminiscences of others, obituaries and tributes. The daughter of William Greene, a retired naval officer, the narrator emigrated in 1842 with her parents and six brothers to Victoria, where they settled at a beautiful property fourteen miles (twenty-two kilometres) from Melbourne. Since the Greene family was friendly with the Brownes, the Macartneys and the Chomleys, this memoir throws an interesting light on colonial life in Melbourne, which expands into the public arena following the narrator's marriage in 1856 to William Foster Stawell, the first Attorney General of Victoria. Reserving the more stirring accounts of bushranging and hunting for male contributors, Stawell confines herself to the personal: a meeting with Burke, the impact of the gold rush on their eccentric butler, or memories of parties. *My Recollections* is also a tribute to the two most important people in her life, her mother who emerges as a woman of personality and spirit and her husband. Unpretentious and expressive as this narrative is, it is too cluttered by memorabilia to be a personally probing account.

A more inward narrative is the later *Family Fresco* (1966)[30] by Nancy Adams. Born in 1890 into an influential Melbourne family of Scots origin, the author was the daughter of Sir Edward Mitchell and the granddaughter of Dr Alexander Morrison. Interesting for its reflection of the structured, English life-style of Melbourne's wealthy class of the period, this autobiography is also a reflection on time. For this family and for the narrator growing up, the present had a stability that was consciously founded on pride in family and pride in Empire. Structured by seemingly irreversible social rituals and unspoken but unbreakable codes, it was a society in which roles and gender expectations were clear cut. Adams effectively represents the extent to which the minutiae of life, from food to furniture, were governed by social class and convention. Claustrophobic as such rigid conformity undoubtedly was, it had a solidity that the narrator values. For the child and girl it was a small but interesting and even challenging world within its well-defined limits and if, at twenty, she was still arguing with her mother about whether or not she should read the news-papers, she grew up within a society which was totally convinced of the rightness of its ends and which valued certain ideals whose passing is perceived as an impoverishment.

Gifted with detailed recall, Adams recreates the firm patterns of her childhood—the regular hierarchy of events on Sundays, the simple routines of nursery and schoolroom which are dominated by the much loved Nanny. At this stage of her life the mother is a distant figure involved in dimly perceived social activities; the father is al-most totally absent and it is the grandfather, in whose residence at Scotch College they are living, who holds the foreground. An in-fluential man and the centre of a wide circle, he delights the children with the sense of a vicarious social life. A description of Scotch College of the period expresses the solidity, conviction and distinctive excess of this world. It is not so much a materialistic excess as an excess of pride:

One either side of the hall lay the drawing-room and the dining-room and, beyond the former, the staircase at whose turn was a monstrous, stained glass window greatly admired by myself as was the stuffed pheasant which stood on a table in an alcove beneath the stairs. The furniture was all solid, cedar or mahogany, the chimney-pieces were black marble, the carpets were Persian or Axminster of the best quality and the wall-papers were dark—either chocolate or maroon. (p. 43)

Looking back, this confident solidity intrigues the narrator, for her central preoccupation is the decay of the old way of life and the paradoxical frail stability of the past. 'What have the Mitchells *done*', she asks herself at one point, 'that the houses which they owned and the gardens which they planted and cherished so should be des-troyed?' (p. 71). Later, when she is researching the earlier history of her family, *Saxon Sheep*, she becomes acutely aware of the past pressing on the present: she is conscious of living 'a queer double sort of existence' as the characters of the past become more alive to her than her contemporaries (p. 179). As the narrative records the gradual narrowing of her life and the deaths of those deities who once filled it, it is impossible to avoid the impression that for this narrator the past is more vigorous and vivid than the present. Yet within her own youth, the present has cancelled out the past and now even goes so far as to ignore it. Thus time is experienced as an oxymoronic phenomenon; it is a dislocated continuum in which she struggles, somewhat despairingly, to maintain her identity.

One aspect of the past which appears to obsess the narrator is dress. Descriptions of clothes proliferate in the text. She has 'only to close [her] eyes' and she can recall her mother's gowns:

She had a pink brocade evening dress as stiff as a board and another of gold brocade, the bodices of which were boned, and a lilac spotted voile with a cerise sash ... But the dress I remember best was the one she wore to the reception at Government House for the Duke and Duchess of York. Of white satin, the chiffon bodice had three narrow black bands—the Court was still in half mourning for Queen Victoria. In her hair she wore the diamond ornament which I have now and, round her neck, the diamond pendant which had belonged to her mother. (p. 58)

The same delight in style flavours her memories of pre-war London, the women 'superbly gowned', the 'slim-waisted officers in sky blue tunics riding sleek, magnificent horses', 'children in charge of English nurses in bonnets or *nous-nous*'. The emotional partiality of such memories is underlined by the fact that the sun always shines in them and the chestnut trees are always in leaf ('I don't remember one wet day' p. 81).

Somewhat embarrassed by this obsession, the narrator at one point seeks to excuse it, tracing it to the ambivalent teaching of her childhood, which simultaneously stressed the importance of looks in winning the social success which was essential for women of her class and the sin of vanity. Looks, however, as the child shrewdly observes, are the *sine qua non* of social existence; without them she is a 'plain girl' of interest to no one; with them she is instantly prominent, interesting to the 'older women and, I suppose, ... the men' (p. 87). Half-convinced of the impractical absurdity of pre-war dress, the narrator is drawn to it as symbolizing the ordered stability and confident style of that era. 'I *love* glitter—the sound of the word and all that it connotes' (p. 153), she confides at one point. And, as a 'perfectionist', reflecting on the arrogance of the pre-war English, 'I felt that if they were arrogant—as some were—they had cause for arrogance' (p. 109). Like the child-self who stares fascinatedly at the lady who cannot remove her hat because she would also remove her hair, she is intrigued by the serious nonsense of the past's concern with externals.

Two events disturb the girl's early impression of permanence, the death of her grandfather and the First World War. The first anticipates the second. The death of her grandfather, who represents the best of the old Scots/Australian way of life, also involves the loss of the homes of childhood and is perceived as a crucial emotional event: 'Such a loss ... was bound to leave its marks ... it formed a bar between myself and our contemporaries'. From that moment she is aware of the 'value of gaiety in order to hide one's feelings' (p. 65). Genuine light-heartedness, on the other hand, is a rare experience: dancing as a child for her grandfather, at her coming out ball in

Melbourne which is akin to a successful graduation, party-going in the few years of frivolity before 1914. 'Now looking back, I am thankful that we *were* frivolous . . . most of the young men with whom we danced had only a few years to live: they died on Gallipoli or in Flanders and their names are forgotten while the girls whom they might have married have not fulfilled their vocation' (p. 94).

Suggestive though this autobiography is, many of the narrator's assumptions are prodded rather than probed with the result that a defensive tone frequently creeps into the narrative; only rarely is the younger self presented with any irony while she is infrequently released from the sad retrospective dimension of the older 'I'. Sometimes on the edge of discovery, the narrator never makes the final leap and the experience of dislocated time is presented rather than analysed. From a feminist viewpoint the text is pregnant with omissions which are as interesting as the inclusions.

3

Four Significant Figures

One of the finest of women's pioneering memoirs is Jane Isabella Watts's *Memories of Early Days in South Australia*[1], issued anonymously 'for private circulation only' in 1882, and in 1890 with the title *Family Life in South Australia Fifty-Three Years Ago.*[2] Both publications are prefaced with a note enjoining the author's relatives not to allow the book to go out of their possession or to allow strangers to read it during her lifetime.

The daughter of William Giles, manager of the South Australian Company's station at Kingscote on Kangaroo Island, and his first wife, Sarah, Jane accompanied her family of six brothers, two step-brothers and two sisters when they emigrated from England in 1837. She was then thirteen. This account of her family, which extends from their experiences on board ship to her father's death and her own widowhood, is a remarkable example of fluent, elegant prose. More Augustan than Victorian in terms of balance and tone, it is a fine example of colonial non-fiction and deserves to be much better known. It is also singularly appropriate that this, one of the earliest, should rehearse so many of the themes, approaches and even characteristic incidents of Australian female autobiographies of childhood. Even its mode of inception and production are representative. Like many other narratives, *Family Life in South Australia* originated as a life-saving device. Towards the end of 'the most calamitous year of her life, when unable any longer to bear the weight of a great and bitter sorrow' (of her husband's insanity and death) the idea occurred to the writer of 'endeavouring to banish the miserable present from her mind by driving back her thoughts to the happier past' (p. 214). And like many other life-histories, the book was also partly collaborative, sustained in an earlier sketchy form by the research of the writer's husband, but ultimately dependent on the encouragement of her sister who gave her 'strength and courage to persevere'. This semi-collaborative aspect is also manifest in the impression in the early pages of a speaking voice, recounting a well-known family legend, seasoned with familiar jokes, incidents and 'characters'. To some extent the narrator sees herself as a preserver of myth, articulating a favourite story known previously only in an oral way. As the narrative proceeds, it becomes more individual in tone and scope but even though the distinctive and attractive individuality of Jane Watts pervades the book, at no time does she present her self as separate from her family, as her second title indicates. Nor does she give space to nationalistic or imperial sentiments; regarding her father's decision to emigrate as a practical one, given his large family (he eventually fathered twenty-one children), she is too aware of the vicissitudes of the family's subsequent fortunes to endorse it completely. She is also too realistic to indulge in naïve aspirations for Australia's future, merely expressing the characteristic hope for the 'righteousness' of the new nation.

There is, however, nothing of the wowser about Watts, and indeed some of the delights of her story are the love of gregarious fun and the display of wit. Constantly shaping the text, nevertheless, is an awareness of life's fragility. Informed by a deep Christian pessimism, which is strongly reminiscent of Dr Johnson's, the narrative rarely loses sight of the reversals of destiny and the ironies of fate. Thus, although the time sequence is roughly chronological, there are frequent time shifts to anticipate or reflect on the characters' subsequent fates. Remembering her role as bridesmaid at a fashionable wedding, Watts cannot resist meditating on the subsequent unfortunate history of the marriage, the early deaths of all those who formed 'a merry party' that day and the dangers of early marriage in general (pp. 89–90); or, recalling an instance of the energy and cheerfulness of one of their hired hands, 'Mark Tapley', she meditates on the fatal accident that was about to befall him:

And yet, in that self-same hour when his prospects were of the brightest, and humanly speaking a useful, successful career was mapped out before him, little as they were aware of it, in the dim distance an ominous black shadow was approaching that would ere long envelope them both ['Tapley' and his fiancée] as with a shroud. (pp. 38–9)

Instances of early death, disappointed love, failed health, family and social cruelty, financial ruin and insanity or depression figure frequently, contrasting with moments of fellowship, family picnics in the Edenic settings of Kangaroo Island and gay social occasions in Adelaide. One of the more poignant of these contrasts occurs in the description of a visit by two young traders, who happen to have a great interest in music. For a week the entire Giles family is involved in making music and other entertainments. Remembering the traders' colourful leave-taking, the narrator reflects that 'those sweet sounds of music on the water still float upon [her] memory

... though long years oft-shadowed over by suffering and sadness have since then passed away' (p. 53).

The theme of time's sad reversals, however, is no more than a broad strand in the narrative. Gifted with a keen sense of the absurd and a great relish for the quirky, ridiculous, pretentious or inconsistent, Watts peoples her story with a range of vividly realized 'characters'. The influence of Dickens, who is often quoted, is obvious here, although Watts is usually careful to temper her more satiric thrusts with qualifying encomiums. From the dour 'John Knox' [David McLaren], whose nature is 'as hard as the granite of his own mountains' except for the chip made there by his opposite and worthless son (p. 43), to the loathsome Dr M. and his equally unpleasant offspring, Watts indulges her deft dramatic flair for distinctive human types. The extensive account of Dr M. and his persecuted wife is a particularly well orchestrated episode. First exposing his insensitivity in his habit of stringing conk shells by 'hooks run into the quivering fish' (p. 56), Dr M. emerges as an incorrigible chauvinist with an 'undisguised contempt for the intellectual capacity of women'. If his insensitivity manifests itself as stupidity in his response to the fatal illness of the child S., it amounts to criminal cruelty in his treatment of his tubercular child-bride. His own death from 'a surfeit of water melon' seems to be one of those instances of life imitating art, and certainly in this whole episode the author's creative energies are intensely engaged.

However distinctive the narrative voice of *Family Life in South Australia*, foregrounding of the self is far from this author's public intentions. Referring to herself in the third person as 'Minnie' or as 'Mr A.'s second daughter', Watts is careful to deprecate her own writing as 'a light gossipy narrative which only skims the surface of things', to justify its inception as a male initiative, and to bolster it with male stories of derring-do in the bush (action-packed accounts of encounters with the blacks by her brother Thomas Giles and of a search party for two lost men by a grandson of William Giles are included at the close). An extensive account of her father's and husband's achievements and the inclusion of obituaries, although clearly labours of love, also have the effect of validating her narrative as supportive female memoir. In fact, so diffident is Watts in the first sections of her story, that she leans heavily on literary or Biblical allusions or familiar proverbs as expressive devices, clearly preferring indirection to self-expression. Fortunately, these encrusting stratagems are soon largely cast off as she warms to her tale. One form of distancing, however, the cultivation of a mock epic style, is more successful. As well as comically reducing the hardships and discomforts of pioneering life without ridiculing the pioneers themselves, it gives scope to Watts's powers of self parody and her unsentimental relish for the ironic gulf between ideal and real.

Discarding the mock epic also enhances the episodes of serious drama, such as the visit by a group of violent, possibly murderous men in the father's absence or the death of a child.

But these are individual effects, the results of a lifetime's reading of Augustan or Romantic writers. Other aspects of this text prefigure more general characteristics. In her preference for a flexible plotless form, her modulating from the general to the inwardly personal, her treatment of landscape, her omissions and elisions and in some of her themes, Watts is significantly a precursor. Even her value system, which is in many ways detached from the public ends of colonial culture, is prophetic. The chronology of the Giles's settlement in South Australia provides the bare bones of the 'family life' which is the foregrounded subject of the book, but the narrator allows emotional interest to determine shape, taking whatever time is necessary to combine incident and reflection. By no means a verbose writer, she nonetheless achieves the impression of free-flowing narration and subtle modulations of mood. Having related the story of the hardships of a group of lost men, for instance, she feels free to call on the Almighty to 'console all such lonely travellers in the wild bush of Australia . . . and . . . preserve them from utter wretchedness and despair' and even to include two verses of an appropriate hymn, before shifting to the more neutral account of the doings of 'Mr A.'s boys' (p. 31). On another occasion, she excuses her concentration on human eccentricities, declaring that she 'simply cannot write at all if she is to be debarred from commenting in a good-natured way, upon . . . oddities' (p. 13).

Like many of her successors, Watts concentrates on the domestic and personal, taking full advantage of her retrospective status as child to indulge acute or subversive observations of her contemporaries, or to expand on the trivial incidents that made up the texture of early settlement life. Thus one of the text's most spectacular attributes is spontaneity, a freedom which gives scope to moments of intense intimacy. This freedom is not often indulged, but it provides some of the narrative's emotional peaks. They include the description of her weariness in her role as nursemaid and her moments of depression when she 'would wonder if she was always to lead this kind of life, and never have an opportunity of resuming her studies broken off at the early age of thirteen', never be able to approach the achievements of her 'well-educated, refined, intelligent mother' (pp. 40–1); or the later account of the death-bed sufferings of an infant and 'the lonely hours she spent with the dying child, walking, ever walking up and down that room the long night through [which] are well remembered to this day' (p. 96).

The freedom which Watts creates for herself in the pioneering genre also allows her to give full vent to one of her favourite topics, the sufferings and courage of other pioneer women. In both men and women she values cheerfulness, courage, self-sacrifice and sensitivity but her most frequent plaudits or expressions of pity are for colonial women. It is the quick-wittedness of a woman, for instance, dousing the candles to frustrate her murderously-inclined husband, which saves Mr A.'s life, and it is the cheerful stoicism of women like Mrs Stow, who bring up a family in the stifling conditions of the tent settlement of Adelaide, which is celebrated as the backbone of the community. Women are perceived as inevitably antecedent but implicated in men's lives; there are numerous accounts of unfortunate or even death-inducing marriages, instances of poverty consequent on the mismanagement of men, of violence, murders and attempted murders. Even if women escape the normal hazards of marriage, there are the emotional hazards of disappointed love, of which the most dramatic is the account of the bridegroom who killed himself on his wedding day, leaving his fiancée devastated.

Family Life in South Australia also anticipates future narratives in the treatment of landscape. The style of this narrator's descriptions is conventional and even formal, but the tendency to invest place with personality and to see the childhood home as an ambivalent Eden is already present. Her descriptions of the first sightings of Australia, for example, have the life of metaphor. On one hand a picture of inhuman desolation:

Not a sign of human habitation was visible; no smoke gracefully curling upwards from the rudest of shanties met their view. All was silent as the grave—dull, dreary, desolation—the only sounds proceeding from the sullen waves that dashed against the shore. (p. 10)

On the other, a suggestion of promise:

just as the good old ship, incommodious as she was, dropped anchor in Nepean Bay, the sun burst forth from behind the clouds with oriental splendour followed by a glorious rainbow, which, stretching from one part of the horizon to the other, formed a complete arch with its beautiful prismatic hues of crimson, green and gold reflected in the water. An omen for good it was hoped to be by some of those wanderers. (p. 11)

And as in other narratives, homes or interiors are almost as significant characters as people. Finally, notwithstanding its freedoms, this narrative like other female autobiographies has its significant omissions. Not only is the central theme of women's fiction, courtship and marriage, shuffled to the sidelines, but certain emotional icebergs are allowed to remain largely submerged. Mrs A., for example, the author's stepmother, appears in only incidental ways, although Mr A. receives extensive room; identifying strongly with her dead mother, the narrator also differentiates between her father's first and second family, clearly bonding far more closely with the former. Whether the second is perceived as more of a burden than an addition is left to the reader's imagination.

An autobiography which was published a year before Watts's but which could hardly be more different is Eliza Davies's *The Story of an Earnest Life: A Woman's Adventures in Australia, and in Two Voyages around the World*.[3] A career narrative in that the author's 'earnest' implies religious earnestness, it was published in Cincinnati. Apart from its religious tone, the book is quite unlike any other Australian account of the period and probably found an American publisher since it happened to fall into the American nineteenth century tradition of exotic literature. Davies, however, was Scots not American and spent some of her youth and adulthood in Australia. Similar to Emily Churchward's *In Paths Directed* and Bessie Lee's *One of Australia's Daughters* in that it presents an assertive personality via the medium of religion, Davies's book far outpaces these as a purveyor of the sensational. It is immensely long-winded (the book has 570 pages), enlivened by a breathless but untiring style, the drama of recalled conversations and vividly described natural scenes. Perceiving herself as the central figure in a long-running melodrama, this narrator overwrites herself as a matter of course.

Born in Paisley into an apparently wealthy family in 1819, Davies was converted to the Baptist faith as a young girl and, following a severe rift with her mother, emigrated with a family of Baptists to Sydney in 1838, arriving appropriately on the very day that eight men were hanged for their part in the Myall Creek massacre. Employed or resident in the house of the Comptroller of Customs for a brief period after her arrival, she soon became acquainted with Captain Sturt, who had been appointed Surveyor-General of Sydney by Governor Gawler. Regarding Sydney as a 'sink of iniquity', Davies agreed to accompany the Sturt family to Adelaide in 1839 in the *John Pirie*, probably as a companion or lady help, although she implies social equality with the explorer (she is presumably one of the two 'servants' listed in the register of passengers). The party arrived in Adelaide in March 1839 after a rough passage and a stay of several days at Preservation Island. In November Davies accompanied the Sturts, Governor Gawler and his daughter, Julia, and a party of men on an exploring expedition up the Murray River and across country towards Gulf St Vincent.[4] The women were apparently included in order to encourage investment in the area. It was a horrific trip on which one man was lost and there were several severe accidents. After returning to Adelaide in 1840, the narrator describes herself as somehow forced into marriage with a master tinsmith, William Davies ('I was so circumvented by Mrs Sturt that I could not but accept Mr Davies. Her taunting manner I could not brook, and my inexperienced youth was no match for her intriguing French ways', p. 171). Five weeks after her marriage, her husband beat her with a Wellington boot and continued to abuse her until January 1842 when he left for New Zealand. During his absence Eliza laid her case before the church and received its protection after her husband returned in September. In the same month she left for Sydney and thence for Europe. A relentless traveller, she returned to Australia in 1858, ran a private school for a time in Sydney and was later befriended by G. F. Angas, who provided funds for another school for poor children at Hindmarsh, which she apparently ran successfully. In 1874 she left Sydney for San Francisco.

Packed with sinister events, supernatural incidents, disasters, near-disasters, storms, violent deaths and accidents, *The Story of an Earnest Life* is a Gothic romance peopled with villains and angels. To this rich brew, Australia of the 1830s adds the ingredients of a primitive 'crime-stained' city, murderous savages, several storms at sea and the perils of a journey of exploration into the uncharted wilderness. A violent husband and an almost fatal illness, suffered within the confines of the prison-like Sydney hospital, are more personal spices. The protagonist of this extraordinary story, Eliza Arbuckle, later Davies, is never slow to particularize every detail of her difficulties or to lament her fate; fortunately, she is equal to every situation and more than equal once she has enlisted God on her side. In this highly-charged atmosphere, the question of truth inevitably arises, and certainly Davies is guilty of embroidering her story on at least one occasion; during her second visit to Australia, for instance, she describes herself as 'wrecked' on a voyage from Melbourne to Adelaide in the *Miami* in 1861, when in fact the *Miami* was only dismasted. What is also certain is that every situation is a superlative one for this narrator; it is not enough for her to tremble, she must tremble 'like an aspen leaf', it is not enough for an Aborigine to look fierce, he must look as if he is 'about to tear me to pieces and eat me'. Equipped with a great love of drama, she attracts disasters like a magnet.[5] As far as the literary value of this autobiography is concerned, however, the question of truth or falsehood hardly matters, as it probably hardly mattered to the author. For it is the psychic drama that is interesting and if some of these events are fictionalized or heightened, they happen as they should in terms of the narrative's emotional integrity. An Australian Moll Flanders in her unwitting absurdity, Eliza Davies is a comic paranoid who cannot fail artlessly to expose her real motives. She is a wonderful example of thick-skinned sensitivity, who is born to survive.

Hysterically coloured as Davies's narrative is, it never fails to live. One reason for this is the narrator's grasp of language. The sea voyage from Melbourne to Adelaide with the Sturts, for example, provides this vivid glimpse of the storm-tossed passengers (Eliza herself is characteristically presented as calm):

I was sitting high up, my naked feet dangling down, holding to a rope to keep myself from swaying about too much. The drunk Captain sat on the corner of the sofa 'nid nodding', and at the other corner of the sofa sat Captain Sturt,

trying to quiet his wife's hysterical cries. She was clinging to him, and calling
to him to save her, while one of her little boys was clinging to her and crying,
but she took no notice of him. The nurse, with the other in her lap, was
sitting on the floor groaning and swaying back and forth, and holding to the
leg of the table. One tall, swarthy figure, enshrouded in a long white robe,
and a red night-cap on his head, from under which hung what looked like
black strings (hair dripping wet), stood in a doorway with arms stretched
wide holding to the side posts. Another crouched in a corner, burying his face
in his hands, his streaming hair hanging over them. Another, with his hands
behind him, leaned his back against the wall. Another lay across the table.
The one dimly burning lamp hung over this spectral group. (p. 105)

Later, an Aborigine is an even more promising subject:

He had coarse, frizzy black hair, not wool, standing away from his head like a
sombrero or mop; his forehead was so low that his hair and eyebrows nearly
met, his head receded from front to back, so that his head behind was
enormous in size; his eyes were large, black, deep-set, glittering and fierce,
and overhung by beetling, shaggy brows; his nose was large and flat; his
mouth huge, with gleaming teeth; his lips thick and hanging. While he sat
on that rock motionless, he was a picture of ugliness that fascinated me . . .
(p. 130)

Verbal energy is matched by physical energy, and the narrator's
preferred scenes are those in which she holds centre stage, engaged in
some admired enterprise. Thus in her early childhood she amazes the
people of the Scottish highlands with her courage ('My mountain
friends marveled much at the fearlessness of the "wee toon lassie",
with her white skin, golden curls and slender form. I was in my
element' p. 11); or, she nostalgically recalls a voyage on which she
was the only child on board ('and the gentlemen all said I was a brave
little sailor, and I was a good deal petted by them', p. 17). Later still,
when she has survived a great storm, she sees herself as 'quite a lion,
or at least a cub . . . I was a natural curiosity to the children who came
to see me' (p. 18). Although rarely a page passes without some peril,
she is quick-witted and resourceful, calm when others lose their heads
and endowed with massive recuperative powers. At one point during
the 1839 journey of exploration, she appears to take over from the
men who are hopelessly incapable of directing affairs; at another,
faced with a hostile group of Aborigines, a moment when 'life and
death were in the balance' (p. 140), she resorts to cutting their hair
and beards. Decisive and inventive, she is never at a loss for actions
or words.

Notwithstanding her expressive powers, Davies rarely presents
an objective description of anyone else. Totally self-absorbed, she
is only able to register other individuals as positive, negative or
sometimes merely useful commodities. Of her two half-brothers,
for instance, one, a handsome soldier 'in his scarlet coat and shiny
epaulets', shows great care for her; the other, of the 'keen blue eye

and cutting glance . . . had forever chilled my love for him' (p. 24). In all her vicissitudes it is extraordinary how many men find time to make Eliza's welfare their chief concern: 'I was delighted to see them. They said they had come to see their "little pet"' (p. 90); 'When I awoke, I was warm and comfortable, and Mr H. H— sitting at my feet to prevent my being pitched into the sea. He told Captain Sturt . . . to allow me to have my sleep out; it would make me well, and he would watch by me while I slept' (p. 103); 'They all made my days pass pleasantly' (p. 148). Some, who are less benevolent, fortunately change their attitude after a longer acquaintance; thus Mr C— and Mr R— abandon their 'teasing propensities' and show an unexpected sensitivity in an extreme situation: 'Mr C— spread my mattress, and Mr R— carried me to it, and laid me down as gently as a tender mother could have done. He . . . covered me up, and left me to sleep or die. I did neither' (p. 162). (The comic irony of the last comment is quite unconscious.) Not surprisingly, large numbers of men are overpowered by the narrator's physical charms and she is hard put to keep such suitors at bay. Evelyn Sturt in particular proves to be a 'wicked tempter', a 'soft-toned, smooth-faced young gentleman' who speaks 'libertine addresses . . . tenderly in my unwilling ear' (p. 169).

In this morally unshaded world, two individuals are dyed in darkest hue. They are the narrator's mother and her husband. 'All through my childhood's loving years my heart yearned for her love', she writes of her mother on the first page; but it is an unrequited yearning. Distant and authoritarian, and apparently engrossed in her 'worldly' social life, the mother perpetually thrusts the child from her. Aware of her daughter's love of music, she forbids her to sing ('The voice of the canary was hushed', p. 21), and on one occasion scars her spirit by autocratically requiring that she wear black to a party.

Strangely veering between indifference and outright enmity, the mother never makes her motives clear and her personality remains similarly opaque. After she has attempted to force her daughter into an unpleasant marriage (an episode that is never satisfactorily developed) she appears to ignore her daughter's flight and period of self-supporting life apart. On the day of emigration, however, she puts in an appearance as a sort of vindictive farewell, standing 'like a pillar of light' among the receding dark crowd on shore. Later still, she suddenly and inexplicably arrives in Australia and joins forces with the husband in maltreating the young bride. As in *Moll Flanders*, individuals with strong feelings for the narrating self, pop unpredictably in and out of the narrative.

Similarly, events often seem shaped to fit psychic needs rather than documentary truth. Thus, the final casting off from Scotland, which is perceived as a casting off from the care of the mother ('I felt that the cords that bound me to family and home were loosened, and I, like the ship, was about to try my strength in unknown regions', p. 50), has been preceded by another curious sea-distancing between mother and self. After a terrible storm in the Irish sea, during which the mother had jeopardized the lives of both the child and herself by remaining on board, the mother leaves the child to go on shore ('I watched the boat as it rose high, and then sank out of sight behind the billows. I feared several times that she had gone down to rise no more; but up she came again and finally she touched the shore', p. 16). Later, the mother sends for the child, who survives the crossing, although another boat capsizes and nearly everyone is lost. Given the extensive sea-imagery which the narrator draws on to define the self, the implications of foiled infanticide are tempting. Certainly, the absence of mother love is perceived as a permanent sorrow, a sad memory that casts its blight on all her after life.

If the mother's antagonism is unexplained, the husband's is equally impenetrable. Tricked into the marriage by Mrs Sturt in another blurred episode, Eliza suffers the sudden transformation of her husband into uncontrollable 'demon'. Again, the inconsistencies and omissions are as intriguing as Moll's; beaten into a pulp one day ('my hair matted with blood; my face and eyes blackened and swollen', p. 176), she does not seem severely handicapped in social life a few days later and indeed is soon irritated by Julia Gawler's assumption that Mr D— is a model husband.

But *The Story of an Earnest Life* is not just an account of personal hardships; it has a didactic purpose, which is to show the workings of God in an individual, pious life. Not surprisingly, Eliza's conversion to Baptism is dramatic. Walking home one evening after she has separated from her mother, she is startled by a sudden light and has a vision 'in bold relief' of a human figure nailed to a cross, the lower part 'concealed by the clouds' and the face illumined by 'large, love-lit eyes, full of pity' (p. 39). From this moment, she clings to God's protection as a physical defence against all perils and as a substitute for the family she has lost. Abandoned by her mother, she prays to God to come near 'for the gulf is wide between me and my kindred' (p. 48), and on several occasions she refers to her reliance on divine love as a substitute for the parental version (pp. 45, 49, 50). If she is denied value by her mother, she finds her value in Jesus who even finds time to care for the sparrows ('I had cost Him too much to be neglected by Him', p. 67). God is a more effective parent, moreover, and time and again she states her conviction that He will literally preserve her in the direst circumstances. The conviction is a wonderful stimulus to courage. God's care even extends to the trivial details of personal comfort; thus several people find themselves directed by God to look after Eliza's welfare and even the head of the arrogant Mr F— is invaded with the God-sent idea of supplying the thirsting girl with quandongs ('I felt truly grateful to Mr F—, as an instrument in God's hand, for bringing me the berries, at the dreadful risk he ran to himself', p. 156). Apart from these implicit tokens of concern, He proves of real practical help in the dispute with Mr D—. Affording her Biblical authority for leaving her husband, He makes sure that the congregation gets the message ('He did not deliver me to my enemies, but he raised up friends for me in my greatest need', p. 201). There is almost no development of religious doctrine in the narrative, however; generally too hard-pressed by life's dramatic events, Eliza is unable to do more than alternate between grateful responses to God's timely interventions and retrospective accounts of calm 'faith' in their arrival.

This perception of herself as one of God's special wards is un-doubtedly this narrator's 'metaphor of self', to use James Olney's phrase.[6] It extends into a wider matrix of meaning, however, in an extensive pattern of sea imagery. Perceiving herself as a restless, wandering spirit ('roaming, unheeded, over mountain-tops, in deep glens, on swift-gliding streams, or on the stormy firth', p. 23), or as a storm-tossed orphan, fated to try her strength alone 'in unknown regions' (p. 50), Eliza has an affinity with ship-board life ('It was delightful on a calm, still day to sit on the spars and peer over the side of the ship and down into the depths of the sea, and feel myself rocked upon the great waves and floating over the dark, blue sea' pp. 53–4). Her early experiences on the Irish sea, moreover, during such a gale that not the 'oldest man' could remember its like, have convinced her that the sea has returned her her life; 'half-drowned', she is received on shore as if the sea had given her up again. A series of curious incidents *en route* to Australia confirm her in this impres-sion. On one occasion, when someone protects her from a wave which drenches the other passengers, she is christened 'Neptune's favourite' (p. 55); later, when the ship is about to cross the equator, she is assured that if Neptune comes aboard, she will be exempt from his ducking. On a hot, still day they cross the line, and she notices that her shadow has disappeared. Then, visiting a sick girl in the hospital, she falls into the bottom of the hold; miraculously, she suffers neither broken bones nor bruises. ('I was the only one on board who had been roughly handled on crossing the line, though I was the only one who was to be exempt. The captain told me that my adventure in the hold was just as good as if "Neptune" had come on board and ducked me' (pp. 63–4).

Revealing as this incident of Eliza's paranoia is, it also sheds light on her real motive in writing her autobiography. More obviously than most autobiographers, Davies is obsessed with what Barrett Mandel has called the 'smell of lilies'. In a persuasive article, Mandel suggests that most autobiographies are existential acts, written to preserve some remnant of the self from the 'superior and relentless forces of non-being'. The autobiographer writes to 'reduce the power of fate and the threat of death as much as possible'. Struggling with death and writing as an act of self-affirmation, the autobiographer's self '"discovers" death in all that is not itself—before, after, and surrounding . . . [the] experience of life. [He] writes not only to affirm, but also to stave off non-being. Death has to be killed'. Impelled to protect the self from extinction by the forces of nothingness, the autobiographer makes of his life a static effigy, a frozen effigy of 'life'; it is an enterprise which produces 'seemingly paradoxical double states of courage and defensiveness', self-admiration and self-pity.[7]

Eliza Davies is preoccupied on one hand with a very powerful sense of self and on the other with the early denial of that self by the mother. Existential fears in her case, therefore, are likely to be particularly acute, and indeed in her account of her pre-conversion days she frequently speaks of her liability to be 'cut down'. And elsewhere in the narrative she conveys a vivid awareness of the extinction that death represents; contemplating the death of a passenger at sea, for instance, she estimates the length of time it will take the body to reach its watery grave:

Five hours alone, unattended, unthought of, pressing steadily on away from all light, passing without a pause the limit where the last ray of the sun becomes extinct, and where the last trace of life forever fails. (p. 60)

Literally half-drowned by the mother's actions, she contrives to survive, and continues to see her particular life experience in terms of voyaging by sea. Indeed, it is impossible to avoid the conclusion that her personality positively requires the constantly alternating drama of storm and calm. She is, of course, given the ultimate guarantee of surviving life's storms when she undergoes conversion, but it is delightfully consistent that she should underpin this with a personal, pagan mythology. Deprived of her shadow, she makes sure that as 'Neptune's Favourite', she is not really extinguished.

Another strong-minded autobiographer of the latter half of the nineteenth century, but one with a much more public consciousness is Mary Gilmore. Born in 1865, she was one of the few Australian women to find a public voice in the early years of this century, writing an influential page in the Sydney *Worker* for twenty-three years from 1907. At least two of her autobiographical narratives, *Old Days, Old Ways*[8] and *More Recollections*[9] were written when she had become not just an accepted public figure, but virtually a national symbol. In 1937, when she was made DBE, the congratulatory telegrams flooded in from all over Australia, and at her death in 1962, she was given a state funeral, the first Australian writer to be given such an honour since Henry Lawson. From the 1920s until her death, she was accorded the role of 'tribal mother' in the public consciousness, a living repository of the national memory. When Douglas Stewart recalled his visits to her, for instance, he described her conversation as 'all about who was related to whom in Australian history'; losing track of the connections, he was left with the impression that 'she was related to everybody'.[10] Like Henry Lawson, her work and life appeared to many of her contemporaries to be quintessentially Australian. At her centenary, for example, R. D. Fitzgerald described her image as 'closely allied to our profoundest thoughts and ideas of our country'[11], while at her death Kenneth Slessor compared her to Queen Victoria, 'a kind of symbol of the century through which she almost lived'.[12]

To readers of the 1980s, however, Gilmore seems a contradictory figure. A champion of feminist causes, she held conservative ideas about marriage, motherhood and the domestic role of women; a frequent defender of the culture of the Aborigines with a keen awareness of their past losses, she was committed to the White Australia policy and fearful of miscegenation; nostalgic about the simplicities of pioneering life in the bush, she described her own adult years of rural living (1902–7) as 'a descent into hell' and ultimately jettisoned marriage and motherhood to live as a journalist in Sydney; a socialist who claimed to have taken part in some of the major strikes of the 1890s and to have been on the first executive of the AWU, she was happy to accept the honour of DBE; a regular contributor to the *Tribune*, she also wrote frequently for the *Bulletin*. Some recent critics have attempted to explain these paradoxes as merely aspects of her kaleidoscopic scope; *Old Days, Old Ways* and *More Recollections*, however, indicate that they were rather unresolved contradictions.

Autobiography is not life *per se*, of course, but merely a partial and even temporary perception of the life, filtered through the prism of subjectivity and thus prevented from ever achieving wholly accurate representation. As William Earle has commented: 'If consciousness is inherently true, it is so only "in principle"; in fact it perpetually retains the power and desire to conceal itself from itself. It is also the great liar, not chiefly to others, but to itself'.[13] Even for the writer who is not burdened with a public self to justify, the autobiographical artifact is only one of many possible bridges thrown across the gulf between the 'I' who is and was and the 'I' who observes the other selves. Like Eliza Davies, Gilmore creates for herself a public persona; she selects, represses and interprets her experience, making herself into an ideal fictional character. In Davies's case the persona is devout and divinely justified; in Gilmore's she is the wise old woman or tribal elder with a unique understanding of the past. The gap between the mask and a more authentic self is comically immense in Davies's narrative, whereas in Gilmore's the chinks are far less obvious, and in other ways the two are not really comparable;

Gilmore is much more skilful and controlled a writer, and her concerns are attractively wide-ranging.

Besides *Old Days, Old Ways* and *More Recollections*, Gilmore wrote two other prose autobiographies; the first, a group of essays titled *Hound of the Road* (1922), which uses the childhood past as a springboard for meditative free-fall, is even more obliquely personal than her later collections. The second is an incomplete, unpublished account, 'My Childhood'. I am only concerned with the 1930s narratives here in that they are both conscious justifications of the public self.

In her preface to the first edition of *Old Days, Old Ways*, Gilmore stresses her interest in personal rather than public history:

So far, this country's writers of reminiscence and recollection have shown events rather than people, have detailed historied hours rather than life. I have written here of life as I knew it, and with the desire to show, not the miles walked, but the feet that walked them; not the oven, but the bread baked in it, and the talk of those who buttered (when there was butter) and ate that bread.

If this is a characteristically female concern, so are the preface's admission that this is a loosely wandering narrative and its apology for the 'impertinence' of thrusting such a 'personal' book on others. Less characteristic are the implications that the writer is a capacious reservoir of general memory which must be drawn on for the nation's good ('with one single thought of recollection come whole battalions . . . there is so much to do and so little time in which to do it') and the linking of the self with a male authority on the national culture, Vance Palmer.

Less characteristic too is the absence of an intimate self in both *Old Days, Old Ways* and *More Recollections*. If, on one hand, the wise voice of the narrator, speaking to the reader with a simple person-to-person directness, dominates the narrative, on the other, the narrator's past self is only obliquely visible. Seen occasionally clinging to the father's hand, or nestled between his knees before a camp fire, the child-self is rarely more than an implied witnessing or listening presence. As receptive auditor, she records not only her own stories but those of her father, Donal Cameron, and grandfather, Hugh Beattie; occasionally the memories of others are pressed into service in this revisioning of the past, but they are always absorbed into the mono-rhythms of the sage over-voice. Omniscient and assured, this voice draws on the authoritative rhythms of the Bible and the simple sequences of fable. Impressed with the mytho-poetic grandeur of its tale, it frequently takes time to reflect on human life in general or to compare the Australian civilization with others of the legendary past. If there is little of the personal quest for self in these recollections, it is because the self is already perceived as having the settled identity of national memorialist and myth-maker. Nevertheless, there are indications that probing the memory brings surprises which unsettle the public rhetoric.

Gilmore's qualifications for the role of memorialist can hardly be questioned. Acutely sensitive to the hidden histories of mute relics of the past, she is also finely aware of the significance of changes in dress or furniture. Clothes, cooking utensils, shoes, farm tools are transformed in her descriptions from inert objects into significant reflectors of social conditions, attitudes and class distinctions. Like Mary Fullerton and Katherine McKell, she is drawn to the simplicities of pioneer life: 'They lived clean in their little huts, so austere in their naked whitewash and the bare scant possessions, the early settlers of our Inland' (*Old Days, Old Ways*, p. 9). Reflecting on a single object, in a way that is reminiscent of Lamb, though without his whimsy, she is able to produce extended melodies; the baby trunk that was in constant use in most households, or the bell, which structured the life of community and family, are the starting points of revealing socio-historical explorations. Clustering around a range of central stimuli, memories follow each other in quick succession, vividly recreating community rituals, domestic practices, social conventions and religious attitudes. Certain glutinous details stick in the mind: the funeral notice nailed to a tree to alert passing riders; the chalk line on the floor to separate the classes at a dance, the valuable china washed with scrupulous care by a woman with no stockings to her feet; the carefully preserved half of a pair of scissors in case another half should ever come to hand; the 'shocking' incident of the woman who leant across her husband to put her offering in the collection plate. Few writers have had so developed a sense of piety for the past.

Fortunately, piety does not imply uncritical nostalgia, and the narratives bristle with pithy comments on the hardships, cruelties, waste and injustices of the past. Men certainly suffered, but women, children and Aborigines were the prime sufferers. 'A woman without a man was defenceless against womanless men once the aboriginals had been destroyed', the narrator comments on the first page of *Old Days, Old Ways*, and the series of cruelties implicit in the folds of that sentence echo through the narrative. Women, who only existed socially and legally through men, and were 'not supposed to have the needs of a man', are perceived as suffering from the deprivations of poverty at one extreme and the suffocating restrictions of gentility at the other. Sometimes used literally as a work-horse in the absence of animals to pull the plough, the wife was immediately imprisoned in the house once money and respectability came along. If she could expect little but hard work and constant childbirth in marriage, widowhood was a semi-death ('only a man could release her from black'): 'It was the day of the man. The woman's day had not dawned. The child's day had not been thought of. The nerves of the man vented themselves on woman and child' (*Old Days, Old Ways*, p. 52). Nevertheless, boys were better off than girls (a boy never answered his mother's indoor bell, 'he called girls to do that . . . Boys were men, and men belonged to out-of-doors', p. 76). And in the extremity of a difficult childbirth, it was frequently the [male] child that was to be saved; (I remember . . . how men argued for the child as a possible heir, and my mother for the woman', p. 134). At the same time Gilmore is careful to document the actual courage and resource of women, including the particularly striking stories in *Old Days, Old Ways* of a woman who saved her family from bushfire by a series of painstaking measures, and of a Spanish woman who took on the role of doctor but who ultimately acquired the reputation of witch: 'That woman was inferior was a regular Church doctrine; and man was constantly told to shun woman as the agent of the devil' (p. 5).

But these injustices pale into insignificance compared with the accounts of white treatment of the Aborigines. Conscious of anomaly in her interest in the Aborigines, the narrator stresses her understanding of their side of the story ('while others had their tales from the persecutors, I had mine from the side of the persecuted—indeed often through my own eyes, in the dead I saw', *Old Days, Old Ways*, p. 161). In *Old Days* this theme is largely contained, the narrator concentrating more on explicating and recording the value and values of Aboriginal culture. In *More Recollections*, however, she gives more scope to accounts of persecution and even massacre, with the result that it becomes more difficult to hold the mask of white myth-maker in place.

Merging into the landscape in *Old Days, Old Ways* by dint of their tribal knowledge of the land, the Aborigines also merge into the general theme of the land's desecration: 'free selection rolled like a tide . . . Like a steam-roller man swept down everything his own will had not planned or decreed. No sanctuary was proclaimed, so the wild went' (p. 171). Lamenting the drying up of waterways, and the destruction of wild life, the narrator at one point builds up a sensuous picture of the land as it was under the guardianship of the black:

In sheltered places where the blue wren was plentiful, he was literally in hundreds, a family flight being like a small jewelled cloud slipping tenuously through the undergrowth. In every bush I dare affirm there was a pigeon or a dove; the grass was a moving mass of parrots and parrakeets; while the trees glistened white with cockatoo, or were flamingo-pink with the galah. Ants swarmed on the earth and trees; native bees, flies, gnats, beetles, spiders, and butterflies, burst from egg; rose from larvae, emerged from chrysalis. Everywhere things crept, swarmed, climbed, hummed, chirped, whistled, croaked, sang, and flowered. The air was full of the scent of life and honey, of the warm rich smell of feathers and fur. (p. 265)

As the 'dare affirm' of the above passage acknowledges, these are more ancestral than personal memories; of at least a third remove, they are no doubt the father's memories of stories. Time and time again, in both books, Gilmore acknowledges her debt to her father's memories ('It is through him that I remember so much that is recorded here', p. 60). Station manager and amateur explorer, Donal Cameron had travelled extensively in outback New South Wales and Queensland, later accompanied by his daughter. Emerging as a skilled bushman, an influential man in the community, a born raconteur and a tender father, he is the male hero of these autobiographies. Undoubtedly part of the narrator's piety towards the father stems from his superior knowledge of the land, but many more intimate touches build up the impression of a strong emotional bond between father and daughter. The mother, by contrast, hardly appears. The narrator clearly regards herself as her father's natural heir, if not his natural male heir, for there are few signs that gender has handicapped her freedom as wanderer and gatherer of the old ways.

Indeed, at one point, she admits that she lived in a 'world of men' when she was small. Men, the wanderers, are described as the 'permanent' ones, those who 'made the world' and contained 'life's continuity, for with them were the roads that went out back'. Women, by contrast, were impermanent and their talk was of 'the things of individual life that were only interesting as they happened, like eating your dinner, but which meant nothing afterwards'. The talk of men, on the other hand, 'was full of the colour of life; talk that went like a broad river, sweeping in times and places and people as it flowed; talk that reached from Sydney to California, and that covered travel, endurance, seas, and oceans' (pp. 102–3). The world of women was 'a world into which I did not go' (p. 103). And there is a sense in which the world of women is still unentered; for all her sympathy with woman's lot, this narrator implies a freedom and authority that are distinctively male. Similarly, she perceives *her* stories, even though they are 'personal', as male stories, permanent, 'full of the colour of life' and linking past and future. Recovering the past is also a recovery of the freedom of a male childhood ('I am again a child on a boundless sea, a child without the need of a compass', p. 101).

Remembering, in fact, is a personal as much as a general liberation. Perpetually intrigued by the strangeness and vanished solidity of the past, the narrator clearly relishes the act of remembering. Sometimes she takes time to observe herself remembering, to register surprise at the quirks of memory as it retrieves events folded away in 'the drawers of the mind'; on other more rare occasions, she puts aside the role of general historian to record one of the sensuous pleasures of childhood, the falling of a poplar's leaves or the strange colours of tree trunks. A curious anomaly in this text, though familiar in other autobiographies, is the experience of cosmic nothingness ('when all would be consumed, and the heavens rolled up as a scroll, and there was nothing—nothing—nothing', p. 98). But it is characteristic that she should dismiss the thought of the self's nothingness, 'though I could imagine the sun and the moon and the stars and the round world of geography all gone, I still never thought of a time when there would not be a solid earth, and two feet, mine of course, standing on it' (p. 99).

More than most autobiographers, Gilmore is possessive of the past. She has, of course, appropriated the Australian past in terms of superior memory, so that the phrase 'I am the only one who remembers' is a refrain through the narrative. But in a more personal sense her individuality is validated by the past, she *is* the past. She is at one with the old days of Australia and the process of remembering has a value which almost cancels out other considerations so that recall is an end in itself. This, I think, partly accounts for a final unsatisfactory fuzziness in these two narratives. Accepting uncritically her initial aim of celebrating the white settlement of Australia, and absorbed in the experience of remembering, she fails fully to confront the undermining effects of memory. William Earle has suggested that the autobiographical consciousness is one which thinks about itself: 'To whatever extent we can know ourselves, we have gathered together in reflection where we have been, where are, and where we can go'.[14] Gilmore's assumption of the role of sage interpreter of the past implicitly comprehends present and future, of course. Yet for all her intimate knowledge of where we have been and her rhetoric on nationhood, she is less certain of the meaning of that journey than she appears; she is more familiar with its topography than its destination.

Patriotism is the unquestioned good which lies at the heart of these narratives, and, frankly proud of her Scots ancestry, the narrator publicly celebrates her association with the pioneers: 'I feel glad that I belonged to those who pioneered and helped set the foundations of this the last of the Wonderful Lands' (*Old Days, Old Ways*, p. 268). Unlike Maie Casey's, Gilmore's persona never seems afflicted by a sense that the white culture may be anomalous. Notwithstanding the diminishment of the natural paradise, the destruction of the Aborigines, the cruelties and the wastage of human talents, white settlement is not just to be accepted but to be seen as a glorious endeavour.

For large sections of *Old Days, Old Ways*, Gilmore manages to avoid the implicit contradictions she sets up for herself. Absorbed in the detail of recording, it is enough for her to relay 'the drama of the human effort' to the present forgetful generation. In *More*

Recollections, however, where she undertakes to explain the more distant past, revaluing the worth of Aboriginal culture and inevitably becoming involved in accounts of white persecution, the earlier assumptions are decidedly shaken. On one hand, consciously writing a 'romance' with a 'pen of fire', the sort of history which feeds patriotism and 'conscious nationhood' and invokes the name of C. E. W. Bean, on the other, she is recording with devastating honesty horrific scenes of genocide. The confusion is apparent in the occasional windy passages of philosophizing. Reflecting on the hardships of the past, for instance, she comments: 'Cruelty is; and in cruelty is charnel. But sometimes out of charnel comes life—life itself a combination of charnel and grist, and above it all moves on in steadfastness the still unconquerable sun' (p. 92). Here, of course, the impression of sagacity is undercut by the empty Biblical phrasing, sonorous repetitions, and vaguely emotive adjectives, while the final affirmation is almost farcical, really affirming nothing more than solar progress.

Confusion also shows itself in several near-admissions of ambivalence. Remembering the tales of the blacks told to her father, for example, 'the same feeling sweeps over me, and I see with their eyes and feel with their feelings'. Reflecting in the next breath on the droving teams of the past, however, and the 'long roads that made this Australian nation's first history . . . The sins and wrong-doings of the elders are forgotten, and only the spirit and the things of the spirit remain, so that the high tide of the heart rises in the thought of those who once far travelled, and in their travelling made our first roads' (p. 95).

In her accounts of atrocities she is careful to dissociate her family from involvement, emphasizing her father's efforts to warn tribes of impending trouble and relating the costs her grandfather suffered by refusing to go on shooting expeditions. Nevertheless, her accounts are too vivid to justify the earlier heady patriotism. In the last chapters of the book, grim memories of killings accelerate, culminating in one that is uncomfortably close to home. The chapter titled 'The Whip', for instance, retrieves the conversations of men, overheard by the child and only half-understood at the time:

the talk . . . wandered to skulls, where thick and where thin, and how to hit with a stirrup-iron in order to get a 'clean' kill. One who had a rounded stirrup always made for across the nose, another with a square iron used it on the temple, another hit behind the ear. (p. 221)

Meanwhile the adult self relates others' accounts of the effects of the Clarence River massacres, of poisonings and hunting parties: 'the water was so polluted with human debris that no one drank it without first boiling it; and . . . the dingoes ceased to attack calves and fattened on babies' (p. 243).

But it is a more personal account that is the most disturbing, not just for its horrific content but for the light which it throws on the narrator's own attitudes. Her grandmother is described as having many memories of the exterminating expeditions; she is pictured on one occasion as mixing dough for scones and simultaneously listening to the wild cries of the hunt outside:

As she mixed up the dough she heard the dogs, the guns, the shouts of the horsemen, and the cries of the hunted who were being driven to the river. It was not the first time, and she went on with her work. Suddenly the door was pulled open and a girl of about twelve rushed in, fell at her feet, clutched her skirts and with agonized eyes and broken words pleaded for protection. There was nothing that could be done, for immediately 'two gentlemen' entered the room, dragged the girl out, and beat in her head at the door. The blood was still there when grandfather came home. (pp. 246–7)

There can be no reconciliation between this and the earlier glorifica-tion of white settlement and the narrator seems at least partially aware of the fact: 'Perhaps the mailed fist is, after all, the sign of civilization and righteous because ruthless. One thinks and wonders' (p. 267). Nevertheless, the acceptance of the contrast between the white woman doggedly mixing her dough ('It was not the first time') and the fatalism of 'There was nothing to be done', are insensitivities which the modern reader cannot fail to find shocking. At other moments in the narrative the sage over-voice *is* sufficiently shocked, even comparing the Australian atrocities to the actions of the 'terrible Spaniards of the fifteenth and sixteenth centuries', but elsewhere it seems bent on explaining the horrific past as one of the inevitable injustices of history:

In the establishment of a new community, as in Australia, there has always followed the destruction of the community in being before the invader came. Such destruction where powers are equal or are equally armed, is war. But where there is inequality there is conquest for one side and massacre for the other. In Australia we were the conquerors. (p. 182)

Wise omniscience, in fact, become untenable in the latter half of *More Recollections* and Gilmore's inability to integrate her multiple roles becomes jarringly obvious. Engrossed in her function as unique memory, the public persona is self-righteously preoccupied with *her* sympathy and understanding of the Aborigines, even seeing herself as a Homer-like figure who will reveal the affinities between the 'natives'' [sic] mythology and that of the ancient Greeks. Anxious to counter white prejudice, she expands on the unwritten civilization and 'fidelity' of the blacks, contradicting her assumptions elsewhere that the white culture is synonymous with progress and civilization. Venerating Australia's history and her own status as interpreter, she must somehow show the past as sanctifying the present. Separating herself from the racism of her time, she unwittingly exposes her own limitations of imagination. And just as she records the oppression of women, but ranks herself with the male, she records the destruction of the Aborigines but ranks herself with the white. In the latter case, however, one has the impression that the memories have a pressing, vivid life of their own, appealing to a less public, more sensitive self. Frenetically invoking Shakespeare, the Greeks, the Bible, the voice attempts to reassert the sanguine conviction of Australia's noble destiny, but memory is an uncertain horse and like other autobiographies this narrative is prey to subversive forces.

Writing, of course, is always culture-specific and it may appear anachronistic to accuse Gilmore of racial insensitivity in the 1930s; my point is, however, that these texts reveal two modes of 'knowing' the past. The most sensitive private form of knowledge, limited though it is, generates ambivalences which the surface rhetoric cannot conceal.

One of the most self-conscious of the autobiographies of pre-1920 childhoods is Maie Casey's *An Australian Story 1837–1907* (1962).[15] In many ways this narrative is characteristically female: in the concentration on the family past reflected in the oblique title; in the personal mode of recreating that past, cumulatively drawing on historical record, family myth and personal memory; and in the perception of audience. Facing both forward and back, the narrator writes to repay a debt to 'those loved persons and places behind me' and to inform her children of the inherited past ('there is much in it my children should know since they are the outcome of it', p. 9). Claiming to keep herself 'out of the story' as much as possible, Casey is nevertheless preoccupied with personal meaning; indeed the meaning of family story and self are inseparable for however unique and independent the latter, the former is perceived as influential as climate:

we are both outside and inside time. We are each of us a core with time flowing by and sometimes through us. The body and the mind develop and grow older, are tempered by personal experience but remain essentially themselves, made up as they are from the inherited past. (p. 9)

Yet Casey is by no means determinist in outlook; sensitive to the submerged currents of time, she is also intrigued by the variety and pace of its changes. Four recurring words—phase, adventure, challenge and sorrow—express her sense of the inevitable links in all human experience, but are particularly evident in the Australian history of her pioneering ancestors.

As interested as Gilmore in the experience of remembering, Casey is also self-conscious about her autobiographical strategy. The book is described as a 'mixture of record and memory', which will preserve the 'essence' of the people and places of the past, presenting them through the eyes of a child. The child's perceptions, however, are merely one thread in a narrative which blends the sharply perceived event with retrospective, mature appreciation, and with the findings of historical research. It is as if the child is the field worker, storing data for the backroom researches and reflections of the older self. Thus the child records her impressions of the intense Ellis Rowan, painting with 'ferocious concentration', oblivious to her bright-eyed niece, while the older self reflects on her aunt's extraordinary life and achievements, given their context. At times, the child-self has been too timid or inexperienced to cull the most from a personality, as in her response to her Grandmother Ryan; very deaf and somewhat offended by her daughter-in-law's implicit refusal to honour the child's inheritance of her own name, 'Marion', the old lady appears to regard her granddaughter 'without favour'. Yet, as the older-self realizes when she reads her letters and reviews her history, 'Nobody could have told more, had I been able to reach her, than Grannie Ryan' (p. 102); articulate and perceptive, she had known life in England and in the bush and the vicissitudes of her life had included 'poverty, sadness, death'. At other times, the child has no means of knowing the people of the past and their personalities have to be created from letters, public documents, portraits, poems, houses, domestic objects and others' memories.

Underlying this painstaking effort to recreate the past as a collage of record and memory, is an assumption that time has insidious but invisible continuities, lying in wait for the dedicated archaeologist. In one of the italicized passages which highlight the narrative's more self-conscious breathing spaces, the narrator reflects on the book as an adventure in exploration: '*My task is beginning to assume the fascination of a detective story, with here and there an illuminating clue*' (p. 24). Two influences, meanwhile, sharpen the urgency of this journey of exploration; one is the awareness of the threatened invisibility of Australia's and her family's brief history. 'They must be remembered and their essence preserved or the waters will have closed over them for ever and they might never have been' is one the book's opening sentences. At the same time occasional references to Australia's lack of a 'record of the mind' before the coming of the white settlers evoke an impression of fragility and even impermanence ('we still rest lightly upon the surface of the earth', p. 182). *An Australian Story* is, as its title implies, an attempt to add to this young record of the mind. Paradoxically 'all of a lovely piece' without the white settler, Australia is seen as presenting a continuing challenge to the European consciousness; to exist as a Europeanized country, it must exist in the imagination, just as the life of Australia's European past depends on that other branch of the imagination, memory. Thus Casey is attempting to retrieve three interdependent identities—her own, her family's and her country's. The other sharpening influence is the awareness of death, not just the author's own death but the memory of all the other deaths which have preceded this story; however timely, they will be untimely if their 'essence' is not preserved.

One apparently mundane sequence at the beginning of the book illustrates the complexity and sophistication of Casey's approach to the concepts of time, memory and identity. A weekly tram journey undertaken by mother and daughter to the maternal grandmother's residence, Stony Park, is the occasion for a series of deft shuffles of memory's pack which evoke the mother's appearance and personality, her family context and history, her difference from the father, her role as daughter of a somewhat repressive matriarch and her challenge to her own daughter. The most intimate of the cards are those expressing the essence of the mother, the tiny details of her physical appearance and personal habits. Meanwhile, conscious of her mother's style, the child has moments of inadequacy: 'Imagine how difficult it was for me to be the one small descendant of this stylish family' (p. 31). Leaving the tram, the two walk from the terminus to Stony Park

each thinking our own different thoughts as we passed the small weatherboard houses, trimmed with iron lace, in the treeless streets that led to the side gate of the park.
. . . The preoccupations of older persons seem boring and incomprehensible to children who cannot understand them or their urgency. How should they, with all the long lush years ahead, each year full of the leisurely beauty of the months, which seem never to end! The time of growing seems so slow. (pp. 34–5)

Given the strength of the child's real bond with the mother, apparent in the latter's centrality in the daughter's growth into adulthood, and given the older narrator's awareness of time's brevity, the conscious irony of the words 'boring', 'incomprehensible', 'leisurely' and 'slow' is obvious. The personal significance of this insignificant journey is further highlighted by an italicized erruption into the text, describing the child's first conscious glimpse of her own face; shocked by its '*fat and potato-like*' aspect, she did not admire herself at all: '*a depression settled on me every time afterwards that I saw myself in a mirror*' (p. 35). Detached and yet invisibly and powerfully bonded, the relationship of mother and child exists on one of those 'mysterious . . . wavelengths [that] cannot be interpreted by words':

The depths of instinct and age-old experience we share with the animals and insects, and the stresses of the mind, are expressed through communication more subtle still. We have very different lives running side by side. (pp. 32–3)

Thus various personae are at work in this narrative: the unthinking but observant and retentive child, the older, more worldly-wise reflective narrator and, behind them both, the observing 'I', who is frequently surprised by the revelations of this journey into self and family.

Probably the most immediately striking illustration of Casey's sophistication, however, is her narrative structure. Consciously composed like a piece of music, *An Australian Story* consists of four quartets, each of which describes a family home and carries a musical sub-title. Thus the story of Stony Park is *andante*; the story of Derriweit Heights at Mount Macedon is *allegretto*; the story of 37 Collins Street, Melbourne, is *allegro animato*; the story of Earimil on the Mornington Peninsula is *sostenuto con amore*.

Stony Park, the maternal grandmother Sarah Sumner's home, is the most convinced of its own Anglo-Saxon solidity and yet the most enervated and frail. A pretentious substitute for an earlier Stony Park which was destroyed by fire after the death of the grandfather, who has been similarly obliterated from memory, it is an incongruous mix of styles lacking integrity. Acutely sensitive to the personalities of houses and gardens, Casey contrasts the lifelessness of her grandmother's 'shell' with the apparent vigour of the earlier Stony Park. Even the furniture of the second house has an emotional affinity with its owner:

What spoiled it was the excess of spindly furniture, small Victorian tables and chairs, without sufficient authority in the big space where they stood awkwardly like guests who have not been introduced and are without life. Even the sofas with their hard backs and slender legs appeared frail and discouraging. No sturdy chairs were there into which man or child could throw himself with confidence. (p. 38)

The 'product of the efforts of her father and her husband', whose lives had been active and hard, Sarah Sumner has led a 'remote, nurtured and comfortable' life. Although she is an authoritative figure, due largely to her material wealth, 'she never seemed to do anything but sit about, giving an impression of mental alertness but none of achievement'. The narrator is careful to qualify her criticisms, but the impression of sterility is unavoidable. Relying on her daughter to manage affairs, the grandmother seems to limit even her writing to a signature on a cheque, 'an easy form of generosity'. Meanwhile there are suggestions that the tranquility of the mansion is unnatural; described as an 'inhuman calm' at one point, it masks a sequence of unexplained, unmourned absences—the son who fails and flees to England, the once welcome James Grice who has had some legal dispute with the family, the grandmother's companion, the once indispensable Mrs Miller, and Aunt Katie's husband. Contrasting with this picture of enervation is the narrator's retrieval of her unknown grandfather, T. T. Sumner, and great grandfather, John Jones Peers, the one living mostly in a charred book of poems and a long birthday ode to his fiancée, the other in his books of hymns, 'words and music carefully written out by him in ink that is now the brown of old blood' (p. 27).

Memory, for this narrator, is spurred in two specific ways. One is by sound:

Recognized sound, like smell, has the power to telescope time, to jerk one back for a moment into an earlier self so completely sometimes that one can look down on a socked leg and see again the long forgotten pattern of the sock. (pp. 39–40)

And there are frequent descriptions of representative sounds from the Swiss musical box of Stony Park with its 'exact and passionless music' to the later one at Collins Street ('Some level of my life is threaded on its remote melodies, where change stands still', p. 147). Melbourne of the 1890s lives in the sounds of its streets, and people are survived by memories of their distinctive speaking and writing voices. The unreachable Grannie Ryan, on the other hand, is remembered as playing vigorous tunes that make no sense. Not surprisingly the language of clocks is particularly significant, often expressing the quality of a time that they have superseded: 'We have his Ellicott watch that still goes, bridging time: while the man with the scythe on its embossed gold case still lies in wait' (p. 97). Even the experience of remembering itself is imaged in auditory terms, described as partly painful, like listening 'for the first time to the recorded voice of someone dead whom [one] had closely known' (p. 9).

Visual impressions are also important and there are some instances of the significant human detail—a glimpse of the hand of her brother, anticipating his future strength and purpose, or of the grandmother's 'fine exact hand' peeling a peach. But it is faces that are most interesting; frequently indulging in detailed descriptions of the physical features of friends and relatives, the narrator also depends on portraits of unknown ancestors as interpreters of personality. Similarly, she is almost as preoccupied with dress as Nancy Adams, but her interest is quite different; clothes bear the stamp of identity and like the trivial relics of the past, give it shape.

If Stony Park imposes itself uneasily on Australia, finally surviving only in the street names which record some of its personalities, Mount Macedon, where the Ryans have their homes, fits them as closely as a skin. 'Rare' individuals of artistic talents and naturalist enthusiasms, the Ryans live in a haphazard way which is very different from the rigid patterns of Stony Park. Dispossessed of their first splendid garden home, 'Derriweit', they nevertheless establish an affinity with the spirit of Macedon while their disinterested enthusiasm for place survives in the paintings of Ellis Rowan and her grandfather, John Cotton. Paradoxically, the Ryans also preserve their European heritage with more certainty than the Sumners and their cottage is filled with relics from both pasts:

[the cottage's treasures] are our background, the details forming the delicate net that holds families together. Details that have given each one of us the comfort of familiarity; objects sometimes as simple as a plate or a spoon we have known all our lives as have others before us. Small things link the past with the present. (p. 94)

Like Stony Park, the Ryan household is a female one, but more closely bonded; duty is the foundation of much of the attentiveness at Stony Park, whereas feeling is the rock of the relationships between the Ryan sisters. Separated in different countries in later years, they are united by their weekly letters which bring 'the contact of life'.

No. 37 Collins Street, the narrator's own childhood home, is by contrast a male household. Dominated by the father's ebullient personality and the demands of his profession as a surgeon, it also reflects his past experience of war; the great Doré engraving which 'haunted the house depicting an angel with an angry open mouth and sword, driving a host of people downhill' expresses the disturbing influences that the father's experience represents. This is also Alice Ryan's 'own territory', where she provides both authority and security. Married to a man of impetuous, quicksilver temperament, she looks after the business arrangements; nevertheless, in this section of the book she is described as 'The Wife' and it is not until she is in the Earimil setting that she comes into her own. Criticisms of Collins Street are kept to a minimum, yet it is clear that the house represents difficulties and confinement; overlooked by the constant flow of her father's patients, the family is also 'hemmed in . . . by the tools and books of his profession, which took up more and more space' (p. 124), or is expected to come into the father's professional 'net' and entertain his patients. Pride in the father's achievement mingles with remembered distress at witnessed suffering; unable to share the surgeon's detached professionalism, the child empathizes with the sadness of his patients, feeling her face 'drooping' with theirs or, accompanying him on his visits to hospitals, is 'filled with terror and distaste'. Not surprisingly, given this narrator's sensitivity to place, the house itself mirrors these impressions of difficulty and confinement; designed by a male architect to fit the external personality of the area, inside it is a labyrinth that has 'the fascination of the difficult, the intricate, the almost impossible' (p. 110).

The book's last quartet, dealing with the mother's childhood holiday home, Earimil, is the most nostalgic. Where Collins Street is aggressively male, Earimil is resistantly female; preserving its unique identity through several generations, it is the mother's natural province:

It had been part of her earliest life, the secret depository of much that I was not to know, except years later and then scarcely through words. She had been there every summer from childhood and the place was filled with her essence (p. 181)

It is also the daughter's ('How can I write about Earimil? I was wrapped in it. I have waited a long time before permitting my mind to go back, to enter into that departed world', p. 153). So intensely is it loved that the narrator prays that if it should leave the family, it would 'slide into the sea and lie there intact like Tyre and Sidon under deep water' (p. 153).

Difficult of access and nestling in a secret part of Mornington Peninsula, Earimil waits nine months every year for repossession of its secluded delights. It offers freedom from the pressures of Collins Street and the more tangible freedom of solitary forays into the bush on horseback. If the house's geography is a more congenial, female one ('the house in Collins street showed the fanciful achievement of some master mind, Earimil must have grown gradually into its fascinating shape', p. 155), its dangers merely serve to deepen the 'benign atmosphere'.

With this last quartet Casey subtly draws the threads of her public theme, the difficulties of European appropriation of Australia, together, for Earimil exists also as a hopeful metaphor of the new Anglo-Australian culture. At the same time it concludes two further explorations, of the self and of the relationship with the mother. Observing her in her different roles and environments, as mother, daughter, daughter-in-law, and wife, and as a strong, self-sufficient individuality, the narrator gradually rediscovers her mother's essence. At Stony Park her personality is subdued ('She was scarcely a wife, a mother herself, much less the Alice Ryan of other settings', p. 33); at Macedon she is ill at ease and out of her element; at Collins Street, she is Alice Ryan the stylish, competent wife of a successful surgeon; but at Earimil she is her quintessential self, at one with a loved environment. Earlier the narrator has commented on the inevitable adolescent rift with the mother, based on the inability of generations to reconcile different points of view, but here she celebrates the final understanding. Understated though it is, this section also appears to celebrate an understanding of the self. It is at Earimil that the child first becomes triumphantly aware of her individuality when she escapes from the family on the beach:

It was, and has remained, one of the most desperate and significant adventures of my life. I had to struggle for a long way over the hazards of the sea-line, then up the narrow precipitous track joining the Byronic cleft at the cliff edge. I can still recall the beating of my heart—stifling me with fear and pleasure—as I entered the smooth safety of the Lovers Walk. The image is intact. (p. 159)

A later incident, when she is pushed by an unknown individual into a cupboard during a bushfire, is remembered as a gross misrepresentation of her sufficiently courageous self. The book as a whole, however, is a celebration of individuality in relationship. If in the Stony Park section the self's reflection appears disturbingly anomalous, by the close it has acquired both relatedness and individuality, framed as it is by the diverse faces of male and female ancestors.

4

Relational Selves

Serious interest in autobiography as a genre in its own right is of relatively recent origin. Georg Misch's massive *History of Autobiography in Antiquity*, published in German in 1907, should have initiated critical studies, but it was not until the early 1960s that Anglo-American interest began to quicken, perhaps in response to two bibliographies which revealed the extent of the field for the first time, William Matthews's *British Autobiographies* (1955) and Louis Kaplan's *A Bibliography of American Autobiographies* (1961). Even then, discussion was bogged down for a long time in questions of legitimacy and genre, in distinguishing autobiography from biography, diaries, letters, history and fiction. The question of genre is still unresolved and likely to remain so, notwithstanding the attempts of such critics as Philippe Lejeune and Elizabeth Bruss[1] to discover the north-west passage to a stable definition of the form. Two roughly coincidental essays had a seminal effect, James Olney's study *Metaphors of Self* (1972) and Francis Hart's 'Notes for an Anatomy of Modern Autobiography' (1970). Georges Gusdorf's article 'Conditions and Limits of Autobiography', first published in French in 1956, is sometimes accorded pioneering status but it was not available in English until 1980, by which time Anglo-American autobiographical criticism had become both prolific and varied.[2] Attempting to impose some order on the mass of criticism which had appeared by 1983, Avrom Fleishman in his *Figures of Autobiography* establishes six main approaches: the concern with the self's truth and its difference from the truth of fiction, demonstrated most brilliantly by Hart's essay; the concern with meaning, or the design which the autobiographer gives to the facts of the self's history in the process of writing, typified by Roy Pascal's study *Design and Truth in Autobiography*[3]; the concern with genre, that is, with the characteristic rhetorical features which might demonstrate the author's sense of writing within a literary tradition; the concern with the linguistic

workings of the text which reveal the 'co-presence in autobiography
of a narrated past and a narrational present', the stylistic essence of
the autobiographer as 'he' holds his pen, typified by Jean
Starobinski's essay 'The Style of Autobiography'[4]; the concern with
myth, that is with the creation of a personal mythos that has a
Jungian, integrating effect on the psyche, pioneered by James
Olney's *Metaphors of Self*; and the concern with post-structuralist
insights into the displaced self of the author, 'the impossible dream of
being alive to oneself in the scriptural', most comprehensively illustrated by Jeffrey Mehlman's *A Structural Study of Autobiography*.[5]
Fleishman concludes his survey with the contention that no approach
can claim to appropriate the protean forms of autobiography,
although all have their uses. Not 'generically distinguished by formal
constituents, linguistic register, or audience effects', autobiography
has no history as a genre, although it is 'steeped in history':

Certain studies look for the defining characteristics of a theoretical genre,
with an essence or eternal nature; others propose historical generalizations of
certain shared features—in a manner approximating the family resemblance
definitions of Wittgenstein. Both these enterprises fail to take hold of
autobiography's protean forms: the one because autobiography cannot be
derived from an abstract theory of genres; the other because a variety of
pragmatic criteria are always introduced to delimit the range of works
considered.[6]

Although Fleishman fails to mention the fact, a major delimitation
of the great range of autobiographical criticism in Europe and
America is the failure of critics to concern themselves with female
texts. It is an extraordinary silence in a field which is both polyvocal
and innovative. On one hand critics have seized on the modernist
implications of autobiography as self-reflexive, self-enacting discourse; on the other, they have virtually ignored the equally challenging potential of feminist theory. If the criticism of autobiography is
pre-eminently concerned with ideologies of selfhood, it must also be
concerned with ideologies of gender, yet autobiographical theory has
consistently turned a blind eye to the relationship. Both Gusdorf and
Olney fail to mention a single female autobiography; Hart includes
mention of one, Anaïs Nin's, in his consideration of a wide range of
male texts; Karl J. Weintraub's *The Value of the Individual* (1978)
values only the male, although his study ranges from Augustine to
Goethe; William Spengemann's *The Forms of Autobiography* (1980)
claims to be a classification based on representative texts but recognizes only male forms, A. O. J. Cockshutt's *The Art of Autobiography in Nineteenth and Twentieth Century England* (1984) implies a
broad cultural reference but deals with only three, oddly selected,
female texts in an otherwise varied gallery of self-portraits; Pascal
offers some discussion of St Teresa's *Life* in a general treatment of

early Christian autobiographies but then restricts himself almost entirely to male texts; Elizabeth Bruss limits her study to chapters on Bunyan, Boswell, De Quincey and Nabokov; and Janet Varner Gunn's *Autobiography: Towards a Poetics of Experience* (1982) is a similar selection of male 'greats'. One study, Paul Delany's *British Autobiography in the Seventeenth Century* (1969), finds that women's texts are in some respects superior to men's. More concerned with intimate feelings and less with *res gestae* than the male writer, the female autobiographer may have stimulated the development of the novel:

female autobiographers strike the modern reader as having generally a more 'unified sensibility' than their male counterparts: their lives seem less compartmentalized, they have a wider range of emotional responses to everyday events and more awareness of concrete realities.[7]

His treatment of female writing is comparatively cursory, however, an afterword to a study which equates the representative with the male and is at home with an androcentric theory of autobiography. As Donna Stanton comments, the absence of women's autobiographies from critical writing sorts oddly with the frequent claim or criticism that women's writing is more autobiographical than men's: she concludes that 'autobiographical' constitutes 'a positive term when applied to Augustine and Montaigne, Rousseau and Goethe, Henry Adams and Henry Miller', but has 'negative connotations when imposed on women's texts', implying a lower imaginative activity, grounded in the factual.[8]

In response to this curious silence, four American writers have attempted to give some account of female autobiography. Patricia Meyer Spacks's *Imagining a Self*[9], a study of English autobiography and novel in the eighteenth century, includes both male and female texts and some lively discussion of features perceived to be characteristic of female versions of the self. Estelle C. Jelinek has written a history of women's autobiography and edited a collection of essays on the topic[10]; the former is necessarily the more concentrated. Dividing her history into three sections, 'From Antiquity to Nineteenth-Century British Autobiography', 'American Autobiography to the Twentieth Century' and 'American Autobiography in the Modern Era', Jelinek brushes in some general trends before concentrating on the four writers who compose her last section, Stanton, Stein, Hellman and Millett. Her book undoubtedly adds to knowledge of the field, but her attempt to cover as much territory as possible in a historical and geographical variety of women's self-writing and a disappointing residue of conclusions. The collection of essays edited by Donna Stanton, *The Female Autograph*, is both more challenging and rigorous than Jelinek's books; representing something of the historical and geographical variety of women's self-writing and interpreting 'autobiography' in a wide formal sense, the overall tone of the collection is deliberately questioning rather than conclusive in accordance with Stanton's own title: 'Autogynography: Is the Subject Different?'. By far the most ambitious attempt so far to elucidate an answer to Stanton's question is Sidonie Smith's *A Poetics of Women's Autobiography*.[11] Smith's first three chapters are a rigorous discussion of the limitations of current theories and historical accounts of the genesis of autobiography; in the second section, however, titled 'Readings', Smith deals with five centuries of female autobiography via a consideration of only five texts. Stimulating though her discussions are, the narrowness of this latter approach, and especially the decision to select texts by women who would have preferred to be men, limit the usefulness of her study. Given the variety and extent of women's life-writing, no critical work can hope to represent the whole field, of course, but at the very least these studies have exposed the extraordinary lacunae in previous theoretical approaches.

The study of autobiography in Australia is still in its infancy; the absence of bibliographies of autobiographies compounds the general gaps in Australian bibliography so that knowledge of both male and female life-writing until the 1950s is necessarily patchy, nor is there any substantial critical study of the known texts of so-called 'literary' autobiography. Nevertheless, it is generally conceded that our literature is particularly rich in autobiographies of childhood and that the genre is remarkably popular with the general reader. As Richard Coe comments, in an influential essay in 1981, 'Proportionately to their numbers, Australian writers write more, and more frequently, and as likely as not *better*, about themselves-as-children, than do those of almost any other cultural group outside France and England'.[12] Coe has included several Australian texts in his broad study of childhoods, *When the Grass Was Taller* (1984), and the recent anthology edited by John and Dorothy Colmer[13] has given some indication of the variety of life-writing in Australia.

An interest in the genre's cultural content has been the prominent feature of writing on Australian autobiography so far; it is the shaping force in Coe's essay, the Colmer anthology and the numerous critical essays on individual texts and the genre as a whole. As the Colmers conclude, 'the quest for personal identity involves asking fundamental questions about national culture and identity'[14], and the recurring fascination with such texts as *My Brother Jack*, *A Fortunate Life*, *Cutting Green Hay*, and *The Watcher on the Cast Iron Balcony* is nearly always a fascination with the question of cultural identity. It appears, however, that the Australian cultural identity is still a male identity, for female texts play a minor role in this quest to relate personal to national meaning. While Coe concentrates mainly on male texts and the Colmer anthology includes extracts from twelve female as against thirty-one male narratives, other commentators muse on the conflict between Australia and the life of the individual spirit.[15] Equating 'individual' with the experience of the male individual and 'interest' with cultural interest, it is not long before the critic concludes that male autobiographies are superior to female.[16] Although numerous articles illuminate such major female texts as *My Brilliant Career*, *The Getting of Wisdom*, *The Man Who Loved Children* and *For Love Alone*, the relationship of these texts to women's life-writing in general is never investigated. Meanwhile, a middle range of autobiographies including such narratives as *Solid Bluestone Foundations*, *Aunts Up the Cross*, and *Beltana—Six Miles* is never granted more than the brief nod of a sympathetic review. On the other hand, male texts of the same range, such as *Cutting Green Hay* and *The Education of Young Donald*, have aroused a spate of articles.

The same tendency to conflate male experience and critical ideology afflicts the theory(ies) of autobiography. A brief résumé of Fleishman's six approaches, for instance, reveals a common basis underlying their apparent variety, that is, the assumption that autobiography is grounded in individualism and in individualism of a certain kind. Gusdorf, for example, is preoccupied with the individual's subjectivity, his singularity and sense of difference: the autobiographer 'believes it a useful and valuable thing to fix his own image so that he can be certain it will not disappear', but at the same time the anxiety of the project assails his consciousness. The autobiographical image is 'another "myself"', a double of my being but more fragile and vulnerable, invested with a sacred character that makes it at once fascinating and frightening'. Recalling the past satisfies a 'disquiet of the mind anxious to recover and redeem lost time in fixing it for ever' and, imposing on the assorted facts of his life his own unity of design, the autobiographer 'structures the terrain where his life is lived and gives it its ultimate shape'. The autobiography is an 'apologetics or theodicy of the individual being', appeasing the author's sense that he has lived 'in vain', it is 'the diagram of a destiny' that is as yet uncompleted and engaged with 'the very arrow of lived time.' Embracing the 'always secret but never refused sense of his own destiny', the autobiographer seeks 'the meaning of his own mythic tale', and wrestles 'with his shadow, certain only of never laying hold of it'.[17] As in other examples of male autobiographical discourse, Gusdorf's 'I' has what Sidonie Smith terms 'the imperialistic designs of a speaking subject intent on "naming, controlling, remembering, understanding"'.[18] The male autobiographer, according to his commentators, is concerned with the enchanting pursuit of the elusive first person singular, with making a coherent system out of his life; according to Robert Sayre autobiography is preoccupied with showing 'how the life has been the fulfillment of ideas' and is written 'out of a desire to see both a shape and an end to one's life, to see the end of everything that has been in flux and process, and at the same time to understand it all'.[19] Other commentators stress the impossibility of the quest for identity and shape; Paul Eakin, for instance, expresses the common dilemma:

all autobiographies are by nature incomplete and they cannot, accordingly, have a definitive shape. As a life changes, so any sense of the shape of a life must change; the autobiographical process evolves because it is part of the life, and the identity of the autobiographical 'I' changes and shifts.[20]

Pascal sees autobiography's centre of interest as 'the self, not the outside world, though inevitably the outside world must appear so that, in give and take with it, the personality finds its peculiar shape'. The best autobiographies are those which suggest 'a certain power of the personality over circumstance ... in the sense that the individual can extract nurture out of disparate incidents and ultimately bind them together in his own way'. And the value of an autobiography depends on its creation of an impression of its 'driving force ... what Montaigne calls a man's "master form"'. Truth in autobiography is not objective truth but the truth that 'grows out of the author's life and imposes itelf on him as his specific quality'. Since the primary purpose of autobiography is not to show us the private individual behind the public man but 'the man within the work', the most interesting autobiographies are necessarily those of men who have led interesting public lives.[21] As in other male accounts of the genre, the concepts of singularity, autonomy, teleological design, unity, appropriation and achieved rhetorical ends are privileged. Texts perceived as particularly valuable are those which are self-consciously aware of the process of self-discovery and comment on the transforming power of the existential journey. If autobiography is necessarily subjective, the writer who maintains a scientific objectivity about the subjective quest, or at least an impression of distance, offers the preferred paradox. According to Hart, the interpretative reader seeks 'an evolving mixture of pattern and situation—pattern discerned in the life recovered, pattern discovered or articulated in the self or "versions of self" that emerge in that recovery, pattern in the recovery process'. Less prescriptive than Pascal on the subject of form, Hart nevertheless relates form or anti-form to the author's search or failure to find purpose and meaning in the life, and privileges individuality and separateness over connectedness.[22] Implicitly committed to the ideals of progress and the coherent self, male commentators are fond of verbs of control, power and agency and quick to recognize them in their subjects; William Howarth, for instance, finds that 'Rousseau searches obsessively for his own "true self", Thoreau wants to "drive life into a corner", Agee vainly hopes to capture "a portion of unimagined existence"'[23]

It might be thought that the recent emphasis on the textuality of the self, and the epistemological instability of language has dislodged the stress on singularity and autonomy. If the 'I' of autobiographical discourse is exposed as no more than a shifty pronominal shifter, the search for unity and autonomy is doomed from the start and speaking the self is as problematic for the male as for the female within his culture. As Ken Ruthven has commented, it is no longer the case that 'whenever a man uses the first person pronoun he produces that "unified 'I'", which (in the words of Mary Jacobus) "falls as a dominating phallic shadow across the male page"'.[24] But far from eroding the emphasis on individualism inherent in autobiographical theory, post-structuralist strategies emphatically reinforce its pre-eminence; if the truth of the individual cannot be realized, the experience of his individual (failed) search for the self has endless fascination. Thus the approved model for the theorist becomes the text which deconstructs itself. John Sturrock, for example, describes Michel Leiris, as 'the new model autobiographer', and *L'Age d'Homme* as a 'thoughtful and adventurous' confrontation with language's writing of the self.[25] As another commentator on Leiris puts it: his text 'is an attempt to produce a *signifié* (a signification) from a plethora of signifiers, and ... the attempt itself becomes in its turn a signifier calling for a new search for a *signifié*—a never-ending more abstract process'. Pondering the question 'Who is that I ... that self of mine around which everything is articulated?', Leiris 'seeks in the materials of his life the central symbolic order that could give them significance'.[26] Thus deconstruction might be regarded as the latest development in the history of individualism in Western culture, romanticizing the fragmentation, the lack of agency, meaning and authorship which has preoccupied man since Freud; de-centring the self, it is fundamentally self-centred. As with other branches of literature, the new ideology concentrates on the few texts which display the required self-conscious 'sophistication' or experimental formalism. Female autobiographies need not apply.[27]

The conspicuous silence on female life-writing suggests several possibilities: that women's writing is innately less complex and crafted than men's, that autobiography is a male generic act, alien to female creativity, that the paradigm of selfhood inscribed by 'normal' autobiography is not typical of women's experience or that the received autobiographical theory is a male construct that fails to recognize the difference of women's texts. My reading of this group of autobiographies indicates that the last two represent the reality. As Sidonie Smith comments, the established theories 'seem to derive from certain underlying assumptions: that men's and women's ways of experiencing the world and the self and their relationship to language and to the institution of literature are identical'.[28] Applying to female writing any one of the approaches analysed by Fleishman, at least in the manner they have hitherto been pursued, is to experience the occasional insight and, in some cases, even the occasional breakthrough. But the main impression is of lighting up odd corners of the text while huge areas remain in shadow. Like their male counterparts, women consciously write problematic narratives, use fictive narrators, are intrigued by the tension between the narrated past and the narrational present, draw on myth and imagery to shape their meanings and are responsive to collaborative, fictive readers. Yet if these are the parts of the female text, it remains stubbornly greater than their sum, skewed from centre, out of focus, or at least reduced from the initial reading experience.

The main difference appears to be one of content rather than style, although it has stylistic consequences; certain foci, characteristic of male writing, are either absent or are replaced by others. Most strikingly of all, the paradigm of selfhood described by the received theory is radically altered, suggesting that the figure is an androcentric one. Indeed, reading the interpretations of male and female development by such object-relations psychoanalysts as Nancy Chodorov, Dorothy Dinnerstein and Jane Flax, brings home the extent to which exploration of the self-reflexiveness of autobiography has been uncritically based on the male experience of individuation. Chodorov's *The Reproduction of Mothering* and her numerous articles on the topic suggest, for instance, that the different relational context of the early years of boys and girls imposes distinct psychic consequences. Identifying closely with the mother as the primary care-giver and role-figure, the daughter has no need to detach herself and to find selfhood in separation as has the son. Thus her experience of self is characterized by 'more flexible and permeable ego boundaries'. The son's maleness, on the other hand, has to discover itself in the external society of the powerful fathers; he becomes male by not being female, whereas his sister enjoys a less equivocal and negatively formed sense of gender. Her difficulty, on the other hand, is likely to lie in the conviction of continuity and similarity, complicating her sense of a separate self. Thus 'the basic feminine sense of self is connected to the world, the basic masculine sense of self is separate'.[29]

[The] relational context contrasts profoundly for girls and boys in a way that makes difference, and gender difference, central for males—one of the earliest, most basic male developmental issues—and not central for females. It gives men a psychological investment in difference that women do not have.[30]

Chodorov further emphasizes the continuing experience of individuation for men, endorsing Margaret Mead's observation that 'maleness is not absolutely defined, [but] . . . has to be kept and re-earned every day'.[31] She is also illuminating on the common equation of male and human in phallocentric society, in a way that is particularly relevant to autobiographical theory. Granted power and cultural hegemony in our society, men have appropriated and transformed the early android experiences, interpreting them as universal: 'Both in everyday life and in theoretical and intellectual formulations, men have come to define maleness as that which is basically human, and to define women as not-men'.[32] Thus it is not surprising that autobiography, the linguistic embodiment of the self, has traditionally been seen as wearing a male mask over its human features.

The insinuating power of this conflation of male and human was recently demonstrated in an article by the feminist writer, Carolyn Heilbrun. Responding to the work of Spacks and Jelinek, Heilbrun argues that women were incapable of writing autobiography until recently, that it is only 'in the last decade' that their life-writing has 'unmistakably found its true form'. Doomed to be 'selves in hiding' in patriarchal culture, women were compelled to present themselves as 'intuitive, nurturing, passive, never managerial . . . they did not tell the truth about their lives'. Dating true women's autobiography from 1973 and the publication of May Sarton's *Journal of a Solitude*, Heilbrun welcomes the full awakening of feminist consciousness:

> The new women autobiographers will probably be the first real mothers of achieving, self-realized women in the history of the world. It is a sobering thought, and one which reveals how new and revolutionary a form we are considering.[33]

Persuaded by the very theoretical works she criticizes, to equate self-consciousness and self-realization with the male experience of individuation, Heilbrun has no ear for the different voices of earlier female texts. Heilbrun's article emphasizes the fact of difference between male and female life-writing, however, even though it privileges the male.

Experiencing difference in reading these texts is inescapable. Defining it is another matter and the problem is intensified by the fact that difference has become a loaded issue, perhaps *the* most loaded issue, for feminists. Lynne Segal, for example, has warned of the dangers of an 'apocalyptic feminism . . . which portrays a Manichean struggle between female virtue and male vice' or which stresses the 'separate and special knowledge, emotion, sexuality, thought and morality of women . . . a type of separate "female world", which exists in fundamental opposition to "male culture", "male authority", "malestream thought"'. Not only does such an attitude reinforce the ideas of polarity which the feminist movement originally aimed to challenge, but it frequently portrays women's powerlessness, poverty and victimization as 'women's timeless history'.[34] It is therefore of the first importance to attend to what women actually write or have written, not to what they should write according to any received ideology; feminist preconceptions can be as imprisoning as male chauvinist attitudes. This study cannot and should not claim to

be a general poetics of women's autobiography, but some appreciation of the question of difference within this group of culturally
defined texts is obviously necessary.

As far as Australian autobiographies are concerned, it appears that
women established a well-defined and distinctive if initially thin
tradition in the nineteenth century, which has swelled to a flood in
recent years. Initially a by-product of an androcentric, pioneering
culture, women's autobiography rapidly developed more congenial
forms of expression, which genuflected only superficially to male
expectations. Probably a literate outcrop of a familiar oral tradition
of story-telling, women's texts established themselves as an alternative, rather than a countering tradition to men's. Initially at least they
represent not so much a subculture as a complementary culture,
expressing areas of experience ignored by men. Although some
Anglo-American critics of women's autobiography see their authors
as inevitably imprisoned in male rhetorical forms and inevitably
silenced on many topics, it seems to me that in Australia at least
women developed a lively and varied range of alternatives for writing
the self. Given cultural constraints, and those of the nineteenth
century in particular, there are, of course, silences, gaps and telling
omissions, but male texts of the same period suffered from even more
rigorous constraints; the documentary pioneering mould effectively
inhibited male expression for a much longer period, while the pre-
dominating secular, materialistic concerns of Australian society imposed more subtle fetters on inwardness. Elaine Showalter's suggestion that women are not confined to two alternatives, either imitating
their male predecessors or revising them, certainly applies to this
genre of Australian writing. Far from being an obverse of male
writing, fitting into a 'crude topography of hole and bulge' with the
'bulging bogeys on one side' and women's writing 'a pocked moon
surface of revisionary lacunae on the other', it is in fact a female
tradition of 'strength and solidarity' generating 'its own experiences
and symbols'.[35] Nor would I want to suggest that the difference
between male and female texts is an innate gender difference; more
reflective of social conditioning than any other form of literature,
autobiography cannot escape from its historical and cultural moment.
In Australia cultural circumstances initially provided women autobiographers with relatively few publishing outlets, but with greater
freedom and opportunity for inward exploration than their male
counterparts. If men eventually secured a like freedom of expression,
the movement merely underlines the general human attractiveness of
the opportunities offered by the genre.

Difference, as it promoted itself historically speaking and primarily
within the autobiography of place, was one of mimesis, that is, the
selection of a certain kind of reality; form, implying structure and

patterning; and genre, that is, the perception of audience and the writing self. Although it is not possible to select any of these configurations as they characteristically appear in female life-writing as inherently and exclusively inscribing the female, since male texts sometimes use some of the same strategies, their relative and much greater consistency in female texts endow them with the strength of a tradition. Furthermore, male treatments of the same configurations have had and continue to have subtle but real differences as I hope to show.

No doubt the first impression on reading a group of mixed nineteenth century autobiographies is the difference in values. As Virginia Woolf remarked, women tend 'to make serious what appears insignificant to a man, and trivial what is to him important'. They remember what men choose to forget and often forget to mention what men choose to remember. My discussion in the previous three chapters should illustrate this impression; whereas men record external events, geographical features and climactic conditions, discoveries, feats of endurance or skill, observations on native flora and fauna, women concentrate on the minutiae of daily life, the pleasures and discomforts of ordinary relationships, the personal aura of the place that is the new or familiar home, the anxieties, griefs, lonelinesses and achieved enjoyments of early settlement life. More sensitive to the cross-grained, cluttered nature of things, women are also often more light-hearted about setbacks and makeshift conditions, ironic about the gulf between aspiration and achievement, observant of human absurdity, not averse to the shrewd or satiric aside, and far more frank about emotional and even spiritual vicissitudes. Place is invariably perceived and valued in human terms while the human costs of any enterprise are invariably privileged. And all these characteristics persist into the twentieth century with remarkable consistency. If women's autobiographies have become more frank about the inward life, the direction of their focus has not changed. Without overvaluing the texts considered here, it is possible to suggest that their representation of 'reality' approximates to Woolf's 'erratic and undependable "reality"' that is paradoxically permanent and that 'remains when the skin of the day has been cast into the hedge'.[36] Equally characteristic and consistent is the absence of design in the male sense. Less optimistic or concerned about the idea of progress, whether national or familial, women's life-writing rarely describes a personal teleology. It is the process of living that is foregrounded, rather than achievement or destiny, demonstrating the fact that women have had 'different ideas about human development, different ways of imagining the human condition, different notions of what is of value in life'.[37] Not only have women found their lives interesting in ways that are different from men's, but time, both present and past, is known differently and the retrospective discovery of a personal arrow-like unity is less common. Jelinek notices the same phenomenon in international autobiographies:

The traditional view of women is antithetical to the crucial motive of auto-biography—a desire to synthesize, to see one's life as an organic whole, to look back for a pattern. Women's lives are fragmented; they start as young women and are successively transformed from without into spinsters, demimondaines, wives, mothers, or matriarchs. The process is not one of growth, of evolution; rather, they enter each stage as a failure of the previous stage.[38]

In Australian autobiography, even the naïve teleology of women's fiction that ends in marriage or motherhood is generally lacking. If the male writer, on the other hand, inscribes an achieving or enduring self and unified destiny, it is a fragmented self, largely silent about the personal and emotional areas of experience. As in the seventeenth century English narratives of Delany's study, women display a more unified sensibility, while that of men is compartmentalized.

A unified sensibility does not equate with a culturally integrated ego or a unified destiny, however. Some contemporary feminist critics, such as Heilbrun and Showalter, privilege the integrated ego and the linear destiny, regarding women's difference in self-realization as a failure or deprivation. Heilbrun, for example, attempts to interest women in imagining for themselves what she sees as 'the full range of human experience, moving through action and quest to achievement or failure', normally ascribed to men.[39] But as Toril Moi points out in her response to Showalter's similar criticism of Virginia Woolf's fluid subjectivity:

What feminists such as Showalter ... fail to grasp is that the traditional humanism they represent is in effect part of patriarchal ideology. At its centre is the seamlessly unified self—either individual or collective—which is commonly called 'Man'. As Luce Irigaray or Helene Cixous would argue, this integrated self is in fact a phallic self, constructed on the model of the self-contained, powerful phallus. Gloriously autonomous, it banishes from itself all conflict, contradiction and ambiguity. In this humanist ideology the self is the *sole author* of history and of the literary text: the humanist creator is potent, phallic and male—God in relation to his world, the author in relation to his text.[40]

And as Judith Gardiner points out, the male model is hardly 'full': it is not that 'women's imaginations fail; rather, women writers re-create female experience in different form'.[41]

Lacking a sense of teleological design, women frequently structure their narratives irregularly, preferring non-chronological, discontinuous, episodic structures. Jane Watts, for example, retains a rough chronology dating from her family's decision to leave England, but her narrative avoids a sense of progression in its fidelity to feeling, and even the religiously motivated Eliza Davies finds experience more a succession of haphazardly linked stages than a progress. Jelinek sees the irregular structure as one of the distinguishing marks of a female autobiography, but unfortunately it is not a stable referent. Just as men's autobiographies in the twentieth century become more inward, they also become more tolerant of fragmented form; indeed, the discontinuous narrative has now acquired a respectable male tradition as the sanctioned form for the modernist, alienated consciousness.

More reliable than structure or an interest in inward experience in defining the difference between male and female life-writing, is an interest in relatedness. The most common and consistent characterisic of women's autobiographies is the characteristic that Carol Gilligan defines in her study of female development in *In a Different Voice*, that is, definition of the self in a context of relationship and judgement of the self in terms of ability to care. Frequently taking up the pen as mother or as daughter, women 'bring to the life cycle a different point of view and order human experience in terms of different priorities'. As Gilligan observes, whereas 'the developmental litany intones the celebration of separation, autonomy, individuation, and natural rights', the 'elusive mystery of women's development lies in its recognition of the continuing importance of attachment'.[42] When Alexandra Hasluck looks at the self in the mirror of autobiography, she finds it crowded with other faces; Maie Casey negotiates her own individuality via the individualities of her mother, aunts and grandmothers; Nellie Stewart declares that the most valuable aspect of her career has been the friendships it created with other women; for Jane Watts the family is the primary reality and the self is inseparable from the roles of daughter, sister and later wife; Mary Gilmore's attempt to appropriate the male role of tribal elder is dramatized in maternal and filial terms and her attempt to preserve links with the past is another expression of relatedness; Eliza Davies is threatened at the root of her identity by her mother's rejection. Nancy Phelan expresses the common sense of the self as contextual in *A Kingdom by the Sea* when she reflects on the death of an uncle:

it is *we*, the survivors, who are diminished. A part of us goes with them. With Uncle Launce's, my own death had begun ... The *I* that I took for granted was only made up of reflections seen in my family's eyes. When they were all gone, all those who knew *Me*, what would be left? We were leaves blown away in the wind.[43]

In Chapter 5 a group of autobiographies which have a more purposive design are considered and yet even in this group relatedness is inseparable from a sense of self. Franklin in *Childhood at Brindabella* mourns the loss of a sense of belonging as she celebrates earlier, positive relations; Kathleen Fitzpatrick perceives her academic career as based on the solid relationships of her childhood and even as duplicating those relationships; Katharine Susannah Prichard traces the development of a strong sense of responsibility, inherited from her grandmother and centring initially on her younger sister, alongside her ambition to be a writer; Barbara Hanrahan recreates an intimate female family and her frustration when certain changes reveal that it has not understood its own special quality; Agnes Gosse Hay and Doreen Flavel in different periods and circumstances find satisfaction in a career which offers significance in relation; Bessie Lee vanquishes her orphan status by becoming a nurturing figure of international proportions; Kylie Tennant treads a hazardous, almost despairing path through a world which fails to value relatedness as it should. Even those well-known autobiographical novels which are frequently seen as duplicating the *Bildungsroman*'s pattern of development are somewhat skewed in their orientation. The conventional pattern of the *Bildungsroman* is premised on separation and a narrative of failed relationships as the hero becomes more emphatically individuated; leaving the repressive atmosphere of home, the hero makes his solitary way to the city, where he will begin his education. As Joyce's Stephen Dedalus leaves childhood he necessarily leaves relationships, David Copperfield's personal growth depends on the removal of a juvenile wife, the hero of George Johnston's *My Brother Jack* seeks to come to terms with the figures of his childhood so that he can successfully leave them behind. As Don Anderson observes, the male heroes of Australian autobiography perceive separation as intrinsic to their development:

They are sensitive (if at times aggressively insensitive), literate, and isolated youths (yes, male!). All feel guilt with respect to their mothers, aggression to their fathers, and ignore their siblings. All lose some form of faith. All choose some form of flight, from family or country.[44]

If both Louie of *The Man Who Loved Children* and Laura of *The Getting of Wisdom* are conventional in that they progress to a finer understanding, celebrated by their rejection of relationships, they also differ from the traditional male hero, for both novels are radical exposures of patriarchal society, conventional goal of the *Bildungsroman*'s male protagonist, while their culminating flights are flights from forms of perverted relatedness. Louie departs in search of a nobler form of love, the search which her autobiographical successor, Theresa, takes up in *For Love Alone*, and Richardson's Laura is explicitly invested with her author's destiny as a writer, whose obsessive subject incidentally will be the family. Miles Franklin's *My Brilliant Career* confronts on one hand, the 'abject littleness' of a woman's life in Australia of the 1890s and, on the other, the romance of the bush myth. The 'virile fascination' of the bush hero is finally no substitute for the ideal of companionship with one who 'had suffered, who knew, who understood', while the heroine's individual frustrations are complicated by her commitment to the fellow feeling of the bush and female ideals of caring: aligning herself with her 'sunburnt brothers' and sisters, 'Daughters of toil', Sybylla concludes her story with a paeon to their suffering and stoical solidarity. In this she is typical of the hero of the fiction of female development analysed by Elizabeth Abel: 'The heroine's developmental course is more conflicted, less direct: separation tugs against the longing for fusion' and identity is seen as residing in 'intimate relationships, especially those of early childhood'.[45]

Factual female autobiographies also emphasize attachment and continuity, while breakdown in relationships is a cause for suffering; if the male hero fears connection, the female hero fears separation. Some narratives describe the failure of relationships as threatening the self's survival: Lecky Payne's *Beltana—Six Miles* is a moving story of a child's attempt to weld her relationship with an equivocal father; Amie Livingstone Stirling's *An Australian Childhood* describes the failure or loss of a series of relationships, culminating in the loss or rejection of Australia itself; Katherine McKell's *Old Days and Gold Days* evokes the deprivation consequent on the death of a mother and a father's emotional inadequacy. Jean Baker Miller's feminist reinterpretation of psychology finds that 'for many women, the threat of disruption of an affiliation is perceived not just as a loss of relationship but as something closer to a total loss of self'.[46]

Rediscovering the pastness of the past is also a different experience. Male narratives characteristically establish the past as a stepping stone or stage in the individual journey; *Life Rarely Tells* is the title Jack Lindsay chooses for the first volume of his autobiography, expressing the insidious design which will make Brisbane intellectually a place of childhood as well as personally; Bernard Smith's 'lucky bastard' treads a journey which will mean leaving the people of his childhood, notwithstanding his unusual piety for the past; the childhood figures of Vincent Buckley's *Cutting Green Hay* are valued purely as supportive figures or as mentors enabling the hero's progress. The past in male narratives is also characteristically subject to the sort of selection that will emphasize the perceived teleology. Pascal assumes much early experience will necessarily be excised by the autobiographer in favour of the unity of his design: 'as the autobiography moves into adult years, much of the childhood may seem superfluous, disconnected from the later man—like those photographs of chubby children in sailor suits that contrast rather painfully with the men of substance and importance they become'.[47] Reviewing the past from his present achieved status, the male narrator selectively reconstructs it so that in Erikson's words, 'it seems to have planned him, or better, he seems to have planned *it*', thus making himself the proprietor or creator of his history.[48] Lejeune describes the final object of every autobiographical search to be the impossible search for origins; the autobiographer penetrates the past in the hope of uncovering the mystery of his beginning.[49] If it is a vain hope or a false certainty, male heroes are nonetheless preoccupied with the should-be story, with its beginning, middle and end. George Johnston's hero ponders the baffling shape of his own ill-defined pattern against that of the ideal Australian hero, his brother Jack; Randolph Stow's concludes that the story he has drawn from his environment has the absurdity of a merry-go-round in the sea. Terrified by the threat of non-identity, the male hero may wonder like Sartre if 'All [his] exploits, laid end to end, were only a string of random events'. Female narratives, on the other hand, seem characteristically bent on cherishing the past for its own sake, recreating its sensuous flavour, rediscovering the nuances of relationships or the sensations of old familiar rhythms. No autobiographer does this so successfully as Hal Porter in *The Watcher on the Cast-Iron Balcony*, of course, but in Porter's narrative, scene is always complicated by the watching 'I', preoccupied with the rush of time around the suffering but impermeable self. The patterns that women perceive in their lives tend to converge around the central early experience; childhood is the heart of the later story, which frequently attempts to explain itself in terms of the early life, to perceive itself as an elaboration on a given pattern, or a reconstitution of given ingredients. Thus the 'characteristic' image of life as a journey is mostly missing from women's life-stories.

Paradoxically, although women writers present themselves as more attached to the past, men are more obsessed with its elusiveness and the intractable project of its recovery. As Louis Renza puts it, submitting the memories to the 'profanation of the fictional world', the male autobiographer is obsessed with the way that language displaces the past and alienates the writer from his present self, which is the true object of his autobiography. Life-writing is 'a unique, self-defining mode of self-referential expression, one that allows, then inhibits, the project of self-presentification, of converting oneself into the present promised by language'. And reliving the past is also to relive the threats to individuation, as writing the self loses the self: 'how can he keep using the first-person pronoun, his sense of self-reference, without its becoming—since it becomes, in the course of writing, something other than strictly his own self-referential sign—a de facto third-person pronoun?'[50] If women see themselves as continuous with the past, men regard the past as another form of the Other, against which the self must strive to define itself.

Two writers who are in many ways representative of the two traditions of autobiography, Nabokov and Woolf, describe their lives in images which sharply illuminate these differences. Appropriately enough their titles, *Speak Memory* and *Moments of Being*, signal the difference, although Woolf's was drawn from her several autobiographical pieces by her editor. For Nabokov, his life is like a unique watermark:

Neither in environment nor in heredity can I find the exact instrument that fashioned me, the anonymous roller that pressed upon my life a certain intricate watermark whose unique design becomes visible when the lamp of art is made to shine through life's foolscap.[51]

Virginia Woolf, on the other hand, sees herself 'as a fish in a stream; deflected; held in place' even though she 'cannot describe the stream'. In an earlier piece of autobiography, she describes life as a piece in a pattern: 'our lives are pieces in a pattern and to judge one truly you must consider how this side is squeezed and that indented and a third expanded and none are really isolated'.[52]

The same distinction between the self in relation and the self as single individual can be immediately seen by comparing the male and female texts in a family group of Australian autobiographies, the Lindsay family. Norman Lindsay wrote at least two fictional auto-biographies, *Saturdee* (1933) and *Redheap* (1930), as well as the 'factual' story of the self, *My Mask* (1970); his wife, Rose Lindsay, wrote two factual accounts of her life, *Ma and Pa* (1963), which describes her childhood, and *Model Wife* (1967), which describes her life with Norman; the autobiographical impulse also seized other members of the Lindsay family, but three of the most significant, which are also directly engaged with the personality of Norman, are Jack Lindsay's *Life Rarely Tells* (1958) and *The Roaring Twenties* (1960) and Jane Lindsay's *Portrait of Pa* (1973). *Saturdee*, as a group of short stories, lacks the well-defined teleology of a larger narrative, although Lindsay makes it plain that the stories, based on his own 1880s–1890s childhood at Creswick, are about growing up: 'All decisive gestures are acts of growing up. An act done by you: an act done to you: a bunged-up eye or a bunged-up love affair.' The equation of love and fighting as similar acts of male proving persists; for the narrator of *Saturdee*, people exist as a field for the demonstrating of mastery, whether it is the mastery of manipulation, deceit, sex or physical force. Others exist merely as reflectors of the self, awestruck, admiring, defeated, temporarily triumphant; adults are not so much the enemy in this text (which divides people into the weak and the strong, rather than the good and the bad) as holders of the high ground, vulnerable to sapping operations from the army of innovative juniors. Jack Lindsay's autobiographies are in a different class altogether. Sophisticated, contemplative, observant, they are important cultural studies of a place and time. They are also the record of the growth of a mind, in which the lately discovered father was—for a time—significant. As in other male autobiographies, siblings are only marginally relevant, love affairs are perceived as necessary interruptions to the main business of life, in this case the life of ideas, and the past is experienced as a series of temporary lodgings, discarded as soon as the furnishings are worn out. The mind that is disclosed is undoubtedly attractive and even benevolent, but it is difficult to probe past the mind to the man, so detachedly abstract is Lindsay's approach. Both Rose Lindsay's *Ma and Pa* and her daughter's *Portrait of Pa* are concerned with recreating the experience of living in relation, of probing the succeeding and failing family relationships which puzzled the child. Jane Lindsay, largely uninterested in her father's reputation as an artist, judges him as father, friend and husband; Rose Lindsay, intrigued by the complex relationship of her parents, tries to cut a path through the past's thicket of emotions and is content to be only half-successful. In both cases achievement is equated with community, and failure with insensitivity, indifference and neglect.

If individuation is represented as a necessary hazard by male autobiographers, relatedness is no less necessary and equivocal for female life-writers. Many of the autobiographies considered here express tension between the need to merge with others and the need for autonomy. Katharine Susannah Prichard is divided between her strong sense of responsibility and her need to find her own vocation; abandoning the latter temporarily in the face of family difficulties and even priding herself on her uncomplaining attitude, she is appalled to hear her father's satisfied conclusion that she is finally cultivating the virtues of the angel in the house. Fairlie Taylor deeply resents her father's appropriation of her unpaid labour and his implicit judgement that girls are not worth educating; Connie Miller records her confusion when attitudes to her suddenly shift and she is regarded as potential woman; Stead's Louie suffers furies daily at the expectation that she will automatically be a second mother to her brothers and sisters; Ella Simon resents her family's assumption that she will give up her life in Sydney to nurse her mother, even though she is a fond daughter. *My Brilliant Career* is the most famous representation of despair at the reductions of gender, but the pattern is a familiar one.

Some commentators and some feminists conclude that relatedness is a handicap that women need to surmount if they are ever to develop a pristine individuality. Erich Neumann, for example, sees women as halted on the road to selfhood by the temptations of pity and writes of women's necessity to learn to *do*, rather than to *be*, if ego stability is to be achieved and maintained.[53] Erikson's famous developmental theory sees the self as progressing through necessary stages of detachment towards an established goal, an end product.[54] Other writers question the equation of maturity with independence. Chodorov, for example, suggests that selfhood does not depend only on the strength and impermeability of ego boundaries and develops the idea of a new kind of individualism, relational individualism, which assumes a fundamental internal as well as external relatedness to the other: 'The relational individual is not reconstructed in terms of his or her drives and defences but in terms of the greater or lesser fragmentation of his or her inner world and the extent to which the core self feels spontaneous and whole within, rather than driven by, this world.'[55] Furthermore, the female core self is less problematic than the male:

core gender identity for a girl is not problematic in the sense that it is for boys. It is built upon, and does not contradict, her primary sense of oneness and identification with her mother and is assumed easily along with her developing sense of self. Girls grow up with a sense of continuity and similarity to their mother, a relational connection to the world. For them, difference is not originally problematic or fundamental to their psychological being or identity. They do not define themselves as 'not-men', or 'not-male', but as 'I, who am female.'[56]

Judith Gardiner takes up the implications of Chodorov's findings and concludes that 'female identity [is] typically less fixed, less unitary, and more flexible than male individuality, both in its primary core and in the entire maturational complex developed from this core'. Perceiving the female personality as fluidly defined and cyclical in formation, she concludes that these traits have far-reaching consequences for the distinctive nature of women's writing.[57]

Certainly, the bulk of the autobiographies considered here celebrate rather than deplore the necessity of relatedness. A large number, however, record experiences of imposed reduction on the grounds of gender. Ironic, subversive, wry, angry or bitter comments on the social constraints, indignities, injustices and humiliations associated with being a girl are common in texts of both centuries. Sarah Conigrave is engaged in a constant battle to prove herself the equal of her patronizing brothers; Amie Livingstone Stirling attempts to align her father's enlightened pronouncements with the cramping actualities of being female; Eliza Chomley dissects the genteel education accorded to young girls of her day with withering irony. There is also a large group of texts which record the contrast between early experience of autonomy and freedom, when in Chodorov's terms the core self was spontaneous and whole, and the sense of being 'driven by the world' once the constraints of gender were imposed, usually at puberty. Granted an unusual degree of freedom and even an equality with the other sex in childhood, the Australian girl and especially the bush girl frequently regards the adolescent years as a form of imprisonment. Judith Wallace and Kathleen Mangan contend with conventional, sterile schools after exceptionally free, stimulating childhoods; Ellen Campbell is parted from her closest companion in mischief when her brother is sent to school and she is relegated to the prickly care of governesses; Miles Franklin loses all the confident enjoyments of Brindabella and is forced to crush her spontaneity into a conventional feminine stereotype; Patsy Adam-Smith has to contend with adult knowledge of her origins, which temporarily sullies the confident freedom of her early years; Fairlie Taylor and Connie Miller have their childhoods suddenly wrested from them when they are thrust into the world of work; Katharine Susannah Prichard confronts the reality of a father's weakness and a mother's dependence; Barbara Hanrahan is confused by the conventional suburban expectations of her mother and grandmother after they have granted her an unconventional childhood; and even the independent Delarue sisters of *A Bunyip Close Behind Me* have to conform to male expectations of their gender in *Ladies Didn't*. For all these narrators the new conditions affect physical freedom, allegiance to nature, the life of the imagination, exercise of the intellect and the ability to form relationships spontaneously. The difficulties they record are not difficulties in knowing what it is to be female but difficulties in responding to social rules about being female. As Jean Rhys observes: 'When you are a child you are yourself . . . . And then suddenly something happens and you stop being yourself; you become what others force you to be.'[58] And as Chodorov comments: 'In the development of gender identification for girls it is not the existence of core gender identity, the unquestioned knowledge that one is female, that is problematic. Rather it is the later-developed conflicts concerning this identity [that] arise from identification with a negatively valued gender category.'[59]

Some commentators on women's autobiography assume that women write within the rhetorical structures appropriate to this negatively valued gender category. Sidonie Smith, for example, suggests that the female autobiographer up to the twentieth century was subject to cultural fictions which represented the ideal woman as self-effacing, effectively silencing her and reducing her to a passive sign:

However much she may desire to pursue the paternal narrative with its promise of power . . . she recognizes . . . that for her, as for all colonized people, the act of empowerment is both infectious and threatening. Her narrative may bring notoriety; and with notoriety can come isolation and the loss of love and acceptance in the culture that would hold her in its fictions.

And it is only in the twentieth century that the autobiographer 'begins to grapple self-consciously with her identity as a woman in patriarchal culture and with her problematic relationship to engendered figures of selfhood'.[60]

But this sense of effective silence is not true to the reader's experience of earlier women's life-writing, I suggest, and stems from two assumptions that Smith seems to make in her study. One is that women write for a male reader, or at least for a mixed audience, subservient to patriarchy; the other is that women autobiographers desire 'the power, authority and voice of man'. Many of the authors considered here are sceptical of male authority, unenvious of male power and unimpressed by the male voice; they write largely for female readers and according to a shared system of values, which allows for freedoms of its own.

Judith Gardiner has come closest to describing the female writer's sense of audience. Perceiving the maternal metaphor of female authorship as clarifying the woman writer's 'distinctive engagement with her characters' and indicating 'an analogous relationship between woman reader and character', she formulates the metaphor: '"the hero is her author's daughter"'.[61] Discussions of female identity inevitably centre on the mother/daughter bond so it is not surprising to discover the centrality of the bond in autobiography. A complicated tie, it frequently expresses much of the writer's ambivalence about relatedness as it is culturally defined and actually experienced. I discuss some autobiographical treatments of the bond in Chapter 11. Gardiner is discussing fiction so her metaphor needs some modification if it is to express the relation between female autobiographer and reader. I therefore suggest the following metaphor: 'The hero is herself as mother and as daughter'. As I have already indicated, and as their titles often demonstrate, many women consciously write as mothers or daughters: *An Aboriginal Mother Remembers the Old and the New*, *Portrait of Pa*, *Ma and Pa*, *The Man Who Loved Children*, *Nobody's Daughter*, *Esther Mary: My Pioneer Mother*. But the relation is more fundamental than this. Since autobiography is generally more emphatically a consoling, therapeutic act than fiction, a form of self-salvation and self-discovery, and since the female self is invariably perceived in relation, writing the self is also to experience the self as 'one's own cared-for child and as one's own caring mother'. Imagining the self being read, is to speak to other women who are also mothers and daughters. Thus even women who are not physical mothers, such as Kathleen Fitzpatrick and Mollie Skinner, speak to the self and the reader as mother and daughter, even as they negotiate the private experience of being a daughter.

One interesting facet of this tendency to see the narrating self as a self in relation, is the extraordinary fluidity of female narrators. If the male writer is obsessed with the gulf between the narrating and the narrational self, the female writer shifts readily and freely between narrators. Jane Watts assumes the third person without any loss of subjectivity, Bessie Lee shifts abruptly to the third person after opening in the first, Sally Morgan includes and orchestrates narrations by her mother, grandmother and uncle, which are stories of their lives, but also, most intensely, stories of hers. In numerous other texts, the shifts in narrative voice and perspective widen the reader's appreciation of complex relations. In Vera Adams's *No Stranger in Paradise*, for instance, a mild irony tempers both the narrator's nostalgia for a past community and her own past self; Emily Churchward's persistent tendency to move from the incisive perceptions of the inward self to a more bland public self generates an unconscious comedy. *Family Life In South Australia* is an early example of the female capacity to view the self simultaneously with irony and compassion, which will be more brilliantly displayed in *The Getting of Wisdom* and *The Man Who Loved Children*, and all three illustrate a common subjective/objective pattern. A fluid narrative persona does not imply a totally merged persona and it is the balance between individual and relation that is so marked a feature of the relational individualism of these autobiographies. Even more extraordinary is a group of narratives which are double-voiced, a duologue rather than a dialogue of mother and daughter, as in *A Bunyip Close Behind Me*, *Ladies Didn't* and Meg Stewart's *Autobiography of My Mother*. In these autobiographies it is the mother's story which holds the stage, but it clearly rests on a history of shared stories and values, just as it depends on the daughter's voice for articulation. *Puberty Blues* is another duologue, in this case implicitly subverting male postures of bonding via the very rhetorical bond itself. Almost the same phenomenon of speaking through and with another appears in early English autobiographies, according to Mary Mason, a practice which she describes as 'delineation of an identity by way of alterity':

the self-discovery of female identity seems to acknowledge the real presence and recognition of another consciousness, and the disclosure of female self is linked to the identification of some 'other'. This recognition of another consciousness—and I emphasize recognition rather than deference—this grounding of identity through relation to the chosen other, seems ... to enable women to write openly about themselves.[62]

This seems to be a uniquely female style of defining the self. Louis Renza, for example, in his analysis of male autobiographies, describes the vicious circle which commonly encloses the (male) writing self:

Except by an act of will, which already implies a separation from his act of writing, the autobiographer cannot rely on the 'others' of discourse to substantiate his references in a phenomenological sense. Writing raises the possibility that these 'others' could have 'existed' the writer's existence, and raises it as he writes. But in doing this, writing also estranges him from his signified referents, his 'life'—an experience he alone is privy to as he writes since he is, quite literally, the only one who can *signify* his life to *himself*.[63]

Some female autobiographies, however, are like bumble-bees and defy the laws of flight, in their integration of essence and existence, speaking and listening, being and doing.

At this point, I would like to make a plea for the special 'self-consciousness' of women's life-writing. Often dismissed as unselfconscious, most women's texts are, more accurately, not self-conscious in the male sense, and in fact play is integral to their mode of writing. As inhabitants of the female covert culture, women writers are appreciative of the subversive or skewed slant on the things of men and often relish the quirky, the absurd, the explosion of pretentions. They are tolerant of discontinuous forms and unsettled closures, content to leave completion to the reader or to let their questions hang. The relationship between the dramatic present and the narrative past is more often perceived as a necessary tension, than as a confrontation that frustrates the writing self's need for autonomy. In the same way, comedy and irony are congenial modes and portraying the self as subject to comic misfortunes is often both another form of collaboration with the reader and a way of trivializing the disastrous. Many texts, such as *My Brilliant Career*, *Your Hills Are Too High*, and *Puberty Blues* move unselfconsciously between comedy and more serious modes. Less preoccupied with maintaining a pristine individuality and even habituated to the self's fluidity, women writers are also trained in the division between the inward 'I' and the gendered self. They are thus less openly concerned with the fictiveness of the narrating 'I', since fictiveness is infused into the air they breathe. Familiar with experience as equivocal, uncertain and untidy, they write narratives whose fabric is seeped in the problematic. Thus Ella Simon titles her autobiography *Through My Eyes* and maintains an awareness of the white perspective, even as she records the Aboriginal point of view; Kathleen Fitzpatrick is conscious that the metaphor that she creates for herself is only one of several alternatives; Mary Drake, intent on nostalgically savouring her childhood, is nevertheless alive to its equivocal echoes and is content to leave them as equivocal. Indeed, many of the strategies which are privileged as 'self-conscious' in male writing are strategies of writing against the stream, confrontations with the fact that unreliability is an inescapable condition rather than a rhetorical option. They create their own kind of stimulus, of course, but it is unfortunate that their 'absence' in female narratives has led to (male) charges of unsophistication on one hand, and (feminist) charges of disabled silence on the other.

Some female narratives, of course, are written for a male or mixed audience, or attempt to emulate male values. In Chapter 7, for instance, I consider a group of autobiographies which strive to absorb the bush myth. Writing for a male audience undoubtedly imposes restraints. Mrs Daly in *Digging, Squatting and Pioneering Life* is hard put to insert her identity into her account of *res gestae* and the pioneering mould in general was inimical to women's deepest interests. Adopting a male rhetorical structure also undoubtedly imposes the sort of doubleness or indirect insinuation of subversive content that Gilbert and Gubar have analysed in their influential study of nineteenth century fictions[64] and that Sidonie Smith sees as typical of pre-twentieth century autobiography. Some of the strident awkwardness of the opening passages of *My Brilliant Career*, for instance, can be traced to an embarrassed awareness of 'unnatural' self-assertion and the confusions of the text arise from the impossible attempt to align a patriarchal ideology with self-realization. And Mary Gilmore's partial adoption of male standards is only achieved by an act of rhetorical ventriloquism and at the ultimate cost of self-deception. Agnes Gosse Hay and Bessie Lee's narratives carry traces of the double-voiced discourse that Smith isolates, privileging a male norm, while undercutting it with a female, submerged norm. Nevertheless, Smith's contention that autobiography generally imposes a double estrangement on the female writer, locking her into the uneasy position of speaking before and to 'man', the representative of the dominant order, 'arbiter of the ideology of gender and its stories of selfhood', the one 'who remains silent and ... exerts power over the one who speaks', is not true of the main body of women's autobiographies in Australia. Obviously, women have not developed the *écriture feminine*, anticipated by such French feminists as Hélène Cixous, but they have not been silenced or even muted by the structures of patriarchy. Male writing, after all, might well be different in non-patriarchal culture and imagining what women's autobiography might be like without the complications of gendered expectations is a Utopian project, best served by linguists. Confronting the limitations of a strongly masculine society, Australian women have succeeded in establishing a different, complementary tradition of remarkable variety and vitality, even if that difference has not been readily recognized. Jean Baker Miller can find in psychology no language to describe the structuring of women's sense of self, 'organized around being able to make and then to maintain affiliations and relationships'.[65] Similarly, in the language of criticism there is no name for the female autobiography. Halfway between 'autobiography', traditionally defined as a narrative in which attention is focused on the self, and 'memoir', a narrative in which attention is focused on others, it refuses to be defined by male standards.

5

Some Distinctive Figures of Self

'To weave the intricate tapestry of one's own life, it is well to take a thread from many harmonious skeins—and to realise that there must be harmony.'[1] Katherine Mansfield's words could well be applied to the vast majority of the autobiographers considered here who have perceived the self as more fluid than impermeably singular, and experience as more a matter of being in relationship than an individual progress. As I have already suggested, this apparently common experience of relatedness has important consequences for women's life-writing: since time is not generally experienced as linear with neatly separated points of reference, the narrative structures with which women compose their lives are frequently discontinuous, episodic, open-ended or circular. Wayne Shumaker has suggested that autobiography is 'the literary simplification of an extremely complex reality'[2], but women on the whole have been more preoccupied with re-experiencing the complexity of their realities than in discovering a distinctive, unifying, shaping design. As in female fictions of development, the 'I' of female autobiography implies a distinctive value system and pattern of development, which are defined not in terms of achievement and autonomy as in male writing, but in terms of interaction. Paradoxically, the harmony in the sense of arrival and integration in the social order, that is so often privileged as the maturity towards which the male hero struggles, does not necessarily conclude the female narrative; more tolerant of untidiness, diversity and opacity, the female writer will sometimes leave her questions about relationships open to the reader's speculation.

Some writers, however, are more preoccupied with design and purpose than others, and this chapter concentrates on a group of autobiographies which are shaped according to well-defined teleologies, or which imply a belief in design. All the writers considered in this chapter express the self by means of metaphor; they create an organizing structural pattern which emerges as a personal mythos. At first sight, therefore, they might be assumed to fulfil James Olney's definition of autobiography as personal metaphor, an expression of the individual's sense of his/her own unique, unrepeatable being. In every instance, however, the personal mythos is also an expression of relatedness; it may be a means of integrating the distinctive self and community as in Agnes Gosse Hay's myth of marriage, or of uniting the achieved self and the communal past as in Kathleen Fitzpatrick's *Solid Bluestone Foundations*, or of vanquishing the solitary, insignificant, youthful self in the myth of the spiritual mother as in Bessie Lee's *One of Australia's Daughters*. Three of these autobiographies, although diverse in every other way, seek to impose a myth that will explain the loss of an earlier, or an ideal, authentic self-in-relationship: Katharine Susannah Prichard's *The Wild Oats of Han*, Miles Franklin's *Childhood at Brindabella*, and Kylie Tennant's *The Missing Heir*. For all these autobiographers the myth proves inadequate or crippling, but the consequences of their grappling with their individual figures are particularly interesting for the reader.

In *My Brilliant Career*, written in her teens, the myth Franklin selects to express her experience, reflected in the structure of the narrative, the imagery, the narrative point of view and even the syntax, is the myth of the Fall. *Childhood at Brindabella*, written at the end of her life but from the same position of exile and 'perpetual homesickness'[3], is an extraordinary illumination of the myth's origins in her early experience and of its resilient power over her imagination. Her selected myth reflects, on one hand, the determining effect of cultural ideologies on the self's fictive patterns and, on the other, the potentially crippling power of cultural mythos, for however perceptive Franklin's criticisms of patriarchal society, they are, I suggest, limited by her uncritical obsession with the primal myth of patriarchy, the myth of Eden.

Arranged more according to a psychological than a chronological sequence, *Childhood at Brindabella* is like a theatre of the mind in which the images of the past present themselves to be questioned by the still baffled consciousness of old age. From the first infantile memory (characteristically an experience of rejection, in this case of being weaned at the age of eight months), to the last image of the post-lapsarian child bound for Stillwater (the place name is a wonderful case of life imitating art), the autobiography is almost a dream-sequence of half-understood symbols. The Eden myth is quite explicit. Edenic titles are used for two chapter titles ('Return to Paradise' and 'Exit from Eden'), paradisal imagery runs as a consistent thread through the narrative, while the self's experience of fall from integrity of being and primal innocence is frequently perceived in Biblical terms. Franklin is not alone, of course, in Edenic patterning of childhood experience and the myth has a venerable history, recurring in such diverse autobiographies as those by Rousseau, Henry James, Edmund Gosse and Edwin Muir. Where *Childhood at Brindabella* and *My Brilliant Career* are distinctive is that they deal only with the Paradise and the Fall, not with the Recreation; Franklin's personal myth is simple, dramatic and tragic and her fall is more than the normal adult fall into self-consciousness. Exile from the Paradisal Garden perpetually baffles and grieves her autobiographical narrators as it structures her pioneering novels and conditions her nationalism and politics. *Childhood at Brindabella* brings home the fact that her political anachronism is involuntary and emotional in origin, an expression of her creative imprisonment within a repressive myth, however romantically and personally interpreted. Coinciding at some points with the national metamyths, and colliding at others, this adherence to an early paradise generates the ambivalences and truncated or confused attitudes that are so notorious a feature of her work.

The most prominent paradisal feature of *Childhood at Brindabella* is the Garden. At her grandmother's farm at Ajinby/Talbingo, the garden is an endless harvest of fruits and vegetables untroubled by diseases ('Australia was as yet an uninfected but slightly infested heaven'). The theme reaches a culmination in the chapter, titled 'Gardening', which hymns the splendour and fragrance of all the gardens of the narrator's first decade. Underlying the horticultural descriptions is a celebration of fruitfulness, amounting to perpetual harvest, and of human toil and the piety of generations, reflected in the careful tending of grafted and seeded plants. For the child the plants are friends, recording poignant or historic events, illustrating nature's regenerative powers or engaging directly with the self. What is remarkable about Franklin's gardens is that they are predominantly English or European; like the English flower gardens of Caddagat, they are transplanted heavens, oases miraculously untouched by the rigours of Australian droughts.

As in the first chapter of *My Brilliant Career*, the child-self experiences a total emotional and physical health in the home of her first decade; 'I have no memory of ever having been left alone, or frightened or being cold or unhappy'. Accustomed to the rhythm of horses before the age of walking, she rides fearlessly around her domain, swims with the father from infancy and even drives the bullocks. These early experiences of freedom and power are bolstered by an awareness of protective, mainly male, deities, while the most tender of memories is of the child-self riding before her father's or uncle's pommel. Unchastened by the later constraints of gender, the bisexual child clearly becomes for the older consciousness a Jungian symbol of the unified personality, in Jung's own words, 'a symbol of the *self* where the war of opposites finds peace [expressing] a wholeness which embraces the very depths of nature'.[4] This intuition of unity is heightened by several quasi-mystical experiences granted to the child, which linger like an elusive fragrance in the older consciousness. The extraordinary tulip, grown from a foreign bulb, which is given a chapter to itself, represents one of these experiences as do the pomegranate, which still has power to transport the older self back to that timeless room 'warmed by natural family affection that never wavered, never waned, as well as a fire of red-gum logs', and the Grandmother's brooch, which fascinates the child with its flickering colours.

Franklin is more like a male autobiographer of childhood in her perception of the child-self as an only child; not only is the child presented as independent of siblings but relegation to the society of other children is regarded as a demotion and there are even suggestions that such associations trouble the child's innocence or threaten her with disinheritance. Nevertheless, relatedness is integral to the paradisal experience, although the important relationships are with a large family of indulgent older relatives. The most important individual in this paradisal microcosm is the Grandmother. It is she who represents God. Invested with male power and authority, she is the radius of the revered order and abundance:

She was ceaselessly industrious, had a head for business and was known as a 'good manager'. Her haysheds and other storehouses were always well-stocked for winter with the yield from her orchards, potato and pumpkin paddocks, her fowlhouses, her dairy and vegetable garden. She grew and cured her own bacon as well as her own beef. Her streams were full of native trout and Murray cod. Order, plenty, decency, industry and hospitality were in the home I so loved.[5]

Enjoining gentility on her female descendants and obedience on her male progeny, it is the Grandmother who has the authority to retain or eject the child from Eden. Although the old lady is perceived with unreserved affection and respect, she emerges as a somewhat minatory figure, threatening the child with her hoe, locking her into the pantry for an imagined misdemeanour, and on one key occasion striking her to the ground with a broom for her childish heresy. The incident, which appears to be central to the emotional history, becomes one of the narrator's photographic memories: 'I can still see the inner back yard, clean swept. Not a footmark or leaf lay upon its smooth face, nothing but one puddle in a depression after the night's rain' (p. 111). Associated with the social and religious conformities which threaten to confine the growing girl, the Grandmother's disapproving description of her as 'froward' is linked to the indefinite but acute sense of guilt which clouds her last days in Eden. So powerful, in fact, is the Grandmother figure that one wonders whether the child's earlier remonstrance—'"I believe you really will kill me some day, Grannie, if you are not careful"'—is not freighted with some unconscious psychological truth.

As in *My Brilliant Career*, the narrator suffers two falls in *Childhood at Brindabella*. The first removal, from Bobilla to Stillwater, fills her 'with a sense of degradation . . . I never forgave it for its inferiority to my birthplace'. Soon afterwards, however, the Grandmother arrives to take her back to Ajinby: 'My one obsessing thought and determination was to accompany her on her return. No Peri could have pleaded more passionately at the gates of Paradise' (p. 99). Her ecstasy is accompanied by a sense that this redemption is unlooked for and even arbitrary. The journey to the 'lusher regions' and 'more opulent way of life of Ajinby' reaches a dramatic peak when the engine of their train is derailed and rams into a coal shed. At this point the narrative clearly approaches mythology, the engine representing some magical beast which attempts to prevent the child's entry into Paradise, but is ineffective in face of the Grandmother's superior powers: 'The engine seemed to hate the coal-shed. It was banged hard against it shrieking in rage, spouting fire and boiling water from which we were warned' (p. 101). Not really daunted, the child welcomes the incident as heightening the anticipated pleasures. After their return she runs out into the spring garden to retrieve her Eden. The familiar plants 'seething with spring' and the old 'beloved nooks' welcome her back: 'All the old delights remained', 'Heaven could be no more magical and mystical than unspoiled Australia' (p. 103).

But this return to paradise is complicated first by an accelerating awareness of its impermanence and then by a sequence of disturbing incidents that combine to suggest that she has become unfit for Eden. The threat is made dramatically manifest by her confrontation with a snake, 'coiled like a whip' and ready to strike, which she discovers at the foot of the great apple tree in the 'Heaven' of her Grandmother's orchard. This incident, in the book's psychological sequence, immediately follows a long account of her abandonment of the 'anthropomorphic . . . bullying God' of her Calvinistic family and the consequent confrontation with her Grandmother described above. The image of the threatening snake is to be a permanent memory, but the guilty child, supposedly confined to the verandah to do her lessons, says nothing of the incident at the time.

'Frantically' aware of the 'diminishing weeks', the child attempts to savour all she can of the 'ethereal wonderland', but now her former freedoms begin to be curtailed. Constantly reminded of her sex, she is appropriately confined to the house and its hen-yards, even though 'I strove to evade the oncoming doom of contraction to the housewife's hen-mindedness, or incarceration in her cage, by escape into nature' (p. 135). The 'slur' of being 'froward' introduces a vague sense of guilt, which is to continue to rankle for half a lifetime. Unable to communicate her natural frustrations to the old lady, she is further cast down when suspected of stealing raisins. Her inward conviction of invincible honesty is affronted when no one believes her denials: 'I was bewildered as when struggling in a bad dream'. She is eventually acquitted when a servant confesses, but this is not followed by any real reprieve: 'My character was restored but not cleansed of frowardness. The slogan that I must go home to be a help to my mother, etc., etc., after Christmas, did not wane' (p. 144).

As Christmas looms ('the frail barrier that stood between me and exile'), the narrator identifies with a chicken, which she had inadvertently injured so that it is unable to feed itself. Closely associated with her feelings of guilt ('I felt like Cain'), the incident becomes a potent metaphor of threat:

I sat in the blossoming clover thick with bees and butterflies, the crime in my hand to make the warm sunlight chilly and the river lullaby sound as intrusively as it did before a storm. (p. 139)

As her own awareness of imminent ejection accelerates, she assiduously feeds the bird. Elaborate plans to carry it with her on the final journey home encounter implacable and baffling opposition from her favourite aunt. Unaccountably, the chicken dies, and is found by the child 'on the pathway in the baking sun. A few scout ants had just found him'. The calamity is etched on her mind, returning years later as a haunting and inexplicable image. 'Erased by a sense of vaster bereavement in the exile from Eden' (p. 158), it is some time before the bird's death is perceived as tragedy. After she has been condemned to a reduced existence among 'new people and children of my own age with whom I had no inner life', the narrator clearly half-perceives the bird as surrogate for the potential self and its destruction. Interestingly, the bird, which turns out to be male, may have been secretly destroyed by Aunt Metta, who in the role of severe angel supervises her departure from Eden. The imagery makes the analogy explicit; comparing her defencelessness to that of 'a bird reared in a boudoir' suddenly released into the wild, she describes herself as exchanging the 'protective aura' of Ajinby for the 'real trials, disappointments and deprivations, and inner gropings and turbulence and furious and agonized beating of wings of a bird not knowing where to fly' (p. 159).

There are obvious links between this account of childhood and *My Brilliant Career* in terms of place, narrative structure, incidents, imagery, characters, relationships and central consciousness; the older self is more resigned than Sybylla, but just as entranced by the sacred place and just as baffled by her exclusion. The ambivalent figures of the adored Grandmother and Aunt, who inexplicably reject the narrator, the former by failing to allow her to return to Caddagat and the latter by refusing even to acknowledge her existence, reappear, and even the changes in other family relationships are changes of degree rather than of kind. There is the same overall polarizing of content in response to the central metaphor of Eden and exile and the same experience of a double fall; in both books the narrator enjoys the ecstasy of a temporary return, which is heightened by a sense of threat and the despair of a final, unaccountable rejection. *Childhood at Brindabella* also goes some way towards explaining Sybylla's ambivalent attitude to gender, which is somehow implicated in her exile, the childish aspects of the relationship with Harold Beecham and the disabling impact of feelings of self-distrust, no less urgent because they are baseless. It also elucidates Franklin's persistent idealization of a remote Europeanized Australia, her inconsistent élitist tendencies and concern with caste, and her commitment to the patriarchal ideology of the 1890s, which was in fact inimical to her deepest needs. More Garden of Eden than actuality, Franklin's Australia is not so much historical locality as psychic domain, whose timelessness is the most important condition of its existence.

Franklin's myth is strikingly individual, but it is also representative of a great number of childhoods which record the loss of an earlier, unitary self after false, socially-approved forms of 'self-expression' are imposed. If the experience is particularly acute in Australian accounts of childhood, it is not, of course, confined to Australia. As one of Ruth Suckow's heroines reflects: 'How queer it was that childhood should seem all the time only a preparation—only a prologue—and then, afterwards, the only part of life that was wholly real!'[6] *Childhood at Brindabella* is the only one of Franklin's autobiographies to admit the existence of design, even if design in this case is a negative and baffling one; *My Brilliant Career*, ideally including the query its author intended, opens and concludes from the same position—a defeated recognition of the lack of purposive shape.

Kylie Tennant's autobiography, *The Missing Heir*[7], is imbued with the author's wisdom after a lifetime as a self-professed 'battler' and coloured by her determination to see life as comedy; it is written, nevertheless, from a similar position of defeat as Franklin's. Responding to the book's verve, reviewers have been puzzled by its title. If it refers to her father's claims to be the heir of the Tennant family in Scotland and his consequent confidence in his significance ('He was surrounded by worshipping women. He expected it. Was he not the Heir, the bearer of the Tennant name?' p. 4), it is a topic that soon disappears from sight. If it refers to the author's missing grandson, the late loss does not appear to feed back into the text. It is, I suggest, Tennant herself who is the 'Missing Heir', consciously separated from her real people and astray in a crazy world, in which the only defences are a conviction of anarchy and the cultivation of a comic persona. Convinced at an early age that she can remember her own birth but that she lost her memory when she was born, the narrator describes herself at the beginning of her story as left behind: 'My own people, I decided, had gone on somewhere else, leaving me behind. I would never overtake them. But I wished someone would come by, as I sat, lonely and bored, on the stone gatepost of Lauderdale, and have an interesting conversation' (pp. 20–1). Although she has many interesting conversations in the course of her life and is extraordinarily supportive of others, writing theses for the incapable, serving on committees, fighting for the rights of the underprivileged, demonstrating against war, mothering her recalcitrant family of male egoists, father, husband and son, she remains true to the description of a psychiatrist-friend, that she is 'gregarious but not social'. There is always a sense that part of her personality is held in reserve, that she observes, enjoys and even participates in a series of dramatic scenes, but that she is partly unengaged. It is not a case of dispassion, for there is much suffering and even despair in *The Missing Heir*; it is rather as if every situation offers multiple possibilities of participating, but that behind every acting self, there is a stable observing self. It is this self which is the Missing Heir, displaced from her real, dimly-remembered community.

The description of her parents' ritualistic rows might be the most accessible illustration of this characteristic. After summarizing a typical family 'scene' over the purchase of a pair of shoes in which 'the Parent' (the father) obtains 'the utmost emotional return for small sums dealt out' and the two daughters fulfil their scripted parts, 'pleading with tearful fervour for whatever was required and falling upon the provider with gratitude, hugs and kisses', the narrator concludes:

I did not always join in the chorus of praise and thanks. I had begun my lifelong distrust of emotion, temperament and lack of discipline. I avoided scenes with distaste and began to go and live at Grandma's on my own account. I would just quietly depart and refuse to come back until they settled down. (p. 38)

It is this uncanny habit or attitude of quiet departure from many of the scenes that she plays with outward gusto that makes *The Missing Heir* such a complex autobiography.

If separation from the contemporary world is implicit in the narrator's prehistoric memory of belonging, a measure of disengagement appears to be necessary, given her consistent perception of that world as crazy. She is early afraid that 'there was something very wrong with the society into which [she] was born' and that 'lurking suspicion' is confirmed by an encounter with a Colonel Blimp of the Gallipoli campaign. The incident initiates her determination to resist those in authority who send men 'to become lumps of mud and blood in some far corner of the world'. Resistance, however, does not include anticipation of victory and in all the narrator's confrontations with the world there is an implicit expectation of defeat. In many ways Tennant's personal myth meshes with the cultural myth of defeat, analysed by Graeme Turner:

The dominant myth of the Australian context sees the imperatives of the self surrender to the exigencies which are imposed by the environment, and this is true regardless of whether the myth is rural or urban in application, or articulated in a celebratory or critical mode.

Describing the myth as depending heavily on 'notions of acceptance, upon the tolerance of frustration, and on the recognition of the levelling nature of Australian experience', Turner suggests that it also exposes the futility of 'any resistance based upon assumptions of uniqueness, of superiority of class, or intelligence or destiny'. The 'difficulty of survival becomes the justification for doing no more than that'.[8] In Tennant's writing, battling, whether it is against the blind elements of nature or the blind elements of society, is similarly a justification for itself.

At the close of her autobiography, Tennant attempts to express her dominant philosophy by relating a newspaper story on the reaction of some expatriate Australians to a Spanish bullfight. To the horror of the local bullring, they barracked for the bull. Seeing this as an affront to centuries of misguided tradition, Tennant celebrates its courage: 'the bull never wins, is never supposed to win. In high finance, in war, in all walks of civilisation, the people who run the bull-rings or the stock exchange ... are powerful in the knowledge that the bull never wins'. Yet these Australians 'a terrible and strange people—[were] encouraging the bull' (p. 170). The situation is a metaphor, of course, of Tennant's admiration for the battling champion of the underdog, but it also metaphors her commitment to a closed circle of action. From within a distant, foreign country and confronting one of its most cherished rituals, based on centuries of history, what could be more futile than the cheers of a few Australians.

Tennant's personal perception of her life as a courageous but unequal struggle against superior and even faceless forces is illustrated by her account of two dreams which appear as keys to her existence. In the first she is a Jewish gladiator, accompanied by two close friends, confronting Roman cavalry:

We fought as a team. I could depend on them and they could depend on me because if you fought as a team you had a better chance of getting out alive ... This time, I knew I wasn't going to get out alive, but I didn't feel upset. I was going to miss Gaius and Nicholas. I hefted my short sword and the dream cut out. (p. 21)

Describing this dream as the most impressive of her experience, she comments: 'somewhere in my personality for the rest of my life prowled the gladiator. It was a part of my persona'. In the second dream, in which she appears as a Puritan woman attempting to restrain four nephews from risking their lives in battle, she is similarly hopelessly trapped in a situation of war.

Numerous childhood experiences affirm this impression of unequal battle. Watching a guy burning on a bonfire, she assumes it is a real man, but concludes she is helpless to save him: 'So must have thought little Celtic girls who saw men burnt in wickerwork' (p. 32). Raped at the age of four by a boy of ten, there is nothing she can do because he is twice her size. Promised some relief from the domestic battles of her youth when her mother plans to divorce her father, she is not surprised when her mother weakens and the battles continue. Most confirming of all is her father's invincible egoism, which combined with his charm, makes him a continuing adversary. If many of her attitudes are formed in opposition to his—in that she cultivates prodigality to counter his parsimony, sincerity and self-deprecation in opposition to his hypocrisy and pretension, and pacifism to his war-mongering—he persists as the major feature of her life until her marriage; indeed, he is in some ways reinforced by her marriage, since he joins forces with the husband who is sometimes seen as resembling him.

At numerous points in the narrative, Tennant conveys her impression of society as naturally unjust and inimical to the self's needs. Her reaction is to structure for herself a comic, anarchic persona, who retains authenticity, if not power, by claiming the extra-cultural liberty of the fool. Doomed to be eternally tripped up by life, or to be perpetually drawn in the frothy wake of more noisy individuals, she has a fatal capacity for doing everything the hard way: 'It had never occurred to me that there was an easier way of going about whatever I was engaged on. I fully expected to make a mess of it and was very surprised when, by a miracle, it proved a great success' (p. 45). Similarly, evil omens are signals to be consistently ignored, even though they prove invariably correct. If she achieves a sequence of extraordinary successes, writing books, raising a family, nursing people through desperate illnesses, they are no more than brave attempts to hold the dyke. Even writing is not an unequivocal achievement of the self, as it is performed first for the 'Parent' and then for the husband.

Early in her story, Tennant describes her discovery of the mask of fool. Learning from a friend, she discovers how to make the catastrophic incidents of life into a comic dirge, with herself as hapless victim, 'the technique of *fausse-naive* and running gag.' It is a technique that she continues in the writing of her autobiography, just as she privileges the fool's reaction to cross-grained life: 'What shall I leave my heirs' (the girls who read her books), she reflects at the close:

The power to smile crookedly at life? Not to fear anything and laugh at disaster? The power to make their own unique pattern on chaos? . . . No:

more potent than all, I will leave them the impulse to make fools of themselves. (p.170)

But the voice of the fool-self is only one of the voices in *The Missing Heir*, for there are at least three narrating voices in this autobiography. There is the jaunty, resilient, entertaining narrator of a comic, picaresque tale, in which the 'I' is the funniest character, a McGoo type who survives and is often miraculously protected. There is a self-justifying voice, which often directly addresses the reader and explains the activities of Kylie Tennant, the well-known writer, in her historical context. And then there is the voice of a more bewildered, lonely 'I', which suffers deeply and often mutely, admits to strange determining dreams and lacks defences against exploitation by those she loves most. This 'I' reveals the most and is the most probing, although the comic 'I' frequently brushes it aside. For Tennant's voices are not integrated. Compare, for instance, her comment that it is toughening to have fighting parents, 'I don't know how people get on who haven't been reared in a battling Australian family where the parents are incompatible', with the anguish reflected in the extract on these same battling parents quoted above. It is as if the private 'I' witnesses, is, suffers, attempts to comfort, thinks. The comic 'I' acts and makes defeat a grand joke. The historical 'I' is somewhere lost between the two. Only in one area of experience are they united, in valuing struggle and stoicism and companionship in struggle.

A writer who is more cogent and articulate in her reflections on a fragmented self is Barbara Hanrahan. Autobiography lurks within all Hanrahan's work, both as artist and writer, but three books focus exclusively on her early experience, *The Scent of Eucalyptus* (1973), *Sea-Green* (1974) and *Kewpie Doll* (1984). *Sea-Green*, a fictional treatment of the artist's life in London after she left Australia in 1962, is a postscript to the primary experiences described 'factually' in the other two texts and is justly regarded as a lesser achievement by the author.

Hanrahan is often considered to be a quintessentially female writer, preoccupied with exploring the female side of experience and inevitably engaged with feminist issues, although she is by no means a programmatic writer. In *The Scent of Eucalyptus* and *Kewpie Doll*, she traces her distinctive knowledge of herself as female and as artist to her childhood in a household of women, made up of her widowed mother, her grandmother and her mongoloid aunt. The self-contained quartet of relationships which comes into its own when the door of their house closes on the outer world, has a reality that is far more real than the realities served by school, church and business. It is a green, innocent, simple world, at one with the secret, growing world of nature, 'strangely original, strangely unworldly' under its 'sham layer of studied conformity':

It was nurtured and protected by the roses and the grape-vines, the ivy and the lavatory-creeper that clung to the fences; by the arching berry bush, the plant that bloomed once every seven years. The real world came into being round the dining-room fire, as we toasted bread on the crooked fork; it lurked in the porcelain basin as my mother washed my hair with rain-water from the well, bloomed in the fusty bedroom as Reece soothed my head with little pats when I was sick, rose from the earth when my grandmother stooped in the garden and coaxed withered seedlings to life. In these sequestered haunts—behind the crinkled green glass and the roses, the grape-vines, the ivy and the lavatory-creeper—my grandmother's and mother's lives blossomed secretly, unacknowledged even to themselves.[9]

Unfortunately, it is also a world unconscious of its own value, and ultimately subject to the stultifying forces of a mundane, materialistic society; it forfeits its authentic reality to the 'wan pretence fabricated by newspapers and politicians; made safe by shops that sold lounge suites and latest season's costumes on hire-purchase, bearable by wireless jingles and long-range forecasts'. *The Scent of Eucalyptus* describes the narrator's enjoyment and loss of the early authentic world; *Kewpie Doll* elaborates on the loss but intimates a rediscovery. Going off on a long 'journey to aloneness' is paradoxically the 'only chance of returning ... of burrowing back through that aloneness to the childhood I thought I'd lost' (pp. 144–5). Moved by the death of her loved grandmother to re-explore the early world by writing it into existence in *The Scent of Eucalyptus*, she reforms the circle of time that had silently bound her childhood days together, even as she records its apparent disjunction.

For the ceaseless flow of time and its permanent, long-term effects are one of the contradictions that Hanrahan loves to explore. She has frequently commented in interviews on her interest in time, and in both her autobiographies and her fiction, she is preoccupied with the contrast between the past's sepia impression of finality and its vivid life in the present. If her father's existence is recorded in a few incongruous school prizes, photographs and old-fashioned garments, and if her great grandmother is survived only by a bleached cameo, a tray-cloth sprigged with iron-mould and a photograph of herself with spectacles, their attitudes and experiences tenaciously survive in the lives of their descendants and their stories. As characters in those stories, partially explained and symbolized by legendary deeds or misdeeds, obscured by prejudices and the received clichés of family memory, they are at once part of the child's sense of herself as an historical phenomenon, and elusively individual. Hanrahan has a remarkable capacity for expressing the sticky significance of heterogeneous mementoes or the way that the dead depend on the rhetoric of their survivors' memories:

My father was twenty-six when he died on the seventh of September, 1940, the day after my first birthday. I had his photo in my pencil box. The girls at school were sorry when they saw how handsome he was. He was picking grapes up the river. He wore a singlet and a cap made of a handkerchief and his arms were shiny.

But my mother said I would never have liked my father. He drank beer and read the racing news; he played billiards and walked with his hands in his pockets. His friends weren't good enough—one of them was a boxer who knew Big Chief Little Wolf, the Redskin wrestler. He could wriggle his chest and do the Indian death-lock. (*Kewpie Doll*, p. 11)

Meanwhile the identities of the living are inescapably bound up with the past which is part of their meaning for the child. Familiar with the facts of her grandmother's life as Iris, the baker's daughter, victim of a second, brutal husband and devoted elder sister of the mongoloid Reece, the narrator also makes her mother's past her own: 'All my mother's past was in her voice and, telling, she made it mine . . . A past she didn't tell to anyone but me—it was safe in my head, had been safe there for years' (*Kewpie Doll*, p. 129).

Hanrahan's concentration on the fluidity of time is typical of her inclusive approach, her interest in the conjunction of the fantastic and the concrete, earthy and spiritual, physical and symbolic. The so-called ordinary world of everyday experience is for Hanrahan's child a fantastic world of extraordinary beauty and ugliness and she loves to celebrate the minute hidden facets of things, the 'shadow-play the rose leaves made on a fence', the 'clipped stems of the valerian', 'bulbs slit by greener spear', the 'pleated linings of mush-rooms', tomatoes 'ruffled by stars, carrots hung with tassels . . . the mould that flecked the lemon'. Inside the house, the hidden facets of things are just as intriguing: 'I came inside, and found the dust that lay under the mat, the stale hair in the brush, the soap's awful underside like a sweating sore' (*The Scent of Eucalyptus*, p. 12).

Several impressions strike the reader of these characteristic accounts of seeing. One is the minute, sensuously grasped detail of the things described, coupled with a freshness of perception that evokes their oddity; another is the contrast between the activity of the described scene in which bubbles 'dance', 'clenched dots turn into lilacs', an ant 'clambers over a pebble', runs under a needle of grass and is lost amongst the ivy, bulbs are 'slit' and soap sweats, and the stillness of the child's observing eye. The child as voyeur is a recurrent figure in Hanrahan's writing, and verbs of seeing, perceiving, observing are sown profusely through the narratives of her autobiographies, while verbs of doing, controlling, ordering are conspicuously absent. It is the self's 'negative capability' that Hanrahan celebrates, describing her child-self at one point as wanting to 'wriggle through the soil with the pink earthworms; lose myself in the pointed leaves with the little pecking birds; merge with the greenness like the grasshoppers in the hills' (*The Scent of Eucalyptus*, p. 107).

Another characteristic is the emphasis on everything as vulnerable to time and minute forms of invasion, which to another eye might appear as imperfections. People are no more immune from this sort of process than plants and animals:

I came closer to the three who were important: to the grandmother, and saw the hair in her nostril, the dirt between her toes, dye spots in her scalp; to the great-aunt, and her parting was thick with scurf, she had wax-buds in her ear, a sour handkerchief up her sleeve. And my mother tried not to cry: face all crumpled, eyes gone blurry, ugly mouth square. I watched unmoved. (*The Scent of Eucalyptus*, pp. 12–13)

The last sentence refers not to the child's heartlessness but to what the author would describe as the 'innocence' of her observations. In an interview, for instance, she has described the child as 'the truest part of you' for the child sees 'purely', whereas the adult's vision is 'hedged and blinkered, weakened by so many half things. But the child that's still innocent can see clearly, unsentimentally'.[10] Thus the child appreciates the physical oddities of her great-aunt Reece, whereas the medical textbooks present an evil lie of her condition, treating her as a case-study, something to be pitied and locked away. The child's intense view also takes in reality's complex blend of the fantastic and the earthy. Hanrahan's child has an unsentimental interest in the odours and colours of human decay and a fascination with earthiness in all its forms. Visits to the run-down home of her friend Carol, for instance, with its innumerable cats, aura of perpetual evening, musky urine-laden smells and bizarre collection of human inhabitants are irresistible. Eating at Carol's house is a sensual experience in 'feckless glamour': 'On torn oilcloth, like an arrangement of holy relics, stood the tomato sauce and vinegar, plum jam and condensed milk that accompanied every meal—their glass and metal sides tattooed with congealing stigmatas' (*The Scent of Eucalyptus*, p. 76). It is this ability to find pleasure in the dirty underside of life that ultimately defends her from the temptation to yield to the insipid lures of being a 'normal' 1950s girl; she is saved from pliancy and ignorance by 'something awkward and unyielding, prickly and resisting deep inside . . . I was saved by the crudity that made me pee into the bath, and revel in the tar-black shit that poured out of me and stank. Therefore I was different' (p. 158).

The fresh, unsentimental perspective of the child, buried but not killed by the later impulse to conform, exposes the craziness of the world that others accept as real; it also reveals the existence of evil, which includes the self's capacity for evil. Thus if the narrator is shocked when her great grandfather attempts to abuse her sexually, the incident is not a permanent scar and her curiosity about sex and female development is open and shame-free until external prescriptions about gender impose themselves. She is also frank about her own occasional cruelties, teasing those in her power, such as Reece and her puppy. And it is clear that the narrator finds these minor aggressions preferable to her later attempts to reject Reece in her efforts to be the Saturday night girl of her grandmother's suburban fantasy.

As Hanrahan's child 'progresses' from primary school to the technical institution which the limited ambitions of her mother and grandmother have selected, the pressures to conform to a reductive female stereotype are insidiously increased. It becomes easy to forget 'the quiet, calm place' she came from and she becomes accustomed to 'a world that others said was real': 'I was seduced by the smooth voices of radio announcers, the banality of soap powder jingles, the empty glamour of film-star buccaneers. I paid homage without question to a sovereign and a flag and a sunburned land that were not mine' (*The Scent of Eucalyptus*, p. 156). Outwardly and in the daytime, she conforms to the unimaginative plan of her family, the expectation that she will settle down and live in a neat suburban bungalow with a substantial mortgage and a sound husband, shopping, cooking, cleaning and watering the flowers through a pretty rubber hose. At night in the garden, however, she abandons this shadow world for the authentic natural one, a wild world that breaks through the prim suburban symmetry: 'With the night, rats wove between the creepers on the fences that divided the yards. With winter, the galvanized iron sheds were lapped by sour-sobs and grass; the houses became Noah's arks, bobbing in a swollen sea'(p. 162). The split in her personality, between an outward conforming self and a private dreaming self, which she had previously known as complementary, now becomes an unbridgeable gulf: there is the pale one she despises at school and the wild one who comes home, takes off the shoes and the hat and tunic and is free. Even the 'fits' which had threaded her life, and 'illumined all [her] ages' become sterile ceremonies, empty of comfort. The old innocence has been lost: 'I masqueraded as a child' (p. 175).

Kewpie Doll records the increase in sterility which her mother's remarriage brings, the abandonment of the old Rose Street house with its green mysteries and the substitution of a red-brick neatness which attempts to erase the past. If the old furniture and the familiar photographs do not fit into this new male-dominated environment, neither does Reece. Interestingly, the narrator describes this conforming dream, which she adopts because of her love of her mother and grandmother, as destructive of the integrated time they had all unconsciously experienced. On one hand, the pursuit of the materialistic suburban dream is an attempt to conquer death and the uncertainty of the unknown; it cultivates a now, which cancels out the loyalties of the past, makes Iris no longer the baker's daughter but merely an old, silver-haired grandmother, Reece an oddity, visited on the family by chance, and her father's death 'a sad mistake'

(*Kewpie Doll*, p. 146). On the other hand, the dream is deathly, frustrating growth and real change: 'The trees and the flowers will grow and we will die. But not to worry—there will be others, always others, to take our place and live out other lives. Lives that are just as nice and proper—and mean as little, as ours' (*The Scent of Eucalyptus*, p. 161).

In her struggle with the false stereotypes of the 1950s, Hanrahan's narrator is sustained partly by her discovery of the release into another, purer dimension that her skill as an artist offers, partly by the resilient power of her memories of the original female childhood, and partly by the image of her father as natural rebel: 'I love him, I think of him picking grapes, his tanned arms shiny in the sun; of him standing before the paling fence in his striped blazer' (*Kewpie Doll*, p. 123). *Kewpie Doll* intimates that eventually the buried, authentic childhood is rediscovered, and the old relatedness restored; going away is also a coming home. Thus in this Portrait of the Artist as a Young Woman the pattern is the reverse of the male model, for achievement is not imaged in terms of the future career nor even in terms of the self's discovery of her vocation as artist, but in terms of integrated being in the world; and not only does authenticity of being depend on the continuing life of the past, but the self's journey is circular rather than an onward progression.

Freedom from conformity and authenticity of being are also prominent themes in Katharine Susannah Prichard's autobiographies, the factual *Child of the Hurricane* (1963) and the fictional *The Wild Oats of Han* (1928).[11] Ostensibly written for children, *The Wild Oats of Han* is confessedly based on the author's Tasmanian childhood and provides some of the text of the later account of the same period. For Prichard the departure from Tasmania, consequent on her father's losing his position as editor of the Launceston *Daily Telegraph*, represented the end of her childhood. The sudden discovery of her family's financial crisis was a major blow: 'My childhood fell from me like the chrysalis from a butterfly'. Dating her political commitment, described as a sense of responsibility for the 'families of mankind', from that moment, Prichard describes herself in *Child of the Hurricane* as having a 'sense of going down into the great mysterious world to take my part in its labour and sorrow'.

Almost the same words conclude *Wild Oats*. Her mother's confession of helplessness coupled with the news that another baby is imminent, induces feelings of pity and responsibility in the child. 'Her mind whirled. She thought of herself as some one she had known a long time ago ... A sense of the helplessness, the tragedy of it, appalled her. The weight of the world seemed suddenly to have descended upon her shoulders' (pp. 158–9). In both books Prichard emphasizes the wild freedom of her young self and clearly perceives her natural nonconformity as an important element in her later political radicalism. In *Child of the Hurricane* she frequently refers to herself as a 'rebel'; left in the wake of the hurricane that raged at her birth, she is destined to have a stormy life and she is recognized as a naturally free spirit, more valuable than 'twenty boy baby', by her devoted Fijian servant. Han, her childhood self in the earlier book, is imaged as similarly untamed: 'Han was the wildest of all the little wild animals who lived in the hills' (p. 1). Initially an amoral child, whose sense of wrong is is tailored to fit the resulting punishment, she is imaged as sowing the wild oats which mark her as a special spirit. Sam, the old man who is presented as understanding her best, sees her as an adventurous and original child, who will avoid the mental paralysis that afflicts others. '"Wild oats"', he explains, '"grow mostly in unbroken ground ... and break it up ... and make it fit for cultivation".' As for Han, '"Her mind's fallow now ... she's sowin' her wild oats ... She's shriekin' mischievous sometimes, but she'll be wakin' one of these days"' (pp. 56, 63). And Han comes to see herself in the same light, telling Sam at the close that she is 'awake': '"I've been 'sowing my wild oats' ... doing what I liked ... not thinking or bothering at all. I want to grow up now ... I want to help"' (p. 159).

But Han's story is not so uncomplicated as her author seems to assume, and in both books Prichard betrays her ambivalent or half-formed response to the idea of freedom. If the image of herself as a free spirit, at one with the wild forces of nature and even privileged in that she has access to secrets that adults cannot share, is a congenial one, the transformation of free self to social-service self is less of an organic sequence than Prichard openly admits. For Han is never as free as she believes herself to be; not only is her early freedom the temporary, casual dispensation to be male, typical of the bush child, but her loss of freedom is also closely bound up with her gender. She is both more and less realistic than Franklin's child; she leaves Eden voluntarily in response to claims of the human world, but she turns a blind eye to the disjunction in her destiny.

In *Wild Oats* Prichard grants her younger self two mentor figures. One is her maternal grandmother, also recognized as an influential figure in *Child of the Hurricane*. Grandmother Sarahy, unlike her daughter whose sensibilities are unfitted for the workaday world, is a woman of great but gentle authority:

Such a sweet face she had, Grandmother Sarahy; such gentle and tender ways. Whether she sewed, or read; whether her shoulders were bowed over her work, or with slow and stately steps she took the air in the garden, and talked of the weather and progress of seeds to Josiah, a hush fell on Han's spirit whenever she saw her. (p. 6)

It is the grandmother who tries to instil a sense of female duty in the child, who teaches her Bible stories, sets her to hem dusters, sends her to school and punishes her when she plays truant. Setting before her the constant example of her namesake, Great-Aunt Hannah Frances, the grandmother frequently compares her unruly behaviour with the blameless life of this dead relative, who at an early age had become a member of a Dorcas Society, and had worked all her days making shapeless garments for the poor and the heathen. Han regards the 'lovely, sad face' of her portrait with enmity.

The father in this autobiography is much less visible than in *Child of the Hurricane*, although he looms in the background as a figure to be reckoned with, and as in the later book, the parents are presented as so absorbed in each other that their children are secondary, 'in the nature of accidents—not unwelcome accidents to be sure—but just circumstances incidental to their love' (p. 10). Rosamund Mary, Han's mother, is so lacking in motherly authority, that the child refuses to call her mother. Contenting herself with playing 'wispish little airs' on the piano, she leaves the affairs of household and community entirely to the grandmother. Enlarging the grandmother figure in *Wild Oats*, Prichard invests her with all the traditional female virtues and transposes her death so that it coincides with the child's discovery of the family crisis. Given the admiration consistently expressed for the old lady, it is impossible to avoid the conclusion that Han is to be seen as inheriting her commitment to social service. In both autobiographies the child-self has two loved younger brothers, whom she frequently leads into mischief, but who are also already set on different, manly destinies. In *Wild Oats* they are presented with different challenges and their companionship in a boyish code of honour is beginning to exclude their sister, a fact which the older narrator accepts as natural. And in both texts the birth of a sister is presented as a key event for the younger self's growth in responsibility.

Han's other mentor is the old woodman, Sam. In *Child of the Hurricane*, Prichard admits that she altered the historical influence of this individual: 'He didn't have much to do with the awakening really. I worked that out for myself' (p. 39). To Han he is more wonderful even than her grandmother, a man who understands the natural world and lives in tune with its laws. As the grandmother is surrounded by the social community and mindful of its conventions and obligations, Sam enjoys the freedom of a solitary outlaw: 'although he had been a runaway sailor, cook's boy, ship's carpenter, Methodist preacher, and fought in foreign parts, he had never turned his sword into a ploughshare, or tilled the soil' (p. 56). His memories of droving and of life at sea, evoke the 'great, dim mysterious "world"' which lies beyond the hills', while his stories of Dyak pirates and tropical islands have the same inspiring effect as the stories of Greek mythology which feed Han's impression of the outside world as a 'huge enchanted island, wrapped round by fathomless blue and green seas' (p. 15). Being free, according to Sam, means 'realising life', knowing the 'rush of joy and sorrow', getting 'to grips with it' (p. 57). To confront life with courage is to defeat its hurts: ' "You've just got to shake your fist at Life and say: 'You can't break me. You can't!' And Life'll get tired of tryin' " ' (p. 133).

There is no doubt that in the moral structure of *Wild Oats*, Sam's attitudes are privileged, and that Prichard intends her readers to regard his wisdom as primary for the younger self. In a central debate with Grandmother Sarahy on the subject of freedom versus convention, the old lady is presented as shaken by Sam's radical views. His discourse about thinking for oneself is described as disquieting for one who has never questioned the faiths and ideas of previous generations. But the story of Han's growth refuses to restrict itself to the parameters of Sam's simple romanticism, however enchanting it appears to the implied narrator. Prichard has a heavy investment in the idea of Han as free spirit, 'set apart' by her sacramental participation in the natural world, and devotes lengthy sections to celebrating her Pan-like vitality. At one point she even indulges the retrospective fantasy of punishing a repressive adult, inflicting an accident that chastens the old woman's censorious spirit; when Han concludes that the accident, which has forestalled a thrashing, is a 'dispensation of Providence', neither Sam nor the author corrects her. After every rebellious sally or downfall, Han hastens to Sam's hut, where her wounds receive the salve of his homely wisdom. It is not a wisdom that intersects with her life in any convincing way, however. Han's attempts to grasp freedom, for example, are all remarkably tenuous; if she is granted a day's wildness among the hills, she is more often confined to bed, school or dull household tasks. Many of her romantic escapades end in fiasco or are cut short by her growing sense of responsibility, and her life is as embedded in a general life and as complicated by contending claims as Sam's patently is not. If her grandmother's wisdom issues as much in her actions as in her pronouncements, Sam's is rarely tested by circumstances. On the few occasions when he takes a more active part—contradicting Miss Whitler's expressions of disapproval, or attempting to warn the local townsfolk of the imminent floods—he is singularly ineffective. The grandmother, on the other hand, responds to the floods in a mission of mercy, which opens the child's eyes to the reality of misfortune: 'She did not feel comfortable among these people who had been flooded out. They were not a bit like what she thought they would be' (p. 141).

The floods, moreover, are the direct cause of the grandmother's death, an event which abruptly fractures Han's romantic speculations; failing to reconcile this loss with the 'beautiful story' of death, Han is 'more disturbed than anybody imagined, and thoughtful in a vague, troubled, childish way when no one had any idea she was thinking at all' (p. 148). Most significantly of all, Prichard occasionally implies that her child-self is troubled by thoughts that are inaccessible to Sam: she is afflicted with doubts about her appearance and the social expectations that being female arouse, and she is sometimes uncertain of her identity and destiny. It is disquieting to see her face reflected in water, for the reflection poses questions she cannot answer: 'Is that you, Han? Who are you? What are you: Where are you going?' (p. 134). Her final 'awakening' to a feeling of helpless responsibility in a world where fathers lose their ability to provide, grandmothers die, mothers are frightened, people lose their homes and babies are drowned, seems to have little in common with Sam's 'Life', which can be conquered with a shake of the fist, even though the narrator is ostensibly unaware of the inconsistency. Thus the 'wild oats' theme is far from unequivocal: privileging one sort of freedom, Prichard unwittingly undercuts it by implying that it is a male freedom and unobtainable, given the female responsibility of caring. As in *Child of the Hurricane*, Prichard fails to resolve the dichotomy she implicitly raises between a romantic perception of the self as free agent and of life as a liberating adventure with more restricting perceptions of the realities of relatedness.

Some autobiographers, however, attempt to combine autonomy and relatedness by reinterpreting traditional roles. Motherhood, for example, is a role that has had a satisfying elasticity. Although marriage is rarely presented as the life's destiny in these autobiographies, and the traditional theme of courtship in women's fiction is largely missing, as I have already mentioned, some narrators perceive marriage and its attendant motherhood as the unique means of achieving selfhood. Agnes Gosse Hay, for example, the author of *After-Glow Memories* by 'Anglo-Australian'[12] has an unusual sense of design in her life, culminating in the 'glow' of wifehood. The mother of the novelist, William Gosse Hay, Agnes wrote her autobiography in late middle age after the death of her adored husband, Alexander Hay. The book has been strangely ignored by historians and literary critics, although it is used as a source in Fayette Gosse's history of her family.[13] Disguising her family's name Gosse as Guest, Agnes Hay casts a thin veil over the places and people of her childhood. South Australia, her home from the age of twelve, is Alexandrina, Adelaide is Lightonia, Bishop Short becomes Bishop Lang, Sir R. G. MacDonnell becomes Sir Charles McCarthy and Port Victor, Port Moira. Agnes herself is rechristened Helen and her only sister Mary becomes Lucy, while the first names of her other five siblings are fictionalized or rearranged. She has a strict regard for literal truth, however, and this account of 1850s Adelaide, filtered through a particularly observant and shrewd consciousness, is a valuable social document. It is also one of the most complex of the narratives considered here, composed of layers of meaning, of which only some are fully accessible to the narrator. Preoccupied and even obsessed with herself, Hay is also partly blind to some of the implications of her revealed nature, so that her journey of self-discovery sometimes skirts sharp precipices of insight with unconscious, comic sang-froid. If her negotiation of the secret self is occasionally circuitous, her narrative style is remarkably direct, succinct and expressive. She has a novelist's interest in people and values strong individualities as she relishes absurd situations. A glimpse of Queen Victoria fails to impress the young child and the older woman is no less surprised by the absence of royalty in the sovereign's appearance: 'I can only say that on close inspection, she owed nothing to natural beauty or even to the picturesque mellowing of time' (p. 306). The ceremony of presentation at court, which is the natural conclusion of this success story, is similarly unimpressive: 'the curious gate leading to the "Throne Room" through which we were admitted to the Presence, one at a time, reminded me of sheep passing into a yard' (p. 297).

The self-confidence reflected here is typical of this autobiography, which is embellished with appropriate literary epigraphs and unusually shaped according to a temporal progression: 'Sunrise', 'Mid-Day', 'Change' and 'Full Glow' are the titles of the text's four 'Books', while numerous chapters project the same perception of life as a journey through time: 'The New Dawn', 'Rainbow Weather', 'Morning Influences'—Hay has a gift for the trite title, which fortunately does not extend to the staple of her narrative. At the same time, she has certain strong convictions that she does not hesitate to ventilate, one of the strongest being that early training is important but that genes will out: '"Ere thou wert born into this breathing world, God wrote some characters upon thy heart"' (p. 25). Writing as a grandmother to her grandchildren, Hay perceives herself as a matriarch, who not only established a new prosperous line by her fortunate marriage to a wealthy, influential man, but also restored her mother's frustrated destiny as heiress. If Queen Victoria is physically unimpressive, as 'Sovereign' and 'Woman', she fills a role that Hay finds appealing and even familiar, for her own marriage brilliantly appeases her dual need for personal significance and relatedness.

Hay's close relationship with her mother is established from the beginning. Drawing on Wordsworth to express her influence, 'the heart/And hinge of all our learnings and our loves', Hay dwells on her selflessness, refinement and loss of fortune. She is somewhat dismissive of her father, on the other hand, critical of his lack of business acumen and 'common sense' and of his irritable temperament which divided him from his children as infants. Indeed, so partial is Hay towards her mother, that she establishes for herself a matrilineal descent, virtually by-passing the unsatisfactory father in favour of the

dimly-remembered maternal grandfather: 'I believe that my character, many sided as it is, and always has been, came to me as much
from my Scotch grandfather, whom I really never knew, as from my
English father, with whom I lived in close contact for many years'
(p. 7). Significantly, her memories of the old man centre on symbols
of his lost fortune, 'a very handsome silver knife, fork, spoon', his
role as giver and as the one who taught her to walk. And equally
significantly she confers his historical name, Grant, on her future
husband, who is also a Scot. The analogy is even explicit:

While my grandfather was teaching my baby feet to toddle their first stage on
the journey of life, a young Scotchman, who was afterwards destined to be
my guide and dearly-loved fellow-traveller through a large part of that
journey, was taking an important step in his career by leaving his native land
and seeking his fortunes in Australia. (p. 6)[14]

Perceiving herself on one hand as most strongly influenced by her
mother, who was 'the very essence of motherhood', to repeat the
maternal role ('I may safely say that the maternal instinct was the
most marked trait in my dawning life'), on the other, she is both more
ambitious and less selfless than her gentle parent ('I feel conscious
that, in my own life, I have fallen far short in what might have been
expected in the daughter of such a mother').

Selflessness, in fact, is an ingredient in the concept of motherhood
that Hay ultimately manages to reinterpret, given the power conferred by marriage to an older, powerful man. Thus her mother's
motherhood is characterized by helpless dedication but her own is a
triumphant giving of valuable gifts: the financial gifts and social
prestige of a wealthy son-in-law, the first grandchildren, even the
father's acquisition of a German degree, negotiated by means of her
own language skills. Psychological explanations can be risky, but it is
possible to see Hay's selected memories of her early manifestations of
maternal feeling (simulating post-natal experience and 'saving' a new
baby in an enterprise which threatened both their deaths) as unconscious protests at the destructive selflessness of her mother figure.

Lively, strong-willed and self-conscious, Hay presents herself as a
personality to be reckoned with. Acknowledging her younger self to
be unpredictable, troublesome and restless, she is conscious of being
different from the crowd: 'Even in these early years I was considered
haughty and stand-off, and if I did not express my difference of
opinion with that of my elders in words, yet I showed it in my face
and manner' (p. 50). She frequently expresses pride in her 'stately'
appearance, in her ability to entertain and her popularity with the
wittier ladies of her parents' acquaintance. On the journey to Australia she takes the 'deepest interest' in mastering knowledge of all the
ropes and sails of the ship, and if she finds a fellow passenger's
romantic interest flattering, his physical attentions are brusquely

repudiated. Persuading her parents to allow her to 'come out' early in Adelaide society, she thoroughly enjoys the social whirl as one of the few eligible young girls; back in London, she is flattered by comments on her dignified, fashionable appearance and reports them verbatim. London, however, accentuates the lack-lustre future of an unmarried lady and she takes up religion with the uncomfortable enthusiasm of a Dorothea Brooke. On her return to Adelaide, it is clear that her ostentatious piety makes for strains in family relationships, a situation she reports with unconscious irony: 'they were frightened of me in my new character' (p. 200).

The descriptions of her bleak years before marrying at the age of thirty-seven convey the unmistakable impression of an energetic, commanding personality, suffocating under the conventions of her time. Religion offers a form of self-assertion and travel grants a temporary stimulus, but the first alternative speedily fades given her worldly inclinations and the second is curbed by her father's rapidly declining fortunes. Well aware of some aspects of her personality, such as her natural worldliness and love of beautiful things, she is also capable of surprising herself. Unlike the reader, for instance, she is amazed, after marriage, to discover a lurking, native ambition: 'I always had liked men who had leading parts to play; in fact, there was a considerable amount of ambition in my character, though I had not recognised the fact before my marriage, but it soon made itself apparent afterwards' (p. 275). It is this odd capacity for the blinkered perception or the half-insight which makes Hay's narrative so stimulating for a contemporary reader. On one hand, she reveals herself with the frankness of a Moll Flanders; on the other, she fails to assimilate the full drift of her honest perceptions. Paradoxically, she is often an unwitting victim of her own acute power of recall and, immersing herself in the immediacy of remembered experience, is largely unaware of the ironies she generates. Thus, the discovery that her beautiful hair will not be jeopardized with the onset of religious piety is reported with all the relief that it created at the time: 'Mr Nagron said it was the duty of everyone to make themselves look as well as they possibly could. It was a comfort to me to hear this, for I was always desirous of looking as nice as was attainable' (p. 154). And a perceptive comment on the strength of her religious conversion is delivered in an off-hand way that implies ignorance of its implications: the extremities of her piety can be traced, she suggests, to the thoroughness of her nature, for 'I was nothing if not thorough, and indeed may claim to have been that in all I have undertaken' (p. 153). On the other hand, the temporary nature of her piety is described in external climactic terms: 'My religion had about it very much of a tropical character. It had come so suddenly, and there was more of the emotional than the practical element in it' (p. 193).

Although Hay reports the history of her religious conversion with the factual accuracy of a case-study, she is bewildered by the memory of her contradictory emotions. The very time when her religious feeling is at its strongest is also a time when she is irritatingly subject to the tug of sexual passion. She has determined to be 'very good' on the passage home, but finds instead that she is rapidly entangled in an affair of the heart:

Here was a situation to find myself in. I had gone through seasons of gaiety without any entanglement, and now that I had given up all frivolities, to be acting the part of a common flirt. It was intolerable... (p. 195)

Equally irritating is the knowledge that the young man in question is socially 'impossible'. The mingling of worldly and spiritual concerns is typical.

Indeed, just as Hay never penetrates to the bottom of her religiosity, she never confronts the contradictions of her attitude to marriage. For, if wifehood is a role she ultimately finds congenial, it is also one she has studiously avoided. Looking back from the vantage point of the indulged Mrs Hay, she is everlastingly thankful that she was 'kept' from less worthy entanglements and works the knowledge into her personal teleology. The reader, however, can draw other conclusions, given the number of negative comments on the institution of marriage which pepper the text. Intimate with her mother's marital problems, she is also familiar with a range of unhappy wives, from Mrs O'Flynn, who had to wait long years before death liberated her from a tyrannical husband, to Mary Anson, tricked into marrying an alcoholic: 'My heart bled for her, and a feeling of disgust and anger arose in my mind against the old man for the trick he had played her' (p. 192). Her own secret engagement on board ship inspires feelings of despair: 'a consciousness of being bound, chained and done for came over me, and all the pleasure of our intercourse was over' (p. 198). At the same time, the women who act as Hay's mentors are all strong, distinctive personalities, who have gained substantial independence for themselves either within or without marriage. Not surprisingly, she has nothing but contempt for the wife who is too insipid to further her husband's career with style, for the old maid who is narrowly conventional or for the religiose wet blanket.

Hay's treatment of her courtship and marriage is one of the comic high points of this narrative. Regarding her younger self with exasperation, she is amazed at her stubborn reluctance to accept the marvellous opportunity of Alexander Hay's proposal. As always, her frankness has unwitting dimensions. If the elderly Hay is unable initially to provide one essential ingredient ('I had a spice of romance about me, and there was no romance whatever in this affair'), a visit to his beautiful property 'Braeside' frames his offer to effect: 'certainly Archibald Grant could never have been seen to greater advantage than as a host in his own home' (p. 271). In the event, marriage to an established, older man able 'to gratify all [her] reasonable desires' provides Agnes with undreamed-of scope for her love of dominance and display. Motherhood, which she recommends in moralistic terms, and a second home at Port Victor fill her cup of happiness to the brim. Characteristically, she feels no qualms about her interest in possessions, complacently recounting her husband's prodigality at the 1880 Exhibition: 'our names as purchasers were to be seen all over the Exhibition, and some lady . . . remarked to one who knew us, that, "she wished she was Mrs Archibald Grant"'. (p. 287).

Also characteristic is this narrator's tendency to trace the workings of a special purpose in her life. The bleak years of spinsterhood are perceived in retrospect as 'the dull antechamber of the palace to the halls of delight that I was shortly to enter', while one event in particular is signalled out as symbolically announcing the change in her destiny. On her family's return from Europe in 1871, they are greeted by two items of news, the deaths of the narrator's old friend and mentor, Mrs Vereker, and of the first Mrs Grant (Hay). One death is emotionally shattering but of negligible practical consequence; the other appears of negligible interest but has far-reaching effects. Such a coincidence, reflects the narrator, would be accounted 'unnatural' in a novel: 'It was the news of the passing away of the old life and the entering of the new, although of course the latter was hidden from me' (p. 265).

My discussion so far will have illustrated the intimacy and even privacy of this autobiography, notwithstanding the narrator's public didactic posture as Grandmother. Far too fascinated by her own wayward personality and spectacular destiny to restrict herself to the conventional subject matter of a society lady's memoirs, Hay cannot resist probing her past selves. But this disjunction between public and private selves has curious, unexpected complications. If the public rhetoric provides a convenient facade for an inward exploration, the public persona is sometimes called on to rescue the narrated 'I' when intimacy proves dangerous. Thus Hay is at her most didactic whenever memories become uncomfortable. Recalling the solace she found in books during the 'dreary' difficulties of adolescence in a new, raw country, she draws a veil over those memories by adjuring parents to keep a keen eye on their book-shelves: 'Many a young life has been made or marred by early reading of good or bad literature' (p. 84.); pondering her close shaves with unsuitable marital prospects, she counsels her readers on the importance of prayer: 'I prayed earnestly to God that my husband, if I had one, might be a good, kind man, and this prayer I can safely say was answered in its fullest, widest sense' (p. 235). A delightfully thick-skinned introvert, Hay complacently shares with her reader her confidence in a God who preserved her for a role that combined motherhood and power.

A much more recent autobiography, which also has a well-defined teleology with motherhood as the ultimate independent destiny, is Doreen Flavel's *The Promise and The Challenge*.[15] A member of a family which had farmed on Eyre Peninsula from the early 1900s, Flavel became blind in 1937 when she was twelve, although in adulthood she regained limited sight in one eye. Her 'Prologue' illustrates her preoccupation with ideas of shaping and design and her sense of having created a countering but related design of her own:

In the chapters that follow I try first to show how my childhood was shaped by the land in what we now think of as primitive conditions. Then I show myself rejecting my father's challenge to accept the land as my heritage (at the price of being bound to it), and instead responding to what I felt was a more valid challenge—to break free and go my own way, in spite of my disability. And after all, my own way will perhaps be seen as continuing the family pioneering traditions.

In the descriptions of her early years, Flavel establishes the interdependence of her family and their land, the seasons determining her father's work, and her father demonstrating his shrewd ability to live in tune with the climate. Hard-working, versatile and resourceful, her father gradually improves his inherited property, implicitly contributing to the narrator's impression of generational progress. The sudden loss of her sight, however, following the death of her mother two years previously, dislodges her from this achieving sequence. Frequently afflicted with feelings that she is 'good-for-nothing', and often ignored by insensitive people who equate blindness with idiocy, she teaches herself new skills, gradually taking over the running of the home. Although she rapidly becomes indispensable to the farm, she suffers from a great sense of loneliness and isolation and longs for a different, more independent future, a longing her father fails to understand. Now more of an inescapable burden than a challenge, the farm threatens to trap her, as it eventually traps her father. Nor are her father's protestations of necessary protection unequivocal: 'I was not sure either, what Father really wanted from me. I wondered was he thinking of my physical well-being by protecting me, or was he thinking of material gain by wanting me to stay on, on the farm' (pp. 40–41).

Eventually securing herself a training at the Royal Institution for the Blind and winning a new independent life that includes marriage, motherhood and running a business, she carves out a destiny that is not dependent on the land. As self-sufficient pioneer and as mother, she makes herself the equal, perhaps even the superior, of her pioneering father. Looking back at her achievements as wife and mother, she reflects that she has shared in the challenge of pioneering, while one of her most tangible rewards is a note of congratulation from her father. Unlike his achievements, moreover, which are partly forfeit when he becomes too old to work the farm, hers rest on a stable foundation: 'With my family beside me ... I knew at last that the Promise—that vague something that had always seemed to be in the clouds of the future—was actually being fulfilled. I did indeed possess a Fortune—one that would go on growing and never be spent' (p. 87).

If secular motherhood can provide a distinctive role for the self, some women find religious motherhood an even more liberating role. Two in particular, Emily Churchward (1853–1944) and Bessie Lee (1860–1950), wrote full accounts of their lives as spiritual mothers. The autobiographies of these women are remarkably similar, although their lives were very different. Both have a strong sense of personal destiny, reflected in the title of Churchward's narrative, *In Paths Directed*[16], and in Lee's choice of chapter titles ('Rungs in the Ladder', 'New Avenues', 'On the Battlefield'); both enjoy dramatic religious experiences early in life; both express their sense of destiny in terms of service and see themselves as selfless individuals, mere vehicles for God's purpose. Humility, however, is more convention than fact and both women project themselves as energetic, dominating personalities, often comically unconscious of their real motives and impervious to the discomforts they occasionally generate. Looking back with barely disguised complacency on the eminence she has achieved, Bessie Lee thanks God for every pain He has permitted to fall on her life: 'Pains have been ladders up which I have climbed to celestial heights; difficulties have shaped into wings on which I have soared to glory's gates'. It all goes to show that the poorest girl who takes Christ's hand, 'trusting her all to Him', can 'rise to any eminence'.[17] Both are well-written accounts, if lesser achievements than *After-Glow Memories*; Churchward's has more interest as a socio-historical document, Lee's has more psychological interest.

Unlike Emily Churchward, Bessie Lee never had children, which is not surprising given her radical ideas on birth control and the sinfulness of all sexual intercourse that had no procreative intention. Nevertheless, she retains the filial/maternal mould with her title, *One of Australia's Daughters*, and her emphasis on her spiritually-nurturing role. After an isolated, deprived childhood, Lee had a prominent career in the temperance movement, spending much of her life in globe-trotting expeditions for the cause. *One of Australia's Daughters* is a curious blend of insight and mystification. About one-third through the text, significantly after her conversion, the 'I' abandons itself to the interpretations of a third, unnamed party and Bessie becomes either 'she' or the 'little woman', presumably emphasizing her identity as God's vessel. Occasionally thereafter the first person takes over, intervening in the narrative without announcement or explanation. From the first, Bessie is convinced that she is an extraordinary child, and indeed the opinion of diverse others that she is different from anybody else runs as a refrain through the text. Perceived at first as a disadvantage, her distinctiveness gradually becomes a source of strength, and what was seen as perverse or odd in her nature is revised as resilience or moral fibre. She presents herself as a naturally loquacious, loving child, doomed, after the age of eight when her mother dies, to live with people who are either alcoholics who maltreat her or are religiously austere and censorious. Her descriptions of her early years at a small mining settlement in the Victorian Alps evoke all the loneliness of an emotional, ambitious nature, forced to repress her natural energies and constantly belittled by a self-righteous, dominant aunt. 'Strong of body, and ten times stronger of will, she had no pity for weakness or shiftlessness, and many a time did I feel as if I must really crumble into dust, so withered and scorched was I beneath the awful rebukes falling thick and fast on my devoted head' (pp. 20–21). Deprived of the chance of an education after she is found to be too weak for the three-mile (five kilometres) journey to school, she educates herself by reading *Paradise Lost* and whatever periodicals the miners take. She finds some emotional outlet looking after the miners, even though her 'dear charges' often get drunk, or in reading her little Bible to them, although here her enthusiasm for the task sometimes carries her beyond their tolerance levels. Her morale is sustained first by her experience of conversion and her consequent sense of spiritual worth, and then by her discovery that she can influence people by writing. She had always admired orators and writers, although she never dreamt of standing beside them, but now she discovers that writing brings the new and 'delicious' experience of finding herself famous in that little 'out-of-the-world place'. Best of all, writing opens hearts to her; even her aunt melts at her poetry, described as the 'key to unlock doors she could never otherwise hope to enter' (p. 52).

Bessie also discovers another means of building her self-esteem, which she describes with characteristic blinkered insight in Chapter 7, titled 'Two in One'. This is a practice of turning herself into two people:

... she formed the habit of conversing with herself, as though she were really two separate and distinct persons. The one self was a very censorious and arbitrary individual, the other self was a very meek and long-suffering creature. They had some wonderful conversations together, and gained great comfort and consolation from each other's society. (p. 42)

At every crisis Bessie's selves engage in a mutually sustaining discourse, which preserves her from the depression and sense of inferiority that otherwise threatens her mental stability. Later, she learns to combine the two in an outwardly projected duality that is 'soft and pretty' externally but 'firm as a rock underneath'. It is clearly a combination that her first husband and her future adversaries find baffling. In the second edition of *One of Australia's Daughters*, Lee bolsters her accounts of her dual personality by providing a striking photograph as frontispiece; surrounded by a circle of five reflections of herself in a swing mirror, she appears to be engaged in animated conversation with her various profiles. An articulate narrative that is psychologically fascinating, Lee's autobiography is a franker exploration of self than its religiose surface might suggest and, like *After-Glow Memories*, deserves to be better known.

A recent autobiography that is well known but that has received no attention beyond a few sympathetic reviews is Kathleen Fitzpatrick's *Solid Bluestone Foundations*.[18] Unlike some of the autobiographers considered in this chapter, Fitzpatrick is in control of her material and writes as if her tale is a familiar one, well seasoned in the wood of memory. She combines the fresh, amoral perceptions of the child with the reflective hindsight of the adult, the educated insights of the historian, aware of the play of socio-economic forces, with an appreciation of the personal impairments they leave in their wake. A gentle irony plays over the people and selves of the past, preserving them from sentimental nostalgia on one hand and dismissive satire on the other. The author is not averse, however, to speaking directly to the reader on occasion, a practice that highlights the narrative's emotional peaks. Fitzpatrick also has graphic powers of description and a keen eye for the significant detail or the subtle discrimination so that her acute descriptions of the gallery of relations that enlarged her childhood underline the reader's consciousness of being in touch with a literary sensibility as well as an historical one.

The solid bluestone foundations of the title belong to her grandparents' mansion, Hughenden, built in the era of Marvellous Melbourne. Hughenden is not particularly old, little more than thirty when the narrator first remembers it, but it has a solidity that is not just physical. Describing it in the first sentence as 'the most solid and permanent fact ever known' to her, the narrator terms it her 'rock of ages'. Contrasting with the nomadic habits of her parents and the tensions that make their temporary homes even more temporary, Hughenden has a reassuring orderliness:

while we came and went 'Hughenden' stood firm: there the ground never quaked under our feet, we felt safe and could count on everything. At 'Hughenden' life was orderly, the gong announced meals at exactly the same time every day, Grandpa sat at his end of the table and Grandma at hers, with the uncles and aunts in between, and it would have been as astonishing if there had not been roast beef for Sunday dinner as it would have been in our house if we had predicted correctly what we might have to eat on any given day.

At home the mother's private personality and the father's struggle to establish the family economically make for restraint and isolation, but at Hughenden there is a marvellously mixed selection of uncles and aunts and a different, more philistine, worldly activity. The narrator blends the child's unformed, artless perceptions with successive strata of knowledge and insight in all this retrospective exploration of Hughenden. The effect is to modify the historical solidities of the place and its human inhabitants, while retaining Hughenden's solidity as symbol. If Grandpa and Grandma are twin planets, essential for Hughenden's continued existence, they are divided by everything except the marriage tie: 'there was almost every other division between them, racial, religious, cultural and personal' (p. 39). Grandpa is a delightful companion for the young child, but he is seen as a demanding egoist by the older narrator: 'a stage version of an Englishman in a play written by a foreigner', he does as he pleases and expects others to adjust. Grandma is wonderfully accommodating, but she is also overly passive under her husband's shows of tyranny, effectively turning her granddaughter into a feminist. Meanwhile, reflecting on the familiar family legends of their immigrant pasts, and fitting them into the general historical jigsaw of nineteenth century Australia, the narrator weaves a thick context for Hughenden. It is one which has many ironies, not least being the unlikely marriage of her Irish, Catholic grandmother and her English, Protestant grandfather. Hughenden itself, built at the peak of the grandfather's fortunes, becomes for a time a burdensome white elephant during the 1890s slump. As she learns more about her relatives, the narrator becomes aware of the impact of social, political and family forces on their lives. Hughenden's sudden reversal of fortune, for instance, has affected her mother, increasing her fears and anxieties; then there is Uncle Jack, a veteran of Gallipoli, who never recovers emotionally from his experiences; and Aunty Dot, who fails in the limited circumstances of her time to make a career on the stage and lives in the shade of her family until her death. And her grandmother's life has been one of excessive hard work, as the mother of nine children, responsible for the running of a large house without servants. Hughenden, the symbol of permanence, shelters numerous disappointments and fragmented lives. Disappointment also clouds the life of her successful, hardworking father, who was compelled to abandon his chance of a university education after the death of his father. Even his selfless dedication to the education of his younger brothers was finally fruitless, when one died and the other was too grief-stricken to continue his course.

But these reminders of general determining forces are balanced by an appreciation of the diversity of human nature represented by these older children of Hughenden, from the gregarious Uncle Ack, whose vitality affects everyone ('he had only to come into the room to make you feel that life was a lark and that champagne was about to be served'), to the gloomily religiose Aunty Doone. Fitzpatrick has a great admiration for wit and style, and dwells on the individuals who put a brave front on their disappointments. She also has a great tolerance for the irregular or uncomfortable practices of adults, whether they are the vagaries of her impractical, unmotherly mother, or the more systematic absurdities of the nuns at her Portland convent. Thus people are subject to the whims of chance but their personalities are their own and may have a permanence beyond their imagining. This blend of historical consciousness and sensitivity to the flow of time, with an appreciation of the permanence of the things of the spirit, is part of the distinctive tone of *Solid Bluestone Foundations*. Hughenden, for example, is threatened by time, having become a Danish club by the time of Fitzpatrick's writing, but its real foundations are in the minds and hearts of the grandchildren and when they are dead, it will persist in this 'record of the impressions of a child who, more than sixty years ago was taking notes' (p. 77). As far as the author's personal life-story is concerned, Hughenden as a complex promise of permanence and as an experience of community, will continue to exert its pervasive influence.

Fitzpatrick's story of her progress to the University of Melbourne and thence to Oxford is far from straightforward. Following her experiences in the numerous homes of her youth, from the unpleasant 'Verona', made ugly by her mother's unhappiness, to the rigours of the convent at Portland, where the children board in 1914, back to 'Verona', to the comparative stability of 'Cluny', to a boarding house when the mother's housekeeping support breaks down, Fitzpatrick charts a map in which there are few oases of permanence. Schools have even less to offer in the way of permanent gifts, and it is only when, by dint of taking her own education in hand, she wins a place at the University that she lays firm hold of her vocation:

During those years I underwent a change of personality in that the aimless drift of my childhood was arrested and I became what I was more or less to remain for the rest of my life, one of the world's workers. (p. 174)

Characteristically, she is sensitive to the personalities of buildings, discovering an affection for the great dusky dome of the Public Library, spanning a rich store of learning and suggesting past generations of scholars, and the old brick Shot Tower with its intimations of Europe.

It is in Europe, however, that she begins to discover the shape of her life, even though a subsequent period of intense disappointment at Oxford threatens this sense of design. For Fitzpatrick, like Hanrahan, leaving home is also to go home. 'When we change skies ... we become aware of alternatives.... The bent of mind which dictates choice is in ourselves but might never have surfaced into conscious-

ness had we never changed skies (p. 196). Sitting in the Piazza dell'
Esedra in Rome, she has her own 'adventure on the way to
Damascus':

Classical form. I now knew what I liked... The Pantheon expresses
stability, not aspiration, and offers shelter to men rather than a ladder to
heaven. But why should I prefer to be earth-bound rather than sky-borne?
Could one trace it all back to those solid bluestone foundations of my
childhood which had seemed to offer some promise of permanence in a world
of flux? I could not find a reason, but knew that I was the kind of person
to whom classical form is more congenial than romantic, not only in
architecture but in painting, sculpture, music, literature, dancing, even
landscape. I can admire waste and solitary places, high mountains and deep,
rugged gorges strike awe into my soul, but I cannot love them and am only
happy in scenes made to the measure of man and humanised by his long
habitation of labour in them. (p. 197)

The years at Melbourne are liberating, but graduation to the more
rigid, sexist, patronizing confines of Oxford reimposes the impermanence that has threatened her childhood. Treated as an inferior, both
as a colonial and as a woman, homesick for Australia and separated
from the sister who has always been more of a mother, Fitzpatrick
temporarily loses confidence. She cannot learn at Oxford, as she has
learnt at those seemingly ill-assorted places, Hughenden and the
University of Melbourne. At the close of her story, Fitzpatrick relates
her elation when a telegram offering her a teaching position at the
University of Sydney erases the sense of failure experienced at
Oxford. If her conclusion that she is naturally more of a teacher than
a scholar ('I was not first-class, not an original or profound
thinker ... I knew myself and my limitations [and] would never again
aspire to a status beyond my capacity'), seems an unnecessary
self-deprecation to the reader, the decision to be a teacher fits the
Hughenden metaphor of her life. Although the narrator is not
explicit at this point on the links between the early place and self, it
appears that fidelity to the humanized habitations of her youth,
determines the Classic, earth-bound, choice of teaching, rather than
the solitary, Gothic path of scholarly aspiration. Hence her conclusion at this moment in her life story: 'I had been "Home" and now
was coming home' (p. 210).

6

Father Figures

The mother-daughter relationship is a well-rehearsed one in recent literature; for daughters writing about fathers, the tradition is more slender. 'We think back through our mothers if we are women', commented Virginia Woolf, acutely. Thinking back through the mother inevitably implicates the father, however; the first, and most authoritative representative of patriarchy, he is burdened for good or ill and willy nilly, with the powerful, male messages of his culture. In a relationship which has been called 'one of the tragedies of patriarchy', the father symbolically represents for his daughter 'many things that are outside the world of women; the world of her mother, the world she is supposed to enter'.[1] It also appears from the great majority of autobiographical narratives studied here, that his messages are largely delivered to the daughter indirectly, via his relationship with her mother. In the intimate drama of the family, it is difficult to say whether his role is perceived as primary or secondary. Whether he is absent or present, weak, shadowy, tyrannical, successful, failed, violent or gentle, his voice, presence and style appear to pervade women's memories of their families. Even death cannot remove him. One of the surprises of this study has been the discovery of the father's extensive, even exceptional emotional power in women's recorded memories. Less surprising is the discovery that he is also an extremely equivocal figure. The daughter/father bond is more often than not a problematic one, complicated by ambivalences and longings, which appear to be as incorrigible and often more visible than the ambivalences which trouble the mother/daughter relationship. Another surprise has been the irrelevance of time to the father as patriarch; although his external power, as far as this body of autobiography is concerned, was greater in the Victorian period, his actual power has depended more on circumstances and personalities than on era. It should be remembered, however, that most fathers described here were active, if that is the right word, before 1950.

One of the most common of the father figures in this group of autobiographies is the austere, distantly severe father. Invariably presented as distracted by the pressures of work, whether he is a struggling farmer like Katherine McKell's father, or a State Governor, like Adelaide Lubbock's, he hovers as a minatory, defining presence on the margins of family life. If he is lucky, like Eleanor Spence's father, who is able to leave the emotional province almost entirely to his wife, he is able to maintain his position as self-righteous balancing power. If he is unlucky, and is suddenly required to provide nurturing qualities, his emotional sterility is rarely forgiven. Katherine McKell in *Old Days and Gold Days in Victoria* sees her father as offering his motherless children a stone in place of the bread they craved; Annie Duncan, on the other hand, who also suffers the loss of a mother, enjoys a brief spell of muddle and smoky comfort in her father's care, before the arrival of a stepmother imposes formal boundaries.[2] Eliza Chomley is almost suffocated by her father's formal respectability, until a lively elder brother liberates her into Melbourne society of the 1870s.[3] Judith Wallace's grazier-father in *Memories of a Country Childhood* is greatly admired by his daughter, although he 'revolved on his own separate, mysterious axis'; after servants become unobtainable during the Second World War, he grows slightly more accessible, but his presence is still silently inhibiting, foreclosing the lively games of mother and children, which flourish in his absence. On one hand, this father is an authority on their region and its past, on bush lore and animal husbandry, and both his library and his tales of his well-travelled past open windows on to other exciting worlds. He offers the attractions that de Beauvoir described so well:

The life of the father has a mysterious prestige ... his pursuits, his hobbies, have a sacred character... As a rule his work takes him outside, and so it is through him that the family communicates with the rest of the world: he incarnates that immense, difficult and marvellous world of adventure; he personifies transcendence, he is God.[4]

On the other hand, Wallace's father is as traditional in his attitudes as Ford Maddox Ford's good soldier, and his conventional notions about gender lead to his own hopeless search for a son-substitute and his daughters' loss of their beloved home. In this autobiography, the common root of the two bereavements is not drawn out, but is allowed to emerge indirectly via silences and incompletions. Adelaide Lubbock's father in *People in Glass Houses* maintains a discreet distance from the turbulent nursery struggles between mother, nannies, governesses and children; almost as dignified and aloof a father as he is a Governor, he has difficulty in understanding the strange, uncouth behaviour both of his children and the Australian 'natives'. Within the family, he shifts uneasily between the roles of autocrat and constitutional monarch, but is able to keep only a surface control of his unruly subjects.

One of the most poignant accounts of the distant father is Hilda Abbott's fictional story of her 1890s childhood in New England and the Monaro, *Among the Hills* (1948).[5] One of seven children, Honora, the narrator, is aware that she really belongs to the sub-family of the youngest four children. Both parents are shadowy figures, virtually emotional counters, expressing warmth and self-sacrificing concern on one side, the mother's, and unresisting severity on the other, the father's. The mother, usually called the 'Little Mother' is the centre of the family circle, but is powerless to prevent a series of disasters—the departure of her best-loved son, the loss of the family property, and, ultimately, her own illness and death. The father, described as 'the big stern Father', appears increasingly impotent externally, although his family power is undiminished. Changes, sometimes vaguely associated with the 'dangerous play-things' of city business, occur unannounced and unexplained; after the loss of their home, the father is employed as manager on one property after another and the family moves annually.

This narrator sensitively recreates the child's vulnerable openness without recourse to retrospective explanations; moods, incidents, landscape, people, houses and animals impress themselves as physical sensations, chilling, terrifying or comforting in their immediacy. The mysterious loss of the family home accelerates the child's sense of threat; she is conscious that her family is at the mercy of the 'serious' men, who suddenly appear as 'Buyers' on the farm, and numerous incidents evoke men as unpredictable and threatening powers. Previously, the child had accepted reluctantly the rough affection of the farm workers and even the vicious teasing of one of her brothers:

the two men named Clifford . . . used to tease the little girls, threatening to burn their dolls' hair when they were lighting their pipes and squeezing their faces tightly between large brown hands when they said good morning. (p. 49)

But later men loom as 'grisly', 'bear-like', unpleasantly intrusive figures, while the brother becomes increasingly powerful and humiliating.

Honora is acutely sensitive to the mother's moods, and deeply affected by her helpless but visible griefs. In the second half of the narrative, her world begins to divide sharply into the unpleasant, threatening sphere of men and the gentle, vulnerable sphere of women. Chapter 5, titled '"A Cold, Calamitous Thing"', initiates the book's emotional change of temperature. Up to this point, threatening elements add spice to life, and the child revels in the physically dramatic delights of her natural playground. A favourite contrast is one between a fireside, warmed by the mother's presence, and an external, snow-bound scene. The intrusion of mysterious misfortunes destroys this emotional balance, however, and the parents' power to shelter is seriously eroded. Emotionally separated from the grown-up world of decision-making, these little girls appear to watch for signs of change as if they are behind glass; they are intensely vulnerable to the activities of men, conscious of their humiliating potential, and their power to proscribe what little freedom they possess:

The working men on the station were definite factors in their lives. So much depended on them. Whether you could play about the stables, or sit on the side of mangers and watch the horses feed; whether you could stand and watch the plodding draught horse go round and round, or listen to the whirr of the chaff-cutter and watch the hay become flying atoms—all depended on the men. (p. 112)

Meanwhile, the men's world is presented as busy with mysteriously serious concerns; it makes a point of ignoring or excluding the children, although they sense that eventually they will be caught up in its coils. A description of a cattle sale is representative. When a wild bullock threatens a man with its horns, he hurls it to the ground by blocking its nostrils; Honora topples from the fence and lies for a 'hideous instant' in the yard among the horses. She has no sooner escaped than the big Father rides up and, 'unaware of these near tragedies', sombrely orders his daughters home. Half fascinated and half fearful, they watch the drama from a distance, the streams of men coming to the house, the wild gestures of the auctioneers and the frenetic activities of the women servants. Later, they watch the men having lunch and 'all the women waiting on them'. In this emotionally charged atmosphere, the meal has the force of a Brueghel painting:

There were big pieces of corned meat, all reddy and cold, huge rounds of roast beef, dishes of potatoes and salads, jellies and creamy things. And [the children] with only rock-cakes! They huddled together and peered. The big Father was pressing a long, thin knife along the beef . . . (p. 73)

Like so many women's autobiographies, this narrative lacks a progressive structure, although it loosely follows the history of the family's fortunes; events are emotional events and the narrator's subsequent realization of a kind of freedom is presented more as experience than achievement, an unexpected gift in the clutter of the present, and one which may well be forfeit to new confinements in the future. In the same way, the determining influence of the father's doubleness is insidious rather than explicit. Offering the security of unquestionable power with one hand, and withdrawing it with the other, he betrays his insecurity by his emotional defensiveness. It is his equivocally powerful presence, which broods over the children's lives, quickening their fears and sharpening their losses.

The representation of the emotionally ill-at-ease father as inherently weak is not unusual in this group of autobiographies, where fathers are generally more weak than wicked. Even tyrants frequently emerge as inwardly frightened men and no doubt the writing act of disinterring and placing the fear is itself a kind or revenge. Louisa's victory over Sam in *The Man Who Loved Children* is mildly duplicated in several autobiographies, while numerous narrators take pride in achieving the very goals which the father attempted to foreclose. Thus Fairlie Taylor in *Bid Time Return* wins for herself the education her father had refused and even beats the old man at his own game, running his shop with a dash and flair that he himself cannot emulate. For some narrators the father's wickedness results in his complete abandonment. Mrs J.S.O. Allen's drunken father in *Memories of My Life* proves an incorrigible source of misery; Dorothy Casey-Congdon in *Casey's Wife* makes a point of ignoring her father with the same casual air as he displayed, when he ignored his dependents, carelessly and unpredictably stepping out of their lives.

Elizabeth Harrower's short story, 'The Beautiful Climate'[6], is one of the few immediate studies of a tyrannical father's oppressiveness. Harrower's representation of a domineering temperament, unable either to control or understand its powerful instincts for cruelty, has a claustrophobic intensity. As in other studies of predatory men within the family, the women are clamped together in a desperate struggle for emotional survival: 'They were not free. Either the hostage, or the one over whom a hostage was held, they seemed destined to play for ever if they meant to preserve the peace' (p. 218). Harrower also understands the conviction of moral erosion, which unwilling collusion brings: 'Something about her situation made her feel not only, passively, abused, but actively, surprisingly, guilty' (p. 219). The description of a fishing scene in which the husband sports, not only with the fish, but also with his wife's fear of deep water and the daughter's repugnance for their troubled triumvirate, is subtly sensitive to the terrors which may lurk in 'normal' family life; in this situation, everyday objects become metaphors of unpleasant emotions:

Stationed in the dead centre of the glittering bay, within sight of their empty house, they sat in the open boat, grasping cork rollers, feeling minute and interesting tugs on their lines from time to time, losing bait and catching three-inch fish . . . The wooden interior of the boat was dry and burning . The three fishers were seared, beaten down by the sun. The bait smelled. The water lapped and twinkled blackly but could not be approached: sharks abounded in the bay. (p. 220)

More often in these narratives, a father's cruelty takes the form of extreme insensitivity, as in Eve Hogan's story of her childhood in outback Western Australia of the 1930s, 'The Hessian Walls'.[7] A matter-of-fact, even bald, account of a family's harsh struggle to survive, it has a plain clarity which rises to eloquence at certain emotional peaks. Hogan's mother died when Hogan was six and before the family left Wales for Western Australia in 1927. On arrival, the father was offered a contract clearing land on a property near Carribin and the family of five young children, father and stepmother, settled in to the first of the hessian-walled humpies, which were to be their homes for several years. Two elder sisters remained in Perth. Hogan's stated intention is to celebrate the spirit of the pioneers and her story is certainly written with verve and wry humour; nevertheless, a more intimate story of grief and loss lurks in the narrative's crevices.

As the only girl still at home, Hogan soon takes on the role of mother to the other children. Her stepmother is often away, earning extra money, and in any event never takes the place of the children's natural mother. The narrator's own memories of her mother are hazy, and her brothers have no recollections at all, but the idea of the mother is clearly an implicit presence in her life, determining her own pride in the nurturing role and in keeping the family unit together. When another child is born, he belongs more to his fourteen-year-old stepsister than to his mother. With her brothers' support, she even wrests the parents' naming power from them: 'Despite threats of beltings and supperless nights, we stood firm in our decision and refused to use the given name' (p. 106). The boy's infancy lacks many things usually considered necessities but he eventually grows into 'a man standing six feet tall in his socks ... a fine monument to stale bread soaked in water and rabbit stew' (p. 106). Meanwhile, the narrator's numerous victories over their recalcitrant poverty increase her pride.

But if physical poverty is perceived as a challenge, another sort of poverty, emotional poverty, is less easy to surmount. The total lack of parental affection emerges late in the narrative and indirectly, in her description of a key incident, her stepbrother's near-drowning. When he hears of her desperate measures to revive the boy, the father takes his daughter in his arms: 'he held me close while I sobbed out my fright and fear. This was the only caress I can ever remember receiving from my father' (p. 107). A later visit by one of her elder sisters, who have remained in Perth, stirs latent embers of resentment at the father's decree that she should stagnate in primitive conditions, 'which would have daunted the most stout-hearted woman': 'I could not help resenting ... my father's rigid, and often unfair, code of discipline and his decision that I, the youngest, should have been chosen to live in hessian-walled shanties' (p. 124). The same resentment seems to underlie her appreciation of a young man, who values her 'budding womanhood' and compels her brothers to show her the respect she is normally denied.

Hogan's account of the final division in her relationship with her father is a moving passage. The betrayal, when it comes, is an emotional one, darkening the father's previous acts of physical toughness, at least for the reader. It is preceded by another betrayal, the desertion of the stepmother with two of the children, leaving the baby behind. At this juncture in their fortunes, the narrator, then sixteen, is left with three children to look after and much of the seasonal work of a busy railway siding. When the work comes to an end, their situation is desperate, and there follows a nightmarish journey to Mt Gibson, where the father has relatives and, he assumes, work. The hardships of the journey are briefly alleviated by the kindness of strangers, who give them rest and food, but at Mt Gibson the relatives prove unbelievably indifferent to the fact that the small family is literally starving. The narrator's anger when she is gracelessly offered a spoilt cake by her 'Christian' cousin, is obliterated by an even more searing betrayal, the discovery that her father had given these distant relatives her precious family Bible, 'the only thing of my mother's I had':

I felt the intolerable weight of my father's betrayal. There were many times when I was called upon to forgive my father, but until this day, that deed was one I still cannot forgive or forget, even though he has been dead for many years. The sheer cruelty of that act, and my cousin's delight in it, has yet, in my life since, to be equalled. (p. 131)

Her subsequent sufferings when she and the baby are virtually abandoned by the father, who makes his way back to Perth, never evoke this depth of grief; clearly the Bible is not only the symbol of her link with her dead mother, but of the implicit morality which underlay all her previous feats of endurance. The father could not have chosen a more expressive way of registering his rejection.

This level of cruel insensitivity is unusual in these narratives, however. More often, fathers are exposed as weak in that they are improvident, uncertain providers, failures in their chosen way of life. As Richard Coe comments: 'the collapsed image of the father, like the total absence of the father, is one of the traumatic shocks of childhood, and one which requires at some stage redress, exorcism or, at the very least, explanation'.[8] For a boy, the father's failure appears to be complicated by his preoccupation with his own developing identity. Just as his rivalry of the father may be appeased by his own greater success, the father's failure may assault his own pride in his maleness. It is possible that fathers of sons are in an even more invidious position than fathers of daughters, and certainly, as Don Anderson has pointed out, would-be parricides are prominent in some of the better-known male accounts of growing up in Australia.[9] Most of the daughters of these autobiographies tend to see the father primarily through the mother's eyes, or at least in terms of his relationship to the mother. And this is particularly true of 'weak' fathers; loaded with the mother's anger, grief, or even her silent suffering, the improvident or careless father is invariably transfixed as the main cause of the family's troubles. His actual, historical remoteness from the family often perpetuates itself as a remoteness in his daughter's subsequent imagining, and many fathers appear to have no individuality beyond their existence as failed husbands. On occasion, his inadequacies as husband become more pronounced as the narrative progresses and the narrator rediscovers, with adult eyes, her mother's experience. This study makes no claims to psychoanalysis, but there is no doubt that most of these autobiographies demonstrate the triangular family relationship which Nancy Chodorov and Helene Deutsch have described. As Chodorov puts it: 'A girl's relation to [her father] is emotionally in reaction to, interwoven, and competing for primacy with, her relation to her mother'.[10]

Not every disillusioned daughter can welcome the father's death with the alacrity of Thelma Forshaw's narrator of 'The Pawn' in *An Affair of Clowns*: 'My father had ... been dead some six weeks and none too soon as far as I was concerned'[11], but several vehemently consign him to memory's dustbin. The narrator of Margaret Trist's *Morning in Queensland* is relieved when her mother finally abandons her romantic interest in her ne'er-do-well father and turns her attention to the economic realities of survival without a male breadwinner. The father in Agnes Melda Prince's memoir of her mother inserts himself briefly and forgettably as one of the hardships his wife learns to surmount. After siring nine children and growing tired of the family's grocery business, he appears to fade out of the picture of the family's pioneering epic, which is composed of mother and four children. His own distinction is confined to his trim appearance and his feats as a teamster. In the latter capacity, he even becomes famous, bequeathing his name to a place where his timber wagon once became bogged for several days, forcing the traffic to detour— 'Henry's Bog Hole'. Fortunately, his lack of know-how and capacity to attract misfortune are reversed in his amazingly capable wife. He reappears only once in the latter part of the narrative, as driver in a buggy accident, which results in serious injury to the mother and temporarily quenches her vitality: 'When Mum used to be singing to me out in the paddocks she would often say, "I want to be able to sing till I die", but now poor Mum found that when she tried to sing her head pained dreadfully.'[12] The reader is not surprised to discover at the close that the parents continued to live separately in retirement. At an opposite social extreme, Alexandra Hasluck's father is no match for her mother in *Portrait in a Mirror*. A shadowy man who died at fifty-seven, when his daughter was seventeen, he spent himself in designing railway lines, which were soon superseded by road transport. The compressions of the section dealing with his death give the unfortunate impression that its main effect was to remove a stumbling block from his wife's ambitions for her daughter's education: 'I am sure she would have battled on and brought him round to her opinion that no amount of education was ever wasted, but his death saved her from possibly painful argument'.[13]

Other autobiographers are more explicitly resentful of the father's limitations. The narrator of Florence Edward's *The Joys and Sorrows of a Migrant Family* (1985) becomes increasingly irritated by her father's combination of improvidence and arrogance. Notwithstanding the superhuman efforts of the mother, the family is eventually reduced to relying on the outside work of the daughters for survival. The section dealing with the mother's death at the age of forty-six, after bearing ten children, elongates into reflections on the father's insensitivity to his wife's suffering, the historical plight of Australian women, who were overburdened with work and child-bearing, and on the current neglect of women's contribution to nation-building. Jane Caverhill, in 'Reminiscences 1840s–1850s', records the father's frequent failures in a matter-of-fact way, but their impression lingers in the narrator's sensitivity to the mother's moods and the descriptions of her as anxious or grief-stricken. Connie Miller in *Season of Learning* traces the graph of her mother's destiny as the lonely wife of an increasingly bigoted man, against her own, expanding life. This narrator achieves a triple effect, capturing the child's external insouciance, her sensitivity to the mother's moods and a retrospective, adult acknowledgment of the mother's griefs. If the results of the father's hasty decisions are slow to release their effects on the children's lives, they have an immediate impact on his wife's, and some of the happiest episodes take place during his absence at war, when the mother's self-reliance and capacity for fun come to the fore. His longed-for return paradoxically results in new confinements for both daughter and mother.

Zelda D'Aprano in *Zelda: The Becoming of a Woman* withholds blame of her father, while recreating the child's fears as the parents ceaselessly quarrel. The father, nevertheless, is as intriguingly elusive as he was in real life, and it is the retrospective reflection on the mother's inward experience which dominates. An exciting figure and another incarnation of 'the world of adventure', the father is perceived as an opportunity which never fulfilled itself:

With dad being absent from home so often, I enjoyed snuggling up to mum in her bed for she was soft and warm. It was only on rare occasions that dad seemed to be happy, but at odd times he would come into our bedroom whilst we were in bed and sing to us. He had a fine singing voice and I would enjoy listening to the beautiful songs and respond to his feeling of well-being.

When he stopped, I would plead with him to continue for these moments were very rare and the only opportunity I had to feel close to him.[14]

Joice Nankivell Loch in *A Fringe of Blue* begins by recording her father's impracticalities dispassionately. He is George Nankivell, the unfortunate, improvident, irrepressibly optimistic son of a sugar grower. Her mother's decision to marry him is presented comically, as a decision to take the second-best offer which an overbearing sister recommends. The parents soon refuse to remain in these comic categories, though, and the narrator's response to her mother's subsequent imprisonment in Gippsland's untamed wilderness is heart-felt: '"It's too isolated!" cried Mother, and there was something in that cry that twisted my heart so that I have always remembered it'.[15] Marjorie Motschall in *Wild Wood Days at Panton Hill* records her mother's disillusionment with her handsome, irresponsible, 'hasty' father with an adult sympathy that totally excludes him. Perceived as a child, but an unfortunately powerful one, he is crassly unaware of the way he contributes to the mother's sufferings. In due course, his improvidence extends to the lives of his children: one son is compelled to leave school at eleven to help in the logging business, the narrator herself to leave at twelve to look after the youngest child, and the eldest daughters subsequently contribute to a household which grows too crowded to include them.

Miles Franklin's treatment of the father-figure is an interesting demonstration of his protean possibilities. In *My Brilliant Career* he is the improvident cause of the family's descent to poverty, the 'support of his family, yet not its support'. Sybylla contemplates his degeneration from his former heroic self to drunken bully with all the fierce contempt of a sixteen-year-old. If she is more outspoken than other daughters of her era, she is characteristic in her concern for her mother: the 'helpless tool of man—the creature of circumstances', burdened with the 'curse of Eve', the mother is a bleak daily reminder of her own likely future. The father of *My Career Goes Bung* is interpreted far more sympathetically. In this book father and daughter are temperamentally alike; a man of wit, ready sympathy and imagination, he has no trace of Dick Melvyn's pretensions or weakness for alcohol, although he shares his failure. He is loved unreservedly by his daughter:

I concede that technically Ma is my primary parent and Pa merely secondary. The question of woman's emancipation and the justice which is her due make this fatally clear in theory, but when it comes to the practice of an affection which springs spontaneously from my human breast, Pa can have no second place; and when it comes to being understood, well . . .

Her mother, a dour figure who regularly quenches the schemes of father and daughter, is much less understanding; nevertheless,

Sybylla accedes that her mother's world-view is unfortunately more accurate than her father's: 'Ma is the practical member of our menage. She has to be, so that we have a menage at all'.[16]

One of the most sensitive recreations of a father is Lecky Payne's *Beltana—Six Miles* (1974).[17] In many ways this autobiography is representative of women's life-writing in Australia. Ostensibly a local history and classified as such by the Library of Congress subject heading, it is actually an inward exploration of a key relationship of the past. Beltana, the place, is more a subjectively realized character in the narrator's personal quest for meaning, than historical actuality. In the concern to retrieve the past self as a self in relationship, the book is characteristic of the great majority of women's narratives. It is also representative of a smaller, but still significant group, in the recreation of an intensely happy, early period, which is dramatically cut off and succeeded by unhappiness. Loosely, and even untidily structured, the narrative is minutely sensitive to the emotional life of the child. Incidents which are outwardly insignificant, but inwardly seismic, are given prominence, whereas long periods of emotionally uneventful time are telescoped. The conclusion is hesitant, barely tentative, and although there are indications that the narrator has accomplished certain *rites de passage*, there is no attempt to withdraw the child's perception of life as cloudy and baffling.

The father of this narrative is an exceptionally charismatic figure. When the story opens, he is a railway ganger at the little settlement of Bruce, near Quorn in South Australia, the father of three little girls, of whom the narrator is the youngest. The time is 1899. The opening scene of the child delightedly running to meet her father, but uncertain of reaching him, is virtually a metaphor of their future relationship; an elusive man, he will both evade, and, occasionally, welcome her. He is also a gregarious individual, presently caught up in the celebrations planned for Federation, and his absences have made him less familiar and secure than the mother. Indeed, much of his charisma is filtered through her eyes and the child perceives him in the beginning as the admired and admiring husband, the handsome hero of her mother's legendary love story. One of the most nostalgic memories, which again has the force of metaphor, is of responding to the mother's delight in the father's singing at the Federation celebrations; already ill, the mother listens from bed, while she cuddles the child.

Some jarring notes disturb the early idyll. Certain equivocal remarks and incidents briefly cloud the bright picture of the father; he appears to have a great many admirers, some of them women, and his increasingly lengthy absences at the hotel threaten the child's sense of security. The parents' past has mysteriously unpleasant aspects, most offensively communicated in a grandmother's dire predictions and open contempt for the father. A horrific incident, in which the child witnesses the death of a man, sharpens her sense of the outside world as threatening and unpredictable. Payne allows all these impressions to impose themselves haphazardly, in the inexplicable way that events in the adult world familiarly impinge on the minds of children.

This approach is particularly effective in the description of the young child's response to her mother's death: the baffled sense that things are horribly awry, the fear of the closed door of the mother's bedroom, the distaste for the rough, well-meaning tactics of neighbours, the nightmare of the funeral, which is only half-understood. After this death, the father's weaknesses emerge more clearly, although even now the criticisms are displaced; presented as criticisms of neighbours, friends and family, they impinge on the child's consciousness and even merge with her own distress at the father's extended absences, but are never explicitly owned. Neither are they disowned by the implied older narrator's emotional drift; the child-self fiercely rejects overt criticisms of the father, but they are more than straws in the wind for the reader. There is a compelling need for the child to believe in the father—he is all she has—and compelling reasons to distrust him. In the harrowing section describing the children's extreme indigence at this time, the prose adopts semi-passive tactics, expressive of this half-evasion of an unpleasant truth:

We saw less and less of him, and I seemed to spend the evenings waiting and watching for his return home. He often forgot to leave money for food. Certainly our meals were different from when mother was there, or even when Doris was housekeeper. But we enjoyed what we had. We poured hot tea over slices of bread, piled on sugar, and loved it. We didn't buy vegetables any more, but our salvation lay in the neighbours' gardens. They grew tomatoes, peas, and turnips which could be drawn through the fence with a piece of bent hoop-iron. (p. 30)

The crisis which culminates this period and results in the splitting up of the family and the father's departure, is handled dramatically; the appalled exclamations of neighbours briefly insert an external picture of the disparity between the children's neglected condition and the father's self-indulgence. Even so, he is presented as more grief-stricken at his own weakness than callous.

The narrator's subsequent years of suffering in the 'care' of first, a vindictive grandmother, and then an exploitative aunt, are graphically but succinctly described; separated from her family, and even ignorant of their whereabouts, it is as if she is enclosed in an emotional bell-jar. Her life suddenly quickens, however, at the age of fifteen, when she is suddenly given an opportunity to rejoin her father and sisters at Beltana in the Flinders Ranges. The place itself has a magic; it is her mother's childhood home, it is the place where the parents' love story began and where her unknown grandparents had worked and died.

At this point, Payne devotes three chapters to the child's train journey to Beltana. The journey is a potent experience, a mingling of intense delights, anxieties, fears and physical discomforts. A series of encounters with other male passengers are at first terrifying and then reassuring; they culminate in her terrified fainting when an Afghan, who is ultimately her sole fellow-traveller, suddenly approaches her with a package, later revealed to be a present of butter. Once again, the naturalistic surface of Payne's writing conceals her symbolic effects. The frightening/welcoming men are clearly representative of the equivocal father, waiting—with what emotions?—in his home-land for her arrival.

Once home, the narrator is delighted to be there, but Beltana too reveals itself as equivocal. Some mystery surrounds her grandparents' history and her father refuses to be drawn on his own childhood. The Flinders Ranges are perceived at first as welcoming: 'The range reared sharply to its top to where ridges of rock shaded its whole length like a bulwark. I stood looking, and knew that this was where I belonged' (p. 82). They remind the narrator of 'a great enveloping cape of soft purple velvet' (p. 142), but later they reveal themselves to be 'other than soft and kindly'. They contain copper mines, which promised to do well, but soon petered out; they hold a false promise of water in Lake Torrens: 'I found it hard to believe that it was a sheet of dry salt without a drop of water' (p. 163). Later, they take the life of a pet goat, which she had previously saved from death, and which has become an emblem of her own hope for a better future.

The father, too, is as equivocal as ever. He happily re-enacts the childhood ritual of meeting, but there are indications that his old reputation as an alcoholic is still justified and later the narrator discovers that he is deeply in debt and that his daughters have only recently rescued him from a period of heavy drinking. An ugly incident with some bullock drivers, the departures of friends and the deaths of loved animals combine to remind her that the external world is no more benign than before. As she uncovers more of the past, she is more willing to accept life as chequered; she becomes more of a 'northerner' in her courage, and begins to take her future in her own hands. But the growing threat of war reinforces her recurrent fear that she is perpetually destined to lose those she loves, and presents her with an immediate personal crisis, when she is given an opportunity to burn the mail bag containing the men's letters of enlistment. Resisting this temptation, and even performing an act of courage to send the bag on its way, she has a sense of a new maturity: '"I feel as though I've grown up"', she tells her aunt. Even so, it is typical of this writer's sensitivity that she refuses to impose an emotionally consoling conclusion on her story. The narrator's last impression of the Flinders Ranges as 'a friendly giantess in a rich gown', is immediately undercut by the howl of a wild dog:

I shivered, and my feet moved urgently to the track, running faster and faster until I saw the lights of home. My thoughts ran anxiously with me. I could not get this last picture out of my mind; for me, it symbolised the danger all around us now. How would it all end? (p. 180)

Lecky Payne's nostalgic search is characteristic of many of these narratives and of an underlying trend which Richard Coe has found in his study of a large number of international autobiographies—that 'beneath all the more everyday accounts of paternal incompetence, bankruptcy and failure there lies a recurrent nostalgia for the *ideal* father'.[18] Sometimes the loss of such a father is the result of death, as in Kathleen Mangan's *Daisy Chains, War, then Jazz*, but, more usually, it is the result of some change, gradual or sudden, in the father. The latter may even be a more painful experience. Once again, *My Brilliant Career* is an archetypal text, but the experience is memorably repeated in Amie Livingstone Stirling's *Memories of an Australian Childhood*, Katharine Susannah Prichard's *Child of the Hurricane* and Connie Miller's two autobiographies of childhood. Christina Stead's *The Man Who Loved Children* opens when the father's clay feet are already visible, but elsewhere she has recorded her delight in their 'long morning', when he was both father and mother as well as a stimulating guide to the world of story.[19]

One of the most poignant of this group is Clara Jackamarra's story, recorded by Sheila Kelly in *Proud Heritage*.[20] The daughter of George Roe and granddaughter of John Septimus Roe, Clara has a happy early childhood on her father's station, *Thangoo*, near Broome. Returning to the station in old age, she recalls the happiest of her memories, 'my father coming home laden with gifts for us, the sound of my mother's happy laugh' (p. 83). In his relationship with his part-Aboriginal, part-Asian wife, George Roe is more of an autocrat than most fathers, although he is greatly admired and loved by the narrator. The extent of his power is brought home in Clara's description of her sudden, unexplained expulsion from the family and removal to Beagle Bay mission in 1909. She was never to return home. In 1912, her two sisters and brother follow her there, and the children subsequently make several futile attempts to return to *Thangoo*. Clara never sees her father again, although she hears of him from time to time. She receives no mention in his will, nor is she invited to a reunion of the descendants of John Septimus Roe. Their mother is inexplicably kept apart from her children, and is not reunited with her daughter for several years. Even then, the two can only communicate through the wire fence of the hospital, where Clara works. Bewilderment, grief and, ironically, pride in the father are the dominant emotions of this narrative.

A common fatherly betrayal is his decision, usually communicated at puberty, that his daughter is less valuable than his male heirs. Amie Stirling discovers that her father's rhetoric about equality of the sexes is not sustained by his actions; Connie Miller is silently appalled that her brothers are granted an education as a natural right, while she is expected to leave school early; Katharine Susannah Prichard sustains a blow from which she never really recovers, when her father confesses during her brother's critical illness, that he had rather she were the threatened child; Doreen Flavel has to surmount two handicaps in the eyes of her father, her gender and her blindness. By choosing, silently or explicitly, his boys as his social heirs, it seems that fathers, at least in these Australian autobiographies, run the greatest risk of losing their daughters' esteem. Once again, Chodorov's comments are illuminating:

a daughter looks to her father for a sense of separateness and for the same confirmation of her specialness that her brother receives from her mother. She (and the woman she becomes) is willing to deny her father's limitations (and those of her lover or husband) as long as she feels loved.[21]

On the other hand, numerous narratives record the enormous power of the father as a stimulating, encouraging figure. Many narrators, who have a strong sense of achievement, link their efforts to a desire to please the admired father. Nellie Melba and Mary Gilmore relate to particularly strong father figures, and like Prichard, although with more success, Gilmore sees herself as the father's natural, intellectual successor. Jane Watts's autobiography resonates with admiration for her father, and all her own feats of pioneering endurance relate to his model; recording his instances of approval as emotional high points fifty years later, she submits her life willingly to his destiny without any loss of independent spirit. Della Edmunds, whose life is a great deal more rugged over a century later, and whose father has none of Mr A.'s refinement, also responds to paternal challenges, consciously fulfilling the father's role after his death. Sarah Conigrave gives a vivid account of her childhood feats of bravery in the hazardous conditions of her family's early settlement on Hindmarsh Island. If the father saves the family's fortunes by a superhuman journey, the twelve-year-old Sarah saves their wheat from a mob of wild cattle during the father's illness:

As I walked along, I began to think how bravely I had acted. If I had played the coward's part, what would have happened—papa would have made the effort—fainted—and probably been trodden to death. Well then, had I not saved his life? Of course, I had—and if a soldier on the battle-field had saved a comrade, so, he would be rewarded with a V.C. probably ... I hastened away to find how poor papa was getting on. I found him waiting anxiously for me. His eyes were shining, and he gave me a look, and said, 'Thank you, my child,' and that was my 'V.C.', and I believe I felt as proud of it, as ever a soldier did of his medal.[22]

Conigrave's identification with a male symbol or ideal of bravery is repeated in other accounts of positive relationships with fathers.

Often competing with brothers, daughters take pleasure in wresting their laurels from them. Conigrave sees herself and her sister as in a state of war with their brothers; they are natural enemies, and their constant attempts to gain the superior ground have to be resisted at all costs. Eve Hogan goes to extraordinary physical lengths to win recognition, but gains scant regard; Amie Stirling is patronized by an insufferably arrogant brother. Like Ernie in *The Man Who Loved Children*, many brothers appear to be aware that time will soon heal their powerlessness; meanwhile, they simulate their future power by 'taming' their sisters, using aggressive tactics which far outdo their father's. Similarly, many brothers resemble Tom Tulliver and define their masculinity at their sisters' expense. Harriet Martineau's conviction that 'in the history of human affections ... of all natural relations, the least satisfactory is the fraternal'[23], seems to be borne out in the great majority of these autobiographies. Jessica Anderson's recent collection of childhood stories, *Stories From the Warm Zone*, is typical in the representation of the brother as a would-be replica of the father, eager to share in his thunder and quenchable only by his superior power.

Other autobiographers relate more positive experiences of the fraternal relationship. Fairlie Taylor's brother accords her the equal status which her father denies, and she is a welcome accomplice in all his exploits; Elyne Mitchell's brothers reflect the same chivalric values which she admires in her father and in her teens their infrequent visits enlarge her somewhat lonely life. A handful of autobiographies record the relationship with the brother as particularly intimate; as Jane Miller comments, the brother 'may ... be the one man [the sister] has unconditionally loved, the one by whom she is known'.[24] Although the relationship is sometimes altered by time, as Ellen Campbell, Adelaide Lubbock, Katharine Susannah Prichard and Joice Loch Nankivell record, it may still be one of peculiar sweetness.

If brothers frequently oppress sisters, fathers may obliterate mothers and it is a curious fact that a daughter's admiration for a father often involves dismissal of a mother. Other commentators have noticed the same phenomenon. As Adrienne Rich remarks: 'a nurturing father, who replaces rather than complements a mother, *must be loved at the mother's expense*, whatever the reasons for the mother's absence'.[25] Ursula Owen concludes that the reasons why daughters who idolise fathers generally undervalue their mothers may be found in our culture: 'mothers and fathers symbolise quite different aspects of experience in children's early lives—far beyond those which biology lays down'.[26] Sarah Conigrave's mother figures rarely in her autobiography, and never in a situation where she is meeting a challenge; Margaret Gifford's mother in *I Can Hear the Horses* is perceived as recessive and socially isolated while the father is ebullient and gregarious; Mary Drake's mother in *The Trees Were Green* is a social butterfly and no match for the father in either charm or energy; Elyne Mitchell's father, Harry Chauvel, is one of the most charismatic of the fathers encountered here. Of immense influence on her own development, he also shapes her perception of her mother; in *Chauvel Country* she is the lady to his knight, the fit recipient of his military honours, and her individuality is somewhat lost in the chivalric role.

Fathers who inhabit the bush are particularly obliterating of mothers. A minor narrative, Sophia Stevenson's *Across the Vanished Years*, describes the father as a 'giant' in physique and strength of character. 'Dressed in his usual garb of khaki shirt and jodhpurs, concertina leggings, elasticide boots, spurs, and wide-brimmed hat, and of course a belt decorated with numerous pouches containing knife, watch, glasses and snakebite kit, he was a typical Queensland bushman.'[27] The narrator's mother is cast in the supporting role of colourless but stoical survivor. This is most evident at her death, which is recorded as the father's loss of 'his wife', and another of the blows of his old age. Dorothy Cottrell in *The Singing Gold* perceives the parent figures as naturally occupying strongly demarcated provinces, even though the narrator herself enjoys a boyish freedom. If the father is less realistically flexible than the mother, his romantic dreams and adventurous aura are granted privileged status and both mother and daughter preserve his prestige as intrepid bushman, even while they suffer from its limitations. Rose Scott Cowen in *Crossing Dry Creeks* identifies strongly with her bush father. Like Sophia Stevenson's, he is constantly referred to as the 'Boss' and his charm and skills excuse him manifold delinquencies. His philandering makes his marriage a 'dangerous mockery', sours the family life indoors and eventually ends in his divorce. Explaining his weakness retrospectively as an inability to refuse the advances of predatory women, Cowen solves the immediate childhood problem by taking to the outdoors and becoming his 'inseparable companion'.

This pattern is not universal, however, and it is heartening to discover that for some narrators both parents are valued, nurturing and stimulating figures; Barbara Corbett's *A Fistful of Buttercups*, Ivy Arney's *Twenties Child* and Ruve Cropley's *Forty 'Odd' Years in a Manse* share this attractive characteristic.

Of all the fathers who stalk these autobiographies, none approaches Norman Lindsay in charisma or enigma. In the culture at large Lindsay is still an equivocal father-figure, questioning some familiar perceptions of the Australian identity and proffering a heady vitalism which numerous writers have found irresistible. His children also appear to have experienced him as irresistible, even though, like Rousseau, he was more interested in his cultural than his natural progeny. Two of his five children have left remarkable accounts of his impact as father, Jack Lindsay's *Life Rarely Tells* and *The Roaring Twenties* and Jane Lindsay's *Portrait of Pa*.[28] Jack Lindsay's autobiographies are important cultural studies and differ widely from *Portrait of Pa* in range and purpose. Nevertheless, *Portrait of Pa* has a value of its own. The Norman who is Jack Lindsay's father is an exciting, cerebral figure, whose ideas and influence have an enormous impact on his son's intellectual development. Arguing with Norman eventually heads Jack towards his own, very different intellectual destiny, just as re-arguing with Norman in the autobiographies confirms his decision. The Norman who is Jane Lindsay's father is an older and more human figure and the standards by which he is measured are those of human feeling, rather than intellect. 'People said he was a genius . . . "A man above the normal level of humanity" . . . But genius is hard to recognise at close quarters', comments Jane (p. 4). Largely unimpressed by Norman as cultural prophet, Jane reduces him to the level of 'normal humanity' and interprets him as a father, as 'Pa'. *Portrait of Pa* is both narrower and wider than Jack Lindsay's autobiographies. It concentrates almost entirely on family relationships and life at Springwood; cultural and political events pass it by, or are only registered in terms of their personal effects. But Jane is less concerned with her personal trajectory of development than Jack and her attempts to understand the father have implications about ways of being in the world, which some readers may find more appealing than Jack Lindsay's specific political solutions. The two approaches illustrate well the differences between male and female life-writing; undoubtedly Jack Lindsay's texts will be valued more highly in the traditional literary canon, but comparisons between the two are not really tenable. Although they deal with the same subject, they ask different questions, confer different pleasures and demand different reading approaches.

Portrait of Pa appeared simultaneously with John Hetherington's biography of Lindsay, inevitably inviting comparative reviews. Many reviewers commented that the autobiography was at least equally valuable as a study of Lindsay the man, but they appeared to hesitate about its individual achievement. Whereas one reviewer described it as lacking in charity, another praised it as a 'droll' account of one girl's growing-up, another perceived it as an uncritical 'romp', a gaily coloured, two-dimensional picture of an artist/writer, and yet another complained that the author either failed to know her father or chose to withhold what she knew.[29]

This last reviewer appears to half appreciate the provisional nature of *Portrait of Pa*. Paul Eakin has described autobiography as 'not merely . . . the passive, transparent record of an already completed self, but rather as an integral and often decisive phase of the drama of self-definition'.[30] For Jane Lindsay self-definition cannot evade definition of this exceptionally ambivalent father; sensitive to the confused cross-currents of their relationship, her autobiographical act is clearly a phase in the relationship's continuing drama and a necessarily indecisive one. Thus *Portrait of Pa* implicitly recognizes the unavoidable presence of the inward father, effectively described by Sara Maitland in 'Two for the Price of One':

I have another father. This one is alive and well and rampaging inside me. He never goes away, although sometimes he is silent; he is never ill, never weakened, never leaves me alone ... In my late teens I fled away from my father's house; it has taken me a long time to realise that I carried with me the Father from whom I could not escape by escaping childhood, from whom I have not yet escaped, and from whom I have had, and still have, to wrest my loves, my voice, my feminism and my freedom. It is this Father that I have hated loving and loved hating. It is this Father that I want to kill, and dare not.[31]

Lindsay perceives her father as disgracefully defective, and even wicked, in normal intimate relationships; even so, as a loved and living figure, he cannot be measured with the just measure of hatred due to abstract wickedness and it is the perplexing difficulty of loving while hating, which she attempts to recreate in *Portrait of Pa.*

The book's language is strikingly informal and even laconic, the judgements of people and events are brusque and matter-of-fact, the self is often presented ironically and self-pity is carefully avoided. Even compassion is guardedly given. Trained in detecting pretension, false drama and self-inflation, Lindsay has retained the shrewd, uncomfortable insights of the child, so that honesty is the book's most immediate impression. It is also remarkably artful, carefully structured to allow the interplay between conflicting emotions and assessments full scope. The book is divided into two parts, each part inferring roughly the same beginning—1940, and Jane's return to Springwood to live with Norman, while Rose, her mother, is in America. The final section of Part I fills in the background to Jane's decision to return in 1940; the final pages of Part II recapitulate the first pages of Part I.

Norman's death in 1969, presented in a tone of wry comedy at the beginning, is a moving experience at the close. But this is not because the writer has won through to a rosier picture of the father through the act of writing; on the contrary, he progresses to a high order of insensitivity in the second part of the book. Although the narrative is roughly circular, 1940 and 1969 are not the poles of its time-scheme, for time is both prospective and retrospective, a complicated criss-crossing, back-tracking to 1913 when Rose bought Springwood, anticipating future events, contrasting past and present and hinting at their hidden ironies. In this text the older narrator is more than implied. She is integral to the retrospective understanding of episodes, which were baffling or ambivalent for the child; and it is her

voice, ironic, caustic, reflective, which interposes between the reader
and the child's experience. At the same time, there is a sense that the
older self is also an implied reader, on the watch for the conclusions
which will emerge from this quest of the father.

Shape or structure is focal to our reading of an autobiographical
text. As Elizabeth Bruss points out: 'the way the autobiographer has
arranged his text is . . . experienced as a "sample" of his epistemo-
logy and his personal skill . . . there is no way the autobiographer
can evade personal responsibility for the shape of his work—even
conventional choices reflect his individual identity'.[32] Lindsay's unconventional treatment of time is a brilliant means of circling her
ambivalent subject; not only is the picture of Norman subtly cumulative, but certain themes and motifs insert themselves unobtrusively
and the inner meaning of ostensibly neutral or seemingly irrelevant
episodes or digressions is released. Thus, the extended descriptions
of horses, birds and animals, of the Stratton family and of Jane's
farming friends are related to the central problem of Norman, even
though he rarely figures in them.

1940 is an important year for Jane's understanding of Norman. As
we discover later, she has recently reached a low point in her own
emotional growth; her ambitions to be a doctor have been frustrated,
her relationship with her mother is at its nadir, and she has the
impression that the other members of the family have abandoned
her. Returning to Springwood presents her with an opportunity to
rediscover both her father and the recent past: 'Pa left home when we
were barely through childhood. I was twenty before I again gave him
any serious attention as a human being, let alone a genius' (p. 4).
Most importantly, Rose is out of the way, and both the younger Jane
and her older, narrating self need this dispensation if Norman is to be
seen in focus. Rose is as powerful a figure in her daughter's emotional
life as Norman, and her sufferings must be kept momentarily out of
the balance, if the father's point of view is to be approached.

Returning to 1940, then, Jane starts a densely-layered portrait of
her own, applying the pigments with the same apparently artless skill
that marked her father's painting. She is impressed once again by his
gaiety and energy, his amazing vitality and versatility. She recalls
the times when his extraordinary talent spilled out to light up her
childhood, when he taught her to read from *The Magic Pudding*,
made an enchanting fairy who danced on the lawn and built the
children a tree house. Looking back, her childhood on 'Olympus'
seems full of colour and movement, even though Rose is a more
visible presence than Norman. This response to his charm persists
through vicissitudes. As she comments towards the end: 'I was long
accustomed to Pa's Jekyll and Hyde personality. I liked him in spite
of it. Even when he was behaving like a demon, no one could deny
the charm' (p. 179). Meanwhile the older narrator watches the 1940
self assess the 1940 Norman and all the other Normans she has known

and is to know. She perceives that his interest in people is superficial, a 'novelist's interest', close to the interest he attributes to Dickens. He enjoys an audience—'as long as someone offered a pair of ears he talked incessantly' (p. 9)—but conversation is absent at his table: 'It was usually a discourse on whatever was occupying his interest at the time. If someone attempted to put in a comment or two he would say, "Exactly, exactly", without bothering to listen, swallow another mouthful and get briskly back into his own orbit' (p. 114). The contrast between his liberal attitudes and his Methodist ancestors becomes less remarkable; like them, he is self-engrossed and single-minded, dominated by the work ethic and wowserish about alcohol and parties. 'It ... seemed best to give him back to the Methodists', his daughter comments with conscious irony after his death. In the second treatment of the 1940 period, the narrator is even more caustic about his exploitation of friends and relations; the selfless Douglas Stewart is more 'suitable' for Pa's purposes than Kenneth Mackenzie—'making use of people was one of the games Pa perfected. He never hesitated to ask if he thought someone could do something useful for him, or run a message or do some boring chore' (p. 120). Underlying the account of Norman's habit of withdrawing his gifts is a sense of personal hurt, while the numerous descriptions of Norman the room-dweller, undisturbed by the claims of people, content with his work, his mice in the mantlepiece and his anti-social cats, build up an impression of the man as extraordinarily isolated. Described often as 'bird-like', he seems to fit the analogy with semi-human connotations.

He is made up of contradictions; a vitalist, who regards early death as an escape; an influential artist, who dislikes other artists; a cultural figure of consequence, who avoids society and substitutes mono-logues for debate; a political cartoonist, who has no knowledge of politics; a father, who regards his duties fulfilled at the point of conception. Springwood itself is seen as a monument to his inconsistencies; a pseudo-Grecian, pseudo-Chinese anomaly, 'posing' majestically on its orderly lawns, it presents a hypocritical front of civilized life (p.103). Although Norman has impressed his personality on it and grandly wills it to the Lindsay Trust, it belongs in fact to Rose.

Norman is at his best in *Portrait of Pa* when his daughter turns her attention to the days when both parents lived as Olympic deities at Springwood. If Norman is a room-dweller, Rose is a house-dweller, and Springwood is dominated more by her presence than Norman's:

Ma was always full of excessive house pride. The floors were waxed deep mahogany and shone richly against the Persian carpets. The big drawing room was ornamented with inlaid tables, brassware and deep, comfortable sofas. The walls were adorned with a series of panels upon which Pa painted compositions in oil ... It had always been a beautiful room and had known years of Ma's cheerful gatherings with a fire in the big grate ... (p. 36)

As impressive a personality as Norman, Rose is equally energetic and involved in creation. She makes his impractical building projects workable; she spends her energies in manipulating the heavy press which turns out his etchings; she has an artist's skill and dedication; she runs the household to suit Norman's tastes and preserves him from the worst effects of his intemperate letters; she manages his business interests with an acumen he lacks. If the accounts of their mutual habits of secrecy are comic and often counterproductive, there is an impression that the two form a productive, and mainly harmonious, union. The narrator makes great play with the Olympian theme, which is almost as ambivalent as Norman himself. The dream turns horribly sour, but the narrative also recaptures the child's delight in the scenes of both parents working at the decorations for the numerous fancy-dress parties, in Rose's pleasure in self-display, whether as a model, or in the imaginative costumes she runs up, or in the 'chariot' she drives to town. Both larger than life, arrogant and self-engrossed as all deities are, they are the centre of a radius of vitality, which the two sisters find exciting. They may be cut off from other children, but they share in the heady atmosphere of Olympus.

Rose's bitterness when Norman abandons her and their heightened life together, singes the life of her daughter as the summer fires singe Springwood. Fire, in fact, begins to play a double role; as literal reality and as metaphor of the dangers that Springwood represents. As the narrator comments: 'Pa's branch of Olympus at Springwood suffered various onslaughts from his Gods' (p. 88). Rose is at her Wagnerian best when fires rage in the Blue Mountains during her Olympian period, but it is she who later suggests a move to Sydney, after Jane and her baby's lives are threatened. A key passage eloquently describes the destruction of all that Jane had found good at Springwood. Horses are her passion, familiar enough in accounts of childhood, and yet in this narrator's case associated with the integrity, freedom and normal, natural pleasures, which Norman's Olympus lacks. The description of her response to the burnt-out stables evokes the contrast between the two ways of being:

Next time I visited Springwood and saw the charred mess, I felt unbearably sad. Horse yards, cow yards, stables and feed shed and all the rest of that crazy old edifice had been so important.

I remembered the feel and the smell of all its odd corners. Musty lucerne chaff never swept from under the bins. Charlie smoking his pipe after lunch. Stockolm tar and linseed oil, gall cure and saddle soap. Horses warm with sweat. Warm milk splashing into the bucket. Horses rugged against cold winter wind. The sweet smell of wet lucerne and warm cow's breath ... The blackened posts made me sick with nostalgia. (pp. 93–4)

The criss-cross time sequence presents several glimpses of the sour years, when Rose drowns her grief with wild parties at Springwood and Norman buries himself in his studio in Sydney. The young narrator is bewildered and hurt but the older one interprets the mother's actions with an adult understanding. The account of Rose's desperate, failed attempt to re-establish Olympus by making Norman's name in America is suffused with compassion for the mother. Rose's grief at the loss of much of his best work in a train fire and Norman's refusal or inability to take her hurt seriously, set the seal on the emotional division between the parents and align the daughter with the mother. Later Norman's 'streak of coldness' widens and the account of his attacks on Rose in his last years is bleak indeed. Rose is incomplete without Norman and never recovers from her passion for him, but Norman seems even more incomplete without her. In his hands Springwood is an uncivilized place:

The scuffed-over boards were nothing like Ma's polished deep mahogany floors which had set off the rich Persian carpets and gleamed against the handsome furniture. There had been a warmth and humanity in that room belonging to a kind of civilised living which had always been foreign to Pa ... Like the house, Ma's drawing room had had an entity and beauty of its own which Pa in his obsession for the glorification of his art, had destroyed—and not even noticed. (pp. 183–4)

Two inter-related themes set Olympus in sharper critical focus. One centres on building. All the Lindsays have a passion for building and both parents impose additions on the house. Inside, the structure suffers from Norman's persistent weaknesses as a builder, small windows and low ceilings. Later he takes to blocking up windows, preferring electric light. The descriptions of his room and style of living while on his own, become cumulatively a metaphor of his self-contained personality. As a builder, he works at fever pitch, using cement for everything—'paths, pillars, walls, pools, flowerpots, statues'. The garden is littered with his statues and stagnant ponds; an ornate fountain spouts water from its shower-rose top months before water is connected to the house; a dam, built of hastily assembled cement, is scarred by cracks. Rose's later comment that 'he always was a dirty little builder', seems to be shared by the narrator and to refer to things other than buildings. There is also another builder in the district—Mick Stratton, who builds patiently and solidly in stone. Taking pleasure in the natural colours of his stones, and working slowly and methodically, he is a strong contrast to Norman as his houses are a silent criticism of Springwood's incongruity. He builds a house for Jane and half-completes one for Rose. Mick's numerous relations also represent the normal, saner, natural world, which Jane seeks as a refuge. The Strattons are 'as much a part of that piece of the mountain bush as were the trees... They had a close affinity with the earth and could make things grow and flourish in that hungry soil when other people toiled fruitlessly and watched their plants die' (p. 97). Fra and Nina, neighbouring poultry-farmers, also offer Jane uncomplicated companionship, and the pleasures of literature and productive work. One vivid memory in particular underlines Jane's perception of her father as contrastingly anti-nature and even anti-life. Pursuing a personal, futile campaign against the extensive weed calliopsis, which 'made a wonderful show of colour in the back-blocks of the garden', he injects each weed individually with weed-killer; he has no sooner finished the acreage than he has to begin again. His liquidation of the weed is compared to his attitude to American Negroes: 'The Negro problem was easiest . . . "send them all back to Africa", he advised' (p. 144).

The last sections of the book are heavy with a sad irony. As Norman plans for posterity, writing the letters that will be preserved, framing the Will, making plans for the Trust, he ignores his human posterity. His grandchildren fail to interest him, his wife is 'abolished' and his daughter is exploited until a minor misdeed leads to her abolishment also. The ironies underlying the first description of his funeral become more apparent: it is attended by a great number of people, 'one daughter, two grandchildren, two nephews and in-numerable television technicians' (p. 3). The conclusion also evokes the narrator's sense of loss which has been a constant undertow; in her hope that his spirit has been searching for hers at the last she expresses her longing for the father who might have been. 'He confused his work with himself and its possible immortality with his own', comments Jane towards the close; he insisted 'that he was more than human' (p. 184). *Portrait of Pa* emphatically redresses the balance.

The death of the mother is often perceived in cataclysmic terms; the death or threatened death of the father appears to be a more ambivalent, delicate topic for the autobiographer. One of the most sensitive approaches to the subject is Jessica Anderson's collection of short stories in *Stories From the Warm Zone*.[33] In this account of a Queensland childhood between the wars, the narrator's earliest memories are overshadowed by her father's illness. As she grows older, consumption takes a firmer hold of the father, 'stiffening and hollowing out his big frame' (p. 14); his return home is often a moment of anxiety and his terrible bouts of coughing frequently inspire a sense of panic in the child that 'the dreaded moment' had finally come. Like Lindsay, Anderson uses a criss-cross time scheme, in which future deaths are anticipated and two separated spans of intimacy with the mother inter-reflect images of the past and its future. Death is a familiar figure to the child and even more so to the older narrator. For the child, reminders of the recent war are everywhere: its 'bloody legend' touches the three sisters despite the mother's pacifism; church, cenotaph, school and a memorial stand of gradually dying trees commemorate it; fatherless children are common in the neighbourhood; and the father's illness is traced to his suffering at Gallipoli. Other deaths loom on the horizon—of the old family horse, of Rhoda, the narrator's sister, at the age of forty, of the father and perhaps the mother, of Mr Gilbert, the Anglican vicar whom Rhoda worships.

The first story, 'Under the House', is a delicate anticipation of the dominant themes. The narrator, aged four, is hiding under the house, while her elder sisters prepare a game, which mysteriously excludes her. Under the house creates unpleasant sensations, 'an uneasiness, a dogged like depression'. The objects stored there are 'sterile', 'grey', 'sombre', and 'dusty':

Broken cobwebby flowerpots were piled in one corner. From a nail in a post hung the studded collar of the dog Sancho, who had had to be shot, and from another hung the leg irons dug up by my grandfather, relic of 'some poor fellow' from the days when Brisbane was a penal colony. (p. 4)

Under the house, the child feels 'imprisoned, put away, discarded'. Clearly the place is associated not only with death but with imprisonments which death may metaphor. It anticipates the various taboos which afflict the child.

Death itself is a major taboo. Both parents refuse to acknowledge the father's illness to the children, who are trained to hide their anxiety. The father even refuses to see a doctor, since doctors are one of his taboo subjects, and this itself brings the shadow of death closer for the child. Conventional religion, which pretends to answers about death, is also a family taboo; the mother's rejection of Irish-Catholic bigotry and the father's free-thinking position make the subject of religion a prickly topic. Past events have also made some intimate relations taboo and the maternal grandmother will not acknowledge the father or his children. Later a Catholic playmate is directed to shun the family. The narrator, Beatie, suffers intermittently from a speech impediment, but this too is not a subject for disussion. Certain disreputable people and places, such as the cinema and the creek, are forbidden. Meanwhile the parents' conversation, which is always guarded in front of the children, intrigues the narrator with 'the tantalising significance of something I felt I was on the very verge of understanding' (p. 18). Death, then, is merely one in the thicket of taboos surrounding the child; but as the stories unfold, it becomes clear that every taboo betrays a preoccupation with death and is itself deathly in its effects.

'Under the House' also anticipates Beatie's victory over taboo, and recapitulates an earlier victory, initiated by her best-loved sister, Rhoda. On the earlier memorable occasion, Rhoda had dressed her in a red wool rug and introduced the forbidden delights of a running gutter in front of the garden: 'I shouted to find myself holding a ball of live water. I was amazed, enraptured by such resilience, freshness, softness, strength' (pp. 5–6). The moment is recaptured in the conclusion to the incident, which is the story's main topic. Admitted to some of Rhoda's secret knowledge about a magnificent grown-up hat which she had squirrelled from some source for dressing up, Beatie is liberated into an exciting dimension of being. The old reminders of death, the collar and leg irons, are literally and figuratively hidden and:

Filled with delight, I flung myself twirling away down the length of the verandah. Once again, as when we ran back from the marvellous torrent, I fully connived, this time by silence, so that together, twirling at different parts of the verandah, we put my new-found cleverness in its place. (p. 16)

The moment rehearses another less riotous, more guarded, but perhaps more lasting liberation, in the conclusion of the last story, 'The Aviator'. On this occasion the child is accompanied by Kenny, a crippled boy, whom she has both helped and unwittingly wounded; free from the constraining presence of adults, they affirm a tentative achievement of friendly independence by sharing a forbidden cigarette:

'Here,' he said, offering it. 'There's no wind today.' So we leaned on the railing, drew the aromatic smoke into our mouths, and expelled it in rings that writhed a little before they were absorbed into the shimmering air. (p. 111)

Between these epiphanies, Beatie traverses a complicated emotional journey. At eight, she is close to her father. When he returns home, she rediscovers his face and hands in a tactile way, venting the anxiety about him, which she is not allowed to express. 'He was a man of unreliable temper, but under these inspections he was always patient and humorous' (p. 18). Sitting under the dining-room table, she taps his toe and keeps his foot 'at a gentle jog'. During the family dispute about whether or not the girls should be christened, Beatie is torn by her loyalty to her father and a desire to share in the mysteries of church, which her sisters discover. Her pipe-filling ritual for the father has a new meaning: 'Thoughtfully I wiped away the ridge I had made across his knuckles; regretfully I stroked the back of his head. In the words he spoke after those first few puffs of his pipe, I heard a new confidentiality, a comradely intonation' (p. 34). Her defection to the church-going party does nothing to lighten her preoccupation with death, and her nights are described as 'disturbed by the dark angel' and occupied with ways of dying. Meanwhile, she senses a new exclusion from the self-righteous world of father and brother. Although time will reverse their situation and the brother will convert to Catholicism, at this juncture, he joyfully choruses the father's dismissal of religion as weakly feminine.

The story 'Against the Wall' deals with a crisis, initially instigated by an insensitive teacher, but clearly related to Beatie's preoccupation with the deathly taboos. Her speech impediment suddenly worsens at school and she is subjected to punishment. The well-meaning mother intervenes, but unwittingly breaks another taboo practised by the schoolchildren and forbidding parental interference. Faced with the intolerable situation, Beatie instinctively takes refuge in the more natural, straightforward, adult-free society of the creek. Initiation to the creek tribe requires a showing of genitals, a symbolic act registering defiance of the convention-bound sphere of parents and teachers. Here, Beatie is free to associate with two albino outlaws, Peggy and Des; the children of vagrants, who belong to a mysteriously exciting camp at Budjerra Heights, they display a laconic tolerance and easy freedom which is irresistible. She always feels joyous after seeing them and they offer a rare sense of 'settlement, of comfort, of having arrived at exactly the right place' (p. 69).

The discovery of her truancy creates new barriers between father and child. In fear of the anticipated beating, she voices the unforgivable, the hope that he will be too ill when he returns home to carry it out. The guilty words block off further speech: 'I had spoken my intention to murder. It was from inside myself, this time, that the word-blocking emanation came' (p. 60). The fragile communication between father and child has broken down and her stammer, which will persistently erupt in his presence, will reflect the 'malign pattern' destined to trouble their relationship until his death. That event is marked by the first and last words he ever speaks freely to the children, without the constraints of fatherhood: '"I am done for"' (p. 90).

As Beatie's relationship with her father becomes more difficult, her relationship with her mother suddenly flowers. Granted a year's absence from school, she discovers her mother's distinctive personality and wins access to her freer, inward self. If earlier she was inhibited by the parents' habit of reserve ('They never tell us anything'), now she has a new sense of intimate knowledge and frank conversation. Watching her mother, she has something of that same sensation of comfort, of having arrived at exactly the right place, which she had experienced in the company of Peggy and Des. Whereas the father's personality is stiff, remote and enervated, the mother's is energetic, variable, accessible. Although the daughter later rejects her mother's assertion that the father had chosen death, she also confirms it: '"That was his right"' (p. 89).

For Beatie herself, Budjerra Heights ceases to be necessary as a place to escape to. The last story, 'The Aviator', celebrates her liberation from the 'paralysis of speech'. Greeting the smiling aviator in his low-flying aeroplane, she is finally free of the 'dark stain', which the anticipated return to school has evoked. Subtly, Anderson suggests that she is also freed of the fear of death and the deathly taboos: the memory of their dead horse, often imprinted on his familiar paddock, is at this moment 'quite incidental' (p.100). Like Kenny, who will eventually defeat his paralysis, she has defeated her inhibiting constraints and is ready for school: '"I can't wait to play Medes and Persians"', she exclaims (p. 110).

Curiously, Anderson's linking of the dying father with images of war and confinement is repeated in two other autobiographies, both dominated by a charismatic father who dies early: Kathleen Mangan's *Daisy Chains, War, then Jazz*[34] and Mary Drake's *The Trees Were Green*[35]. Neither has the sophistication of *Stories from the Warm Zone*, but they are sensitive explorations of the subterranean, emotional meaning of a father's death and its long-term consequences. The 'War' section of Mangan's autobiography describes Melbourne during the First World War through a child's eyes; war, both literally and as an ominous symbol of change, is linked to her father's (Frederick McCubbin) early death. Sensitive to her father's moods and apprehensive of the change in his normally cheerful temperament, she identifies with his fears and anger. Both father and child seem to share the knowledge that the romantic Melbourne necessary for his art has been destroyed. A particularly striking incident describes the unexpected arrival of a present from Gallipoli, where her brother is serving, and her parents' horror when it is revealed to be three machine-gun bullets. On the home front, violent or unpleasant emotions seem to have been unleashed, and women, no less than men, are revealed as vindictive. These emotions even invade the narrator's home, and McCubbin's death is linked to a particularly unpleasant incident, the blatant aggression of a pro-German sympathizer. The woman's insults are 'a victory for the Germans in the end . . . that unfinished sketch of father's was his last attempt at a city landscape. It remained in his studio, facing the wall, until the day he died, a haunting reminder of Mrs Tulberg' (p. 51).

Mary Drake's *The Trees Were Green* describes an exceptionally wealthy and sheltered childhood in Sydney of the same period. The narrator has a strong rapport with her father, who is perceived as a man of great charm, elegance and business skill. His death at fifty-six occurs late in the narrative and yet overshadows it from the beginning, deepening the significance of the narrator's memories of war and her obsession with the theme of transience. The narrative's public theme is one of nostalgia for a simpler, warmer past; but there are more probing, disturbing undertones, which come to a head in her descriptions of the war and the depression. The underlying sense of threat is sharpened by the retrospective knowledge that this childhood was exceptionally sheltered. Dreaming of the past, Drake is preoccupied not just with its disappearance, but with the ominous signs and symbols of its erosion, which the child-self barely absorbs. The present is like the noise of the cicadas, whose deafening chorus 'was so much a part of summer that we only became aware of it when it stopped' (p. 65). Describing the sequence of her memories as unpredictable as raffle tickets drawn from a hat, she retrieves one in particular which symbolizes the external threat to her charmed world: it is the memory of a male doll, made in Germany, which is condemned by an unpleasant uncle and buried out of sight by the gardener each week when the uncle visits. The suggestive memory mingles with memories of the drowning of another much-loved uncle, of the anxieties provoked by war in general, and looks forward to that other death which will signal the end of this romantic childhood.

Another important group of narratives deals with fathers who predate the author's memories. Eugénie Delarue of *A Bunyip Close Behind Me* (1972) and *Ladies Didn't* (1984) can just remember her father as 'a vague figure in a purple smoking jacket', who dies when she is six. As their mother is a naturally cheerful, resiliently practical individual, the Delarue sisters survive the death of Father, despite Victorian attempts at gloom and melodrama:

We were given black sashes to wear and taken, solemn and wide-eyed, to View the Corpse. In an age when children and young girls were 'spared' the facts of birth and a wife's 'duty' was often explained in terms so ambiguous that its exact nature remained obscure, it's amazing how anxious their elders were to acquaint them with the facts of death ... However, with his curly beard and surrounded with flowers ... father looked quite life-like and we weren't a bit afraid. (p. 5)

The sisters' subsequent childhood is delightfully eccentric and varied, even though their mother remains colourfully convinced that they are 'Ruined!'. The absence of a father in 1890s Bankstown is no tremendous handicap. In *Ladies Didn't*, however, the mother begins the inevitable quest for husbands and external, gender-laden values intrude into their destinies and limit their freedom.

Barbara Hanrahan's *The Scent of Eucalyptus* (1973) and *Kewpie Doll* (1984) are more seriously concerned with a dead father. This father, who dies when the narrator is a year old, is a mix of individuals, part-larrikin and part-good-Catholic-son; his various identities, preserved in a few, ill assorted mementoes, trouble her thoughts and intervene in her adolescent struggle with suburban conformity. His reported insensitivity links him to the bullying actions of other men: the sexually predatory Great Grandfather Collins, the divorced grandfather whose cruelties darken her mother's childhood, the teacher whose beatings make his class a daily battleground, the municipal workers who blind the family dog with weedkiller. On the other hand, his rebellious spirit is an inspiration when she begins to resist the sterile suburban future of her mother's imagination. Depressed by her mother's acceptance of suffocating values, she takes refuge in her father's self-assertive image. In *Sea-green* (1974) Hanrahan creates a father who might have been, the dull preferred husband of her mother's dreams.

A narrative which is strong in content but bristles with unresolved anger and suffers from some slack writing is Josie Arnold's *Mother Superior Woman Inferior* (1985).[36] This narrator's father is killed in the Second World War, shortly after her birth, and she is the only member of the family not to have known him. The privileged knowledge of the other children makes her doubly fatherless and she pieces the jigsaw of family memory together in an attempt to retrieve the 'golden father' she never knew and to acquire some family equality. But it is the mother's sense of loss that is the determining experience. The earliest image of the mother is of her mourning the father:

I was standing in the cold passageway at home, in the darkness of a winter's day. My brothers and my sister were all at school . . . I shrank from the sharp sand-blasted walls. I could see my mother lying on her bed and hear her crying the most mournful keening: she lay on her back and held out her arms and called my father's name in a heart-broken voice. I knew then that I was cold comfort, and this added a deep unworthiness to my already felt distress at not having been good enough to keep my father alive. (p. 10)

A remarkably capable woman, who raises her family of eight children in conditions of great poverty, the mother remains bewildered by her loss until her death. The author's admiration for her strength is troubled by memories of her incorrigible sadness. She identifies with the mother's harsh childhood, and laments the prejudice and bigotry she encountered as a young woman. Dominant and yet broken, she is an ambivalent figure for both the child and the older self: 'She was myself, yet both less and more than myself. Her force and colour intrigued me. I spent as much of my time trying to figure her out as I spent trying to get away from her influence' (p. 160).

The ambivalence she generates resonates in an implicit sub-text. On one hand, the father is a longed-for figure; he is associated with his homeland, Walwa, which to the children is 'little short of para-dise'. Whereas the city is perceived as 'cheap, tinny and narrow', the country is 'deep and rich with a significant expansiveness' (p. 33). The father's identity is merged in the country where he grew up, which is seen as the children's rightful home. At Clifton Hill in Melbourne, on the other hand, they are in exile. Even the rigidities of the mother's personality soften in the country as she loses some of the anxieties which preoccupy her in the city. The father's absence is perceived as a presence, even a sexual presence, for the mother is seen as incom-plete, as are some of her widowed or deserted relations. Losing her husband and becoming dependent on the cold charity of a war pension, the mother has been caught in the unjust system which she entered at birth and the narrator shares her anger at 'Them': 'One understood from earliest childhood who "They" were: the powerful, the wealthy, the government, the employers, land-owners' (p. 57).

On the other hand, there are more equivocal notes undercutting the narrator's received view of both Walwa and the father. There are fears that had the father returned, he might have been a less likeable, changed, even violent father. Other fathers, some of whom belong to Walwa, are highly unpleasant: Old Man Hunt is a drunken father who frightens his children for fun; the children's paternal grandfather is an improvident drunkard, a murderous bully with incestuous pro-clivities; an aunt is deserted by a philandering husband and left with three young children; a neighbour preys on the young girls that his wife 'adopts' and prostitutes. The families on both sides of the childhood home have regular orgies of violence, and 'bad men' trouble the children's journeys to school. Whereas men have some amusements and a lighter work-load, women endure lives of unre-lieved drudgery, while the church affirms their disparate burdens and conditions the children in sexist attitudes. Just as the father becomes equivocal, Walwa the place is undercut with more specific accounts of vindictive relationships and unpleasant events. On one hand the story is fuelled with resentment of the fathers who control the social, political and religious systems; on the other by resentment of a personally fatherless destiny. And both have their root in an ambiva-lent relationship with the mother. Disarmingly, the narrator partly admits her ambivalence and allows it remain unresolved:

I allowed my work-worn mother nothing, never giving an inch in my need to dominate and destroy her individuality by binding her to me at the very same time as, paradoxically, I wanted to free her from her dark sorrow and her hard life. These irreconcilable needs and desires were not to leave me until she was killed; and, as I grew older, they were to be joined by my own need to free myself from her at the very same time as I turned to her for support and sustenance. (pp. 152–3)

7

Mother Images

'... it is difficult for me to write of my mother now ... I struggle to describe what it felt like to be her daughter, but I feel myself divided, slipping under her skin.'[1] Adrienne Rich's words are implicitly or explicitly echoed by many of the autobiographers studied here, for the idea of the mother is both powerful and ubiquitous in women's life-writing. Many autobiographers pick up the pen as mother, whether consciously assuming her authority, like Mary Gilmore, or passing on the experiences and wisdom of a lifetime as one of the duties of old age, like Sarah Musgrave, or in response to a daughter's demands that family stories be preserved, as Sarah Conigrave. Motherhood is frequently the rationale or excuse for writing and the mother's or daughter's voice the most congenial, so that the good-mother narrative is almost as common as the good-daughter one. In the nineteenth century one or other of the two positions *vis à vis* the reader was often as not adopted, although the two are really interdependent. In recreating her childhood, the autobiographer is both daughter and mother, duplicating many of the functions of the actual, historical mother, and becoming the mother's literary parent; in this retrospective relationship of the text it is the daughter who controls, or at least seeks to control the mother.

Recreating the self as daughter, drags in the idea of the mother in more profound ways still, however, and again Rich expresses the common phenomenon succinctly: 'The "childless woman" and the "mother" are a false polarity ... We are, none of us, "either" mothers "or" daughters; to our amazement, confusion, and greater complexity, we are both'.[2] If retrieving the self as daughter is one of the most common motives for women's stories of childhood, it is nearly always an ambiguous and ambivalent retrieval. 'You look at yourself in the mirror. And already you see your own mother there. And soon your daughter, a mother. Between the two, what are you?

What space is yours alone? In what frame must you contain yourself? And how to let your face show through, beyond all the masks?', asks Luce Iragaray.[3] Whether it evokes feelings which are painful or pleasant, exhilarating or cramping, bitter or nostalgic, and sometimes all by turns, the mother's identity with the female self is apparently inescapable. Some autobiographers make a virtue of the condition, writing the self in the form of a mother/daughter conversation, which is in turn or synchronically inscribed as a daughter's biography, as in Eugénie McNeil and Eugénie Crawford's autobiographies and Meg Stewart's *Autobiography of My Mother*. Others, like Cherry Cordner in *A Mavis Singing*, immerse the narrator in the storied selves of grandmothers, mother and even aunts, presenting the self as a variation on a theme, rather than autonomous individual. Autonomy, in fact, even for the justifiably angry daughter is not possible—or rather, least of all possible—as the autobiographies of Eliza Davies, Connie Ellement and Kathy Brown testify; the indifferent or rejecting mother is the hardest and most baffling of all internal parents, far more burdensome than the prematurely dead mother. But whether or not the conversation is openly acknowledged, many autobiographers imply an interchange with the mother, perhaps reflecting an inward interchange that is characteristic of women's attempts to know the self: 'We could play catch, you and I', reflects Iragaray. 'But who would see that what bounces between us are images? That you give them to me, and I to you without end. And that we don't need an object to throw back and forth to each other for this game to take place. I throw an image of you to you, you throw it back, catch it again'.[4]

At first sight, the identity of autobiographical self and mother indicates that mother/daughter relationships are typically perceived as more harmonious than father/daughter ones, but the pattern is more apparent than real. Anger, bitterness and guilt trouble this relationship as well and if the twentieth century daughter is often more open about her feelings, her nineteenth century predecessor may rely effectively on eloquent silence. For it is the mother who frequently binds the feet of her daughter in obedience to social law, as it is the mother who consciously and unconsciously educates her daughter in the duties of nurturing and self-sacrifice. Even if her lessons are silent, the mother instructs and burdens her daughter with her powerlessness. While on one hand a figure of enormous emotional power, usually the primary emotional power in a child's life, on the other hand, the mother is invariably and soon exposed as socially powerless. As Sara Ruddick comments: 'Children confront and rely upon a powerful maternal presence only to watch her become the powerless woman in front of the father, the teacher, the doctor, the judge, the landlord—the world'.[5] Confronting a mother's powerlessness and chafing under her education in obedience are probably the most common of the negative experiences of mothering recorded in these narratives.

Once again Miles Franklin's texts are archetypal. In *My Brilliant Career* where the father's drunken mismanagement is presented as the main cause of the family's sufferings, the mother's delimiting role is displaced to the margins. Overburdened and understandably irritable, the mother is experienced as a positional, rather than an individual figure. It is true that Sybylla has an uneasy relationship with her and is expelled from Caddagat at her fiat, a betrayal which is condoned by her grandmother and Aunt Helen, but the mother/ daughter bond is an unexplored given of the situation. In *My Career Goes Bung*[6] the relationship is central.

The mother of this autobiographical novel is a far more formidable individual. A remarkably capable woman, whose achievements as housekeeper and amateur doctor are legendary in the district, she is acknowledged to be 'perfect' by both daughter and husband. Although she fits the parts of lady with practised ease, dispensing circumspect small talk as required, she is invariably outspoken within the family. Here she makes no bones about her resentment at being 'dragged in the backwash of man's mismanagement' (p. 20). Regarding herself as cursed with an impractical husband and a feckless daughter, she is consistently cynical about men and women's lot. Her cynicism is untouched by ideas of revolution, however, and indeed much of her practicality consists of dogged acceptance of the status quo. Her 'common sense' lectures on submission to the female yoke settle on her daughter's spirits like 'a dead, dank gloom'. It is the mother's voice which holds the stage in this second picture of Possum Gully; the sympathetic father in the wings may share some of his daughter's dreams but her experience makes his voice more and more irrelevant. Protest as she may, Sybylla instinctively accedes to her mother's views that protest is useless.

Denied the management role which would have challenged her skills, this mother exerts herself in managing her daughter. Dreams and ambitions are carefully scoured. '"What a waste!"', is her comment on the ream of paper which is to become *My Brilliant Career*, and both acting and piano-playing are similarly dismissed:

> there was no appeal against Ma. She disabused my mind of any notion that I could go on the stage. She ridiculed my every feature and contour. Ma believes in finishing things. She says it is a sign of a weak mind to begin things and leave them half done. Ma has no weakness of mind. She always finishes the hardest task. She finished me to squashation like a sucked gooseberry. I often longed for death or a nunnery as an escape from my depressing lack of desirable attributes. (p. 44)

According to the mother, circumspection and tractability are necessary to snare a suitable husband, and under present circumstances marriage is the only destiny for a girl; but it is a poor destiny at best, soured by men's sexual demands and unwanted children, for sex is presented as the first of the sequence of disappointments that marriage inevitably brings.

The unconscious revenge underlying her systematic depression of her daughter is half-perceived by Sybylla. On one hand, she grants the mother a full measure of her self-righteousness, on the other she undercuts it by comically exposing her inconsistencies. If the mother adopts a posture of religious fatalism, she fails to recognize that her God is the apex of the patriarchy she deplores. Her martyrdom to housework is more than slightly sado-masochistic. Hard work and worry have driven the piano-playing out of her and she rejects her daughter's alternative of driving out dullness with the piano; preferring spotless floors and windows, she is determined to enslave her daughter as well as herself: 'My thumping on the piano irritated her as a love of idleness, and I had to desist' (p. 48). She is also briefly perceived as re-enacting the role of scathing critic practised by *her* mother: 'Ma was passing on this piece of heredity' (p. 100). Sybylla claims that her mother lacks the egotism which drives herself and her father but the novel's implied narrator allows the mother's corrosive resentment to emerge at every point. It deadens every initiative and stifles every hope. Writing her autobiography grants Sybylla a brief interlude of authority, but the mother's gloomy predictions as to its consequences are fulfilled.

Comedy is the only vehicle for such a destructive mother, but laughter fails finally to disarm her, for guilt and pity are emotions not easily deflected and it is the mother's disgrace which most troubles Sybylla in the aftermath to the publication of *My Brilliant Career*:

I was in an agony of disgrace. I did not sleep that night. I lay awake shivering with ignominy and listening to the mopokes and plovers. I did not mind what people thought or were so silly as to mis-think about me, it was Ma. To have brought disgrace upon her and to be compelled to remain there and be tied to it in 'Possum Gully was a deadly tribulation. (p. 61)

Thus intellectual dissent is not accompanied by emotional dissent, nor can comedy obscure the fact that the older Sybylla comes to share her mother's cynicism. 'More and more I understand Ma' is a refrain that occurs with increasing frequency in the Sydney section of the novel. If the Sybylla of *My Career Goes Bung* begins as the older, more fatalistic narrator of the close of *My Brilliant Career*, she completes her cycle as dream-shorn, middle-aged woman, an echo of the mother she feared becoming. As in the earlier autobiography, her journey is a circular one, no more than an escapade from Possum Gully, the place of the mother's martyrdom and the self's reality. Back there, the 'withering actuality' of the mother's dismissal of her Sydney career exposes it as the nebulous dream it was from the beginning: 'I sat amid the debris of hopes and expectations—only nebulous ones it is true, but all that I had—and I had to grope my way out'. Franklin's texts implicitly illuminate the way 'the mother stands for the victim in ourselves, the unfree woman, the martyr'.[7]

Amie Livingstone Stirling's *Memories of an Australian Childhood 1880–1900*[8] explores a contemporaneous childhood from the perspective of late middle-age. A sensitive rediscovery of a mother's influence, this autobiography attempts to recapture the sharp, dramatic impressions of the child, with a minimum of retrospective comment. But memory is 'a great artist', making the recollection of life both 'a work of art and an unfaithful record'[9] and Stirling's account rapidly shapes itself into story; if the child-self, like David Copperfield, makes no more provision for growing older than for growing younger, the reflective older narrator is preoccupied with change and endings. Inward events soon assume more significance than outer ones and there are signs that the autobiographical act has been a surprising journey for this writer and that some of its discoveries are not fully assimilated. Certain integrating themes are partly embedded in a distracting clutter of impressions, and certain intriguing sequences of images and incidents, which a more self-conscious writer would have teased out, are allowed to remain tentative and half-posed.

The daughter of James Stirling, Government Geologist of Victoria at the turn of the century and a man of some stature, and Elizabeth Reid, a botanist and painter, the narrator enjoys one of those romantic bush childhoods which figure frequently in these autobiographies as never-to-be-forgotten experiences. Her first memories are of Omeo in the Australian Alps, where her father was Lands' Officer. As beautiful as it is wild, Omeo is perceived as a sacred place: it is said to be named by Chinese settlers after one of their sacred mountains, it is the home of the Biblical Manna tree, 'probably the only specimen of its kind in the world', and fossils found in the area reveal that it has once known deep-sea monsters. Both parents possess the area in that they are involved in discovering and naming its plants and minerals and even the children are granted special status, corresponding on their own behalf with Baron von Mueller and winning the names 'Geology' and 'Botany'. The father is far more prominent than the mother, but the mother belongs to Omeo in more deep-rooted ways: 'I knew, even then, that the people of Omeo loved my mother. We felt it wherever we went . . . Father was loved too, but in a different way. He was popular with everyone, and the men were proud of his scientific attainments . . . he could sing all sorts of songs, grave and gay; and he had a penchant for telling good stories' (p. 49). When the narrator is seven and the family leaves for Melbourne, she is profoundly conscious of her mother's silent grief and retrospectively aware that for her, too, the move is reductive:

'Little did I know then that I was leaving the greatest freedom I would ever know, the freedom of the primeval forest, of untamed plant and animal life, of the vast silence of snow-covered mountains' (p. 50).

The parents could hardly be more dissimilar as personalities. Ebullient and gregarious, the father is brimming with ideas and intellectual enthusiasm. The cause of Science claims a great deal of his attention, but he has time for other causes, such as the brotherhood of man and the equality of the sexes. The narrator's juxtaposition of the two is not intended to be ironic in this unconsciously revealing narrative. The mother is outwardly unemotional, laughing rarely and crying only once in her daughter's memory; dignified and quietly discriminating, she is also religious and obedient to social convention. There are indications that her own work and selfless support, which have made the father's achievements possible, are taken for granted. Despite his advanced views on equality, the father autocratically disposes his family and, unlike his wife, enjoys a life of prominence and independence. Later, he even escapes the money worries, which are a constant preoccupation for the overburdened mother. Nothing reveals their difference more than their naming of the Stirling children. The narrator's mother had wanted Eleanor for her after her own mother but she is called Amie, in honour of the father's belief in human brotherhood, and Livingstone, after the 'intrepid explorer and friend of all the coloured brothers'. Her elder brother, Victor, is named after Victor Hugo, whose works the father was reading at the time, and two younger brothers receive Kosciusko Omeo and Australix Alpinae respectively, once again evading the family names preferred by their mother.

The father is no Sam Pollit, however; genuinely interested in his daughter's development, he includes her in the daily lessons in natural history, encourages her skills and saves her from the sewing instruction her mother regards as proper. Dressed like a boy and granted a boy's physical freedom, she is, for a while, her brother Victor's equal. Victor soon attempts to destroy that equality, though, in his own aggressive struggle for differentiation, frequently pouring scorn on her achievements and ambitions. An incident in which he tortures and executes her favourite doll symbolizes his inclinations, however unconscious. His winter with a tribe of Aborigines, after the father absent-mindedly leaves him behind on a trip into the wilderness, results in the first of the several separations which this narrator is to suffer. Although his absence has been deeply felt, his arrival is a bitter disappointment; grown taller and more patronising, he boasts of the exclusively male skills he has acquired. The experience leaves the narrator with the feeling that 'this business of being a girl was not right somehow', however persuasive the father's rhetoric on equality.

But there are other more subtle influences at work. Sensitive to the mother's moods and especially to her silent eloquence, Amie is subject to a kind of porous learning, in which she is quietly taught to curb her assertive impulses, to study the feelings of others and to foster a nurturing self-image. If she provokes laughter in certain good-humoured men by her irreverent quips and ridicule, she also learns that ridicule is an unfeeling act, which fails to acknowledge her own implication in frail humanity. The father's ideas are exhilarating, but she is conscious of an unspoken complicity between herself and the mother, which is ultimately more revealing of the real, gendered world. There is great excitement when the father buys a new micro-scope, but the child is moved by the mother's silent concern that the purchase represents a year's salary. Absorbed in Science, the father fails to notice that his preoccupation cramps the mother's spirit, providing her with insoluble economic problems and an uncongenial environment. Like Ernie in *The Man Who Loved Children*, the child is appalled to discover that her mother has sold some of the jewellery which belonged to the first years of her marriage. Thus in her implicit posture of sad stoicism, the mother teaches that woman's experience is confined and vulnerable, reactive to the man's flamboyant destiny. The stories of her grandmothers, women who are quite dissimilar in temperament, predict the same pattern; married young and widowed early, they have both suffered from the recklessness of their menfolk. Emotionally stronger than men, women are perceived as wholly confined in their orbit.

One particular incident expresses the child's ambivalent lessons. Filling in time before a promised outing, Amie and a brother practise walking the plank; inevitably, her brother tumbles into the water and is rescued by onlookers. The mother's reaction, to scold and punish her daughter, is deeply puzzling:

Being a girl, I could not do all the things I wanted to do; I could not go to bat unless they were a boy short on the team; I could not be an engine driver or a sailor; but if one of my brothers did anything stupid, I could be blamed, because I was a girl and should know better. It was very difficult to understand. (p. 60)

This specific lesson in gender difference is succeeded by a more subtle education in female relatedness and acceptance versus male adven-ture and aggression. Relenting from her severity, the mother takes the two children to the bluff, where they can watch the sailing ships. The bluff is dominated by the large granite gravestones of two un-named shipwrecked sailors, which are the subject of one of the mother's poems. The sad beauty of the poem makes Amie want to cry, until she remembers Victor's pronouncement that 'only silly girls cried'. Victor had recently been teaching her to endure pain by inflicting various forms of physical torture adopted from his reading of Fenimore Cooper. It is typical of this narrator that she allows the suggestiveness of this sequence of incidents and reflections to answer for itself; selection and juxtaposition are interpretation enough.

The sea plays a major role in this narrative, both literally and figuratively. As the background to the children's lives at Melbourne and even more so during an extended stay at Western Port Bay, it represents beauty, danger, excitement and variety. The child's first sight of the sea, significantly granted by the father, is one of the most intense in her experience, and she is enthralled by a visit to the docks: 'I now knew that I had found my life: I would be a sailor and go on a ship to far-off lands' (p. 59). When she is convalescing from a severe illness, the sea plays a part in her recovery of health and on several subsequent occasions she intrepidly sets out in a boat, either alone or with her brothers, while on four occasions, her life is seriously threatened by the sea.

Although this narrative's symbolism is understated, it is not a distortion to suggest that the sea and its mythology become associated with the young girl's ambivalent inner life. Many of the human suggestions traditionally evoked by the sea are here—wildness, mystery, solitude, fruitfulness, adventure, excitement, danger and death. In one curious incident in which she is eventually isolated in a flood, like a sea-bird on a post, she compares her frail vessel to 'the boat of Charon drifting on the waters of the river Styx' (p. 63). At another point, she attempts to draw the associations together into a reflection on the meaning of death. Running along the shore and 'glorying' in the waves 'dashing' on the rocks and the 'flight of the sea-birds', she comes across a dead bird, which cuts short her mood of exhilaration. 'I thought of my mother and father. Would they too end like this bird?' Pondering her parents' different beliefs, she develops a pantheistic belief of her own, which unites the protective theology of her mother and the freedom of her father's rationalism: 'I knew that I was part of God's plan, that I was wind and sea and sky and cloud and grass and water' (p. 78).

This level of controlled self-consciousness is rare in this narrative, though, and indeed the text becomes increasingly responsive to subconscious or semi-submerged forces as the memory of the mother's early death begins to impinge. This occurs when Amie is fifteen and at the end of the seventh chapter, 'Life in Melbourne'. The death itself, which is reported with a minimum of description, is preceded by a lengthy passage, praising the father's achievements and acknowledging the mother's role in his success. It is virtually the author's farewell to both her parents, for from this point the father is also lost to her. His speedy remarriage to a dominating, neurotic woman effectively erodes his power as fostering, inspiring parent. Incapable of controlling his new wife, he is perceived from this point as weak and even bumbling; even his free pursuit of Science is now curtailed. Oddly, a literal event anticipates the break in the relationship. A few days before the mother's death, the narrator herself is nearly drowned at Lorne; the father's reaction to the news is strangely indifferent, a forecast of his future betrayal.

Chapter 9, 'Living with a Stepmother', is a reliving of dark, psychic experience. Some reviewers have commented that the narrator's stepmother is too much the wicked stepmother of fairy tale, which is to miss the interesting aspects of the analogy, for however unpleasant this individual in real life, the selectiveness of Stirling's account reveals the psychic compulsions of its retelling. As usurping figure, the stepmother is perceived as the reverse of the real mother in every respect and her existence threatens not only the memory of the mother but the daughter's appropriation of her mother as her self. After her mother's death, for instance, Amie describes herself as 'dead inside' and large stretches of time are erased from memory. Even before the stepmother arrives, the mere announcement of the engagement is enough to darken the sun: 'Everything went dark; it seemed as if a cloud was over the garden'. The new wife's visit to the mother's sacred place, Omeo, is a desecration, tarnishing the father's relationships there, while she seems bent on trampling on all her predecessor's household gods. Meanwhile, a curious pattern, probably unnoticed by the narrator, establishes a series of strong, supportive women, in contrast to the sequence of unpleasant, narrow women of the narrative's first half; it is as if the mother's protective genius survives her death and is refracted in her relations and friends. Significantly, it is the stepmother's explicit attack on the memory of Amie's mother that inspires Amie's final flight from home. Salvaging the few possessions of her mother not appropriated by the usurper, she runs away to her aunts. The separation from home repeats the previous separations, from Victor, Omeo, father and mother. It is also the most final, including in its scope the separation from country which concludes the book.

The experience of indivisibility with the mother and the countervailing need to separate is also apparent in twentieth century childhoods. 'And the one doesn't stir without the other. But we do not move together. When the one of us comes into the world, the other goes underground. When the one carries life, the other dies';[10] Iragaray's description of the ambivalent tug between mother and daughter seems to be a continuing experience. Lark, the narrator of Glenda Adams's *Lies and Stories*, shares with her mother's younger self a yearning for overseas, even as she is propelled into a sharper need to leave by her depressing, suburban narrowness. Stella Bowen recalls that her mother 'was a simple person whom it would have been easy to make happy', provided one were willing to fulfil her limited expectations: 'my mother's daughter could never have become a golf champion—or even, it seemed, a painter!'[11] Barbara Pepworth's narrator resents her mother's 'conditional love', dependent on her achieving: 'I hated performing but I couldn't help it. I loved being loved. I loved being loved but I also hated it. I hated being loved because I know what it means, I know my mother's terms'.[12] The narrator of Elizabeth Riley's *All That False Instruction* angrily relives a 1950s childhood and the effects of a mother's frustrated ambitions and partiality for a male sibling; the unresolved resentment spills out in expletives: 'she got over her pride bloody fast but it did flash on for a day or so, sometimes. Like sunshine. Like love. Surrogate, but good enough. So I tried, thirsted for the teachers' questions, longed for the exams that proved me top, knew damned near everything'.[13] Mature understanding of her mother's emotional deprivations, however, ultimately unites her in near-complicity of feeling. Gail Morgan's Lucy is torn between pity and rejection:

Lucy felt that her mother, in spite of a redoubtable profile, was to be pitied. She was vulnerable, reacting to people as if they were about to hit her. And just as she seemed to love her daughter, she spent much of her time teaching her how to minister to failure.[14]

In Jennifer Dabbs's *Beyond Redemption*,[15] an autobiographical novel about growing up in the 1940s and 1950s, the struggle with the mother-figure, which is also a struggle with a repressive religion, is clearly unresolved, even though the narrator is consistently dismissive. This narrative shares the confession's tone of special pleading, but it is more a denunciation than a confession for the narrator confronts her arraigned characters with the rhetoric of a court-room prosecutor, allowing them little life beyond their forensic function. The book's fictional status cannot disguise the pressure of an autobiographical motive nor the fact that Dabbs's narrator is preoccupied with justifying a lingering bitterness, for she has a simple rhetorical purpose, which is to reverse the crude moral polarities of her childhood.

The villain of her story is a primly conventional mother, dominated by her Irish-Catholic family and their primitive faith. Retiring and even colourless, this mother is nevertheless a powerful emotional figure, whose wickedness is only fully confronted at the narrative's close. The cast is made up of familiar types: on the enemy side there is the Irish-Catholic Clancy family, made up of a clutch of puritanical aunts and headed by the revered maternal grandmother, hovering on the edge of senility. Husbands are ineffective figures, whether evasively finding pleasure in extra-family male pursuits like Uncle Bernie, or literally succumbing to a wife's malevolence like Uncle Pat, who dies of tuberculosis after being relegated to sleep on the verandah. The Clancy sideboard guards the photographs of other dead men; one, a riotous, improvident grandfather, fortunately dead, and a son, killed in the First World War and now no more than a pious memory. For a time the narrator's father, away at the second war, threatens to become part of the collection, but he returns to join the meagre ranks of anti-Clancy sympathizers. Frequently associated with all that is life-affirming and natural, he is a vaguely reassuring figure who largely fails to reassure in this maternal environment. He is, of course, excluded by his different religion and he is rendered doubly helpless by the 'mothers' at school, the nuns whose religion, interpreted literally by the children, arouses confused feelings of guilt and inadequacy. A more effective ally is Hannah, a good-time girl, who resists the attempts of the Clancys to appropriate her by working at the Tivoli and marrying at a registry office. If the father is ultimately alienated from his wife and daughter by a display of female vengeance, Hannah is a more robust supporter. In this simple drama of opposites, even Melbourne and Sydney have polarized roles, the former expressing the drabness of Clancy existence, the latter the warmth and vitality of Clancy-free life. The beach at Melbourne confronts a 'sluggish sea' and is tainted by the smell of seaweed, but it recalls the happier time before the father left for the war: 'I could recall the sensation of my father's arms around me and his large hands holding me safe in the waves of another beach' (p. 4).

The description of the small child's introduction to the Clancy ménage typifies the emotional weightings which skew this narrative. The mother's attempts to clean the gritty child prefigure the wrenchings and manipulations, which will be a feature of her Irish-Catholic existence:

Mother tried to polish me up a bit by spitting on her hanky and wiping the night's soot from my eyes, nose and ears, raked her comb through my tangled hair, then unable to contain herself for another minute, she tugged at the little wrought iron gate, ran up the steps to the narrow black and white tiled verandah and rang the doorbell. (pp. 2–3)

The appearance of the grandmother, a 'ghostly figure' in the 'gloomy passageway', brings into play the new set of relationships—the child turned towards the mother, who is turned towards *her* mother, largely ignoring the child. Meanwhile, a closer inspection of the grandmother reveals her to be an embodiment of the Clancy life-denying spirit:

My eyes were fixed on my grandmother's feet. She was wearing slippers with holes cut out of the sides, thick stockings wrinkled around her ankles and she was dressed from head to toe in a drab coloured dress. Her eyes were set back deep in their sockets and the bones of her face showed sharply through yellowish, papery skin. (p. 3)

Her predictable comments on her granddaughter's anomalous appearance anticipate the child's position in this repressive household. Grandma Clancy never emerges as more than symbol. Although she is described at one point as sitting 'in her corner like a spider in a web, watchful and still', her malevolence is never concretely established, and she soon degenerates into an inert burden, imposing unnecessary sacrifices on her daughters:

Mother still adored Grandma and I couldn't understand how she could love someone so old, who didn't even know who was who anymore, got everyone's names mixed up and had to have Father Shannon bring Communion to her at home. She was too disruptive at Mass ... I wondered how there could be a soul ... when the brain was finished? (pp. 171–2).

Curiously, there is no attempt to distance the older narrator from the child's cruelty here. Yet there are indications that the hostility directed at the grandmother is not specifically personal, but rather a displaced hostility, reflecting the narrator's anger versus the mother. Less intimately known and physically repellent, the grandmother carries the main burden of odium for the Clancy way. It is even possible that her helpless senility does service for a wished-for helplessness in the mother. As Jane Flax comments, women are slow to express anger against the mother, and 'tend to feel guilty that they are somehow betraying their mother in the attempt to resolve and terminate the symbiotic tie'.[16]

The mother of this narrative is charged with restricting her daughter's opportunities, imposing feelings of guilt and shame and even threatening her life by consenting to the primitive surgical practices of a hospital of the right religious persuasion. On one hand, she is her daughter's only guide to her potential as woman. As Sara Ruddick has observed: 'it is because we are daughters that we early receive maternal love with special attention to its implications for our bodies, our passions and our ambitions. We are alert to the values and costs of maternal practices whether we are determined to engage in them or avoid them'.[17] Given her peculiar religious weighting in both family and community, this mother is especially powerful. On the other hand, she refuses the responsibility of mature mothering, preferring the role of good Catholic daughter. The years in Sydney are for her an exile for she only knows herself as daughter. Living in Sydney '"just wasn't right. We'd both be much better off in Melbourne. With the family. Where we belonged"' (p. 1). What is more, she cannot know her child as individual, only as a replica of her ideal self, a good Catholic daughter. An example of the hyper-symbiotic mother, described by Chodorov, she sees her daughter as a narcissistic extension or double of herself, and vainly expects the same infantile dependence as she displays towards her mother. And it is partly this expectation that makes her so alarming; Judith Gardiner points out that the 'mother-villain is ... frightening because she is what the daughter fears to become and what her infantile identifications predispose her to become. One way in which the author may dispose of this fear is by rendering the mother so repulsive or ridiculous that the reader must reject her as her fictional daughter does'.[18] In this instance, the grandmother is repulsive as a love-object, the mother is ridiculous in her love and the relationship is thus deprived of its coercive power. Thus, the narrator of this novel is at once angrily disappointed in her powerless mother and resentful of her powerful will. If her perception of the grandmother appears emotionally distorted, the distortion is authentic as an image of this set of malformed relationships.

In the dramatic conclusion to the story, the narrator chooses a subtle revenge by selecting a lover who is the polar opposite of the Clancy way and relates to the Italian inheritance she derives from her father. Furthermore, by threatening the mother with her own illicit maternity, she chooses the powerful female weapons of her particular environment. The mother's reaction is a naked exposure of her own neurotic urge to be the good daughter, but the narrator's revenge also creates a gulf between herself and the father. The Clancys appear, at least temporarily, to have won: 'There was nowhere for me to go; except back into the house. I knelt down in the loungeroom, head suitably bowed as befitted a humble penitent' (p. 258).

Beyond Redemption deals with the mother's ambivalent power in terms of moral absolutes, but other narrators appear intent on the paradoxical mission of re-experiencing ambivalence from an impartial retrospective. Two particularly fine rediscoveries of the mother, which measure the child's immediate impressions by the reflections of maturity, are Rose Lindsay's *Ma and Pa* and Nene Gare's *A House with Verandahs*.[19]

Gare's study of an Adelaide childhood between the wars is as sensitive as it is unpretentious. The supple, conversational style, which is capable of modulating a range of tones from comedy to pathos, is the perfect vehicle for the author's naïvely wise narrator. Presented as a younger, less street-wise sister, she is both an ironic observer and the object of her own irony since she is granted the partial status of outsider by her position in the family. While the attitudes of her older sisters and brothers, aunts, uncles, neighbours and friends are inevitably part of her landscape of opinion, she is also capable of independent insight; both sheltered and independent, solitary and crowded, she relies heavily on her own observations and experience. Gare also skilfully interweaves drama and scene, often allowing conversations, gestures, expressions to speak for themselves and she has a particularly discerning eye for an individual's moment of dramatic self-expression, or for the gesture which registers emotional nuance more tellingly than words. When Aunt Liz grows impatient thinking of all the foolhardy things her brother has done 'her needle shot in and out of her mending like a swift and shining sword'. Her own well-stocked garden is an implicit criticism of her brother's mix of jungle and junk yard:

'Snaps!' Aunt Liz called . . . 'I've brought you some of my snaps', she would call down our passage when she came to visit, and would push the flowers ahead of her like some kind of admission ticket . . . Aunt Liz always smiled broadly at Mother's children but her eyes never followed suit. (p. 54)

The narrative opens with a mental image of the mother, sitting beneath the well-loved cooking-apple tree in the backyard, which the family at the time rented for a shilling a month:

As usual Mother's glasses are on crooked; they have been sat on and the frames are bent. She is peering intently at the hem of my blue and white gingham dress as she lays down a line of tiny stitches. I could have done this job but it is a way of getting Mother to oneself. While she is working for you she is yours, and there are so many of us to share her. We never feel we get enough; we are always fighting and scrambling around telling her what has happened to us during our days, claiming her ears, her hands, her eyes, and if she sits, her lap. (p. 1)

The passage rehearses one of the book's unifying themes, the narrator's fear of losing the mother. When Aunt Liz indicates that seven children is a 'sinful indulgence', she resents the implied relegation to limbo: 'I had to be wanted . . . I envied the older ones. They were safe' (p. 55). The birth of another child, which results in a stay with relations, also inspires fear that she may have been given away; the odd one, too young to be grouped with the older girls and too old for the younger children, she may be the dispensable hyphen between. A dress sewn by the mother reassures her: 'All round the hem I saw her smallest finest stitches, like little bits of herself that she was sending to me' (p. 61). And a visit to see mother and baby is an epiphany of love: 'She reached out her hand to me and I felt loved and understood and forgiven all in one. Alongside her, on another pillow, lay the baby. My own personal baby whom I was determined to take charge of the minute I was allowed home' (p. 62).

The mother is the salient planet in this child's small cosmos and the child is acutely sensitive to changes in the maternal atmosphere. Watching her face, learning her gestures, responding to her tone of voice, the child absorbs knowledge of the mother at the subliminal, preverbal level that Adrienne Rich has described.[20] Not only is her growth in self-knowledge dependent primarily on her understanding of the mother, but the education she receives from siblings and others is nearly always related back to the primary relationship. As the description of her response to the new baby implies, identity with the mother and female identity are interdependent; and female identity implies relationship. Chodorov's observations on female development as building upon the 'primary sense of oneness and identification with [the] mother'[21] are particularly relevant to this narrative. For this narrator, being like the mother necessarily implies marriage, and much of her education is stimulated by watching the mother/father relationship and other male/female alliances.

The father of this narrative is a colourful figure, who makes a virtue of improvidence; he is a Peter Pan in the commercial world, who has frequently changed occupations on the grounds of principled avoiding of ruts. Oblivious to appearances, he is expressed by the ramshackle house he rents, with its sagging, bulging, cracked walls, spilling a 'porridge of coarse sandy mortar mixed with pebbles'. For the mother, the inconveniences of the house are a daily purgatory, and all the children are aware of her alternative ideal house, a house with verandahs. On the narrator's walks, she keeps a look out for one that measures up: 'If I found one, I would feel as elated as if I had actually purchased it and placed the deeds in her lap' (p. 19).

But the house is also an expression of the love that unites the parents and a measure of the mother's love in particular. For the father is attached to it in a child-like way and numerous attempts to dislodge him fail, largely because the mother always defers to his feelings. The bond between the parents is a tangible presence in the family, even though in many ways the father is the mother's eldest and most important child. Affectionate, demanding, uninhibited, unworldly and charming, he has the child's power to evoke protection. Worrying upsets him, so the mother struggles along as best she may; minor borrowings and gifts of food and clothes from relatives and neighbours eke out the small budget. The house, with its stinking rubbish heap, piebald lawn, outside lavatory negotiated via the stable, external water supply, inadequate drains and gaping walls, testifies to his impracticality. It is also a generous, prodigal household, finding a place for a motherless niece, entertaining numerous visitors, providing a refuge for unhappy aunts, feeding numbers of guests, whether adults or children.

The part-adult, part-childish relationship of the parents is well expressed in the description of the father's weekly bath:

Dad enjoyed his bath and he bathed as he washed, like a grampus, heaving and splashing so that the water sucked and plopped about him as if he had been a ship. During the bathing he conversed with Mother in the kitchen where she was standing guard.

'Coming in to do my back old girl?'

'In a minute.'

'What about getting me the soap? I think it's under the bath.'

'Do be quiet Adam. And why do you splash like that? You've wet your clean towel and there's water everywhere.'

'Of course there is. That's what a bathroom's for, isn't it?' (p. 17)

The sexual overtones are instinctively absorbed by the child; the parents' eyes exchange secrets and the mother is described as proud of her husband's physique, his broad shoulders, flat stomach and 'well-shaped legs which flashed whitely' as he made his way to the bath.

The strong love between the parents and its unequal costs partly inspire and partly baffle the child-observer. It is a difficult mix, in which it is hard to say who is protected and who is protector; like a familiar puzzled facial expression of the mother's, which may turn out to be either laughter or tears, it tugs at the child's deepest emotions: 'Mother believed in love and showing it and so did my father. Dad never passed Mother in the house without stopping to give her a hug or to ask her, "All right, old girl?" Mother always said "Yes". She almost believed it too and Dad certainly did' (p. 83). Retrospectively, the narrator concludes that this love was made up of great tolerance and emotional confidence in each other. The mother never blames the father for his numerous business failures, only his associates; the father unquestioningly condones the mother's decisions about the family.

Interestingly, the disadvantages of the father's eccentricities and the mother's compliance are not glossed over. The children are often conscious that they lack the amenities of other children; decent clothes are a rarity, dental care is haphazard, school books have to be borrowed, money for music lessons and art school runs out, some key aspects of education are scamped and talents remain untapped: 'one did not mention ambitions—there might be laughter'. At the same time, external and even internal criticisms are allowed a place as aunts, uncles, neighbours, growing siblings express more jaundiced views of the family's economy. The situation seems ripe for bitterness, but in this case transcendent concerns firmly shift what is negative to the picture's edges.

Constantly refining, comparing, and observing other family relationships, the growing child carefully distils the essence of her parents' education. In this process the house with its gaping walls plays a major if understated figurative role. Walls and boundaries, in fact, are central to this narrative, which is concerned with ways of owning, sharing and giving. A key chapter, which precedes the most extended interpretation of the parents' relationship, deals with the children's loss of a near-opportunity to acquire a better house. The conviction of a better future revives the mother's youth: 'her eyes . . . shone and glowed. She had never doubted that some day she would get her house' (pp. 70–1). The scene in which the father scotches the project is a painful one, sensitively expressed according to the child's alert observation: '[Mother] was leaning on her rolling pin as if she needed to, and she was pale but her eyes were the darkest blue I'd ever seen them' (p. 75). At the time, none of the disappointed children understands and their hostility towards the father takes fire, until it is effectively quenched by his irresistible charm.

Later still, the father's refusal to live in the world of owning and his eccentric assumption that everyone shares his own natural generosity, lead to more serious consequences. He turns down a generous offer to purchase the half-acre of land he had rented at a peppercorn rental, believing that longevity of possession has made it his. After the land is sold to another, the family's garden is turned into a small, square gaol. The 'dear old apple tree', the quince, almonds and grapes are ploughed under, and a high brick wall prevents the afternoon sun from striking the soil. 'Mother often wiped her eyes when she thought nobody was looking. It was miserable' (p. 110). Surveyors discover that the stable wall intrudes into the neighbouring land and it is demolished. Shortly afterwards, the father is drawn into a petty dispute with a brother-in-law about the ownership of the 'family' piano and again loses possession.

The death of Aunt Liz seems set to be another demonstration of his refusal to think about money. Subtle changes are in process, however. Supported by her daughters, the mother is firm about receiving a rightful share under the will. For the narrator too the death provides an opportunity. If her previous attempts to fill the old house's cracks have failed, she is granted an opportunity to give her mother the house with verandahs, when she remembers the family cottage carefully preserved by Aunt Liz. As her father's childhood home, it represents a return to origins which satisfies his deepest needs: 'As often happened with me I seemed to have struck gold without having done any really thorough fossicking' (p. 143).

In all this latter section of the text, the association between walls and boundaries and attitudes of owning and being owned, giving and taking is strongly marked. The father's attractive generosity of spirit and love of freedom have unfree aspects and consequences; the mother's attractive tolerance, her permeable boundaries of self, have cramping implications. The child has to find a middle way between assertion and acquiescence, independence and dependence, and indeed there are indications that she has already discovered a different destiny and that marriage will not be her ultimate and only goal.

Rose Lindsay's story of her 1890s childhood in Sydney, *Ma and Pa*, has some affinities with Gare's autobiography. Once again the mother is the salient parent and her relationship with the father intrigues and baffles the child. This father is much more the reprobate, though, and the parents' marriage is both more intense and more unstable. Lindsay's narrator remains baffled and her story deliberately avoids conclusions, the structure of her narrative reflecting her tentative, piecemeal approach to her parents' truth; sketching in episodes, personalities and memories of places, she colours her canvas in an apparently random fashion, following only a roughly linear chronology and relying on the short, sharply etched scene and the pungently expressive conversation. Lindsay has a fine comic gift

and a Rabelaisian sense of fun, which may owe something to Norman
Lindsay, and she certainly shares, at least superficially, his perception
of the 'nineties. Not only is her social scene just as colourful as his but
the same types perambulate for the author's amusement: the wowser,
the wimpish husband with the nine-to-five occupation, the languorous maiden, the young buck on the make, the old roué, the dominant materfamilias, the irreverent schoolchildren, the sanctimonious
parson, the Sarah Gampish gossip. Like Norman Lindsay's, this
society is class-conscious, superficially genteel and preoccupied with
respectability, while sexual and other Dionysian energies seethe
below its surface. Certain incidents, especially those dealing with the
children's 'care' of their younger siblings, have the hard-boiled tone
of Lindsay's descriptions of his young larrikins in *Saturdee* and
Redheap; somewhat anomalous in this narrative, which is preoccupied with relatedness and betrayal, they may indicate the author's
intention to emulate her husband's style. The intimacy of Rose
Lindsay's ideal memory of her mother, on the other hand, which
introduces the book, underlines her individual emotional investment
in the 'nineties. It is also a perfect reflection of the autobiographical
impulse of this narrative—the child in pinafore and bare feet watching the mother, a vision in blue and gold, walk down a long stretch of
sunlit, sandy road, turning to wave a gloved hand in farewell.
Dressing up for an expedition to the city from the family home at
Longueville recurs frequently in *Ma and Pa*; an anticipation of
enjoyment and sometimes of more specific good fortune, it may also
signal a betrayal or a secret assignation, or be an attempt to uncover
or undo the betrayal of another. Ada, the eldest daughter, frequently
sets out on spuriously innocent missions and returns bearing gifts of
dubious origin; the mother on one occasion decks herself in unusually
elegant underwear before leaving on a similar mission, although
more usually she is setting out to retrieve her dissolute husband from
one of his numerous scrapes; the father invariably slips off to drown
his thirst. Waiting for the return of the absent one, listening for the
click of the gate which announces that he/she has returned after all, is
an even more familiar occupation.

Lindsay's mother is delightfully picturesque. She has the same
vitality and irreverent spirit of Laurie Lee's mother in *Cider with
Rosie*. Gossipy, clannish, earthy, curious, spontaneous, slightly disreputable and hugely generous, she accepts the arrival of her nine
children as if motherhood is a legal obligation. The early scenes
present her as the focus of the local life. The policeman, sent to
complain about the father's timber-gathering, stays to take off his
boots and confide his marital troubles; if the advice he receives has
disastrous consequences and he returns with a black eye, he obtains
substantial consolations. The postman, inspired to momentary vengeance by a dispute amongst the children in which his child was

worsted, is forced to return by his need for gossip. The butcher is a constant, curious visitor. His intentions are mildly dishonourable, although the entertainment value of the Soadys is enough to make their house a natural waterhole; regarding the father's rustic furniture and eccentric building activities with wonderment, he has a natural sympathy for the family's implicit subversiveness:

Ma liked the rose arch, and so did the butcher.

'I like walking through it,' he said to Ma, holding out a handful of steak like a bouquet, and curtseying with fingertip lift of his blue-and-white-striped apron.

'Go on with you and your antics,' Ma said, smiling, for the butcher was a humorist, in which his meat joined with much frivolity.

'Now, Fido, be quiet,' he would say to a string of sausages, as he sliced off the required number; or he would play pitch-and-toss with a piece of roast beef as he advanced, whistling a lively tune. Sleek and dark, his skin shone as if it had been rubbed with olive oil.

'He's one for the girls,' Ma said. (p. 18)

During the father's extended absences and after his ultimate betrayal, he is also one of the family's most loyal mainstays. The sexual undertones of the mother's relationship with the butcher are typical for sexual energy is perceived as an irrepressible force. One of the narrator's first memories is of her mother entertaining a male friend, who slips quietly off as the husband arrives; a mentally backward girl at school discovers that the dispensing of sexual favours can be a profitable business; the milk-boy suffers from a sexual drive that is uncontainable and a constant embarrassment to his watchful mother; Grandma Cotton's talk is centred on her own daughters' facility for unmarried pregnancy and on the downfalls of other 'maidens' in the district; Ada's apparently active sexual life is watched with fatalistic misgiving by the mother. The mother herself, of course, exudes sex as naturally as she breathes, and her ready tolerance is a part of her uninhibited earthiness.

If sex is perceived as a vitalist force, a colourful expression of individuality, it is also threatening and associated with selfishness and betrayal. For the child it is a mystery, underlying the shifting alliances of family life, resulting in suffering, both emotional and physical, associated above all with the shifty unreliability of the father. The older, narrating self retains the impression of mystery, to some extent. Relationships are interpreted from the outside, through the eyes of the wondering child, and motives remain unexplained; whatever further knowledge of events the narrator possesses is withheld and the impression of unpredictable activity is maintained. Some past, partly explained events still have a potent influence and certain individuals from the past reappear haphazardly, bearing powerful secrets which are never fully divulged. On one occasion, the child wakes to discover unusual activities in the house, Grandma Cotton hurrying to and fro between the mother's bedroom and the laundry with strange bundles under her apron, the father anxiously stoking the fire. A cry of a new baby illuminates the situation and explains an earlier, less happy one:

'That last miss come against her, I don't like misses,' [Grandma Cotton] added, sipping her tea.

So that was why Ma was sick last time when Granny was here in her white apron, and the doctor came in the night, and Pa buried his head in his arms and the table was wet with his tears after the doctor left, and Granny washed all the blood-stained clothes early in the morning, shooing the kids away from the laundry.

That silence from the bedroom—making me fear that something like that had happened again. (p. 79)

The scene is almost a metaphor of a recurrent state of mind, for the fear of implicit violence or disruption, associated with sex, persists in other less specifically recognizable situations. The father's past evokes dark hints of unthinkable betrayals, which seem 'to whisper through the years as we grew up'. His habitual drunkenness is frequently given as an excuse for acts of gross inhumanity; on one occasion, he is said to have left the mother alone for days with a stillborn child, and another crime, which only occasionally comes to the surface, is enough to bring on a mood of gloomy remorse: 'the kids wondered what it was that Pa wouldn't have done but for the drink, and decided that he must have killed someone' (p. 66). Sometimes, the mother flings up at him the reminder that he got another girl into trouble before their marriage. Ada's sly capacity for alliances, flights and broken promises seems to duplicate the father's unreliability. The passions she arouses result in a vengeful attempt to burn the house, an action which the Soady family is strangely anxious to cover up. Similar betrayals are visible in the lives of others; one mother guards her daughter in the house until she is adult and contrives to elope with the postman, and then refuses to see her until she (the mother) is dying. Another family rejects their pregnant daughter, who is forced to live in a cave surviving on plants and fish, until she is rescued by Grandma Cotton.

On the other hand, people can be just as unpredictably kind. The narrator receives unexpected gifts from one of her father's employers, and neighbours and friends rally round the family after the father's desertion. But it is the parents who most exhibit this ambivalent mix of tolerance, care and betrayal. Several scenes evoke the mother's deep concern for the father and even, on occasion, his concern for her. When he leaves for the West Australian gold-fields, she worries more about his welfare than about her own consequent financial problems and when he returns she cares for him like a child. Even more worrying than his drinking are his occasional moods of black depression, and on these occasions the mother will even resort to alcohol to cheer his spirits. On the other hand, any activity which keeps him busily engaged, however manic, is valuable if it keeps him from drink. It is clear that he is the centre of her life and many of their rough scenes have an underlying lusty camaraderie. At the same time, the mother is concerned about her relations in the old country and assumes the same concern in her husband, shielding him from bad family news. If the father receives the news of the death of a sister with equanimity, he seems genuinely concerned about his mother's blindness and on other occasions he is presented as a caring father. In this ambivalent moral climate, two betrayals seem to be critical. The first occurs when the father leaves the narrator and her brother without explanation at Windsor and returns to Sydney for a drinking bout. The children survive for a week on tinned fish and condensed milk, before a neighbour informs the police and their mother arrives to retrieve them. The second, which may or may not be a reaction to the first, is the mother's betrayal when she re-ignites the mysterious relationship with 'Uncle Dick' which has dogged the marriage from long before the narrator's birth. The father retaliates by leaving for New Zealand with his eldest son and selling the house before his departure: 'A month's notice was given Ma to hand over possession' (p. 192). Another letter much later, consisting merely of a small money order without any news, quenches the hopes with which she had watched boats arriving from New Zealand: 'she seemed to grow harder about Pa after that—just a few words would have made such a difference' (p. 197). Nevertheless, when she runs into him four years later and discovers he is seriously ill, she nurses him with infinite care until his last moments. Uncle Dick, who is thereafter perceived minus the attraction he has had as a marital irritant, dies soon afterwards to everyone's satisfaction. It is hard to say whether it is merely a coincidence or an intriguing illustration of the tenacious mother-daughter symbiosis that Rose Lindsay's portrayal of extraordinary ambivalence in *Ma and Pa* should be repeated by *her* daughter in *Portrait of Pa*.

No author has had such an intense preoccupation with ambivalent feelings towards the mother-figure as Henry Handel Richardson. It has often been remarked that nearly all her work is autobiographical, a reworking of the childhood, which she described as 'bitten with acid' into her memory[22], although the centrality of the mother in all her retrospections has been infrequently acknowledged. Autobiography, whether fictional or factual, was an act of personal salvation for Richardson, a means of effecting a peace treaty with the self and, for one with such a powerful and even 'fatal' mother-fixation[23], such a treaty was necessarily one with the mother as well. In this struggle to free herself from the mother, Richardson, of course, was doomed to failure and hence the number of her attempts to 'fix' the figure in fiction. She illustrates particularly effectively Gusdorf's contention that the autobiographer, striving only to embrace more closely the always secret but never refused sense of the personal destiny, never achieves the 'final word' which will complete his or her life. It is ironic that this protean wrestling with the shadow of her own life, 'certain only of never laying hold of it'[24], should have marked her as an unduly factual writer, lacking in imagination.

Richardson was acutely aware of the intricate roots of the mother/daughter bond. One of the protagonists of 'Two Hanged Women' comments, for instance:

Oh! mothers aren't fair—I mean it's not fair of nature to weigh us down with them and yet expect us to be our own true selves. The handicap's too great. All those months, when the same blood's running through two sets of veins—there's no getting away from that, ever after. (p. 81)[25]

As Dorothy Green has sensitively demonstrated, the circumstances of Richardson's childhood were particularly productive of emotional instability. Walter Richardson's illness and death left both his children with terrible memories and unusually prolonged feelings of dependency: 'What Richardson would learn about men from observing her father would be ... that males were essentially untrustworthy, or at least unpredictable'. At the same time she would have learned that 'it was the mother who was the source of food, clothes, and shelter, of the visible, material necessities of existence'.[26]

In all her various representations of her mother as mother, in *The Getting of Wisdom*, *The Way Home*, *Ultima Thule*, 'The End of a Childhood', *Myself When Young* and even 'Mary Christina', Richardson presents her as preoccupied if not obsessed with her motherhood role: 'to these small creatures, bone of her bone and flesh of her flesh, links bound Mary that must, she felt, outlast life itself. Through them and her love for them, she caught her one real glimpse of immortality'.[27] In 'The End of a Childhood' she takes the fatal decision to refuse another father for them: 'No one but the father they were so like would be capable of understanding them ... On no one but herself should their lives and happiness depend' (*The Adventures of Cuffy Mahony*, p. 9). Persistently perceived as earth-bound and practical, the mother has all the attributes of instinctive female nature, she is the earth-mother *par excellence*, so that Dorothy Green's discovery that Richardson exaggerated her practicality at the expense of her actual interest in things intellectual is intriguing. As Richardson often admitted, the personality of Richard Mahony was based substantially on her own and no doubt she invested her father with her own resistance to maternal interference in the name of practicality. Thus in *The Fortunes of Richard Mahony*, Mary's incorrigibly materialistic outlook afflicts her other-

worldly husband, in *The Getting of Wisdom* and *Myself When Young*
her practicality is sometimes at odds with her daughter's imaginative
nature, and in 'Mary Christina' she dies unblessed by any spiritual
belief. She consistently finds her identity and her immortality in her
motherhood; if she is not mother, she is nobody. Nor is she alone in
this belief, for her daughter shares it, appearing in all the versions as
egocentric child, who accepts the mother's protection and devotion as
a law of nature. 'Just how Mother contrived to meet the expense of
my schooling I don't know, I never enquired. Nor would she have
wanted me to. That was her own business', she comments in *Myself
When Young*[28], and both Cuffy and Laura accept the mother's selfless
dedication and vicarious ambition as natural, even as they resent her
interference. Thus all Richardson's young selves perceive the mother
as object, 'a narcissistic extension, a not-separate other whose sole
reason for existence is to gratify [the child's] wants and needs', and
fail to grant her the particular selfhood, which Chodorov sees as
essential for mature emotional growth.[29]

'The End of a Childhood' is the most condensed and complex
of Richardson's attempts to come to terms with the mother, to be
'purged once and for all of [the] mother's bondage, to become individuated and free'.[30] Imagining the mother's death, or what it
would have been like if the childhood dread she describes in *Myself
When Young* had been fulfilled, the dread that when mother went out
she might fail to return, is a dramatic excising of the mother's desperately needed presence, and typical of Richardson's practice of
confronting the minds' 'cliffs of fall' in her writing. In this short story
she confronts a complex mix of ambivalent feelings, all of which flow
from her overwhelming dependence on the mother. These feelings
include the element of panic which characterized both that relationship and its later substitute, her bond with her husband[31]; the fear
of engulfment and the need to abandon the self completely; the
desire to revert to infanthood and the fear of doing so; the need to be
free of the need for her mother/husband and the guilt that this need
provoked coupled with pride in the mother's stoicism and selflessness; the fear of death and resilient joy in living; the fear of loneliness
and need to be solitary; the fear not of the mother or even of
motherhood, but that she might become like the mother; the fear of a
mother's responsibility and the need for relatedness. Several readers,
offended by the story's departure from the sustained tragedy of
Ultima Thule and by the apparently abrupt ending, have suggested
that the work is a clumsy afterthought which should never have been
published. Certainly, a knowledge of *The Fortunes* is necessary for a
complete understanding of the story's action, which detracts mildly
from its self-contained integrity, but it has a power of its own. The
experience of personal disaster filtered through the immediate impressions of a sensitive, uncomfortably honest child is brilliantly

handled, while Richardson's fine modulation from external to internal perspective and masterly control of tempo should on their own defend her from allegations that she is no stylist. But it is above all her insight into the oddities of a child's mind, especially when such a mind is under unbearable stress, that makes the story a small masterpiece.

The beginning section of the story, dealing with Mary's response to the letter from Henry Ocock proposing marriage, establishes her familiar oneness with the children. If for a moment she allows herself to contemplate what marriage might mean for her personal comfort, she quickly abandons the thought:

Oh yes, she knew quite well what she was doing when she wrote; *Deeply as I appreciate your kindness, I cannot marry you.* Besides condemning herself to poverty . . . She was also, in a sense, taking leave of her womanhood. Many a year must elapse before either of the children could come to her aid. By then she would be old in earnest, and long past desiring. But she did not waver. Once more it had been brought home to her where her heart really lay. (p. 9)

In this story, Cuffy is the main representative of the childhood self, although it is possible that Richardson has located some of her shock at the thought of the mother's death in the female child, Luce. Certainly Cuffy bears a strong resemblance to the 'dark and spidery self' of *Myself When Young*, sharing some of the experiences and attributes of that self—the nervous tic, the solitary games and those with Luce, the dislike of the isolated Victorian town in which the mother's new profession as postmistress has landed them. The reasons for Richardson's choice of a male narrator/observer in *Ultima Thule* and 'The End of a Childhood' and in particular the reduction of her relatively gregarious sister to psychotic dependence have aroused much speculation. As far as the story is concerned, the choice adds enormously to the dramatization of ambivalence about separation and connection; as male child Cuffy can be expected to be preoccupied with differentiation and ashamed of dependence, his assertiveness and independence of mind are more acceptable, while the full burden of the disaster falls more appropriately on his shoulders as older brother. At the same time, his 'Mammy-fed' style of existence in a household of women excuses the female aspects of his personality.

Proud as he is of his nine years, Cuffy is still locked in an infantile relationship with his mother. Often he finds himself sitting on her knee in the evening, even though he is really much too big and his legs hang down to the ground:

And there they'd sit, just Mamma and him, nobody else knowing about it; and it was most awfully comfortable, when you were tired, quite the most comfy place, with a kind of shelf for your head, and Mamma's arms keeping you from falling off, and her chin against your hair. You just sat there and didn't talk, not at all . . . you wouldn't have liked to; it was too close for talking. Besides, there was nothing to say. (pp. 14–15)

Mary is well aware that the father's illness and death, the death of Luce's twin sister, the racketing from place to place and the collapse of one home after another have made Luce excessively dependent on her mother's presence and have produced nervous traits in Cuffy. Her identification of herself as the mother of Richard's children leads her first to turn down Ocock's generous offer and then to concentrate her energies on securing for Cuffy the sort of education he should have as Richard's son. At this point, her uncompromising pursuit of perfection, compounded by her determined stoicism and independence, is her fatal error and it is finely appropriate that she should die of the after-effects of a broken leg suffered while whitewashing walls that barely needed it.

Richardson's treatment of the dying woman's experience and her questioning of the meaning of existence for the first time in her life, is analogous to the short story based on the actual death of her mother, 'Mary Christina'. First published in 1911, titled 'Death', it was re-named 'Mary Christina' and appeared in *Two Studies* in 1931 and *The End of a Childhood* in 1934. Its location as the final story of *The End of a Childhood* completes the circle which that collection describes on the subject of motherhood. '"It all seems so stupid. What's the use of it? What good can it do anyone?"', ponders Mary as she struggles against her fever. Mary Christina endures a more prolonged disillusionment with the meaning of life and a mother's struggles in particular:

Nothing of them had persisted; nothing been real or lasting: her hand had caught the frayed edge of no perdurable garment. The wonders had been a chimera; the evils, too. And their hold upon her had been an imaginary one: her inmost self, the vitalest part of her, had remained unmoved by them, and unharmed. She had not striven in mortal combat; for there had never been a combat to engage in. That was still another illusion—perhaps the greatest of all. Life, tapped at its core, stripped of its rainbow gauds, meant—she knew it now—a standing dumbly by, to let these dream-things pass. (p. 194)

Richardson later distanced herself from the nihilism of this story and numerous readers have protested at its unrelievedly negative spirit. What the story is dramatizing, however, is the despair felt by the daughter when the part of herself that is the mother dies. Although the memories are those of the mother herself, there is also an emphasis on the watching adult children and their emotions, and it is the death of the mother's protectiveness that is the appalling truth confronted in this story, the fact that her self-sacrificing care has frozen into indifference: 'the withdrawal of her warm affection seemed, to those who had been used to shelter beneath it, like the first significant victory gained by death over life' (p. 190). Like the 'living shadows' thrown on the wall by the candle in her death-chamber, the mother's death induces a fear of nothingness; it assails the identity, the value and the reality of the self as no other event can. In 'The End of a Childhood', the shocked reaction of both Cuffy and Luce to the experience of no-value following the death of the mother is the most searing. Cuffy's eavesdropping on the wrangling of Tilly and Uncle Jerry as to responsibility for their future has terrible consequences: 'Behind the cactuses which was the most secret place he knew, he flung himself face downwards on the ground. His heart was full to bursting. Nobody . . . *nobody* wanted them, him or Luce, any more' (p. 31).

At the same time, Richardson weaves into her story feelings of relief, guilt and resentment at the removal of the mother. Although Cuffy misses his mother after her departure for Melbourne, he is half-glad she is gone: he dislikes to look at her in her newly disfigured state even though the manner of her parting, on his bedroom door used as a stretcher, is 'a *very* exciting going-away'. At first Mamma's going leaves 'a sort of hole in him', but later he is 'really rather glad':

For when she wasn't there he didn't need to think so much about her. She wasn't *nice* to think of, since she fell off the steps—not able to walk properly, and her face so red and swollen. He wanted her to look like she always had. (p. 22)

The passage is reminiscent of another story in the collection, 'The Bathe', which deals with a child's shocked reaction to the ugly, naked bodies of a mother and aunt. The little girl's violent determination never to grow up is partly an aesthetic distaste but also a response to the meaning of motherhood and the anomalous idea of change. The ideal mother is one whose slight signs of ageing are static, who is not threatened with change; the ideal self is the child-self, unburdened with the ugly costs of motherhood.

Cuffy's dislike of change in his mother is exacerbated by guilt, for one of his most loathsome anxieties is that his mother will return with a wooden leg. His imagining of her future ugliness and the ridicule she will inspire is more than he can bear: 'And when he went to school . . . she might come and see him, and then the other boys would laugh and make fun of her behind her back, and he'd feel so ashamed he believed he'd die' (pp. 22–3). Later, memory of this imagined betrayal induces a prolonged fit of guilty weeping. Fear of the mother's powerlessness to resist ridicule is an unbearable reflection on the dignity of the identical self.

The boy's response to his bereaved sister is also the vehicle of highly ambivalent feelings. On her departure for Melbourne, the mother needlessly reminds Cuffy of his responsibility as surrogate protector. It is a responsibility he takes seriously, standing up to Tilly Beamish with admirable selflessness and frequently putting Luce's interest before his own. The thought of what will happen to her when she is separated from him is intolerable, and worse even than 'Mamma being dead'. All of which makes the change in his feelings as he leaves with Tilly quite remarkable. Although he is assailed at first by a fit of weeping, after a time his tears, 'as tears will . . . ran dry and other and pleasanter thoughts insinuated themselves'. There are the excitements of the journey and possible reunions with Luce to contemplate and then the perfume of the wattles, always associated with new life in *The Fortunes*, assails his senses:

he sniffed and sniffed, till the dust all but choked him, and his head went giddy.
And, from now on, his spirits continued steadily to rise, hope adding itself to hope, in fairy fashion. Just as mile after mile combined to stretch the gulf, that would henceforth yawn, between what he had been, and what he was to be. (p. 36)

Richardson is exploring several familiar emotions at once here. The most obvious is the resilient human tendency to affirm the self's survival in the face of the death of others. Like Sterne in his treatment of Bobbie's death in *Tristram Shandy*, Richardson is observing this instinctive reaction, rather than moralizing on it. Cuffy's reaction also expresses the grim relief induced by a death, in that at least the anxiety lest the loved one die is at an end. In a diary note, entered fifteen years after her husband's death, which itself may well have inspired some of the mood of 'The End of a Childhood', Richardson described the cessation of her anxiety for him: 'Odd to think that I shall never need to be troubled about his whereabouts again. Death has *had* him; it is over; he is safe now for ever. My heart can be at rest in his eternal absence'.[32] At the same time the boy's resilience punishes the mother for dying and celebrates his and the author's achievement of liberation from her.[33] He/she has also been prevented from taking up the responsibility for his sister, the seductive anxiety of the mothering role which the mother thrust upon him; he/she has eluded the solidarity with the mother by refusing to join 'that long chain of women who sacrificed themselves for the good of their children, their husbands, and the continuation of society as we know it'.[34]

The complexities of this story are expanded by the multitude of reflections on mothers and mothering and the issues they raise, which are contained in the other stories in this collection. If 'Succedaneum' is a positive reply to 'Mary Christina', 'Life and Death of Peterle Luthy' probes the meaning of a mother's indifference and 'The Professor's Experiment' the meaning of her caring; '"And Women Must Weep"' relives the resentment of a girl forced into a conventional form of female proving by mother-figures, 'Two Hanged Women' explores the cramping impact of a mother on her daughter's sexuality and 'Sister Ann' the way that mothering is a barrier to authenticity. When one considers the crucial role of the equivocal mother image in Richardson's writing, it is odd to recall that her greatest work is a fictional study of her father. Or is not *The Fortunes of Richard Mahony* the most subtle of her autobiographies, an identification of self with the long-dead father in the hope that together they might come to terms with mother?

But Richardson is not alone in finding the mother a rich topic and indeed Australian women have produced an immensely varied gallery of mother images in their autobiographies. There is, for instance, a large group of 'good' mothers, who are genuinely perceived as positive role-models. Although there is apparently no blueprint for the good mother, and certainly no specific lesson for child-care theorists, it seems that it is essential for a mother to have a strong sense of self and an interest in the child that is free in that it is generous, and free from narcissism. Eleanor Spence, for instance, draws strength from her mother's sturdy independence, even though this mother is dependent in an economic sense; developing her skills as a writer, she is consciously following in the footsteps of the mother, who has always valued the life of the imagination. Alice Henry's ambitions appear to have been nourished by a similar mother in unlikely socio-economic circumstances, while Alexandra Hasluck takes great pride in emulating the unusual intellectual achievements of her mother. More often though, it is not what the mother does, but what she is that entrances the child, the distinctive flavour of her personality, the integrity of her being. Insincerity, whether it is conscious as in Adelaide Lubbock's mother or unconscious as in Barbara Hanrahan's, tarnishes the mother's image more quickly than any other quality. Several intimate portraits of the mother, such as Maie Casey's, Nancy Phelan's, Mary Stawell's and Eugénie McNeil's, evoke the mother's personality in a musically resonant way, establishing her existence in her gestures and tone of voice and all the significant minutiae of daily living. The good mother, it appears, may even be absent for long periods, providing her personality is sufficiently strong. Nancy and Janet Mitchell approach their mother late, but appreciably nevertheless; if their nanny is their first strong role model, the mother's personality appears to have been bolstered rather than diminished by the mother-substitute. Dame Agnes Hunt records in her *Reminiscences*[35] her understandable gratitude for long rests from the demanding energies of her stupendous mother. Indeed, this mother is one of the most gargantuan of the mothers that inhabit these narratives, an upper class match for the working-class mother that Mary Rose Liverani celebrates in *The Winter Sparrows*. Agnes Hunt, the co-founder of an orthopaedic training college, was a woman of remarkable foresight and energy whose efforts initiated a new era in the treatment of the handicapped. She was one of eleven children born into a family with large holdings of land in Shropshire and was herself handicapped. Her mother, described in the Preface and Foreword as having 'nothing petty about her' and as pursuing her family with 'malignant fidelity', brought seven of her children to Australia in 1883, after the death of her husband and having conceived the notion of breeding angora goats on a Queensland island. She returned to England in 1886, followed a year later by her daughter. The opening paragraph of Hunt's autobiography initiates the reader into her talent for comedy:

My poor mother disliked children intensely; she disliked them when they were coming, during their arrival, and most intensely after they had arrived. It seems, therefore, distinctly hard lines that between the ages of twenty-one and forty she was doomed to produce eleven children. At two weeks old we were consigned to the nursery and the bottle. In after years my mother told me she had tried to nurse one of my elder brothers, but the little wretch had bitten her without a moment's hesitation, and so sealed the fate of his numerous brothers and sisters. (p. 9)

The parents' eccentric ideas on child-rearing, combining Spartan discipline and total freedom out of school hours, appear to have produced offspring of extraordinary resilience and hardihood. No concessions are made to the narrator's handicap, a fact she later accepts with gratitude, although she is less grateful when her mother demands she accompany her on a trip into outback Queensland, notwithstanding an illness. When this turns out to have been typhoid, her ever-sanguine parent congratulates herself on the effectiveness of plenty of fresh air. Queensland, in fact, is barely a match for this mother and her daughters, whose riding is equal to the meanest buck-jumper and whose hunting, fishing and shooting skills come in handy in the bush. Indeed, no challenge can surpass the challenges offered by this energetic, restless mother, bent on one manic scheme after another. If she 'weakens' on islands, she is determined to sample as much of the authentic Australia as possible. Everything about her is excessive, from the number of her children to her physical bulk, and her personality engrosses every situation. Bemused, fascinated and eternally helpful, the local populace appears to have accepted the family's antics as an unlooked-for circus. The narrative reaches a comic peak in the descriptions of the mother versus the Tasmanian bush. Undaunted by the primitive conditions, she refuses to allow her children to make any concessions to its deficiencies, so that producing meals according to her exacting West End standards is a problem of huge proportions. Fortunately, the narrator soon discovers that the Tasmanian horse, which performs the functions of 'guide, philosopher and friend', generally knows its way from one settlement to another, and she is able to cull produce from their distant neighbours. Underlying this lively account runs a great affection for this stupendous mother and a characteristic concern with relatedness. When her mother returns, Agnes stays behind as companion for her almost equally energetic brother, well aware of the dangers for the solitary bush-dweller. Her decision turns out to be justified when he survives a logging accident only with her help.

But in autobiography as in other literature, it is invariably the devil who has the best tunes, and some of the most memorable mothers are dominant or destructive figures. Oddly, the rejecting mother, although apparently the most insidiously powerful of mothers, is frequently presented as a shadowy figure, reflecting perhaps her refusal to be known in life. 'As she beat me I cried to her, "Beat me, mother, but love me ... O love me"', recalls Anna Wickham[36], expressing a common need to have the mother's attention, for her indifference is the most dreaded of misfortunes. Eliza Davies's unpredictably malign mother, who is more elemental force than individual, is typical in her shadowiness. Kate Rodd's mother reveals something of herself indirectly in her actions, but her daughter makes no attempt to develop a coherent picture and clearly it is the impact of her rejection that stings the memory; Connie Ellement in *The Divided Kingdom* accords her mother a few well-chosen moments of self-betrayal, and concentrates with damning effect on the consequences of her dereliction; Kathy Brown's *The First-Born* is a poignant, baffled account of her search for the meaning of a mother's abandonment.

The interested but dominantly destructive mother, on the other hand, is invariably a vividly realized figure. The most memorable of these in this group of narratives is Anna Wickham's, described in her 'Fragment of an Autobiography'. An original poet and an extraordinary personality, Wickham or Edith Hepburn as she was also known, was familiar with such figures as Natalie Barney, Dylan Thomas, Malcolm Lowry, Harold Munro and D. H. Lawrence. In her childhood she made two visits to Australia, the most extended lasting from 1890 to 1904, from the ages of six to twenty.

A remarkably frank piece of self-analysis, Wickham's autobiography was written in 1935, as a piece of 'house-cleaning', prior to her intended suicide. This, in fact, did not take place until 1947. The entire tone of the autobiography is one of despair and yet it is spirited despair: 'I feel that I am myself a profound mistake and that I was doomed from my conception by being myself', she writes at the beginning (p. 52). Autobiography is 'an expedient for survival', but the act merely lights up the reasons for her despair and in her closing paragraph she refuses all consolations:

As I look back over this long and melancholy road, I am ashamed. I try to think why I endured so much futile pain, and the truth is that I believed in pain. I believed that by suffering and endurance I was working out some salvation. Nearly all the relationships of my life have been tawdry, insincere and unsatisfactory. Many people were attracted to me, but I was intimate with nobody. I was not sufficiently like anyone to invite that self-identification which is the essence of true friendship and love. (p. 157).

Dark as the mood is, it is shot through with wit and humour; Wickham has a gift for the incisive aphorism, the satiric insight: 'She filled me with her virus as a spider does a fly'; 'Our life was easy, but without ambition or plan—I felt like an eternal pensionnaire at a creditably equipped seaside boarding house'; 'My mother liked death: it was spectacular. She liked diseases: they were a definite departure from the normal'.

As the last quotation illustrates, Wickham's mother has a huge appetite for drama. A woman of enormous, frustrated energy, she needs a constant audience for her melodramatic roles. Fake suicides and fits are common devices for this personality which constantly craves sensation. At the same time she has 'a peculiar charm', which is like a scent and in her moods of tenderness she has remarkable healing powers; her moods of rage, on the other hand, have 'a universal effect of paralysis'. Constant companionship with the mother invariably induces illness in the narrator as a child and even as an adult, her mother's impending arrival is enough to send her to bed for days. Finding a surrogate theatrical audience in her only daughter, the mother frequently exploits her emotions and her need for her physically comforting presence: 'something seemed to click with satisfaction in my mother when I cried' (p. 84). A moment of genuine shared emotion is perceived as an epiphany of pleasure, however, and on another occasion the daughter makes contact with maternal feelings which appear to be semi-erotic, a brief respite from the unconscious will to destroy which normally underlies this mother's behaviour: 'She opposed my existence with her will. In regions below the conscious she desired to destroy me' (p. 96). Descriptions of the mother's impact on other people make it clear that this woman has extraordinary power. Setting herself up in Queensland as a teacher of elocution and then as a fortune-teller, she rapidly makes enough money for the family to buy several houses in Sydney; she is renowned for her psychic powers and even as a contact healer and her lectures are well-attended public events. Touring North Queensland without any advance publicity, she is instantly able to attract clients.

The mother's capabilities are hardly matched by the father, Geoffrey Harper, at least in the eyes of his wife and daughter. Although the editor of this narrative suggests that Harper was far from ineffective, he is presented by Wickham as having an inveterate talent for failure. At the same time he makes large claims on his daughter's pity and love. Wickham's analysis of the ambivalent feelings of the only child, exploited as 'a virgin field' by the contesting emotional claims of the incompatible parents, has a clinical acuity. She is sensitive to the 'pathos' of the father's dissatisfaction with life, and eager to provide him with a vicarious sense of success in her own achievements. Recognizing that she is a substitute for a son who died at birth, she readily complies with his efforts to make her as boy-like as possible. Already at four she feels a companionship with him in enduring the mother's rages. Later, she pities the mother's inability to find a commensurate heroism and eroticism in her husband. To some extent the familiar gendered stereotypes are reversed: she is dismayed by the powerlessness of the should-be-powerful father and sensitive to his emotional claims; she admires the masculine power of the mother but is repelled by her rejection of genuine feeling. Above all, she resents the fact that her mother imposes her dismissive view of her husband on her own perception of him. If the mother's contempt is seen as having its seeds in an elder sister's amused reaction to Harper during his courtship, the narrator is equally incapable of rejecting the view that she receives in her turn.

While still young, she has an impression that she is older than her parents, that she manages them and is responsible for them: 'Looking back to this time it seems that our roles were reversed and that I regarded their rages and their cruelties as a mother would regard the black moods of two adored children. I had the feeling of wanting to make up to them for what life had done to them, and for what they did to each other' (p. 85). Not surprisingly, in trying to realize their conflicting ideas of her, she seems 'somehow to lose possession of a self' (p. 102). Again and again, she describes her sense of being an isolated foreigner—within the families of both her parents, at her various schools in Queensland, and in Sydney. Just as the small family never escapes its own emotional hothouse in Australia, making contact with society in the most fragmentary manner and constantly on the move, it is clear that Wickham sees herself as eternally trapped in its unnatural climate. Exhausted by irreconcilable emotional claims and used up by roles demanded of her in the family melodrama, she is unable to cultivate the 'new will', which occasionally takes root in her personality, so that all her later life seems a stale repetition of the earlier static pattern.

Extraordinary as Wickham's narrative is, it shares some characteristics with other autobiographies. The lengthy descriptions of maternal and paternal families, for instance, and her interest in their determining influence, is a fairly common feature. Wheareas male narratives return to genealogical origins to establish the authenticity of the self, female narratives appear to be more interested in the particular patterns of relatedness that influenced the relations of the narrator's immediate family. Wickham's narrative is also curiously similar to a recent, fictional autobiography, Jean Bedford's *Love Child*.[37] Bedford's novel lacks the sharp insights of Wickham's and her mother-figure is far less remarkable, but the same pattern of relationships emerges and there is the same sense of a determining family past. Once again, the vibrant mother deprives the father of his appeal to the only daughter, the incompatible parents are locked in endless war and the narrator's identity suffers a similar diminution as a result of their contesting emotional claims.

Discussion of the mother-figure inevitably leads to reflection on the family figure who is often a substitute for the mother, that is the sister. Many of these narratives describe sister-relationships as the most tenacious ever experienced. Mary Edgeworth David's sister, far more accessible than her Victorian mother, is both friend and mother and her untimely death inspires a sadness that is never completely erased; Hilda Brotherton's sister tacitly provides the education in relationships that her mother neglects; Laura Todd and her two sisters instinctively form a tight knit group in order to survive in a hostile institution; Patsy Adam Smith looks back with nostalgia and pain at the spirit and sufferings of her elder sister; Clara Campbell supports her sister through the terrible ordeals of living with a violent husband and although her own story is ostensibly the traditional one of courtship, the sisterly relationship emerges as the strongest. Several narrators, such as Katharine Susannah Prichard and Nene Gare, describe the urgent sense of responsibility that the birth of a younger sister brings, while others dwell on the comic ups and downs of the experience of being a duo. However competitive and even turbulent, the relationship is invariably perceived with keen nostalgia. Some autobiographies virtually exist to celebrate the sisterly companionship. Of these, Sarah Conigrave's *My Reminiscences*, Eugénie McNeil and Eugénie Crawford's *A Bunyip Close Behind Me* and *Ladies Didn't*, Ruve Cropley's *Forty 'Odd' Years in a Manse*, Mary Edgeworth David's *Passages of Time*, Mary Fullerton's *Bark House Days* and Eve Langley's *The Pea Pickers* are the most striking, but the relationship is prominent in numerous others. Like women's friendship, the topic of sisterhood is a rich one that feminist critics of literature have only just begun to explore.

8

The Man Who Loved Children:
Mermaid and Minotaur

Without doubt, *The Man Who Loved Children* is the most astounding outcrop in Australia's autobiographical tradition. Retrieved from the obscurity into which it sank after its first publication in 1940 by Randell Jarrell, and republished in an American edition in 1965, it was received as a text of international stature. Jarrell's own enthusiastic estimate of it as knowing 'specifically, profoundly, exhaustively—what a family is' and knowing this as few books have ever known it, has become one of the tenets of critical lore generated by Christina Stead's fiction. Even so, we are only just beginning to grapple with the complexities of Stead's understanding of the family.

Two seemingly contradictory impressions appear to affect most first-time readers of the novel: one, that this family is the most melodramatic and bizarre of families and two, that it is the most familiar. Stead herself expressed surprise at the widespread identification, concluding that it was a devastating comment on the institution. A more likely conclusion is that melodrama and eccentricity are endemic to families and that however civilized the surface of domestic life, extraordinary passions swirl in its depths. As Lowell put it, 'No one like one's mother and father ever lived'. In Stead's case, she counted herself lucky that the melodramatic emotions of her family were daily and thoroughly aired. She also described the book as a *'celebration* of an unhappy family', emphasizing perhaps the peculiarly fortunate configurations of family misery for her discovery of herself as an artist: 'I have always thought that it was very lucky'.[1]

Few writers have had such a gift for recreating the sensuous, daily texture of childhood experience, the uniquely familiar amalgam of sounds, smells and physical sensations that are the stuff of family living. The description of a typical Sunday/Funday in the Pollit family early in the narrative initiates the reader into this intimate world. 'A slippery sound like a fish flopping on the stairs' announces that four-year-old Tommy has moved down to his mother's room and barely perceptible noises reveal that everyone is now awake, waiting for the first ritual of the day, Louie's tea-making. Later, the other children gather in their mother's room:

A musky smell always came from Henrietta's room, a combination of dust, powder, scent, body odors that stirred the children's blood deep, deep. It had as much attraction for them as Sam's jolly singing, and when they were allowed to, they gathered in Henrietta's room, making hay, dashing to the kitchen to get things for her, asking her if she wanted her knitting, her book, tumbling out into the hall and back, until it was as if she had twenty children, their different voices steaming, bubbling, and popping, like an irrepressible but inoffensive crater.[2]

At a deeper level, this recreation of teeming activity lays bare the sundry woundings and humiliations, large and petty victories, public and private defeats, vengeances and retributions, attractions and repulsions that are the quotidian fare of any family, but particularly of a large family with dominant parents. Retrospectively, one can trace patterns in the apparent chaos of impressions: the insidious, weedy growth of unpredictable allegiances, understandings, attitudes, differences, and the impact, delayed or immediate, of specific incidents, words, books, facial expressions, retorts, gestures. It is partly this combination of prolific, telling detail and keen psychological insight that makes *The Man Who Loved Children* such a challenging work of art. As she often emphasized. Stead's eye was trained early by her naturalist father. Regarding herself primarily as a psychological writer, she often described her creative method as one of focusing on a group of interesting characters and allowing them to spin their own story:

I wait and wait for the drama to develop. I watch the characters and situation move and don't interfere. I'm patient. I'm lying low. I wait and wait for the drama to display itself . . .[3]

At the same time, and almost to the same degree, Stead is a political writer, although this aspect of her genius has received less attention. In numerous interviews, for instance, she expressed her agreement with her husband's Marxian views, although she was always careful to stress that she was not a 'go to meeting type' and strenuously rejected any suggestion that she wrote polemical novels.[4] The contradiction here is more apparent than real. For someone with such an ingrained awareness of the way in which ideology lies within each of us and is reproduced in our intimate social relations, polemics were irrelevant. Seeing 'what's going on' included seeing the curious and various ways in which psychic experience and ideology are interpenetrated. Thus, ideology is always part of the texture of life for Stead's characters, although *The Man Who Loved Children* is her most thorough study of the impact of ideologies of sex, family, economics, politics and culture on a single family. But Stead's understanding goes much deeper than this. She understands the psychic needs which support and prolong ideology's grip, the symbiosis between self and a range of destructive cultural 'norms', the invisible hegemony of feeling over thought. Cultural ideology invades family life in all its aspects, but equally powerful is the family's penetration of cultural thinking. We often speak of the 'parent culture'; Stead's observation of her own family led to the perception that the family was and continues to be the first and real parent.

More than thirty years later, this same perception led Dorothy Dinnerstein, Professor of Psychology at Rutgers University, to develop her analysis of traditional familial organization in *The Mermaid and The Minotaur*. The two books, separated generically and by the social changes of over three decades, are in fact an extraordinary meeting of minds. Dinnerstein's bold and wide-ranging thesis centres on the early infantile experience common to most of the human species and its fostering of an unhealthy form of dependent heterosexuality. This unhealthy interdependence, she argues, has not only affected humans' relation to nature, but also the character of history itself and now threatens the very survival of the human species. Dinnerstein sees 'the most potent sources of sexual conservatism [as] buried in the dark silent layers of our mental life'. The two mythological figures, which appear to her to express the internal inconsistencies of our species' nature and its mysterious differences from and continuities with the earth's other animals, are the mermaid and the minotaur:

The treacherous mermaid, seductive and impenetrable female representative of the dark and magic underwater world from which our life comes and in which we canot live, lures voyagers to their doom. The fearsome minotaur, gigantic and eternally infantile offspring of a mother's unnatural lust, male representative of mindless, greedy power, insatiably devours live human flesh.[5]

The submerged power of these two mythic figures also lies at the heart of *The Man Who Loved Children* and results in the same radical, cultural insights.

The household gods of the Pollit family, Sam and Henny, are a striking sexual contrast. Henny is the first to be presented and she comes alive with marvellous particularity in the first few pages; Sam, appropriately, is allowed to exude his intrusive presence in a more seeping, pervasive way. Dark and vinegary, Henny has a salty style that is the direct opposite of Sam's sweetness. She has a more comforting rightness, nevertheless. She belongs to the house and her marriage in a physical way, registering their shortcomings with habitual fatalism. The walls of the house are covered with the rhymes of her life-sentence 'invisible . . . thick as woven fabric' (p. 8):

She had the calm of frequentation; she belonged to this house and it to her. Though she was a prisoner in it, she possessed it. She and it were her marriage. She was indwelling in every board and stone of it: every fold in the curtains had a meaning (perhaps they were so folded to hide a darn or stain); every room was a phial of revelation to be poured out some feverish night in the secret laboratories of her decisions. (p. 7)

She is frequently described as 'vile', meaning that she has a frank acceptance of life's scabby grubbiness that never fails to intrigue the children. 'Henny was beautifully, whole-heartedly vile: she asked no quarter and gave none to the foul world' (pp. 10–11). Henny's world and Sam's converge only in violent conflict. The inhabitants of Henny's world are 'grotesque, foul, loud-voiced, rude, uneducated, and insinuating, full of scandal, slander and filth, financially deplorable and physically revolting, dubiously born, and going away to a desquamating end'. The inhabitants of Sam's are 'good citizens, married to good wives, with good children (though untaught)' (p. 10). The father sees 'a moral, high-minded world', the mother 'a wonderful particular world', which the children love to share. Henny's intriguing possibilities are reflected in her room which the children frequently invade, and above all in her drawers, her *'treasure drawers'*, a jumble of delightful objects which are anathema to Sam but a 'joyous mystery' to the children (p. 32). Resigned to the chaos and even the 'muck' of womanhood, Henny is in touch with an invisible, intriguing sphere, a 'tragic faery world'. She is 'a cave of Aladdin' to Sam's 'museum'; 'Beyond Sam stood the physical world, and beyond Henny—what? A great mystery' (p. 33).

In her mystery, Henny is an archetypal, oceanic figure, an intriguing mermaid. She is in touch with the personal in ways that de Beauvoir describes as typical of the female:

From the depths of her solitude, her isolation, woman gains her sense of the personal bearing of her life. The past, death, the passage of time—of these she has a more intimate experience than does man; she feels deep interest in the adventures of her heart, of her flesh, of her mind, because she knows that this is all she has on earth. And more, from the fact that she is passive, she experiences more passionately, more movingly, the reality in which she is submerged.[6]

Sam, on the other hand, prides himself on living in the 'real' world of reason. 'Greedy for the daylight', which dispels the dark creatures intuited by the sixth sense in the small hours, he stands 'on feet of clay in a world of clay' (p. 25). A large, golden man, brimming with energy and optimism, he is the white to Henny's black:

Sam was naturally lighthearted, pleasant, all generous effusion and responsive emotion. He was incapable of nursing an injustice which would cost him good living to repay, an evil thought which it would undo him to give back, or even sorrow in his bosom; and tragedy itself could not worm its way by any means into his heart. Such a thing would have made him ill or mad, and he was all for health, sanity, success, and human love. (p. 47)

He has much in common with Stead's later description of her father, David Stead. Like him, he is 'floodlit', his natural fairness enhancing his 'vitality, his self-trust and restless inner and outward life'. And his appearance of 'whiteness, fairness and all that goes with it', dazzles himself.[7] At the beginning of the story, his minotaur-like qualities are visible only to Henny and, in an early glimmering way, to Louie; unmasking and confronting the monster in the man will be a vital part of the latter's self-discovery. For the present, however, Louie perceives the struggle between the household gods as a bewildering melodrama, where feelings are given full vent. It is, of course, an unequal struggle, given Sam's full assumption of patriarchal power, but Henny is a powerful adversary and her vociferous struggle accelerates Louie's understanding of the situation. But even the younger children understand the relative power of the opposing forces: 'their father was the tables of the law, but their mother was natural law; Sam was household czar by divine right, but Henny was the czar's ever lasting adversary, household anarchist by divine right' (p. 34).

As the indulged daughter of a wealthy man, Henny had been trained for marriage to another wealthy man. In the event her father, David Collyer, sentimental about his own 'self-made' past, had selected struggling young men as his sons-in-law. The situation has many ironies although they unfold slowly: Sam also prides himself on his self-made career, but is dependent on David Collyer's influence and the presumption in everyone's mind that he will inherit wealth. What is more, Henny's status as heiress allows him the double pleasure of feeling 'moneyed' and of avoiding the responsibility of facing the financial difficulties of raising a large family. He is unaware of it, but the family scrapes by on loans that Henny raises from her family. Even Tohoga House in prestigious Georgetown, Sam's personal Eden and symbol of his success, belongs to David Collyer and is loaned to the family for a meagre rent. Sam's irresponsibility takes on manic proportions after David Collyer dies, virtually penniless, and he loses his position; he now enjoys a self-righteous poverty while leaving the 'heiress' to provide for the family. When, after Henny's death, her desperate measures to secure money are exposed, Sam enjoys general commiseration as the suffering husband of a spendthrift wife. Thus, the self-made men are not self-made, nor are they even good managers. Their promises to provide are even more destructive than their failures to do so. Henny, on the other hand, who sees herself as incapable of managing or making money, is a magnificent provider.

Henny's function as object of exchange is most marked on her father's death. Sam complacently appropriates the news as naturally of the greatest importance for himself, even withholding it from Henny. His concentration on the economic implications of the event, rather than the feelings of the bereaved daughter, exposes his subservience to the prevailing materialist ethos; as he rightly perceives, *he* has lost a father, not Henny. Henny too accepts her slave status. She is resigned to the fact that motherhood, the marriage laws and her exclusion from money-making have denied her rights. Time will not heal her as it will heal her son Ernie. Nevertheless, she frequently reflects bitterly on her lot: 'life was a rotten deal, with men holding all the aces' (p. 36). ' "Isn't it rotten luck? Isn't every rotten thing in life rotten luck? When I see what happens to girls I'd like to throttle my two, or send them out on the streets and get it over with" ' (p. 168). When she perceives the subtle change in Louie's allegiance from her father to herself, she rejoices in their unspoken, growing complicity of hate, the 'hate of woman the house-jailed and childchained against the keycarrier, childnamer and riothaver' (p. 36).

Henny's static rebellion makes her typical of one form of female reaction to patriarchy described by Dinnerstein. Excluded from 'making history', she takes the role of 'outsider court jester' ridiculing the 'pompous, dangerous, stupid games' and the history-making men (Dinnerstein, p. 157). Henny's favourite name for Sam is the 'Big-I-Am' and she has nothing but contempt for his public enterprises. But she is not a true revolutionary. She is rather what Dinnerstein terms 'a house-trained menial', who collaborates in her own subjection because of circumstances, children and upbringing. Upbringing even injects an element of willingness. Her sabotage is 'harmless to what it purports to assault' (Dinnerstein, p. 225). In a brilliant image, Stead captures the stagnant cycle of the parents' struggle and its archetypal echoes:

In this light, Louie and clever Ernie, who observed and held his tongue, saw, in a strange Punch-and-Judy-show, unrecognizable Sams and Hennys moving in a closet of time, with a little flapping curtain, up and down. (pp. 34–5)

Judy can irritate and tease Punch and even occasionally outwit him, but is her fate to be beaten; meanwhile, Punch must beat Judy if he is to continue to be Punch, the 'Big-I-Am'. The contest is timeless and endless.

At one point, during a lull in the marital war, Henny's sullen but willing collaboration in this sordid contest becomes clear even to herself. Suddenly noticing the wedding ring on her left fist, she is struck by the power it gives her:

As she looked dully at the band of gold that was with her night, day, in her washings and cleanings, in the children's sickness and at their birthday parties, that went into the bath water, the dough bowl, and the folds of the new cotton print running over the sewing machine, that went to the maternity ward with her and to the manicurist and fortuneteller's, that she saw when drinking cocktails with Bert and when signing away her every cent on some scrap of paper at the moneylender's, that stayed with her as stayed the man she had taken it from, she took a grip on herself. If this plain ugly link meant an eyeless eternity of work and poverty and an early old age, it also meant that to her alone this potent breadwinner owed his money, name, and fidelity, to her, his kitchen-maid and body servant. For a moment, after years of scamping, she felt the dread power of wifehood; they were locked in each other's grasp till the end. (p. 145)

Powerless though she is, the wife does possess a sullen, perverse power; if she is his creature, he is also hers. The passage invests the familiar marriage vow 'till death do us part' with murderous meaning. Unlike Sam in her sensitivity, Henny is like him in that she is made semi-human and 'monstrous' in Dinnerstein's terms, by consenting to one of the 'pernicious prevailing forms of collaboration between the sexes' (Dinnerstein, p. 5).

Henny's sad entanglement in the invisible snares of her culture is underlined by implicit and explicit authorial criticism on several occasions. She is shown, for instance, as regularly discontented with the sagas of 'upland Georgian gentility', which are her staple reading, because of their distance from real life, but is unable to surmount the lack of confidence that such books exploit. She had '"no fancy big buck niggers to wait on her and lick her boots"' and 'Where . . . was she to find heroes to succour her and how could she succeed in business with her spendthrift ways' (p. 443). Her thoughts about her children's future are similarly contaminated at their root: 'About the girls she only thought of marriage, and about marriage she thought as an ignorant and dissatisfied, but helpless slave did of slavery. She thought the boys would get on by the brutal methods of men' (p. 457).

If Henny's impotent struggle at Tohoga House is solitary and even eccentric, the cultural and familial roots of her individual defeat are established in the superb female drama that takes place at her father's old home, Monomacy, during Sam's absence in Malaya. Here, in company with her sister and Ellen, her cynically irreverent mother, veteran of several decades of marital war and fourteen pregnancies, Henny takes comfort in the 'natural outlawry' of women. Henny's previous history is filled in to some extent, but it is the tone of the whole section that is important. Here, in the very heart of patriarchy (for the name, Monomacy, clearly expresses male money-making), the women enjoy the frank, upstairs freedoms of servants when the master is away. The discussion of dissolute men, sex, pregnancies, women's ailments, miscarriages, conjures up a fascinating, seamy, female world for the listening Louie. At the same time, Ellen's own history and brand of salty fatalism amplifies the reader's understanding of her daughter. As so often, Stead's families talk their pasts into full-bodied existence.

> 'Life's dirty, isn't it, Louie, eh? Don't you worry what they say to you, we're all dirty . . . Only it's all over now; I'm clean now . . . Now it's different. I'm a decent body, fit to talk to my washerwoman. No more milk on my bodice, mud on my skirts, only snuff on my moustache.' (pp. 181–2)

But the Monomacy episode, often criticized as too long, has more extensive implications, which both include Henny and transcend her. In the first place, the episode dramatically presents the female covert culture, which is traditionally sceptical of the male. Dinnerstein defines this as an 'everyday folk-knowledge . . . that personal truth, one's own intuitive grasp of what is going on, is ignored at one's own grave risk; that large-scale politics are pompous and farcical' (p. 267). Ellen, in particular, has a 'spicy cynicism' about man's mystifications, which both de Beauvoir and Dinnerstein see as the special gift of the old woman. Henny, of course, is well on the path to the same set of attitudes, frequently displaying a contempt for Sam's world of 'big bluffs and big sticks'; but her criticism is intermittent, flickering and undeveloped. Louie can only guess at the reasons and extent of her dissension. The full meaning of Henny's sense of 'the personal bearing of life' and her suppression of that knowledge in the face of Sam's know-all talk comes alive in this episode. Compared with Sam's empty rhetoric on universal brotherhood and the new socialism, the talk of the women deals with the real, gritty problems of living, giving birth and dying. It is submerged in the now, not in some abstract future.

Elsewhere in the novel, Henny's harmonious submersion in the real is presented descriptively. Propped up in bed while the children hold their little parliament on her flowered carpet, brooding over the inevitable cup of tea on her debts and the worn defects of the house, reflecting on the sleeping form of a child, Henny has a 'rightness' that the children unconsciously breathe in: 'everything that she did was right, right, her right: she claimed this right to do what she liked because of all her sufferings, and all the children believed in her rights' (p. 368). Whereas Sam confuses the children by the conflict between his professed intentions and his actions, Henny has a natural integrity of being in the world that reassures them. Beset by problems though she is, she is more at rest in the present; she instinctively discovers a self-suffcent reality in the living moment. Sam, however, has to fill every moment with projects, things, talk of the future. Quietly, and even unconsciously, Henny subverts Sam's 'wisdom'. It is this daily dramatized opposition of two ways of knowing the world which is part of Louie's silent education and helps to define her own world-view. At Monomacy, she is given a wonderful glimpse of the solidarity of female knowledge.

Another important aspect of this episode for the novel's larger issues is that it dramatizes the helplessness of the female covert culture when faced with patriarchy's cut-and-thrust power, a help-lessness which even becomes collaboration. The arrival of Henny's brother-in-law, Archie Lessinum, come to arrange a loan to cover her debts, coincides with Louie's casual disclosure that Ellen's little maid has called her a bastard. Immediately, the situation, which had the potential of being enjoyable, becomes serious and the women are confused and divided by Archie's decision to dismiss the girl. In the subsequent sordid debate as to whether the girl's bags should be searched or not, 'Archie's male authority won' (pp. 185–6). The other women truckle loudly or reluctantly to his decree, but Henny clearly identifies with the girl: '"I'd steal if I had only her threadbare rags, and rich rotters swanked their things under my nose"'. She disgustedly hands him a pair of brass tongs for the task: 'But it was an insult to Archie, not the girl' (p. 186). It is a minor illustration of the female/male collaboration which, according to Dinnerstein, helps 'to keep history mad'. But the Monomacy episode as a whole is a marvellous example of the way Stead immerses the political in the personal and the personal in the political.

It is Sam, the father, who is the most complex figure in this archetypal drama of the sexes. Sam is not just a father, he is *only* a father, having made the role as capacious and various as any man might. Although he sees himself as a scientifically enlightened man, the old-fashioned patriarchal role fits his emotional needs like a glove. As Jennifer McDonnell comments: 'he plays all the traditional comic roles assigned to the father . . . the heavy, the pantaloon, the benign, friendly but firm parent, who has starred in hundreds of domestic TV dramas'.[8]

But, as critics have often pointed out, he is also a child. In the words of Terry Sturm:

He has a child's petulance and optimism, a child's sense of being aggrieved when things go wrong, a child's astonishment that schemes he has thought up *can* go wrong, a child's desire to see the world in terms of heroes and villains. Even his egotism has much in it of the ego-centredness of a child, just as the games he perpetually plays with the children have to be games *he* has thought up, in which *he* acts the role of leader.[9]

Sam also has the child's or even the baby's need for constant sensual gratification. His enjoyment of his children is always intensely physi-cal. The opening description of Sunday/ Funday is the first dramatiza-tion of this side of his nature. Lying in bed, Sam wheedles his favourite daughter, Evie or 'Little-Womey', to join him, his voice falling 'to the lowest seductive note of yearning'. When she half-pleasurably, half-doubtfully submits, massaging his head and twisting his thick silky hair, he closes his eyes in ease. It is a scene destined to repeat itself many times. But Sam mostly needs all his children around him for perfect contentment: '"Bring up your tea, Looloo-girl: I'm sick, hot head, nedache [headache], dot pagans in my stumjack [got pains in my stomach], want my little fambly around me this morning"' (p. 30). Sam's powerful sexual drive is evident from the first. His intrusiveness and his manipulations are nearly always sexually loaded, no less powerful because he exudes his sexuality unconsciously. 'Working' in the garden, clad only in his overalls, he is inescapably phallic: 'When he waved his golden-white muscular hairless arms, large damp tufts of yellow-red hair appeared. He kept on talking . . . He was not ashamed of his effluvia, thought it a gift that he sweated so freely' (pp. 49–50). He brandishes his sultan's potency like a weapon, frequently indulging in polygamous and paternal fantasies: '"I wish I had a hundred sons and daughters . . . Yes the Mormings [Mormons] had the right idea altogether: fifty women and their children and no work for the old man." He grinned wickedly at Louisa . . . ' (p. 48). He is not averse to confiding the fantasy to adults, to his Indian associate, Naden, and even to the shrewd Lady Modore.

The gratifications of sultanhood reach their height on the morning of the birth of his seventh child, which coincides with his return from Malaya and with the death of the older patriarch, David Collyer. Reclining on the settee 'on a billow of silks and cottons', he exults in the arrayed treasures which he has collected from the 'age-old shores of the East'. Responding with surprise to the luxuriousness in himself which Eastern things evoke, he has filled several crates with his purchases and has been careful to keep them out of the hands of his Pollit relations. As he complacently receives the homage of neighbours and relatives, he contemplates his likely inheritance of some of his father-in-law's power. 'What with the new baby and the splendours from Malaya, it was a morning of satisfactions' (p. 303).

The uneasy restlessness of Sam's emotional life is as pervasive in his family as the fishy smell with which he later pollutes Spa House. Indeed, as I argue below, the analogy is no accident. Sam, however, has trained himself to ignore his darker self. 'Some time the secret life rises and overwhelms us—a tidal wave. We must not be carried away. We have . . . too much to lose . . . Forget, forget!' he tells himself (p. 18). 'Greedy for the daylight', he keeps the gods and trolls of his underworld at bay by his faith in the floodlit world of science, by his powerful fun as father and by his endless talk. Cheerfulness is a goal he strenuously tries to achieve and with the talk of the bright new world of brotherhood and freedom, he lectures himself and others into a stupor. Unlike Henny, he has buried his less civilized self, in

Dinnerstein's words, 'that wordless alogical being who lives inside each of us' and, as a result, this repressed self exerts a 'dark, rebellious, chaotic power' over the shape of his life (Dinnerstein, p. 11). Enveloped in facts and science as he is, he discloses a powerful sub-humanity. Dinnerstein remarks that 'the subhumanity of women is proverbially obvious . . . the sub-humanity of men may in fact be more ominous' (p. 15).

Sam, in fact, is an extreme example of the human inability to recover from the infantile illusion of omnipotence that Freud describes. His sexuality 'resonates . . . with the massive orienting passions that first take shape in pre-verbal, pre-rational human infancy' (Dinnerstein, p. 15). And his most basic, unacknowledged urge is to recover as far as possible the infant illusion of omnipotence when child and mother merged in delightful harmony. He is remarkably successful in repressing the 'discovery that circumstance is incompletely controllable, and that there exist centres of subjectivity, of desire and will, opposed or indifferent' to his own, which Dinnerstein describes as 'an original and basic human grief' (p. 60). But the repression can only be effected at great cost to himself and his family. Indeed the children, who exist primarily to satisfy his attempt to regain vicariously the lost infant delight, are doomed to suffer the full brunt of his yearning. And to suffer it more intensely as their growing threatens his hopes of gratification.

An early scene which graphically illustrates Sam's need to invade his children under the guise of nourishing them is his siphoning of a chewed sandwich into the mouth of infant Tommy. The incident recalls his feeding of the motherless Louie when she was a baby and his retrieval of infantile harmony via his closeness to the child: '"she could hardly speak, but we knew what the other was thinking"', he reflects, voicing a familiar theme. Sam has a great need to get inside the minds (and bodies) of his children. At this point, the impulse to force Louie back into an infantile receptacle is too strong: 'Mottled with contained laughter, he stretched his mouth to hers, trying to force [a] banana into her mouth with his tongue' (p. 58).

Sam's drive for omnipotence, literally irrepressible, colours every aspect of his life and thought. Only in his rare moments as disinterested ichthyologist does he transcend the stunting emotions. Convinced of hs own goodness, he sees himself as a special, naturally deserving object of Providence: 'he smiled at Fate, for he believed Fate was on his side' (p. 265). He is an acknowledged freethinker, but he has retained all the religious egoism of the New England Fathers: 'Fate always had a lesson for him, just as every book that fell on its face open, and every scrap of muddy newsprint blowing in the wind and even every shop sign might hold a message for him' (pp. 264–5). Tohoga House provides him with a wonderful chance to be God: his 'sunflower coloured head' could often be seen 'spying out of the attic

windows . . . for some toddler who might be making for the Garden
of Eden, Tohoga House . . . he beamed, he bloated with joy, to see
how they feared and loved his great house' (p. 47). The rambling
gardens have become his infantile paradise, furnished with his own
created children, his small zoo, his aquaria, his museum and his
pond: 'What a world of things he had to have to keep himself
amused!', reflects Henny (p. 41).

At the same time, his doctrine of love and espousal of brotherhood
are the reflexes of a nature which wishes to insert itself into every
cranny of the universe.

'Mother Earth,' whispered Sam, 'I love you, I love men and women, I love
little children and all innocent things, I love, I feel I am love itself—how
could I pick out a woman who would hate me so much!' (p. 21)

In Sam's ideal future, all differences of nationality, creed and education will be 'respected' and, ominously, 'gradually smoothed out' (p.
49). The contradictions of his commitment to freedom comically
escape him: 'Why did he feel free? He had always been free, a free
man, a free mind, a freethinker. "By Gemini", he thought, taking a
great breath, "this is how men feel who take advantage of their
power"' (p. 17). '"No one who knows me could doubt my motives"',
he tells Henny, with unconscious irony (p. 148).

Although Sam prides himself on belonging in, and even eventually
leading, the big male world, he must have contact with the world of
woman. Only woman can retrieve that sense of oneness with the
'other' natural world; only the mermaid-woman can recreate the
oceanic harmony of infancy. Thus it was inevitable that Sam should
choose Henny, a woman who powerfully evokes the age-old mystery
of her sex, the 'Old Woman of the Sea', as he privately calls her. The
identification of woman with the Other, with Nature, is, of course, as
old as time. De Beauvoir, for example, describes the way man assigns
the role of 'other' to women in order to console himself for his
loneliness in nature.

For Sam the female sex is divided into mothers and daughters. The
idea of woman as an independent individuality cannot lodge in his
imagination. Thus Henny has been thoroughly reduced to mother;
she has become her function, as his favourite name for her denotes—
'Mothering'. Her destiny in Sam's eyes is perfectly represented in the
heavy china cup, wreathed with roses and labelled *Mother*, which he
made the children buy. As Louie grows from child to woman, he
begins to cast her too in the role of mother, dismissing her 'discontent' as immature womanhood: 'All girls were discontented till they
married and had men and babies' (p. 377). The aggression which
fuels this desire to slot Louie into instant motherhood is horribly
exposed in his suggestion that the fourteen-year-old girl assist at her
stepmother's confinement. Meanwhile, the world of work charmingly

supplies him with several child-women, secretaries or younger col-
leagues, who are drawn to his potent charisma. Occasionally, he
plays with the idea of substituting 'sweet little beauts ... seventeen
years old' in place of the old wife, but better still is the comforting
idea of a child-woman waiting for him '"in the back street of life,
without children ... that is even better than children, perhaps—and
besides I have children"' (p. 479). Within the family, Evie provides a
licit sexual gratification, although even she finally avoids his bed.
Polygamy is more than a fantasy in Sam's life.

For the rest, woman's function is that of ministering angel, a phrase
he uses often. Sam thus perceives woman as identical with nature, in
Dinnerstein's words, 'a bottomless source of richness', a being not
human enough to have primary or self-evident needs; if, like Henny,
she withholds her bounty, or refuses to mirror his self-perception of
worth, power and significance, she is perceived as 'a monster, anomalous and useless', and he is justified in using any ruthless tactics
whatever. Thus Sam is frequently outraged and bewildered by Henny's refusal to reflect his sense of his self-importance. Sam's ideal
female is necessarily kept 'in live captivity, obediently energetic,
fiercely protective of [her] captor's pride, ready always to vitalize his
projects with [her] magic maternal blessing and to support them with
[her] concrete, self-abnegating maternal help' (Dinnerstein, p. 169).
Thus Louie's demonstrations of her growing individual, independent
power are always threatening to Sam and may even induce infantile
attempts to desecrate them in excremental ways. Her sublime quotations from Confucius on friendship, for example, evoke a string
of sordid analogies from her father, culminating in '"A chamber
pot was given me and in return a toilet bowl I gave"' (p. 276).
'"Women is trouble; women is cussed; you have got to learn to
run women ... "', he tells Ernie (p. 472).

Sam's need to control women is reinforced by his puritan upbringing and tendencies. The little we learn of his mother is the fact that
she suffered from a dissolute husband and secured a promise of
premarital sexual purity from her son on her deathbed. A man of
powerful sexual drives, Sam attempts to ignore them or rationalize
them as 'love', denying the body and hence, unlike Henny and Ellen,
separating himself from acceptance of its dirtiness. Priding himself on
his whiteness/fairness, in contrast with dark women or the dark Asian
men he patronizes, Sam assures himself that he lives in the mind, not
the body. His cultivated cheerfulness, willed belief in a bright destiny, universal brotherhood and the pure world of science, his dislike
of literature or the stained fabric of history, his fear of alcohol, are all
expressions of his repressed sexual life. Perceiving himself as 'a kind
of Livingstone', a pure soul venturing into the dark heart of the
world, he looks forward to a Golden Age, comically summed up by
the narrator as 'permeated by simple jokes and ginger-ale horseplay,

tuneful evenings, open-air theatres and innumerable daisy chains of naturalists threading the earth and looking, looking . . . ' (p. 226).

Denying the body, of course, affirms it with redoubled power. Dinnerstein, drawing on the work of other writers, sees the repression as having two major effects:

a compulsive concentration of attention and energy on that which can be predicted, controlled, manipulated, possessed and preserved, piled up and counted. And it consists on the other hand of the ashamed eruption of a dirty interest in this rejected body. (p. 135)

Both tendencies are displayed to grandiose effect in Sam. His intrusive fascination with Louie's adolescent change of life, for example, is acutely presented:

Louie was his first adolescent, too: he was full of the mystery of female adolescence, of which, in his prim boyhood, he had been ignorant. He poked and pried into her life, always with a scientific, moral purpose, stealing into her room when she was absent, noting her mottoes on the wall, and investigating her linen, shivering with shame when suggestive words came into her mouth . . . and all with a shrinking niceness, a qualmish sensibility which surprised and repelled her . . . With mental lip-licking, he followed her in her most secret moments. (pp. 329–30)

If Sam regains something of infantile bliss in his relationship with maternal and childish women, these relationships are also threatening. '"I need a woman to understand me. That is my softness. I want you to understand me"' he tells Henny in one of their lulls in fighting (p. 149); nevertheless he clearly fears her witch-like or devilish power and spares no pains to reduce her physically and morally to the status of slave. As Henny clearly perceives, the numerous children are effective fetters on her independent energy. Invested with the power of the mother, Henny is also potentially destructive. On more than one occasion, Sam sees her as a Medea and shudders at her threats. As Dinnerstein comments:

while she provides . . . vital support for the early growth of the self, the mother is inevitably felt as a menace to that self. She is the outstanding feature of the arresting, sometimes overwhelming, realm within which the self's boundaries must be defined. The multiple rhythms of this outside realm, its pulls, pressures, and distractions, can threaten to swamp the nascent self's own needs and intentions, to blur its perception of its own outlines, to deflect its inner sense of direction and drown out its inner voice. (p. 111)

'Sam the Bold's' endless talk may thus be the chatter of an inwardly frightened man.

Sam's unease at Louie's obvious sexual growth ('he wanted a slim, recessive girl whose sex was ashamed', p. 329), his frequent attempts to shame her, his inexplicable anger on behalf of a father accused of incest and his strange, exultant reaction to Henny's birth pangs, forcing the frightened children to listen at the bottom of the stairs, all expose his deep fear and resentment of women. Interesting too, is his Sam-language, an infantile version of Artemus Ward's idiom, which he often uses to express emotions too outrageous for normal speech: females are 'hannimiles' or 'crazy she-males' who should not have the vote, '"Becaze they know nuffin! Becaze if they aint got childer, they need childer to keep 'em from goin' crazy; en if they have childer, the childer drive em crazy"' (pp. 74, 113). At times these submerged feelings of anger become more wide-ranging and erupt into his public euphorics, in notions of permissible murder, eugenics and the weeding out of misfits and degenerates by means of the gas chamber.

This repression of instinctive life has a wider meaning, however, which reaches into the heart of the novel's moral dialectic. Sam sees himself on the side of all that is vital and good; in fact, he is on the side of death. Preoccupied with his immortality in the duplicates of himself, his children, and unable to come to terms with his carnality, he suffers from the neurotic denial of death, which Freud perceived as the heart of civilization's discontents. Sam keeps sturdily to the daylight world of science, avoiding the snakes and dragons of his dreams, and building elaborate defences against the knowledge of early loss. But the bitter knowledge is at work in his life, nevertheless, souring all his relationships, thoughts and enterprises and effectively shutting him off from genuine joy. In this, he typifies what Dinnerstein and others see as the central failure of our species, the failure to leave childhood behind and take one's fate in one's own hands. Unable to live erotically in the present, as his daughter will do, he fouls his own Eden and like Saturn or the minotaur gobbles up the living flesh of his young people. In this he is representative of excremental, life-denying forces in society at large.

If Sam represses what D. H. Lawrence described as the 'dark forest' in himself, Henny is instinctively in touch with it, as I have already mentioned. She knows, without articulating her knowledge, what is wrong with Sam's version of life; she daily and mutely criticizes it simply by being Henny. It is this instinctive knowledge that Louie is seeking to understand from the beginning of the novel's action. Almost the first picture we have of her is her reaction to Henny's mock strangling: 'Louisa looked up into her stepmother's face, squirming, but not trying to get away, questioning her silently, needing to understand, in an affinity of misfortune' (p. 20). By the close of the story, Louie has absorbed Henny's mute form of knowledge and moved on to an understanding that eludes Henny herself. Not only does she finally understand what is wrong with Sam's world view, she understands Henny's unwitting collaboration in his neurosis. She has freed herself from the pernicious past and from the fate of repeating the destructive dependency of her parents. It is therefore appropriate that the novel closes with her abandonment of the family, for the knowledge that she carries in her bones is that the family can initiate, feed and endlessly perpetuate destructive forces. It is the particular symbiosis between the two parents—would-be Apollonian Sam and Dionysian Henny—which is the rotten core of the family apple. Dinnerstein and Stead appear to agree that man uses woman to support him in his free creation of his own existence, keeping her unfree for that purpose, and that he also uses her to help him cope emotionally with *un*freedom:

The main use man makes of woman in the face of unfreedom is to hide from himself the depth of his capitulation to societal coercion, the depth of his failure to leave childhood behind and take his fate in his own hands. (Dinnerstein, p. 188)

But there is another wider vision than Louie's embedded in this extraordinary novel. It is a vision which is dependent on hers but links her understanding of a particular family to broader political apprehensions. Rarely explicit, it breathes through the pores of the text, emerging in subtle analogies, images, literary and historical clues, juxtapositions, pauses, emphases. The larger world of governments and nations and the historical past are barely realized by the characters, yet they are there by implication, shadowy presences which are also engaged in this 'storm in a teacup'. At this point Stead and Dinnerstein seem to come even closer together. What happens when man evades the dark instinctual life within himself, by relying upon woman as the 'other' to represent it, is that he maintains what Dinnerstein terms the 'blind drivenness' of his exploits; the misgiving that 'there is something trivial and empty, ugly and sad in what he does' is kept impotent within the covert culture (p. 214). Writing in 1939, at a time when she was deeply unhappy and surrounded by political activists, Stead had the same sense of urgency as Dinnerstein in 1976 and, I suggest, the same conviction that the small world of the family was profoundly relevant to the world crisis.

Extraordinary as Sam is, he is by no means an isolated phenomenon; indeed, in the last third of the novel he resonates with echoes of 1930s' ideologies and there are implications that his pathology is a distorted image of the external one. The decision to locate the novel in America, rather than its historical home, Australia, is significant here. *The Man Who Loved Children* is by no means an anti-American novel, but it is wholly appropriate that Sam should be American. The popular ideology of the United States, especially in the 1930s, is particularly explicit and familiar, self-conscious and even ambivalent about itself, so that as an American, Sam clearly evokes a wider range of cultural/political resonances than as any other national. Stead frequently maintained that the novel was set in America to 'shield the family', although she also admitted that Sam had something of the American in his make-up. To see him wholly as American would be disastrously reductive, but his American attributes are a useful political shorthand, deftly making the link between man and society, repressed sexual energy and destructive political forces. Sam's political notions are, of course, a general grab-bag of emotive ideas that happen to fit his peculiar sexual pathology. His ideas are also latently Fascist, particularly when he is under threat. Gross exaggeration though he is, many of Sam's crudities and inconsistencies are recognizable as received American traits; he swims very well in the waters of the New World. As Puritan, materialist, optimist, 'self-made man', believer in brotherhood, science, progress, democracy and constitutional rights, Sam has ideals that are familiarly American. Interpreting his own progress as one of log-cabin to White House, he complacently appropriates Washington as his rightful home. Washington is his 'New Jerusalem', 'built on a definite plan for a definite purpose and not by the worst cases in a madhouse', it is 'the great white city of brotherhood' (pp. 130, 244–5, 205). This 'heart of the democratic Athens' with its 'flashing colonnades' is a metaphor of his success, its advertised fairness and freedom a guarantee that his self-conviction of fairness and freedom will be rewarded. '"I sometimes think I live in the White House—or I think Samuel thinks so . . . I can't understand why he never went into politics, with his gift of the gab and greensward style!"' reflects Henny (p. 90). And Sam himself on one occasion smugly identifies with the 'Great White Father', object of the reverence of numbers of multicultural American infants (pp. 72–3). Patriotism and paternalism and even polygamy are delightfully wedded in Sam's transparently murky consciousness. Henny, of course, sees a different Washington: 'She detested perennial Heaven, Sinai's thunder, the new Jerusalem's powerful hierarchy; she felt it was the Eden of fleshpot men and ugly women striving for God knows what ugly, unhewn, worthy ends, not for the salvation of miserable creatures like herself' (p. 87). Temperamentally unfitted for money-making and competition in the adult world, Sam implicitly reveres Darwinian notions of survival and has great reverence for money and beautiful possessions; inherently impractical, he makes a fetish of practical tasks; a deeply sensual man, he values a muscular Puritanism. Even his own names and his heroes have ironic potential. Named Sam and Clemens after David Stead's favourite humourist, he has something of Twain's early enthusiasm for the machine-age and aspires, vainly, to his folksy, heart-warming humour. His boyish innocence recalls Tom Sawyer, and perhaps Huck Finn's dark quest is ironically intended here as a silent question mark. That Artemus Ward is the source of his would-be-comic Sam-language also reflects on the crude aggression which the language frequently projects. Sam is regularly as manipulative, self-serving and falsely emotional as Brer Fox. For the rest, his heroes are Faraday, Clerk Maxwell, Einstein, Theodore Roosevelt and Woodrow Wilson. '"If my children can't distinguish between Grimm and Clerk Maxwell, let them go and jump in the lake ... !"', he remarks with unconscious Freudian significance (p. 112). His regard for the scientists is self-explanatory; Woodrow Wilson is selected because prohibition came in during his Presidency. The choice of Theodore Roosevelt is significant. Louie, who is trained to recite Roosevelt's strictures on the 'strenuous life', has quickly uncovered his sexism, but the analogy is more extensive. Roosevelt has been described by one history, roughly contemporary with the novel, as a man of 'tremendous energy', a 'defiant robustness' and 'an unquenchable desire to shine in public':

He had essentially 'a boy's mind': The adolescent quality of his thought and action is very apparent and very striking. His mind was one of extraordinary elasticity, cheerful egoism and self-confidence. He did not hesitate in praising himself.

Even his decline into 'youthfulness soured by disappointment', which 'expressed itself in a vindictive and continuous stream of fault-finding' is close to Sam's destructiveness in disappointment.[10]

But it is above all Sam's innocent, Adam-like self-righteousness which gains from the New World transference. In 'A Waker and Dreamer', Stead described her father as 'an Adam', who 'believed in himself so strongly that, sure of his innocence, pure intentions, he felt he was a favoured son of Fate (which to him was progress and therefore good), that he was Good, and he could not do anything but good'. Stead is obviously drawing on and no doubt exaggerating certain aspects of her father for her own creative purposes; it was not her habit to make literal studies of people. Nevertheless it was a happy coincidence that her father's dream of innocence, grounded in secularism, science and ideas of progress, meshed so well with American ideals. Louie very early absorbs the link between patriotism and self in her father's make-up. Advised to learn '"good American grammar"', she replies: '"I know that ... there's no one as good as me"' (p. 136).

In the last third of the novel, the destructive aspects of Sam's New World/Utopian identification come to the fore, even though the explicit analogies are few. One brilliant touch draws out the connection between Sam's specious, paternalistic philosophy and the worst aspects of Western popular culture. Encouraged to get on to a radio programme, he begins to think of himself as 'Uncle Sam'. Either foreign policy or the children's hour would suit him, but in any case he plans to tell 'the people' folk tales or 'tales of our revolutionary past', which will emphasize America's moral difference from 'crooked old Europe' (p. 518). The cumulative effect of the identification of Sam with America is to establish his would-be

Houyhnhnm tendencies and those of his culture, or any culture that prides itself on a 'rational' or benevolent ideology. Swift, who frequently lurks in the text as a sarcastically bland presence, saw it all long ago, and Sam has much in common with Gulliver. Shrinking from his Yahoo self, preserving his 'whiteness', channelling his sexual energy into paternalism, he is doomed to hate.

Sam's capacity for destruction is frequently apparent, but in the last third of the novel his aggression is fully and dangerously unleashed. The move to Spa House and his loss of his position change the balance of power between the two household gods. Henny loses ground in the 'war', as Sam gains it. The whole brunt of their desperate financial situation falls on her, as he retreats into his Swiss Family Robinson. His repressed insecurities emerge in the fevered pursuit of his children's secrets and the wild aggression of his public policies. Meanwhile his invectives against women increase in frequency and openness. His fascinated fear of Louie's sexuality, in particular, leads to an act of implicit rape—his gift of James Bryce's propagandist book on the Belgian atrocities, ostensibly to make her ideas of procreation more 'scientific'.

The desperate family situation becomes critical after Sam receives an anonymous letter suggesting that his last child is not his. It is a blow that Sam's frail control of his sexual fears cannot absorb. The situation becomes literally murderous, for Henny has lost the real hold she had on him. Unequal though she was, Henny until this moment, has been a dominant, balancing power in the family, and this power has now been wrested from her. The hold is not just the legal claim, represented by the gold band, although Henny explicitly sees this as lost, repeatedly expressing her fears that Sam can now jettison her. The hold was also an emotional one. As Dinnerstein comments in her explanation of the persistent double standard in sexual relations, man's fear of adultery is 'supported . . . on that stubborn wordless level of adult feeling which is continuous with infant feeling'. The wife's adultery 're-evokes for him the situation in which mother, unbearably, did not belong to baby'. At the same time the act disrupts the male solidarity that evolves during a boy's Oedipal period 'by establishing a principled independence, a more or less derogatory distance from women' (pp. 38, 41, 53). Sam's most agonizing memory, it will be remembered, is of a past flirtation between his wife and his best friend.

Sam's unregenerate infantilism now becomes murderous. All the children immediately notice the difference in the parents' quarrels but it is Louie who bears the main burden of awareness. The morning after their first quarrel over the letter, she expects to find their bodies on the floor, and in the days that follow she is the chief witness of Henny's despair and her chief intermediary between Sam and the objects of his uncontrollable aggressions. Thrashing around in her new desperation, Henny tries, hopelessly, the traditional source of help by appealing to her one-time lover. The scene with the shallow Bert is a finely modulated dramatization of her extremity; her eyes have a strange glow, her hands tremble and her breast heaves with painful breaths; 'she turned her head aside and hid her eyes in her hand. He heard her whispering, "Oh, God, Oh, God, this is terrible!"' (p. 450). To the embarrassed Bert she implies that this may be her last day on earth. At this point it is impossible not to see the analogy between Henny and the marlin which has been caught for Sam and which he now boils down to extract its oil. 'Its great eyes were sunken; it looked exhausted from its battle for life; there was a gaping wound in its deepest part' (p. 464). The manic chopping up and boiling process which follows is clearly fuelled by Sam's wild hurt; contrary to his own description of its economic utility, it is an 'angry stew' (p. 473).

The first night of burning is a 'night of jamboree', as Sam tends his brew, burning Henny's insult out of existence, and chanting his Freudian chant '"Good name in man and woman, good my Lord is the immediate Jewel of their Souls!"'. The obliterating stench of the fish, which is destined to linger in the house for years, is his stench: '"When you fellers snuff my mortal remains, it won't be half what this is!"', he tells his boys (p. 469). All the children have to take watches to tend the fire, but Sam reaches the height of sweet vengeance when Henny herself takes a turn. Even nature seems to take part in the immensity of what is happening, presenting a sort of celestial family drama:

Somewhere beyond the world, an enormous voice shouted, whips cracked, and sheet-iron clanged through space, while every few minutes the flares of an open hearth, distant and beneath, lighted the entire sky. (p. 471)

Although all are affected by the desperate game, only Louie understands that the minotaur is at large: '"When Moloch in Jewry munched children in fury, 'twas thou Devil dining with pure intent"', is her response to her father's chants. Meanwhile the truth that Henny's life, like the marlin's, is played out is brought dramatically home in the final speedy working out of her game of double patience. The symbolism is almost too obvious:

Henny forgot the storm and the fish in the copper and looked helplessly at the eight stacks of cards before her, each with a king on top. The game that she had played all her life was finished; she had no more to do; she had no game. (pp. 471–2)

The full force of Sam's fury is not realized until several hours later. Strangely, all his efforts have not assuaged the obscure sense of loss that the accusation of adultery has opened up:

Wasn't his life empty, always amusing the kids, thinking up projects for them, teaching them to be good men and women when they ran off upon their own bents and a woman was always twisting them, snatching them away from him? (p. 474)

In a scene of appalling cruelty, he turns his anger on the child who is, he feels, most like himself. When Little Sam refuses to shovel the remains of the fish because it makes him sick, his father covers him with a dipper-full of the cauldron's mess: 'He stood dripping with the juice, fish tatters on his head, one long shred of skin hanging down over one eye, making him look like the offspring of a mermaid and a beachcomber' (p. 492). The scene is carefully configured to evoke the submerged sexual forces at work in Sam, Henny's grief and her new inability to intervene, Louie's helpless understanding, and the varying responses of the other children from shock to collusion to outright rejection. The culminating touch of Sam's threat to do the same to 'Mothering' and his attempt to draw Ernie into the act emphasize the root cause of his anger and the pernicious effect that this new manifestation of neurosis is having on the children's natural affections.

Incidental to the whole episode, although by no means laboured, is the association between Sam's manic attack on nature and nature's desecration by industrial society. Sam, of course, usually sees nature as a mother; at this crucial moment in his emotional life, he sees her as like a Magdalen or slave 'licking at his feet . . . like a woman, that he had read of somewhere, that washed the feet of the man she loved and dried them with her hair' (p. 475). Dinnerstein also sees a relation between 'the murderous infantilism of our relation to nature' and 'the murderous infantilism of our sexual arrangements'. Sam's burning of the fish duplicates the mother-directed anger, which Dinnerstein sees as central to the modern desecration of nature: 'the son has set his foot on the mother's chest, he has harnessed her firmly to his uses, he has opened her body once and for all and may now help himself at will to its riches' (Dinnerstein, p. 104). Certainly, the farcical collection of bottles of marlin oil which confront Henny in the wash-house, neatly labelled fish-fry, bike-oil, and just oil, which are the end-product of Sam's labours, along with the permanent traces of grease and smoke in the house, resonate with social overtones.

The conclusion of the drama, with Louie's decision to kill both parents and liberate the children, has puzzled some readers. The decision is readily understandable, though, if we are alive to the development of this psycho-sexual crisis. Louie's decision to kill Sam rarely presents a problem—his minotaur properties are only too recognizable; but why Henny?

Louie's growth in understanding and discovery of herself as an artist is, of course, a complicated story and there is no space here to deal with it in detail.[11] But, briefly, her development is dependent partly on the gifts that both parents indirectly bequeath her. From Sam she learns to observe with a naturalist's dispassionate concentration; she also inherits his independence of thought, originality, confidence and even creativity. She inherits, in fact, the gifts that Sam assumes in himself but that in him only exist in embryo. Sam's story-telling is cramped by his moralizing bent, his originality is pathologically twisted and cracked-brain, his independence is stunted by his repressions. He offers his child these gifts and then withholds them, or presents her with warped versions, but he has had the effect of stimulating her own creative energies. She is forced to resist, question and define the terms of her dissent; she creates her own language and presents her father with a rebellious drama, acted by all his children. The drama is unintelligible to him even in translation, but it presents the truth about him, as all the children delightedly recognize. It is almost as if Louie's growth in understanding, creativity and self-knowledge feeds on Sam's failures. At the same time, of course, her stepmother's acrid perceptions help her to see her father in the round:

Whenever her irritations got too deep, she mooched in to see her mother. Here, she had learned, without knowing she had learned it, was a brackish well of hate to drink from, and a great passion of gall ... something that put iron in her soul and made her strong to resist the depraved healthiness and idle jollity of the Pollit clan. (p. 258)

In addition, the daily melodrama casts constant light on the sexual issues. As the eldest child, verging on puberty, she arouses all the powerful energies of the father; potentially cast in the role of mother herself and often actually a substitute mother to the youngest children, she is particularly alive to Henny's sufferings. And Henny is also drawn to Louie's female predicament, mourning that she too must be dragged into the 'muck' of womanhood. Louie is also gifted with the partial status of outsider. Not only are her annual visits to Harper's Ferry and her mother's people a valuable insight into other ways of living, but Henny's gruff treatment is paradoxically useful. She is trained in dispassion and saved from sentimentality. '"I beat her, but I don't lie to her"', says Henny' (pp. 126–7). The shift in her allegiance from father to stepmother is itself an index of her rapid growth, given the great charisma her father can exert. The chief victim of her parents and their declining fortunes, she is also the greatest beneficiary.

Louie's discoveries in the world of everyday are also remarkably extended by her discoveries in the world of literature and, above all, by her confidence in her burgeoning creativity. She delves into poetry, philosophy, history and fairy-tale, reading in the shower, over the washing up, during the mild passages of her parents' rages, while looking after the children. Literature is both a refuge and a discovery. Stead refrains from explicating Louie's growth, allowing it to emerge in the fragmentary and even confused way of Louie's own experience. From her patterns of reading, her own story-telling, her cryptically angry responses to her father, it appears that she wins through to a vision of erotic possibility, which is the direct opposite of the thanatos that her father unconsciously worships. It is clear, for example, that she is inspired by Nietzsche's call to self-love, pinning his injunction 'Throw not away the hero in your soul' to her book-case, and, like Nietzsche's, her quest will involve a rejection of the family. 'If I didn't know I was a genius I would die: why live?', she mutters to herself early in the narrative. Perennially clumsy and physically lumpy, she is well aware of her growing mental power and the other children know it and respect her natural superiority. She draws strength from the friendly night-rider, that no one hears but herself, and knows that she walks to a different drum. However sordid the family squabbles, she quickly recovers from them by retreating into her own fantastic world. 'Spreading glass but subtle wings, wide as the world, Louie, meandering through flowery mazes of metaphysics, was walking out with beauty and destiny' (p. 190).

After Sam's return from Malaya, the battle with him passes more directly into Louie's hands, and in many scenes she is shown as baffling and defeating her father with weapons drawn from her reading. One interchange, in particular, reveals the distance she has travelled from him:

'I know something,' said Louie, 'I know there are people not like us, not muddleheaded like us, better than us.'

'What do you mean?'

'But I know something else: if it is chaos, it will not be chaos forever: "out of chaos ye shall give birth to a dancing star!" Nietzsche said that.'

Sam blushed, and he said gently, 'You mean, out of confusion we will bring order.'

'No,' cried Louie, 'no, no; you understand nothing. People like us understand nothing. I know people at school better than us, better in their minds than—' she stopped in deep embarrassment. (p. 302)

Sam's response is typically Apollonian, but Louie already recognizes the Dionysian energies within herself and their roots in creativity. Her growing confidence in her powers increasingly makes her Sam's match: seeing his humility at her creative efforts, Louie 'would strike at him verbally, or flash a look which said, plainer than speaking, "I am triumphant, I am king"' (p. 341). The more she understands of his predatory motives, the more she is able to despise him. His gift of Bryce's book inspires an adult passion of loathing for him. At the same time, she grows confident of her power to confront the 'infernal middle kingdom of horror ... she felt sure that she only *felt* what was going on under the ribs of the visible world' (p. 381).

Just before the final crisis of Henny's death, there is another important interchange with Sam about life, death, sex and love (pp. 476–8). Louie's protestation that she only knows about love ('I love, I love, I only know about love'), seems to imply that she understands that her father's ideology of love is really one of hate, and that she has discovered a different way of loving or of being in the world, that is similar to the erotic passion celebrated by Blake and Nietzsche. Louie thus sees herself as confronted with the responsibility of ending this destructive conflict: 'it fell to her, no one else would do it or understand the causes as she did' (p. 503). The quarrel, Louie perceives, 'is ruining [the children's] moral natures'. The terrible divisions imposed on them by the parents' conflicting claims, their degeneration to objects in the savage tussle between the two, are warping their chances to grow. The family has become a deathly crucible, creating in the lives of the children the neurotic dependencies which have already ruined the lives of the parents. A whole series of incidents exposes the sudden unleashing of vicious forces and their eroding effects on the children's attitudes. Ernie is already turned towards death, as his hanged self, the doll attached to his bedstead, dramatizes. His mother has tampered with the springs of his nature when she broke an unwritten trust with him by stealing his last dollar; 'to see the empty box there was like the end of his world'. From that moment a new vacancy enters his life and he thinks 'something strange: he did not know what it was'. His pathetic hoarding of lead and the subsequent struggle with Sam over its storage are a searing demonstration of his impotent misery. Henny herself understands the change in their close relationship, symbolized by the lead, so that the scene of his discovery of emptiness is given tragic dimensions. She is aware that they have lost the old intimacy for ever, and her terrible beating of the boy in her last days is really an expression of their mutual grief. Even Sam is aware that he is witnessing 'Eleusinian mysteries'. Henny's relationship with Tommy also suffers a 'great shock' when she realizes that he is already imitating his father's predatory tactics with the other sex. The dependent Evie is drawn more and more into her father's incestuous embraces, rapidly evolving into miniature mermaid. The identical twins, Little Sam and Saul, reflect reverse aspects of the same confused reaction; Little Sam is impotent in his rages, Saul rejects the whole world in disgust. Even the baby is not safe. Sam's encouragement of his attempt to eat his own excrement and Henny's inability to prevent it, is virtually a metaphor of the self-dirtying impulses that the parents' hate has unleashed.

Louie's decision to kill both parents reflects her sense that they have both become monstrous. 'She no longer thought of Sam as her father; she had not thought of him as anything but a mouthy jailer for months.' As for Henny, 'she did not see how her fate would be better if she went on living' (p. 503). Henny's life is played out; the energies of her great struggle to keep Sam's deathliness at bay have failed; her access to the instinctive sources of life has dried up and she has become a destructive force herself. The scenes of her wild attacks on Louie and Ernie are furies of self-punishment: '"I'll beat you to death"', she cries, later warning them to stay out of the house 'for she might do herself a mischief if she looked at them' (p. 441).

The change in her relationship with Sam forces her to duplicate his use of the children as objects of power. They have always been her hard but loving destiny, but now that destiny is threatened with destruction—Sam has the power to take them away. The children are also her only way of punishing Sam, who fears her special relationship with them; like Medea she knows that the threat of child-murder is a powerful attack on the father's power. As Louie reflects: 'Those two selfish, passionate people, terrible as gods in their eternal married hate, do not care for [the children]' (p. 503). Thus Louie realizes that Henny, in her desperation, has abandoned the humanity and respect for her children's freedom which has always been an implicit part of her motherhood, and become monstrous. She has become the mermaid to Sam's minotaur.[12]

The final section of the novel, describing Louie's departure on her 'walk round the world' is, I suggest, more mythic than real, a dramatization of her liberation into a vision of love that is self-loving.[13] Free of the self-hate and the collaborative hate of her parents' marriage, she is 'rotten with innocence'; as artist and as woman, she has achieved the dolphin's playful enjoyment of the present, a Blakean childishness. 'She smiled, felt light as a dolphin undulating through the waves, one of those beautiful, large, sleek marine mammals that plunged and wallowed, with their clever eyes' (p. 525).

9

Seasons of Learning

Not surprisingly, education plays a large part in female autobiographies of childhood of both centuries. Although it would be absurd to claim that these texts are comprehensively representative of women's educational experience, they have much to offer the historian, supplementing the painstaking documentary findings of such studies as Coral Chambers's *Lessons for Ladies*[1] with experience at the grass roots. It may be useful to know that in 1875 women were first admitted to the University of Melbourne, but the historical fact has a new reality when one is presented with the effects of the previous bar on an individual life.

In terms of class, period and region these narratives are, of course, remarkably diverse, and it might be thought that the daughter of a wealthy Melbourne family in the 1850s, such as Eliza Chomley, might have little in common with a girl in a semi-charitable institution in 1915, such as Laura Todd, but in fact the similarities are more surprising than the differences. If women's autobiographies have a common complaint, it is the inadequacy of educational opportunities, and of all the narratives studied here, only four are consistently positive about their experiences; of these, two are accounts of private education (Nancy Adams and Janet Mitchell) and two are written by headmistresses, who use their life-stories partly as vehicles for their own educational philosophies (Constance Mackness and Vera Summers). With only a few exceptions, the autobiographers who are the subject of this book put a very high value on education and see school as a crucial, if not the crucial, experience; they are retrospectively perceptive of the limitations and reductive ideologies of the educations they were offered, scornful of negligent, tyrannical or fraudulent teachers, and sensitive to the hidden agenda transmitted by both peers and authority figures. For many writers the school years appear to have been fraught with acute but ambivalent challenges, on one hand offering a new, enlarging life and on the other imposing undreamt of barriers.

It is often school which first imposes the social grid of gender difference. Some writers see school as imprinting this sense of difference with unsurpassed severity, while others describe their bewilderment in terms of the immigrant learning the ways of a foreign country. As we have seen, many narrators represent the early years of childhood as a period of confident freedom which is seen in retrospect as a privileged male freedom, inevitably forfeit sooner or later, and it is often the school which imposes or at least justifies the forfeit. In Ellen Campbell's case it is the brother's school which teaches the difference between masculine and feminine, creating a division between the two which effectively brings their equality as 'Twin Pickles' to an end; Judith Wallace ultimately evades the restricting lessons of her school, but she is eventually taught that only men can inherit the land and that her farming skills are not appropriate long-term achievements for women of her class. Thus for many women school represents the sort of 'growing down' experience which Barbara White has described as typical of the female novel of development.[2] Other narrators record their rejection of the restraints of gender, which even at the time seemed absurd to the point of insanity. Reflecting on the nuns' practice of washing the children in a bathing robe, for instance, Kathleen Fitzpatrick comments: 'Our view of the matter was that all adults were mad and nuns the maddest' (*Solid Bluestone Foundations*, p. 91).

There is no scope here for a detailed comparison, but female accounts of school experience appear to differ markedly in some ways from male accounts: relationships with teachers and friends appear to be far more important and determining than the school curriculum or ethos and although intellectual adventures are important, human adventures are in the foreground. Indeed intellectual development is nearly always perceived as dependent on a human context or some human stimulus. Thus Connie Miller sees herself as mathematically ineducable, given her own timidity and an unperceptive teacher at school, but immediately discovers a strong bent for the subject under a later more sympathetic one. Nor are women retrospectively interested in the general social or political ideology of their education, although they are often alive to patriarchal assumptions; the sort of observation that Donald Horne makes of his 1930s State school education, for instance, as 'optimistic, progressive, and radical . . . on the side of revolution, exploration, and innovation'[3] is quite uncharacteristic of the female account. Nor are women so incisively critical of the content of their courses. Less confident of their relevance to the educational purposes of the nation, women seem to have been more impressed with the random, insignificant, determining event or the inspiring/depressing individual. School is perceived as more of a training than an educational experience, interspersed with few moments of intellectual illumination, which might explain why nearly all the accounts of university life are contrastingly enthusiastic; few of the few women who won a university education seem to have outgrown their initial sense of lucky privilege.

Numerous early autobiographers preceive education as the most precious of the benefits denied by a pioneering life. Relegated to the role of nursemaid, Jane Watts despairs the waste of her young years: 'The possibility of growing up an ignorant woman, with no knowledge of books save what she had acquired in childhood—the very opposite, too, of her well-educated, refined intelligent mother—was unpalatable to her in the extreme' (*Family Life in South Australia*, p. 41). Christiane Hiller receives one precious year of schooling in the 1840s and finds it impossible to describe her sorrow when the year was over. As the only daughter, she is required to help her mother from the age of fourteen, 'but there was a constant yearning for more knowledge as well as to serve the Lord in his kingdom'. Unable to confide in anyone, she often gives vent to her grief at night: 'Under this strain my spirit suffered greatly for several years, and I was repeatedly asked whether I was ill' ('Autobiography of Frau Pastor Christiane Hiller', p. 9). Bessie Lee, in a remote mining village in Victoria in the late 1860s, has to walk three hazardous miles to school, 'But I was blithe and fearless, and hungering with intense hunger for knowledge'. When her health proves frail, however, her aunt keeps her at home: 'She was inexorable as Fate, and I had to submit with bitter tears to grow up without schooling, church, religious teaching or child companionship'. Self-education is the only recourse and she gleans what she can from *Paradise Lost* and such magazines as *The London Journal, The Family Herald* and *Bow Bells* (*One of Australia's Daughters*, pp. 23–4). Agnes McEwin, employed as an unpaid mother's help from the age of ten, records her lack of schooling as an insistent refrain: 'neither Sarah nor I went to school', 'I was not getting any schooling', 'I only attended about a week, I found there was no place for me' ('The Girlhood Reminiscences of Agnes McEwin 1858–1942'). Frances Purcell goes to inordinate but impossible lengths to be in time for the schooling which distances her from her degrading role of milk-girl and invariably suffers public disgrace in the process (*A Surry Hills Childhood, 1870*, p. 10). Kathleen Lambert is grateful for a year at a small boarding school: 'That year at L— was truly a resting-place for me before the real battle of life began, and it was well-spent, for it drew together the threads, a little tangled, of a rather exceptional education' (*The Golden South*, p. 18). Tilly Aston is encouraged to go to the University of Melbourne by the Austral Salon and is even given a theatrical benefit for the purpose but is forced to abandon her course because there are few books in Braille; the failure was a 'bitter disappointment . . . more terrible perhaps because I had unwillingly betrayed the confidence of my sponsors' (*Memoirs of Tilly Aston*, p. 48). Alice Henry is able to matriculate because the University of Melbourne's relaxation of its rules coincides with the end of her schooling; girls are still excluded from University courses, however (*Memoirs of Alice Henry*, p. 8).

Many girls who live later, fare no better. Eve Hogan's West Australian childhood of the 1930s is one of the most impoverished; battling to survive by helping their father to scrub out an acre of land a day, the children have as little chance of schooling as they have of parental affection: 'I remember the feelings of relief I had when night fell and we were all safely tucked inside, free of snake bites and axe slashed legs. How lucky we were that nothing had happened that we could not cope with' ('The Hessian Walls', p. 109). Della Edmunds in Northern Queensland in the 1920s is adept at hunting, mining and droving but is totally innocent of institutionalized education: 'I was never taught to read and write, but I picked it up as the years went by'. Convinced of the value of education, she makes valiant efforts to teach herself and makes sure that her son gets a good education (*Della, the Drover*, p. 16). Dorothy Casey-Congdon is unable to continue her schooling after her brother achieves the age of fourteen since the Department of Social Security deems he is old enough to begin supporting the family:

My last day at school . . . was one of great sadness. I couldn't bear to tell Miss Lowry that I was starting work on Monday . . . I sat staring at a blank sheet of paper and chewing the end of my pencil. Then I looked out of the high windows and resented the freedom of the clouds floating by . . . I hated the thought of having to leave a school I had grown to love so much. (*Casey's Wife*, p. 68).

The sense of hurt pride is characteristic. Katharine Susannah Prichard is unable to prepare for a university exhibition because of her mother's illness and her parents cannot afford to pay the fees. 'It seemed disastrous at the time; but Father and Mother never knew how deeply I was disappointed' (*Child of the Hurricane*, pp. 63–4). Determined never to ask her parents for money, she subsequently helps pay for her sister's education and for a recuperative trip for her father. Although her mother understands something of her predicament, her father is 'delighted to see [her] becoming more of a home-girl and mother's help' (p. 66). Prichard is typical of many of these writers in her tenacity of purpose; like Kathleen Fitzpatrick, she even takes command of her own secondary education, insisting on going to a State school, and one that would give her a good chance of winning a university scholarship. Prichard's account of the response of her parents is also representative, for many a father has unwittingly created a great gulf in his relationship with his daughter by insensitivity on this topic. Fairlie Taylor in *Bid Time Return* is removed from school at the age of eleven to help run her father's ironmongery during the 1890s depression; her father is not only incapable of understanding her grief, he is unable to recognize it, assigning her unpaid labour to the shop with the unconcern of a Southern slave owner. Six years later, the old man has to be gradually won round by the womenfolk to the idea of the daughter continuing her education. Connie Miller, who faces a similar situation in the 1920s depression, feels more pity for her father than anger, but the effective breach is almost as wide (*After Summer Merrily*). Roslyn Taylor, on the other hand, is held back in the 1930s by the old-fashioned ideas of her mother: 'She tried to fit me into a mould of her own choosing ... Like many people of her generation and upbringing, she strongly resisted change'. Committed to the convention that men make the decisions, she nevertheless has no difficulty in ignoring the more enlightened ideas of the father: 'In spite of all her protestations about the duties of a married woman, it was becoming increasingly clear to me that it was my mother who really ran the show'. Eventually slotted into business studies instead of art or literature, Taylor bitterly resents the decision for many years. (*Your Hills Are Too High*, p. 83). Other narrators are less frank about parental prejudice and one of the curiosities of Patsy Adam-Smith's *Hear the Train Blow* is her description of the effects of her mother's blanket ban on books with her silence on its reasons.

If poverty of income or attitude deprives many of these autobiographers of education, genteel prescriptions of womanhood can be even more frustrating. Marjorie Butler's *Time Isn't Long Enough* implicitly highlights the pathos of women who are equipped only with the sort of girlish instruction which George Eliot describes in *Middlemarch* as 'comparable to the nibblings and judgement of a discursive mouse'. Faced in the 1920s with life as a single woman and the erosion of the family's wealth ('To be a spinster without occupation or purpose was to me not only depressing but terrifying' p. 54), Butler is eventually absorbed into poorly paid secretarial work and considers herself lucky when a position which is at least interesting comes her way. Eliza Chomley has nothing but scorn for the education she is offered in a genteel establishment in Melbourne in the 1850s; memorable mainly for the 'copious records' of their own personal histories and the 'untoward events which necessitated their teaching', her teachers provide lessons of stupefying dullness: 'writing—in a copy book—one or more pages a day, with moral or didactic copy steps, reading—*Little Arthur's History of England*— later on, *Mrs Markham's English History*, with conversations at the end of each chapter between her and her ineffably priggish children' ('My Memoirs'). Sixty years later, Kathleen Fitzpatrick's education in a Catholic convent seems remarkably similar; long hours are devoted to copying into a copy book and there is a great deal of learning by heart (*Solid Bluestone Foundations*, pp. 88–9). Enid Moon's education in Moss Vale and Sydney from 1911 to 1918 is largely a matter of copying down passages from the *Encyclopaedia Britannica* and memorizing books by rote ('Myself When Young'). Emily Churchward, writing of Adelaide in the 1860s, describes the chaos that ensues when teachers fail to bolster a miserable intellectual diet with physical discipline; she and her sister attend 'Miss Gilbert's Select Seminary for Young Ladies', run by an elderly widow 'professedly very religious, but the "Seminary" might better have been styled "Bear Garden"' (*In Paths Directed*, p. 27). Mildred Snowden, the daughter of Sir Arthur Snowden, recalls that her education in 1870s Melbourne consists of about two hours' daily instruction in which books seem to have been used more as weights for the encouragement of posture than for their content ('Reminiscences'). Mary Drake in 1920s Sydney is sent to an excellent school but is so discouraged from studying that homework had to be done during the chauffeur-driven rides to and from school (*The Trees Were Green*).

Numerous narrators are taught privately for at least some of their education and the accounts of ineffective governesses are legion. 'Pale shades who passed without leaving a single trace of their persons or their teachings' in the words of Henry Handel Richardson (*Myself When Young*, p. 16), governesses are often regarded as fair game for the pranks and evasive tactics of children. Rose Scott Cowen records an extreme instance of children's attempts to rid themselves terminally of a nagging governess by engineering a riding 'accident': 'The Boss [the father] tried to act the stern parent and reprove us but the break in his voice and the twinkle in his eye gave him away' (*Crossing Dry Creeks*, p. 48). Adelaide Lubbock and her brother have to contend with parents with more rigid ideas, but they effectively achieve the departure of several governesses. Their greatest triumph is the dismissal of a much-hated German governess, an effort in which they are abetted by the outbreak of the 1914–18 war: 'I considered it a major contribution to the war effort that my insubordination had caused the enemy within our gates to have been unmasked and deported out of the country' (*People in Glass Houses*, p. 62). For the Delarue girls in 1890s Bankstown, governesses come and go with the regularity of the seasons and are usually more interesting as examples of the infinite variety of human eccentricity than as teachers. They represent the mother's attempts to give her girls the 'thin veneer of culture' necessary if they are to take their place in society: 'She herself had received little schooling and done very well, so she hadn't rebelled against the beliefs of her parents that to be thought clever was almost as damaging to a girl's chances as to be thought "fast"'. Thus Miss Fox, who teaches the children two things, the game Puss-in-the-Corner and a four line verse about

Big-bellied Ben, is succeeded by Miss Reynolds 'a Lady in Reduced Circumstances, who knew absolutely nothing about anything, but had very refined manners'. Having established the foundations for the narrator's chronic bad spelling, she is succeeded by a tartar who believes in Latin verbs, straight backs, rote learning and much brushing of the hair. On the whole, however, governesses do little to interrupt the excellent education in human nature which the narrator amasses for herself and she at least is preserved from the negative lessons which her sister acquires during a brief period at school: 'Lydia ... had developed an inferiority complex (though the term was not then known), because her clothes were never as elaborate as other girls' and the young barbarians teased her by changing her beautiful name, Lydia Victorine, to "Lid o' yer Soup Tureen"' (*A Bunyip Close Behind Me*, pp. 37, 38, 89).

Some positive accounts of governesses exist, however, and both Nancy Adams and Janet Mitchell gratefully record the challenging education they receive from remarkably cultured women. For Mitchell, in particular, her relationship with her governess seems to have been almost as essential for her future sense of an independent self as those with the two other strong-willed women of her childhood, her nanny and her mother. Adelaide Lubbock appears to regard the one governess who is a match for her rebellious personality as of the first importance in her own development, softening 'the asperities of my nature' and helping to control 'my headstrong disposition'. Her brother, on the other hand, who is sent to boarding school, at the same time undergoes the change that is typical of several brothers in these narratives: 'Edward soon became insufferable after he went to Melbourne Grammar—boastful, arrogant and contemptuous of girls' (*People in Glass Houses*, p. 118).

Stress on the impact of personality is not confined to accounts of private education, however, and many autobiographers reflect on negative or positive encounters with teachers. Often the incident itself is minimal, although its effects are profound. Thus Anna Ey's memory of an unjust punishment from her otherwise respected teacher and her partial recovery of justice is one of the most vivid of her youth: 'When next we went to Confirmation lessons, the pastor called me aside, and I thought I was in for more trouble, but instead he commended me for having done the right thing. This, of course, pleased my "Old Adam", but I had received my slap never-the-less' (*Memoirs of a Pastor's Wife*, p. 35). Marjorie Motschall records her suffering at the hands of a dyspeptic teacher: 'God help the children unlucky enough to have chilblains on their fingers as many of them did on frosty mornings. Swollen purple fingers clumsy with pen or pencil would be sharply rapped'. Nevertheless in retrospect she appreciates his energy and dedication (*Wild Wood Days at Panton Hill*, p. 42). Many narrators recall that self-esteem and even the sense of identity are highly sensitive to a teacher's approval or disapproval; often parched for attention, the girl-self appreciates any notice, provided it denotes interest. Jennifer Dabbs, for instance, describes herself as deeply disheartened when a nun whom she admires indicates displeasure after she has cut off her long hair: 'Was there nothing about me for her to admire except what I no longer possessed? ... I couldn't bear to think that she was capable of such pettiness and cruelty; towards me, who adored her.' Later, when the nun recants her disapproval, the child responds with repressed emotion: 'I stumbled away from her, blinded by tears, and rushed to the toilet where several weeks of pent up injustice, resentment and wounded love poured down my face in hot streams' (*Beyond Redemption*, pp. 122–3, 126). A teacher's refusal to acknowledge the child as individual may be perceived as cataclysmic, on the other hand. Patsy Adam-Smith, for instance, is terror-stricken when a vindictive teacher hints at her dubious genealogy: 'A fear grabbed me and my heart shook "Smith is my name, isn't it?" I appealed to the kids, who of course remembered me' (*Hear the Train Blow*, p. 143).

An autobiographical short story by Eileen Haley in *Memories of an Australian Girlhood* focuses on the ambivalent relationship between teacher and children. Titled 'Sixth Grade', it is a study of the shifting balance of power in a class dominated by a tyrannical nun, Mother Agnes. Under her reign of terror, the children frequently attempt to draw God into the situation, but He seems more often to be on the side of Mother Agnes: 'We'd always suspected that God wasn't on our side, and now we knew we were right'. Thoroughly initiated in the playground into the competitive nature of existence and the unjust system of winners and losers, the children attempt to weather their teacher's unpredictable aggressions in the classroom environment where all are losers but some lose more than others: 'We sat there quiet as mice; we felt like we were in a mined field: we didn't dare move even half an inch for fear of setting something off'. Gradually, the teacher's punishments fall into an even pattern, although one child in particular takes on the role of scapegoat, satisfying the children's barbaric need for theatre and ritual: 'It was a show for us. A thrill, something we looked forward to. We were getting a taste for blood'. All the same, their sense of justice is outraged when Giovanna, the victim, receives sixteen cuts for only fifteen spelling mistakes and they take up her cause. Although the nun shows remarkable restraint when she discovers their criticism, she completely loses control when Giovanna persists in making a Freudian blunder in a poetry reading. Implicated in the teacher's violence ('I felt guilty. I felt responsible'), the child-self evades the perception of the older narrator that both teacher and class are victims of a repressive, patriarchal ideology.

This partial understanding of a teacher as human and vulnerable is particularly characteristic of accounts of Catholic educations. Most narrators perceive nuns as highly ambivalent role models; both confined and free, governed and autonomous, practical and unworldly, gentle and tough, sympathetic and intransigent, female and sexless, they seem to present an alternative way of being even as they suggest its impossibility. Kathleen Fitzpatrick realizes that the nuns mean well by the children but their attention is slightly skewed from them:

Convents, in my day, were not child-oriented institutions: they were dedicated *Ad Majorum Dei Gloriam*. This was no mere form of words as in the Latin mottoes of many private schools, but quite literally true ... Perfection was the standard and it was immutable. But young children, engaged in the discovery of the world, are not perfectionists but empiricists, taking up this and casting that aside, leaving a trail of deformed or maimed objects in their wake. Therefore, according to the convent ethic of my time, they had to be forced to be perfect, just as Rousseau held that men must be forced to be free. (*Solid Bluestone Foundations*, p. 85)

Josie Arnold is only able to see the nuns as individuals when she leaves the rough primary school for a more elite secondary convent: they are 'intelligent, strong, vigorous and capable women', whose lives have an order and beauty which is strongly appealing. Nevertheless their inability to reconcile the demands of the world with the 'inner life of prayer and sacrifice' and their denial of the body, make their way impracticable for the narrator, nor can they offer a preparation for later life: 'Santa Maria was an oasis of simplicity and goodness. While it in no way prepared us for "the world", Santa gave us four years of harmony before it launched us, innocent and unformed, into a life which was irreconcilable with what we had left' (*Mother Superior, Woman Inferior*, p. 103). And both Kathleen Fitzpatrick and Patsy Adam-Smith retrospectively value convent life; for Fitzpatrick the 'firm routine and unvarying reliability of every element' of life compensates for the sexism, prudery, discomforts and dullness of the nuns' education, while Adam-Smith discovers a delightful freedom, security and companionship in her brief experience of convent life.

Two autobiographical narratives which are centrally concerned with education are Connie Miller's *After Summer Merrily* and *Season of Learning*.[4] Deceptively artless and emotionally restrained, these texts chart the narrator's uncertain progress to the Elysium of a university education. Born in 1904 into a farming family which had been established in Cheshire for generations, the narrator grows up with an impression of permanent rural and social rhythms: 'the sounds and seasons and repetitions of nature had been bred into their blood for aeons of time', she comments of her family (*After Summer Merrily*, p. 14). In this familiar world, books are one of the most reassuring of possessions and she particularly treasures infant memories of her father reading to her in the evening: 'Some of the poems that I liked specially he would read over and over. I expect all this, along with Mother's help a little later, made it possible for me to read long before I began school' (p. 13). Perceiving this interest in books as one of the most abiding patterns of her life, the narrator frequently discusses her earliest experiences of them as if they are of relationships, while one of the most precious memories is her mother's preservation of her favourites after a bout of diphtheria (pp. 65–6). Meanwhile the apparent stability of these early years is threatened by the father's restlessness and in 1911 he sells up the farm and emigrates to Western Australia, followed by the mother and three children a year later. The exchange of permanence for impermanence is never explicit but allowed to emerge in the narrative's general drift and in the obvious contrast between the hessian-walled 'house' the family inhabits in Western Australia and the solid stone farmhouse they have left, while the family's subsequent history has the muted theme of constant change and progressive diminishment. Driven out from their market garden by fire and then flood, they move to a three-roomed hessian shack on the outskirts of Perth, where the father finds a series of makeshift occupations: 'The first Australian house had been a surprise. To us children this second one was an even greater surprise. To Mother, it must have been the greatest shock she'd ever had' (p. 99). Lacking even the amenity of a cooking stove, it is inhabited by carpet snakes. Although they subsequently find a more substantial home, their tenure is always insecure and eventually only the father's enlistment in the army in 1916 saves them from complete destitution.

This theme of diminishment is bolstered by the photographs in *After Summer Merrily*. The solid brick farmhouses of the narrator's grandparents, which are as substantial as manor houses, and the stone structure and classic lines of her father's old farmhouse, 'Sharston Mount', are a powerful contrast with the verbal descriptions of the hessian-walled dwellings in Australia. Even more poignant are the changes in the family photographs taken before the father's departure for Australia and his later departure for war. Confidently speculative in 1911, the mother's expression has changed to one of great wistfulness in 1916, while the father's assurance has been replaced by a rigidity which has more of anxiety than military pride. In another photograph he is bolstered by an ammunition belt, swagger stick and 'Greek' balcony which fail poignantly to cancel the bewildered expression of his eyes.

By this stage of the family's fortunes, the child has conceived an ambition to be a teacher and is flourishing at school notwithstanding a series of illnesses. The only lesson she detests is needlework and it is typical of the restraint of this autobiography that her dislike is absorbed into the general narrative and is barely referred to in the greatest crisis of her young life when she is forced to become an apprentice in a tailoring firm. Just as an external decision had removed her from her first home in England, another external decision begins to threaten her security in Australia, although this decision is the more general social one that she is to be a woman. Vaguely threatened by her friends' growing interest in sex and her own bodily changes, she attempts to hold on to the childhood world: 'Life was hurrying on far more quickly than I wanted it to' (p. 150). But external conditions become increasingly reductive; she is warned by a teacher of literature not to give full scope to her imagination ('[it] will get you into serious trouble, one of these days' p. 155) and she enters a spiral of defeat in mathematics when an unsympathetic teacher fails to realize the effects of a two week absence. The sense of failure culminates in her near-drowning when she accepts a dare and jumps into deep water. Curiously reflecting on a triad of disasters with water, she resolves to 'ponder all future dares carefully' (p. 166). The cessation of hostilities in Europe coincides with her own temporary defeat by society's prescriptions on gender and a sequence of incidents inflicts the fact of secondary status. Travelling into Perth for the victory celebrations on a lorry, she is appalled when her underwear is exposed on alighting: 'My dress and petticoat caught on a hook at the rear of the vehicle, and for a moment I hung there, my toes just brushing the pavement, my navy-bloomered thighs exposed to the entire world' (p. 161). The shameful incident recalls another a year earlier, when she had been made aware that her 'world was beginning to change dramatically; that my brothers and their friends no longer regarded me as one of them, as an equal' (p. 162). This memory of the unwelcome advances of a young man invokes a 'strange bleakness' of mood. The distance she has unwittingly travelled from the secure expectations of childhood is finally brought home in 1919 when her father returns from the war and faces the impossibility of getting work. On the verge of taking her Junior exams, she is forced to leave school and earn her living at tailoring. The narrator rarely makes her criticism explicit, but at this point her father's sudden omission of his persistent nickname for her, 'Little Woman', takes on a profound significance. Since infancy the child has grown closer to the mother, identifying with her hardships, acquiring some of her fatalism about the blunders of men and relying on her for support in her intellectual life. At this juncture, however, the mother, who believes herself to be pregnant, is defeated and the child feels more pity than anger towards her parents: 'a strange sympathy filled my mind and heart. I was fifteen years old; but just then I felt sad for them both, and—in some way, older than them both' (p. 177).

   Season of Learning, Miller's next volume of autobiography, records her gradual recovery of her earlier ambitions. From the age of twenty she picks up the threads of her education, eventually winning a place at the University of Western Australia in 1927. Her resentment at the contrast between her own treatment and the uninterrupted education of her brothers is rarely expressed, but the contrast between her own widening life and her mother's narrowing one is very marked. If the mother finds a vicarious achievement in her daughter's success, her own is limited to success at bridge. Increasingly alienated from her conventional and rigid husband, she settles into a resigned sadness, whereas her daughter enjoys the variety of her new life in which her independence of the marital state is a key ingredient.

If school is perceived as opening doors and holding the key to intellectual and economic freedom, it is also perceived as closing them and offering another kind of key. In fact, images of keys and doors and analogies with prison are common. The external architecture and interiors of their schools appear to many narrators to cultivate a deliberate affinity with prison, while their routines and disciplinary tactics are retrospectively seen as those of the jail or military barracks. Eliza Chomley's school combines genteel intellectual inadequacy with rough living conditions:

We had our meals down in the basement, a cobble stone floor, two long narrow tables with a coarse cloth, and the commonest crockery and table appointments. We had forms instead of chairs—for breakfast and tea, roughly cut bread and butter—dinner equally plain. At breakfast there was a dish of some kind of meat or fish, sufficient for the teachers and about six of the girls, and in rotation we had this addition to our meals—about once in every week. There were no baths, no hot water for washing—in the coldest weather we would put our heads under the pump in the yard. ('My Memoirs', pp. 18–19)

Kathleen Fitzpatrick recalls the bleakness of her convent boarding school of 1914: 'bare, gleaming, terribly clean linoleum-covered floors, a great deal of empty space, minimal furnishing and, even on the most bitter winter days, no heating whatever' (*Solid Bluestone Foundations*, pp. 82–3). Sealed off from the outer world, many of these schools impose restrictions which a convict would find familiar: common uniforms and hair-styles, meagre or dull food, intrusive supervision and the denial of privacy, and the application of rigid routines to the most trivial of activities. Kathleen Fitzpatrick learns that even folding one's clothes at night must have a common pattern and Kathleen Mangan discovers how to repress her hair's exuberance in the total absence of mirrors. Exercise is confined to exercise yards or the boredom of the strictly supervised crocodile (reminiscent of the chain gang), visits from friends and relatives are confined to visiting days, sometimes parental rights are even suspended in favour of the school's authority and incoming and outgoing mail is often inspected. Both Fitzpatrick and Mangan reflect on the repression of self that results from conforming to the nuns' concept of the dutiful letter home and both record that other practice associated with imprisonment, forced feeding. If the practices of the boarding school are prison-like, those of the semi-charitable institution correspond to the punishment block for hardened offenders; Laura Todd and her sisters in the School of Industry are subject to every indignity from cropped hair, to forced doses of castor oil, to whippings, to solitary confinement, and Connie Ellement records practices which are almost as alienating in *The Divided Kingdom*.

Undoubtedly boys' memories of school are as rich in cruelties and indignities, but the girls of these accounts appear to have been particularly subject to conformist ideologies. Again and again, school is presented as the place where gender roles are enforced, a process which involves unlearning or at least temporarily discarding an earlier, freer self. In many ways, school imposes that sense of the world as a foreign land in which the child-self is an immigrant with an immigrant's fear. It is the sort of fear which Jane Miller has described as characteristic of women's experience in general: 'the disorientation of anyone who leaves the place where they were born, its people and its language, to enter a foreign country alone'. In this strange new environment

the bedrock of expectations about the world, effortlessly garnered in childhood, is allowed to seem worthless even as a provisional model for learning to understand a new one, and mastering a new one appears to entail the abandonment or even the desecration of the old.[5]

Thus many autobiographical narratives reflect on the dramatic differences between the childhood 'kingdom' and the school where the self becomes an 'inmate'. The beginning section of *The Getting of Wisdom* is probably the best known treatment of this experience but the experience is a common one. Judith Wallace can find no correlation at all between the freedom of her bush childhood and the claustrophobic guilts of school and compares the plight of girls like herself to that of country heifers 'cooped up and herded together in a few dreary acres'. Later, under the influence of the school's punitive religion, she becomes depressed and fearful of the 'terrifying world outside':

I began to realise something must be wrong with me. All around were people living normal, apparently happy lives, in spite of their certain knowledge of inevitable hellfire. I realised that the constant, unremitting depression that I felt must be a kind of illness. (*Memories of a Country Childhood*, pp. 87, 131)

Vera Adams exchanges an individual experience of rapid intellectual growth at home with her mother for reduction to a cultivated uniformity of dullness (*No Stranger in Paradise*). Some narrators are so uninterested in the conformity of their school experiences that they omit them altogether. Nellie Melba comments: 'Of my school-days I do not wish to write at length. They were much as other girls' schooldays, though perhaps some of them may have been more Spartan than nowadays' (*Melodies and Memories*, p. 14); Mrs Hughes concludes her extraordinary story of childhood at the point when her story becomes ordinary and, an 'untamed harem scarum', she goes to school (*My Childhood in Australia*); Lady Wynford perceives the aridities of her 1850s education as typical: 'hot days when learning to sew and the needle was damp and sticky and the cotton black' ('Memories of her Childhood, 1847–1860'). Nellie Stewart remarks that her school was much like any other:

[a girl's] real education begins after she leaves school. The things one learns to one's real profit are the things one learns of one's own free will and initiative. The world taught me far more than the school did. (*My Life's Story*, p. 19)

Others record the difficulties they face in conforming to the myths and pieties of the host community. Like Laura Rambotham, Anna Wickham is painfully aware of her difference from the mass:

Back at the convent . . . I went out into the grounds, knelt down, pressing my knees against the earth, and prayed that the people at school would never know I was not like them. But they did.[6]

Others, like Josie Arnold and Kathleen Fitzpatrick, reflect on the unstated sexism of their school with enlightened hindsight: separated from her brother at their Portland convent, Fitzpatrick is neverthe-less aware that his life is different from hers. Boys go on more exciting outings, their rebellions win them more concessions and they escape the full brunt of the nuns' stress on trivial conventions. Laura Todd, on the other hand, undergoes such a reduction of self that even her sense of sexual identity is extinguished; deprived of everything that might express their femininity, subject to severe physical hard-ships and ignorant of physical difference, the sisters wonder, with unconscious irony, in what way they are different from boys (*A Place Like Home*, pp. 84–5). Roslyn Taylor resorts to the extraordinary recourse of inventing another persona; wearing a wig, and inventing a foreign history, she attends school under another name, temporarily mystifying both teachers and children (*Your Hills Are Too High*, p. 87). 'You think that girls are just turned out in batches, all made in the same pattern as if they had been set in the same jelly moulds', protests Myra Morris's heroine of 1915 (*Us Five*, p. 224), echoing the feelings of many of her sisters before and since.

Resistance to the unimaginative rigidity of gender roles is particu-larly marked in accounts of Irish-Catholic educations. As some of their titles indicate (*Mother Superior Woman Inferior* and *Beyond Redemption*), most of these texts deal with the sort of intense experience which resists emotional resolution. In Josie Arnold's words: 'My Catholic childhood in the 1940s was a world of sharp contrasts, a world which by its very nature could never be accommodated, a world which was to dominate my life' (*Mother Superior Woman Inferior*, p. 66).

One of the most striking of this group of autobiographies is Kathleen Mangan's *Daisy Chains, War, then Jazz*.[7] The youngest child of Frederick McCubbin, Mangan grows up in the 1900s in an environment which stresses freedom and aesthetic enjoyment. Her childhood is symbolized by her first hat, a 'cream straw hat, trimmed with blue forget-me-nots':

Whenever I think of it I recall many events that I would have otherwise forgotten. I see myself walking along the windy Esplanade at St Kilda with father because I seem to relate the blue forget-me-nots on my hat to the blue waters of Port Phillip Bay. I remember men and women promenading in their Sunday-best clothes: the men in blazers, white flannel trousers and straw-decker hats; the women, whose complexions always looked fresh-washed and rosy, in wide-brimmed hats and long dresses. I see gulls, and the blue sea lapping the pale sand, little girls with their dresses tucked into their drawers, and little boys in sailor hats with their pants rolled up, paddling in the water ... (pp. 11–12)

Mangan is an unselfconscious and even naïve writer, but she reacts to experience in a spontaneously aesthetic way. Educated to enjoy colour, life and energy by her ten years with her much-loved father, she discovers that the convent to which she is sent after his death is a negation of everything she has grown to love. Worse than repressive, it offers a form of death. Before her arrival there, however, she fosters romantic notions of the life: midnight suppers, pillow fights, dances and dresses. The day of departure brings a new realization of separation and like Laura of *The Getting of Wisdom*, she bids farewell to the lares and penates of her childhood world—the broken vase still filled with her father's brushes, his easel and paintbox, the enormous blue and white Chinese fish bowl, the Wedgwood plates on the dresser. Implicitly comparing her fate to the sun-loving swallows of her father's stories, she appears to have a presentiment that she is going to an existence which ignores the sun. Her first glimpse of 'Sacre Coeur' does nothing to contradict this impression: 'a three-storey fortress', it has rows of silent windows that appear to be passing judgement on her. A further prophetic incident has the novelistic force of metaphor:

As we stood silently waiting for someone to answer our ring at the front door, we were suddenly startled by a very loud grinding noise above our heads as a chiming clock geared itself to peal out three. The vibrations from the clock hung on the air after it had ceased to chime, so much so that we were taken by surprise when the front door was silently opened. (p. 84)

The impression of Gothic menace and forced mechanical energy are inescapable and are typical of Mangan's effective style of writing to the moment. Overpowered by her meeting with the formidable Reverend Mother (a Mrs Gurley in her command of parents and children), the child is quickly separated from her relatives and inserted into the prison-like system:

My locker was marked number 6. And for the rest of my time at the convent I was to remember that number well. It was in marking-ink on everything I possessed. Even my tooth brush had a little 6 on it, and in time I came to regard myself as number 6, just as if it were my name. It was my first lesson in regimentation. (p. 88)

Meanwhile, other impressions on this first day enforce her sense that the self is threatened with cancellation: the voiceless flocks of nuns and children who walk along the corridors, the absence of mirrors, mention of the strange practice of showering in a bathing suit, the impersonal cleanliness of the dormitory and the pervasive cold. The nuns' chanting of vespers draws these sensations together into an impression of death, reminding the narrator of 'the sun going down, the tide going out, and the mournful shriek of the gulls as they fly low over the darkening sea' (p. 91). In the next chapter, 'Sacre Coeur' is compared to the Snow Queen's palace in Hans Andersen's story and the narrator describes herself as undergoing the emotional suffocation of life in a prison. Resisting a nun's attempt to force feed her with porridge, she is less able to resist other restraining influences; a square peg in a round hole, always homesick and restless, she can make no sense of this sudden disjunction in her experience. She is deprived of visits from her family in an attempt to encourage settling in and her letters home are scrutinized and rejected. Instructed to write a cheerful letter, she is 'mortified': 'The impression that I had lost the last vestige of self-esteem and the right to determine my own affairs was weighing heavily upon my mind. I suddenly felt lost' (p. 97).

When her mother finally pays a visit, the child responds by screaming until exhausted. At this point, the juxtapositions of Mangan's reflections are interesting and, as so often in her narrative, take on the power of metaphor; on one hand she notices that the samll parlour in which she is incarcerated with an attendant nun is the priest's room ('Essentially a man's room—the only one in the convent'). On the other, she can hear the Benediction upstairs and the sweet voices of the girls ('To me, they were as unworldly as the nuns who taught them, those girls; meek, dedicated, accepting the regimentation of their daily lives without question. I wished that I could be like them.' p. 103). Later, she discovers that 'even Father complained about her screaming'. The point is not explicit, but the narrator's sensitivity to the patriarchal nature of this repressive 'life' is obvious. Later still, it is the tyranny of a priest which impels her to flee.

After she has endured the life for two years and feels as inanimate as the convent's trite plaster statues, she is galvanized into action by the punitive response of a priest when she confesses that her family failed to attend mass during the holidays. Condemned to various public punishments, she feels an intense sense of shame. When the next opportunity to escape presents itself, she seizes it without hesitation. Mangan is subsequently sent to another convent, but on this occasion she barely gives it time to open hostilities, escaping homewards with a fourteen-mile (twenty-two kilometres) walk in drenching rain.

Mangan's openly hostile reaction to the negative environment of school is unusual in these accounts. A naturally confident and spontaneous child, from a home with a relaxed attitude to religion, Mangan's narrator knows that school is the inverse of her family's values and that she is the temporary victim of her mother's unimaginative adherence to convention in this instance. A silent acquiescence to the cruelties encountered at school is a more common pattern, however. This phenomenon is not confined to female narratives, of course, and probably reflects a common insularity between generations. As Hal Porter comments in his autobiography of childhood:

I am a child of an era and a class in which adults are one tribe and children another, each with its separate rights and duties, freedoms and restrictions, expected gentlenesses and condoned barbarities, each with its special reticences and sacred areas.[8]

The cruelties described in these narratives, however, are usually emotional rather than physical, inducing fear or guilt and creating a vague but real barrier of shame between home and school. As Richardson comments in *The Getting of Wisdom*, the uninformed obsession with sex of Laura's peers, described as 'dabbling in the illicit', 'had little in common with the opener grime of the ordinary school-boy'.[9] A representative text in many ways, *The Getting of Wisdom* is perhaps most typical in presenting the powerful sexual undercurrents of school life. On the edge of womanhood, and yet denied the knowledge that is essential to their future well-being and even their survival, the girls of Laura's school garner as much information as they can. Such a situation is ripe for ingenious surmise and unpleasant theories grow like bacteria.

A topic that is common and even ubiquitous in these autobiographies is sexual ignorance; sometimes simply recorded and at others explicitly criticized, the deliberate mysteries which are used to veil the facts of life are everywhere resented. If infant brothers and sisters arrive unannounced and unexplained, menstruation may be a similarly inexplicable and unwelcome arrival. Menstruation is also sometimes associated with guilt or the vaguely shameful fact of being woman as in Jennifer Dabbs's *Beyond Redemption* and Connie Miller's *Season of Learning*. Several narrators also comment on their dislike of the prurient gossip of their school peers. Paradoxically, a less inhibited response to sex may cancel out some restraints but impose others, as in Gabrielle Carey and Kathy Lette's *Puberty Blues* and Barbara Pepworth's *Early Marks*. In both texts sex is the dominant ingredient and indeed so engrossing are the alternative sexual careers of these narrators that they virtually obliterate the school career as a topic of interest.

Even in the case of asexual anxieties, narrators often reflect with wonder on the strength of the past emotions and their inability to communicate their problem. Annabella Boswell records her persecution at the hands of a girl who used to slap her and her eventual retaliation: 'I never had been in a passion before and never have been since; murder was in my heart, fury in my eyes. I was only eight; she was twelve or fourteen, but I was victorious, and thoroughly ashamed of myself for long afterwards'. In addition, some of the bigger girls terrify the younger ones with stories of ghosts and murders: I professed to have no fear, but I had a severe illness in that house and thought I saw a ghost in my bedroom and wonder now that it did not more seriously affect me'. Although she eventually informs the teacher, who puts a stop to it, there is no indication that she tells her parents of her misery and her eventual removal more than a year later appears to have been the effect of the family's decision to move to Bathurst (*Early Recollections*, p. 16). Mary Edgeworth David describes her misery when she becomes the perpetual butt of a teacher's ridicule: 'Being a shy and sensitive child, I suffered agonies, and though my sister was worried about the situation, it never occurred to either of us to confide in our parents'. Only when a visiting uncle is appalled at her hysterical behaviour on leaving for school, does the trouble emerge (*Passages of Time*, p. 21). Frances McGuire is humiliated by an act of 'real, deliberate, and even organised' hostility at her school: 'This was no girlish prank, thought of and carried out as a lark. This was planned malevolence. I never found out who was responsible and I never spoke of it to anyone' (*Bright Morning*, p. 151).

One of the most vivid accounts of childhood anxiety is Katherine McKell's description of her loss of a key, which incurs the reproaches of her severe teacher: '"A new key would have to be bought and fitted to the padlock, and that would cost five shillings!" Five shillings! Quite a large sum in those days when people studied thrift to the smallest detail.' Retrieving the key, after a ritual of washing and prayer and an intense search, is a sacred experience for the child; it had been silently watched over by her friend, the guard dog. The discovery is received coldly by the teacher, however, ('my joy, chilled like a flower in the night air, folded itself up') and the child is left to cherish her secret knowledge alone: 'Child as I was, not a word did I tell about the face and hand washing, the earnest prayers in that little corner bedroom, but hid these things in that inner sanctuary of the mind, where none may enter and trample' (*Old Days and Gold Days*, pp. 89–90).

Kathleen Fitzpatrick's early schooldays are overshadowed by an 'infant sadist . . . a skilled and practised pincher to whom it gave positive pleasure to inflict pain. My sole occupation was watching her and keeping out of her range.' She fails to tell her parents, retrospectively ascribing her silence to the school ethos against tale bearing (*Solid Bluestone Foundations*, p. 130). Whether or not this common pattern of silent acquiescence stems from taboos imposed by a peer group, it appears to be a highly reductive experience, enforcing a solidarity that is at best unpleasant and at worst shameful. Compelled, it seems, to probe old wounds, few narrators can explain the younger self's complicity in her pain.

One common experience of externally induced guilt which is fiercely resented and not always resolved is the fear of eternal punishment, usually conveyed by an over-zealous priest. Most accounts of Irish-Catholic childhoods include this experience, although they dispose of it variously. Judith Wallace records her unhappiness as an illness which is cured as soon as she goes home; Kathleen Fitzpatrick describes her attempts over several years to prevent herself falling to sleep, having been terrified by the hell-fire predictions of Redemptorist Fathers: 'Horrors make a deep impression which is not commensurate with the time they actually occupy' (*Solid Bluestone Foundations*, p. 95); Josie Arnold still resents the ritual of confession, the 'powerful men [who] told you that you were bad' and the doctrine that consigns her non-Catholic father to Hell (*Mother Superior Woman Inferior*, pp. 66–70). Two autobiographical narratives in particular are fuelled by resentful and unresolved anger: Jennifer Dabbs's *Beyond Redemption* (1987) and Gail Morgan's *Promise of Rain* (1985). Both interesting autobiographies, they are nevertheless uneven achievements. Morgan's novel is particularly unbalanced. A study of a 1950s childhood, it is distinguished by some graphic scenes and dramatically realized encounters between adults and child. Morgan has a gift for subversive comedy but unfortunately she allows the book's finest comic moment (the impact of an Irish nun's lugubrious story of a girl in a no-win situation on the practical minds of healthily sceptical children) to become a metaphor of the narrator's defeat; protesting at the climate of defeat in which her heroine grew up ('It was no use talking to parents. They soaked up misfortune like a sponge, and never did anything about it', p. 43), she deals her a fate which justifies the nun's ridiculous story. In white, patriarchal Anglo-Australia, God will find some way to punish you for the sins of your fathers, the novel's conclusion seems to imply.

The most famous account of school experience is, of course, Henry Handel Richardson's *The Getting of Wisdom*. Like *My Brilliant Career, The Getting of Wisdom* is one of those archetypal texts, which seem in retrospect to have been virtually produced by their cultural moment and which continue to resonate with cultural implications. More coherent than *My Brilliant Career, The Getting of Wisdom* is also more certain of its feminist meaning. It belongs to that class of literature which, in Adrienne Rich's words, provides us with:

a clue to how we live, how we have been living, how we have been led to imagine ourselves, how our language has trapped as well as liberated us, how the very act of naming has been till now a male prerogative, and how we can begin to see and name—and therefore live—afresh.[10]

Described by Richardson herself as 'ironic throughout'[11], and by her husband, J. G. Robertson, as 'decidedly subversive'[12], the book is one of the most radical in Australian literature. So radical, in fact, that readers have been slow to accept its intentions. For a long time after it began to receive critical attention (which in itself was long after its publication in 1910), the book was regarded as a female portrait of the artist, an account of the writer's discovery and refining of her craft. Concentrating on Laura's romantic fabrications and subsequent findings about truth and fiction, this interpretation narrowed the novel's focus to a question of aesthetics and led inevitably to its comparison with Joyce's *Portrait*, to its obvious detriment; as potential artist Laura is only mildly interesting, as representative young girl undergoing an intense experience of socialization, she is fascinating.

More recently, the insights of feminist criticism have opened up the text to some extent but readers have seemed loth to pursue their observations to their logical conclusion. Brian McFarlane, for instance, is dismayed to find that Richardson 'seems not to believe in or, at least, is unable to show an exciting interaction of individual impulses and social claims' and sheets this disbelief home to her individual dark vision.[13] Delys Bird perceives some of the feminist wisdom at the heart of the book ('The lessons women must learn in *The Getting of Wisdom* ... those disseminated and perpetuated by the conservative, patriarchal, puritanical, masculine Australian dogma ... to be female is not to get wisdom, not to be free, not to achieve'), but refuses the author full knowledge of her own message, describing the novel's conclusion as a 'vaguely conceived' romantic freedom.[14] Bewilderment at the general subversion of standards, as Robertson perceived, is undoubtedly one of the reader's first impressions, but bewilderment does not necessarily imply authorial confusion and it is unfortunate that the book's *avant garde* nature should still be overlooked. As a study of the artist as a young child, as a fictional autobiography which reflects both on the life and on the factual narrative, *Myself When Young*, and as a text which throws light on *Maurice Guest, The Getting of Wisdom* has undoubted value. But the book also responds to the new, different questions of feminist criticism and stands on its own as a powerful, radical statement.

Of recent feminist critiques, a collection of essays titled *The Voyage In* (1983), which deals extensively with the genre of the *Bildungsroman*, is particularly relevant to *The Getting of Wisdom*. In their introduction the editors point out that critical definitions of the *Bildungsroman* (seen as represented most fully by *Wilhelm Meister*) have never assimilated gender as a pertinent category, 'despite ... the fact that the sex of the protagonist modifies every aspect of a particular *Bildungsroman*: its narrative structure, its implied psychology, its representation of social pressures'.[15] Originating in the Enlightenment and characterized by a belief in human perfectibility and progress, the *Bildungsroman* assumes the possibilities of individual achievement and social integration. 'Through careful nurturing, the hero should be brought to the point where he can accept a responsible role in a friendly social community.' As Marianne Hirsch observes in the same collection, the *Bildungsroman* valorizes 'progress, heterosexuality, social involvement, healthy disillusionment, "normality", adulthood'.[16] *The Getting of Wisdom*, on the other hand, subverts almost every one of those terms, and like other female novels of development such as *The Mill on the Floss* and *The Awakening*, substitutes 'inner concentration for active accommodation, rebellion, or withdrawal'.[17] Laura discovers that the roles which are sanctioned for women are enemies to selfhood, and her final flight is a rejection of the distorted values of her society. If Richardson is consciously writing in this tradition, she is subverting it and exposing with ruthless clarity the incompatible break between female selfhood or achievement and social accommodation.[18]

One of the reasons for resistance to the novel's radicalism is probably Richardson's air of ironic detachment, both within and without the text. Deprecating the book to Nettie Palmer as 'just a merry and saucy bit of irony', Richardson seems to have come closer to the reader's appropriate reaction with the quotation from Nietszche which she scrawled on the flyleaf of a first edition copy: 'Wer hier nicht lachen kann, soll hier nicht lesen' ('Who cannot laugh here, shall not read here'). Committed to European models of naturalism, which demanded the author's invisibility, and to a comic reduction of the heroine's 'crimes' and quandaries in this the most 'personal' of her novels, Richardson intended her book to be nonetheless satiric. Like Swift's Gulliver, only more perceptive, Laura is trapped in a petty, Lilliputian world, comically convinced of its own significance; the older self, meanwhile, implicitly inhabiting a world of fitting standards, derives a wry amusement from watching the wily twists and turns of the young protagonist. In this story of a complex, developing individuality at odds with an environment that is both baffling and simplistic, irony becomes the pivot for the frequent shifts in perspective and tone. In many ways an uncomfortable text, *The Getting of Wisdom* challenges the reader with its cool wit, and the avoidance of value judgements or moral signposts.

The power of Richardson's 'cool and curious eye'[19] is most obvious in the presentation of Laura herself. Articulate, intelligent and observant, Laura is also 'passionate' and 'unexpected'; incorrigibly individual, she has a mind 'like a clean but highly sensitised plate' (p. 131)[20] and 'sharp, unkind eyes' (p. 169). In some ways she is an unpleasant individual, capable of gross acts of 'toadying' when necessary and even of inflicting on others the cruelties she herself has only recently suffered; on the arrival of another new girl she rejoices 'in barbarian fashion' that this girl 'should have to endure a like ordeal' and even accentuates her part of old girl (pp. 98–9). She is eager to be accepted by the group but conformity is not her only goal; in every situation, Laura needs to count. Equal to any outward deception, she is nevertheless incorruptibly honest at heart so that there are frequently two Lauras at work, the outwardly conformist girl and the inward self which watches and reflects. As convincing as Huckleberry Finn's, Laura's honesty is a given of her nature, an effect of her invincible individuality which eventually detects and resists what is fraudulent. Fidelity to her individual sense of self is perhaps the only virtue Laura retains from her schooldays, but it is a powerful one.

Laura's gift for originality has been nurtured, of course, by her previous experiences. In her fatherless childhood home in the country, Laura has been used to leading her siblings and occupying the centre of attention. Enjoying an unusual physical freedom, she has known and dominated her garden home, its natural features, trees, animals, birds and children. Even the grown-ups regard her as a force to contend with. Intellectually, she has 'absorbed the knowledge of [the] whole house', having devoured her father's well-stocked library. Although Richardson heightens Laura's dominance in *The Getting of Wisdom*, the picture is basically the same in *Myself When Young*; carefully nurtured by a selflessly devoted mother and confined to the society of her younger sister for several years, Ethel Richardson enjoyed a childhood that was unusually free and unusually sheltered.

To this naturally spontaneous, confident child, the school appears first as prison-like. 'Vast in its breadth and height' and 'appalling in its sombre greyness' outside, the school inside is oppressively still: 'it must be like this to be dead, thought Laura to herself' (pp. 34–5). Contact with the 'awful personage' of Mrs Gurley reinforces these first impressions and immediately begins Laura's education in self-repression. Indeed, so blatant are the snubs that Laura receives from girls and teachers alike, that the whole episode of her entry into school life smacks of the familiar group rite of initiation whereby the 'fresher' is subdued. The attack on her identity takes its sharpest form in the ridiculing of her name, and the subsequent interrogation as to her antecedents and property.[21] Unusually resistant to conformist ways of knowing, Laura continues to transgress the unwritten taboos of the tribe, and it is a long time before she learns to curb her impulsiveness, crush her spontaneity and understand that shyness is expected of her. She is guilty of displaying a forward musical talent on a visit to the Principal, but is disciplined by the cold treatment of her peers and by a humiliating interview with Mrs Gurley: 'The lesson went home; Laura began to model herself more and more on those around her; to grasp that the unpardonable sin is to vary from the common mould' (p. 98). Although in due course the 'natural easy frankness [is] successfully educated out of her' (p. 139), the 'aroma of eccentricity' continues to cling and Laura is frequently aware of her difference from the herd. Plagued by fears of exclusion, she prays that 'she might be preserved from having thoughts that were different from other people's'. Her greatest 'crime' stems ironically from the pressing need to conform ('it seemed that some one had to be loved, if you were to be able to hold up your head with the best' p. 158), and ironically brings about the very fate of rejection she had feared. For the most part, however, she learns circumspection and becomes 'a regular little tactician', weighing her words before uttering them, keeping her real opinions to herself and making those she expresses tally with those of her hearers. She learns, in short, the way of 'Mr Worldly Wiseman' (p. 211) and gives a politician's cast to the first of the Biblical texts she learns at the school: '*I wisdom dwell with prudence and find out knowledge of witty inventions*' (p. 54).

Meanwhile, the author makes it clear that this education is not just peculiar to one cloistered institution, but is in fact the way of the world. Composed of a great mix of classes, the society of the school duplicates the snobberies, barriers and prejudices of society outside. In the sorts of pressures it imposes and the roles it elicits, it is merely a smaller, more intimate replica of the parent world. Even its rituals of punishment are borrowed and the assembly which meets to witness the public disgrace of Annie Johns is explicitly compared to a mob witnessing a hanging. In terms of cultivated insensitivity, unthinking conformity and triviality, the teachers are as implicated as the girls, goggling at Laura's unfortunate purple dress and decrying her lack of *comme il faut*. Ridiculous and bigoted though it is, the society of the school is essential to Laura's development. Subsequently describing these early years as 'bitten in as with acid' and as incomparable 'for vividness and vitality', Richardson also stresses the importance of all experience for the writer: 'to a writer, experience was the only thing that really mattered. Hard and bitter as it might seem, it was to be welcomed rather than shrunk from, reckoned as gain not a loss'.[22] Laura is largely unconscious of the nature of the deposits she is storing up, but she is aware of the necessity of this experience; at her nadir in popularity she contemplates the possibility of a return to the old home of childhood, but categorically rejects it: 'No: badly as she had suffered at her companions' hands, much as she dreaded returning, it was at school she belonged. All her heart was there' (pp. 205–6). School is essential, first for self-education—it provides the worldly knowledge which she must confront if she is to grow—and also for her subsequent profession as writer; the second is wholly dependent on the first.

The school is also crucial for Laura, given its coincidence with her entry into adolescence. It is here that she learns the world's requirements of her gender. On the 'threshold of womanhood' like her peers, Laura is to be educated in the facts of patriarchy, for one of the school's profoundest implicit lessons is the inescapable dominance of men. Presided over by a male Principal, whose power is measured by his effortless exercise of it, the school reinforces the importance of fathers and, potentially of husbands, as economic providers. Marriage is the universal goal 'and the thoughts of all were fixed, with an intentness that varied only in degree, on the great consummation which ... should come to pass without fail, as soon as the college-doors closed behind them' (p. 152). Laura manages to evade concentrating on this single end, but she fails to retain her earlier unconcerned freedom in relation to the opposite sex, undergoing a severe blow to her pride when a potential flirtation turns into a fiasco. Her feelings are not alleviated by the knowledge that she had done nothing to deserve it, never having sought the boy's regard; nor does her uninterest in the opposite sex release her from the competitive quest for male attention. The distance she has travelled from the spontaneity and freedom of childhood is measured by two scenes where her incapacity to propitiate men is contrasted with the disparaging tactics of mere children.

This subject of initiation into gender, which is the most sustained of all the novel's topics, is also interesting for what it reveals of levels of knowledge, for Laura is constantly involved in breaking through strata of 'wisdom'. On the surface is the 'received' wisdom, the conventional Edwardian matrix of attitudes based, however shakily, on Christianity and Biblical authority; perceived as sexless in terms of sexual feeling, women's lives are nevertheless determined by their sex according to this implicit world view. Just as love in marriage is eventually conferred on the 'nice' girl, motherhood is compatible with sexual innocence. Both the teachers and the girls see through most of this layer of 'wisdom', although unlike Laura, they fail to question the more fundamental implications. The inconsistencies of their attitude are borne out in the following passage:

Man was animal, a composite of lust and cruelty, with no aim but that of brutally taking his pleasure: something monstrous, yet to be adored; annihilating, yet to be sought after; something to flee and, at the same time, to entice, with every art at one's disposal. (p. 131)

Instinctively perceiving the economic grounds of the marriage game and well aware of the necessity 'by fair means or unfair' of acquiring sexual information, the girls throw all their energies into winning in a system which has declared them the losers from the start. As for Laura, she is puzzled by the purpose of this competitive game, dubious of the worth of the ultimate prize, and aware of the real absence of relationship: '"But you never get to know him!"', she protests to Maria Morell's elucidation of the purpose of flirtation ('"it's only for getting lollies, and letters, and the whole dashed fun of the thing"' p. 149). Although she fails to articulate the crux of the matter, she has instinctively grasped its essence; at the same time, of course, the more sophisticated enlightenment of the older narrator mediates her point of view, subtly enhancing its subversiveness.

By emphasizing conformity, the school thus encourages the sort of general self-deception which is necessary if patriarchal values are to be internalized. As in *Jane Eyre* the girls do not significantly expand their options or realistically anticipate taking an active part in shaping society; they may be receiving the same formal education as their brothers, but the hidden agenda instructs them in reactive and supportive roles.

The sort of blinkering which women unwittingly impose on each other is nowhere more apparent than in the exchange of letters between Laura and her mother and sister early in the narrative. As yet untutored in the necessary circumspection, Laura frankly conveys her thoughts on Mrs Gurley and the girls' obsession with boyfriends. '"I do want you to have nice feelings"', replies her mother, criticizing every item of her honest account and employing all the sanctions at her disposal. The emphasis on 'niceness' is a continuing refrain: '"I'd much rather have you good and useful than clever ... Try and only think nice things about other people and not be always spying out their faults"' (pp. 59, 85). Wisely tailoring her letters to suit these parental injunctions, Laura sees through at least part of her mother's unconscious bad faith: 'Laura took the statement about the goodness and cleverness with a grain of salt: she knew better. Mother thought it the proper thing to say [but] ... Mother's ambitions knew no bounds' (pp. 85–6).

Intelligent and original as Laura is, she is not always able to

penetrate the obscuring fog around her and for a long time she is
caught up in the question of truth. This inward debate, terminating
in her discovery that honesty is the best policy in everyday affairs but
that 'you might lie as hard as you liked' on paper, has been seen as
the central discovery of the book, essential to her future career as a
writer: 'To be true to one's art one must be false to the facts' is thus
regarded as the aesthetically liberating peak of the narrative. Coming
as it does before the key discoveries about love and God, however,
this discovery of what is true can also be seen as more of an
epistemological than an aesthetic breakthrough. In all this middle
section of the book Laura is preoccupied with 'ways of knowing'.
Equipped with a lively imagination, which allows her to recreate the
feel of historical periods, she is nevertheless made aware of her
resistance to male ways of knowing and includes herself in a teacher's
criticism of another girl's 'woman's brain':

" . . . vague, slippery, inexact, interested only in the personal aspect of a
thing. You can't concentrate your thoughts, and, worst of all, you've no
curiosity—about anything that really matters. You take all the great facts of
existence on trust—just as a hen does—" (p. 88)

This has often been taken as having authorial approval, but Richardson is more even-handed that she appears at first sight. In *Myself
When Young* she praises a friend's 'woman's eye [which] seized and
held just those intimate personal details that the male eye is apt to
miss, or think of no account' (p. 194) and in *The Getting of Wisdom*
she is far from endorsing male perception. The limited M. P., after
all, is described as having a 'male exactness' of vision. If female ways
of knowing are personal and inexact, male ways can be arid and
irrelevant. A knowledge of facts is certainly a help in winning school
prizes ('highly gilt volumes of negligible contents'), but their general
uselessness is apparent in the irony which plays over the following
passage:

it was not the least use in the world to her to have seen the snowy top of
Mount Kosciusko stand out against a dark blue evening sky, and to know its
shape to a tittlekin. On the other hand, it mattered tremendously that this
mountain was 7308 and not 7309 feet high: that piece of information was
valuable, was of genuine use to you; for it was worth your place in the class.
(p. 90)

What is more, Laura discovers that the barrier between fact and
fiction in no way correlates with that between truth and falsehood.
Fiction-making is woven into every aspect of life and those who
consider themselves the most 'rigidly truthful' of individuals often
base their lives on the greatest book of fiction of all. '"You can't do
away with truth, child"', M. P. tells her sententiously. '"The Bible is
truth. Can you do away with the Bible, pray?"' (p. 214). The

quotation from Nietzsche which heads Chapter 17 makes Richardson's position clear: 'Inability to lie is far from being love of truth . . . He who cannot lie does not know what truth is'. And in this climate of sophistries and self-deceptions, it is the girl with the liveliest facility for fiction-making who sees the truth most keenly. Even her most elaborate fiction is truthful in that it accords with the girls' unhealthy speculations about men's sexuality. What they cannot forgive is the 'extraordinary circumstantiality' of the fictions with which she gulled them.

Laura's liberation from the prison of self-doubt created by this incident comes during the period of her great friendship with Evelyn. Innately well-balanced, Evelyn advises her to 'never mind that old jumble sale of all the virtues' and reinforces Laura's own instincts when she concedes that the girls are 'mostly fools'. Richardson spends little time on this episode, deliberately toning down the real emotional strength of this lesbian relationship. As she explains in *Myself When Young*: 'The real thing was neither light nor amusing. It stirred me to my depths, rousing feelings I hadn't known I possessed, and leaving behind it a heartache as cruel as my first' (p. 70). In terms of Laura's development, however, the episode is emotionally liberating, reviving some of her spontaneity and faith in her own perceptions.

At the same time, however, it initiates her into the sad knowledge of transience:

she began to grasp that, everywhere and always, even while you revelled in them, things were perpetually rushing to a close; and the fact of them being things you loved, or enjoyed, did not, in the least, diminish the speed at which they escaped you. (p. 248)

This discovery invests Laura with a maturity far beyond her years, but she is to make yet another emotional leap before leaving school. Having neglected her studies during her love affair with Evelyn, she is hard pressed to pass the final school exams and makes a pact with God, promising him life-long devotion if He ensures her success. In the event, God does take a hand but it is via a ruse which compels her to cheat to succeed. It is a measure of her retrieved independence of mind that she is able to perceive the fraudulent nature of the patriarchal God she has been taught to worship, dismissing such a cold and calculating Deity from her personal cosmos:

She could not go on loving and worshipping a God who was capable of double dealing . . . Nor would she ever forget His having forced her to endure the moments of torture she had come through that day. (p. 264)

So advanced is Laura in some of her knowledge of life by the time she leaves school, that the few years there might be described as a lifetime in an emotional sense. The knowledge is unrelievedly comfortless, however, and few readers have been able to accept it. One reader, for instance, complains that Laura is a 'congenital misfit' in a world unresponsive to individuality and suggests that for Richardson 'to grow is to suffer a loss of innocence without any reassuring gain in experience'.[23] Certainly, the older narrator makes it plain at the close that there can be no reconciliation between Laura and the world represented by the school:

> She went out from school with the uncomfortable sense of being a square peg, which fitted into none of the round holes of her world; the wisdom she had got, the experience she was richer by, had, in the process of equipping her for life, merely seemed to disclose her unfitness. (p. 270)

Uncertain of where she belongs or even 'under what conditions she might be happy', Laura has only her own uniquely feeling, perceiving self as comfort. On the other hand, this is a great deal; she has, after all, freed herself from the blinkers which will hamper the development of her fellows and she has retained and sharpened that innate integrity of mind which detects what is fraudulent. If she perceives her society as 'unresponsive to her individuality', it is a tonic perception, and remarkable in that it is decades ahead of its time. Laura's final flight down the avenue, then, is neither a 'vaguely conceived' romantic freedom nor a 'misleading gesture'; it is simply an expression of the freedom of her inner self, wonderfully preserved from this essential trial by ordeal.

Reflecting in *Myself When Young* on 'the raw slip of a girl who was thrust forth from school to find her own feet' (p. 73), Richardson feels some sympathy for her. The 'old innocent self-confidence' (p. 64) was permanently crushed, but the education in outwardly conforming to the ways of the world was entirely necessary: 'I cannot remember ever being really happy at school. None the less I should have been sorry to miss a day of the four to five years I spent there' (p. 65). If for an artist, the time was time wasted ('Irreplaceable time, too, for never again would the mind be so like putty for taking impressions'), as a compressed education in the received fraudulent wisdom of patriarchal society it was, I suggest, invaluable.

There is, of course, another far more positive future awaiting Laura, which the older narrator of *The Getting of Wisdom* perceives: 'She could not then know that, even for the squarest peg, the right hole may ultimately be found; seeming unfitness prove to be only another aspect of a peculiar and special fitness' (p. 270). The fitting role that Laura ultimately discovers is the role of the artist, one which initiates her into that:

> freer, more spacious world, where no practical considerations hamper, and where the creatures that inhabit dance to their tune: the world where are stored up men's best thoughts, and hopes, and fancies; where the shadow is the substance, and the multitude of business pales before the dream. (p. 271)

This is not just the free world of the artist, it is an ideal female world where the male terms of everyday are inverted. In this way Laura/ Richardson recovers that emotional resource which had preserved her from the worst effects of her father's breakdown. In *Myself When Young* she describes her youthful practice of making up stories while bouncing a ball against a wall, a refuge which was unavailable to her sister, who consequently suffered the full brunt of the period's anxieties and insecurities. At school, Richardson herself was deprived of this creative therapy. Later, of course, she was exceptionally fortunate in discovering her talent and the right circumstances in which to nourish it, but this does not reduce the representative wisdom of this remarkable book. As the previous discussion of other autobiographies of school experience has shown, I hope, Richardson is more typical than exceptional in her response to school; it is her thoroughgoing exposure of the institution which is remarkable.

10

Love Stories

With a few remarkable exceptions, the autobiographies which are the subject of this book are not structured according to the quest for true love, the traditional staple of women's popular fiction. It might be expected that autobiographies written in old age and focused on the memories of childhood, as many of these are, will view the passions of early adulthood with detachment, but many written early in the author's lifetime are also preoccupied with concerns which transcend the theme of love. Barbara Hanrahan, for instance, is concerned to recover the integrity of childhood, and retrospectively discards early sexual relationships as inauthentic and uninteresting; Miles Franklin's quest includes a temporary dalliance with the ideal bushman, but rejects the possibilities he represents. And both Franklin and Hanrahan represent a characteristic experience of alienation caused by men's attitude to women as primarily sexual beings, for many writers reflect on the reductions of social perceptions of gender and the loss of an integrated childhood self. Franklin also anticipates a common need when she expresses her yearning for a mate who will have the empathy normally attributed to women. Eve Langley in *The Pea Pickers* invests her lover with female qualities and *Barbara Halliday* by Marion Miller Knowles distinguishes the true from the false lover in terms of sympathetic feeling. As Maureen Craig comments in *All That False Instruction*: 'I hoped that I would meet a man unlike any other on my travels, a man who would want me as I was, who would be as gentle and understanding as any woman'.[1] In some twentieth century autobiographies, as in fiction, the heterosexual theme has had a distinctly anti-romantic treatment. In these narratives the situation resembles that described by Judith Kegan Gardiner:

Women in recent novels do not fear loss of their lovers, nor do they seriously resent male infidelity. The husband who goes off with another woman leaves

his wife poorer but freer. The sexually active women heroes are not guilty,
nor do they find sexual love redemptive. At best it offers women temporary
warmth and sensual exhilaration: more often, it confuses women and
alienates them from themselves.[2]

In *Monkey Grip*, *Dancing on Coral*, and *Early Marks* falling out of
love is, as Stella Bowen observes in *Drawn From Life*, a more
liberating experience than falling in love. Meanwhile, numerous
narratives include descriptions of sexually threatening incidents
ranging from rape to male exposure; if the incidents are more frankly
described in later texts, they are unequivocally implied in earlier
ones.

In an intriguing study of typical love fantasies in men and women,
Sex and Fantasy[3], Robert May finds that two myths are profoundly
expressive of the different experiences of the sexes. The myth of
Phaethon represents the most striking common quality associated
with the male fantasy pattern: pride. Pride best describes 'a cluster
of attitudes and wishes that includes an inflated view of oneself, a
touchy vulnerability to feelings of shame and inadequacy, a worship
of will and willpower, and a restless urge to achieve something outstanding'. The typical female fantasy is well expressed by the myth
of Demeter and Persephone, with its emphasis on enduring, caring
and attachment. Both myths have negative and positive aspects. The
acknowledgment of pain, the acceptance of suffering and the maintenance of hope celebrated in the story of Demeter are most obviously privileged in *For Love Alone*, but they are also part of the
love experience explored in *Monkey Grip*, *The Pea Pickers*, *Dancing
on Coral*, *Puberty Blues* and *All That False Instruction*. May's description of typical differences in the initiation of a love affair is also
relevant to Australian male and female autobiographies. For the
male, the relationship is initiated by the sexual urge and 'the sexual
urge . . . provides the emotional capital to maintain it'. The female is
more likely to explore her erotic feelings 'as an outgrowth of an
intense emotional investment in another person' while the 'interper-
sonal context remains more important than it typically is for men'.[4] In
The Boy Adeodatus, *My Brother Jack*, and *Redheap*, for instance, the
first sexual encounter is more a test of masculinity than a relationship
while numerous other male autobiographies display the characteristic
pattern of valuing the female, not for herself but for the transcendent
qualities she appears to represent. As Don Anderson asks, 'are all
Australian women [in male autobiographies] either Mothers . . . or
not so much Whores as Free Spirits?'[5]

But perhaps the most striking difference between male and female
autobiographies of growing up is that not a single male text is
exclusively concerned with the passion of love, whereas some of the
finest studies of erotic love in Australian literature are included in this
female genre. Only some of these can be considered here.[6]

One early autobiography, superficially in the tradition of the pioneering narrative, is an extraordinary demonstration of the creative space that the woman author could achieve for herself within this most unpromising of genres. This is Clara Ellen Campbell's *Memoirs: 1861–1872*, published in 1919[7] by the author's son, although the date of writing is uncertain. Two-thirds of the narrative is presented in diary form but several clues, such as anticipations of future events, indicate that it was written consecutively, although undoubtedly based on a journal. A dramatic account of a brother-in-law's tyranny, this narrative is reminiscent of *Pamela* in terms of tension and Gothic atmosphere. Like Pamela, the narrator, Clara, is virtually held prisoner by a man of uncontrollable temper and menacing sexual intentions, although unlike Mr B., he is not an object of love and never reforms. Clara does have a reforming role, as far as her true lover is concerned, however, and like Pamela she perceives her ordeal as a moral proving of self. Clara Campbell also resembles Richardson's heroine in her early artful artlessness, her wit and confidence, her dramatic style of writing to the moment and even her reliance on letters, secret messages and hidden records. Her story is a remarkable revelation of male power in the nineteenth century, a sensitive record of the loneliness and isolation of bush women in this period and a testament to their courage and resourcefulness.

Beginning in diary form in 1861, when the narrator is sixteen, the narrative resorts to the past tense and the autobiographical form in Chapter 3. In Chapter 14, dated Christmas day 1869, the diary form appropriately takes over again as the brother-in-law's threat intensifies. Entries, which are 'recorded' irregularly and include copies of letters, vary greatly in length. Although the general conditions of life are frequently described, there is little of the diary's episodic character in this section of the text for everything focuses on the central drama. Preoccupied with the urgent problem of finding her true love and then securing him from the threats and malign schemes of her evil brother-in-law, Clara spends little time on retrospective reflection. She begins her *Memoirs* with a brief account of her English forebears, in a style which belies her claim that these are the thoughts of a sixteen-year-old girl. Reflecting on the past of her parents, she is trenchantly critical of her father's delinquencies. A 'reckless spendthrift with a strong taste for drink', he wastes his English inheritance and is forced to emigrate to Australia to a small station in Victoria, bought for him by relatives. After five years he tires of country life, sells the property and rapidly loses the profits by living at a great rate in Melbourne. The family is saved from ruin by a marriage arranged between their eldest daughter, Emma, then seventeen, and Thomas Raines, a partner in Cobb & Co and owner of properties in Ballarat, Lyneton and Sandhurst. As part of the marriage settlement, Raines buys his parents-in-law a farm at Swan

Hill and 'adopts' Clara, the narrator, agreeing to provide for her education and settle £1000 on her at marriage. Although initially more paternalistic than concupiscent, he has almost absolute power over her life, supervising her correspondence, dictating her movements and even regulating her visits to her parents. During the course of her eleven-year-long servitude Clara frequently contemplates escape, but is always deterred by concern for her gentle sister, the chief butt of Raines's uncertain temper.

From the first, Clara presents herself as a strong-willed, spirited and capable girl. Enthusiastic about farming and horse-riding, she resents the restraints of boarding school, bribes the butcher's boy to have a ride on his horse and is expelled after a farmer complains that she has damaged his crop of peas. Later she describes herself as 'a wild bush shrub [that] can always brave a storm', compared with the delicate plants that are amongst her acquaintance. In 1861 she is a light-hearted girl, unaware of the 'nearness of sorrow', delighting in a close friendship with a neighbouring girl, Carrie, and indulged by Raines and her governess. Nicknamed 'Heart's Delight', she generates merriment in the family's circle of friends at Swan Hill and receives proposals from most of the young men of her acquaintance. Only one, the first, from the shadowy James Campbell, stirs her heart and initiates her experience of steadfastly loving in the face of uncertainty. For the rest, she is direct in her rejections and visibly irritated by those who refuse to accept a refusal, such as the unfortunate whom she names 'Anyhow' and who suffers a sequence of humiliating reversals to his energetic wooing. The impression of social charisma and sexual attraction persists, for Clara leaves a dual trail of broken male hearts and enduring female friendships wherever she goes. In the Barrier Ranges, which is her home for several years, she experiences the paradox of extreme isolation and a steady sequence of proposals from casual workers, visitors, passers-by.

The apparent general willingness to found marriage on the slightest of acquaintance is part of the shadowiness of society both at Swan Hill and in the Barrier Ranges. Little appears to be known of the background of young men, while money is the sole criterion of eligibility. Even this is an uncertain attribute, though, and Clara is for a time pressured to marry a man of means and then mysteriously released from pressure:

the mystery was soon solved. On Wednesday night Carrie and I went to the post office for the letters and papers, as we had done for years. The first thing I saw in the *Australasian* was that Mr Beveridge had gone insolvent. He had lost Tyntyndger and everything he possessed. He was not even allowed to take his favourite mare Vixen off the station, so that now the 'King of Swan Hill' was on the same level as other men. (p. 25)

Shortly afterwards, he has a riding accident while intoxicated and when she last sees him some months later, he has become an old man, leaning on a crutch; 'He had neither money nor friends'. Raines also loses his fortune and moves from Swan Hill mansion to crudely constructed shed in the Barrier Ranges. Distance and the apparent mobility of men adds to the general shadowiness; rumours are rife, and both fortunes and affairs of the heart wax and wane on the waves of gossip. The accepted hazards of bush life and the difficulties of communication mean that people are falsely reported to be engaged, ruined, married or even dead. For several years Clara assumes that her first lover has been drowned and is then surprised to discover that he is living close by; when she arrives at Dunbar's Well in the Barrier Ranges she is amazed to receive a letter from her brother, Willie, whom she has not seen for some years, to the effect that he too lives in the area and when he arrives she fails to recognize him. A woman who is reported to be seriously ill turns out to be well, a girl who is reputed to be engaged reappears as the wife of another. At the nadir of her emotional life, Clara agrees under pressure to an eighteen-month engagement, which her fiance spends in a distant part of the bush. His ardour expresses itself in two brief letters during this period and he fails to reappear at the end of the agreed time. His reply to her letter of rejection is in the handwriting of another. At the same time, there is a general assumption that young men will be unreliable and dissolute, although Clara never explicitly comments to this effect. Raines is frequently the worse for drink and Clara is well aware that Peter Beveridge suffers from the same 'folly' as she puts it, and is surprised to find herself speaking to him 'on a subject that was not at all to his favour'. In the ranges alcoholism is more open and on her journey there Clara is warned by an old woman of the dangers she will meet: '"Treat everyone with respect and keep them at a distance."' On several occasions when men visit their settlement they camp down by the creek for a long drinking bout, and on others Clara avoids unknown male visitors by hiding outside. The real dangers of the area are emphasized by the nervousness of both men and women if forced to travel alone and in fact Clara's horse is first stolen by a bushranger and then ridden to death. Placed in a superior moral and economic position, men frequently abuse their power, and if Raines is an extreme example of abuse, his behaviour is duplicated by others, by the vicious Dan Stewart who lets his wife die on the Darling and abandons his daughter, and by Clara's guide to the Barriers, Curran, who steals one of her horses. Even courtship can be an act of aggression, as Clara realizes, valuing those of her suitors who do not 'bother' her again and resenting the manipulative 'Anyhow'. In this hazardous environment where respectability is the thinnest of veneers, it is obviously difficult for a girl to find the true love and the strong sustaining arm that Clara seeks, and much of the tension of her story springs from her justifiable uncertainty about the sincerity and reliability of James Campbell. Like Pamela she has to reform her lover and undergo a bewildering ordeal in which he often fails her. One of the most intriguing aspects of their courtship is the change in his letters, recording a gradual increase in maturity; his decision to sign a five-year pledge to abstain from alcohol is regarded by both of them as an important step toward his winning of her as wife.

Clara's concern about alcohol might make her seem wowserish, but nothing could be further from the reader's impression of this narrative's spirited and sensitive recording 'I'. If she frequently reflects on the loneliness of the bush and longs for the friends of the past, she meets hardship and privation with amazing cheerfulness. Often the extent of the hardships which she and Em encounter in the ranges emerges indirectly. Awakened by a sense of cold when they are camping in the bush, she is relieved to discover it is not a snake, only a flooded tent; a few nights later their tent is invaded by a wild pig which refuses to be dislodged, an event which the men of the party find hilarious. On another occasion she mentions that the shed that is their home at Euryowrie is too cold at night so they sit round a fire outside, and even the loss of the shed's roof during a wild dust storm arouses more of a wry than a despairing reaction.

Although Raines forbids visiting as much as possible, especially after he has begun to spin a web of rumours designed to keep her for himself, she is clearly in great demand by the few married women in the district. Her sparse visits to these friends are highly valued, literally liberating experiences, while her centrality to these gatherings as entertainer is obvious. There are occasional indications that her power to charm is irresistible and she half-inadvertently causes a rift between a girl-friend and her fiance (inevitably one of Clara's cast-off suitors) by reining him in again, or almost upsets her ultimate engagement to Campbell by inflaming yet another suitor. The main impression, however, is of an energetic, gregarious nature, starved of the company that is her natural medium. Her enjoyment of a Christmas outing shortly after their arrival at Euryowrie in 1869 is typical. Their shed is half-finished, the tents are flooded, the horses which are unyarded take an hour to catch and her mount is so wild that he has to be blindfolded. Nothing daunted, she sets off for the nearest property with an Aboriginal boy as a companion, steadying her horse a little with an eight- or ten-mile gallop:

we were not long in going the sixty miles. They were all very pleased to see me, and after supper we spent the evening in dancing and singing. Annie and I slept together, so you may be sure there was more talk than sleep. (p. 101)

As Clara's story develops, so does she, changing from the unsophisticated, heedless girl of the beginning to mature woman. The most remarkable change is from urban girl to hardy bushwoman. Tracking horses for long distances, kangaroo hunting, cutting mulga, building sheep yards, killing snakes and dingoes, horse-breaking, droving, wielding hammer and nails, Clara is obviously indispensable to Raines and it is not surprising to discover that his property deteriorates rapidly after she leaves; nor that the possibility of her departure inspires him with horror, quite apart from the disappointment of his sexual hopes. Attempting to hold her by promising her half-ownership of the stock, or as a last resort suggesting a partnership to Campbell, he does his best to cause a rift in their relationship. Clara herself is surprised at the change in her capabilities:

They used to say in Victoria that I would never make a bushman's wife, and that I should marry a wealthy man, so that I should never have to work, but if they could have seen me this morning chopping down mulga trees and assisting to load the dray, they would have altered their opinion. They would scarcely know the Miss Harrod they knew in Victoria; in fact, I often wonder whether I am or not. (p. 111)

Nor is she immune from pride, taking pleasure in impressing a nervous male rider with her courage and skill and carefully recording her many feats of horse-catching or of riding with an improvised bridle of stockings and belt. She also has time to enjoy the wild landscape, to gather wild flowers with which she decorates herself in Ophelia-like display, or to indulge her domestic and artistic skills. Perhaps the most characteristic scene is of her crocheting and minding the sheep:

I have been shepherding today, and a cold showery day it has been. I carried a stone to sit on, and another for my feet, so I managed to keep fairly dry. I had just commenced some crochet work—for I always crochet when I am shepherding—when a heavy shower came on and wet me through. (p. 139)

But her increased maturity is also emotional, for her ordeal strengthens her belief in loyalty and fidelity in love. If she is loyal to her much loved but less resilient sister, refusing several opportunities to escape, she values loyalty in others, determining to marry for love alone and chastening her lover when he falls short of the ideal. Wealth, compliments and kindness are well enough, she reflects, 'but they do not satisfy the heart' (p. 147).

Raines, the villain of Campbell's *Memoirs*, is physically a shadowy figure and even his moral nature emerges indirectly for Clara is more concerned with the impact of his personality on their lives and too contemptuous of him to spend time in analysis. Nevertheless, he emerges as a weak individual, naturally drawn to alcohol and low company, prone to conceal his sense of inadequacy by tyrannizing those in his power. He is at his most unpredictable and violent when things go wrong. After losing some valuable stock, for instance, he breaks Clara's concertina in an outburst of temper and humiliates the girls in front of a visitor; convinced on another occasion that Campbell has visited the station during his absence, he threatens to

knock her down. Again, Clara is not specific, but it is clear that after
the failure of his business at Swan Hill he takes to the ranges like a
whipped dog. When the girls join him there after a horrific journey,
made without any of the help he promised, he behaves either with
surly indifference or terrifying violence. Living in a crude dwelling
cut into the side of a hill, which serves as the local bar, he is carrying
on an affair with the slatternly maid of all work. When a mob of the
Barrier 'roughs' arrives, Raines drinks and races with them all day,
racing Clara's saddle horse to let her know 'that my noble little horse,
as well as myself, was in his power'. Later, he locks the girls in the
house and threatens to kill them:

I took up a butcher's knife that was lying on the table as I passed into my
room, and was determined to use it in self-defence if necessary.

I had no door to my room, so I placed two old pannikins, my books, and
several other articles across the doorway, so that I would hear him if he came
in. I hardly slept a night for three weeks; I slept during the day, and at night
watched while Em. slept. (p. 61)

After they move from Umberumberka to Dunbar's Well, they are
joined by their brother Willie and Raines's behaviour improves. In
addition, Clara rapidly becomes indispensable, frequently working
alongside her brother-in-law, so one assumes the improvement is
partly linked to a shrewd assessment of his own interests. Even so, he
reads or confiscates her mail, rifles her few possessions when she is
out, dictates her social behaviour, begrudges her small pleasures and
restricts her movements. And always, he holds the powerless Em as
hostage. The situation deteriorates rapidly after he quarrels with
Willie and realizes that marriage between Clara and Campbell is a
real possibility. Spreading rumours of Clara's involvement with
others in the hope of deterring Campbell, Raines even advertises his
intention of making her the second Mrs Raines, notwithstanding
Em's good health. His violence becomes a daily hazard and Clara is
convinced that he would rather take her life than allow her to marry.
Her communications with Campbell have to be delivered secretly and
she hides his letters on the bank of the creek. Although she is now
twenty-four, he declares that he will refuse his consent unless she
promises three things. There is not much mystery about his demands:
'It is better to die innocent than guilty', she replies to his threat that
he will kill her if she does not submit:

'I can carry out my wishes whenever I like, and then please myself as to
whether I give my consent or not.' I felt cold all over when I thought how
much I was in that man's power, and yet, had he lain a hand on me I fully
believe God would have given me strength twice as his. (p. 159)

In the event, thanks to Willie's watchfulness and her own resource,
all his stratagems fail and she is safely married. Nevertheless, leaving

her sister is a terrible grief and a constant trouble to Clara after marriage. One is grateful for the epilogue added by Clara's son to the effect that Raines died in 1874 and that Em married again and ended her life with her sister.

As for Campbell, the somewhat elusive object of Clara's passion, he appears to have finally made good, although he and Clara seem to have lived their last years apart. If he is initially lacking in tenacity, failing to visit the Raines's menage for twelve months although he lives only thirty miles (forty-eight kilometres) away, Clara soon stiffens him with the starch of her own resolve. The turning point comes when he signs the five-year pledge and takes his mother's name, Stewart, in memory of her previously neglected wisdom: '"Your refining influence has worked a change in me"', he tells Clara (p. 181). Looking back on the first year of their marriage he is 'very grateful to the old year, 1871, for it has brought me my greatest happiness, and given me a start in the world. It has also opened my eyes to many a folly'. With Clara beside him how could he fail and indeed, even before their marriage, her letters are careful not to neglect farming and business advice. As she reflects with disarming confidence in one of her last letters to him, 'I see no reason why we cannot prosper in the world'.

No account of the place of love in women's autobiographies would be complete without a study of Christina Stead's epic novel, *For Love Alone*. Stead frequently emphasized in interviews that her novels, especially *The Man Who Loved Children* and *For Love Alone*, are her autobiography, and these two are undoubtedly based on her own formative years; but both books are also remarkably impersonal, on a par with Lawrence's *Women in Love* as ambitious attempts to link personal, psychological and political. As Terry Sturm has pointed out, Stead's novels are saturated in ideologies of sex, family, economics, politics and culture but her mode of realism is not a reductive discovery of typical political configurations in individual lives. She discovers instead the logicality hidden in 'idiosyncratic behaviour and extremities of feeling' and the 'violent grotesquerie lurking within apparently logical attitudes'.[8] Observing even her own life with the dispassion of the naturalist (always her preferred analogy), she is minutely sensitive to the symbiosis between psychological needs and anxieties and political structures. As I have already argued, ideology in *The Man Who Loved Children* is not just a mix of ideas, imposed on the individual, but ingrained in the mental and emotional texture of living. As Teresa comments at one point:

Where we have passions that are uncontrollable as in sex, a difficult social web is consciously spun out of them, with the help of oppressor and oppressed, so that practically no joy may be obtained from them, and I believe that it is intended in society that we should have little joy. (p. 254–5)[9]

'They' who impose the joy-defeating social taboos are hard to define 'But I am trying to get by them—whoever they are'. As her difficult journey illustrates, 'they' includes Teresa herself, for even such a free spirit as she is cannot avoid being an accomplice in her own victimization.

For Love Alone is also that rare phenomenon, a female epic. Teresa has no doubt that her quest is a heroic one and that she has the heart of a hero. She knows that she has 'some kind of a great destiny' for 'Glory and catastrophe are not the fate of the common man', and like the hero she must undergo a sequence of ordeals, perform tests, take a solitary path and even risk death itself. She is like 'those princesses in Grimm and Andersen . . . who had to make twelve shirts out of nettles' before they could be liberated, but she is also like the male hero, consciously taking on the bold male pursuit of the loved one. She 'felt that she was behaving as behaves a gallant and a brave man who passes through the ordeals of hope deferred, patience, and painful longing, to win a wife' (p. 250). Although later, during the miserable contest with Crow in London, she reflects on 'the rigmarole of her buffoon Odyssey', neither she nor her author persist in this detraction. For the epic nature of her struggle is constantly underlined by literary analogies and the use of traditional epic devices, while the leisureliness and poetic licence of the narrative infuse it with a constant sense of the legendary.

As Joan Lidoff has pointed out, Teresa's affront on the limitations imposed on love requires 'the active self-assertion of a traditionally male style of heroism rather than a passive feminine one'[10], most obvious perhaps in her adoption of a male concept of honour. In the brilliant first scene, a dramatic representation of the fierce revolutionary, Teresa, surrounded literally by uncomprehending, conventional males but figuratively by many of the visible and invisible forces she will have to resist, she defends her 'honour'. Andrew Hawkins, a latter-day Sam Pollit, is the chief instigator of her anger when he characteristically emphasizes that the only female honour is sexual chastity. Teresa makes it clear that honour has a much wider definition for her, '"Honour is more sacred than life"' (p. 13), and later after a fight with her brother she reflects that she would kill for honour: 'A scene flew up in her mind in which she killed in hot blood, for honour and was glad of it, saw the spilt blood spreading' (p. 79). Honour is close to the determination not to compromise, another resolution which she declares early, and expresses her refusal to accept the conventional stereotype of sexual relationship, tarnished by ideas of owning and paying, and by conventional attitudes which are nothing more than an expression of territorial rights. Nothing will induce her to succumb to the dishonourable, unchaste 'marriage-sleep' with a husband she does not want, for Teresa, like her predecessor Louie, is committed to a vision of love as the 'real life', the essential creativity of the self. Since school she has ravaged libraries in her obsession with 'this boundless love of love, this insensate thirst for the truth above passion' (p. 76). Like the male hero of the traditional *Bildungsroman* in her boldness and willingness to be singular, she is unlike him in her sense of being connected to the lives and passions of others. She recognizes that she is not alone in 'this insensate thirst', that it is felt by her brothers and sister, although it is 'neglected, denied, and useless; obnoxious in school, workshop, street':

She smelled, heard, saw, guessed faster, longed more than others, it seemed to her. She listened to what they brought out with a galling politeness, because what she had to say she could not tell them. It was not so that life was and they were either liars or stupid. At the same time, how queer that she understood what was going on in their minds so well! For it seemed to her that they were all moved by the same passion, in different intensities. (pp. 76–7)

At the same time Teresa glimpses what is obvious to her author, that sexual repression is part of the poverty that afflicts 1930s Sydney in particular and capitalist society in general. Sensual poverty is part-fruit and part-cause of all the other poverties which make exploitation a natural law: as Teresa comments, '"we prey on each other, but we don't want to "'. In an interview Stead once described the novelist as a vivisector who 'uses the pen as a scalpel for lifting up the living tissues, cutting through the morbid tissues of the social anatomy'[11] and in Teresa she has created a hero who is singularly fitted to distinguish the living from the morbid, even though she is almost destroyed by her engrossment with the latter.

The link between creativity and love was frequently emphasized by Stead in interviews (Love 'brings out the creative powers. It is intended to be creative. I mean by nature. And it is creative'[12]), although no interviewer was ever bold enough to take up her assertion that her ambition was to love not to write, for writing was as inescapable as breathing. In *For Love Alone* she suggests that finding the right lover is the most crucially creative act of life, although love underlies the most ordinary acts, from selecting clothes to cooking to house decoration. Thus the extraordinary trousseau that the elderly Miss Smith-Wetherby commissions for Malfi March is an expression of all her thwarted creativity, just as her choice of recipient, a girl marrying in a desperate shot-gun situation, is a metaphor of creativity's generally stunted issue in this sort of society. Somewhat similar is the cruelly termed hope chest, an apparently spontaneous social metaphor of the buried creativity that the intrusion of ideas of property into love imposes.

In the first fourteen chapters of the novel Stead brilliantly orchestrates in a series of contrasting, interlocking movements her central theme of love and Teresa's commitment to its hazardous quest in a society bent on its suffocation. The first chapter, 'Brown Seaweed and Old Fish Nets', returns to the small family world of *The Man Who Loved Children* dominated by the voice of the old mermaid-catcher, the father. Appropriately displaying his physical potency from the first sentence ('Naked, except for a white towel rolled into a loincloth, he stood in the doorway, laughing and shouting ...'), he luxuriates in the rhetoric of male domination. With a few deft contrasts, Stead places the man and his old patriarchal nets in Teresa's moral context. His descants on his life-long service of truth and beauty and the attractions of the angel in the house, for instance, are accompanied by Teresa's laying of the 'worn damask cloth' for the family's miserable meal and his own peremptory reminders to Kitty to clean his boots. Susan Higgins has pointed out the subtle implications in the contrast between Hawkins's concept of love as the harmonious attraction of opposites forming one '"blessed circle, perpetual motion"' and Teresa's remark, '"We will never be finished"', referring to her sewing but anticipating her final vision of the endless repetition of perverted love stories.[13] But the contrast also looks back ironically to the vicious circle of mermaid-minotaur struggle in *The Man Who Loved Children* (see Chapter 8). Teresa takes up Louie's position in the family; 'unappeased ... relentless, ferocious', she stirs the family into an awareness of the smallness of their lives, while she shares Louie's perception of them as 'enemies'. And she resumes Louie's final position of total rejection of the father:

'I am informed, on the moral side. You're ignoble. You can't understand me. Henceforth, everything between us is a misunderstanding. You have accepted compromise, you revel in it. Not me. I will never compromise.' (p. 14)

In her bedroom which she has decorated with unusual designs symbolizing fertility, she indulges in sessions of creating fantastic garments which emphasize her sexuality, or in night-long dreaming by the window looking out to sea. In this secret life of profound pleasure, she is in touch with the 'active creation going on around her in the rocks and hills, where the mystery of lust took place'. She perceives the universality of the drive to love, feels the lovers at her back like a 'swarm of locusts' and revels in her own, half-formed vision of future love, which must be like 'a strange walking in harmony, blood in the trees' (p. 73). The wedding of Malfi March, which the sisters attend at the opening of the novel, echoing *Women in Love*, is a richly toned picture of the strength of the universal love instinct and the ignoble diversion it suffers under social pressures and constraints. The day is hot, undoing the efforts at outward respecta-bility, increasing the effect of the wine and contributing to a general loosening of corsets. The knowledge of the bride's circumstances, shared by some guests, stimulates a crop of innuendoes, while the usual *risqué* humour associated with weddings bubbles irresistibly to the surface. The 'irritated lasciviousness of the girls, on whom the heat and the thought of the wedding night worked as an aphrodisiac' combines with their 'impatience, curiosity and discontent' to throw them into a fever. Aware that they, unlike the men, are pressed for time, before the 'long night of spinsterhood' comes down, they are stalked by 'three hooded madmen ... desire, fear, ridicule' (pp. 74–5). Malfi's tossing of her bouquet, which ends up under Teresa's feet, dramatically exposes the pain and indignity of their common situation, forced to compete for a husband to stave off the social stigma of the solitary state. Teresa, witness of 'the awful eagerness' of the others observed by the circle of patronizing men, is conscious that 'They were laughing at them, at her, because they had been struggling for a husband'. She roughly rejects the remains of the bouquet, exclaiming: '"You're cruel to us, making fun of us, this is cruel"'. The scene is a demonstration of the miserable inner life of the girls of her acquaintance, which has previously insistently pressed on her imagination: 'writhing with desire and shame', they grovel before men 'silent about the stew in which they boiled and bubbled, discontented, browbeaten, flouted, ridiculous' (p. 18).

The following four chapters greatly expand the theme of universal yearning and universal disappointment. Shut up with her cousin Anne and her mother, Aunt Bea, in their pathetically poor rented room, Teresa participates in an intense drama of dreaming and loss. On one hand, Aunt Bea's irrepressibly bawdy innuendoes and reflections on the incredible trousseau extend the mood of sexual excitement and yearning, while on the other, the moon pours into the room bringing the romance of the summer night with it and whitening the outline of Anne's hair. '"Oh, you young things, you do not know what you have. These are the happiest days of your life. When you're my age, you'll catch up with an old woman on the street, it will be yourself"', muses Aunt Bea, unwittingly pressing on her daughter's bruised sense of time's passing. The strange story of the landlady's husband, rendered insane because of sexual deprivation, and Teresa's interview with the half-mad woman herself, anticipate the general madness that her flight to Harper's Valley discovers, and that is sharply dramatized by the shrieks of the clinically mad young man. '"Why, we would all go mad, if we were shut up and not allowed to get married"' (p. 161), exclaims Teresa, and her response to the grotesque distortions of life in Harper's Valley, culminating in her pursuit by an old man who exposes himself, is that 'It was a shame and disgrace'; like Ellen, her cousin, forced into a loveless marriage with a boorish countryman, and like the madman, the old man is pushed into making himself an obscenity. '"There's something I don't understand in the whole arrangement"', reflects Teresa, '"No,

I'm not mad, they are"' (p. 92). The general acceptance of social taboos puzzles her: 'How can we all suffer when none of us wants it?' and 'Why do men make the laws . . . about marriage, decency and the like, to shackle themselves?' (pp. 92, 93). For she perceives clearly that men suffer under the system of laws as much as women.

In all these early chapters the power of the love force in human lives and the dangers of Teresa's quest are constantly emphasized. Like the sea which floods the reefs and chokes the headlands, love is an irresistible tide. Threading her way through the 'strange battle-field' of love on her way home, Teresa is conscious that the 'sounds of the dying' will mean that children will be the result of this night and perhaps some real deaths: 'There were often bodies fished up round here, that had leapt when the heart still beat, from these high ledges into waters washed round these rocks by the moon' (p. 61). Down on the beach the body of a woman, deserted in love and drowned in the sea because of her 'great thirst', is concealed in a fishing boat. Like Queen Dido, she has suffered death, a fate that Teresa is prepared to accept if her quest fails. 'This was the truth, not the daily simpering on the boat and the putting away in hope chests', she reflects, recalling the preoccupation of the girls of her acquaintance with getting a providing husband rather than a lover. And the total absence of erotic writing by women puzzles her; if her world is recognized and illuminated by the writings of men, there is 'nothing in the few works of women she could find that was what they must have felt' (p. 76).

Given the grandeur and boldness of Teresa's dream of love, it is extraordinary that her first love object should be a man who is her polar opposite, Jonathan Crow. As some readers have commented there is something even comical about her idealization of this preda-tory figure, and even her most sympathetic observer, Quick, is at first disposed to wonder about her intelligence. A poor boy, who has won his way into the academic world by hard work and deprivation, Crow has surrounded himself with a circle of female admirers when Teresa first meets him. Fitfully aware of his own emotional poverty, he takes refuge in exploiting the yearnings and pity of women. If he is poor, women are poorer still and he assuages something of his resented poverty by tyrannizing his unsuspecting admirers whose sufferings he has 'tabulated'. Rasche describes him well:

'Mr Master-of-Arts Crow . . . back from a trip to the nearer suburbs with lectures on free love in Croydon, contraceptives in Strathfield, and sterilizing the unfit in Balmain . . . I congratulate you, sir, on the love of woman, fair woman. Nobly cutting himself off from his equals, he goes out among the women and will prove to anyone—if she wear a spirit—that she must modify herself for men . . . No, she must accommodate herself to being the universal mother.' (p. 171–2)

Superficially, he has attributes that are bound to attract the inexperienced Teresa. He is associated with all the romance of the University, which seems to her to be a place of unusual male/female companionship, and he speaks boldly of free love and the unequal ordering of society. He appears to reject the property basis of relationships that she rejects and insinuates that there are alternatives; he is shortly to set out in quest of his fortune overseas, suggesting that, like her, he has something of the stormy petrel in his make-up. To the young girl, stifled by the chalk dust of a dull classroom and the prospect of a career as an unmarried teacher, he is a figure of hope. Above all, he is poor and makes constant calls on her pity.

Nevertheless, he is her moral opposite in every way. Whereas Teresa is convinced of her singularity, he is gloomily aware that he is 'an ordinary man who had got to the top by observing and following the rules' (pp. 172–3); whereas she delights in her creativity, he knows himself to be barren; 'he saw his bareness. He not only wanted nothing but he had nothing' (p. 199). Stifling his dreams instead of revelling in them, he has 'reduced himself to a miserliness of mental life' (p. 198). His solitariness is a condition to be endured, rather than an energetic acceptance of freedom and difference, for he knows that he can only be real to himself in a crowd, 'he was nothing by himself' (p. 200). Spending himself in a few insincere letters to a group of women, he achieves a mild, cost-free sexual relief. Teresa abhors notions of owning, but Crow can only think in terms of profit and loss; his discovery that Teresa derives pleasure from her love for him fills him with resentment: 'It irritated him to give this great naked slobbering joy to one who could not make payment in kind; the wretched woman could get pleasure out of him when she wished merely by looking at him; he did not own himself' (p. 196). On the other hand, his manipulations of her emotions give him the delightful impression of owning her. In his conviction that the female sex has been created to succour the male, should be gracefully recessive and reserved for motherhood, he is a duplicate of Andrew Hawkins. Whereas Teresa is a bold lover, he is sexually timid, expecting women to 'do the work of passion'; in answer to her belief in love, he offers the cynical conviction that there is only lust. Above all he differs from her in that she is free whereas he is bound. Although he initially responds to her statement that she is a free woman by interpreting it as a freedom for him, an offer of love without claims, he resents his deeper apprehension that she knows a freedom that he is denied: 'Only to wipe that expression off her face and make it droop, as he liked to see it, thoughtful and wretched, wearied, with the spurt of resistance breaking through' (p. 197).

Crow has fabular dimensions but he is also an acute psychological study. He perfectly fits Karen Horney's analysis of the misogynist, the man whose infantile anxieties centring on the mother have issued in a fear of rejection by women and an attempt to evade that fear in derision. Quick, for instance, recognizes that he carries the classic 'sign of the misogynist' in his perception of his mother as a madonna figure and there is the curious scene of his anger at his brother's wedding and his refusal to allow his mother to attend. His dislike of marriage is not just a rational dislike of ties. By restricting his sexual life to women of inferior class he runs less risk of rejection, while by playing on women's feelings of pity and yearning for love, he wins for himself the illusion of conquering, the only form of love he can know. At one point, Crow unburdens himself as if on a psychiatrist's couch, admitting his sadistic impulses as a boy and their continuation in his adulthood and his ability to know only lust, not love. '"Boys—all boys and all men—are sadists. Women offer themselves as victims, it's the sexual difference. Sex makes us suffer and men don't like to suffer, so we pick the wings off flies"' (pp. 359–60). In Horney's terms he is expressing the twofold fury caused by his infantile frustration, 'the thrusting back of his libido upon itself' and the wounding of his masculine self-regard; 'his phallic impulses to penetrate merge with his anger at frustration and the impulses take on a sadistic tinge'.[14] Afraid of sex as he fears the sexual power of the mother, he takes vengeance by inflicting suffering. Similarly his passivity as a lover, which frequently surprises Teresa, is a manifestation of his infantile desire to receive the love of a mother.

But Crow is much more than an accurate psychological case-study. As Teresa's moral opposite and as a crystallization of the evil of the system she fights, he is her fitting adversary in the legendary quest that is *For Love Alone*, even though she only half knows him as an adversary. As several readers have pointed out, Teresa is a twentieth century Saint Teresa seeking fulfilment in human love as Saint Teresa sought it in divine love. The shadow of *Middlemarch* lies across the book as well as that of *Women in Love*, for like Dorothea, Teresa is determined not to compromise, invests her ardour in a man incapable of love, and discovers a new, worthy love that depends on an enlightened form of compromise and includes a new vision of connectedness. It is as if Teresa's heroic self selects Crow as the enemy who must be defeated even as she makes him into a romantic love object. Several passages, for instance, suggest that she cold-bloodedly selects him as potential mate: 'She cast about for a man to love; the nearest man was Jonathan, but she ran over the others' (p. 225). Once she has cast the die by writing to tell him of her love, she resents having to concentrate on him rather than on love: 'It isn't that half-starved, half-grown man I want. It's passion' and 'If she won him, she would succeed, and in some mysterious way conquer her life and time' (p. 226). Occasionally she sees her affair with Crow as 'only a step to the unknown man'. Later in England, she perceives that he has provided her with a purpose: '"it was for you I came here, without you I might never have come. I would have failed"' (p. 379). And at the close she realizes that he was just the illusion of a love-hungry girl: '"Love him!" she cried in horror. "I never loved him at all. I thought I did, though. He helped me. I will always be grateful to him"' (p. 450). In many ways it is appropriate that the affair in Sydney should be of short duration, followed by a four-year long ordeal of commitment to his ideal, for there are indications that even in Sydney Teresa begins the process of disillusionment that is hers in London. She begins 'to dread meeting him, even though these meetings had become the whole reason for living through days and nights' (p. 231). There are even indications that he is as much her victim as she is his, held in the forceps of her will, and certainly he rapidly loses any grandeur he had after the affair is concluded, scuttling off to London with almost comical haste after the final confrontation at the sawmill. Indeed, the resolution of this fine Lawrentian scene of opposed wills emphasizes Teresa's superior power:

They looked at each other by the light of the flare with unveiled dislike. Teresa, looking at him, released him from her will; it happened suddenly. The harness of years dropped off, eaten through; she dropped her eyes, thought: 'How stupid he is! How dull!' He looked sullenly at her, with hatred, crueller and more vicious than teased lust. He half shut his eyes and turned his head away. When his eyes returned to her, they had a natural look, but he was a stranger. (p. 408)

Some readers have seen the conclusion of the affair as dependent on Quick's influence, who is interpreted as a life-enhancing figure as his name suggests. Certainly Teresa tells him that he has brought her back to life, but the affair with Crow is something she knows she must prosecute independently to the end; Quick sets the seal on her decision by his judgement of the man, while his large interests and work in 'the Hanseatic world and the Baltic outpourings' revive her own interest in outer things. Thus those readers who interpret Teresa's ordeal of near-starvation in Sydney as enforced masochism under the influence of Crow have missed the point of her struggle. Joan Lidoff, for example, concludes that Teresa makes herself the very image she rejected of 'the female hero as martyred saint' and 'inadvertently treads the path of masochism and martyrdom. The most violent action Teresa ever takes is against herself'.[15] It is certainly true that Teresa frequently suffers assaults on her self-esteem during their relationship, but like the representative hero she is, she confronts powerful foes and she is no less representative in that the cause of her temptations to repress the self is irrational and even ridiculous. But, as she subsequently recognizes, her ordeal is a magnificent victory of will, saving her from the conventional fate that threatened before she met Crow. Without the holy grail of love she would have fallen into the marriage sleep or into 'loveless love affairs with no conclusion' and 'the great desire to go abroad' would have withered, 'her will ruined' (p. 243). She needs Jonathan as an aim so as not to fail, 'even if he rejects her', and by fixing her will to a transcendent purpose she confirms her impression that she is strange: 'and to strange persons, strange visions, strange destinies' (p. 265). Being hungry and paring her physical needs down to the absolute minimum to stay alive, she makes life more interesting than it had been for years. When Crow concludes that her years of self-denial must have been empty, she replies proudly, '"Empty? No, full! A burning full life, I had, while I was saving—"' (p. 379). And to Quick she confesses '"I couldn't give up, be beaten by fate . . . It was never Johnny"' (p. 450). The real contest with Crow is postponed until she arrives in London, but her ordeal has armed her morally for the struggle.

The final stages of Teresa's quest are a series of rapid leaps forward. 'Saved' by Quick according to his own definition of his role, it seems that she will subside into the conventional end of women's fiction, marriage with Mr Right. Instead, she hazards another love affair within three months of settling down with Quick. Although she loves Quick deeply, she must retain her freedom to think, resist his desire to 'make her over' into another, more socially brilliant woman, resist even the natural feelings of pity which might muddy love. She needs also to know men from whom 'she had been wrongly, feloniously separated' (p. 458). The insidious influence of social conventions intrudes into even this revolutionary marriage of wanderers and she soon discovers that Quick wants only a woman's love. The discovery threatens to frustrate her ideal of open companionship and to initiate their confinement in 'the labyrinth of concealment and loving mendacity' (p. 460). She is embarrassed 'by this devotion of the man whose idea of heaven was the rapture of married love . . . he had no idea of how his constantly proffered love, sympathy, and help troubled her; she was used to thinking for herself' (p. 463). If her quest has been for total freedom in loving, she must not abandon her goal, however much she respects Quick's devotion and loyalty. Women have the same right to happiness as men and the only way they can defeat 'the false lore of society' is by having 'the right to love':

In the old days, the girls were married without love, for property, and nowadays they were forced to marry, of themselves, without knowing love, for wages. It was easy to see how upsetting it would be if women began to love freely where love came to them. An abyss would open in the principal shopping street of every town. (p. 464)

Still 'unappeased' and 'hungry', Teresa exercises her right to love freely in her brief affair with Harry Girton. Paradoxically, her infidelity is her most chaste act ('I was never chaste till now'), for she retains her initial honourable quest of free love and avoids the 'mere tranquility and the death of the heart' which threatened to be the fate of her alliance with Quick. Choosing to love Girton, she breaks through the 'insanity' of taboos and finds the happiness denied in the name of morality. As she had foreseen, she finds her own destiny and conquers time, watching the passing of her necessary affair with Girton with the same tranquility as she watches the passing of an immense dusk-white flower on the river the next morning. Making her heart 'unselfish' when she thinks of Quick, she freely chooses what there is of compromise in their relationship and returns to him with the 'milk and honey' that she has won in her secret romance with Girton. She recognizes that this is 'the only love, but not the first and not the last', and in future she will know how to cultivate her heart and mind in secret while loving this loyal and generous man.

The last chapter, titled 'I am Thinking I am Free', reflects on the meaning of Teresa's experience for her struggling companions in the world, for as Diana Brydon has commented, 'Stead elaborates a fiction of connection that affirms our essentially social nature as human beings while criticizing the social conventions we have developed to accommodate this need'.[16] Several incidents that are also images come together to reaffirm the poverty and insanity of human society that Teresa has confronted with the revolutionary insights of passion: a last view of Jonathan, representative of the deathly forces at loose in the world, 'sucked into himself like a sea-anemone' and a reminder of the eternal vicious cycle of perverted love relationships ('"It's dreadful to think that it will go on being repeated for ever, he—and me! What's there to stop it?"', reflects Teresa. p. 502). And a familiar sight, the departure of an old beggar and his parasite, a vicious slum youth, 'one bent back following another', evoking the eternal bent backs of all those made poor by the sinister 'abracada' of the human community. Teresa herself experiences an intense realization that her quest has only just begun, and that she must continue restless while there is 'something on the citied plain for all of them, the thousands like thin famished fire that wavered and throve around her, pressing on':

suddenly as a strange thought it came to her, that she had reached the gates of the world of Girton and Quick and that it was towards them she was only now journeying, and in a direction unguessed by them; and it was towards them and in this undreamed direction that she had been travelling all her life, and would travel, farther, without them; and with her she felt many thousands of shadows, pressing along with her, storming forwards, but quietly and eagerly, though blindly. She even heard the rushing and jostling of their patched and washed clothes and the flapping of their street-worn shoes, their paper-stuffed soles. (p. 494)

If *For Love Alone* has been an influential book for women writers, one 1980s writer, Glenda Adams, has virtually re-written the epic in her own autobiographical novel, *Dancing on Coral*.[17] Like *For Love Alone*, *Dancing on Coral* is a self-consciously literary text, drawing on previous versions of the myth of the journey and assuming a cultural community with the reader. More playful than *For Love Alone*, it is a richly comic work, exuberantly parodic of its time, the 1960s, but no less political in intention than its predecessor, for Adams is preoccupied with subversion, especially the subversiveness of language and its fictional constructs. Her play with the idea of fictiveness marks her as a modernist, but she is also alive to the arid delusions that can sprout from a preoccupation with the fictive, which makes *Dancing on Coral* as relevant to the 1980s as the 1960s. Lévi-Strauss and Barthes stalk the text as well as Camus, Joyce, Stead and Aristotle and it is no accident that the male protagonist and his mentor are anthropologists. ' ". . . [T]he world itself is my text, the spectacle" ', declares Donna Bird, Lark's sophisticated rival, whose diaries contain 'nothing of importance', nothing with meaning, but merely exist to 'affirm the spectacle': ' "I try to stay on the surface, that is true freedom, and to eschew the psychological" ' (pp. 106, 107). For Donna Bird the lie is always a political stratagem, a joke subversive of the dominant culture's fictions, but Lark, who can lie like a trooper if a personal occasion arises, remains committed to the idea of meaning, especially the meaning of love.

Like Teresa, Lark, the heroine, is in quest of love and determined to leave Australia for overseas, although in her case America is the natural mecca, not England. Her ideal of true love is as concerned with sincerity and fidelity as Teresa's but she is less fortunate and in many ways her story enacts the disillusionment with heterosexual romance common in women's writing of this century. Like many a modern heroine, she finds that integrity and her culture's versions of love, whether inside or outside marriage, are incompatible and the eventual departure of both husband and lover leaves her 'poorer but freer'.

At the beginning of her story, Lark is the young impressionable colonial, bored with the garden of Australia, where there is 'too much nature' and dazzled by the idea of the great American city, and by its quintessential representative, Tom Brown. Her ennui is exacerbated by her parents' conviction of failure, especially her father's serio-comic attempts to fulfil his dream of travel, and the departure of a potential lover, Solomon Blank. The opening chapters brilliantly establish the imperializing impact of Tom Brown, patronizing Harvard graduate and articulate social theorist, on the self-consciously inexperienced Lark. She is admitted to the group of student notables, which he heads, and which includes Donna Bird, the cosmopolitan editor of the student newspaper; Perce, a libertarian who wears no shoes, ties his khaki trousers with a piece of rope, writes lewd columns for the newspaper and makes the 1960s permissiveness an excuse for abusive chauvinism; and the leader of the student conservative club who wears a monocle, is known only by his initials and approaches women with the tactics of an exacting quizmaster. 'Lark knew she was very lucky to be sitting in this restaurant with uninhibited, politically aware students. Seminal, she guessed they were' (p. 49). The contrast between their rhetoric on the evils of imperialism and the White Australia policy and their raucous, destructive behaviour in a Chinese restaurant (behaviour that is fatalistically accepted by the waiters) escapes her. Nor does she explicitly relate the dismissive chauvinism she experiences in interviews with two prospective employers, Qantas and a newspaper editor, with the chauvinism of her peers, but in both cases her physical attributes are emphasized at the expense of her intellect. Flattered to be useful, Lark is drawn into Tom's schemes to make money and manipulate the manipulative media by concocting bizarre stories of 'barbarian' Australia for an American magazine, *Strange but True*. As part of his stance of sibylline omniscience, Tom never asks questions or volunteers information, but transmits it piecemeal, according to Lark's questions. As a result, she is mystified about the staged kidnapping of a 'schoolgirl', in which she participates, and slips inadvertently into illegalities which will make her departure from Australia a necessity. With his usual air of casual, imperial disposal, Tom turns her danger into a virtue, or a joke, anticipating the central joke of the book, the dancing on coral.

Lark's odyssey includes the ordeal of travelling on a German cargo ship with only Donna Bird as companion. The captain (a stereotypical Nazi and physically reminiscent of Hitler) forces the two women on to a coral reef in the middle of the ocean, leaving them there while the tide rises to waist level: 'Lark stood in the middle of the Pacific Ocean and sobbed' (p. 119). As the tide rises, the two are forced into a weird dance:

They stood braced, their arms outstretched for balance, their legs apart and vaguely outlined beneath the water. The horizon, dividing blue water from blue sky, encircled them. They looked into the distance, expectantly, urgently. As the water swelled and pressed against them they were forced to take little steps, first this way, then that, in unison, two women dancing on coral. (p. 121)

The image extends its suggestions into the corners of the text. As well as an obvious expression of the loneliness, danger and emptiness of contemporary life, it evokes the humiliating impression, familiar to Lark, of being the butt of ridicule which is a thin mask for brutal aggression. Women, as the German sailors never fail to remind Lark, have no place within the male community of the freighter. Dancing to

keep upright in the water and cutting their feet on the sharp edges of
the city of living coral, is a physical metaphor of the dance they must
perform in the human city and the wounds they suffer. As several
people comment, Lark's sneakers could have been just as damaged
by walking the streets of New York, the Big J[oke] or Joke City. The
incident exposes the weakness of Lark's only male ally, the Australian steward, who detachedly watches their helplessness, and the
inhumanity of Tom who is also inclined to treat the affair as spectacle. ' "You lucky devil . . . That's called really getting your feet wet" '
(pp. 173–4). The phrase is one of a group which recurs and extends
itself; for Lark, getting her feet wet in the ways of the world will be
like the bad joke of dancing on coral. True to her policy of taking 'the
current when it serves', Donna Bird is also inclined to treat the
incident as spectacle, a practical joke consequent on crossing the
equator and a useful story for dinner parties, and for a time Lark
simulates a similar unconcern in order to keep in step with Tom. But
water, with its associations of danger, opportunity, adventure, voyaging and even piracy is an extensive figure. If Donna, Tom and
Manfred are natural vagabonds roaming the world, Lark is a land-
lover who is grief-stricken when she loses the bracelet her mother has
made her of polished pebbles from home, while in the latter part of
the novel ideas of settlement and travel take on far-reaching moral
connotations. And if America is the natural home of the pragmatic
relativism, which Lark rejects, water seems to be the natural habitat
of nascent Americans. In snow-bound Chicago, Lark is amazed to
discover that her motel window looks over the swimming pool where
dozens of 'Children of the American Revolution, all of them remarkably chubby', cavort in the water while 'the parents of the revolutionary children' chat contentedly on the green carpeting.

' "It's all friable, wherever you are" ', comments Tom early in
the story, implying his thesis that all realities and value systems are
incurably subjective. Donna Bird informs Lark that everything recurs: ' "Every tragedy, every humiliation, every image that imprints
itself on the mind, every incident, even every word that is spoken or
heard in a certain context will recur in a different form and be
relevant much later on? That's why there is no such thing as tragedy
or error? No such thing as meaning?" '. Tom always dismisses Lark's
question ' "Do you love me?" ', with the response that it is a question
without meaning. In a world where everything is relative, the anthro-
pologist, who categorizes differences, sees all value as culture-specific
and places people in their cultural context, is king. The world is his
oyster, as Tom frequently claims, or his text, as Donna Bird would
say. Manfred Bird's game of names is a farcical metaphor of the
arrogant imperialism of certain contemporary ideologies, which place
the author/individual's identity and his/her life-text in the hands of
the reader/interpreter:

Professor Bird cried out, 'Times's up. Let me have your names.' He seized Elizabeth's list, and Jean-Claude's. As he held his hand out for Lark's, she found herself holding onto it.

'I'll keep mine. I haven't finished.'

'But I will interpret your life. It's a game, for you. For me, it's my work. I need your list.' (p. 200)

He resembles the German captain, not only in the rapacious acquisition of native works of art, which the 'natives' themselves fail to appreciate, but in his lack of humanity: '"he talks like a Nazi"', remarks Lark. Like the king who calmly watched the drowning of a servant bringing him food on his island on the Rhône, he treats the natives as serviceable laboratory rats and his destructiveness is reflected in the deathly debris that clutters his apartment. Donna Bird follows in his example when she exchanges a useless plastic raincoat and black umbrella for valuable artefacts. The bad joke is ubiquitous.

Lark had always longed to travel to an island, but the island on which she finally settles, Manhattan in Joke City, is unlike her dream of knowing real life. Here she frequently has the impression of being at a work-in-progress play or a drive-in movie or of participating in a game whose rules she does not understand. Outside, life and death dramas play themselves out while she and Tom watch, helplessly in her case, passively and fearfully in Tom's; inside, even the furniture of their apartment has the function of props in a ritualized scene for the enlightenment of visitors. Donna Bird literally regards the world as her stage and, like the seasoned sea-going rat she is, 'has to keep moving, engaging in new enterprises. To her, that is freedom' (p. 248). Tom has developed a series of roles, which he plays with versatility, to keep the threat of emptiness at bay. In France, he tells the same stories in French as in America, with a few appropriate expletives thrown in; even the pauses are the same. His insane commitment to joke and spectacle comes to a head on their wedding day, when he stages a piece of theatre for *Strange but True*, in which Donna Bird appears to accuse the unsuspecting Lark of abandoning her on a Pacific island. At this point, Lark realizes that she has inadvertently been duped into playing out Donna's text of her, that she is part of 'a mighty, pedagogical practical joke' in which, as Donna predicted, she has consciously decided to break the law and destroy property; convinced earlier by Donna's suspicions that the freighter on which they were travelling might be carrying nuclear weapons, she had attempted to set it alight. In her wedding day 'trial', however, she almost defeats Donna with her spirited defence and, as events unfurl, she realizes that she too has written an alternative script for Manfred Bird, defining him as plunderer, when she instigated investigations of his cargo. For a very brief period, after their marriage, Lark breaks through Tom's joking, playing roles to the essential man: 'for the first time, Tom was quiet, not performing' (p. 249). But the habits of the past quickly reassert themselves and, offered the chance to play saviour to an old girl-friend, he immediately responds, leaving Lark with a quick 'stage hug'. After this Lark realizes that she has lost him, that he has gone from her, although his infidelity after barely three weeks of marriage is the culminating blow, marking the emotional end of their relationship.

A literal-minded individual, who invariably interprets figures of speech with ridiculous, literal effect, Lark is preoccupied with essentials, with empirical conclusions. Frequently analysing stories in terms of their essential and episodic elements, she describes the essentials of her own during the scene of the break up of her marriage: '"I left home, traversed half the world, and have now settled down, with my baby. That is essential, the rest is episode"' (p. 280). The exclusion of the story of her relationship with Tom is significant, for like Solomon Blank, he is entirely and wilfully episodic, having turned his life into a role in a farce. Even the break-up of his marriage is appropriately enough perceived as staged by a visiting journalist. Episodes can be lengthy, essentials swift: 'In the space of a baby's afternoon nap, Lark had separated from her husband and rejected a lover' (p. 289). Travelling, she has realized, can 'be a form of weakness . . . To put down some roots, and to make friends, that can be a brave thing to do, for some people"' (p. 280).

If romance is not a common topic in women's autobiographies, sex is almost ubiquitous. Growing up female, many writers imply, is to be educated in the self as gendered, to arouse expectations, assumptions and perhaps threats, and numerous writers record the shock of seeing themselves through male eyes as an accessible sexual commodity. Earlier writers may be more reticent but the experience is a consistent one, whether strikingly brought home by acts of sexual aggression as it is for the narrators of Nene Gare, Barbara Hanrahan, and Josie Arnold's autobiographies, or more insidiously via a local culture, as it is for the young Annabella Boswell and Laura Ramsbottom at school. Some more recent autobiographies, such as Barbara Pepworth's *Early Marks* and Helen Garner's *Monkey Grip*, intimate that while the relaxation of taboos in contemporary society has made for freer sexual experience and treatment of sexual matters, it has not diminished the vulnerability of women and may even have made their relationships with men more equivocal than ever. A comparison of two seemingly disparate autobiographies, Gabrielle Carey and Kathy Lette's *Puberty Blues*[18] and Eugénie McNeil and Eugénie Crawford's *Ladies Didn't*[19], suggests that the changes brought about by seventy years have been more rather than less imprisoning. *Ladies Didn't* is set mainly in Glebe of the early 1900s, *Puberty Blues* in Cronulla of the early 1970s. Both narratives are written with wit and relish the comic; both are collaborative texts, *Puberty Blues* a collaboration of friends and *Ladies Didn't* of mother and daughter; and both celebrate a close female friendship, surfie chicks in 1970, unmarried sisters of genteel, impoverished background in 1902. Both also have a semi-anthropological flavour, since Eugénie McNeil looks back on the quaint practices of Edwardian society from the enlightened feminist perspective of the 1980s and Lette and Carey have almost the same sense of distance in their reflections on the surfing subculture that they knew at thirteen.

Puberty Blues is a brilliant exposé of a well-defined subculture, that is as rigidly governed by conventions and formalities and as hierarchical as Victorian or Edwardian society. To join a surfie gang it is necessary to have the right attitudes, the 'in' knowledge, cigarettes, clothes, posture, skin colour, argot and hairstyle. To graduate in the same gang is even more exacting:

you had to be desired by one of the surfie boys, tell off a teacher, do the Scotch drawback and know all about sex. You had to be not too fat, but not too skinny. You had to be not too slack, but not too tight. Friendly but not forward. You had to wear just enough make-up but never overdo it. You had to be interested in surfing, but not interested enough to surf. The surfie girls had a special walk. It was a slow and casual meander. They slouched their shoulders, sunk into their hips and thrust their pelvises forward. (p. 7)

If surfie gangs differentiate themselves from each other by territory (on the beach, in the school bus and on the playground), distinctive argot and minor details of dress, they combine in a common contempt for 'Bankies', that is anyone who comes from Bankstown or is in any other way 'uncool'. At school, short uniforms and black underpants are in, long socks and singlets out, while surfie boys make a point of never appearing in full uniform. On the beach, surfie boys are careful never to be seen in their scungies and slink modestly out of their board shorts behind a towel; surfie girls are careful to be seen only sitting in their halter-neck bikinis, never walking, which would signal a moll-status. Surfing is a sacred religion with its secret rituals (banned to surfie chicks), funeral ceremonies and God (King Huey). The boys, who have to be good surfers, are faithful to the sea; the girls, who have to be good screws, are faithful to their surfies. On Saturday nights in 1970s Cronulla the panel vans on the Point do the same rhythmic dance as their occupants perform the necessary sexual exercises, whereas in 1900s Glebe sex is still disguised in euphemisms and voluminous clothing. Nevertheless, the girls have a similar innocence; sex for all of them is a mystery, shrouded in disinformation. Deb and Sue believe that pregnancy can only take place during menstruation: 'We never thought much about getting pregnant. We didn't know anything about it. We didn't do sex in Science till third form. It was too heavy to *really* think about' (pp. 70–1). Lydia and Eugénie are educated in the naïve half-knowledge of their French cousin, Lulu, and the peasant superstitions of their maid, Marie. While all four are totally absorbed in pursuit of the male, all are also indirectly informed that sex is a male pleasure and a female duty. There is a convention in the surfie subculture that the girls never discuss the sexual attributes of their 'lovers', while the males on the other hand talk of nothing but the girls' differences while waiting for a wave. Lydia and Eugénie are circumspect about their romantic relationships, while half-aware that the young men of their acquaintance have a free sexual life and are familiar with ladies of easy virtue. They learn to look up from under their lashes with interesting effects, and undergo tortures of bodily suffering to achieve the correct S bend; waving, crimping, teasing, curling the hair before adding the crowning touch of an enormous hat takes up large parts of the morning: 'An old photograph shows me very pleased with myself with what looks like a tame hedgehog clinging to my scalp' (p. 80). Sue and Deb coat themselves in oil and bake for hours trying to achieve the correct shade of suntan; 'Sylvania Heights is full of nineteen-year-old girls looking like shrivelled up ninety-year-olds' (p. 7). Ladies in 1900s Glebe are expected to be frivolous and silly, to be ignorant about business, decorously inactive and timid lovers. Surfie chicks are expected to converse in monosyllables, wait to be asked to go steady and avoid the water until the surf has subsided. If Edwardian men never smoke in front of the ladies, surfies are shocked if their chicks smoke anything but Marlboros and are unable to do the drawback. Surfie chicks wait avidly for the friendship ring, which is due after a certain decent period; Edwardian ladies anxiously look forward to the engagement ring and the newspaper announcement. Lydia and Eugénie are embarrassed when they misinterpret a French custom whereby 'ladies' could gain free entry to the music hall:

Mother motioned away a waiter, who arrived with a bottle of champagne, and then two gentlemen, who seemed to think they could sit at our table. The pretty ladies around us started giggling and when Mother waved away another gentleman, who was a complete stranger, they laughed outright. In such a friendly atmosphere, we laughed too, though we didn't quite know why. However, we decided to get our coats and go home early. (pp. 46–7)

In the surfie culture the distinctions are even more fine:

You had to 'go out' with a guy for at least two weeks before you'd let him screw you. You had to time it perfectly. If you waited too long you were a tight-arsed prickteaser. If you let him too early, you were a slack-arsed moll. So, after a few weeks, he'd ask you for a root, and if you wanted to keep him, you'd do it. (p. 24)

The difference in physical proximity, if not intimacy, between the two cultures is immense, even so females in both are not expected to have natural functions. If Lydia and Eugénie suffer acute discomfort because they are not supposed to have bladders, so do Sue and Deb. The sufferings of the latter are compounded by the taboo on eating: 'We were . . . busting to go to the dunny, but that was too rude for girls. Our stomachs rumbled and our bladders burst. It was a great day at the beach' (p. 2). Lydia and Eugénie have to submit to tightlacing of their overweight figures, but at least Edwardian genetlemen liked a full 'armful'. Male behaviour in both cultures is equivocal. In the surfie gang, there is a taboo on affection and even articulate communication: 'The only way you knew you were some-one's girlfriend was because he'd root you every week-end' (p. 81). A girl knows she is dropped when the weekly phone call to arrange the weekend's predictable events suddenly ceases. Lydia and Eugénie are discarded by two swains but receive a bouquet of flowers, signifying according to their book *The Language of Flowers*, eternal devotion, folly and indifference. A week later Lydia receives another bouquet from a new admirer: 'It contained forget-me-not, True Love, and mignonette, Your Qualities Surpass your Charms. Really, growing up was a very complicated business and relations with the other sex even more so' (p. 61).

Underlying the wit and humour of both books is a serious criticism of the way of life and a personal sense of loss. *Ladies Didn't* records the wastage of the girls' natural talent, their lack of opportunity, the loss of the family home and the foundering of the Delarue business due to the cultivation of female silliness. In this book the Delarue girls are initiated into the absurd restrictions of gender, after the remarkably free female world of their childhood, celebrated in *A Bunyip Close Behind Me*. The conclusion of *Ladies Didn't* empha-sizes the point as Eugénie totters to the front door to meet her destiny, her future husband, literally fettered by the new hobble skirt. *Puberty Blues* ends on a personal note of liberation as Sue and Deb throw off the restrictions of the surfie gang, but the book is permeated by an even more acute sense of loss, best summarized in the list of deaths, addictions, breakdowns, disappearances, gaol sentences, unwanted births and adoptions which is its conclusion.

Sex in *Puberty Blues* is a barrier to intimacy, a public sign of proving and conforming, which has nothing to do with personal feeling. Arbitrarily selected by the appropriately named Bruce Board, Deb is the brand new chick he needs to complement his car and his brand new board. Talking is not part of the contract, as the ludicrous reported telephone 'conversations' between the girls and their paramours illustrate. For the male, sex is a function like eating carried out with military precision and a minimum of emotional commitment. For the thirteen-year-old Deborah, one year out of primary school and not yet menstruating, sex is a bewildering, necessary ordeal: 'I let go and clutched the bedspread, digging in my fingernails. I waited in agony to pass out' (p. 41). At the drive-in Sue strains to get a glimpse of the movie over her boyfriend's pumping shoulder, and Kim and Dave, who are different in that they like each other, force themselves to graduate from the despised state of virginity. Meanwhile, the girls try desperately to make contact with their boyfriends, performing a dance to bring on the rain which will make the beach impossible or mothering them when a member's 'olds' go away for the weekend, leaving their house available. For a brief while Deb has a loving relationship, although ironically it is misinterpreted by teachers and parents and comes to an end when the boy becomes a heroin addict. For the most part, however, love is unattainable: 'All our attempts at romance failed miserably and the only time we ever got close to our boyfriends was when they were on top of us panting. It was hopeless from the beginning' (p. 72). If being in the gang is frustrating, being outside is to know only two alternatives, the familiar God's police/whore choice. As in Edwardian Glebe, the double standard operates and the boys can 'screw as many molls' as they like during the week, while the girls have to learn 'to fuck just enough not to be called slack or tight' (p. 74). Girls who are overweight, pimply, migrant or unattractive are offered the choice of being a prude or a moll. The former is even more boring than being a surfie chick, the latter offers the distinction of notoriety at a terrible price. Dirt, ignominy and even death are the lot of the moll, as the following death-laden passage emphasizes:

There were a lot of molls where we grew up. They grovelled around with their pants off under the bowling alley—in the dark and dirt and spider-webs; in the cold, damp caves at Cronulla Beach; in the prickly lantana bushes down the paddock and on the grotty banks of the Georges River behind the Ace-of-Spades Hotel. (p. 74)

The misogyny that underlies the surfies' code is appallingly illustrated in the graphic scenes of exploitation of reputed molls, followed by physical vilification, spitting on one girl at the end of a 'gang-bang' or prodding another with their feet as she lies grovelling with pain on the footpath.

Apathy, mindless conformity, and boredom characterize life in the surfie gang, alleviated only by spurts of rivalry, point-scoring and the fanning of easy dislike for those outside the group. Time hangs heavy on Saturday nights even if in the panel van there is an illusion of doing something. The weekend rituals have a repetitive emptiness that makes alcohol, marijuana and heroin natural addictions for numerous members of the group. The acquisition of a car does little to mend the futility of existence: 'It was the same old story of getting all dressed up and having nowhere to go. We were one step further than a year ago, because now we had nowhere to go in a car' (p. 106). Meanwhile, the world of home and school remains farcically oblivious of the children's activities and wholly irrelevant to their real experience. More important tests than school tests have to be passed, just as there is another uniform to be worn and other rules to be observed. The purple curtains that Bruce's mother made for his panel van frequently and incongruously part on lurid physical scenes or conceal the details which groans and screams imply, while Deborah's bikini top, 'crocheted-by-Auntie-Janet', underlines the pathos of this loveless adult childhood. All the same, adult society displays the same apathy, conformity and materialism as surfie society, for the narrators build up an acute Humphries-like satire of suburban life. Bruce's visit to the Vickerys, for instance, is a marvellous piece of comedy, juxtaposing the 'respectability' of the new shag-pile carpet and the Keith Lord lounge suite with Bruce's rough-hewn builder's-labourer's speech, sandy thongs and luridly decorated panel van. Similarly, the constant use of brand-names (Jupiter Bar, Chiko Roll, Big Ben Meat Pie, Sara Lee Apricot Danish), and of place names (Arizona Milk Bar, Roberto's Pizza Hut) evokes the larger plastic, Coca-Cola culture which deadens any creativity the children might display. Indeed, Carey and Lette use names and lists as a means of satire in a way that is reminiscent of *The Great Gatsby*: if personal names evoke a period (Cheryl Nolan, Danny Dixon, Darren Peters, Tracey Little, Wayne Wright), the names of television shows and even animals reinforce the impression that a general cultural aridity is being criticized. In this satiric atmosphere even factual names (Miranda, Sylvania Waters, Sylvan Headlands) become loaded terms:

We dropped our towels and collapsed. There was Strack, the Brown-Eye chucker. Gull, short for Seagull. He could stay in the water longest. Wayne Wright, Cheryl's boyfriend. Tall, spunky, top-surfer, Dave Deakin. Glen Jackson, the doll, Johnno, Hen, a few others and Danny and Bruce, our boyfriends.
Soon the other girls arrived, galloping up the beach on their frothing horses. There was Kim on Cochise, Tracey on Rebel, Vicki on Prince, Cheryl on Randy and Kerrie on Candy. (p. 29)

It is the comic world of Barry Humphries, made sad in that it is a lived reality, with destructive consequences. At the close Sue and Deb walk off into a freer future, having deliberately broken the surfie code by surfing themselves; as the Epilogue discloses, many of their friends are not so lucky. *Laides Didn't* exposes the absurdities of a convention-bound society, dedicated to the principle that women are helpless creatures, but at least it is a society that knows what cherishing means. Indeed at one point, Eugénie McNeil comments on the difference in values, almost as if she is thinking of *Puberty Blues*, comparing the 'astonishing' willingness of the contemporary teenager to 'shack up' in a tenuous relationship and to regard viriginity as an 'abnormal condition about which she should be consulting her psychiatrist' with the protected lives of middle-class Edwardian girls. Whateverever else changes, she concludes, the vulnerability of women is a permanent fact of life.

Although women's friendship figures large in the autobiographies studied here, homosexual love is a thin stream as yet. Henry Handel Richardson, with her usual boldness, explores the subject in some of her short stories and *The Getting of Wisdom* but a similar boldness did not appear until 1975, when 'Elizabeth Riley's' *All That False Instruction*, set mainly in the 1960s, was published. Beverley Farmer's novel, *Alone* (1980) deals with the grief caused by the loss of a lesbian relationship and a recent novel, *What Are Ya?* (1987), touches on the topic, but is too split between two different protagonists to be consistently or identifiably autobiographical. Farmer's novel is virtually a prose poem, a delicate, poignant exploration of the internal world of intense, individual emotion, specifically the emotion of loss, which is central to all Farmer's fiction. Death and the incurable loneliness of the spirit are as much the subject of *Alone* as the narrator's love for Catherine, for the novel focuses on the terminal point in the narrator's story, her last day on earth, and weaves this particular loss into a general vision of life as dispossession and bereavement. 'Elizabeth Riley's' novel, on the other hand, is a study of the difficult *rite de passage* of a lesbian, a journey which has many diversions and an uncertain conclusion. It is both fascinating and disappointing, marked by some fine passages and some slack writing, and by some half-insights which fail to develop and patterns which fail to cohere. Much of this would accord perfectly with the narrator's experience of lesbian love as threatened and hazardous, if the distance between author and narrator were firmly controlled, but sections of the novel are skewed by an identification which is too immediate and self-pitying to allow for judgement. The latter half of the novel, however, is a brilliant serio-comic dramatization of the narrator's attempt to inhabit the male world, in which the poignancy of her situation is enhanced, rather than diminished by her context. In this section Maureen, or Craig as she often refers to herself, is the true versatile *pícaro*, which the novel's chapter titles have intimated from the first ('Maureen at bay', 'Maureen against the wall', 'Cripple Craig', 'In which Maureen begins to see'); at the beginning, however, she is the sentimentally interpreted child, victim of a vindictive mother and an inadequate father. It is as if the author literally but unconsciously relives the progress from experiencing the self as simply an isolated site of suffering to experiencing the self in a longer view, related to a social and historical context and involved in sophisticated role-playing. In the latter part of the novel, the self is presented as a series of Craigs, which partly obscure, partly defend the authentic 'I' ('Free-Ranging Craig, Liberated Craig, or, beat this, Detached Craig'), whereas in the first the author uncritically iden- tifies with a resentful, passively reactive, bewildered 'I'. Parents, teachers, grandmother and brother are realized in an elementary way, as forces impinging comfortably or uncomfortably on the child- self, while the mother, in particular, is realized as mystifyingly unsympathetic. Later, the narrator reflects on the antagonism be- tween herself and her mother, valuing its formative astringency, but none of this retrospective assessment feeds into the first few chapters.

The lesbian novel is inevitably one of coming out, recognizing the feeling of homosexual love, acting on it and publicly affirming the identity. But as Karla Jay puts it, 'We spend our lives coming out, and the reality is that none of us is completely "out" or "in"'.[20] *All That False Instruction* is for the most part a sensitive recording of the liberating experience of homosexual love and of the series of blocks which inhibit the process of coming out. If Maureen delightedly recognizes her sexual identity during the relationship with her second lover, she is not allowed to retain that liberating sense of self for her lover is unable to withstand the disapproval of family and peers and complies with their college's decision to outlaw Maureen as the older, evil seducer. 'Riley's' interpretation of the petty-minded, claustro- phobic world of the women's college is particularly acute, surpassed only by her interpretation of the male world of beer, roots and cars. It is the familiar environment of the drama of Williamson, Buzo and Hibberd, but 'Riley' uncovers the sadness and inbuilt loneliness that the tradition of male proving and inarticulacy promote. Paradox- ically, it offers a sort of dignity and integrity that the women's strait-laced community of the college denies, even though its prom- ises of empathy are strictly limited. Loneliness and loss may be the lot of the lesbian, given the homophobic reactions of conventional society, but the committed heterosexual may be even more lonely; for the inarticulate, love-hungry Max the only supports are beer and the ritualized conventions of male camaraderie. Maureen has at least the hope that she will rediscover the wholly liberating sense of con- nection that she briefly achieved with Libby and Cleo. However successfully she fills the virile male persona, Maureen knows that she is the paradigmatic woman, 'Self-effacing and loyal . . . always caught and strangled by considerations for the interminable others' (p. 196). Choosing exile rather than the more violent solution of death, which is the frequent ending of the lesbian novel, Maureen finds strength in her last experience of love with Cleo: 'Our foreheads rest together, our minds flow into one another. There is no gap. Tonight perhaps no gap at all' (p. 246). Like the female quester for heterosexual love, the lesbian is preoccupied with connection rather than possession and conquest and perhaps one of the greatest attractions of the lesbian relationship is that as a revolutionary, outlawed mode of loving it promises to ignore the powerful ideologies which constrain the conventional alternative.

11

National and Personal Myths

The few general studies of Australian autobiography so far have all been concerned with the genre's cultural implications. John and Dorothy Colmer, for instance, see the quest for personal and national identity as interdependent and anticipate that a study of Australian literary autobiography will 'create an ineradicable scepticism towards the official myths offered us by our literary critics and social historians'.[1] If we define national myth as the symbolic embodiment of a general idea often buried too deep to be neatly apprehended by the analytical mind, but manifesting its continuing relevance by a tenacious life in the national consciousness, then it is clear that Australia's most powerful myth is the myth of the bush. Usually associated with the 1890s, the myth has been most succinctly expressed by Russel Ward in *The Australian Legend* (1958). Although Ward's account of the genesis and influence of the legend has often been criticized, his summation of its basic ingredients in the popular mind is generally conceded. Male camaraderie, taciturnity, irreverence for social pretension and authority, physical mobility, stoicism in the face of hardship, a talent for rough and ready improvisation and a valuing of all that is non-urban are the recurring shibboleths. It is, as Dorothy Jones has remarked, a myth which has 'accorded women little place, generally dismissing them with indifference or hostility'.[2]

Given the intimate connections between autobiography, personal identity and cultural myth, the question of women's response as autobiographers to a perception of Australia that either excludes them or shifts them to the margins, is a fascinating one. Have they evaded the myth and, if so, in what ways? Have they treated it with scepticism? Have they attempted to re-articulate the legend in female terms?

In fact, surprisingly few women autobiographers have attempted to embrace the national myth. As we have seen, women are less concerned with large-scale national experience than men and even in autobiographies which include adult life it is the personality of the small, intimately-known place of childhood which fascinates the female writer; in Barbara Corbett's case it is a stretch of river, in Vera Adams's a Victorian village, in Ivy Arney's a suburb of Melbourne. In the group of narratives which are the subject of this book and which are constrained by time and the narrow boundaries of a child's experience, the place which is celebrated is likely to have idiosyncratic myths, with may be strikingly at variance with the larger legend. Thus the 1890s Bankstown of the Delarue girls has a cultural variety that is totally ignorant of the concurrent *Bulletin* ethos and the 1930s Carlton of Amirah Inglis's childhood is coloured by European myths, a potent mixture of Polish nationalism, Judaism and Communism.

Some women writers have been drawn to the bush myth, however, and have even attempted to appropriate it, running a special sort of risk in the process. Myths, of course, are as complex as they are powerful. As Richard Coe comments, they 'incarnate anxieties, or drives, or urges too deeply-buried to be clearly and rationally apprehended by the individual'.[3] Superficially, in the implicit love of the land and the emphasis on relatedness, the yearnings underlying Australia's bush legend gesture towards general human values. It is only a gesture, however, for the drives are also profoundly and exclusively male. Indeed the true bushman, like Miles Franklin's Harold Beecham, who has not the least trace of 'effeminacy', knows himself to be male and therefore Australian, because he has attitudes and qualities that are not-female. Mary Gilmore solves the problem of gender implicit in the celebration of the legend by adopting the role of tribal elder, although the device imposes a self-deceiving rhetoric. Dorothy Cottrell's *The Singing Gold*[4], attempts to implicate the reader in a mood of cosy nostalgia for the outback heroes of North Queensland. A curious book, which received an enthusiastic response when it was first published, it demonstrates the extraordinary contortions which some women writers underwent to accommodate the noble Bushman. Cottrell could cast the figure as elder brother or, preferably, as son, but was inevitably confronted by his limitations in the role of father or husband. For the present day reader, Cottrell's men emerge as *Boys Own* heroes, emotionally retarded children, who must be cherished for their 'dear' but impractical dreams.

Other more complex writers have also indirectly intimated the negative aspects of the legend. As 'outsiders' in the popular culture, women are powerful transmitters of a covert culture, which is inherently if unconsciously sceptical of the overt ethos. The covert culture I am referring to is similar to the common female experience described by Dorothy Dinnerstein and Simone de Beauvoir. In *The*

Mermaid and the Minotaur, for instance, Dinnerstein comments that 'woman, by virtue of her non-participant's perspective on world-making activity, has more leeway than man to see what is arbitrary and false in it'.[5] Dorothy Hewett sees the woman writer's role as 'doubly subversive' of the male culture: 'She *thinks* subversively by nature and experience, and she writes from that other country of spirit and physicality, which still remains ... largely uncharted'.[6] If some women writers openly embrace the covert culture, others indirectly intimate its presence even while apparently celebrating male, public myths. Several female autobiographies, which outwardly endorse the Australian legend, reflect this sort of ambivalence. Ostensibly projecting the overt myth, they unconsciously undermine or subvert it. I have space here to discuss only three writers, but the autobiographical novels of Dorothy Cottrell and Eve Langley are in the same category and traces of the same pattern can be found in other texts. Some, such as Jean Bedford's *Country Girl Again*, openly challenge the myth in the tradition of Barbara Baynton.

The most celebrated response to the bush myth of the 1890s is, of course, Miles Franklin's *My Brilliant Career*. Published in 1901 with the support of Henry Lawson, the book was initially welcomed by the *Bulletin* school for its nationalism; in the words of A. G. Stephens, 'the author has the Australian mind, she speaks Australian language, utters Australian thoughts, and looks at things from an Australian point of view absolutely ... her love of Australia is positive rapture'.[7] Both Lawson and Stephens seem to have remained blind to the book's feminist content. To readers of the 1970s, however, the feminism was inescapable. Republished by Virago Press in 1980, the novel was hailed as an *avant garde* protest against the patriarchal system of the 1890s, while its heroine was seen as mouthing 'the fears, conflicts and torments of every girl, with an understanding usually associated with writers of the 1960s and 1970s'.[8] Other commentators have been less willing to include Franklin in feminist hagiography, troubled by her strident adherence to a naïve version of the 1890s myth of Australia, and her inability to articulate fully her perceptions of the myth's exclusion of women.[9] John Docker sees her dilemma as evidence of the ideology's contemporary power:

It shows the strength of the desire for Australia to be a unified community that female intellectuals like Franklin accept a tradition which either excludes them, as in the case of 'mateship', or limits them by projecting predefined sexual roles.[10]

As I have suggested in Chapter 5, *Childhood at Brindabella* indicates that there are other, more compelling personal reasons for Franklin's notorious ambivalence, although the clues are already present in *My Brilliant Career*. In the first autobiography as in the last, Franklin is involved in an effort to uncover an essential inner truth and unity of being, to give the meaning of her own mythic tale. For the teller, it is as baffling and fascinating a tale at seventeen as at seventy, and possesses the same basic configurations. Perfect happiness is followed by perfect misery, a heaven of innocence, power and plenty is succeeded by a sudden, disabling descent to poverty and self-division. *My Brilliant Career* is the author's first version of her Edenic myth and if *Childhood at Brindabella* testifies to the lifelong tenacity of the early memory of exclusion, *My Brilliant Career* expresses its initial mordancy. Even more than *The Getting of Wisdom*, *My Brilliant Career* sets the seal on an eventful emotional history; as Verna Coleman puts it, 'It was as though all [Franklin's] life was a charade after the idyll of childhood and the anguish of adolescence'.[11]

In many ways, Franklin's personal myth coincides with the national one. Both have their home in the bush and both posit unspoiled innocence, natural confidence, spontaneity, equality, youth, solidarity, freedom and physical activity. Mateship, the keystone of the public myth, where it implies male camaraderie, also fits snugly into Franklin's personal metaphor, expressing the uncomplicated sexless bonding which her narrators seem to prefer to mature sexual relationships. If the national myth values qualities that are often implicitly childlike, the personal myth is literally one of childhood. Both, of course, are threatened, whether it is by the disjunctions of growing up, or the contradictions of actuality. Both also belong in the past, in Franklin's case in the personal past, and in the national case in a more uncertain, visionary past. As Leon Cantrell comments, literary images of bush life as Arcadian are frequently placed in the past; even in the 1890s the idyllic Australia was perceived as 'belonging to a bygone age, now lost'.[12] In Franklin's case, it has often been remarked that her imagination is fixed in the period of her own youth and even her parents' and grandparents' youth, returning to this era for the 'Brent of Bin Bin' novels and *All That Swagger*, for as Havelock Ellis noted, she is 'ardently devoted to Australia, but to a remote, ideal Australia'.[13] Paradoxically, both myths implicitly sanction defeat; like Tennant, Franklin endorses the national myth's dominant trope of failure, which several cultural historians have analysed. In the words of Graeme Turner, for instance, in the pioneering myth of the land, 'the difficulty of survival becomes the justification for doing no more than that . . . the environment is tough but survivable if one accepts its basic dominion over the self'.[14] Thus the dual national tradition, implying on one hand innocence, freedom, space and energy, and on the other, solidarity and stoicism in the face of inevitable defeat, meshed with Franklin's personal myth, a coincidence which had stagnating consequences for her fiction, her political outlook and possibly her life.[15] Described by Marjorie Barnard as 'perpetually homesick'[16], she was locked in the static situation of endorsing the national dream, which implicitly endorsed the self's exclusion. If the Legend reinforced the first personal Fall, Franklin was unable or unwilling to accede to the fact, becoming more stridently chauvinist the older she grew.

Even more than in *Childhood at Brindabella*, an unremitting polarizing impulse is visible in *My Brilliant Career*, while both texts are tethered to a frustrated acceptance of defeat. From the first, there is a distance between the bravura of the posturing, acting heroine and the fatalism of her author/observer. The Sybylla of *My Brilliant Career* is more of an actress than most autobiographical narrators; if acting is one of her most conscious party skills, she also exercises her talents in everyday situations, diverting herself, her observers and the implied older narrator. Nevertheless, however dramatic or even melodramatic the self-cast roles, histrionics can only provide a temporary respite to the dull groundnote of monotony which appears to be the fixed autobiographical 'reality' ('how my spirit frets and champs its unbreakable fetters—all in vain!' p. ix).[17] As Sybylla learns and as the older narrator knows from the beginning, the only escape from Possum Gully is by means of fantasy ('I was ... forced for ever to live in a desert, ever wildly longing for water, but never reaching it outside of dreams' p. 191). Eden may be repossessed by the mind, but the correlative Fall is the keener experience. Thus fantastic release succeeded by descent to impoverished reality is the characteristic emotional pattern and as in *Childhood at Brindabella* the repetitive selection of inimical contraries and arbitrary reversals suggests that this is a landscape of the mind which pretends to a documentary 'reality' only at the surface level.

Thus, it is as if there is only one sort of movement possible in the emotional climate of *My Brilliant Career*, an oscillation between opposing poles of pleasure and pain. Bruggabrong, the home of activity, significance, community, prosperity, confidence and interest, is replaced by Possum Gully, the place of restraint, poverty, isolation, insignificance, tedium and self-distrust. A landscape of rugged peaks, substantial gums and clear, running streams is succeeded by a confined, semi-rural slum, depressingly flat and treeless and watered only by a 'few round, deep, weedy waterholes'. Time runs cheerfully and benignly at Bruggabrong; at Possum Gully it stagnates and erodes, changing the once beautiful, cultured mother to care-worn shrew and the jovial, supportive father to drunken wastrel. At Bruggabrong there is a congenial, male cross-section of society, 'Doctors, lawyers, squatters, commercial travellers, bankers, journalists, tourists ...' (p. 2); Possum Gully offers only the small change of 'common bushmen farmers and their equally uninteresting wives'. With her occasional gift for crudity, Sybylla describes the change as one from 'swelldom' to 'peasantdom'. For Sybylla herself the freedom and significance of a male world give way to the petty restraints and imposed reductions of a female one. At Possum Gully she confronts first her secondary status as female and then her lowly ranking (on the grounds of ugliness and cleverness) even within that inferior category. Personal integration and solidarity are replaced by a conviction of anomaly and alienation. The frequent refrain that she is 'woefully out of [her] sphere' expresses not just her sense of gender reduction, but her awareness of exile from home, position, rightful identity and even religion. 'Religionless' from the age of ten, when her father abdicated his position as 'hero, confidant, encyclopaedia, mate, and ... religion' (p. 4), Sybylla grows to see God as either absent or malevolent (pp. 27, 37).

This polarizing of experience continues throughout the novel while the impression of a wildly swinging pendulum is reflected in the destinies of others besides Sybylla. Fortunes are made and lost with a rapidity which few find surprising. Women suffer in the wake of their men; Aunt Helen is abandoned by her husband and left as 'neither wife, widow nor maid' and the life of Sybylla's mother is a constant warning to the narrator of the perversity of fate. Meanwhile, experiences of pleasure are perpetually framed, if not shadowed, by reminders of fortune's fickleness[18], just as the heaviest blows fall at moments of greatest happiness.[19] Even chapter titles record the same, perversely inane fluctuations; of a piece with the novel's correct title, *My Brilliant? Career*, they summarize the inevitable reversals of sarcastic fate. And, of course, the novel's anti-form, its pretensions to be a burlesque of conventional autobiography, a parody of popular romance and even a sarcastic comment on the idea of story, are all part of the same emotional dialectic. The principle of oscillation affects every aspect of narrative structure, syntax, diction, prose rhythms and imagery[20], while short chapters, rapid succession of incidents, pithy verbal confrontations, ironic apostrophes and even the stylistic crudities combine to evoke a context of mercurial change and inevitable reduction.

The novel's use of imagery is interesting. Although the narrator uses some well-chosen images, the surface language is not strikingly figurative. A deeper figurative pattern can be detected, however, in terms of landscape or location. In each of Sybylla's landscapes, for instance, climate, scenery, animals, people, incidents and even furnishings present themselves as diametric opposites. The 'pair of fat horses in splendid harness' which draw Sybylla to Caddagat is compared with 'our poor skinny old horse at home, crawling along in much-broken harness, clumsily and much mended with string and bits of hide' (p. 40); the refined Aunt Helen contrasts with the blowsy, ignorant Mrs M'Swat; the distinguished Harold Beecham with the care-worn farmers of the Gully; the well-tuned piano and large library of Caddagat with the M'Swats' 'tin dish' and their single book (Mr M'Swat's illiterate diary).

So unremitting is the pressure of this polarizing impulse that it is impossible not to see the general pattern as having the combined coherence of psychic metaphor. How often, for example, is the outer scene a correlation or even an outward manifestation of the inner mood. At Bruggabrong the happy infant records its first memory in an idyllic landscape that is clearly bi-sexual:

I was barely three. I can remember the majestic gum-trees surrounding us, the sun glinting on their straight white trunks and falling on the gurgling fern-banked stream, which disappeared beneath a steep scrubby hill on our left. (p. 1)

At Possum Gully, the external scene often acts as an expressive metaphor of the self's reduction: 'Crooked stunted gums and stringy-barks, with a thick underscrub of wild cherry, hop, and hybrid wattle, clothed the spurs which ran up from the back of the detached kitchen' (p. 6). In fact, landscape and mind are so deeply and extensively interpenetrated that it is hard to find a scene without a psychic connotation. Landscape is both personal and other, figuring variously as an embodiment of all that baffles, tantalizes, thwarts, extends, mocks or sustains the self. Furthermore, as metaphor for Australia, it expresses the remote yet challenging spirit of the land itself, a powerful presence which both fascinates and disables the narrator.[21]

Sybylla, the reflecting and suffering centre of all this antinomic pattern, is more than emotionally equal to its vicissitudes. Regarding her alternations of mood as proof of her artistic sensibility, she takes pride in the description of herself as 'very variable—one moment all joy and the next the reverse'. She veers wildly from self-love to self-disgust, elation to despair, confidence to self-distrust, idealism to cynicism, naïvety to worldliness, submission to revolt, interest to boredom. Convinced at one moment that she is completely 'mistress' of her life ('It was like an orange—I merely had to squeeze it and it gave forth sweets plenteously' p. 137), at another she is dizzied by the gulf between aspiration and opportunity ('I was too much for myself' p. 36), and at another she longs for extinction or even idiocy (p. 27). There is a certain amount of self-indulgence in all this. Inveterately opposed to the humdrum, Sybylla defeats the threat of boredom by watching herself in the part of mercurial temperament, confounding the 'unmanly' Frank Hawdon or shocking the local wowsers with her daring appropriations of male roles. Several scenes are really variations of one set piece—Sybylla, confronted with male observer (Everard Grey, Frank Hawdon, Harold Beecham), performs an elaborate dance of attraction and rejection, tantalizing her audience but keeping him at bay by verbal wit and physical speed. In the most curious scene of all (the scene of Beecham's proposal) this quality of self-observation is very marked. Running through a gamut of emotions in an hour (she times the scene and even records an interval), Sybylla reaches a dramatic climax when she unexpectedly strikes her lover a blow with a riding whip. Her immediate descent to self-humiliation is not untouched with picturesqueness:

The enormity of what I had done paralysed me. The whip fell from my fingers and I dropped on to a low lounge behind me, and placing my elbows on my knees crouchingly buried my face in my hands; my hair tumbled softly over my shoulders and reached the floor, as though to sympathetically curtain my humiliation. (p. 125)

In nearly all these scenes the male observer's attention is at least temporarily caught. Perplexed and intrigued by the heroine, he momentarily abandons his larger purposes to watch her performance. He may attempt, vainly, to grasp her quicksilver being. In three cases he even contemplates annexing her as wife, but Sybylla's fierce selfhood refuses to accept such a reduction. Real equality is not possible, but she wins a temporary equality with these spirited displays. Hence her strange gratification at discovering that she too is bruised following another violent interchange with Beecham; bruises are proof of her impact.

Self-indulgence is undoubtedly an element in Sybylla's role-playing, but self-discovery plays a more important part. Baffled by the discrepancy between her promise and her reality, she is close to the Dickens of *David Copperfield* in her sense of outrage at the injustice of her sudden loss of caste; she has the same dismayed 'wonder' that a 'special' spirit should be 'ignored'. Role-playing gives her the frail illusion of printing herself on a world that allows her no role. But, like the reflected mirror image that almost attests to her beauty, happiness and youth ('I felt pleased with myself, and *imagined* as I *peeped* in the looking-glass, that I was not *half* bad-looking after all' p. 61)[22], her more positive versions of the self are always close to shattering, whether by outer voices or by the pre-emptive inner voice. She oscillates between extremes of hope and hopelessness, but the latter appears to be close to the natural resting place of her emotional pendulum, as Frank Everard recognizes.[23]

Meanwhile, the impression that Sybylla's reverses are irreversible is increased by the reflections of the implied older consciousness. The older narrator speaks from a more world-weary perspective, some-times commenting on Sybylla's unrealistic or ill-judged activities, sometimes judging the events and emotions from a position of greater wisdom. Inexperience, 'conceited, blind Inexperience', fails to show the younger protagonist the 'impassable pit' between herself and her aspirations (p. 17). Perceived as young and heedless ('a chit in the first flush of her teens' p. 88), she is not equipped with the older narrator's awareness of widespread hardship and poverty (p. 99), nor with her appreciation of the foolhardiness of 'asking the why and wherefore of things' (p. 127). She reasons with the 'one-sided reasoning' of fifteen (p. 21) and has a 'childish intelligence' (p. 29); and her lack of self-reliance and early regression to cynicism are matters for concern 'I was as rank a cynic and infidel as could be found in three days' march' (p. 37). Sybylla may veer between belief and unbelief in love (p. 73), but the hopes of the older self have long since jaundiced, killed like 'the dairyman's surplus calves'. The older consciousness watches the comedy of the unladylike Sybylla's confrontations and enjoys the fun of her sharp-eyed observations and youthful self-deceptions, but there is a sense in which this narrator never leaves Possum Gully.[24] As the narrative proceeds and as Sybylla comes full circle to the Gully, the two voices coincide in a hopeless present. At the end of the novel, Sybylla describes herself as struggling to do her duty, although doomed to a 'peasant existence' and surrounded by 'peasant ignorance':

A note from the other world will strike upon the chord of my being, and the spirit which has been dozing within me awakens and fiercely beats at its bars, demanding some nobler thought, some higher aspiration, some wider action, a more saturnalian pleasure, something more than the peasant life can ever yield. Then I hold my spirit tight till wild passionate longing sinks down, down to sickening dumb despair, and had I the privilege extended to Job of old—to curse God and die—I would leap at it eagerly. (p. 205)

My Brilliant Career should be read with its partner, *My Career Goes Bung*, written in 1902 but not published until 1946.[25] The heroine of *My Career Goes Bung*, also called Sybylla and also living at Possum Gully, has some emotional affinity with the implied older narrator of *My Brilliant Career*. Shrewder and more level-headed than the first Sybylla, this second selected 'I' has a wry sense of humour and a taste for situational comedy that is close to Steele Rudd's and that frequently undercuts the serious pretensions of events and people. Much of the emotional urgency of the earlier novel has dissipated and this Sybylla writes from an ironic, historical perspective that soft-pedals the dramatic content of her experience. In this book there is a sense that battles have been fought and lost and all that remains is to re-explore the experience of writing her auto-biography and record the impact of the published book on self and community.

The narrator of the second book greatly expands the earlier self's reflections on the nature of autobiography. *My Brilliant Career*, of course, opens with an unequivocal challenge to the author's 'dear Fellow Australians': Just a few lines to tell you that this story is all about myself—for no other purpose do I write it'. The book, she avers, is not a romance, nor a novel, but 'simply a yarn':

a *real* yarn. Oh! as real, as really real—provided life itself is anything beyond a heartless little chimera—it is as real in its weariness and bitter heartache as the tall gum trees, among which I first saw the light, are real in their stateliness and substantiality. (p. ix)

Even at this early stage the emotional symbiosis of two 'realities', the positive Australian landscape of the early self and the despairing perspective of the later self, is apparent. An inveterate binary thinker, Franklin usually defines negatives in terms of failed or lost positives.

The Sybylla of *My Career Goes Bung* makes it clear that the first book is concerned with an essential inner truth, a deeper reality than history. If the intended audience of *My Brilliant Career* is often questionable, the second narrative reveals that the book was largely a dialogue with self, 'a secret delight', a 'twin soul', a 'confidant', demanding solitude and creating a bewitched state of mind (p. 38). Sybylla also waxes lyrical about the therapeutic, consoling effect of autobiography, comparing it to the shedding of a snakeskin; once the magical experience of writing the book is over, she returns to the old life with the former distaste. The implied author of *My Brilliant Career*, engrossed in the white-hot furnace of her heroine's self-discovery, has little time to reflect on the autobiographic experience itself. She may throw off a defiant aside to the reader, or point out the 'difference' between this down-to-earth narrative and popular romance, or send up Sybylla's histrionics. But the strangeness of this self-reflexive activity is largely implicit. It is quite a different matter for the second Sybylla, who identifies herself as the author of *My Brilliant Career*. Recognizing the bond between egotism and creativity, she is alive to the fictional quality of the self's reality, to its flickering, unstable truth, and she endlessly reflects on the strange act of writing the self. This Sybylla is much more of an auto-autobiographer, telling the story of herself telling the story of herself. She is also fairly frank about the distance, even the ironic distance, between author and narrator. The heroine of *My Brilliant Career* is 'the girl of her admiration', capable of boldness that the older, more circumspect Sybylla lacks. She describes herself at one point as standing apart from her subject 'impersonally . . . aloof like a scientist in his laboratory' (p. 145) and as 'fashioning [her] characters and acting their parts' (p. 42). And within *My Brilliant Career* itself, there are plenty of indications that the implied author knows more about Sybylla and her world than Sybylla herself and even enjoys ironically exploiting the comic differences.

The apparent distance between Franklin and her heroine has led some commentators to a defence of the author's stylishness and self-consciousness in *My Brilliant Career*; irony suggests that Sybylla's confusions, inconsistencies and posturings are not Franklin's.[26] But distance, even ironic distance, does not necessarily preclude sympathy or identity. The retrospective act of autobiography inevitably imposes an impression of the self as other. Indeed the self is not only other; it is also others, a protean and baffling identity that perpetually eludes the writer as it eluded Rembrandt in his sixty-two self-portraits. No doubt this is one reason some autobiographers choose the novel form. The objective hero may resolve the core of darkness that always lurks within the autobiographical self; only another who is self and yet not self, whether more ideal or less, can unlock the mystery of the personal myth. Thus Dickens both is and is not David Copperfield and George Eliot both is and is not Maggie Tulliver. But the element of acting a part is inescapable for any autobiographer.

It is instructive to compare Franklin's ironic treatment of her narrator with Richardson's controlled response to Laura in *The Getting of Wisdom*. Often treated as analogous, the two books are really dissimilar in terms of insight and achievement. Richardson wrote, of course, from a position of artistic self-confidence and achievement whereas Franklin, at the time of writing *My Brilliant Career*, had only the vague aspirations of a young girl for a creative life. Whereas Richardson's older narrator understands the hypocrisies of the system which seeks to exploit and subdue Laura, Franklin's is confused about the reasons for Sybylla's sense of exploitation. Thus, she registers rather than articulates her resentment. Her protagonist is more of a self-indulgent figure of fantasy, a temporary means of liberation, doomed to deflation and to the experience of life as enigmatic, while the circle which she describes is the circle of defeat. Both Sybylla and her older observer are united in their sense of bewildered injustice[27], unable to penetrate 'the meaning of this hollow, grim little tragedy—life' (p. 225).

One of the reasons for Franklin's comparative failure of insight is that her feminist protest is complicated by an even deeper resentment—the resentment of lost status. Inwardly convinced of her aristocracy, which is interpreted variously as breeding, culture or simply owning the soul of a 'poet' or 'artist', Sybylla constantly uses a vocabulary of class; words such as 'plebeian', 'commoner', 'peasant', 'swell', 'superior', 'inferior', 'vulgar' and 'pauper' pepper her narrative. In her social context of 'wounded pride' and 'humiliation', gender is only one of the determinants of powerlessness and in fact Sybylla at one point reflects that poverty is the most hampering condition: 'Had my father occupied one of the fat positions of the land, no doubt as his daughter my life would have been so full of pleasant occupation and pleasure that I would not have developed the spirit which torments me now' (p. 37). And in the paeon to Australia's 'peasants' which concludes the novel, Sybylla includes gender as only one of her infirmities: 'My ineffective life will be trod out in the same round of toil,—I am only one of yourselves, I am only an unnecessary, little, bush commoner, I am only a—woman!'

(p. 232). Perceiving the world as one of fierce competition, Sybylla's complaint is that she has been deprived of 'every advantage and opportunity', 'thus I was helpless' (p. 36). The implication is that the social convention of gender has refused her male weapons of retaliation, thus exacerbating her situation. Men, on the other hand, are to be envied in that, in the aggressive terms which Franklin favours, they 'take the world by its ears and conquer their fate' (p. 33). Sensitive to the reality of hierarchy, she resents her own rejection from the 'congenial sphere' of the squattocracy, not the fact of hierarchy itself ('I was always desirous of enjoying the company of society people who were well bred and lived according to etiquette' pp. 64–5). Occasionally, Sybylla flagellates herself for the inability to adjust to 'peasantdom', but her prevailing emotion is resentment at an unjust loss of status. On one hand, she identifies with the common poor; on the other, she equates money with worth and much of her sense of inadequacy is associated with poverty.[28] The political stance of the novel is thus élitist and conservative rather than radical, even though Franklin allows her narrator a few moments of vaguely socialist philosophizing and clearly enjoys her protagonist's irreverent posturing ('My organ of veneration must be flatter than a pancake, because to venerate a person simply for his position I never did or will' p. 3). Even if Sybylla were as unimpressed by station as she claims, irreverence is not rebellion, and like McAuley's Australians, she is more 'independent' than 'free'. It is the loss of caste, even more than the reduction of gender, that dismays the Sybylla of *My Brilliant Career*.

Loss of caste is particularly disastrous given Franklin's assumption that competition, exploitation and manipulation are human constants rather than ideological constructs. Enmeshed in binary patterns of thought, Franklin is most preoccupied with binaries of power. Men are 'the dog on top' (p. 34), woman 'is but the helpless tool of man', marriage is the 'most unfair to women' institution because it completely deprives women of power, and Sybylla rejects Beecham because he 'offered . . . everything but control'. Striking as these are as feminist protests, they also reflect Franklin's perception of the world as one in which manipulation and control are universally desirable ends. Control is perceived as an unavoidable ingredient in sexual relationships. 'You are not the man who could ever control her', Aunt Helen tells Everard (p. 67), and even Sybylla herself occasionally reflects on her need of a 'master hand': imagining herself at one point as the classic clinging vine 'without a pole', she describes her need of 'a master hand to train and prune' (p. 15). Similarly, individuals are 'manly', 'unmanly', 'womanly' or 'not effeminate' according to their degrees of dominance or passivity. Social relations between the sexes are perceived exclusively as power plays so that Sybylla measures her success in terms of her 'mastery' of situations and individuals; since marriage represents the ultimate denial of power, the proposal scene in which she strikes her lover can be seen as a dramatic metaphor of her violent response to that supreme abdication.

Thus, much of Sybylla's attraction for her author stems from her ability to win a temporary dominion over men by retreating to a pre-adult, tomboy state, where teasing tactics are given scope. If she nostalgically recalls the time at Bruggabrong when she was allowed a childish dominance, and was 'both the terror and amusement of the station' (p. 2), she frequently attempts to recreate that experience of infantile control. Situations which fall into this self-indulgent category include the teasing scenes I have already discussed in which a large male is bemused by the quicksilver, bantering child-woman. One of the most curious is the account of Beecham's relationship with the infant tomboy, O'Doolan. Feminist critics have seized on this episode as further illustration of Franklin's exposure of sexist attitudes. But its link with earlier images of the infant self, coupled with indications that the child is surrogate for Sybylla, providing a preferred relationship with Beecham, suggests that the incident is more sentimental than satiric. Beecham himself makes the link; '"One little girl at a time is enough for me to care for properly"' (p. 93). Embodying a complicated pattern of personal memories and cultural myths, Harold expresses an ideal love—protective, sexually undemanding, indulgent and somehow redolent of the manliness of both bush ethos and infant Eden.

The pressure of infantile memories is also apparent in the whole Caddagat sequence. Frequently described as her natural 'home', Caddagat restores her childhood to Sybylla, recovering her youthful looks and making her once again the pampered child. Given only a few light tasks, she is showered with presents from Uncle Jay. The latter persists in treating Sybylla as small child, resorting to physical teasing at their first meeting and providing her with a doll on her birthday. Although she is 'disappointed' at the last present, there is no indication elsewhere that she resents her resumption of juvenile condition. Numerous faceless girl-visitors fill the house for her 'pleasure' and parties, outings and birthday-teas emphasize that Caddagat revolves around the self as child. More pleasurable fantasy than real place, Caddagat belongs to the landscape of memory from the beginning. It is an irrigated oasis of indeterminate economy (unlike Possum Gully where the difficult economics of dairy farming are graphically illustrated), representing the 'pleasant life . . . [of] the past' and as hazy as the blue hills into which it fades on Sybylla's leave-taking. It is a tenacious memory, nevertheless, reinforced by all the positive aspects of the bush myth which it naturally attracts and preventing Sybylla from recognizing its own internal contradictions: unlike the more democratic Possum Gully or Barney's Gap,

Caddagat is the apex of a rigid, excluding hierarchy, which demands the qualification of money. Even more disabling, however, is the memory's blinkering effect on the narrator's response to the real frustrations of her situation; if Caddagat is the rightful 'home', Possum Gully is no more than an accident of fate and any thorough-going analysis of the opposition between culture and creativity is evaded.

Caddagat's shadowy but real representation of the Patersonian ethos is extended in the person of Harold Beecham. Noted for taciturnity, bush skills, tamped down emotions and 'manly' physique, Beecham is as organic to the bush as a gum tree. He is 'redolent of the sun, the saddle, the wide open country—a man who is a man, utterly free from the least suspicion of effeminacy, and capable of earning his bread by the sweat of his brow—' (pp. 217–18). Invested with the same romantic aura as the Caddagat landscape, he is the focus of Sybylla's struggles with the impossibilities of the 1890s myth. While he offers a form of mateship, or at least an adolescent type of companionship, Sybylla revels in his company; when it comes to practical jokes, droving or horse-shoeing, she is almost his equal, for he is more protective elder brother than demanding lover in the early stages of their relationship. His devolution into potential husband dramatically changes the emotional atmosphere, presenting Sybylla with a 'mature' alternative, chilling to the spirit, and incidentally exposing her author's inability to project the received cultural myth into a personal future. The relationship with Beecham dramatizes Franklin's emotional fixity as nothing else. If the word 'wife' appalls Sybylla, she nevertheless tries hard to accept Harold, extending their bantering relationship as long as she can by a form of flirtation. When he mysteriously reverts to poverty, she grits her teeth and agrees to a long engagement, since his misfortune evokes feelings of mateship and Lawsonian sympathy for the underdog. Sybylla registers the dichotomy between mateship and female self-determination in no uncertain manner, but Franklin is unable to perceive the contradiction with clarity. The confusion is apparent in the twists and turns of the narrator's thoughts. Normally articulate on the subject of marriage at this point she is unable to explain her opposition to the state of wife: 'What was there to understand? Only that I was queer and different from other women' (p. 156). The situation is resolved by restoring Harold to Five-Bob Downs and his condition as 'chum'; more an idea than an individual, Harold passes in and out of Sybylla's life with the convenience of a thought.

Harold's shadowiness is even more evident during his visit to Possum Gully. Obviously a reflection of the narrator's musings, he exists to conclude the relationship between self and context. The narrator comes closest at this point to articulating her dilemma. If Sybylla's experience has taught her anything, it is that self and loved land are irreconcilable; it is only a little point at which she boggles, but it is an overwhelming one: 'for the point is myself' (p. 224). And the novel closes with the union of the two narrative voices in a song of defeat:

And my heart is weary. Oh, how it aches tonight—not with the ache of a young heart passionately crying out for battle, but with the slow dead ache of an old heart returning vanquished and defeated! (p. 231)

The novel's penultimate paragraph is an astonishingly expressive trope of the ambivalence of Franklin's response to Australia. An elegiac description of a sunset, it rephrases once again in light/dark imagery the polarities that have structured the novel, and echoes the depressive ground-rhythm which has been such a persistent trait. 'The great sun is sinking in the west . . . Down, down he goes', 'the long shadows eagerly cover all,' 'the clouds fade . . .'. The 'great sun', mocking, powerful and enigmatic, grins and winks 'knowingly' at the denizens of his scorched land, the 'starving stock' and 'drought-smitten wastes of land', before lighting up the sky with his transitory but glorious 'garish . . . pageantry'. The merry, mocking laughs of the kookaburras, the softly calling mopokes, the 'shyly peeping' stars and the fading clouds of the rapidly darkening sky, figure the final baffled consciousness of the self and the resigned acceptance of enigma.

Another writer who consciously perceived her childhood as Edenic was Mary Fullerton. Born in 1868 in a remote part of Gippsland, Fullerton belonged to a family which had been compelled to resort to pioneer farming after a financial collapse had robbed the father of the fortune he had made on the goldfields. She experienced an exceptionally sequestered childhood in a forested landscape of prime-val beauty and witnessed its rapid destruction in the name of pro-gress. Memories of her bush childhood stimulated Fullerton's finest prose writing; she returned to it at least twice in 'factual' autobiog-raphies, *Bark House Days* (1921)[29] and the subsequent, unpublished 'Memoirs'[30] and drew on it for some of her novels. Of these, *The People of the Timber Belt* (1925)[31] is the most thoroughly autobiogra-phical. Like Franklin, with whom she became very friendly, Fullerton had strong feminist convictions and undertook the same migratory sequence, leaving the bush for the city and then the city for Europe. In 1922 she left to settle in London and never returned.

Less entranced than Franklin by the 1890s myth, Fullerton was nevertheless attracted to the romantic notion that the Bush offered innocence, simplicity and resources of spiritual strength not found in the city. In this she coincided with her contemporaries in Australia's literary community, of course. As Richard White has commented, the bush in the 1890s became 'an imaginative refuge. The contrast between the cramping, foetid city and the wide open spaces became a cliché for that generation'.[32] Fullerton also shared the Bush mystique, the sense that it was 'a sacred, inspiriting power, influencing for good'[33], although her sentiments were closer to the personal nature-communion of Shaw Neilson than to the nationally-directed optimism of O'Dowd. Sharpened by exile and illness Fullerton's Wordsworthian memories of the 'Genius of the Bush' became a conscious defence against pain. 'Keep the "vision splendid" of the early hours of life's day, the Heaven that lies in the bush about you in your infancy', she adjures the self as bush-child in *The Australian Bush:*

keep the dreams given by the compensating bush, the mother-lore that she sings to you in the strange language of the she-oak boughs, that she shows you in the sweet deep gullies, on the wide-horizoned plains ... Keep those dreams, let them be the soft velvet under the hard harness, so it shall gall you never.[34]

At the same time, Fullerton was alive to some of the internal contradictions of the idealization of the Bush and dramatized them in her autobiographies and fiction. *Bark House Days*, narrated by the grown-up bush child, maintains its note of nostalgic reverie by largely excising the pioneer in favour of his landscape; *The People of the Timber Belt* is an alternative version, narrated by a sophisticated urban outsider, and peopling the landscape with rural types of violence, bigotry and ignorance. Considered together, *Bark House Days*, *The People of the Timber Belt* and 'Memoirs' perceive the Bush as offering both isolation and freedom, imaginative starvation and spiritual nourishment, for their author is remarkably tolerant of ambivalence and sensitive to the dissonant, covert culture and the dualities of the Bush myth. If she anticipates White, Herbert, Stow and Keneally in finding a spirituality or significance in the Bush that is explicitly absent from society, she invests the contrast with an additional distinction in that the land is consistently perceived as female, while its few heroes are women or have female attributes. Meanwhile, land and women are united in their large generosity and helpless suffering.

Nevertheless, *Bark House Days* is one of the most nostalgic of Australian autobiographies. The mood of dreamy, distancing nostalgia is deliberately cultivated as the later 'Memoirs' makes clear. Here she reflects on the experience of writing the past, and describes herself as currently 'laid low':

Memory—how richly its associations play a compensating part for one's later years. Living over again is a very real thing. A very idealizing thing too. It give the plus to the actual that makes it the perfect it was not 'as we moved therein'. And so the compensations mount up, one is never left bare. ('Memoirs', p. 122)

Recognizing that some memories are 'not welcome', she implies that it is autobiography's function to 'starve with neglect' the unpleasant asepcts of the past, presumably retrieving and heightening its quintessential nourishment of the self (pp. 142–3). As she expresses it in her poem titled 'Past':

> The solid cubes of Fact do not remain
> The things they were,
> The darkest hour with lovely lie
> Puts garlands on her hair.[35]

Bark House Days sounds the same self-conscious note of fond reverie. Conceding that Fullerton's memories of the hills are always of spring, she describes the mental picture as 'illusory', a consciously mutable device to defeat the mutability of time (p. 24). There are no wet days in the Eden of memory: 'all things waited upon us, regal young barbarians that we were: sky and air and earth . . . ' (p. 30). Like the bark house, which sturdily shelters the child-self from the wilderness, autobiography offers a haven for the older self: 'I like to dream occasionally on this other side of the world . . . of my last days spent under a roof of the ancient stringy bark, and walls of the same, closing me in snug and safe from sun and storm' ('Memoirs', p. 168). Similar in mood to George Eliot's rural novels, which are sometimes alluded to, *Bark House Days* casts a golden glow over the past, consciously simplifying what is perceived as an admirably simple life. As the narrator of 'Memoirs' comments: 'Our simplicity . . . was part of us, a thing not to be ashamed of (as some of us were later) but a distinction, and a precious thing' (p. 184). Thus this is not escapist fantasy but an attempt to distil the past's spiritual essence, discernible only by the mature, retrospective consciousness.

Fullerton's bush child is like Franklin's in her freedom, energy and equality, but she is more alive to the romance and mystery of the Bush. Sensitive to the signs of the vanished Aboriginal past, which escape adult faculties blunted by toil, she responds to the sufferings of the ring-barked trees and the secret language of the creek. Unlike Franklin's child, she is invariably accompanied by a loved younger sister, Claribel, and the preferred experience is almost always a shared one, its empathy heightened by several minor conflicts with brothers and cousins. Thus Fullerton's Eden is less of an individual kingdom that Franklin's, while the Wordsworthian relationship between children and Nature is extensively developed.

For Fullerton there is no question about the land's gender; it is consistently female. In her description of the local creek, for example, the narrator of *Bark House Days* evokes the fluid, dreaming intimacy between self and landscape that is so characteristic of female writing:

In the cool shades of the ferny banks . . . how many an hour have I lain and dreamed or drifted in that state, half-thought, half-feeling, which is as truly a time of growth as are the hours spent in toil or study. It was in those hours that I most belonged to her, and she to me; that whispering creek of many voices. You could bathe childlike in the shallows, fish in the deeper pools, picnic amongst the grots, ramble along the cobblestone strands; the every mood of childhood was met; her invitations were continual; her hospitality inexhaustible. (p. 42)

The nurturing connotations are consistent; providing materials for writing 'the sign manual of our uncivilized youth', the creek is the source of other means of naming and marking in the form of white and golden gravel. She contrives the first catch of fish, and nourishes the climbing plants and fruits which enhance the children's play. An unsuccessful attempt to discover her source initiates the children into 'another world' of flora and fauna, which is exciting, mysterious and even unlawful. On one awesome occasion she floods her banks; seen at first as a 'bold prank', a burst of 'wickedness, through sheer ennui of well-doing', it produces a great abundance, manifesting her 'power and mystery' and correcting the children's impressions of familiarity with the 'ultimates of her nature' (p. 49). Like other female writers, Fullerton celebrates a state of being which is an inter-relation with Nature and has nothing to do with owning or subduing. In *The People of the Timber Belt* the narrator, a schoolteacher, shares with two bush children an experience of listening to the female Spirit of the Bush. The description is contrived or even crude but the irresistible attraction of the childhood memory is obvious: 'What a pretty picture they were of childish innocence (shot through with wisdom) those two little Bush children there among the tall white gums, listening to the Genius of the Bush!' (p. 155). Given these perceptions of the Bush as mysterious and mothering, both physically and spiritually, it is not surprising that Fullerton's narrators are ambivalent about the destruction of the great forests. The sentiment is one of grief, rather than anger, a fatalistic acceptance of the universal heritage of pain, which is one of the refrains of 'Memoirs'. In *Bark House Days* the narrator frequently gives vent to her sympathy for the felled trees, 'The natural primal owners of the soil—inheritors of it from Darwinian eras of time' (p. 121).

When the hewing axe goes into their sappy flesh, do they not groan and make protest? When deprived of their life-blood, and swaying gaunt and grey in the autumn winds, are they not moaning for the green life lost? (p. 39).

Frequently referred to as 'virgin', the land has to submit to the power of the male: 'My father intended to get on, to subdue the scrub, to woo the virgin soil of his selection' (p. 2). The links between male authority and destruction are muted and complicated by a countering impulse to revere the stoicism and labour of the pioneer; nevertheless, a series of vivid incidents and character sketches combine with personal lamentations at the passing of the wilderness to subvert the pioneering panegyric. There is the story of the strange 'Andy', a 'terrifying-looking creature', who has a self-appointed 'contract to destroy' an ancient stump and spends six weeks on the task before disappearing once more:

Sometimes he sawed, sometimes dug beside it, and always he burned, stoking his fires with smaller logs piled against the huge one. They said that he rose muttering at night, and went out to his fires, stoking and levering. And so it was worn away at last. (p. 37)

Or the procession of half-mad or alcoholic itinerants, who occasionally terrify the children with their murderous appearance. Abandoning the goldfields, they have transferred their restless impatience to the surface of the land and the endings of their lives—in insanity, suicide or alcoholic decay—are emblematic of their latent violence.

Those men who are more settled are presented as limited by religious bigotry or ideology. Rigidly confirmed in their opinions and prejudices, they appear to meet only to argue. Even the gentle and inspiriting John Parker (the only male who is granted a separate chapter) is confined in 'walls of granite': 'He himself, who would succour a fly, believed hardily in a Power that doomed utterly' (p. 156). His commitment to the doctrine of predestination and original sin frightens the children as much as his gentleness inspires happiness. In such a Calvinistic community, it is not surprising that they dislike the faces of the old patriarchs in the Bible, scratching the face of Abraham 'because of his cool preparations for the offering up of Isaac' and associating Moses with Owen, 'the old man who did odd jobs about the place, and of whom we were for some reason frightened' (p. 19).

The narrator's father is a shadowy but minatory figure in *Bark House Days*. Clearly an authority who will brook no rebellion, he checks the children's proclivities for mischief by consigning them to the hated toil of the vegetable garden, and his taboo on the orchard's fruit can only be circumvented by the utmost guile. Even his 'one betrayal of sentiment', a buttonhole of verbena in memory of his mother, is more critical in its implications than conciliatory. One particularly vivid scene describes his practice of moulding bullets:

Bright and glittering from the moulds they would roll, at a tap on the hob, upon the hearth, whence, with gingerly touch, we children would lift them. It was great entertainment, that bullet-making; but not its result for the poor native denizens of the valley whose home we had seized. Back and farther back to the ranges they went, such of them as escaped the cruel despatch; back they retreated for ever somewhere beyond the distant sky-line. And so was the valley won from beast and bush. (p. 41)

The ambivalent notes of the above passage are accentuated by the frequent expressions of sympathy for animals in general and the hunted in particular and by an incident in which the two sisters save a pet calf from slaughter. 'Memoirs' extends the opposition to hunting, by describing a personal experience of shooting a leveret, which screams in pain; feeling like Cain, the narrator determines never to go hunting again. This narrative also extends the picture of the father, linking him to the goldfields' itinerants before misfortune and a growing family impelled him to farming.

More of an unfinished fragment than the other two texts, 'Memoirs' is interesting in that it is another rethinking of the same experience and sheds light on its contradictions. It includes several invocations to the craggy Bushman ('I find over all the years a closer brotherhood in my nature with the real Bushman than I have ever been able to feel with the human products of polished culture. It answers to the gipsy feelings of the wind on the heath' p. 128). Vaguely associated with the general nostalgia for far away and long ago, these sentiments are less convincing than the acerbic comment on an Aboriginal who had chopped off his wife's toes ('Still, the noble savage-child of God in keeping himself master of his [nomadic] household differs, but in method, from his civilized brother. The white man's fist or his boot has been known to exercise a like authority' p. 151); or the indignation which fuels the account of the illiterate, drunken, self-important farmhands on polling day and the mother's exclusion from voting (p. 61).

If men are implicitly oppressive or threatening figures in *Bark House Days* and 'Memoirs', women are presented as strong, nurturing individuals. Although their lives are far more confined than the men's, they are powerful, refining influences, transmitting an alternative, softer but more enduring culture. Jessie McDermott, the narrator's Sunday-school teacher, dies young but the influence of her life 'still hangs over many a spirit. Outside, she never taught directly; but there was a ministry about her life' (p. 21). Miss McGregor inspires the children with her wealth of Scottish lore and her gifts of the monthly *Good Words*. The mother-figure is particularly attractive to Fullerton and like Katherine McKell she is drawn to the Scots ideal of the thrifty, hard-working, home-keeping woman. The first chapter of *Bark House Days* celebrates the mother's transformation of the rough home with pasted newspapers and pipeclay ('Such an effect! It tutored our savage little souls' p. 5). But the strongest evocation of the nurturing woman is the study of Mrs Dwyer McMahon. An immensely generous individual, ('Strong, confident, self-reliant, a true soul and a brave one' p. 77), she valiantly takes on the role of breadwinner when her husband succumbs to tuberculosis. 'Memoirs', which includes a more intimate account of the narrator's mother, celebrates the friendship of women which mitigates hardship. Male mateship is absent, as it is in *Bark House Days*. 'How those women clung to the blessing of each other through those early years of isolation and of child-bearing! . . . My mother and aunt and Mrs McFarlane chimed like three mellow bells' (pp. 44–5).

The landscape of *The People of the Timber Belt* is the same as *Bark House Days* and the later narrative even repeats some of the characters and individuals of the earlier, but the emotional climate is vastly different. In this novel Fullerton appears to have released the negative memories which are filtered in *Bark House Days*. The human community is in the foreground in this narrative, an ugly contrast to the inspiring forests. The urban narrator has fled the city in search of moral simplicity, only to encounter brutality, bigotry and cultural isolation. An ignoble version of *Wuthering Heights*, the novel traces the sordid passions which afflict two branches of a family. There are signs that the author's intent is to demonstrate the universal nature of human nature, whether urban or rural, but less explicit intentions quickly subvert this theme and the drama's resolutions depend on the Herculean efforts of the exiles from the city, the narrator and a curate. Indeed the narrator becomes so busily involved in the affairs of her neighbours in her efforts to avert a 'tragedy' that the novel degenerates into black farce. By no means Fullerton's best writing, the book nevertheless has fascinating repercussions for *Bark House Days*.

The narrator speaks from a position of superiority from the beginning. A successor of the dedicated schoolteacher in *Bark House Days*, who brings education to the unschooled children, she brings music and poetry to the benighted citizens of the timber belt. She is drawn to the daughter of the house, where she is boarding, repeating one of Fullerton's favourite themes, the impact of poetry on a virgin mind. The men of the family are dismissed from the beginning as ignorant, vainglorious boors. The father's firmness is merely that of an ox and he quickly responds to the narrator's sophisticated manipulation ('Even super-bulls have their weak spot; their vanity' p. 20). Not surprisingly, he is totally mystified by his guest's conviction that it is sacreligious to clear trees. He is worse than insensitive, however, beating a cow unmercifully with a bill-hook on one occasion when the narrator is a concealed spectator: 'Trembling in every limb, I left my easel and ran to where the brutality had taken place. I think that I almost expected to find a limb of the cow there; hair and blood were scattered about in profusion' (p. 40). Her dismay is enhanced by the parson's information that Lurcher has been known to beat his wife 'almost to death'. His brother also bears the mark of his violence—'a hideous scar, all puckered and red and white' (p. 37)—the brand of a bite on the neck. The son of the house is even more dangerous; mocked by the narrator as a 'great, clean-shaven heavy faced son of vanity', he is nevertheless a sexual predator, who pursues his cousin and a mentally retarded girl simultaneously, and ruins both. Literally threatened by the gallows, he is unconvincingly rehabilitated by the curate's superior riding skills and charismatic personality. A history of murder and execution hangs over the drama, ostensibly reflecting the narrator's theory of genetic determinism, but also coinciding with the vague fears that men arouse in *Bark House Days*; of uncertain origin, these itinerants often carry signs of a violent past.

In this community women are the helpless victims of their menfolk. Mrs Lurcher fatalistically accepts her husband's brutality and her son's exploitation: 'The poor woman, so far from being negative, is a tragic figure; the central, silent, weakly-strong object against which the clash and swirl of the natures of those of her household circle' (p. 53). Mrs McGuiness is unable to protect her daughter from the sexual advances of young Lurcher and receives no support from her weak husband during the family crisis. When her daughter's baby dies, an ugly rumour of a grandmother's infanticide circulates in the community, scotched only by the narrator's intervention. Property descends from father to son, avoiding wives and daughters and leaving a legacy of bitterness and exploitation. Sullen and resentful, daughters find relief in petty acts of vengeance, while mothers accede to the local ethos which prefers the male, or simulate the inflexibilities of their husbands. Indeed the theme of motherhood is hedged with ambivalence in this narrative, culminating in the curious story of the hermit woman who creates an imaginary child and suicides when a real child she has fostered is taken from her. Apart from the incredibly managing narrator, this Gothic picture of a primitive community stirred by sordid passions anticipates in many ways Jean Bedford's *Country Girl Again* (1979). Landscape, meanwhile, is far less prominent in this narrative than in *Bark House Days*. An incongruous backdrop to the ugly human scene, it provides a temporary refuge. 'There is a gracious spirit moving in the soul of things just now, making one forget the sinister spirits in the world. In the Bush one is not allowed to remember the darker side of things' (p. 153), the narrator comments during a brief escape into the forest. Her last sentence could be a comment on *Bark House Days*. Drawn to the idealized memory of the Bush as a natural paradise for the child-self, Fullerton was unable to project the romance into adult experience. If *Bark House Days* celebrates the innocent potential of the bush, *The People of the Timber Belt* exposes the myth's hostility to women.

A more recent autobiography, which is steeped in the bush ethos, is Patsy Adam Smith's *Hear the Train Blow* (1964).[36] An account of her childhood as the daughter of a railway fettler in the Victorian outback of the 1920s, Adam Smith's book has gained a wide readership. Frequently reprinted, it has appeared in several editions, the latest of which is an illustrated version, including photographs of the family taken by the mother's brownie camera and typical advertisements of the 1920s. Reviewers have praised the book as an authentic period study, expressing the 'true' Australia of the pioneers: 'Life as the young Adam Smith recorded it doesn't exist any more—neighbourliness, true mateship, the battlers' concern for those having a tougher time than themselves'.[37] 'It is an earthy, nostalgic book, full of the joy of life and genuine feeling for what is truly Australian'.[38] 'The portraits [present] a life full of fun and laughter and a lot of love.'[39]

In the edition of 1981 Adam Smith included an epilogue describing the genesis of the book and the public response. On one hand, it is clear that she regards the book as an act of piety, recording the lives of the humble workers of the outback: 'In some ways it is as though we never lived. There is no monument to the toilers of a land and they wouldn't expect it. But a nation will be poorer if it forgets them'. On the other, she describes a more personal motive. Encouraged by Kylie Tennant to record her experiences of twelve years at sea, she wrote a long account of them but showed it to no one. The writing stimulated childhood memories, which apparently had to be relived before the author's creative life could proceed. 'It was as though I was waiting for something else. And then it came: I sat down and began to write the story of my childhood and the fear that hovered like a wraith about me . . .' The book was written in three weeks.

The fear that Adam Smith refers to, is the fear of not belonging. It was an understandable fear given her discovery in mid-teenage that she was not her parents' natural daughter. Previously, her status in the family had occasionally been the subject of innuendo on the part of her aunts and grandmother, but it had remained an uneasy wraith until her mother broke the news with well-intentioned insensitivity. *Hear the Train Blow* is thus a probing of old wounds. It is also a conscious attempt to lay the personal memory of estrangement, and is preoccupied with ideas of belonging, kindred and even clannishness, which make the bush myth a particularly consoling one. As declared outsider, the narrator has an emotional affinity with the outsiders and underdogs of depression Australia and with the defensive egalitarianism of the familiar myth; as the disinherited member of a family, she identifies with the larger family of bush and railway workers: 'Whatever we were, the soil had made us' (p. 221). The emotional investment in this recreation of community manifests itself at every level of the narrative. In the hearty chapter titles ('They're Off!', 'Kindness and Courage', 'Getting our Irish Up', 'Ho! Ho! Tallygaro!'); in the broad brush scenes which express the fellowship of a tribe; in the frequent emphasis on knowing and being known ('There was a camaraderie about navvies . . . We had the feeling of "belonging to a big family" . . . To say you were a navvy or the family of a navvy on the line was a passport into companionship' p. 101); in the descriptions of the fond farewells and reunions as the family moves around the little country stations of Victoria; in the cheerful, Dickensian lists of festive foods. Adam Smith loves to describe gatherings which centre on the small family and evoke neighbourliness, egalitarian goodwill and unstinted generosity:

When Mick turned nineteen Mum gave a party for her in the Waaia hall. No invitations were sent out, word was merely spread around that it was on. Eighty people turned up; some from outlying areas who couldn't get in sent gifts. There was a trestle table piled high with presents. Fettlers came and sleeper-cutters and wheat-buyers and farmers and retired people and the aboriginal girl who worked at the hotel. Waaia had missed out on the division the Depression had brought to other places. There was no working class here, no gentry. (p. 184)

At their final leave-taking all Waaia turns out, a memory which the narrator cherishes as demonstrating beyond doubt the self's belonging: 'I'd shared in the camaraderie of people working hard, playing with gusto. Others may speak of the "working class". We were aristocrats. We had a whole town turn out to bid us farewell' (p. 222).

Like other devotees of the Bush myth, Adam Smith celebrates the freedom of the outback and the physical skills the life requires. A favourite mental image is of her sister's daring riding ('a bush girl with her hair flying out behind her, her dress tucked in under her knees in front and fluttering out at the back' p. 50); a repetition of an aunt's exploits in her grandmother's familiar story, it evokes the courageous spirit of the pioneers which the narrator finds so appealing. The men of the railways have the same spirit. Faced with the same hostile landscape and the same difficulties of isolation, they demonstrate the same qualities of stoicism, mateship and 'bush initiative'. The tolerance shown to the men who ride the rails during the depression and the widespread response to her father's accident express the familiar male solidarity. Adam Smith is also drawn to the idea that the bush represents freedom, especially freedom from the petty restraints of the city, but solidarity is the value she most reveres.

The family fable of her birth, which begins the book, is really an account of her adoption by the extended family of railway workers. Assuming from the mother's cryptic letter that the child is a boy, they vie for his future: '"We'll keep your kid in the gang." "Too right!" said the men' (p. 11). Kelly the ganger, who tenderly takes mother and child in a Casey Jones to the health clinic's nurse twenty miles up the line, knows 'more about bringing up dingo pups than she does about babies' (p. 12), a remark that attaches itself to the Smith family and is absorbed into the general folklore of the railway workers. As a member of this family, the narrator feels herself to be linked also with the Gallipoli heroes. Wearing her father's medals to an Anzac celebration, she wins a nod of approval from the engine-driver. The sense of patriotism, which she later describes as 'a sheath', is born that day:

I felt the reputation haloed about us that the deaths of these men and the buoyancy of their spirit had earned, a reputation that every Australian from that day on has been born with as his inheritance. Tears coursed down my cheek as they have often coursed since that day, tears not of sorrow but of pride. (p. 138)

The occasion also provokes a rebellion against her Irish-Catholic heritage. Thrashed by her mother for attending a Protestant cere- mony, she tells the priest that she would still have gone had she known what the ceremony was. The fraternity of the bush has its natural enemies, but these are the faceless, heartless wealthy of the city, rather than the British who are the object of the Grandmother's hatred.

Attractive as the myth is for Adam Smith, it fails as a telling of the whole story. Certain incidents and individuals erupt into the text and evade the myth-making process. The most striking of these are the accounts of the Marvel and Moran families. Both stories are grim descriptions of inhumanity, which appear to puzzle the older narra- tor; far more graphic than the group scenes of fellowship, they also lack the philosophical summary which frames the more fabular elements of the narrative. The Marvel sequence begins as a descrip- tion of the children's attraction to a family which has abandoned all civilized standards, living in a squalor that intrigues the young visitors. With the account of the death of the eight-year-old Peter, however, the story takes on an anomalous grimness. An unattractive child, known to tear living fledglings to pieces, Peter is totally neglected. His bed is a horse rug at the end of the parents' double bed. When he develops rheumatic fever, he is ignored by everyone except some compassionate neighbours:

Mrs Young and Mum went across to see him and found him huddled under the horse rug ... in his work shirt and socks. Mrs Young made a red flannel night-shirt and took bottles of warm broth to him. He died early one morning and the parents found him at lunchtime. Next day the Marvel kids turned up at school. (p. 56)

His death registers not a ripple in the family's existence; there is no funeral and the father even returns the sheet in which the neighbours had wrapped the body.

The story of the Morans, 'Message in Green', is an even more horrific tale of murder, suicide and insanity. The account of Joan Moran's reversion 'to the animal' and her isolation in a sordid little house filled with the carcasses of calves she had slaughtered, is oddly juxtaposed to the Smiths' experience of hearty community at a mission. As in the Marvel sequence, the narrator reverts to her own experience of fellowship as if to cancel out the destructive scenes and the intimations that family love may be an uncertain quality. 'Message in Green' ends with the death of one of the participants in the sordid drama and the vain attempts of a neighbour to reach the woman's spirit with the Confiteor.

But there are more direct threats to family solidarity in the form of ignorance and bigotry. The child is an avid reader, but reading is forbidden at home, and books have to be hidden in the outside dunny. And contrary to other suggestions that the Smith family has a gregarious life, it is revealed that the children are prevented from forming friendships. Although the narrator elides over the reasons, ('the reason neither my sister nor I could have friends has no place in this book or on my tongue' p. 43), it is clear that the mother's Irish-Catholic prejudices erect barriers around the girls. A few weeks in a convent preparing for confirmation is ironically a period of intellectual liberation for the narrator. Another of the text's silences concerns the family's constant movements around the State. A result of the mother's initiative, who dislikes staying long in one place ('We were never in one place longer than two years. Often our stay was only for a few months' p. 28), it is erected into a virtue, equated with 'fun', implying that the whole outback of the State is home and perhaps acquiring something of the rolling stone characteristic that Ward noted as typical of the bushman.

The bigotry which confronts the narrator is most offensive at her maternal Grandmother's home. Although she admires the Grandmother's pioneering achievements, the child is alienated by her inexplicable hostility, unpleasant superstitions and complacent ignorance. The description of her bedroom with its multiplicity of starched white linen covers (pp. 189–90) is a fine expression of the old woman's alienating prudery. Having grown tired of her husband 'long ago', she combines stress on physical chastity with a prurient interest in the disreputable. The talk which filters through the scrim walls at night epitomizes the fetid atmosphere of this home:

One night I heard Grandmother telling Mum about some neighbours. 'The daughter—well, she looked about fourteen and she had a miscarriage and the mother left home because of course as you might have guessed with a family where there'd been a divorce it was the father's, what more could you expect? And the father he fed the pigs . . .' I put my head under the blankets so as not to hear what was fed the pigs and then I lifted them so I could hear. Yes, the police had come and the people had moved. (p. 190)

At Grandmother Adams's place the child is never at ease. Aware of a vaguely speculative attitude on the part of her grandfather towards her, she is conscious of her grandmother as frankly hostile. 'Love, love, love. It was everywhere, but I know one place where there was none for me' (pp. 187–8). It is here that she first begins to suspect that she does not belong as firmly as she had supposed.

She is nicknamed as 'Paddie-the-next-best-thing' by her father, but the implications never worry her. Convinced that she is her parents' child, she feels pity for her elder sister who was adopted and finds her mother's fondness for the proverb 'Blood is thicker than water' consoling: 'How few years were to pass before I knew how false that old wives' tale was. How few years before Mum was to repeat that remark so fearfully' (p. 134). In the middle section of the narrative, the fears and innuendoes thicken, often erupting into documentary accounts of events. They culminate in her overhearing a conversation between mother and grandmother which is a fierce blow to her sense of identity; describing herself as 'swallowed up' and as 'only a small part of the stranger who lay dry-eyed, numb, cold as stone in the bed', she has lost her sense of life and wholeness: 'Had anyone called out, "Where's Jeanie?" I could have answered truthfully, "She's not here"' (p. 193). Her mother's blundering confirmation of the truth ends her childhood and her sense of being at home. Pursuing an intensive course of study and work, she seizes the opportunity offered by the war and joins the Voluntary Aid Detachment by falsifying her age: 'All the wheels of all the trains on all the journeys we had made never sounded so loud as the turmoil within my head' (p. 196).

The book ends on a triumphant note of emotional resolution, a recovery of the earlier belonging:

if the love and the lack of humbug in my life had taught me one thing it was to recognize the value of people, places and things. Now I began to see that there was no dilemma. If others wanted to weigh themselves down with whispers and aged feuds, that was their burden, not mine. I'd had everything. None could have had better. (p. 222)

Within the local economy of the book, the conclusion is more wished-for than real, given the vivid dramatization of a personal war with a faceless enemy. Just a few pages earlier, the narrator has described life as a battlefield where fog conceals foes and the most one can hope to do is to parry the enemy's thrusts as they assail the self through the swirling mists; and it is this description which persists if one penetrates beneath the bush rhetoric.

Far from a simple, heart-warming celebration of the Bush ethos, as many reviewers seem to suppose, *Hear the Train Blow* is a complex response to a deep personal wound. If myth and memory coincide in consoling assumptions of solidarity, which evade the gender difficulties afflicting Franklin and Fullerton, the text is by no means unified. The coincidence is asserted rather than realized and the intensely experienced personal truths shift the heroics of the overt theme to the margins.

12

Black Narratives

In his 1969 Boyer lectures, *After the Dreaming*, W. E. H. Stanner
dwells on the national cult of forgetfulness about the Australian
Aborigines, an inattention of over 150 years, which 'cannot possibly be explained by absentmindedness'. Defining the complicity of
silence as a 'structural matter, a view from a window which has been
carefully placed to exclude a whole quadrant of the landscape', he
remarks on the tremendous imaginative difficulty encountered by
whites who now seek to break the cult of disremembering. How are
we to recover 'the story of the things we were unconsciously resolved
not to discuss with [the Aborigines] or treat with them about ... the
story ... of the unacknowledged relations between two racial groups
within a single field of life', he asks; he suggests that what we need is
a different kind of history, based on the personal experiences of
Aboriginal people. Such a history or ethno-history, retrieving the
Aborigines from their traditional status as a 'melancholy footnote',
would be far removed from conventional histories of the coming and
development of British civilization.[1] Stanner does not develop the
implications of his proposal at any length, but it is clear that such
an enterprise must profoundly qualify not only conventional histories but conventional formulations of our national identity. Mary
Gilmore's attempt to boost a national mythos, for instance, soon
found itself in a moral quagmire, once she moved from the
'melancholy footnote' approach to the actuality of family memory.

As if in answer to Stanner's call, an accelerating number of
Aboriginal autobiographies have begun to appear since the early
1970s. Not only are women well represented in this outpouring, but
one narrative, Sally Morgan's *My Place*, has been hailed as a major
cultural event.[2] There are also, of course, a great number of
interviews with black women, included in such collections as Kevin
Gilbert's *Living Black* (1978) and Bill Rosser's *Dreamtime Night-*

mares (1985). Valuable as the interview is as a social document, it lacks the considered, extended character of the autobiography and even its spontaneity, given the inevitable tendency of the interviewer to structure the interview according to external preconceptions and considerations. An editor can be even more intrusive than an interviewer and many black autobiographers have depended on an editor's skill. But editors on the whole, at least in the group of narratives considered here, have been remarkably sensitive to the integrity of their authors' texts and attempts to intervene between author and reader are rare. I discuss the exceptions to this practice below.

Ranging from the 1890s to the 1960s and concerned universally with black/white relations, these autobiographies are a staggering endorsement of Stanner's observation that racial attitudes remained virtually unchanged until the 1960s. Indeed, as Les Murray comments in his foreword to Ella Simon's *Through My Eyes* (1987), perhaps the worst years of the oppression, when various State Protection Acts systematically controlled the lives of Aborigines, were from the 1930s Depression until the 1960s; if the earlier massacres and murders are horrifying to contemplate, at least the oppression was 'sporadic, unorganised, full of exceptions and special arrangements'.

No document has a greater chance of challenging the cult of forgetfulness than a black woman's autobiography. Speaking with a frankness that cuts like a knife through white ignorance, these narratives capture the imagination, compelling the reader to experience with the narrator the pain, deprivation, and bewildered shame of being black, young and female. They expose the thoughts and emotions behind the stereotypes of the boong, the gin, the half-caste, the mission child, and the fringe-dweller. Unlike anthropological studies which endeavour to 'explain' the Aborigines to us, these texts indirectly compel the reader to 'explain' the white culture, to perceive it through the puzzled eyes of an excluded and neglected outsider. Thus the white reader undergoes the curious experience of finding the anthropological role reversed, and the contention of one historian, for instance, that autobiography 'is the highest and most instructive form in which the understanding of life confronts us'[3], is vividly borne out. Extraordinary as it may seem, given the grim experiences that they describe, none of these texts is vehemently angry or even lastingly bitter; written from a position of achieved strength and pride, they celebrate the triumph of will and the resilience of the human spirit. They are elegiac rather than declamatory, hopeful rather than vengeful; taking the white world 'gravely but not seriously'[4], they have room for wit and even light-hearted humour. Thus in many ways they differ from black American autobiographies, although they share the American writer's experience in one important particular, in the equality of loneliness that the author/reader interchange imposes. Roger Rosenblatt has described this condition well:

The self in autobiography is alone, but so is the reader. The autobiographer wishes the reader to be alone and counts on it because whatever else may separate them from each other, their states of loneliness are mutually recognizable. For the black autobiographer this is a central connection; he is after all not a minority in relation to his lonely reader. They are equal in the exchange, equal because of the experience of the artifact. On this level—which is the one level where men may help each other—the artifact and the polemics are one.[5]

That all the narrators of this group of texts are remarkably strong women is an incontestable impression. Articulate and independent, they speak from a position of autonomy which many white women might envy; it is clear that autonomy has been won with great difficulty, but it is also clear that for these women at least, daily grappling with the shadowy underworld of black/white society has been a profound education in the authentic dignity of the self. Although none of them refers to the injustice, they vindicate the recent work by female anthropologists which retrieves Aboriginal women from the belittling assumptions of previous Anglocentric, male-oriented studies. If white pioneer women have been limited to a supportive, observing role by male historians, Aboriginal women have suffered the effects of a twofold prejudice from male anthropologists. Diane Bell's field work in Central Australia, for instance, has challenged previous assumptions that women in tribal society had an impoverished and male-dominated role; emerging as social actors in their own right, the women of Bell's study have a distinct structural importance in that their religious rites complement the men's. Bell points out that although many scholars have felt confident about categorizing Aboriginal woman's place in her society, few have attempted to examine her life from her perspective.[6] It appears furthermore, that white sexism has even affected recent relations with post-traditional Aboriginal society and underwritten a change in the status of women. Men have become the political spokespersons and women have been restricted to the traditional female roles preferred by white society. Other observers, however, have commented on women's relative ability to survive in transitional society[7] and certainly the autobiographers considered here place enormous value on the nurturing power of women; men are largely absent, temporary or powerless in their narratives.

Although every voice is distinctive and each autobiography preserves its own unique shape, these texts are united by several common characteristics. Stylistically, thematically, aesthetically and conceptually, black women writers manifest a common tradition. As in white women's autobiography, the initial impression is of diversity in sameness. What is more, black autobiographies share the fundamental features and biases of white women's texts, although in black writing the features are even more sharply defined. If white women value relatedness, it is a religion for black women; if white women privilege the personal over the public sphere, black women transform the public into the personal; if white women prefer the informal voice of conversation and the discontinuous structure, black women employ these strategies with a fresh spontaneity and conviction. Like black American texts, these narratives have a common moral topography, although the physical features are different. Rosenblatt isolates two constant elements in black American autobiography: an 'expressed desire to live as one would choose and the tacit or explicit criticism of external national conditions that work to ensure one's freedom of choice is delimited or non-existent'. Slavery and the desire for freedom are still the key experiences which shape black life-writing in America. Two overriding elements also dominate autobiographies by Aboriginal women, which one might describe as the ideal value of relatedness and the bewildering experience of silence. At home in the land and mindful of a past rich culture based on kinship, the Aboriginal autobiographer writes according to different co-ordinates. Like the American writer, however, the Aboriginal author apprehends the white world as 'consistent and unique, if dreadful' and, like the American, the Australian autobiographer never needs 'to invent a nightmare' to make her point. The catalogue of crazy inhumanity is less violent perhaps but it includes, like the American's, 'unfairness, poverty, a quashing of aspiration, denial of beauty, ridicule, often death itself'.[8]

In one significant way this group of texts differs from white narratives—black women write with a consciousness of their historicity. The individual story, sharp and even unresolved as it may be, is perceived as describing a general experience; it is both unrepeatable autograph and cultural archetype. 'This story is true. It did happen and I was part of it', writes Marnie Kennedy[9], speaking for her fellow writers, for all these books consciously address the ignorance of the white reader. Just as they all record a variety of silences (the ominous silence which invariably accompanied white plans for the disposal of the blacks; the palpable silence of the half-forgotten past; the silence of white ways of living, reflected in the reductive routines of the mission, the home, the training institution; the silence of contempt; and the silence of the oppressed themselves in the face of alien structures), they all seek to break the silence of ignorance that has afflicted two centuries of white/black relations. As Anne Ruprecht comments in her 'Afterword' to Ella Simon's autobiography, seeing the world through black eyes makes a difference: 'It can never be the same again. It is so much better; somehow bigger, deeper'.

****

We were all accepting that ahead was the unknown—just as well we did not know. (Margaret Tucker)

Margaret Tucker's words could apply to any one of these autobiographies, for they all recreate the experience of living under a vague but real sense of threat. The threat is not of economic misfortune or even homelessness, whch are in most cases givens of the situation, but of the destruction of close relationships. Monica Clare's autobiographical novel, *Karobran*, is a particularly sensitive account of a child's loss of family.

The novel, which is closely based on the author's life, opens in southern Queensland in the 1930s, when the child is seven and her brother five. Her white mother, disowned by her family after marrying an Aboriginal shearer, has just died in childbirth and the children are in the temporary care of a kindly white woman. Hampered in finding work by both the Depression and his colour, the father has been forced to travel long distances, accompanied by his family; the talk of the adults makes it clear that the mother's death has been brought about by these harsh conditions and that the father will now encounter great difficulty in keeping his family together. Even if he finds a station willing to take him on, his children will not be welcome. For the moment, however, the child is ignorant of the full extent of their tragedy; hiding underneath the verandah while the women's sad voices swirl overhead, she tries to work out the puzzle of their weeping and assuage her feeling that something is 'terribly wrong': 'Why had she and Morris been brought to this big house? Why had the Browns carried her Mother inside, and not allowed her or her brother to see her since?' (p. 1). The situation is a figure of the future, for a bewildered sense of being at the disposal of superior powers and subject to arbitrary, unexplained removal from loved ones is to be the dominant pattern of her life. Confronting another's helpless kindness, on one hand, and deliberate mystification about a loved one's whereabouts, on the other, are to be recurring experiences; on this occasion it is the adults' desire to protect the children from the grim truth which is baffling, but the subsequent, less explicable silences of officialdom also appear to be well meant. The welfare officer who ultimately separates father and children cannot explain to them why the father has suddenly lost his right to live with his children, but 'All three of them knew, each in his own heart, that it would be a long, long time if ever, before they would be all together again like this'. Later, she hears from a relative that the father has frequently attempted unsuccessfully to retrieve his children from 'welfare' but has been refused information about their whereabouts in his own interests. After a period in a Sydney institution, where the children live under the threat of separation, they are cared for by a kindly white farming couple on the lower Hawkesbury River, but this idyll comes abruptly to an end when 'welfare' deems that it is time for the narrator to be 'put to work': 'Isabelle was dumbfounded . . . Never did it occur to her that one day they would have to leave this Aunt and Uncle, that they both loved so dearly' (pp. 41–2). Back in Sydney, the children are placed in separate homes and visits are infrequent and unannounced. When Isabelle is offered a domestic job, she accepts because she will be able to see her brother once a week but then he suddenly disappears from his foster home and she discovers that he has been sent to another, unnamed institution. Sitting on the steps while she puzzles over his disappearance, she has come full circle from the moment when she sat on the verandah steps puzzling over the sudden separation from her mother. If 'welfare' is parsimonious in the information it releases, a relative who has made great efforts to find her is more forthcoming and his visit promises to link her once again to Morris; disappointment inevitably ensues with the news that Morris has been suddenly sent to a training institution, again unnamed: 'It always seemed to Isabelle that just as everything was going along well, something had to happen to alter things for her' (p. 56). The children of *Karobran* only experience one instance of outright cruelty and indeed often encounter great kindness; nevertheless, a power which is blind, deaf and dumb seems perpetually bent on meddling in their lives. It is as if they are enveloped in a fog, occasionally emerging into patches of sunlight but always overtaken by the white mist and eventually separated by it. The narrator finally loses contact with both her father and brother.

My analysis has only given some indication of this narrator's experience of life as capricious, but the unequal tug between the personal need for continuity and rootedness and the abstract system's need for disruption structures the whole text. Letters fail to arrive, are unposted or are powerless given the illiteracy of relatives; people who are genuinely kind are either economically or legally helpless; the closest of relationships are the ones most at risk, according to 'welfare''s unstated social priorities; birthdays, which remind the system of one's existence and place on the unseen schedule, are events to be dreaded for they may signal partings, endings and unpleasant beginnings; holidays, which must be spent in the sterile 'home', are grim reminders of one's lonely powerlessness; even the earnings derived from the domestic position, which the inscrutable white system has deemed suitable, are arbitrarily garnered and banked.

Notwithstanding the bleakness of its story, this narrative is remarkable for its moments of lyrical expression. During the period of quiet happiness on the Hawskesbury River, for instance, the narrator identifies with a particular feature of the landscape: 'Above the vegetable garden Isabelle found a flat rock with a big hole in the middle of it, which still held water from the last rains. As she stood on top of it, she found out that she could see for miles and miles everywhere ...' (p. 38). Watching herself in the rock's pool and surveying the landscape, she has an unusual sensation of integration and control. Later, when they are forced to leave this home, Isabelle's parting from the landscape is granted an extensive passage, which unites the natural scene, loved ones and memory:

The next morning as the sun came up, Isabelle was standing on her rock looking over the land that had become so very much a part of her self and her brother. She looked down at the big old house. She closed her eyes to keep the tears away. In her mind she could see the verandah all round the house, with the flower garden in front, the weigela tree shading the square red water tank, and the big thorny mauve bougainvillea vine dominating the other corner, where the hens loved to lay their eggs.

After imprinting all the features of the house on her memory, she rests her eyes on the flowering wattles and the Christmas bushes 'waiting patiently to show off their blooms', on the mountain sides where some of the most beautiful of Australian wildflowers had their secret places, and on 'the sleepy river with its mirror-like surface reflecting everything that was growing along its banks'. Finally staring at her reflection in the waterhole, she is joined by the reflection of her brother. Although the foster parents are helpless to console their grief, 'Isabelle and Morris found comfort in the fact that, no matter what happened to them from then on, a part of these people who had from the start given them so much of their love would always remain with them' (pp. 42–3). The natural piety of this scene is a strong contrast to another, more formal religious scene in a mission church. On this occasion, she is struck by the stiffness of the congregation 'every one ... sitting as rigid as the statues in the church', and feels the same stiffness invading her body:

she had not had this feeling for many years, not since she had been discharged from the welfare. This sensation was difficult to explain to anyone who had not experienced it, but it was a feeling that there was always somebody watching what you were doing. It was a feeling that was deeply imprinted and hard to get rid of ... She knew then, that no matter how sincere white people might be in trying to help the Aboriginal people ... there was nothing that the white people could do for them. While ever Aboriginals remained under this inhuman fear of what Isabelle had come to call establishment authority, they themselves would be able to do nothing either. (p. 84)

The same fear of the powerful system hangs over Margaret Tucker's memories in her factual autobiography, *If Everyone Cared*. Born in 1904, Tucker was brought up in an Aboriginal settlement on the Victorian/New South Wales border. The Aborigines Protection Board of New South Wales is perceived by the children's parents as an intrusive, unpredictable deity, difficult to placate; her father's youngest sister had been removed from the family as had other children from parents on Brungle and elsewhere. A visit from representatives of the Board terrifies the children and explains why there are so few boys and girls on the settlement. Tucker's mother is presented as a singularly strong woman, although her father is mostly absent in an effort to earn a living. On this occasion the family closes ranks, however: 'I edged nearer to Father, who I felt for the first time really belonged to us and would help my mother protect us' (p. 82). Shortly afterwards the family's worst fears are realized when three of the daughters are physically taken from school and forced into the Cootamundra Domestic Training Home for Aboriginal Girls. The narrator at this time is thirteen. Another daughter in hospital is also threatened, but the police rescind this decree as capriciously as they enforce the removal of the other children: 'Mother simply took that policeman's hand and kissed it'. Tucker's description vividly recreates the terror and helplessness of the situation: the confused headmaster who fails to realize 'that Aboriginal hearts could break down with despair and helplessness, the same as any other human hearts'; the sympathetic ruses of his wife to stall the proceedings and inform their mother; the silently grieving group of Aboriginal women and old men who watch this familiar, uniquely humiliating ritual; the desperate attempts of the mother to save her children, literally holding on to them and only releasing them when it appears that they are threatened with shooting. 'I cannot ever see kittens taken from their mother cat without remembering that scene', comments the narrator. The mother is allowed to accompany them as far as Deniliquin, but is left to return as best she may without food or money. She is found by the road the next day, moaning and crying: 'They heard the sounds and thought it was an animal in pain'. At Cootamundra the train is met by the girls' father and uncle but they are powerless to help against the police. Typically, Tucker surrounds her story with accounts of other children removed from their homes: 'Some girls did not ever return'. Her story is also typical in that it is a series of separations and, after the move to Cootamundra, of treacherous events. Like Isabelle of *Karobran*, she becomes a pawn of the system, depressed to the point of suicide by its ignorant workings.

'Oh, it was hard to live to understand that life. I hated to think of that life', reflects Elsie Roughsey at one point, in her narrative, *An Aboriginal Mother Tells of the Old and the New*, which recalls her years in a dormitory mission on Mornington Island in the 1930s and 1940s. When the children are first placed in the dormitory no one tells them why they are there: 'no one ever mentioned to us and told or explained who was our relation by sister, auntie, uncle or other relatives, or friends. Everything was quiet' (p. 7). Unlike the other narrators, Roughsey retains some conviction that the white way must have some purpose, which has so far eluded her. Aboriginal law makes sense but the white system is mystifying: 'Perhaps it meant to do with law of being in the dormitory' (p. 21). Marnie Kennedy in *Born a Half-Caste* shares her impression of a senseless system: 'We feared our own laws too but we knew what we were punished for' (p. 24).

A more recent account, Glenyse Ward's *Wandering Girl*, which describes her experiences as a domestic servant in Western Australia in the 1960s, has the same background of inscrutable, silent power. Brought up in a mission, she has grown used to the fact that she is not allowed to see her mother, but her months of labour on a Western Australian farm are a painful exile. She is immediately cut adrift from the small world she has known and even her letters receive no reply as the priest dislikes the way she writes about her employers. Other girls who leave the mission are never heard of again and only determined efforts retrieve some of the old links. Meanwhile, the outside white world reveals itself as baffling and unpredictable; even its few unexpected acts of kindness are a form of cruelty since they sharpen her need for love or are performed so negligently they are acts of contempt. Deliriously happy when she is allowed to return to the mission for a holiday, Ward is bewildered when she is left to find her own way there. A later holiday on Christmas day is more a contemptuous dismissal than a treat.

Ella Simon's experience of silence in *Through My Eyes* emerges as more complicated. She is the victim of two kinds of shame, white shame that she is part black and black shame that she is part white. It is not until she is eleven that she discovers the identity of her white father and the discovery changes her entire world. Secure in the love of her grandfather, the relationship of father had seemed superfluous and she is told something of her mother who died young. The discovery coincides with the death of her grandfather and a time of severe struggle in her family. Like Patsy Adam Smith, she suffers the pain of illegitimacy and a new sense of not belonging. If some of her black relatives are uneasy in her company, her white ones, apart from her father, choose to ignore her existence completely. Homelessness even becomes a physical reality when she is forced to leave to live with unsympathetic relatives on the Barrington: returning there sixty-two years later she can still 'feel the loneliness; I could still remember lying there dreadfully homesick and listening to the cry of the curlews' (p. 49).

****

Everything went the white man way—quiet and lonely, also friendless.
(Elsie Roughsey)

If the white system is ominously silent about its purposes, it also seems bent on imposing a silent way of life on its subjects. Elsie

Roughsey's free style of language becomes lyrically expressive when she attempts to convey the contrast between the rich culture of the black way and the unnatural stillness of the white. Indeed, attempting to understand the contrast between the two ways after the white culture 'crept in . . . with all its different hard life', is one of the motives for her story. She describes the dormitory life as tough, sad, lonesome, quiet, dull, 'friendless of families' circle . . . hardly any happiness to make us feel were contented of everything nice being in the dormitory' (p. 23). It imposes 'frightness' and 'shyness', it replaces freedom with the padlocked door of the dormitory, meaningful laws with strict rules which have no coherence: 'All I knew . . . the rules. Not all things as I should have learnt, but rules' (p. 12). Laughter and fun have to be enjoyed out of sight of the missionaries. At the same time, the rigidity of white ways allows no room for black initiatives: 'hopeless if there is hope for you to get along with something new, for you to try and give it a go' (p. 86). During the war years when the children are released back into the tribal way of life, she discovers that the black way is less easy physically but that it is full of colour and interest. Best of all are the stories which their father tells around the camp fire; stories of good and evil, they make sense of the relationship between the tribe, the land and time.

Storytelling, dancing and singing are remembered with pleasure by nearly all these narrators. Ella Simon's sense of not belonging is assuaged by her grandmother's stories from the Bible and of the Dreamtime, which seem to have many similarities; Mumshirl recalls the happiness, laughter and music of her childhood and the talk of her grandfather which fills the night with meaning; Margaret Tucker remembers clamouring for stories of 'the olden times' and relays several that filled the children's imaginations with awe; Monica Clare's narrator describes the contrast between the free life with her father and the imposed silences of the 'home', broken only by sharp commands: there, the quiet makes everything unreal and she seems to be dreaming everything that is happening to her. Pearl Duncan's fondest memories are of 'yarning' around the fire, listening to her mother's stories of her childhood and her uncle's songs of his youth ('A Teacher's Life', p. 44). Most engaging of all are Glenyse Ward's memories of filling the empty mansion of her employers with lively tunes pounded on their piano and royally entertaining her friend, an elderly orchardist. If she is normally a shadow in this house, consigned to the kitchen and garage, she fills it with her personality when her employers are absent: 'As I ran my fingers over the piano keys, I felt real glad that I had some company. It was so much more fun!' (p. 94).

****

It was like a disease. (Margaret Tucker)

But the white silence has other more humiliating implications. It implies incomprehension, rejection, contempt. Stanner refers to the white tendency to regard the Aborigines as 'free goods of nature'; these narratives introduce the reader into the insulting experience of being classed as such a good. Marnie Kennedy, the most angry of these narrators, describes the stupidity of the white's self-fulfilling perception of the black; equating the Anglocentric with the human, the white could punish, destroy or ignore the black. The part-Aborigine, according to this binary assumption, inspired shame, fear and guilt, emotions which inevitably clung to the children themselves. 'This new breed the white man created is considered to be dangerous.' (*Born a Half-Caste*, p. 4). Kennedy clearly sees her childhood as a punishment: 'I am neither white nor black but of a new breed, to be punished along with our mothers for what we are'. On Palm Island in the 1930s, the hessian bag dress is both the first item of clothing given to the child and, along with a shaved head, a punishment dress; when tourists visit the island, the inhabitants are on display, much as the inmates of mental asylums in the eighteenth century: 'Captain Firth would throw lollies all over the ground and the white people would get a big kick out of watching us scramble for the lollies. That was part of the entertainment' (p. 15). Imprisonment, sexual segregation, solitary confinement, public humiliations, hard labour, meagre rations, and compulsory examinations for venereal disease, are regular features of this life which is structured by bells and padlocks: 'bell to start work, bell to stop, two bells at night'. Education is minimal and at the age of fifteen employment as a domestic 'under the Act' is the rule; 'I could never understand why Aborigines were sent to Palm for punishment, for something the white man created in the first place', Kennedy comments with conscious irony. Several narrators describe their distress when schooling is arbitrarily cut short, however good their school record, and others record the humiliations of working for whites, whose treatment grants them the status of domestic animals. Frequently locked out of her employer's house, underfed and underclothed, beaten, and often humiliated, Tucker discovers that even her physical suffering is not regarded as human, for the doctor declares that Aborigines have no feeling and that like animals their wounds just heal without any trouble. Ella Simon grieves over a deeper emotional hurt: prevented from attending her father's funeral by his white relatives, who had previously left his care entirely to her, she remembers the feeling of helplessness: 'I couldn't even stand by and just watch. I was still a secret that had to be kept from the world—something that was shameful, something whose very existence was distasteful' (p. 23). Like most of these narrators, Simon frequently comments on the impenetrable ignorance of the whites, which is more a matter of not wanting to know than not knowing: 'They don't *think* about what they're doing' (p. 168). And one of her saddest insights is that that this form of ignorance feeds upon itself: 'Nobody seemed to care. The Aborigines didn't care; and the whites didn't care about the Aborigines not caring about themselves' (p. 138). Elsie Roughsey has the same criticism: 'They are too much of careless of love towards each other' (p. 195).

****

We lived low and sad, calm people. (Elsie Roughsey)

Living within a group which had been confronted with a wall of silence for generations, these narrators all struggle with the experience of anomie, the paralysis of spirit, which white 'civilization', with its fatal propensity to invest the black race with its own sins, has often termed apathy. For these writers, finding the autobiographical voice is a proud achievement, a victory which helps to assuage the memory of all the times when the self was voiceless. In nearly every narrative, personal memories of aphony still trouble the mind, as does the consciousness of the general Aboriginal silence. As Pearl Duncan asks: 'What does an Aborigine do when his whole life style has been destroyed? He takes the line of least resistance, thus becoming an object of scorn and derision for the very persons responsible for his situation' (p. 54).

Several look back with remarkable frankness to a time when they internalized the white derision. Ella Simon is amazed in retrospect at her passivity in the face of the massive insult inflicted by her father's white relations. Margaret Tucker recalls her desperate stratagems to get food when she was employed as a servant: 'I feel awful when I think of those days and the thieving I was practising. God seemed far away as did . . . all my people' (p. 114). Glenyse Ward, on the other hand, saves her self-pride by deliberately taking from her employers those things they deny her. When she first arrives at the farm where she is to work, she is assailed by a barrage of reductive messages. The attack on her identity induces a feeling of panic at first: 'I couldn't quite focus my mind, or pay attention to her', 'I felt frightened as I didn't know how I'd keep my energy or strength of mind up', 'I was beginning to feel like a zombie, beginning to feel that my sanity was slipping'. Very soon, however, her spirit and even her sense of humour assert themselves. 'I sort of overlooked the situation. I could see the funny side of things.' Indulging her sense of the comic to the full, she exults in situations which secretly or semi-openly cock a snoot at her would-be authorities. Assigned to a tin cup and plate, she dines off the best china when her employers are away; prohibited from entering the palatial dining room, except to clean it, and denied a social life, she takes pleasure in entertaining a friend there and in imagining her employer's horror; bacon and eggs and other delicacies from the fridge heap her plate in place of the cheap alternatives she is relegated. Eating, in fact, becomes a way of assertion and there is an extraordinary emphasis on food and enjoyable meals. It is as if she tries to eat herself into notice, to obliterate the insulting assumption that she is a natural beast of burden and therefore should eat as a beast. Food incidentally, or rather its absence, figures largely in other narratives and several writers recognize and resent the subtle discipline of keeping children half-fed. On another occasion, Ward finds her employer's luxurious bedroom suite an irresistible place of carnival and disturbing its cathedral quiet is as much an act of satisfying rebellion as sensuous pleasure: 'The beautiful bedroom looked like a whirlwind hit it. I didn't mind. I was smelling so nice, it made me feel so good' (p. 87). Other rebellions are more open: directed to clean the inside of the car with Pine-O-Clean after she has been sitting in it, she vigorously hoses it out; granted an unexpected holiday, she hangs the soapy clothes on the line unrinsed: 'it looked as if it had been snowing'. Amazed at her skill in hoodwinking the family, she casts a half-wry, half-shrewd glance at the mission values which she has shrugged off: 'Being brought up in a strict environment I was never allowed to tell lies; but since I had been working there for her, I found myself really good at it' (p. 57). By degrees, she surmounts not only the effects of her employer's racism but the inadequacy of her mission upbringing: 'There was no looking back for me'. Enforced duplicity is an experience reflected in several autobiographies; Gladys's story in Sally Morgan's *My Place*, for instance, describes the necessity of lying for survival: 'Usually, I managed to get out of trouble by making up a good story, there were only a few occasions when I wasn't quick enough to think up something convincing ... We learnt it was better not to tell the truth, it only led to more trouble' (p. 264).

****

... with their noses to the ground and their arses in the air they hunted and destroyed everything in their path. (Marnie Kennedy)

Marnie Kennedy's words reflect a common response to the white culture, which to Aboriginal eyes appears to reflect an alien, bewildering value system. Colourless, violent, confused, it appears to many of these observers to be crazy, somehow askew from what is human and not even responsive to the needs of its own people. Kennedy is caustically witty about the craziness. The obsession with scouring, for instance, which appears to grip the administrators of Palm Island, scouring the soul with three visits to church on Sunday, and scouring the body with weekly doses of castor oil are explicitly equated: 'Lord, we must have been wicked people. Whoever sent us there thought we needed a good clean-out: inside and out' (pp. 8–9). Then there is the brass band, the *chef d'oeuvre* of Palm Island:

Their uniforms were khaki trousers with a red stripe on the legs and their instruments were shining, something Mr Currie was very proud of. He taught them to play and he drilled them. When they marched they never missed a step or played off key. Most of them could not read or write. (p. 10)

White morality on Palm Island is strictly sexual morality, a neurotic obsession with things of the body which ignores things of the heart: 'Alice, the cook, got herself into trouble . . . She was sacked, then married. Later, she died having the baby' (p. 20). Reflecting on this insane 'prison', where Aborigines are punished for being displaced by the whites who displaced them, Kennedy is not surprised that the superintendent finally went mad and killed his children. Her matter-of-fact description of the tragedy is similar to the treatment of the two world wars in other autobiographies; to the black observer, the wars appear no more than peaks of hysteria in a society that is consistently hysterical. Providing the Aboriginal with the opportunity of being killed in a new equality with white men, soldiering changed nothing when the soldier returned. Even citizenship was still denied. Mumshirl recalls the general feeling among Aborigines during the Second World War, the anxiety about men overseas and the feeling of relief amongst mothers if a son was in gaol and safe: 'Everybody seemed frightened of something around this time, and there was uneasiness everywhere, but somehow I always thought of it as somebody else's war' (p. 26).

Again and again, the Aboriginal writer questions the purpose of the toughness displayed by the white system. What possible reasons could the whites have for breaking up families? Education in the white way could not be the reason, for several narrators comment on the arbitrary break in their education imposed by the white system, and others are resentful that education was a euphemism for domestic service. Commenting on Facey's *A Fortunate Life*, Ivor Indyk remarks that his world is 'marked by dislocation and fragmentation, in which in the absence of established social structures, the family provides the only haven of security'.[10] For the Aborigines, matters were a great deal worse: the traditional tribal structures were destroyed, white social structures both excluded and condoned their exploitation and, most terrifying of all, the family was the chief target of attack.

Many of these narrators record their futile attempts to make the white system mean something, once they were separated from the Aboriginal group. The prison-like routines and practices of mission and training home are as bewildering to the retrospective observer as they were frightening for the child: comparing their nightly imprisonment in the dormitory to the caging of negro slaves shipped to the USA, Elsie Roughsey comments: 'I cannot understand why all these things had to be done in a hard way . . . today, I still just can't understand why it all meant . . . to be so tough with us' (p. 13). In her graphic way she puts her finger on the human values which the white system seemed intent on negating: 'Friendly humbleness of mankind was now gone or taken away from them. The new settlers thought these kind of things were no good' (p. 63). Ida West terms the white way as 'ignorant', 'as ignorant as the pigs from Schouten Hill' (p. 23). Both Mumshirl and Ella Simon criticize the whites for failing to abide by the teachings of their own religion. When Mumshirl's grandfather is dying, the parish priest refuses to cross the river, although he demands the same feat of his congregation every week; later she is refused communion by a priest, an act which alienates her from Christianity for many years. Ella Simon's white father is prevented by the Aborigines Protection Board from living at Purfleet with her, and is thus condemned to a lonely old age by his own laws. A more comical inconsistency characterizes the actions of successive managers of Purfleet. One, a soldier to his bootstraps, tidies up the entrance to the reserve and erects an arch on which the new title proclaims itself in 'big, daring letters'. 'It read "Sunrise Station". They even erected a flagpole!' The next manager had all this ripped down. 'We were at war then and he reckoned the new name was Japanese!' (p. 74). Elsie Roughsey compares the puzzling laws of the Europeans, which scare the blacks with their empty severity, and the tribal laws, which are even more severe but have purpose and meaning: 'My tribes' laws were so strict. You could not fool around with any of their laws . . . But that only helps to keep the law . . . runs straight and good for all to live as one good people on the island' (p. 183) And in every autobiography, the police are described as terrifying, eternal enforcers and messengers of bad tidings, potentially violent and naturally inimical to the black way: Elsie Roughsey remarks of them: 'Uniforms within the law is where they can hide and be unfair with justices' (p. 209) and Margaret Tucker describes the invariable response of her family to flee at the sight of a helmet: 'we had reason to believe that contact with anyone in those uniforms was not good for us' (p. 20).

****

. . . everything went too, with them, left us all with the life of sadness and unhappiness . . . only memories now you can see and think of.
(Elsie Roughsey)

Elsie Roughsey is the only one of these narrators to recall anything of the tribal life and she can only piece together a patchwork of fragments. None of the narrators is in full touch with the old culture, as are the women in Diane Bell's *Daughters of the Dreaming*, but all are aware of loss. Apart from Roughsey, the life they know before the mission or the training school is the life of the settlement or the fringe-dweller. Even so, it compares well with the coldness of the white way, notwithstanding real physical hardships. Listening to stories around the campfire, they are aware that these stories are precious relics of what was once a network of informing myth and magic. For some, such as Pearl Duncan, experience of the black culture is ironically dependent on the researchers of white academics; others, such as Roughsey, are stimulated by the new interest in Aboriginal culture or, like Tucker, keenly interested in archeological finds which restore their people's lost pride. 'We had to learn both ways, more so than the whites because we had to live with white people', comments Ida West, 'I only wish I could have learnt more about our own culture. Some of that has come back to us, and we're not ashamed of it now' (p. 46). Roughsey sometimes seems to feel that the two cultures were incompatible, that co-existence was impossible:

I have seen, met with this strange life amongst my people. Feelings of mixed life have changed into a drifting clouds . . . good and bad laws could not really settle in the hearts and minds of our people. Then for all times we had to cling to the laws of an European. (p. 185)

And her narrative is largely a threnody for the lost, ritually-structured way of life: 'The customs and laws and cultures are gone with the greatest people of the past' (p. 57). Happiness in Roughsey's story is a comprehensive term, signifying cultural cohesion, religious awareness, tribal relatedness, finely regulating tribal law, the commonality of distinctive language; in a word, wholeness. When the old languages and legends died and the great singers and dancers who trod and sang their meaning were gone, the 'real thing that kept up the Spirit of the tribes' died with them: 'Happiness was gone, many troubles took its place' (p. 181). Marnie Kennedy is almost as expressive: 'Their stories were so beautiful and had a meaning and depth but are now ashes, lost forever' (p. 5).

Piety is often a word applied to cultural loyalty; for these writers, the term shades easily into religious piety. Of all the gifts of the white culture, it seems that Christianity is the only one perceived as valuable, even though Christian and white ends are often explicitly described as incompatible. For Tucker, Simon and Mumshirl, religious faith is a fundamental support and all three find a common meaning in the traces of Aboriginal religion and the Bible. As the editor of *Through My Eyes* comments, 'Ella had a clear insight into the ways her Christian beliefs were built up from Aboriginal lore'. Roughsey has the closest contact with a spiritual dimension, and an appreciation of the reality of fable, but most relate experiences which an Anglo-Saxon writer would avoid or rationalize. Ida West describes the other-worldly emanations provoked by the evil doings of the past on Flinders Island; Margaret Tucker is conscious of the presence of the 'Good Spirit' in her life; Mumshirl's religious experiences include a visitation from her grandfather on her wedding day. Like Sally Morgan's grandmother, these women imply that the 'white fella only believes what he sees. He's only livin' half a life', and like her they imply spiritual powers unrecognized by the white culture. If Daisy believes she has healing powers, which cure her daughter's polio, Elsie Roughsey corroborates her belief, relating many stories of healing and warnings from the spirit world:

It's something that you see but you really cannot explain. So it's a skill of healing from dream land, given to them while they are asleep. So many things to man are given in dreams. While he sleeps he receives dances, songs, bad things in dreams that mean something awful will happen to him or his loved ones. Then again, good luck will be given to him. All that is told to him from someone who has died, so he can help others to save others, warn others of some evilness of mankind life that will or can hurt you . . . Not all receive these gifts, only very few of them. (pp. 73–4)

White Australian literature is predominantly secular and concerned with the material world, but Aboriginal literature in English fluently unites the natural and the spiritual. In this as in so many other characteristics, Sally Morgan's *My Place* is typical.

****

In time to come/There will be no white man/There will be no black man/They will all be one. (Verse quoted by Ida West)

All autobiography inevitably invokes an ideal, an implied absolute perfection of self and world. Whether the narrative is nostalgic or naturalistic, the author's apprehension of a gap between actual and ideal is embedded in the interstices between self and other; indeed, the more bitter or disillusioned the mood, the keener the implied vision of a better condition. This common phenomenon is particularly marked in black writing. All these autobiographies of Aboriginal women are concerned with a common, impossible ideal, the ideal of relatedness. 'Care' is a ubiquitous and complex term in these texts, connoting the ideals of respect, consideration, understanding and nurturing which have been so glaringly lacking in white responses to the blacks. Aching for the lost kinship systems of the past and yearning for harmony between black and white, these women write as mothers whose identities are bound up with their nurturing roles. Stanner remarks on the persistent inability of the whites to grasp that the Aborigines have always wanted 'a decent union of their lives with ours' on terms which would allow them to preserve their own identity[11], and certainly for these women union is the ideal, not separation. Ironically, this has irritated some white reviewers, who distrust any suggestion of compromise and are happiest with black power militancy. But one of the most attractive features of these narratives is that however grim the suffering and humiliation, there is a constant referral to another, more human standard; the protest is a protest at the lack of feeling, at the stupidity of prejudice rather than its wickedness. It is rare that individuals are presented as thoroughly malevolent even though their actions are maleficent. Again a comparison with Facey's *A Fortunate Life* is instructive. Facey is also concerned with simple human values, specifically the value of kindness, but he accepts the variegated nature of relationships fatalistically: 'We used to share and share alike but now I feel as if I have been graded down to the level of the dogs. Well, that is the way of life, one day a manager, next day a tramp'.[12] The female Aboriginal autobiographer has a clearer picture of alternatives and a stronger didactic purpose. Possibly this derives from the persistence of women's responsibility for harmony in transitional society. Diane Bell comments that in settlement life, 'women's role in the domain of emotional management is, like their role in the maintenance of health and harmony, truly awesome'. Responsible for the complex relationships between people and land in tribal society, women in settlement society, according to Bell, have taken over the role of resolving conflicts and restoring emotional and physical harmony.[13]

Once again, Elsie Roughsey is an expressive interpreter. In the old way of life 'Everybody were real people', 'The old tribe really meant relationship, and loved each other as their own families', whereas now relationship is discounted. Describing modern life as 'the reckless life', Roughsey enlarges on the 'unhappy, sad, tired feeling' that persists, 'people don't know how to be happy and be friendly, with no respect or politeness'. Like other narrators, she describes the incapability of whites to grasp the intimacy of kinship-bonded social life:

I know many white people have someone to call them friend. Some also have a kinship with us. But really, I often thought if the whites really know the love that a black fellow has for them. To me, I think they really don't understand our way. They think we just call them this and that, but really have no idea that my people want to love you as their own. (p. 196)

As for the other writers in this group, it is extraordinary how the emotional dialectic repeats itself; if the nadirs of experience are always associated with loneliness, separation and neglect, the high points are experiences of community, respect and care. What is more, the life is seen as having or not having meaning as it has or fails to have relationship; notions of success as equating with social, business or career success are even more notably lacking in these texts than they are in white female autobiographies. Margaret Tucker is typical in that she exchanges the happiness of the group for the loneliness of exile in the white world. She is anguished when her white employer withholds a letter from her mother and experiences feelings of acute relief when she discovers it under the woman's mattress: 'I felt strangely comforted now I knew where the letter was' (p. 114). Her memory of a brief, unexpected visit from her mother during this period of exile is still overwhelming: 'Oh the joy, I can feel it as I write. I experienced it. I kept thinking how? how did she find me? How did she manage it?—all this I thought in the space of a second. As I think of it now, I cry ...' (pp. 121–2). The visit heightens her loneliness to intolerable levels, however, and she contemplates suicide: 'I was like a crazy person'. Unable to muster the courage to throw herself under a passing train, she takes rat poison. When she is reunited with her sister, she discovers that her similar experiences have led her to keep a gun; if she was beaten again, she intended to shoot herself. Two women figure in Tucker's narrative as polar opposites: the strong, supportive figure of her mother, renowned for her dedicated care of animals and people, and the neglectful, viciously cruel white employer, who locks her out of the house on the coldest of days, aggressively frustrates her pathetic attempts to hoard a little extra food and consistently treats her with contempt. Desperate as Tucker's memories are, she is determined to 'forget . . . not to keep [them] sizzling in my heart', and never tires of elaborating on the meaning of her title, *If Everyone Cared*.

The title of Monica Clare's novel *Karobran* is similarly didactic. Signifying togetherness, it encompasses the book's emhasis on kinship and harmony between the races. If the narrator is unable to locate her father and brother, discovery of some black relations who acknowledge her as 'Dave's girl' eases 'the ache she had carried in her own heart for so many years' (p. 95). Although the conclusion of this novel is probably strained to fit the socialist ideals of its editors, the theme of an ideal togetherness in which whites allow humanity to blacks is dominant from the first.

Both Mumshirl and Ella Simon record special relationships with grandfathers and both men are revered for their caring qualities. 'My Grandfather was different', writes Mumshirl, 'To him, I was special. He cared about everybody too, but he especially cared about me . . . I feel I lived my early years always under his watchful and loving eyes' (p. 2). Reflecting on her handicap of epilepsy, she is certain that it was God's way of directing her to a life of caring: 'all people help each other at some time or another and . . . everybody really owes everybody' (p. 12). Ella Simon recalls several instances of her grandfather's selfless dedication to his family and dates her period of intensest misery from his death. Sent to stay with unsympathetic relations on the Barrington, she undergoes a time of acute loneliness and feelings of worthlessness. Like other narrators, she selects the memory of an animal's pain to express her feelings of ignominy and alienation: in Margaret Tucker's case the animal is a new-born lamb, trapped in a burrow and ignored by a white squatter; in Alfred's story in Sally Morgan's *My Place* it is a devoted dog, which is callously destroyed by its master after an accident; in Ella Simon's it is a pig she has befriended which is slaughtered: 'I thought I was killing the only friend I had left in the whole wide world. I had to hold its hind legs while he slit its throat. The pig screamed and so did I' (p. 50). On the other hand, the dedication of an admittedly severe white teacher is a delightful memory: 'I used to appreciate her *efforts* at trying to help me. It was important that someone was trying to do something for you' (p. 44). Rejected by both blacks and whites, and conscious of her grandmother's near death as a baby, when she was left by her tribe to die, Simon has more reason than most to welcome the erosion of some of the old barriers. And like Mumshirl and Margaret Tucker, she sees her own suffering as a necessary preparation for her future life of caring:

I've suffered in life. I feel I have. And because of that I've been able to visit all those different kinds of people in different kinds of hospitals and, yes, gaols, and been able to understand their 'sicknesses', what they were really feeling. (p. 172)

The treatment of relatedness in these texts has two further common characteristics. As might be expected, the nuclear family is strikingly absent; parents are often important but grandparents are sometimes more important and aunts, uncles, cousins and other more distant relations are valued. Children pass from one set of relations to another, usually quite happily, and always the memory of living as an extended group is one of the most precious. Love, or the experience of finding a mate, on the other hand, is barely raised. Ella Simon elides over an unhappy love affair, Mumshirl describes her large wedding but passes lightly over the breakup of her marriage, Monica Clare omits all treatment of her unhappy marriage and both Marnie Kennedy and Margaret Tucker frankly describe their decision to marry as an escape route; for the former it represents an escape from the 'Act', for the latter it is an opportunity to enter white society. Although Elsie Roughsey refers affectionately to her husband, Dick, she refuses to sentimentalize the marriages made by her friends in the dormitory; as the only legitimate way of leaving that life, marriage had little to do with Western notions of romance. White female narrators are also sometimes hesitant to deal with sexual love, but the blanket suppression of the topic in black narratives says something of the perceived need to merge the individual in the general; it is the group which matters to the black female writer.

****

Both Fanny and Lulu were excellent house girls. (Thonemann/
'Bunny')

All these narratives are Anglicized to a greater or lesser degree.
Addressed to the white reader, they are tender of white sus-
ceptibilities and it may be some time before the Aboriginal equivalent of a Rosa Cappiello can find a voice and an audience. They have
also been formally Anglicized, with varying degrees of skill and tact.
As the editors of *Fighters and Singers* comment, editing an
Aboriginal autobiography is a delicate balancing act; excising
sections or re-shaping the narrative to fit European expectations
jettisons the style which is part of the story and impoverishes the full
flavour of the lived life.[14]
   This is an insight which the editors of Elsie Roughsey's manuscript
have obviously perceived and their editing is an attempt to retain the
rare qualities of the work, the unusual, individual flow and expression. Ella Simon's editor has also remained faithful to the oral
style of telling that is characteristic of Aboriginal culture. Even so,
her 'Afterword' is an exposure of some late instances of white
arrogance which intervened between Simon and the telling of her
story. Mumshirl and Bobbi Sykes's collaboration is an interesting
Aboriginal replication of a form common in white female autobiography but so far absent in white male writing. Monica Clare's
autobiographical novel, which was edited after her death, shows signs
of editorial interference. The last section of the novel, in which
Isabelle fortuitously discovers a common fellowship with the white
working class after a chance meeting with strangers in a city milk bar,
rings false, although the main editor, Jack Horner, comments that
the omission of Clare's unhappy marriage and loss of her daughter
accounts for the elisions here. Clare's voice is a distinctive one,
nevertheless, as are the other voices of these autobiographies, and in
nearly every case of an oral account, taped by a white editor, the
actual writer keeps successfully in the background.
   If editors have been on the whole tactfully aware of their
responsibilities, white reviewers have sometimes fallen into the trap
of insensitivity; hypersensitive to any traces of 'Uncle Tom' attitudes,
reviewers have also objected to the retention of non-standard
English. Pidgin English in particular is sometimes regarded as a
corrupt language, which should be 'translated' into an Aboriginal
language or into standard English. The eccentric lyrical power of
Elsie Roughsey's autobiography and the appropriateness of its discontinuous form as a vehicle for her style of free-ranging meditation,
however, are enough on their own to defeat such strictures. Listening to the Aboriginal voice is an education in empathy which
requires the suspension of many European literary assumptions.

By far the worst case of editorial manipulation is W. E. Thone-mann's *Tell the White Man*, published in 1949. Claiming to be the life story of a woman of the Mungari tribe who lived near The Elsey station, it strives hard to represent the black point of view, but is hopelessly bogged down in the Anglocentric and gendered prejudices of its time. Recorded by W. E. Thonemann, managing partner of The Elsey with thirty years' experience of the Aborigines, the narrative is ostensibly the story of Buludja or 'Bunny'. According to Thonemann, Buludja conceived the idea that her story should become a book to be read by white men and told 'true fellow and no gammon' (p. 16). If the narrative's anthropological content is mildly boosted by an introductory note by A. P. Elkin, its sympathetic approach is endorsed by a brief note from Mrs Aeneas Gunn. Nevertheless, the editor unwittingly betrays his manipulation of the story in his statement that 'All the events are authentic and based upon historical and anthropological research, the records of white men and the memories of the blacks'. Interestingly, Elkin appears to recognize the distance between this narrative and one that might be told in the future; conceding that 'telling the story through a native' was a good idea, he anticipates that 'One day . . . an Aborigine will write a book in his own language or in English. On that day we will learn much—about our ignorance and conceit' (p. 9).

Thonemann's book can by no means be admitted into Aboriginal literature, but it is historically interesting in that it illustrates the difficulties faced by the most consciously sympathetic of white men in understanding the Aborigines. Sensitive to the destructiveness of the white civilization for the blacks and even favouring the Aboriginal culture at some points, Thonemann is nevertheless unable to cut the paternalist cord. Like Mary Gilmore, he has an historian's interest in the black race and a collector's pride in knowledge of their customs; but the radical leap in sympathy, which would allow him to experience alienation as Sally Morgan experiences her grand-mother's, for instance, is beyond him.

The black criticism of the whites which he allows 'Bunny' is either so general as to be completely toothless, or is an indulgent record of the quaint reactions of wild blacks to the sophisticated technology of white society. A great deal of space, for instance, is allotted to their comical reactions to the coming of the 'Red Devils' or motorbikes, and other interpretations of black thinking are implicitly dismissive. The chapter titles ('Tribal Divisions', 'Native Customs', 'Modern Tribal Conditions') and the terms ('piccaninnies', 'lubras', 'boys') are obvious reflections of the author's limitations. One chapter, 'A Royal Visit', is devoted to the visit of the Duke and Duchess of Gloucester to The Elsey, a visit which inspires the Muranji tribe with a seemly loyalty. In 'Tribal Divisions', Thonemann appears to forget his black author completely as he delves into the subject of skin groups, illustrating his discussion with diagrams. On another occasion, his description of the public hanging of a tribal chief is presented through the eyes of a white settler preoccupied with deterrence. And on others he parades his enlightenment as he unwittingly undermines it. Castigating the whites for their ignorance of black customs, for instance, he reminds them that the sexual favours of 'lubras' belong not to themselves but to their husbands:

Often the white man takes a black lubra from her own boy for himself, and escapes punishment. Sometimes the white man not only steals the lubra for his own satisfaction, but, which is worse, gives her a present in return. How little he understands that the lubra belongs to some native whose duty it is to protect her, and that any present should be given to him and not to his lubra. (p. 64)

Allowing 'Bunny' to watch initiation rituals in secret and to recall in detail the activities of the white men in the area, he conducts his reader on a Cook's tour of the black culture. Only at the end, as 'Bunny' sadly leaves for a leper's colony, does her voice find a place in the narrative. For the 1980s reader, the account is patently a piece of gross ventriloquism.

****

My Place

Sally Morgan's *My Place* is the most literary of this group of narratives. A younger contemporary of Glenyse Ward, Morgan came late to her Aboriginal heritage and suffered the indignities of her race more vicariously than personally. For the white reader familiar with Aboriginal autobiography, her book has a marvellous comprehensiveness. On one hand, it resumes the themes and preoccupations of its predecessors and retrieves the experiences of two previous generations of Aboriginal women; on the other, it is more than the means of the reader's rediscovery of white culture through black eyes—it shares and even orchestrates that rediscovery. Morgan's dramatic search for her heritage is a personal one, but the poignancy of her discoveries has a broad cultural relevance, which has often led reviewers to compare the book to Albert Facey's *A Fortunate Life*. If the latter is seen as a microcosm of man's historical experience of Australia, it is wonderfully appropriate that a woman's narrative should express the recessive experience of the black Other.

A major ingredient of Morgan's success is her creation of a distinctive and credible narrating 'I'. Blessed with a discomfortingly observant nature and a strong sense of self, the Sally of *My Place* is a born leader. She is instinctively rebellious and non-conformist, sceptical of authority and, on the whole, confident of her scepticism; almost totally innocent of pretension, she has a healthy interest in the physical and the earthy, while her fertile sense of humour gets her over many a rough passage. While she is still in primary school, she makes an important discovery about herself, when a painful bout of rheumatic fever teaches her that she is 'strong inside': ' "Don't worry, Mum", I said confidently, "I'll survive" ' (p. 64). Shame is an emotion that Sally has to struggle to understand and thus it is entirely characteristic that her belated discovery of the family's Aboriginal heritage inspires her with keen interest, whereas her younger, more streetwise sister has long nourished a secret dismay.

In one sense, though, and at a deeper level, Sally has always known her origins. Her instinctive values and aversions are the traditional Aboriginal ones. She has, for instance, always known that she is different from the other schoolchildren: 'They were the spick-and-span brigade, and I, the grubby offender' (p. 26). Retrospectively for the reader and for Sally, certain familiar school experiences take on archetypal overtones: the child, disgraced by a smelly accident and by the grubby contents of her desk or loudly protesting at the departure of her parent ('I stood firmly rooted to the bitumen playground, screaming and clutching for security my spotted, plastic toilet-bag and a Vegemite sandwich' p. 18) is a small repetition of black anomaly in the white world. The rejection of the rule-ridden school is sustained. Contemptuous of this 'factory' or 'army', which depends on bells, boredom and regimentation, Sally chooses the more interesting world of home, swamp and garden: 'I always felt better inside after I truanted' (p. 87). Like Glenyse Ward, she resists reduction by cocking a snoot at the self-important routines of the white system:

Jill, Billy and I loved rude songs . . . Billy beat on his old tin drum and Jill and I pretended to blow army trumpets. I could play reveille, too. By placing a piece of paper tightly over a comb and blowing on it, I could produce a high pitched, farty sort of sound that I could then manipulate into a recognizable tune. (p. 24)

And like Marnie Kennedy, she finds authority's prudery inexplicable; asked to draw her parents, she does a magnificent life study of them, much to the discomfort of her teacher. She also resembles other Aboriginal narrators in her love of the natural world, especially as it is interpreted by her grandmother, and in her enjoyment of yarning around the fire: 'There was something about an open fire that drew us all together. We felt very secure in front of an open fire' (p. 74). Here the ritual is unconscious, but as in the other narratives, it is perceived as a ritual survival. Sally is also characteristic in her valuing of the imaginative and the spiritual; rejecting the limited, primly conventional school readers, she opts for a book of fairy-tales: 'I knew fairy tales were the stuff dreams were made of. And I loved dreams' (p. 77). Later, dreams play an important role in her quest for the people of the past and forge an even closer bond with her spiritually sensitive mother. And even as a small child, she invests great value in relatedness. Whereas the white children avoid their brothers and sisters at school, Sally's stick together according to their perception of the family as the most important thing in the world. As with numerous innuendoes in this narrative, the full resonance of a schoolmate's criticism, 'Aah, you lot stick like glue', is only realized retrospectively. The most ironic perhaps is the schoolchildren's reaction to the information that the family is Indian. The explanation satisfies them. If they cannot quite believe they are Indian, they are relieved that they have ceased to pretend to be Australian.

Sturdy as her sense of self is, it is not strong enough to resist all the cultural messages of evasion and self-effacement that she unwittingly receives from her mother and grandmother. She is surprised, for instance, by her reaction to the questions of authority figures: 'I felt incredibly stupid. I wanted to explain my feelings, but whenever anyone questioned me directly about anything, I automatically clammed up' (p. 79). When she visits a more affluent schoolfriend, she finds it impossible to talk to the girl's parents and when she is warned off another friendship by the friend's father who is also deacon of her church, she accepts his veto passively.

This experience of voicelessness is central to her quest for truth, however; she begins to understand how her own attitudes and feelings have been shaped and even fettered by her mother and grandmother. Although her grandmother retreats hurriedly into her shell of silence whenever the question of the past is raised, Sally realizes that the words of admission must be spoken if the family is ever to surmount the disabling shame. For Sally, knowing her place in the Aboriginal culture and living as a whole person are interdependent, as they must be for her family. Later, when the family has begun to break the bonds of silence, she is armed enough to defend herself against accusations of fraud from the Department of Education. Incidentally, this victory in assertion also measures the extent of her grandmother's imprisonment in traditional fears: terrified of Sally's confrontation with the authorities, the old woman worries that her name has been brought to their notice. If the sadness of her grandmother's situation becomes increasingly obvious as the past is uncovered, it is a sadness that the child has recognized from the first. Finding an outlet in drawing, she is surprised to discover that she always draws sad things: 'I was shocked to see my feelings glaring up at me from the page' (p. 45).

But the child's precocious understanding of adult sadness is not solely the fruit of her black inheritance. Living with her war-damaged father, she is initiated early into the inertia of hopelessness. The regular visits to the veterans' hospital are coloured with her appreciation of his despair, his existence on the other side of hope. Pushing through the heavy ward-doors, which image the heavy doors of the past she is destined to confront, she knows that this particular past is a dead end: 'There was no magic in The Doors, I knew what was behind them'. Anticipating that 'magically the view would change' if she first peers through their windows, she is always disappointed: 'All I accomplished was bruises to my knobbly knees and smudged finger-marks on the bottom of the glass' (p. 11). She is also acutely sensitive to her father's knowledge that he is finished: 'Just a frame, that was Dad. The heart had gone out of him years ago'. Frightening as his violent moods are, she understands the self-hatred they express: 'I found myself feeling sorry for Dad. He was so lost, I blamed myself for being too young' (pp. 43–4). The grandmother has retained an appreciation of the world's magic, but the war is a waking nightmare for the father, hence it is no accident that Morgan's first chapter compares the ghostly, shattered world of the veterans' hospital and Nan's faith in the dreaming of the garden and the magic of her special bird.

The war for Sally, as for so many other black narrators, is a supremely expressive image of the craziness of the white world; it has reduced her father to a ghost of himself and shattered the bodies of his fellow-patients: 'all of these men were missing arms or legs. Dad was the only one who was all there'. Visiting the hospital induces fears of a similar shattering: 'I felt if I said anything at all, I'd just fall apart. There'd be me, in pieces on the floor. I was full of secret fears' (p. 12). Above all, the war expresses the delusions of the white Australian way: 'It was a strange thing, because he'd told me how important it was to be free, and I knew that Australia was a free country, but Dad wasn't free' (pp. 20–1).

Sally's father is a powerful teacher, partly because she knows she is like him. She understands him more intimately than anyone else and it is she who is always sent to negotiate the family's return after one of his black drinking bouts. She recognizes his frustrated creativity and is not surprised to discover traces of his personality in her own; she owes her anti-authoritarian streak to him and, oddly, her determination. Events and incidents in this text often have a dual literal/figurative function, so that the father's reversal of the family van on a difficult mountain track anticipates her own reversal of their inner journey. It is one of the paradoxes of *My Place* that this broken father should so enable his daughter, in contrast to the impairments inflicted by the absent, powerful white men or man, who had fathered her mother and grandmother.

Another quirk is that it is the white culture which inadvertently provides her with a model. At primary school she discovers Winnie the Pooh, the character who is like herself in his self-confident individuality, obsessiveness and fascination with magic and adventure: 'In a way, discovering Pooh was my salvation. He made me feel more normal' (p. 45). Winnie the Pooh is an appropriate analogy in other ways. A remarkably resilient bear, with a great capacity for getting into scrapes, he tolerates the oddity of others as he tacitly assumes tolerance for himself. If the world frequently fails to live up to Pooh's expectations, he never ceases to believe that it will and much of his fun derives from his attempt to distil his tubby-bear dreams from unpromising ingredients. Morgan's Sally also lives according to individual co-ordinates, and her author similarly enjoys the comedy of her unconcerned confrontations with 'normal' society. An obsessive, she appreciates obsessiveness in others, whether it is the grandmother's determination to keep the children safe from fire by frequently hosing them down or her mother's affection for a dog with a mania for sniffing crutches. The fun, of course, lightens the book's inevitable sadness and retrieves it from self-pity, but it also subverts convention and welcomes the reader to a way of life which answers to a different drummer: 'My wedding day, the ninth of December, 1972, dawned bright and sunny. I nicked into town early that morning to buy a wedding dress' (p. 131). The humour also sustains the tone of optimism. We know that Sally, like Pooh, will finally succeed in her quest.

Nevertheless, her task is formidable, given the two-generation-deep silence that confronts her. The key, of course, is the grand-mother; her past is inevitably tied up with her daughter's and only she can fill in the yawning gaps, while her tacit shame, inherited by the succeeding two generations, must be challenged if not uprooted. As Arthur comments, Nan has lived too long with the shame that the white people inflict, and for Sally learning to understand that shame is a difficult but essential process. To her mother's demands that she 'make something' of herself, she infers that she must first remake all their identities: ' . . . it was me, and her and Nan. The sum total of all the things I didn't understand about them or myself. The feeling that a very vital part of me was missing and that I'd never belong anywhere' (p. 106). Both mother and grandmother have lived so long with fear and the necessity of self-effacing tactics, that they are terrified of disturbing the status quo: 'There's no point in digging up the past, some things are better left buried', comments Gladys (p. 99). The daughter is wiser than the mother, however, and Morgan delicately establishes the links between Sally's emotional growth and her mother's. Anxious for her daughter to make her way in the white world, the mother fails to realize at first that Sally's belonging depends on her retrieval of the authentic past; the more the mother insists on white ambitions and values, the more the daughter retreats, pulled back by the voiceless past. The mother's final admission that they are Aboriginal, on the other hand, releases the daughter into a freer destiny, which will embrace white opportunities. Even so, it is not surprising that an individual interest in schizophrenia should trigger her interest in psychology.

Cutting through the walls of silence is saddening, exhilarating and bewildering. Just when individuals appear to have achieved a new openness, further discoveries uncover yet another unadmitted wall. The silence of 'shameful' knowledge is compounded by white ignorance or negligence about the past. Thus Nan is wounded yet again by the refusal of the contemporary Drake-Brockmanns to acknowledge her paternity and Gladys is distressed to discover both the blank against her father's name on her birth-certificate and white explanations of *her* paternity.

Sally's quest is enormously assisted by her great-uncle Arthur, who agrees to allow Sally to tape his story. Arthur has the same parents as Daisy, but unlike her, he is proud of being black; indeed, he traces many of his difficulties to the fact that he is part-white. If he had been a full-blood the whites would not have removed him from his mother when he was eleven and sent him to a mission. His memory of that event recalls the memories of Monica Clare and Margaret Tucker; once again, the whites are silently ruthless, concealing the permanence of this separation, and once again, the white education proves nebulous: 'I thought they wanted us educated so we could help run the station some day, I was wrong' (p. 182). Arthur suffers extraordinary exploitation, cruelty and humiliations and yet his sense of self is strengthened rather than weakened. Like his great niece, he is aware of his inner strength: 'I'm like rubber, you can bounce me anywhere' (p. 183). Not only does he beat the white man at farming in the Depression, but he achieves several moral victories over his exploiters. What is more, he has a firm set of values, which he frequently invokes to measure the inhumanity of the whites. Contemptuous of those who would use him as a 'free good of nature', Arthur knows his own value as a Christian and stores a series of omissions in his memory: the woman who drinks lemonade in front of him on a hot day and never offers him a glass; the squatter's son who eats, smokes and drinks with bare-faced disregard for his hunger and thirst; the employer who fails to pay him for three years; the partner who opts out to join a white man; above all, the white upper class father, who never gives him anything except some old photos.

Arthur had attempted to intervene in Daisy's life in 1927 but had been prevented by her white family; now years later, he intervenes to help her granddaughter, who is in many ways his successor. If Arthur's story inspires a return to Corunna and the discovery of lost relations, it also prompts first Gladys and then Daisy to tell their stories. Gladys's is the familiar one of separation from her mother, loneliness and ill-treatment in a white institution, humiliations and indoctrination in shame. At the Home the children are taught never to speak openly of their Aboriginal heritage and the Drake-Brockmanns' treatment of her mother and herself is a continual lesson in inferiority, all the more devastating because it is negligent or tempered with a little careless kindness.

But it is Daisy's story which plumbs the depths of black humiliation. Tacitly denied her paternity by her white family ('that's the trouble with us blackfellas, we don't know who we belong to, no one'll own up'), she is used as feudal serf, except she lacks even the serf's security. Sent to work in the big house as a child, she is kept apart from her mother and suffers hunger and cold; the promised education proves to be domestic work and she remains illiterate. Like other autobiographers, she longs for the friendliness and culture of her own people; like Glenyse Ward she is given a tin mug instead of the beautiful china used by her 'family' and, like Margaret Tucker, she eats alone. Unlike them, however, she receives no payment:

Alice kept tellin' me, 'We're family now, Daisy'. Thing is, they wasn't my family. Oh, I knew the children loved me, but they wasn't my family. They were white, they'd grow and go to school one day. I was black, I was a servant. How can they be your family? (p. 334)

If Daisy retrieves some pride in her race, she is still defeated:

'You know, Sal . . . all my life, I been treated rotten, real rotten. Nobody's cared if I've looked pretty. I been treated like a beast. Just like a beast of the field. And now, here I am . . . old. Just a dirty old blackfella.' (p. 352)

Nor has she defeated the conspiracy of silence; refusing to reveal some of her secrets, she allows them to die with her. One of the strengths of this narrative is its Chinese-box structure, one box containing a replica of itself and so on. Daisy's story is sadder than Sally's but lest we should dismiss it as a historical, unrepeatable destiny, there is the repetition of her experience in the white man's hospital; reduced to a nothing in an earlier blood-letting, she is reminded several decades later of her subhumanity when she is exhibited to medical students.

In *After the Dreaming* Stanner suggests that we spare a moment to consider the theory of the Aborigines about *their* troubles with *us*, instead of concentrating as usual on *our* troubles with *them*. He sees two of their strongest ideals as to be 'one company' and to 'go level', to be one company on equal terms. The reader of these narratives is bound to agree with his conclusions and to experience the sort of radical revision that he recommends. Even more disturbing, though, is their challenge to the white culture; as Veronica Brady has suggested the question is 'ethical, existential, even . . . theological'.[15]

13

A Sense of Place

Time after time there rises before me that land of my childhood. I live again in the atmosphere of that early home, all in fresh and striking contrast with today. I play no part in the scene myself, but am rested and refreshed by the convincing sense of its extreme simplicity, its nearness to the sources of life and living.[1]

Alice Henry's description of the inward permanence of the childhood home is unfortunately not expanded in her memoirs, but her words express an experience that is common to many of the autobiographers who are the subject of this book. As we have seen, authoritative knowledge of place was the most important of the enabling rhetorical strategies for the nineteenth century autobiographer, and rediscovery of the childhood home has continued to be the major motive of female writers of the self. Indeed, many autobiographies begin from the premise that the place's identity is the co-subject and place and self are presented as interdependent expressions of each other. For the author like Franklin, Prichard or Hanrahan, whose childhood self has an authenticity that is later lost, the early home is invested with a special aura; it has, in Dorothy Hewett's words, 'the peace and harmony of the psychic garden'[2] and rediscovering its magic has resulted in some of the finest writing in the genre.

John and Dorothy Colmer in their recent anthology of autobiographical writing have concluded that 'the quest for personal identity involves asking fundamental questions about national culture and identity'[3], but the most striking aspect of the autobiographies studied here is that there are many Australias. Not only is 'national' inappropriate as a descriptive term, but even 'regional' is too prescriptive, for as George Seddon has commented, 'there is no such thing as an Australian environment', but rather 'a great variety of different places'.[4] Donald Horne in *The Education of Young Donald* describes himself as writing 'sociography', but it is doubtful if the Australia that the sociologist knows is available to the writer. As

Randolph Stow points out: 'this abstract "Environment" is really nobody's environment. It has no observer'.[5] Place depends on the 'logic of the perceiver's state of mind'[6] and certainly one of the most liberating features of women's autobiography is the diversity of their subjective Australias. Preoccupied with knowing the native place as one knows an intimate relation, these writers have rarely paused to consider the national import of their knowledge and are generally alive to the interdependence of place and mind. Eugénie McNeil, for instance, is surprised to discover in adulthood the received view of Sydney's 1890s according to the *Bulletin*, when she has lived through the same decade in a Bankstown with a distinctly European flavour. And the Sydneys of Nancy Phelan, Robin Eakin, Mary Drake and Christina Stead are only superficially recognizable as the same place. Kathleen Mangan's Melbourne is close to the Heidelberg Melbourne of her father's paintings, Ivy Arney's is enclosed in the narrow streets of Collingwood of the 1920s and patterned according to the social rhythms of a small working-class community, Maie Casey's is divided between several different psychic places.

The childhood place may be a house, rather than a locale, as in Kathleen Fitzpatrick's *Solid Bluestone Foundations* and Annabella Boswell's reminiscences. Indeed the importance of interiors is a vast topic in itself. For some autobiographers, such as Vera Adams, Jean Thorne and Marjorie Motschall, the natural home is a particular community, known almost exclusively by its human personalities and even more stranded in time than the past place. Memory of place inevitably involves contemplation of time, however, and numerous writers muse on the changes produced by the years, while identification with the destructiveness suffered by the landscape is a common theme. Some writers, such as Judith Wallace, Katharine Susannah Prichard and Mary Fullerton, perceive the bush nostalgically as a place of freedom, 'freedom to grow at one's own pace with no pressure to be "fashionable"', as Dorothy Hewett puts it.[7] Others, such as Jean Bedford in *Country Girl Again* and Betty Bell in *Mermaids Maybe, Flying Fish Never*, evoke the bush as stultifying and crude. Numerous others are preoccupied with defining the peculiar sadness and yearning implicit in the splendours of their particular 'ain contree', for contrary to the famous indifference of the Australian landscape, many writers perceive the land as emotional, and as speaking to the inner self. If for some authors their Australia has been a place of extraordinary challenge and excitement as for Rose Scott Cowen, Rosa Praed, Joan Colebrook and Della Edmunds, for others, such as Stella Bowen, Christina Stead and Mary Rose Liverani it has represented suburban suffocation. Then there is the vast question of the overseas culture which figures large in these autobiographies from Jane Watts to Joan Colebrook. In one sense the migrant experience is universal and even (or particularly) the Aboriginal writer writes from a position of strangeness. If no other writer has faced a task of the same dimension as Mena Abdullah's in *Time of the Peacock*, of assimilating the oppositions of the Indian Hindu/Muslim culture with Australia, the ambivalences of new and old have confronted the majority. Undoubtedly subsequent commentators on women's autobiography will want to pursue the subject of place, given the richness of the topic. This chapter can only indicate something of the diversity of the places rediscovered by autobiographers of childhood.

A particularly subtle rediscovery of the place of childhood is Barbara Corbett's *A Fistful of Buttercups*.[8] Corbett's early years have that idyllic Wordsworthian quality, often conjured up by the term 'childhood', if rarely in fact experienced. To describe such a childhood is to risk sentimentality, but this author successfully skirts the danger on the whole by a delicate treatment of time and by subtly modulating from the figurative to the documentary. Dora Creek, a broad backwater of Lake Macquarie in the 1920s and 1930s, is the place where the author grows up as the only child of struggling orchardists. Life moves slowly on the river and although memories of the latest external crisis are still sharp ('Memories of the war echoed in the songs we sang round the piano. Pale photos of lost brothers-in-uniform stood on sitting-room dressers, lawned with ribbons and medals') and the next crisis, the Depression, is imminent, old ways of living persist. The contrast is evoked in the first chapter, titled 'The Scene', between the groaning bullock teams, moving slowly through the town, the urchins swimming on the river bank and the city-bound train filled with people who belong to a busier, more homogeneous time. Dora Creek is a backwater in more ways than one; lush and lonely, it is 'sparsely peopled with characters who'd drifted in from other places, other eras'. In this first chapter, the narrative follows the widening circles of events impinging in a strange, tangential way on the life of the child, before returning to her particular place in time, the verandah of her home where she watches the rhythmic ritual of her father's ploughing. It is a pattern that is repeated.

But it is the intense, small, time-world of the child that fascinates Corbett—a seemingly permanent dimension of keen sensations, sharp emotions, sensual pleasures, deep mysteries. A chapter titled 'The Secret Garden' contrasts the immediacy of her imaginative, secret place, her garden on the cool side of the house, where 'the grass was deep and soft to lie in, with a rich earthy smell tinged with the honey sweetness of white clover', with events in the outside world—Burley Griffin creating his garden city, the opening of the new Parliament by the royal newly-weds. The trivial contends with the significant and defeats it:

On the swampy edges of *my* lake were little insect-eating plants, pinkish with flat daisy leaves clothed in long honey-dew hairs. To communicate, I'd carefully put my finger on one leaf and it would curl up and try to hold me. Lovingly. Sometimes I would feed it, definitely my friend, with a succulent mosquito or a struggling ant. Then the magic hours of adventure would drift and whirl around me. (p. 42)

Recreating the solitary child's sense of priorities, capacity for wonder and imaginative freedom, Corbett develops her dependence on the things and stories of the past. At Dora Creek certain relics of the past have been washed up on the shores: the old fisherman who was once sailing master to the Austrian royal family and lives in a humpy made of kerosene tins, the Livingstone sisters who inhabit a dilapidated Victorian mansion and still wear Victorian clothes. Like the pickled monsters on the shelves of the post office, these people evoke a time that is just as real as the external present, marked by the death of Phar Lap and the opening of the Harbour Bridge. The Maxwell family, for instance, lives in the sort of poverty which belongs to the early years of the previous century, at a time when jazz and the talkies have invaded Sydney. Meanwhile the family stories which fill in the long evenings around the kitchen fire evoke a legendary, exciting time, linking the backward-looking present of Dora Creek with the remoter past of migratory sea voyages and pioneering. Thus the narrator is perpetually dipping into various time levels, blending the personal time of the child with regional time, the remembered times of others and impersonal public time.

Death plays a major role in this narrative, sharpening the poignancy of the golden hours and retrieving nostalgia from sentimentality. Past deaths flurry the surface of regional memory—the legendary drowning of a pair of young lovers and the deaths of the recent war. The floods that Dora Creek suffers from 1927 sometimes bring the possibility of death close, while the mother's ill-health is a shadow on the family's happiness, occasionally developing into crisis-proportions. Another death, of the narrator's baby sister, is a daily reality since the child from the age of four is conscious of the dead child's presence as a playmate. But other deaths are humorous affairs, the comic demise of Paddy O'Flaherty, for instance, which is the subject of one of her father's stories and given a chapter to itself, and the death of one of the Livingstone 'girls', which is overlooked by her surviving sister and degenerates into a farcical episode after the neighbours take the affair in hand. Preoccupied with places and times that are somehow sheltered from outside 'reality', whether it is the childhood, sheltered by devoted parents, the secret garden, the quiet backwater, or the preserved nature of memory itself, *A Fistful of Buttercups* is saved from sticky nostalgia by a rich vein of earthy humour.

One of the most remarkable explorations of a past place is Eve Langley's *The Pea Pickers*.[9] When the book was first published in 1942, it was enthusiastically reviewed by Norman Lindsay and Douglas Stewart, both of whom welcomed in Langley a kindred vitalist spirit, and was well received by the public. Apparently giving a new twist to the bush realist school of fiction, *The Pea Pickers* was valued for its lively comedy, its expressive style and above all for its fine appreciations of the Australian landscape. It was reprinted in 1943, went to its second edition in 1958 and its third in 1966. It is strange, therefore, that the book has made hardly a ripple in the general literary consciousness and has attracted only three significant essays, all of them recent and all attempts to come to grips with the posthumous enigma of Langley and her book.[10] Nor were the skeletal facts of her extraordinary life generally known until recently; as Harry Heseltine comments, the biographical record is 'pitifully thin' and it was only after her death in 1974 at the age of sixty-six that her obsession with Oscar Wilde and her solitary last years in a shack in the Blue Mountains became common knowledge.

Few prose writers have evoked the Australian landscape with such passion. Rarely a page of *The Pea Pickers* passes without a poignant insight or a keen reflection on the natural world, for Gippsland the region is sewn with minute stitches into the fabric of the novel. The scene of Langley's adventures as a pea picker in the mid-1920s, when she and her sister, June, adopted male clothes and male names, Gippsland is far more than background: it is character, field of action, myth, lover, talisman, ancestor, destroyer. For the pea-picking adventure is also a perilous personal quest, whose end is a discovery but not a liberation.

From the beginning, Langley is frank about her unconventional younger self. She knows she is a woman, but she should have been a man; she also knows that she is 'comical . . . but serious and beautiful, as well': 'It was tragic to be only a comical woman when I longed above all things to be a serious and handsome man'. She has a desire for freedom ('never to work') and she has a desire, amounting to obsession, to be loved: 'I suffered from it, as others suffer from a chronic delicacy of health. It haunted my sleep and impeded my waking hours' (pp. 3–4). Contradiction and duality are thus integral to her persona, and her adoption of the name Steve, along with male clothes, is an obvious symbol of her doubleness. But doubleness in Steve's case is not androgyny, nor even bi-sexuality, for neither gender identity is perceived as fulfilling. Once adopted, the male name and clothes are not discarded, since duality effectively imposes stasis on her personality, which, as I argue below, she appears to accept and even welcome. Constantly changing from the comical to the tragic self and from the male to the female self, Steve achieves a mercurial life which cancels out the possibility of growth or even change.

The narrator fails to mention the fact in this early analysis of her self, but her real passion is not freedom or love but time. Indeed time is the author of all her obsessions, implicated in her ambivalence about gender and her comic/tragic division. As the older Steve of the later autobiographical novel, *White Topee*, remarks' 'I thought of nothing but Time. Time was my passion'.[11] And in *The Pea Pickers*, her overwhelming desire is to escape the power of clock time. 'I don't want anything to leave a trace on me', she tells Macca, 'I want no change at all, in myself' (p. 105). Being of marriageable age and, worse, being reminded of the fact, is to be reminded that she is 'the victim of slow moving time' (p. 28). Longing to be 'joined to time', she hates an autumn evening because of its reminders of time's passing; 'I hated the day because the meaning of life was full in it, and richer than we could ever be. It retreated, taking with it that which it was intended we should know' (p. 40). Tiring of her passion to 'place a mad fantastic meaning on all things', she is aware that the 'unbelievable day' throws her presumably believable self and energy aside 'into limbo', wasting her and calmly setting her aside 'for destruction' (p. 165). 'Leave us alone, thing, time!', she cries as she exults in her love for Macca and on other occasions she literally tries to stop the 'unendurable' tick of the clock by taking the pendulum off the hook or punching the hands until they cease, 'bruised in their cruel theft' (p. 63). She identifies strongly with the European Romantic poets who have written poignantly of time and sees herself ideally as another Werther, a spirit 'who has been thrown aside by the vortex of time and is able to survey it with a free, clear eye'. Such freedom is quickly exposed as an illusion, however, and it is the experience of being sucked into time's maelstrom, 'tethered' to the movements of the earth and the 'male sun' or fixed in time's 'socket' (pp. 130, 137–8) which predominates.

Given such acute, existential anxiety, it is not surprising that the narrator should be preoccupied with youth, the past and the power of memory. Clinging to every moment in an attempt to distil its essence, she uses up her 'entire mind' in the effort to chain the present in memory. 'A certain grain of earth, a peculiar wind blowing, a look on your face, the very sole of my shoes, with their polished edges, haunts me. I am astounded by the intricacy of their being' (p. 176). She is appalled by the thought that 'all our self-importance is just self-preservation gone mad' (p. 176), and clings to memory as the single means of controlling time, of discovering coherence in 'oblivion's lunacy' (p. 41). On one hand, she is inspired by the power of mind to shape everything to itself, and on the other, terrified by the knowledge of its insignificance in an indifferent world. Thus she is transfixed in the time of the narrator of Tennyson's sonnet, 'Tears,

Idle Tears', forever savouring the sad pleasure of the 'days that are no more' and feeling the 'slow tears rise'.[12] 'All my years shall be dedicated to mourning for our youth', she tells Blue (p. 175) and she is frequently conscious of the way that her memory-making intervenes between herself and the now: 'O God, to stay the flow of time. How could I be happy? Even in that far youth, secure in it, I was crying, "You are passing, passing. I shall soon be old and this will be no more"' (p. 55). The opening theme of disinheritance and exile from the promised land of Gippsland is thus a perfectly appropriate backdrop for this narrator; it is inevitable that she should feel the force of her mother's memories of the old days, that she should try to emulate the male personalities of the 1880s, even that she should take the name of a doomed young outlaw, Steve Hart. The sadness of the national legend infuses the personal despite the contradictions of gender.

Gippsland in the event fails to measure up to Steve's prevision of it as a mixture of Henry Lawson and her mother's stories, but she quickly peoples it with her own myths and characters. Every return home is a time of consolidation, fixing the incidents, landscapes and people of the latest excursion into the amber of memory, while the phrases and jokes of past forays become a stock of delightful lore. If the present is forever transforming itself in the mill of time into the remote past, nothing ever happens just the same again, and perhaps even memory may prove unreliable, the shared legend of quips and phrases is a reassuring bulwark.

In all the narrator's confrontations with time, the landscape of Gippsland is intimately involved. Savouring its beauty is to experience its strange melancholy: 'all about was the silence of the Gippsland bush, the triumphant silence, the hypnosis eucalyptean, giving me indolence and dreams and sorrow for I knew not what' (p. 26). A spray of orange blossoms blowing 'clear and sharp' hurts the heart with the wildness of its perfume (p. 64), an 'awful sadness' hangs over the hillside, rusty with ferns, 'it is living and suffering and breathing out despair, quivering with it' (p. 135).[13] But the bush is more than passively melancholy; at times it intersects almost aggressively with Steve's personal preoccupations. It is a constant reminder of time's passing and the relative impermanence of the self:

In the twilight ... mother Australia laid hold of me; she, with her twigs around the gate, thin and aromatic they smelt; she, with her big white chips sliced from trees that had been ringbarked years ago, with her sad twilight, brown, outward curving, full of dry smells and the first star. Desperately in the agony of brief human flesh I laid hold of her and mourned, while I was young, that I must grow old; and wept, while I was free, that I must marry and bear children; and was maddened to think that, while I lived, I must die. (pp. 74–5)

Its beauty crystallizes the beauty that makes the self long for immortality: wattle is 'so golden and fluffy soft that I felt as though my eyes were hands, that grasped and felt it, pressing it hard and cruelly to crush it into a mass that would end desire' (p. 281). Clouds and stars declare the self's exclusion from 'the rites of the hours' and at times the bush becomes a place of fantasy that mocks the human with its inhumanity: 'The long clay road, in its dampness, was like the frozen floor on which little Kay walked in the palace of the Snow-queen, and on the black and hairy legs of the gum-trees, the small beads of red sap showed' (p. 40). Steve is nothing if not inconsistent in her response to the bush, seeing it as offering and denying immortality, attempting to shape her life, declaring her irrelevance to the scheme of things, rejecting, welcoming, promising meaning and withholding it. Even so, it is far more indifferent to the self than friendly. As the bell at Moe foretells, at the beginning of each journey into Gippsland, 'love is not there ... nor is time to be recaptured ... O come not again to Gippsland! Return not, lest she give you sorrow that will bear you down even unto the grave! Give her farewell forever if you are wise!' (p. 182). On other occasions, the wattle bird warns Steve to go back, a message that she accepts, even if she is unable to obey it. At the beginning of her quest, she is implicitly rejected by a kiss from Kelly, which is also a kiss from 'the earth of Gippsland': 'while I endure I shall bring to me and send from me, lovers, wives, sons and daughters unending. But you, I do not need' (p. 39). And at the end, she reflects that she is doomed to repeat the dispossessed destiny of her mother: 'I am nothing to Gippsland; I just wander through her, being hurt by her and used by her in menial toil' (p. 300). Beautiful, wild and challenging though this, her ancestral home, is, it constantly evokes the unloved, existential loneliness of the spirit: ' "I am unloved," I cried, and ran scream-ing out of sight ... down the soft dry grass; leaping naked, crying, sobbing, cursing and dancing in the terror of the lonely red morning' (p. 130).

At times, on the other hand, the landscape appears to be on the edge of meaning. Since 'nothing is empty or barren, no one thing walks alone' and even the 'tender clouds ... brush against the sky and lip it most gracefully' (p. 283), is it not possible that the self will eventually be loved? Gazing into the sky-filled water, she fancies that in its movements 'lay the whole secret of life. In a moment, while I watch, all will be divulged'. But disappointment inevitably succeeds: 'never, never did the angel descend and ripple the pool' (p. 211). Or the range of mountains staring down into her eyes, begs her 'to cling to it and follow it, none other, pleading that it had a mystical "Yes" which it would one day shout to me, so bringing me to blend with it forever' (p. 235). At another moment, however, the ranges make the heart ache 'with their aloofness, with desire for their ungraspable forms, crumbling in grey, blue and purple against the sky' (p. 266).

Steve, in fact, is obsessed by 'ungraspable forms'; on one hand preoccupied with the otherness of the landscape, on the other she is aware of its dependence on mind, for Gippsland can only live in the eye of the observer. The thought offers her no consolation, however, and if she finds inspiration in fusing mind and landscape, she is always conscious of the tenuous nature of her imaginings:

... with sorrow I saw that these things scorned me, and in the scorning almost denied themselves being.

For I had brought to the country of Gippsland a great marking power which held and judged all that I saw there, and any overturning or dismissing of that power by those I found saddened me, for it meant that they stayed outside my strength. (p. 15)

Just as she has a serious, handsome male self, that is constantly contradicted by a comical female self, her dreams of ideal harmony are constantly contradicted by more mundane reflections. In many ways she veers between the typically male pattern of responding to landscape and the female pattern as Annis Pratt has defined them. Drawing on male and female *Bildungsromane*, and extending the insights of Simone de Beauvoir, Pratt concludes that the male hero tends to see the landscape in terms of symbols, and as a vehicle of inward states of being, a female kingdom to be known, usually through love for a woman; he is characterized by a 'living pour soi', a desire to transcend the natural world and to make it submit to his mind. The female hero, on the other hand, tends to see nature as co-extensive with herself, and is preoccupied with immanence and 'living en-soi'. 'Communion with the authentic self, first achieved ... in early naturalistic epiphanies, becomes a touchstone by which she holds herself together in the face of destructive roles proffered to her by society'.[14] Although Langley's Steve longs for immanence, and frequently steeps herself and the reader in the landscape's sensuous glories, she is also characteristically bent on appropriating the land and bending it to her personal needs. And she never tires of reflecting on the symbolic potential of natural things: trees express 'the vowelled moaning of lost heroes', the 'dry and sedgy grasses' are images of loneliness, a tree's clutching of the marl an allegory of human clutching of hope: 'what is the hill? What are those trees upon it? They are not trees, but symbols' (p. 283).

This urge to find personal meaning in the land also colours Steve's relationship with her lover, Macca. More shadowy even than Harold Beecham, Macca is clearly tailored to fit the narrator's imagined picture of lover. Successor to Kelly, who quickly slips out of the role, he has the sole function of fulfilling Steve's need to love and be loved and, most significantly, her conviction that she is rejected. From the first, there is a clear division between Macca the ideal and Macca the real, who is taciturn and matter of fact, given to rabbit shooting, dancing the Charleston and getting drunk. In the latter identity, he sometimes loses his false teeth. Steve is aware of the discrepancy, but characteristically overlooks it: 'Here . . . was my opportunity to differentiate between the false and the true. The thought of a man raking through the bush and combing the gum-leaves for a set of false teeth, is odious. But, I, loving in the spirit, was undismayed' (p. 286). The phrase 'loving in the spirit' gives the game away; Macca is more necessary feature of the novel's emotional landscape than man, fulfilling several functions at once; he may even be no more than a dramatized element of Steve's inward life. Indeed, on several occasions the narrator more or less admits that she has 'made' this lover figure, shaping him into the preferred poetic image. If he rejects her first attempts at lyrical conversation by asking her to say 'bucket of firewood' as quickly as possible, she soon makes him 'worthy': 'I have made you . . . the poet-youth, ideal and innocent-thoughted' (p. 174). The older Steve of *White Topee* is even more frank, toying with the idea of creating another Macca, 'with his white sad face turned moonward' (p. 93). Macca is not merely twin poet, he is also the spirit of Gippsland itself. Steve's love for him is sparked by the recognition that he is a poetic expression of the region, even though outwardly 'none save his mother could have loved him' (p. 73). And later she pleads with him: '"You must love me. I demand it. You are Gippsland; you are Patria Mia: and you must love me. If you don't, I feel that I shall be lost"' (p. 136). Like Gippsland, Macca is intermittently welcoming and finally rejecting and like the natural landscape, he promises to defeat time. Being involved in an ambivalent love affair gives Steve opportunities for a poetic drama which temporarily arrests time: thus, companionship with Macca is described as 'an exquisite torment that always hovered on the brink of a *dissolving* peace'[15] (p. 166). It is clearly the state of being in love that is important, not the loved individual, and this is reinforced by Langley's obvious capacity to create vivid characters elsewhere in the novel; Macca's shadowiness is a psychic necessity, not a creative deficiency.

Steve's attitude to physical love is interesting. Although she flirts with the idea of marriage and even illicit love, she much prefers the idea of herself as virginal, more spirit than body. At one point, she admits that it is not marriage, love or fame that she wants but the defeat of flying time, '"I only want to sit and behold beauty forever and know that it will never die"' (p. 265). In *White Topee* when Macca finally proposes marriage, she is forced to choose her 'One Love', time, 'I wished only to be alone and worship the past for the sake of it, and poetry' (p. 69). This rejection of the female part of physical love, coupled with her perception of the loved one as part of nature, uncovers a fascinating aspect of Steve's sexual identity. Like the male hero of Pratt's study, she seeks not to be known but to know, and to know the loved one as an extension of the natural world, for to the male hero 'nature and woman are corollary goals, the contained and the container'. And a closer look at Macca reveals that despite his superficial insignia as male, he is also partially cast in the role of recessive, mysterious earth-woman. Indeed at one point Steve confesses that part of her desire to be man is that she should ' "have woman to work my will on; and she is tractable" ' (p. 149). Similarly, much of her passion for the woman she calls the Black Serpent, which is often accompanied by unusual longings for marriage and children, is not, as usually supposed, a contradiction of her 'virginal' attitudes, but an urge, conceived as impossible, to play the role of husband. Steve is even explicit on the subject: 'If I had been a man I should have married just such a woman and toiled for her thankfully and she would have enriched my body as she enriched my heart now' (p. 167). In reality, though, she can be neither male nor female, since the claims of both genders are in unresolved combat within her nature. In the latter part of the novel, for instance, she decries her descent to a more aggressive maleness: killing a hen with 'an exaggerated courage and callousness', she is aware that she is 'putting into brutal acts an intensity and cruelty out of proportion to the simplicity of the moment and, far ahead, I knew my power would rebound hideously on me' (p. 275).

My analysis so far has not touched on the comic passages of the book, which have endeared it to readers and which undoubtedly save it from tedium. Langley's gift for the ridiculous situation or the absurd character is undeniable, but it is the integrity of the comic effects for the overall emotional scheme of the novel that I want to stress here. However ideal Steve's flights of thought, they are inevitably doomed to be contradicted by mundane reality. Italians and Indians inhabit the bush in place of the Lawsonian heros of old; the bark hut's ideal name 'Avernus' is altered to 'Averdrink'; Steve's tragedy of love is often played as an inverted comedy; the noble depression turns out to be no more than a reaction to an unusually heavy meal; and yearnings for the profound are contradicted by the actuality of petty thieving. 'Do not think . . . that the eating of . . . stolen food had lowered the heights of my thoughts', Steve cautions the reader, putting her finger on the curious serio-comic balance that characterizes *The Pea Pickers*, for however mock-heroic her world, she manages consistently to privilege the heroic. She is at once threatened by the mock-heroic and spurred on by it to finer effects. As she comments towards the end of the novel:

When I am in the full impetus of imaginative, passionate flight, I look . . . winged, fiery, a very god, swifter than all the rest. But when I stop, a plain deformed deadness sets in. My limbs grow cold and sad, my faults are noticeable and I am, physically, a thing to be despised. Therefore, I have to burn all the time if I want to get the things I desire from life. (p. 300)

In *White Topee* the image of burning has become more of a self-immolation: watching a burning log, Steve reflects on the satisfying roar of the fire:

satisfied, I thought, to be burning, immersed in its own destruction and licking its lips over it, and partaking of it, thinking, 'O glorious death-bed of fire! Ah, how good it is to be destroyed with a living fire! Roar ... roar ... roar ... roar ... sink into me, eat of me ... ' (p. 78)

In this later novel, the impression of a brooding consciousness convinced of its own metaphysical absurdity is overwhelming. What had been intimated in the serio-comic contradictions of *The Pea Pickers* is made explicit. Like Wilde, the author's future alter ego, the narrator is both in love with an ideal beauty and convinced of its impossibility. Acting a part temporarily keeps anguish at bay, but it cannot conceal the emptiness for ever. 'I love acting; it is so much more real than life', comments Wilde; 'In the face of Macca's love, I had to strike an attitude', comments Langley's Steve, 'though ... being a writer and poet, I had fundamentally no feeling about anything save literature and poetry. But in order to be human one must strike an attitude' (p. 67). The comment has the sadness of *Waiting for Godot*. At the close of *The Pea Pickers* Steve is described as alone in her hut in the bush, but in an important sense she has always been alone. Locked within a pattern of counterbalancing contradictions, which are tethered to the central contradiction, her passion for an ideal permanence and her conviction of death, she can only commune with herself:

Time is flying, and we are going with it ... into what? Into what, O God? I don't want marriage, or love, or fame, really, in my very soul. I only want to sit and behold beauty forever and know that it will never die. (p. 265)

An early autobiography that has a localized fame on the grounds of its regional interest, but is otherwise undeservedly neglected is Sarah Conigrave's *My Reminiscences of Early Days*.[16] Born in England in 1841, Sarah accompanied her parents and five siblings to South Australia in 1853. Her father, Charles Price, was clearly short of capital but bought a run on Hindmarsh Island, which he subsequently had to protect from the unscrupulous tactics of other settlers, but which he ultimately developed into a thriving enterprise. Conigrave's autobiography, written in old age, is dedicated to her daughter Isla ('named after the dear old Island') and the Preface makes it clear that the author writes at her daughter's request and not, as she puts it, out of a desire to blow her own trumpet. Conigrave has a strong sense of self, however, and traces her proven hardihood and bravery to the challenges presented by the island and her heroic father:

The hardships and discipline I encountered in my young days enabled me in after life to face difficulties and trials that otherwise I would have sunk under. I have braved many a stormy blast since, and the thought of how my father battled against all odds has many a time encouraged me to persevere and win through.

The island's distance from Adelaide, difficulties of access, size and lack of internal transport make it both a free and challenging environment. The family appears to have been without horses for some time and later boats and horses are always at the prior command of the menfolk so that for Sarah and her two sisters, walking is the usual way of getting about and her narrative includes several accounts of superhuman expeditions by foot. Wild and isolated, the island offers an unconventional life which Conigrave takes full advantage of: 'The wild life suited us children splendidly. No schools to bother us, and black piccaninnies to play with, we enjoyed life to the full'. The early pioneering days are also fiercely challenging and the narrator takes great pride in her youthful achievements, setting out intrepidly into the bush at night to get help for a seriously ill sister, saving the family's first crop of wheat and perhaps her father's life from a mob of cattle (a feat for which she awards herself the V.C.), preserving the feeble life of her baby sister:

I often look back now, and wonder how I got through, I was only 12 years of age and a child myself. Apart from the invalids, I had the anxiety of my youngest brother, whom I was afraid would wander into the timber, and get lost. However, I stood to my guns, and came out on top at last. (p. 10)

Identifying strongly with her strong-willed father, Conigrave has a great admiration for bravery and the martial arts. She recalls the formation of volunteer regiments during a scare that the Russians would attack and describes her pride in the fine-looking soldiers going through their manoeuvres: 'I almost wished the Russians would come. Ho! those were stirring days' (p. 17). Allowed to carry her brother's rifle home, she is sure that if ever girls are needed to defend the country, she will be ready.

The preferred male image continues through her narrative, for Conigrave loves to recall her physical feats of daring, her skills as gymnast, horse-rider and sailor. Astride a bolting horse that had previously killed two riders, she solves the crisis by somersaulting into the air, amazing her male onlookers. Lodged in a favourite tree for a quiet spell of reading, she is nearly 'winged' by a gun-happy visitor. Even an expedition on behalf of the Bible Society becomes a feat of physical and verbal endurance. With her sister, Jane, she vaults fences, climbs hedges and assails the ears of possible donors.

As in nearly all Conigrave's expeditions, the girls are faced with a near-hopeless obstacle, this time in the form of a huge brushwood fence 'composed of enormous trees, felled and placed together so closely that neither pigs, dogs nor bulls could get through' (p. 52). Undaunted, they climb it like squirrels. Characteristically, this expedition is greeted with amazement, although it is difficult to know whether the missionary or the physical achievement is the most cherished:

We were somewhat tired when we reached home, as we reckoned we had walked fully twenty miles that day, but we felt very satisfied with ourselves, and the Bible Society people did, too, when we forwarded them a nice sum of money. It was larger, I think than they expected and we were thanked most kindly for the effort we made.

The owner of the high fence heard that we had been around the district collecting, and wished he had been near at the time, as he did not believe, until we told him we had done it, that it was possible for anyone to have scaled that fence. (p. 52)

On several occasions Conigrave has near-brushes with death but she reports herself as always outwardly calm and dignified, however terrified her inward state. Her description of venturing into the mouth of the Murray is a good illustration of her intrepid, determined self-image. One of the assets of this narrative is the author's strong dramatic gift and her habit of reporting all her adventures with a great deal of vigorous dialogue. Not surprisingly, she invariably gives herself the last word, frequently leaving her contestants speechless. On this occasion, she is determined to experience crossing the Murray's bar at first hand and refuses to go below with the other ladies, even defying the captain: 'I felt I did not care what punishment I received from any of them'. Sheltering within an enormous coil of rope, she achieves her object, and is relieved to discover that the captain is a 'sensible man' who refrains from informing her papa.

Several of her subsequent misadventures take place on water, but she prides herself on being a good sailor, equal to any storm, quoting a verse by Eliza Cook to express her younger, spirited self:

> For mine is a soul that defies control,
> Too proud for the palace or throne;
> And I was glad that the water had
> A spirit to match my own.

And it is clear that her delight in her island home springs partly from her conviction that it has 'a spirit to match [her] own'. Several scenes recall her enjoyment of its wild beauty, open stretches and lonely shoreline, and although she refers to the household duties which are the natural lot of daughters, she concentrates exclusively on outside activities and events. Not surprisingly, she has little patience with the inhibiting restraints of her time and invests much energy in subverting

and eluding convention. Indeed, part of her pride in physical achievement is the confounding of conventional expectations, for she nearly
always provides herself with an admiring or stupefied audience. A
delightful memory is of terrifying a party of visitors with a display of
hair-raising gymnastics or, with her brothers and sisters, emulating an
Aboriginal corroboree with realistic effect. If she is scornful of a
young lady who fancies herself to be aristocratic and delicate, she
dwells lovingly on a picnic when the ladies of the party removed their
stockings to fill them with 'montrees', returning with bundles resembling amputated legs: 'The roars of laughter from the gentlemen, who
were waiting for us at the boat can be better imagined than described'
(p. 62).

Although she and her sisters encounter few parental restraints,
they conduct a running war with their patronizing and restrictive
brothers, and some of Conigrave's most cherished memories are of
confounding, subverting or defeating these would-be tyrants. Not
above manipulating them with feminine wiles and a show of weakness, she also takes great pleasure in matching them physically. Her
closest relationship is with her sister Jane, but it is made closer by the
implicit need to combine forces against the social power of the male.

Conigrave is never explicitly critical of patriarchy, but her whole
posture is one of defiance. Although she scrupulously obeys her
father's requests, according to her enormous admiration of him, she
subverts every other representative of the male order. But her chief
enemy is convention itself. On one occasion, for instance, she and
Jane miss the horse-drawn truck which is to take them to a concert six
miles from Goolwa, largely due to Sarah's chattering:

[Jane] was very upset, and said she did so much wish to hear Mrs L . . . sing. I
knew that was all nonsense. What she really did wish was to meet some
young fellows at the concert, who had told us they would be there . . . and of
course, they were going to escort us home. I was as disappointed as my sister
was at the turn of events, but was too proud to show it. (p. 48)

In the event they decide to walk, arriving just after the first part of the
concert and arousing great surprise and interest in the audience.
Other incidents, which include 'choking' the parson with Sarah's
leaden pastries, disturbing the congregation in the middle of the
sermon when Sarah mistakenly believes Jane is about to faint and
threatens her with a glass of water, or climbing into the barn in the
middle of the night after getting locked out of the house, have a
Lindsay-like appeal. Clearly regarding her island self as exceptionally
free, resourceful and hardy, Conigrave writes with a verve that
contemporary feminists would find inspiriting.

North Queensland has inspired several notable autobiographies,
two of which, Rosa Campbell Praed's *My Australian Girlhood* (1902)
and Joan Colebrook's *A House of Trees* (1988), have some striking

similarities, although widely separated in time. Both are particularly fine, carefully crafted narratives, written late in life after their authors had achieved overseas reputations as writers, and both present the self as distinctively shaped by the childhood place. For both women, North Queensland is rediscovered after years of familiarity with Western urban culture and for both the region has a Gothic aura which challenges the imagination. It is both a physical and a metaphysical frontier, stretching the powers of the body and starkly confronting the human with a vast non-human dimension.

Joan Colebrook, one of the six children of a pioneer-farmer on the Atherton Tablelands, explores her 1920s childhood in *A House of Trees* from her early years at Kureen, to boarding schools, to the University of Queensland, concluding with her departure from Australia in 1937 after marriage to an American. The book is roughly chronological, but Colebrook's method is more a criss-cross weaving of people and places into a dense, temporally layered fabric. Acutely aware of the formative influence of the region on her consciousness, she is equally sensitive to the partiality and limitations of memory and frequently appears to be more speculative than dogmatic about the past. This impression of openness is heightened by the peculiar contradictions of her personal past, shaped on one side by Anglo-Saxon, semi-imperial values, and on the other by the exotic, tropical-rainforest world, which silently questions the very idea of the human. Describing her family as standing 'on the horizon of the world', Colebrook frequently evokes the brave loneliness of their house in the trees:

Now I realize that the great distance separating us from the heart of the Empire of which we were supposedly part had been deeply impressed upon us always. Vastness and a doubt of belonging make us all seem small, and here we swam in a vacuum—aware of the sky, of the silence, of the slow journeys which faced us before arrival; possessed by that doubt which is the inheritance of those born in lonely places. (p. 6)[17]

As she rediscovers her younger self, she muses on the mixed influences which insidiously shaped the careless child and children like her. Gradually, certain strands in her web begin to stand out and her questions transform themselves into tentative conclusions. The last chapter, titled 'Departure', is also a coming home, as the gifts of the past are finally understood.

Although Colebrook is never explicit about her symbolism, the rainforest with its spidery, man-made tracks, intermittently lit at night by the handful of settlements, is a metaphor of memory in general and of this memory of Australia in particular—exhilarating, mysterious, unique, dangerous. Like North Queensland, 'the lost and discovered and lost again', the past has a distinctiveness that is hard to define. In what way did this wild place, 'where the stars seem to hang low, and where men feel close to a long-ago spinning of the planets', speak to her spirit, she asks herself. What was it about the particular Australian essence, expressing both 'sweetness and a terrible dessication ... nothingness and a rocklike reality', that made departure so difficult:

I was leaving the innocence of the environment into which I happened to have been born. I was leaving the broad horizon, the crudity of spontaneous action; in a sense I was leaving the very power to live. (p. 247)

Responsive to the Gothic quality of her childhood place, its weird cliffs and trees haunted by strange animals reminiscent of the griffins and unicorns in medieval tapestries, and alive to its dangers, the narrator is also retrospectively attracted by the pristine, physical pleasures which give time the illusion of being a 'satisfactory continuum'. The children who grow up in such an environment are naturally wild and confident in their wild freedom. Freedom, in fact, becomes one of the strands that grows in significance, so that the reader is not surprised to discover the narrator treading her own individual path at university or choosing to have a love-affair with a married man or keeping her most private self apart when she herself marries. When she contemplates leaving the tropic world of her youth for the overseas world of discipline and taboos, she has an uncomfortable sense of becoming 'respectable', and one of her clearest principles is that she must never cede any control over her life to others with different values.

Freedom does not mean hedonism, however, and knit into the child's growing self-consciousness is an acceptance of struggle. She watches the unceasing efforts of her parents to create a farm in the wilderness, efforts which seem to have little to do with materialistic or status-seeking ends, but are true to an inner vision. If their father is sometimes dismissed as a dreamer and an odd man out in the farming community, the family lives according to the values of a simpler, more human and neighbourly time: 'Our parents, separate and reserved as they were, joined hands with the other pioneers. They belonged to a communal time' (p. 249). The bravery and pathos of their lives are most movingly suggested by the harness room with its battered hats and well-worn saddles. Contemplating these manifestations of pioneer life, the narrator can only conclude that life is 'mostly action ... a kind of courage' (p. 23). Struggle, hardship and defeat are also prominent features of the stories of the remoter past, retailed by their parents and uncles. As in Praed's recollections, the verandah is the place where the past of the Queensland bush becomes most tangible, and in both narratives that past is exposed as a time of extraordinary brutality as well as courage and selflessness. Praed's autobiography gives more immediate and graphic descriptions of violent events; in Colebrook's the impressions of past horrors and struggle unite with the closer impression of the parents' difficulties, while the sombre rainforest looms over the human dramas, intimating a complex symbiosis of good and evil, civilization and barbarity. Deftly interspersing the retrospective insights of the narrating present, the instinctive knowledge of the 1920s child, the more bewildered questioning of the 1930s young woman growing away from the child, and the stories and storytellers of the pioneering past, the narrative assimilates a thick wedge of time.

Just as time-levels impinge on each other, so do value systems. Countering the Gothic colour of North Queensland is the alien familiarity of the simplex British culture: 'upon our innocent and instinct-prone condition, British, especially Anglican, influences had been imposed'. Some English ideas, especially ideas of propriety, have difficulty finding a place in Kureen, and British visitors, with their pink cheeks, white hands and good manners strike the children as quaintly anachronistic. Nor do the few English expatriates, refugees from British India or Malaya, assimilate readily into the Queensland environment. A visit from some English aristocrats has its flattering moments, but a barrier of incomprehension ultimately separates the two cultures: 'Perhaps there was a certain recognition that they were allied to us by political structure rather than consanguinity; and even—in a complex way—that we were justified in putting up a certain resistance to what was so politely proprietary toward us. We were, after all, tough colonial products' (pp. 136–7). English values and myths, nevertheless, have a potent influence on the children's attitudes. Their father often seems genetically related to the traditional English squire, who worked with his men, while the manly, heroic values of Kipling and Haggard seem a natural part of their cultural baggage. And at school, the disciplines worked out over centuries on that 'small, fertile, sea-surrounded island' still enfold the children. Imperial pride infuses religion and nationalism, and makes itself felt in the classroom, on the playing fields and in the annual Anzac ceremony. Even so, the sense of having a distinctive regional identity, which is not British, persists: 'The truth was that we did not really know *what* we were, for no one had yet told us, and we certainly did not see ourselves as playing a part in a drama of conquest' (p. 12).

For the young woman and the older narrator, the question of values is crucial. Acknowledging the beauty of her parents' idea of themselves, even though that idea is hard to define, she is drawn to other individuals who live for the inner self: John Moffat who lives his religion, the Anglican bush brothers at her boarding school, and J.O.N.Q., the headmaster who had 'an aura of saintliness'. On one hand, the idea of belief is attractive; on the other, influences in the wild and in the city sometimes seem to cancel out the possibility of believing. An expedition to Low Woodie island with a group of

scientists opens up a pagan, Darwinian vista on life. Brisbane paradoxically poses an emptiness, a cultural void, which is more disturbing than the loneliness of the North: 'Where was the real world, I
wondered, which, promising to be more a question of spirit than of
matter, had beckoned me long ago?' (pp. 159–60).

Ultimately, although there is nothing dogmatic about this narrator,
she appears to return to the implicit values of her childhood: the ideas
of hard freedom, struggle and social justice. If the simple communal
past of her parents is already in 1937 part of history, the communal
ideals that had impinged on her youth as unwritten laws persist. And
knowledge of the hardships of the past fuses with pride in the socialist
history of her state: 'In some strange way I was part of the state's
noisy, rambunctious, and distinctive history. I was proud of this'
(pp. 242–3). But perhaps the major inheritance of this strange
part-Gothic, part-Puritan childhood is the interest in what she terms
'internal travel'; interested not so much in goodness but in the nature
of intelligence and 'what such human intelligence could mean for men
in the future', Colebrook inevitably focuses on her own childhood in
a part of the world and a time when the human was most sharply
thrown into relief.

Although Rosa Campbell Praed's *My Australian Girlhood* (1902) is
separated from *A House of Trees* by more than eighty years, the two
books have a family resemblance. Praed's reminiscences are of their
period and hence much less intimate than Colebrook's, but they are
no less inward. For both authors the Australian landscape poses
philosophical questions about human existence and their books are
shaped more according to a quest for meaning than by the circum-
stantial details of the lived life. Like Colebrook, Praed left Australia
as a young woman and muses retrospectively on her remarkable
youth from the standpoint of a travelled consciousness; there is a
similar blending of time-levels, a similar exploration of the remoter
past of parents and grandparents and a similar dependence on stories
and verandah talk. Like Colebrook, Praed sees herself as trained in
unconventionality by the Queensland bush ('conventionality is a
burden to me and society a penance. The wild cawing of rooks is
sweeter to my ears than the song of the nightingale'[18]) and is
attracted to the incongruous blend of the practical and the romantic,
the real and the fantastic in that 'odd, lonely, unconventional life'
(p. 155).[19] In retrospect at least, the childhood home appears to have
an exotic, otherworldly aura which challenges the imagination.

The daughter of Thomas Lodge Murray-Prior, a member of the
Queensland Legislative Council and Queensland's first Postmaster-
General, Rosa Praed was born in 1851. At three she was taken with
her family to Naraigin station in the Burnett district and later, after a
period in Brisbane, to Maroon on the Upper Logan. In 1872 she
married Campbell Praed and lived for a time on his station on Curtis

Island, off Gladstone. They sold the property in 1876 and went to England, where Praed developed her talents as a novelist, drawing on her Australian experience in at least half of her numerous novels and writing of it directly in *Australian Life: Black and White* (1885) and *My Australian Girlhood* (1902). Her later life was even stranger than Langley's, dominated by an extraordinary series of personal tragedies and by her beliefs in reincarnation, astral bodies and telepathy.

My Australian Girlhood shows the effects of a return visit to Australia in 1894, which stimulated her childhood memories and contributed to the 'then and now' passages which frequently intersect the narrative. Acutely aware of the differences that eighteen years had effected, Praed tends to exaggerate the time gap, sometimes referring to herself as a Rip van Winkle, thus distancing and sanctifying her childhood with the romance of a lost era. Revisiting the station of a friend after thirty years, she comments:

The scrub is gone—the lonely, beautiful scrub which can never be made again. One cannot now hear the dingoes howling and the melancholy note of the morepork, nor the faint crying of the native bear. Instead of the long gum-stretches, there are patches of maize and millet, and where the gum-trees have been cut down on the ridge one has a more distinct view of the mountains. They at least are not defaced. (p. 132)

The weird, melancholy landscape still evokes a pre-Adamic time, however, which dwarfs the human with its immensity. Indulging her familiar fantasy that Australia is a remnant of the prehistoric continent, Lemuria, Praed expands on the Gothic character of her region, peopling it with legendary creatures, the antediluvian crocodile and iguana, the eccentric kangaroo and the curious platypus. The bunyip's existence is more than likely: 'I can well imagine that only monsters could have inhabited those gruesome pools locked in the grotesque arms of hoary gums and shadowed by she-oaks—the most dismal of trees, with their straight, black stems and thin, dropping foliage' (p. 43). Adjectives which constantly recur in her lengthy word-pictures are: wild, desolate, melancholy, queer, lonely, strange, weird, antediluvian, primeval, impenetrable. At times the natural scene takes on human characteristics: a white gum has 'spotted, scaly bark', gum 'oozes and drops like congealed blood' from a red iron-bark, a tree slants along the side of a ridge in an 'odd, expectant way' and its dead arms have a 'human look', a kookaburra shrills in 'devilish merriment' (pp. 9–10). But it is the idea of ancient time that she most frequently evokes, the notion that the bush is a primeval survival 'like nothing else in the known world'.

As harsh and challenging as it is primeval, the bush is a place of shocking violence and cruelty. Stories of cannibalism, massacres, poisonings, acts of vengeance and deaths from starvation and thirst proliferate and, like Colebrook, Praed is fascinated by the casual bloodiness of the past: the memory of young, beautiful Miss Frazer, on the brink of marriage, massacred along with the rest of her family, or of the child consumed by ants after her lost mother tied her to a tree for safety, or of the man, speared in the thigh, who pursues his attacker and then pins his bleeding hand to his saddle, or of the cruelty of the black trackers towards their own people: 'all the flimsinesses of life are torn into shreds by the wild forces of nature which reign in the bush' (p. 104). If the cruelties are human and mostly localized in time, they are perceived as virtually inevitable given their natural backdrop: 'the terror of the wild Blacks [blends] in imagination with the oldritch shapes' of the old gum trees, draped with grey moss and the stalactites of red blood-like gum drooping from the branches. Meanwhile, Praed delicately evokes the pathos of her parents' attempts to establish a station in this wilderness. Drawing on their old, yellow-stained love letters, she sets the personal tenderness of their story against the inhuman hazards of their harsh environment. The old-fashioned restraint of their letters, full of 'quaint sobriety' and 'sweet stiffness', reminiscent of the world of Jane Austen, makes the contrast even more impressive.

The dichotomy between human time, which to Praed is European time, and the primeval time of Australia continues to tease her imagination. Later on Curtis Island, she is intrigued by the odd sense of connection with European destinies which the telegraph station brings. The connection is nearly always presented as tenuous, though, for Praed's Australia wears its Anglo-Saxon mask in an off-hand way, forever threatening to remove it. Listening to traditional Christmas merriment, for instance, she reflects:

Ice, snow, the Great Bear, holly and mistletoe, and Christmas waits. What have these to do with the languorous southern night, in which the soul faints and cries for something which it has never known?—something distant, awesome glorious, yet vaguely melancholy—something—the soul knows not what; it is only conscious that it yearns and cries. (p. 151)

The contradiction is symbolized by the picture of the nineteenth-century representation of Time which hangs on the wall of her Naragain humpy and haunts her childhood. Linked in memory with the face of a hostile black, peering through the slab shutters, the picture of Time implies a European order and civilization that are alien to the 'crude bush life' known by the child. For the older, expatriate self, the Australian difference is even more obvious and acute and nothing in Europe can compare with its grandeur.

Fantastic and cruel though Praed's Queensland is, it is an intensely spiritual landscape, infused with a force that she terms God, but that seems to be more pagan than Christian. In an extended section titled 'In a Hammock', she describes an experience of rocking under an old tree and of being absorbed in the 'enchanted kingdom of Nature':

as one rocks and muses, the great oversoul of the tree seems to absorb into itself the human past and present, and there remains only the sense of an all-embracing life, neither of flesh, nor of spirit that had ever to do with mortality, speaking, in curious inarticulate sounds, a language that only the forest gods have understood. (p. 141)

Undoubtedly, Praed's sibylline posture, spiritualist interests and convictions of reincarnation are linked to her imaginative appreciation of Australia's antiquity. But it is also curious that she should anticipate in some ways the time-conscious obsession with landscape of Eve Langley.

As one would expect, Europe, or more often Britain, looms large in Australian autobiographies by women. If the narrator is born in Europe, she is sometimes divided between the two places, experiencing the complex fate described by Henry James, or she has a sense of belonging that is qualified by what might have been; returning to Europe, either physically like Roslyn Taylor or via the mother's stories like Connie Miller, she is conscious of having lost a community of close relations or at least another tradition. Where she is born in Australia, she is frequently conscious of European roots and the European visit is an inevitable *rite de passage*, particularly for the writer born before 1950. The discovery of Europe is nearly always ambivalent; the European landscape may be as picturesque and historical as anticipated, but it is also often perceived as disfigured by slums and visible poverty. The social hierarchy is alienating and its conventions are often experienced as personally cramping so that the narrator soon longs for the relative freedom and openness of Australia. Rose Scott Cowen is oppressed to the point of suffocation by her aristocratic English relatives and gains a new appreciation of her father's rebellion, Kathleen Fitzpatrick suffers the double exclusion of the colonial woman within the privileged walls of Oxford University, Adelaide Lubbock has great difficulty adjusting to the narrow world of a society débutante after an Australian childhood and even the Anglophile Nancy Adams finds the chaperoning requirements of pre-World War I society claustrophobic. The reverse journey can be equally ambivalent, however, and two autobiographies in particular are fine expressions of the experience of the transposed European child: Mary Rose Liverani's *The Winter Sparrows* (1975) and Amirah Inglis's *Amirah* (1983).

The Winter Sparrows, which describes a 1940s to 1950s childhood, is one of the literary peaks of women's autobiography in Australia. Gifted with a keen sense of drama and lively powers of expression, Liverani is a vigorous interpreter of her two opposed places, Glasgow and Wollongong, and takes full advantage of her persona, the wily, observant, irreverent, tenement child. The recreation of life in Glasgow is written from the perspective of the older, Australia-wise self, who perceives in the grey slums of her childhood a range of colourful positives missing in the bright landscape of New South Wales, but the older narrator often adopts the immediate impressions of the child with great effect. An uncle's insincere smile is described as 'just an outing for his teeth'; the voice of a sexual predator is 'like snakes sliding over you'; a first set of spectacles, destined to invite ridicule, announce their malevolence directly: 'The case was dark brown and as hard and sharp as stone. It had a savage lid that slammed shut on your fingers if you left them there unawares and bit into them until you clawed it off with your uninjured hand ... The glasses were lying across their folded legs whose feet hooked round like scythes' (p. 112).[20]

The combined voices of adult and child are heard at their most expressive in the first part of the autobiography, titled 'My Ain Countree'. The older narrator understands the mix of Calvinism and capitalism that founded the granite tenements; 'a triumphant expression of laissez-faire and Scottish thrift', and home for more than one entire line of 'undersized, undernourished, bugbitten, bandy-legged Glaswegians' (p. 16). The child enjoys the drama of the violence they foster, the tension of evading the fighting Muirs or the odd, elderly pervert, the Hogarthian combination of vitality and filth. Climbing their stairs is like climbing a magic faraway tree, crowded not with the bland figures of Enid Blyton's fantasy but with 'hobgoblins and foul fiends, spitting cats, jellied legs that stuck out whitely from smelly corners' (p. 17). The lavatories on each floor, shared by four families, are invariably disgusting: 'One peered at the grimy walls, tracing out the graffiti with an *eager* forefinger, or sniffed disgustedly but with *satisfaction*[21] nonetheless at the accidents on the seat or the floor' (p. 17). The appreciation of the sheer gusto of Glaswegian living, implicit in the above, is typical of this section of the text. Liverani's child is most herself when watching the domestic brawls of neighbours, spying on their surreptitious sexual adventures, participating in her mother's loud feuds or initiating her own, investigating her father's clandestine scrap-iron gathering, vainly attempting to conceal from a bus full of people her little brother's messy accident, even observing an old man's act of exposure. If this last event is disturbing enough to be referred to her mother for judgement, it offers scope for drama and even the mother toys with the interesting thought that the incident may have affected her daughter's mind. But the older narrator is clearly at one with her grandmother; looking at her 'skeptically over the chicken bone that she was sucking with zest', the old lady declares: '"ah'm thinking it hasnae done anything tae her mind. She's gey crafty that big yin ..."' (p. 25). In this fierce environment, passions run high and hating is enjoyed as much as loving. Self-defence is a necessity and survival is the first priority. '"It's the iron in the blood that makes a fighter ... no' his size"', comments the narrator's father and her teacher advises her to fight if she can and if she can't, to run. The children who emerge from the tenements into the summer light have white faces and bodies, but 'all tough and alive-o'. Those not tough enough have been excreted during the winter.

Liverani's Mary Rose is often frightened, cold or hungry, but she has a fierce pride in her own survival skills and a huge enjoyment of the human comedy of her city:

Light and darkness in the city held me continually in thrall, impinging on my consciousness almost every waking minute as supernatural forces that were at work enchanting the buildings and the people, springing changes from minute to minute so that nothing ever remained as it seemed: Jekyll was always in the procress of turning into Hyde. (p. 31)

In a key image, she describes her life as like 'a high tension wire slung out in a void', along which she crawls with fear and hesitation. School and home are a 'perpetual challenge not only to your intellect, but to your survival as a free being' (p. 88). If the self is often threatened, at least it has a sense of its own reality and it is this conviction of an effective, knowable self, a self to be reckoned with, that the older narrator most values. At the high school to which she progresses as an achieving student, for instance, she feels more 'concretely something' than at any other time. One of her teachers at primary school advises her to dismiss the insults of her peers that are only meant to be embarrassing—'"They come from people who're either envious or miserable"' (p. 136), just as an Australian teacher later advises her to give in to her impulse to bite rather than to return the meaningless smile.

In this forthright society sex is as frankly accepted as other bodily functions. Couples hug together in the close notwithstanding the overpowering smell of urine, an uncle has a reputation for philandering and is later revealed to have an extra-marital child, the paternal grandmother may have erred in the same way and during the father's absence in Australia the mother is pursued by several hopeful suitors. Love is a more difficult matter. 'In our house, the only four letter word never voiced aloud was love.' The outside world of church, pop songs and books has a great deal to say on the subject, but Mary Rose finds their messages uninviting. God's love seems to have resulted in a sad sacrifice, the love of the pop songs is a miserable wail, the love of the American series *True Romances* seems to be a competitive game based on being pretty, and the love of the *True Love Magazines* satisfies a salacious instinct while prudently denying it at the end. Although the narrator is not explicit here, it appears that the obvious sexual passion and real affection which unite her battling parents is the genuinely true love. Threatened by the strain of supporting seven children on wages which provide only for an hour-to-hour existence,

and subject to the mercurial highs and lows of the mother's temperament, this love has a tough instinct for survival, even though it is
unostentatious. Thus it is appropriate that it should be the mother
who matter-of-factly enlightens the child as to the meaning of Solomon's Song, which has delighted her with its joyfulness.

Mary Rose's mother is one of the most prodigious of mothers in
Australian autobiography, if one can include such an incorrigibly
Glaswegian figure in the genre. Caustic, shrewd, resourceful and
inflammable, she has ferocious energies that are 'expended in cyc-
lonic gusts' as she whirls through her housework. Tired of coping with
an infested house, she threatens the local council to gas herself and
her seven children if another is not provided and is granted her
'request' within a week; appalled by her husband's decision to plead
guilty to a charge of stealing scrap iron, she circumvents him with a
lawyer and a plea of not guilty; determined to give her children wider
opportunities, she writes to Australia House and arranges for their
migration. Even her numerous children are 'planned', if the planning
has been misguided. She is warned of eventual breast cancer by a
Catholic doctor after she has had two children and has successfully
practised birth control for three years, whereupon she steadily in-
creases her brood until a Presbyterian doctor intimates disastrous
consequences for the womb. Overwhelming, irritating or embarrassing though she often is for her children, she has a reality that is
reassuring. Sensitive to her problems, Mary Rose is aware that her
mother copes with strains and failures that the father knows nothing
of, preoccupied as he is with the external drama between men and
bosses which makes 'Titans' of the participants.

As eldest child, burdened with the business of 'borrowing', while
the father pursues the other means of making money, working and
stealing, Mary Rose is in many ways her mother's satellite. Her
moods determine the child's comforts and discomforts just as her
perpetual craving for the hard-to-get Woodbines thrusts her out into
daily foraging expeditions; her expressions have to be watched and
gauged like weather signs, her occasional depression forestalled and
her tempests weathered. But there are other strong women in this
working-class community and Liverani catches their craggy individualities as she establishes the unwritten constitution which rules
their co-operation in the common struggle. The scene of the grandmother and mother enacting their ritual of marital discontents 'like
weird sisters taking part in a religious ceremony', or of the group
gathered in a small tenement room to discuss the sexual waywardness
of an old father, are particularly rich in comedy and sympathy.

As her mother's 'Chancellor of the Exchequer', invested with the
shameful weekly business of taking her father's suit to the pawn, or of
'tapping' friends and relatives for a loan, Mary Rose bewails her
function, but carries it out with style and even pride. Scrounging a

few Woodbines or trapping her elusive grandmother into disbursing a few shillings, she has a real sense of keeping the wolf from the family door. One of her greatest triumphs takes place when her father is in Australia and the cupboard is literally bare. Stealing a bag of briquette dust and then producing a few Woodbines and some tea which she has hoarded against a rainy day, she is able to reverse her mother's mood from depression to elation. At school she is also taught the value of effort and cajoled along the narrow road to excellence, if the cajoling is heavily embued with the values of John Knox:

'Whatsoever thy hand findeth to do, do it with thy might; for there is no work, nor device, nor knowledge, nor wisdom in the grave where thou goest.'
Some of us found this a little discouraging and wanted to drop our pens straight away, but Miss Brown would never let you. (p. 67)

At Bellastoun High School, she is in the company of children who are as enthralled as she is with books and intellectual debate. Meanwhile in the community at large and the family, she is taught alternative standards, subversive of the establishment. Borrowing and pawning is merely a private version of the big borrowings carried out by governments, to steal scrap metal is to recoup some of the injustices handed out by the big companies who are bent on swindling the post-war government: 'the biggest charities are given tae the richest beggars', comments the father. Poverty, at least for her family, is a condition that is an intellectual challenge, not a disease or a sin as it is for others and Mary Rose has difficulty in understanding attitudes that endorse the social hierarchy, just as she is resentful of the least sign of patronage. Thus she is instructed in subversion in at least five ways: as child, as female, as working class, as Scots and as potential Communist, for her father preaches his political views with fervour.

Jettisoned into suburban Australia of the 1950s, she exchanges Grand Guignol drama for light operetta. Part II, titled 'Hostel', begins: 'I am waiting for Australia to enchant me. To distract me from the past. To become the hypnotic present' (p. 195). In the event, Australia never does make itself real to Mary Rose and the second part of her story is a sustained attack on the country's bland niceness, the cult of cheerfulness and the quest for normality. The bus driver who first drives the hostel children to school is an anticipation of this cheerful unreality; if his bus is bright blue and red, 'like a toy out of a fairy story', there is something toy-like about him, with his cleanliness and bonhomie, 'his gleaming oiled hair and snow white side parting a manifestation of an uncluttered and readily coherent world. His wide open smile was an act of faith and assurance' (p. 216). The narrator's descriptions of this early landscape are infused with her irritation at the dullness and enervation of its people: the houses and shops crouch along the edges of the highways, 'their tired gardens, linked and roofs almost pressed together', reflecting the empty camaraderie that will perpetually baffle the family. The suburbs are marked by uniform signs, 'the chemist shop, the milk bar and green-grocer and by the few streets that strayed timidly away from the highway into the unknown' (p. 218). At the school, which cultivates niceness and sport at the expense of intellectual achievement, she encounters the ignorant assumption that, as a migrant, she must be intellectually at a disadvantage and wins a minor revenge when she tops the class. She quickly learns the unwritten rules that determine acceptance: the cultivation of niceness at the expense of wit, Australian-ness at the expense of other cultures, the banal in place of what is individual or colourful. Drawing on her Glaswegian gift of derision, she satirizes the mindless cheerfulness of the family's Wollongong neighbours with an acidity worthy of Patrick White: the appropriately named Glims with their genuine Axminster carpet and heavy, dark radiogram, and their dual cult of fishing and beer, or Shirley's family engaged in a typical Saturday afternoon's enjoyment of the radio, the parents sitting like old trees, 'aged solid, ringed round with whorls of fat' like annuli, and the entire group looking deep down into the mesh of the receiver as if they had been mesmerized by a great mouth.

Although the narrator makes a few more interesting friends after she has abandoned niceness for candid criticism, she never ceases to miss the earlier, significant way of being. If she was scared on the 'high tension wire', at least her nerves were twanging and she knew she was alive: 'I won't retreat from pain. How else should I know pleasure?' (p. 326). In her Australian school, she begins to feel 'like a pencilled dot, almost invisible, at the centre of an infinity of lines of circumscription' (p. 228). The confident entrepreneuring self is not a possibility and when total poverty ensues due to constant strikes in the steelworks, the family lacks the multiple means of raising loans which they had known in Glasgow. Poverty in Wollongong is not a temporary siege, likely to be relieved at any moment, but a long-drawn-out, imprisoning and battering campaign. Six weeks before her Intermediate examination, it is decided that she will have to get employment; it is a reality that her mother grasps with characteristic energy, although her father is overwhelmed by the decision, sitting in his chair, staring hopelessly at the fireplace.

In the event, the siege is relieved and school goes on but the incident is typical of a whole series which manifest a form of betrayal. It is as if the migrant's experience of personal fragmentation in the Australian nothingness induces infidelities, betrayals, and diminutions. Liverani describes the international life of the migrant hostel with her usual gusto, but underlying the descriptions is a preoccupation with disappointment and breakdown. It is reflected in the events, in the stories of desertion and infidelity. the sporadic outbursts of pointless quarrels and in the accelerating disappointment of the colourful Italians with this society which assumes they are fit only for picking grapes. In the equivocal environment of the hostel, the narrator has to protect even her mother from the threat of an illicit affair. Although the social outings are invariably gay, tensions, 'fine and grit-like' begin to invade relations. On one occasion the Italians light a fire in front of their section and morosely beat garbage tins for hours, meanwhile casually throwing flying foxes on to the fire. One motif in particular seems to have the function of metaphor in this climate of defeated hope; that is the story of the narrator's own undeclared passion for a beautiful Italian, Emilio. The owner of a superb voice and a finely proportioned face, Emilio has almost the value of a talisman for the narrator, but he turns out to have a capacity for minor cruelty and betrayal. He is last seen making love to the noisily virtuous mother of their Dutch friends. As in 'My Ain Countree', Liverani juxtaposes the voice of the growing girl, self-righteous on the subject of sex and preoccupied with her own changing physical emotions, with the voice of the older narrator, but there is little indication that the older voice dissents from the younger's conclusions about the general erosion of loyalty.

In many ways *The Winter Sparrows* is a study in different kinds of poverty, in the physical poverty of a working-class community in Scotland and what is seen as the willed poverty of imagination of suburban Australia. If the narrator's mother concludes at the end that there is 'a worse kind o' poverty than an empty tea caddy', and that the faces around here have 'Nae fight left in them. Nae joy. Nae sense of adventure', the narrator herself uncharacteristically suspends judgement for the moment.

Amirah Inglis was born in Belgium, although her parents were Polish Jews and had spent some years in Palestine before emigrating to Australia in the late 1920s when Amirah was still a small child. They were also Communists and their political life inevitably involved their child. Although she lived in Australia as a child, her Australian self was for many years no more than an outer shell; as Inglis has expressed it in an article on her early political life: 'like one of those wooden Russian dolls which my father brought me back from Moscow, I often felt like one person inside another inside another'.[22] *Amirah* has a similar shape. In the first place, there is the voice of the retrospective consciousness which questions the younger selves, for Inglis is sensitive to the metamorphoses that the immigrant child undergoes, and transparently edits their experiences. The child-self is curious about the new culture and the old, watches the human scenes and listens to the talk of her dichotomous world; her awareness of the relative 'oddity' of both old and new is perpetually sharpened on the grindstone of her expanding consciousness, while the reader's response is expanded by the retrospective knowledge of the present, narrating 'I'. This older consciousness sympathizes with the parents, especially the mother, and is both more and less detached than the child, less immediately involved in their experiences but more at one with them in her mature understanding. And always the reader experiences the oddities and anomalies of the child's experience first, and then the modifications introduced by the older consciousness. If this child is more preoccupied with a quest for identity than many autobiographers, she must find the self within the family and make sense of the tangled root system she has inherited. She seeks a reconciliation between her Jewishness and her Australian-ness, and is bent on retrieving a whole sense of self that will express all the diverse aspects of her experience and her parents' experience.

This narrative thrives on contradictions and opposites. One motif centres on ideas of fear and confidence. The mother is naturally anxious, the father naturally confident, and both attitudes have their strengths and limitations. Another reconciliation that Amirah has to make is between the backward-looking concern for roots and family that is her mother's way and the pragmatism, innovation and thrust for autonomy that is her father's. Australia too has an easy-going confidence and a seductive ordinariness that makes the events in Poland seem unreal; but the parents' return visit just before the outbreak of the war makes them real enough, and of the two realities, Europe's is the more vivid. Another motif of enclosure and expansiveness expands the fear/confidence strand. The small family is living theoretically in the vast continent of Australia but in fact in a small ethnic area in Melbourne; meanwhile they are in constant contact with the Europe which is still their emotional home and lead a life that is rich in a cultural sense and stimulating in a political one. The watered-down British culture of 1930s Melbourne, on the other hand, is relatively confining and has a steak-fed ignorance that makes it far less real to the child than the European world contained in her small terrace house. She is soon aware of difference: that her parents are Jews, not Christians; foreigners, not Australian; and that they read books instead of the *Sporting Globe* and *New Idea*. The older narrator puts her 1930s Melbourne education in historical perspective:

The school syllabus provided an education which was in essence a British pathway alongside the main road of European history and European high culture along which my parents—especially my mother—had travelled. (pp. 79–80)[23]

And is amused at the ironic contradictions which the child had easily assimilated: in Melbourne's 1934 centenary celebrations she is present at a celebration and a counter-celebration, as a daffodil in a pageant welcoming the Duke of Gloucester and at a torch-light meeting in the West Melbourne Stadium during the Egon Kisch affair. 'The complications of being at the same time a communist by upbringing and a non-religious Jew in Australia in the thirties are baroque' (p. 64).

In the second half of the book, the contradictions begins to reverse themselves and the dominant contrast is between the ghettoes, prisons and camps of the family's relations and the freedom and opportunity to grow that Australia offers. If Europe is culturally sophisticated, it spawns a bigotry that is far more ignorant than the ignorance of Australia. Thus the European home expresses continuity, family and culture but also danger, ignorance, limitation. There are other significant contrasts in the second half of the text: between the family's economic progress and the surrounding Depression, between the European war and Amirah's expanding world and educational ambitions; between the destruction of the family in Poland and Amirah's founding of a new family as the mother of 'several Australians'. Unlike *The Winter Sparrows*, *Amirah* ends on a note of achieved reconciliation.

Conclusion

Endings, as George Eliot frequently observed, are difficult and this ending is no exception. Indeed, titling this section the 'Conclusion' belies my impression of having come to an arbitrary full stop, imposed by limitations of space and the tolerance of publishers. As I survey the discarded chapter titles and the numerous potential subjects which suggested themselves during the course of writing, not to mention the equally numerous texts which clamoured for attention, I am conscious of pausing in the project rather than completing it. The chapters which might have been—comic representations of the self, deconstructive readings, structure and the treatment of time, narrative voices, responses to Europe, the treatment of other familial relations, and women's friendship—will have to wait for another occasion. Writing this book also suggested other books and other approaches: a study of adult autobiographies by women, or by men, or of men's autobiographies of childhood, a comparative study of men's and women's life-writing, or of texts from different Commonwealth or other cultures, or of representations of the self in autobiography, fiction and children's literature. Deconstruction as practised by such feminist writers as Kay Schaffer, Carole Ferrier, Susan Sheridan and Elizabeth Lawson also offers rich possibilities in reading both male and female texts, although it has not as yet been pursued to any great extent in the study of women's life-writing either here or overseas. It is an unfortunate fact that deconstruction as a theoretical approach to the genre in general, especially as practised by such critics as de Man and Mehlman, has been more preoccupied with the displacement and eclipsing of the self by language, the defeat of the (male) individual's quest for autonomy and authority, traditionally seen as the central purpose of autobiography.

Possibly as a result of its comparatively recent settlement by

Europeans, Australia is particularly rich in autobiographical narratives and it is no accident that one of our first novels, *Quintus Servinton*, is a disguised autobiography, nor that some of our most significant and culturally challenging texts, such as *My Brilliant Career* and *The Man Who Loved Children*, are in the same genre.[1] As I have tried to show, the archetypal texts are shouldered by numerous narratives which make convincing claims to literary status; if numerous authors have borne out Christina Stead's contention that the story of the self can transform the most inarticulate of women into an eloquent Medea, others have shown that the extraordinary childhoods of Franklin, Richardson and Stead herself are also ordinary and representative.

The number of autobiographies which I regret eventually omitting even within the terms of this study is also large; it was increased almost weekly by the flood of publishing in 1988. In practice, the attractions of close reading invariably implied making a selection so that numerous interesting and deserving texts, such as Robin Eakin's *Aunts Up the Cross* and Jean Bedford's *Country Girl Again*, escaped intensive attention. Some, such as Ruby Langford's *Don't Take Your Love to Town* and Faith Richmond's *Remembrance* were published too late for inclusion. I hope, however, that my discussion of the variety of women's autobiographical writing will have whetted the literary critic's and the historian's appetite for the genre; given the popularity of autobiography with 'ordinary' readers, they are in no need of encouragement.

One topic which many readers might have expected to receive greater attention in a study of this sort is that of 'Australian-ness'. John Colmer, for instance, in the only selection of autobiographical prose to be published so far, comments that 'the quest for personal identity involves asking fundamental questions about national culture and identity'[2], and most of the few essays on the subject have all pondered the cultural implications of this form of writing. In Chapter 11 I consider the treatment of the bush legend by three significant writers and the discovery of the idea or *an* idea of Australia as a major part of some authors' self-discovery, such as Maie Casey, Mary Gilmore, Jane Watts, Mary Rose Liverani, Barbara Hanrahan and Joan Colebrook, receives attention, but this book does not attempt to extrapolate general conclusions about Australian culture from the given range of autobiographical texts. Much as I admire such semiotic studies as *Inventing Australia, National Fictions* and *Women and the Bush*, I have been more concerned to explore the range of 'ordinary' women's life-writing as well as the well-known cultural texts. The tendency of the few articles on autobiography to draw large generalizations about Australian culture from a few well-known texts, to the effect that it is exceptionally philistine, racist, bigoted, egalitarian, repressive or whatever, is, I maintain, tendentious on several counts. Not only does it overlook the wide variety of life-writing by authors of both sexes, but it also overlooks the problematic, provisional nature of autobiography; stories are told, not lived and memory acknowledges several editors as well as social conditioning, such as heredity, temperament and the individual configurations of specific experience. As Maurois comments (in characteristic male-specific terms), by choosing to write, the autobiographer becomes an artist, bent on creating a life more in keeping with his desires than his historical life has been. To endow himself with this life, he acquires the creative freedoms of the novelist: 'The only difference between him and the novelist is that, as he creates [this life], he will say, and perhaps even believe, that it is his own, while the novelist is conscious of his creative act'.[3] The cultural questioning of autobiography (at least as it has been practised so far) also has other limitations; by inducing the stock of familiar tropes of the so-called homogenous Australian legend, it also inadvertently depresses the variety of the genre and reestablishes the unified national identity even while claiming to explore the relevance of the concept.

But I have another more compelling reason for avoiding the question of 'Australian-ness', and that is that the autobiographers studied here are largely uninterested in the androcentric myths, even though they frequently register the frustrations of living within an androcentric culture. Kay Schaffer, for instance, has observed that the masculine bias which we constantly confront in media representations of Australia bears little resemblance to 'the diverse and rich experiences of strong and colourful women encountered daily in interaction with friends, neighbours, workmates, and students'. She concludes that the country is struggling with contradictory impulses, to both 'accept and deny the diverse nature of Australian culture; to ignore and uphold its masculine bias; to come to terms with and reinvent a national identity'.[4] There is hardly any need to re-establish the masculinity of the received version of the 'real' Australia, which has been ably presented by numerous cultural commentators since Russel Ward's *The Australian Legend* (1958), but with some striking exceptions, few of the authors which are the subject of this book have directly confronted either the self or the land as it has been defined by the Lawsonian tradition. This is not to say that they are uninterested in the idea of Australia, since the sense of place and the sense of individual identity are frequently intimately related. But the Australias they have known are remarkably diverse and even personal. A city, for example, has as many personalities as the subjectivities which find a home in it; Ivy Arney's Collingwood has as little in common with Amirah Inglis's Parkville or Kathleen Mangan's South Yarra as they have with each other, and Kathleen Fitzpatrick's Australian self is known via the personalities of a variety of Melbournian houses and a variety of adult relatives. Maie Casey negotiates her identity by meditating on her relationships with the distinctive Victorian cultures established by members of her family. Regional differences are even more extreme and the Australias experienced by Rose Scott Cowen, Della Edmunds, Anna Ey, Mary Edgeworth David and Barbara Hanrahan emerge as more diverse than the countries of pre-1914 Europe. Not only do these texts dissolve the notion of a homogenous culture, but collectively they establish Australia as an exotic amalgam of alternative cultures.

Another striking aspect of these narratives considered collectively is the predominance of female communities. Again and again, the autobiographer recreates a female past in which men figure variously as marginal, troublesome or only incidentally supportive. Granted official authority on one hand, they are often shorn of effectiveness with the other. Thus, Mary Fullerton's narrator acknowledges that her father's word is law within the family, just as the men's interpretation of the Bible dominates her community's religion, but her key experiences are those found in company with her sister and through her relationship with a mothering land. Barbara Hanrahan celebrates an intimate female community, that is later invaded by the alien androcentric culture. Clara Ellen Campbell recreates a female solidarity that is strong enough to resist both the predatoriness and the weakness of the male. Sarah Conigrave re-explores her beloved island in company with her sister and re-experiences victory over the reductive tactics of her brothers. Nene Gare joins her sisters in a series of attempts to rescue their mother from the impractical attitudes of their child-like father. Schaffer has brilliantly established the normative elements within Australian discourses which have produced the entrenched negative meaning of 'woman' in our society. These autobiographies, however, suggest that women have frequently inhabited a space beyond the limits of the Australian tradition, at least in the rediscovery of their early identity. Exiles from power and less certain of their place in national history, or perhaps certain of their exclusion, these authors have discovered freedoms which the male writer, preoccupied with imperatives of male proving and caught up in the processes of 'becoming', has been largely denied. Colmer's conclusion that personal and national identity are interrelated, in the sense that the personal must come to terms with the received idea of the 'real' Australia, is based on his experience of male autobiographies and reflected in his selection of largely male narratives. Only a few autobiographies by Australian women confront their exclusion from the national tradition in a militant way, but many are implicitly radical in their assertion of the value of the inner being opposed to the outer and in their respect for the intuitive, the spontaneous, the different and the complexly simple.

The woman writer's independence of the national tradition is nowhere more obvious than in her response to the land and to the public goals of domination and exploitation of the continent. As Schaffer has noticed, physical, sexual and economic conquest of the land is an alien concept for the woman writer and certainly most of these autobiographers have perceived the childhood place as a loved and loving environment; if like the male writer they figure the land as female, they also perceive it as more of an extension of the self than as a potentially hostile other, a manifestation of the powerful, unpredictable mother who challenges the identity of her sons even as she threatens to withhold her wealth. For some writers, such as Franklin, Prichard, Wallace and Hanrahan, the early experience of the childhood place is presented as a touchstone, confirming the authenticity of the self in the face of inauthentic, reductive roles proffered by society.

Schaffer suggests that when the Australian woman looks in the cultural mirror she sees 'a redoubled image', not only her own image, but man's image of her: 'Australian women have already begun to turn their backs on the mirror, or turn the mirror to the wall'.⁵ It is probably the case that of all these autobiographers only Richardson and Stead have the strength to turn their backs on the mirror. Franklin tries but fails, so seductive is the national reflection. Many like Wallace, Mangan, NcNeil, Chomley and even Hanrahan contemplate the double image, but concede that it is at least double, that there is another self that is different from the cultural sign. A few like Mrs Dominic Daly and Eve Langley are eclipsed by the cultural trope of self-reference. Although most, as I have suggested, write as mothers and daughters, they write for a female community which places a different value on motherhood and daughterhood than the traditional culture and which suggests that the Australian woman is greater and much more interesting than her cultural representation. More at home in their multiple Australias than the Lawsonian hero of the national legend, these writers of the self are also more alive to V. S. Pritchett's observation that we are all 'historical specimens and immigrants in our own society'.⁶ If the Australian woman has been more obviously a migrant than most autobiographers, the imposed status has conferred the opportunity to pursue an alternative or covert perspective, which most have exploited to the full.

Notes

Chapter 1

1 Kay Daniels, Mary Murnane & Anne Picot (edd.), *Women in Australia: An Annotated Guide to Records*, 2 vols (Canberra, AGPS, 1977), vol. 1, pp. vi–vii.
2 Kay Daniels, 'Women's History', *New History* (edd. G. Osborne and W. F. Mandle, Sydney, Allen & Unwin, 1982), pp. 33, 34.
3 Wilhelmina McKerron, 'Foreword', *The Wheel of Destiny* (Devon, Arthur Stockwell, 1980).
4 Jane Miller, *Women Writing About Men* (London, Virago, 1986), p. 39.
5 Marion Simms, *Labour History* 34 (May 1978), p. 95, and Stephen Murray-Smith, 'Messages from Far Away', *The Colonial Child. Papers presented at the Eighth Biennial Conference of the Royal Historical Society of Victoria, Melbourne, 12–13 October 1979* (ed. Guy Featherstone, Melbourne, RHSV, 1981), pp. 73–74. Jane Watts's autobiography receives a brief mention in Paul Depasquale's *A Critical History of South Australian Literature 1836–1930* (1978), but neither Agnes Gosse Hay's nor Sarah Conigrave's rate a mention. None of the three is recorded in E. Morris Miller's *Australian Literature* (1940) nor in H. M. Green's *A History of Australian Literature* (1961), nor, it must be conceded, in *The Oxford Companion to Australian Literature*. Watts and Conigrave, but not Hay, are listed in *Her Story* (comp. Margaret Bettison & Anne Summers, Sydney, Hale & Iremonger, 1980), while none is listed in *Women in Australia*.
6 Ellen Messer-Davidow, 'The Philosophical Bases of Feminist Literary Criticism', *New Literary History* 19 (1987), p. 76.
7 The incidents occur in Adelaide Lubbock's *People in Glass Houses* (Adelaide, Nelson, 1977), Janet Mitchell's *Spoils of Opportunity* (London, Methuen, 1938), Margaret Gifford's *I Can Hear the Horses* (North Ryde, Methuen, 1983) and Kathleen Mangan's *Daisy Chains, War, then Jazz* (Melbourne, Hutchinson, 1984).

8 Patricia Grimshaw, 'Women in the 1888 Volume', *Australia 1888 Bulletin* No. 6 (November 1980), p. 37.

9 Jessie Ackermann, *Australia from a Woman's Point of View* (First published 1913. North Ryde, Cassell Australia, 1981), pp. 71–2.

10 John & Dorothy Colmer (edd.), *The Penguin Book of Australian Autobiography* (Ringwood, Vic., Penguin, 1987), p. 6.

11 Miriam Dixson, *The Real Matilda* (Ringwood, Vic., Penguin, 1976) (p. 12).

Chapter 2

1 Miles Franklin, *My Career Goes Bung* (Melbourne, Georgian House, 1946). Written soon after *My Brilliant Career*, this second autobiography failed to win publication in 1910 as potentially libellous and was rediscovered by the author on her return to Australia in the late 1920s.

2 Barrett Mandel, ' "Basting the Image with a Certain Liquor": Death in Autobiography', *Soundings* 57 (1974), p. 177.

3 Dennis Dugan, 'Adventurous Digger from the States', *Age*, 2 June 1979, p. 26; Maurice Dunlevy,' The Joy of Primary Sources', *Canberra Times*, 5 May 1979, p. 16.

4 Sidonie Smith, *A Poetics of Women's Autobiography* (Bloomington, Indiana University Press, 1987), pp. 49, 50.

5 Mrs Dominic Daly, *Digging, Squatting and Pioneering Life in the Northern Territory of South Australia* (London, Sampson Low, 1887).

6 Mary MacLeod Banks, *Memories of Pioneer Days in Queensland* (London, Cranton, 1931).

7 Mary A. McManus, *Reminiscences of the Early Settlement of the Maranoa District in the Late Fifties and Early Sixties* (Brisbane, E. A. Howard, 1913).

8 'I think I may justly lay claim to a little self-knowledge, as I am the oldest woman now living and the first with my mother who came to the district' (p. 3).

9 Eliza Chomley, 'My Memoirs', MS 9034, Box 142/6(a), La Trobe Library, Melbourne.

10 Betty Malone, Volume 3 : 1851–1890 (Melbourne, Melbourne University Press, 1969), p. 9.

11 K. McK., *Old Days and Gold Days in Victoria (1851–1873) being Memories of a Pioneer Family* (Melbourne, Vidler, 1924).

12 Sarah Musgrave, *The Wayback* (Parramatta, printed by *The Cumberland Argus*, 1926).

13 Anna Ey, *Early Lutheran Congregations in South Australia: Memoirs of a Pastor's Wife* (transl. by Dorothea M. Freund, Payneham, SA, A. P. H. Freund, 1986).

14 'Autobiography of Frau Pastor Christiane Hiller', MS 10199, MSB 182, La Trobe Library, Melbourne.

15 *Annabella Boswell's Journal* (Sydney, Angus & Robertson, 1965).

16   Herman also omits Boswell's account of a return visit to Lake Innes in 1853, a section on bushrangers and an account of the 1844 flood of the Lachlan by Mr Boswell; the last two are typical additions to women's autobiographies of this period, presumably to meet the expectations of male readers.

17   Kathleen Lambert, *The Golden South: Memories of Australian Home Life from 1843 to 1888* (London, Ward & Downey, 1890).

18   'Even if fortune had proved kinder, she would never have liked the colony, and her five years there, spent wearily and sadly, I am certain helped to kill her' (p. 31).

19   'Memoirs of Margaret Emily Brown (Youngman). A Recording of 58 Years of Life Mainly in Port Fairy', MS 11619, Box 1833/4, La Trobe Library, Melbourne.

20   Kate Rodd, 'Lisdillon: The Story of John Mitchell MHA, JP 1812–1880 & his Family'. Held by the Tasmaniana Library, State Library of Tasmania, Hobart.

21   Ellen Campbell, *Twin Pickles* (London, Blackie, 1898).

22   *Mrs* F. Hughes, *My Childhood in Australia* (London, Digby, 1890?).

23   Jane Caverhill, 'Reminiscences 1840s—1850s', MS H15903 102/1, La Trobe Library, Melbourne.

24   'Their themes are often repetitive, like all good music; there are minor keys, variations, trills and flourishes. *Lento, presto, piano, forte*. Women make this music out of their daily lives, their emotions, their shrewd understanding. Women colour themselves in, and their friends and their lovers, endlessly...' 'Colour Him Gone', Jean Bedford and Rosemary Creswell, *Colouring In. A Book of Ideologically Unsound Love Stories* (Fitzroy, McPhee Gribble, 1986), p. 19.

25   Paul Eakin, *Fictions in Autobiography* (Princeton, New Jersey, Princeton University Press, 1985), p. 9.

26   Barbara Hardy, 'Towards a Poetic of Fiction: 3) An Approach through Narrative', *Novel* 2 (1968), p. 5.

27   Paul Eakin, *Fictions in Autobiography*, p. 225.

28   Mary Brennan, *Better Than Dancing* (Richmond, Vic., Greenhouse Publications, 1987).

29   Mary Stawell, *My Recollections* (London, Private Print).

30   Nancy Adams, *Family Fresco* (Melbourne, Cheshire).

Chapter 3

1   Jane Isabella Watts, *Memories of Early Days in South Australia* (Adelaide, The *Advertiser* General Printing Office, 1882).

2   Jane Isabella Watts, *Family Life in South Australia Fifty-Three Years Ago* (Adelaide, W. K. Thomas & Co., 1890). All references are to this edition.

3   Eliza Davies, *The Story of an Earnest Life: A Woman's Adventures in*

Australia, and in Two Voyages around the World (Cincinnati, Central Book Concern, 1881).

4 Part of Davies's autobiography, as well as Julia Gawler's diary of the 1839 expedition, are reprinted in *Charles Sturt: The Mount Bryant Expedition 1839* (Adelaide, Sullivan's Cove, 1982). Edgar Beale in his *Sturt: The Chipped Idol* (Sydney, Sydney University Press, 1979) also draws on Davies's account.

5 Beale does not doubt her veracity.

6 James Olney, *Metaphors of Self* (Princeton, New Jersey, Princeton University Press, 1972).

7 '"Basting the Image with a Certain Liquor"': Death in Autobiography', *Soundings* 57 (1974), pp. 177, 181, 185.

8 Mary Gilmore, *Old Days, Old Ways* (Sydney, Angus & Robertson, 1934).

9 Mary Gilmore, *More Recollections* (Sydney, Angus & Robertson, 1935).

10 *Sydney Morning Herald*, 4 August 1965, p. 15.

11 *Mary Gilmore. 100 Years. Invitation to centenary tribute.*

12 *Daily Telegraph*, 4 December 1962.

13 William Earle, *The Autobiographical Consciousness* (Chicago, Quadrangle Books, 1972), p. 40.

14 William Earle, p. 40.

15 Maie Casey, *An Australian Story 1837–1907* (First published London, Michael Joseph, 1962; all references are to the 1965 imprint by Sun Books, Melbourne).

Chapter 4

1 Philippe Lejeune, *L'Autobiographie en France* (Paris, Seuil, 1971); *Le pacte autobiographique* (Paris, Seuil, 1975); Elizabeth W. Bruss, *Autobiographical Acts* (Baltimore and London, Johns Hopkins University Press, 1976).

2 Gusdorf's essay was published in *Formen der Selbstdarstellung: Analekten zu einer Geschichte des literarischen Selbstportraits* (Gunther Reichenkron & Erich Haase (edd.), Berlin, Duncker & Humblot, 1956), pp. 105–23; translated into English in James Olney (ed.), *Autobiography: Essays Theoretical and Critical* (Princeton, Princeton University Press, 1980), pp. 3–27; Hart's essay appeared in *New Literary History* 1 (Spring 1970), pp. 485–511; James Olney's *Metaphors of Self* was published at Princeton, New Jersey, by Princeton University Press, 1972.

3 Roy Pascal, *Design and Truth in Autobiography* (Cambridge, Mass., Harvard University Press, 1960).

4 Seymour Chatman (ed.), *Literary Style: A Symposium* (New York and London, Oxford University Press, 1971), pp. 285–96.

5 Jeffrey Mehlman, *A Structural Study of Autobiography* (Ithaca and

London, Cornell University Press, 1974).

6   Avrom Fleishman, *Figures of Autobiography* (Berkeley and London, University of California Press, 1983), pp. 36, 37.

7   Paul Delany, *British Autobiography in the Seventeenth Century* (London, Routledge & Kegan Paul, 1969), p. 158.

8   Donna Stanton (ed.), *The Female Autograph* (Chicago & London, University of Chicago Press, 1984), p. 4.

9   Patricia Meyer Spacks, *Imagining a Self* (Cambridge, Mass., and London, Harvard University Press, 1976).

10   Estelle C. Jelinek (ed.), *Women's Autobiography: Essays in Criticism* (Bloomington, Indiana University Press, 1980); Estelle C. Jelinek, *The Tradition of Women's Autobiography: From Antiquity to the Present* (Boston, Twayne Publishers, 1986).

11   Sidonie Smith, *A Poetics of Women's Autobiography* (Bloomington and Indianapolis, Indiana University Press, 1987).

12   Richard Coe, 'Portrait of the Artist as a Young Australian: Childhood, Literature and Myth', *Southerly* 41 (1981), p. 127.

13   John & Dorothy Colmer (edd.), *The Penguin Book of Australian Autobiography* (Ringwood, Vic., Penguin, 1987).

14   John & Dorothy Colmer, p. 7.

15   Don Anderson's 'Portraits of the Artist as a Young Man', *Meanjin* 42 (1983), pp. 339–48 and Fay Zwicky's 'The Mother of Narcissus: Autobiographical Reflections in the Australian Water-Hole', *Island Magazine* 18/19 (Autumn/Winter 1984), pp. 66–72, demonstrate this tendency.

16   Thus Don Anderson with uncharacteristic dismissiveness reflects that 'Australian (male) autobiographies are . . . a jewel in the nation's republican's crown'. *Times on Sunday*, 10 May 1987, p. 32.

17   'Conditions and Limits of Autobiography', Olney (see note 2), *passim*.

18   *A Poetics of Women's Autobiography*, p. 8.

19   'Autobiography and the Making of America', Olney (see note 2), p. 150.

20   '*Malcolm X* and the Limits of Autobiography', Olney (see note 2), p. 192.

21   Roy Pascal, *Design and Truth in Autobiography*, pp. 9, 10–11, 19, 83, 95.

22   'Notes for an Anatomy of Modern Autobiography', (see note 2), pp. 492, 502–3.

23   William Howarth, 'Some Principles of Autobiography', *New Literary History* 5 (1974) p. 378.

24   Ken Ruthven, *Feminist Literary Studies* (Cambridge, Cambridge University Press, 1984), p. 62.

25   John Sturrock, 'The New Model Autobiographer', *New Literary History* 9 (1977), pp. 51–63.

26   Germaine Brée, 'Michael Leiris: Mazemaker', Olney (see note 2), p. 199.

27   Some of the historians' papers at the conference on feminist biography

and autobiography (Adelaide, 1–4 February 1989), however, suggested more liberating possibilities for deconstruction in the study of autobiography than those pursued so far by literary theorists.

28 *A Poetics of Women's Autobiography*, p. 14.

29 Nancy Chodorov, *The Reproduction of Mothering* (Berkeley, University of California Press, 1978), p. 169.

30 Nancy Chodorov, 'Gender, Relation, and Difference in Psychoanalytic Perspective', in Hester Eisenstein & Alice Jardine (edd.), *The Future of Difference* (Boston, Mass., G. K. Hall, 1980), p. 14.

31 Nancy Chodorov, 'Being and Doing: A Cross-Cultural Examination of the Socialization of Males and Females', in Vivian Gornick & B. K. Moran (edd.), *Woman in Sexist Society* (New York, Basic Books, 1971), p. 183.

32 'Gender, Relation, and Difference in Psychoanalytic Perspective', p. 15.

33 Carolyn Heilbrun, 'Women's Autobiographical Writings: New Forms', *Prose Studies* 8, 2 (1985), pp. 14, 17, 27.

34 Lynne Segal, *Is the Future Female?* (London, Virago, 1987), pp. ix, xi.

35 Elaine Showalter, 'Feminist Criticism in the Wilderness', in Elizabeth Abel (ed.), *Writing and Sexual Difference* (Brighton, Harvester Press, 1982), p. 204.

36 Virginia Woolf, *A Room of One's Own* (First published 1929; London, Grafton Books, 1977), p. 104.

37 The words are Carol Gilligan's, used to describe her perceptions of the difference in male and female consciousness in the course of psychological research. *In a Different Voice* (Cambridge, Mass., Harvard University Press, 1982), p. 5.

38 *Women's Autobiography: Essays in Criticism*, p. 37.

39 Carolyn Heilbrun, *Re-inventing Womanhood* (New York, W. W. Norton, 1979), p. 88.

40 Toril Moi, *Sexual/Textual Politics: Feminist Literary Theory* (London and New York, Methuen, 1985), p. 8.

41 Judith Kegan Gardiner, 'On Female Identity and Writing by Women', *Writing and Sexual Difference*, p. 185.

42 *In a Different Voice* (Cambridge, Mass., Harvard University Press, 1982), pp. 22, 23.

43 Nancy Phelan, *A Kingdom by the Sea* (Sydney, Angus & Robertson, 1969), p. 169.

44 'Portraits of the Artist as a Young Man', p. 340.

45 Elizabeth Abel, Marianne Hirsch and Elizabeth Langland (edd.), *The Voyage In: Fictions of Female Development* (Hanover & London, University Press of New England, 1983), p. 11.

46 Jean Baker Miller, *Towards a New Psychology of Women* (Boston, Beacon Press, 1976), p. 83.

47 *Design and Truth in Autobiography*, p. 85.

48 Erik Erikson, *Young Man Luther: A Study in Psychoanalysis and History* (New York, Norton, 1962), p. 111.

49   *Le pacte autobiographique*, p. 201.
50   Louis Renza, 'The Veto of the Imagination: A Theory of Autobiography', *New Literary History* 9 (1977), pp. 6, 9, 22.
51   Vladimir Nabokov, *Speak Memory* (London, Weidenfeld & Nicolson, revised edn, 1967), p. 25.
52   Virginia Woolf, *Moments of Being* (New York and London, Harcourt Brace, 1976), pp. 80, 30.
53   Erich Neumann, *Amor and Psyche: The Psychic Development of the Feminine* (New York, Pantheon Books, 1956).
54   Erik Erikson, *Identity and the Life Cycle* (New York, International Universities Press, 1959).
55   Nancy Chodorov, 'Towards a Relational Individualism: The Mediation of Self Through Psychoanalysis', in Thomas Heller *et al.* (edd.), *Reconstructing Individualism* (Stanford, Stanford University Press, 1985), p. 203.
56   'Gender, Relation, and Difference in Psychoanalytic Perspective', pp. 13–14.
57   'On Female Identity and Writing by Women', p. 183.
58   Jean Rhys, *After Leaving Mr McKenzie* (London, Deutsch, 1931), p. 158.
59   'Gender, Relation and Difference in Psychoanalytic Perspective', p. 14.
60   *A Poetics of Women's Autobiography*, pp. 54, 56.
61   'On Female Identity and Writing by Women', p. 179.
62   'The Other Voice: Autobiographies of Women Writers', Olney (see note 2), p. 210.
63   'The Veto of the Imagination', p. 21.
64   Sandra M. Gilbert and Susan Gubar, *The Madwoman in the Attic* (New Haven, Yale University Press, 1979).
65   *Towards a New Psychology of Women*, p. 86.

Chapter 5

1   *The Letters and Journals of Katherine Mansfield: A Selection* (C. K. Stead (ed.), London, Allen Lane, 1977), p. 35.
2   Wayne Shumaker, *English Autobiography: Its Emergence, Materials, and Form* (Berkeley, University of California Press, 1954), p. 40.
3   The words are Marjorie Barnard's, *Miles Franklin* (New York, Twayne Publishers, 1967), p. 16.
4   C. G. Jung and C. Kerenyi, 'The Psychology of the Child Archetype', *Introduction to a Science of Mythology* (transl. by R. F. C. Hull, London, Routledge & Kegan Hall, 1951), p. 116.
5   Miles Franklin, *Childhood at Brindabella* (First published 1963; Sydney, Angus & Robertson, 1979), pp. 24–5.
6   Ruth Suckow, *The Bonney Family* (New York, A. A. Knopf, 1928), p. 285.
7   Kylie Tennant, *The Missing Heir* (Melbourne, Macmillan, 1986).

8   Graeme Turner, *National Fictions* (North Sydney, Allen & Unwin, 1986), pp. 51–2.

9   Barbara Hanrahan, *The Scent of Eucalyptus* (London, Chatto & Windus, 1973), p. 182.

10 Interview with Julie Mott, *Australian Literary Studies* 11 (1983), p. 43.

11 Katharine Susannah Prichard, *Child of the Hurricane* (Sydney, Angus & Robertson, 1963); *The Wild Oats of Han* (Melbourne, Lansdowne, 1928).

12 [Agnes Gosse Hay] 'Anglo-Australian', *After-Glow Memories* (London, Methuen, 1905).

13 Fayette Gosse, *The Gosses: an Anglo-Australian Family* (Canberra, Brian Clouston, 1981).

14 Alexander Hay was eighteen years older than Agnes.

15 Doreen Flavel, with Donald S. McDonald, *The Promise and The Challenge* (Adelaide, Author, 1986).

16 Emily Churchward, *In Paths Directed* (Hawthorndene, Investigator Press, 1984).

17 Bessie Lee, *One of Australia's Daughters* (London, Ideal Publishing Union, 1900), p. 172.

18 Kathleen Fitzpatrick, *Solid Bluestone Foundations* (Melbourne, Macmillan, 1983; references are to the 1986 edition published by Penguin).

Chapter 6

1   Lusie Eichenbaum and Susie Orbach, *Understanding Women* (Harmondsworth, Penguin, 1985), pp. 65, 66.

2   Annie Duncan, 'Reminiscences', State Archives of South Australia, PRG 532/6, p. 72.

3   Eliza Chomley, 'My Memoirs', MS 9034, VSL Box 142/6(a), La Trobe Library, Melbourne.

4   Simone de Beauvoir, *The Second Sex* (First published 1949, Harmondsworth, Penguin, 1972), p. 314.

5   Hilda Abbott, *Among the Hills* (Sydney, Australasian Publishing Company, 1948).

6   Elizabeth Harrower, 'The Beautiful Climate', in Geoffrey Dutton (ed.), *Modern Australian Writing* (London, Collins, 1966), pp. 217–30.

7   Eve Hogan, 'The Hessian Walls', *Selected Lives* (Fremantle, Fremantle Arts Centre Press, 1983), pp. 81–139.

8   Richard Coe, *When the Grass Was Taller* (New Haven, Yale University Press, 1984), p. 144.

9   'Portraits of the Artist as a Young Man', *Meanjin* 42 (1983), p. 346.

10 *The Reproduction of Mothering* (Berkeley, University of California Press, 1978), p. 192.

11 Thelma Forshaw, *An Affair of Clowns* (Sydney, Angus & Robertson, 1967), p. 83.

12   Agnes Melda Prince, *Esther Mary, My Pioneer Mother* (Fremantle, Fremantle Arts Centre Press, 1981), p. 35.
13   Alexandra Hasluck, *Portrait in a Mirror* (Melbourne, Oxford University Press, 1981), p. 87.
14   Zelda D'Aprano, *Zelda, the Becoming of a Woman* (North Carlton, Vic., Z. D'Aprano, 1977), p. 6.
15   Joice Nankivell Loch, *A Fringe of Blue* (London, John Murray, 1968), p. 13.
16   Miles Franklin, *My Career Goes Bung* (Melbourne, Georgian House, 1946), pp. 19, 21.
17   E. Lecky Payne, *Beltana—Six Miles* (Adelaide, Rigby, 1974).
18   *When the Grass was Taller*, p. 141.
19   'A Waker and Dreamer', *Ocean of Story* (Ringwood, Vic., Penguin Books, 1986), pp. 481–93. First published *Overland* (1972).
20   Clara Jackamarra, in Sheila M. Kelly, *Proud Heritage* (Perth, Artlook, 1980).
21   *The Reproduction of Mothering*, p. 195.
22   Sarah Conigrave, *My Reminiscences of Early Days* (Perth, 1914), p. 12.
23   Harriet Martineau, *Autobiography* Volume 1 (London, Virago, 1983), p. 99.
24   Jane Miller, *Women Writing About Men* (London, Virago, 1986), p. 101.
25   Adrienne Rich, *Of Woman Born* (New York, Norton, 1976), p. 245.
26   Ursula Owen (ed.), *Fathers: Reflections by Daughters* (London, Virago, 1983), p. 13.
27   Sophia Judith Stevenson, *Across the Vanished Years. Memories of a Pioneer Pastoral Family of Central Queensland* (Rannes, Queensland, Author, 1981), p. 97.
28   Jane Lindsay, *Portrait of Pa* (Sydney, Angus & Robertson, 1973).
29   Cyril Pearl, *Nation Review*, 26 October–1 November 1973, p. 61; Ross Campbell, *Bulletin*, 6 October 1973, p. 54; Ruth Park, *Sunday Telegraph*, 25 November 1973, p. 83; Adrian Mitchell, *Advertiser*, 24 November 1973, p. 26.
30   *Fictions in Autobiography* (Princeton, Princeton University Press, 1985), p. 226.
31   In Owen (ed.), *Fathers*, p. 33.
32   Elizabeth Bruss, *Autobiographical Acts* (Baltimore, Johns Hopkins University Press, 1976), p. 13.
33   Jessica Anderson, *Stories from the Warm Zone* (Ringwood, Penguin, 1987).
34   Kathleen Mangan, *Daisy Chains, War, then Jazz* (Melbourne, Hutchinson, 1984).
35   Mary Drake, *The Trees Were Green* (Sydney, Hale & Iremonger, 1984).
36   Josie Arnold, *Mother Superior Woman Inferior* (Blackburn, Vic., Dove Communications, 1985).

Chapter 7

1 Adrienne Rich, *Of Woman Born* (London, Virago, 1977), p. 223.

2 Rich, pp. 250, 253.

3 Luce Iragaray, 'And the One Doesn't Stir Without the Other', translated by Helene Vivienne Wenzel, *Signs* 7, 1 (1981), p. 63.

4 Iragaray, pp. 61–2.

5 Sara Ruddick, 'Maternal Thinking', *Signs* 6, 2 (1980), p. 343.

6 Miles Franklin, *My Career Goes Bung* (Melbourne, Georgian House, 1946).

7 Rich, p. 235.

8 Amie Livingstone Stirling, *Memories of an Australian Childhood 1880–1900* (Melbourne, Schwartz Publishing, 1980).

9 André Maurois, *Aspects of Biography*, trans. by S. C. Roberts (Cambridge University Press, 1929), p. 142.

10 Iragaray, *Signs* 7, 1 (1981) p. 67.

11 Stella Bowen, *Drawn from Life* (First published 1941; Maidstone, George Manus, 1973), pp. 23, 27.

12 Barbara Pepworth, *Early Marks* (Sydney, Angus & Robertson, 1980), p. 253.

13 Elizabeth Riley, *All That False Instruction* (Sydney, Angus & Robertson, 1975), p. 20.

14 Gail Morgan, *Promise of Rain* (London, Virago, 1985), p. 55.

15 Jennifer Dabbs, *Beyond Redemption* (Ringwood, Penguin/McPhee Gribble, 1987).

16 Jane Flax, 'Mother-Daughter Relationships: Psychodynamics, Politics, and Philosophy', in Hester Eisenstein and Alice Jardine (edd.), *The Future of Difference* (Boston, Mass., G. K. Hall, 1980), p. 35.

17 Ruddick, p. 346.

18 Judith Gardiner, 'On Female Identity and Writing by Women', *Critical Inquiry* (Winter 1981), reprinted in Elizabeth Abel (ed.), *Writing and Sexual Difference* (Brighton, Harvester Press, 1982), p. 186, n. 18.

19 Rose Lindsay, *Ma and Pa* (Sydney, Ure Smith, 1963); Nene Gare, *A House With Verandahs* (Melbourne, Macmillan, 1980).

20 *Of Woman Born*, p. 220.

21 See Chapter 4.

22 Unpublished letter by Mrs Kernot. Reported in Dorothy Green, *Ulysses Bound: Henry Handel Richardson and Her Fiction* (Canberra, Australian National University Press, 1973), p. 342.

23 The suggestion is Dorothy Green's, *Ulysses Bound*, p. 403.

24 'Conditions and Limits of Autobiography', in James Olney (ed.), *Autobiography: Essays Theoretical and Critical* (Princeton, New Jersey, Princeton University Press, 1980), p. 47.

25 Henry Handel Richardson, 'Two Hanged Women', first published in *The End of a Childhood* (1934) and reprinted in *The Adventures of Cuffy*

Mahony (Sydney, Angus & Robertson, 1979). All references are to the last publication.

26   *Ulysses Bound*, pp. 494–5.

27   *Ultima Thule*. First published 1929. The quotation is from *The Fortunes of Richard Mahony* (Ringwood, Vic., Penguin, 1982), p. 800.

28   Henry Handel Richardson, *Myself When Young* (Melbourne, Heinemann, 1948), p. 63.

29   'Gender, Relation, and Difference in Psychoanalytic Perspective', in Hester Eisenstein & Alice Jardine (edd.), *The Future of Difference* (Boston, Mass., G. K. Hall, 1980), p. 7.

30   The words are Adrienne Rich's, *Of Woman Born*, p. 236.

31   Dorothy Green suggests at several points in *Ulysses Bound* that Robertson fulfilled the role of mother for Richardson and describes the element of panic in both relationships.

32   Edna Purdie & Olga Roncoroni (edd.), *Henry Handel Richardson: Some Personal Impressions* (Sydney, Angus & Robertson, 1957), p. 103.

33   Dorothy Green, for instance, in *Ulysses Bound* comments on Richardson's attitude of resentment towards both her mother and Robertson for their abandonment of her by dying.

34   Jane Flax, 'The Conflict between Nurturance and Autonomy in Mother-Daughter Relationships', *Feminist Studies* 4, 2 (1978), p. 180.

35   Agnes Hunt, *Reminiscences* (Shrewsbury, 1935).

36   Anna Wickham, 'Fragment of an Autobiography', in R. D. Smith (ed.), *The Writings of Anna Wickham* (London, Virago, 1984), p. 80.

37   Jean Bedford, *Love Child* (Ringwood, Penguin, 1986).

Chapter 8

1   Interview with Rodney Wetherell, *Australian Literary Studies* 9 (1980), p. 438.

2   Christina Stead, *The Man Who Loved Children* (First published 1940; Sydney, Angus & Robertson, 1979), pp. 31–2. All references are to this edition.

3   'Christina Stead in Washington Square', Interview with Jonah Raskin, *London Magazine* (February 1970), p. 72.

4   See for example the interviews with John B. Beston, *World Literature Written in English* 15 (1976), pp. 88–95; with Guilia Guifree, *Stand* 23, 4 (1982), pp. 22–3; with Rodney Wetherell, *Australian Literary Studies* 9 (1980), pp. 431–8.

5   Dorothy Dinnerstein, *The Rocking of the Cradle and the Ruling of the World*. First published in 1976, with title *The Mermaid and the Minotaur* (London, The Women's Press, 1987), p. 5.

6   *The Second Sex* (1949). Quoted by Dinnerstein, p. 222.

7   'A Waker and Dreamer', *Ocean of Story* (Ringwood, Vic., Penguin, 1986), pp. 485–6. First published *Overland* (1972).

8 'Christina Stead's *The Man Who Loved Children*', *Southerly* 44 (1983), p. 399.

9 'Christina Stead's New Realism: *The Man Who Loved Children* and *Cotters' England*', in Stephen Knight & Don Anderson (edd.), *Cunning Exiles* (Sydney, Angus & Robertson, 1974), p. 18.

10 W. E. Woodward, *A New American History* (London, Faber & Faber, 1938), pp. 588–9.

11 Louie's growth has been meticulously analysed by several critics. One of the most sensitive discussions is Shirley Walker's 'Language, Art and Ideas in *The Man Who Loved Children*', *Meridian* 2, 1 (1983), pp. 11–19.

12 This analysis of *The Man Who Loved Children*, I suggest, explains Stead's persistent refusal to be classed as a feminist: 'Men and women are made to love each other. It is only by loving each other that they can achieve anything. This separation of women is the most disgraceful thing and the most disorderly thing in the (women's) movement.' Interview, *Age*, 28 February 1980.

13 Thus, readers who are distressed at Louie's 'abandonment' of the children are distressing themselves unduly.

Chapter 9

1 Coral Chambers, *Lessons for Ladies* (Sydney, Hale & Iremonger, 1986).

2 Barbara White, *Growing Up Female* (Westport, Connecticut, Greenwood Press, 1985).

3 Donald Horne, *The Education of Young Donald* (Sydney, Angus & Robertson, 1967), p. 76.

4 Connie Miller, *After Summer Merrily* (Fremantle, Fremantle Arts Centre Press, 1980); *Seasons of Learning* (Fremantle, Fremantle Arts Centre Press, 1983).

5 *Women Writing About Men* (London, Virago, 1986), p. 19.

6 Anna Wickham, 'A Fragment of Autobiography', in R. D. Smith (ed.), *The Writings of Anna Wickham* (London, Virago, 1984), p. 107.

7 Kathleen Mangan, *Daisy Chains, War, then Jazz* (Hawthorn, Vic., Hutchinson, 1984).

8 Hal Porter, *The Watcher on the Cast-Iron Balcony* (London, Faber, 1963), p. 13.

9 Henry Handel Richardson, *The Getting of Wisdom* (First published in 1910; London, Heinemann, first Australian edition 1946), p. 131. All subsequent quotations are from the 1946 edition.

10 Rich is actually outlining the effects of an ideal feminist critique but her words are too appropriate in this context to be omitted. 'When We Dead Awaken: Writing as Re-Vision', *On Lies, Secrets and Silence* (New York, Norton, 1979), p. 35.

11 Henry Handel Richardson, 'Some Notes on My Books', *Virginia*

Quarterly Review (Summer 1940); reprinted in *Southerly* 23 (1963), pp. 8–19.

12   J. G. Robertson, in 'The Art of Henry Handel Richardson', *Myself When Young* (London, Heinemann, 1948), p. 171.

13   Brian McFarlane, '*The Getting of Wisdom:* Not Merry at All', *Australian Literary Studies* 8 (1977), pp. 51–63.

14   Delys Bird, 'Towards an Aesthetics of Australian Women's Fiction: *My Brilliant Career* and *The Getting of Wisdom*', *Australian Literary Studies* 11 (1983), pp. 171–81.

15   Elizabeth Abel, Marianne Hirsch & Elizabeth Langland (edd.), *The Voyage In* (Hanover and London, University Press of New England for Dartmouth College, 1983), p. 5.

16   Marianne Hirsch, 'Spiritual *Bildung:* The Beautiful Soul as Paradigm'. *The Voyage In*, p. 27.

17   'Introduction', *The Voyage In*, p. 8.

18   Carol Franklin in an interesting comparison between *The Getting of Wisdom* and Bjornson's *Fiskerjenten* concludes that Richardson is in fact writing the first genuine female *Kunstlerroman* (*Southerly* 43 (1983), pp. 422–36). I contend, however, that *The Getting of Wisdom* is concerned more with a thoroughgoing exposure of the heroine's society and less with her discovery of her future as an artist and is therefore not a true *Kunstlerroman*.

19   The words are Richardson's, *Myself When Young*, p. 73.

20   *The Getting of Wisdom* (London, Heinemann, 1910).

21   Richardson was highly sensitive to the question of names.

22   Letter to Mrs Kernot in 1934, quoted in Dorothy Green, *Henry Handel Richardson and her Fiction* (Sydney, Allen & Unwin, 1986), p. 223; *Myself When Young*, p. 62.

23   Brian McFarlane, pp. 54, 55.

Chapter 10

1   Elizabeth Riley, *All That False Instruction* (Sydney, Angus & Robertson, 1975), p. 238.

2   'On Female Identity and Writing by Women', *Critical Inquiry* 8 (Winter 1981); reprinted in Elizabeth Abel (ed.), *Writing and Sexual Difference* (Brighton, Harvester Press, 1982), p. 190.

3   Robert May, *Sex and Fantasy* (New York, W. W. Norton, 1980).

4   May, pp. 61, 139.

5   'Portraits of the Artist as a Young Man', *Meanjin* 42 (1983) p. 345.

6   Two of the finest, *Monkey Grip* and *Maurice Guest*, are excluded in that they are largely outside the terms of this study.

7   Clara Ellen Campbell, *The Memoirs of Clara Ellen Campbell 1861–1872* (Brisbane, Gordon & Gotch, 1919).

8   Terry Sturm, 'Christina Stead's New Realism: *The Man Who Loved Children* and *Cotters' England*', in Don Anderson & Stephen Knight

(edd.), *Cunning Exiles* (Sydney, Angus & Robertson, 1974), p. 13.

9 Christina Stead, *For Love Alone* (First published 1944; Sydney, Angus & Robertson, 1966).

10 Joan Lidoff, *Christina Stead* (New York, Frederick Ungar, 1982), p. 63.

11 'The Writers Take Sides', *The Left Review* I, 11 (August 1935), pp. 453–63.

12 Interview with Guilia Guiffre, *Stand* 23, 4 (1982), p. 24.

13 Susan Higgins, 'Christina Stead's *For Love Alone:* A Female Odyssey?', *Southerly* 38 (1978) p. 432.

14 Karen Horney, 'The Dread of Woman', *International Journal of Psychoanalysis* 13 (1932), p. 356.

15 *Christina Stead*, p. 85.

16 Diana Brydon, 'Resisting "The Tyranny of What is Written": Christina Stead's Fiction', *Ariel* 17, 4 (1986) p. 9.

17 Glenda Adams, *Dancing on Coral* (Sydney, Angus & Robertson, 1987). References are to the Sirius edition, 1988.

18 Gabrielle Carey and Kathy Lette, *Puberty Blues* (Fitzroy, Vic., McPhee Gribble, 1979).

19 Eugénie McNeil and Eugénie Crawford, *Ladies Didn't* (Ringwood, Vic., Penguin, 1984). The two sisters in *Ladies Didn't* are Eugénie McNeil and her sister Lydia, who were born with the surname Delarue.

20 Karla Jay, 'Coming Out as Process', Ginny Vida (ed.), *Our Right to Love* (Englewood Cliffs, New Jersey, Prentice-Hall, 1978), p. 29.

Chapter 11

1 John and Dorothy Colmer, 'Introduction', *The Penguin Book of Australian Autobiography* (Ringwood, Vic., Penguin, 1987), pp. 7, 11.

2 Dorothy Jones, 'Mapping and Mythmaking: Women Writers and the Australian Legend', *Ariel* 17, 4 (1986), p. 64.

3 Richard Coe, 'Portrait of the Artist as a Young Australian,' *Southerly* 41 (1981), p. 129.

4 Dorothy Cottrell, *The Singing Gold* (London, Hodder & Stoughton, 1928).

5 Dorothy Dinnerstein, *The Mermaid and the Minotaur* (New York, Harper & Row, 1976). The reference is to the 1987 edition, titled *The Rocking of the Cradle and The Ruling of the World* (London, The Women's Press), p. 222.

6 Dorothy Hewett, 'The Garden and the City', *Westerly* 4 (December 1982), 102.

7 A. G. Stephens, 'A Book Full of Sunlight', *Bulletin*, 28 September 1901.

8 Carmen Callil, 'New Introduction', *My Brilliant Career* (London, Virago, 1980).

9 Frances McInherny in a pioneering article ('Miles Franklin: *My Brilliant Career* and the Female Tradition', *Australian Literary Studies* 9 (1980), pp. 275–85) sees her as straddling feminine and feminist categories, that

is, partly internalizing male ideologies and partly protesting against them and advancing minority rights and values. Delys Bird, in a response to this article ('Towards an Aesthetics of Australian Women's Fiction: *My Brilliant Career* and *The Getting of Wisdom*', *Australian Literary Studies* 11 (1983), pp. 171–81) sees her as imprisoned within an aggressively male social structure and disabled from developing a coherent viewpoint; possessed of a limited understanding of the male manipulative world, and attempting to write within a male literary tradition, Franklin, according to Bird, produced a chaotic text which is structurally indecisive, thematically ambiguous and shifting in its modes of discourse. Susan Gardner ('*My Brilliant Career*: Portrait of the Artist as a Wild Colonial Girl', in Carole Ferrier (ed.), *Gender, Politics and Fiction* (St Lucia, University of Queensland Press, 1985), pp. 22–43) is more sympathetic to Franklin but also sees the novel as flawed and ambivalent: a racist, national-chauvinist and conceptually and ethically garbled narrative, which fails to come to grips with questions of class.

10　John Docker, *Australian Cultural Elites* (Sydney, Angus & Robertson, 1974), pp. 110–11.

11　Verna Coleman, *Miles Franklin in America: Her Unknown (Brilliant) Career* (Sydney, Angus & Robertson, 1981), p. 191.

12　Leon Cantrell, 'Introduction', *Writing of the 1890s* (St Lucia, University of Queensland Press, 1986), p. xx.

13　Havelock Ellis, *Weekly Critical Review* (Paris) 1903.

14　Graeme Turner, *National Fictions* (Sydney, Allen & Unwin, 1986), p. 52.

15　It is generally agreed that there is a marked difference in quality between the autobiographical books and her other writing; the 'Brent of Bin Bin' novels may be an advance on the thin absurdities of *The Net of Circumstance* and *On Dearborn Street*, but Franklin never recaptured the fresh energy of *My Brilliant Career* and the first part of *My Career Goes Bung*.

16　Marjorie Barnard, *Miles Franklin*, p. 16.

17　Miles Franklin, *My Brilliant Career*. First published Edinburgh, 1901. References are to the 1965 imprint (Sydney, Angus & Robertson).

18　'Ah... What a warm-hearted place is the world, how full of pleasure, good, and beauty, when fortune smiles! *When fortune smiles!*' (p. 98).

19　Thus Sybylla receives the news of her imminent exile to Barney's Gap at the moment when her fortune looks the most promising (pp. 159–60).

20　The following are representative: 'Was I always, always, to live here, and never, never, never to go back to Bruggabrong?' (p. 6); 'Ah, those short, short nights of rest and long, long days of toil!' (p. 16); 'I wasn't anxious to patronise the dull kind of tame nobility of the toad; I longed for a few of the triumphs of the butterfly' (p. 35).

21　The idiosyncrasy of this response to place and its part in the manifest emotional pressures of the narrative illustrate the difficulties of attempting to erect Franklin into a representative figure.

22　My italics.

23　He comments that her face is like a kaleidoscope, 'sometimes merry, then stern, often sympathetic, and always sad when at rest' (p. 65).

24　There is no space here to develop the point, but there are identifiable moments in the text of *My Brilliant Career* when fantasy manifestly fails to satisfy the implied author and there is a distinct drop in the emotional temperature. See, for example, pp. 21, 36, 37, 56, 65, 99, 164, 191, 205, 216.

25　Miles Franklin, *My Career Goes Bung* (Melbourne, Georgian House, 1946).

26　Sanjay Sircar, for instance, stresses Franklin's description of the auto-biography as a 'burlesque' and asserts that she 'was aware of the absurdity of some of Sybylla's more exaggerated outbursts'. 'Artfully Artless: Miles Franklin and *My Brilliant Career*', *Folio* (Folio Society, London) (Winter 1983), pp. 20–7. Elizabeth Webby in an unpublished paper delivered at the 1985 ASAL Conference finds an affinity with the narrator/author relationship of *Such is Life*.

27　The editor of the Virago edition, on the other hand, claims that Sybylla 'knows her problems'.

28　Thus her grandmother's warm welcome is a surprise to this 'useless bad little pauper'. She is anxious not to be identified as the daughter of Dick Melvyn and is relieved when she is regarded as 'granddaughter of Mrs Bossier of Caddagat and great friend and intimate of the swell Beechams of Five-Bob Downs station' (p. 139).

29　Mary Fullerton, *Bark House Days* (Melbourne, S. J. Endacott, 1921). References are to the paperback edition (Melbourne, Melbourne University Press, 1964).

30　Mary Fullerton, 'Memoirs'. Held by the Mitchell Library (MS 2342) and by the La Trobe Library.

31　Mary Fullerton, *The People of the Timber Belt* (London, A. M. Philpot, 1925).

32　Richard White, *Inventing Australia* (Sydney, Allen & Unwin, 1981), p. 102.

33　William H. Wilde, Joy Hooton and Barry Andrews, *The Oxford Companion to Australian Literature* (Melbourne, Oxford University Press, 1985), p. 129.

34　Mary Fullerton, 'The Bush Child', *The Australian Bush* (London, J. M. Dent, 1928), p. 53.

35　*The Wonder and the Apple: More Poems by "E"* (Sydney, Angus & Robertson, 1946), p. 20.

36　Patsy Adam Smith, *Hear the Train Blow* (Sydney, Ure Smith, 1964). All references are to the paperback edition (Adelaide, Rigby, 1971).

37　*Sydney Mail*, 28 March 1987.

38　*Canberra Times*, 19 February 1972.

39　*Australian*, 19 December 1981.

Chapter 12

1   W. E. H. Stanner, *After the Dreaming* (Sydney, A. B. C., 1969), p. 25.

2   The following deal, at least partly, with childhood and adolescence: Monica Clare, *Karobran. The Story of an Aboriginal Girl* (Chippendale, N.S.W., Alternative Publishing, 1978); Theresa Clements, *From Old Maloga: the Memoirs of an Aboriginal Woman* (Victoria, Fraser & Morphett, n.d.); Pearl Duncan, 'A Teacher's Life', in Isobel White, Diane Barwick and Betty Meehan (edd.), *Fighters and Singers* (Sydney, George Allen & Unwin, 1985), pp. 40–54; Evonne Goolagong, with Bud Collins, *Evonne! On the Move* (New York and Sydney, E. P. Dutton, 1975); Clara Jackamarra, in Sheila M. Kelly, *Proud Heritage* (Perth, Artlook, 1980); Marnie Kennedy, *Born a Half-Caste* (Canberra, Australian Institute of Aboriginal Studies, 1985); Magdalene McIntosh, with Elaine Rothwell, 'Maddie', *Aboriginal History* 3, 1–2 (1979) 3–24; Janet McKenzie, *Fingal Tiger* (Blackwood, S. A., New Creation Publications, 1982); Sally Morgan, *My Place* (Fremantle, Fremantle Arts Centre Press, 1987); Patricia O'Shane, 'A Healthy Sense of Identity', in Heather Radi & Madge Dawson (edd.), *Against the Odds* (Sydney, Hale & Iremonger, 1984), pp. 28–37; Elsie Roughsey, *An Aboriginal Mother Tells of the Old and the New* (Paul Memmott and Robyn Horsman, edd.), Fitzroy and Ringwood, McPhee Gribble/Penguin, 1984); Ella Simon, *Through My Eyes* (Adelaide, Rigby, 1978), references are to the 1987 edition published by Collins Dove; Shirley Smith, with Bobbi Sykes, *Mum Shirl* (Richmond, Heineman Educational, 1981); Margaret Tucker, *If Everyone Cared* (Sydney, Ure Smith, 1977); Kath Walker, *Stradbroke Dreamtime* (Sydney, Angus & Robertson, 1972); also contribution to Terry Lane (ed.), *As the Twig is Bent* (Melbourne, Dove, 1979); Glenyse Ward, *Wandering Girl* (Broome, Magabala Books, 1987); Lilla Watson, 'Sister, Black is the Colour of My Soul', *Different Lives*, ed. Jocelynne A. Scutt, Ringwood, Vic., Penguin, 1987, pp. 44–52. Ida West, *Pride Against Prejudice* (Canberra, Australian Institute of Aboriginal Studies, 1984). An earlier autobiography by 'Buludja', edited by H. E. Thonemann and titled *Tell the White Man* (Sydney, Collins, 1949) is probably inauthentic as I discuss below. Faith Bandler's narratives, *Wacvie* (Adelaide, Rigby, 1977) and *Welou, My Brother* (Glebe, Wild & Woolley, 1984) are usually included in bibliographies of Aboriginal writing, but are excluded here as neither fits the terms of this study. Ruby Langford's *Don't Take Your Love to Town* (Ringwood, Vic., Penguin, 1988) was unfortunately published too late to be included in this chapter.

3   William Dilthey, *Meaning in History* (New York, 1961), p. 85.

4   The phrase is Stanner's.

5   Roger Rosenblatt, 'Black Autobiography: Life as the Death Weapon', *The Yale Review* 65 (1976), pp. 515–27; reprinted in James Olney (ed.), *Autobiography: Essays Theoretical and Critical* (Princeton, New Jersey, Princeton University Press, 1980), pp. 169–80.

6 Diane Bell, *Daughters of the Dreaming* (Melbourne, McPhee Gribble, George Allen & Unwin, 1985), p. 229.

7 See for instance Fay Gale, 'Introduction', *Women's Role in Aboriginal Society* (Canberra, Australian Institute of Aboriginal Studies, 1980).

8 The phrases are Rosenblatt's.

9 Marnie Kennedy, *Born a Half-Caste*, p. 1.

10 Ivor Indyk, 'A. B. Facey's Australian Autobiography', *Australian Literary Studies* 13 (May 1987), p. 31.

11 *After the Dreaming*, p. 28.

12 A. B. Facey, *A Fortunate Life* (Ringwood, Vic., Penguin, 1981), pp. 188–9.

13 *Daughters of the Dreaming*, pp. 144, 145.

14 *Fighters and Singers*, p. xvi.

15 Veronica Brady, 'Something that was Shameful', *The Age Monthly Review* (October 1987), p. 3.

Chapter 13

1 Alice Henry, *Memoirs of Alice Henry* (Melbourne, Alice Henry, 1944), p. 1.

2 Dorothy Hewett, 'The Garden and the City', *Westerly* 4 (December 1982), p. 100.

3 John & Dorothy Colmer (edd.), *Australian Autobiography* (Ringwood, Vic., Penguin, 1987), p. 7.

4 George Seddon, 'The Evolution of Perceptual Attitudes', *Man and Landscape in Australia*, edd. George Seddon and Mari Davis (Canberra, Australian Government Publishing Service, 1976), p. 9.

5 Randolph Stow, 'Raw Material', *Westerly* 2 (1961), p. 3.

6 The phrase is Leonie Kramer's, *Man and Landscape*, p. 152.

7 'The Garden and the City', p. 102.

8 Barbara Corbett, *A Fistful of Buttercups* (Kenthurst, Kangaroo Press, 1983).

9 Eve Langley, *The Pea Pickers*. First published 1942. References are to the paperback edition (Sydney, Angus & Robertson, 1984).

10 Marion Arkin, 'Literary Transvestism in Eve Langley's *The Pea-Pickers*', *Modern Fiction Studies* 27 (1981), pp. 109–16; Joy Thwaite, 'Eve Langley: Personal and Artistic Schism', in Carole Ferrier (ed.), *Gender, Politics and Fiction* (St Lucia, University of Queensland Press, 1985), pp. 118–235; Harry Heseltine, 'Eve Langley. Oscar Wilde in the Blue Mountains,' *The Uncertain Self* (Melbourne, Oxford University Press, 1986), pp. 112–30.

11 Eve Langley, *White Topee* (Sydney, Angus & Robertson, 1954), p. 69.

12 The narrator in fact quotes from the sonnet at one point (p. 261).

13 Langley's Steve is not alone in this response to Gippsland, for several writers have reflected on its peculiar impact on the spirit. Grace Jennings, for instance, recalls 'the intense feeling of loneliness and

melancholy' that she felt as a child in 1870s Gippsland: 'It had a magic
kind of fascination, blended with a feeling of perplexity that is somewhat
difficult to define'. 'Carmichael, Jennings' [Grace Elizabeth Jennings],
'My Old Station Home', *Centennial Magazine* (February 1890), p. 556.

14   Annis Pratt, 'Woman and Nature in Modern Fiction', *Contemporary
Literature* 13 (1972) p. 488.

15   My italics.

16   Sarah Conigrave, *My Reminiscences of Early Days: Personal Incidents
on a Sheep and Cattle Run in South Australia* (Perth, 1914).

17   Mary Drake, *A House of Trees* (London, Chatto & Windus, 1984).

18   Rosa Praed, *Australian Life: Black and White* (London, Chapman &
Hall, 1885), p. 28.

19   Rosa Praed, *My Australian Girlhood* (London, T. Fisher Unwin, 1902),
p. 155.

20   Mary Rose Liverani, *The Winter Sparrows*. First published 1975. References are to the paperback edition (Melbourne, Nelson, 1978).

21   My italics.

22   Amirah Inglis, 'An Un-Australian Childhood', *Island Magazine* 18/19,
p. 73.

23   Amirah Inglis, *Amirah. An Un-Australian Childhood* (Richmond, Vic.,
Heinemann, 1983).

Conclusion

1   The study of Australian autobiography is still handicapped by the lack of
bibliographical guides, however, a gap which Kay Walsh and I hope to
fill, thanks to a generous grant from the Australian Research Council.

2   John & Dorothy Colmer (edd.), *The Penguin Book of Australian Autobiography* (Ringwood, Vic., Penguin, 1987), p. 7.

3   André Maurois, *Aspects of Biography* (transl. S. C. Roberts, Cambridge,
Cambridge University Press, 1929), pp. 144–5.

4   Kay Schaffer, *Women and the Bush* (Cambridge, Cambridge University
Press, 1988), p. 8.

5   *Women and the Bush*, p. 183.

6   V. S. Pritchett, Presidential Address to the English Association, June
1977.

Bibliography of Autobiographies

The listing includes published and unpublished prose autobiographies written by Australian women, or women resident in Australia, as well as fictional autobiographical narratives. Short stories are included only where these form a cycle or group. Narratives which deal exclusively or in the main with adult years are not included. The date cited is of the first edition, although in some cases subsequent editions are cited. Birth and death dates are also given where these are obtainable.

Abbott, Hilda. *Among the Hills*. Sydney, Australasian Publishing Co., 1948.

Abdullah, Mena (1930–) and Mathew, Ray. *The Time of the Peacock*. New York, Roy Publishers, 1965.

Adam, Jane E. (1851–1951). 'Reminiscences of Early Days in Perth by Jane E. Adam (née Leake) completed in 1949 when she was in her 85th year'. Battye Library. PR 3555.

Adams, Glenda (1940–). *Lies and Stories*. New York, Inwood Press, 1976; *The Hottest Night of the Century*. Sydney, Angus & Robertson, 1979; *Dancing on Coral*. Sydney, Angus & Robertson, 1987.

Adams, Nancy (1890–1968). *Family Fresco*. Melbourne, Cheshire, 1966.

Adams, Vera Mary. *No Stranger in Paradise*. Sydney, Australasian Book Society, 1976.

Adam Smith, Patsy (1926–). *Hear the Train Blow*. Sydney, Ure Smith, 1964; illustrated edition, Melbourne, Nelson, 1981; 'The Road from Gundagai'. *Australia Beyond the Dreamtime*. Richmond, Vic., Heinemann, 1987.

Ahearn, Maude. *I Remember*. Greenough, WA, Author, 1977.

Airy, Joan. 'Rural Life Between the Wars'. Ed. S. W. Dyer. *South Australiana*, 14 (March 1975), 3–19.

Allen, *Mrs* J. S. O. *Memories of My Life: from My Early Days in Scotland till the Present Day in Adelaide*. Adelaide, J. L. Bonython & Co., 1906.

Alsop, Florence A. 'The Wheel is Turning. An Australian Autobiography'. Written 1956. La Trobe Library. Part I H17292 Box 115/4, Part II H17292 Box 115/4. 'Journeys and Journals. The Story of My Family'. H17289 Box

115/1. 'The Wheel is Turning' is accompanied by a volume of illustrations drawn by the author. H17293 Box 115/4.

Anderson, Jessica. *Stories From the Warm Zone*. Ringwood, Vic., Penguin, 1987.

Archdale, Betty (1907–). *Indiscretions of a Headmistress*. Sydney, Angus & Robertson, 1972.

Arney, Ivy V. *Twenties Child*. Melbourne, Collins Dove, 1987.

Arnold, Josie (1941–). *Mother Superior Woman Inferior*. Blackburn, Vic., Dove Communications, 1985.

Aston, Tilly (1874–1947). *Memoirs of Tilly Aston*. Melbourne, Hawthorn Press, 1946; 'Gold from Old Diggings'. *Bendigo Advertiser* (August 1937); *Old Timers*. Melbourne, Lothian Publishing, 1938.

Attrill, Glorie. *Sunset Serenade: Autobiography of Glorie Attrill 1911–1975*. Author, 1975.

Baker, Mary Lou. *I Remember*. Adelaide, Griffin Press, 1960.

Balsamo, Eileen. 'A Conspiracy of Forces'. *Sweet Mothers, Sweet Maids*. Ed. Kate Nelson and Dominica Nelson. Ringwood, Vic., Penguin, 1986. pp. 45–50.

Ball, Shirley (1926–). *Muma's Boarding House*. Adelaide, Rigby, 1978.

Bandler, Faith (1918–). *Welou, My Brother*. Glebe, Wild & Woolley, 1984; *Wacvie*. Adelaide, Rigby, 1977.

Banks, Mary MacLeod (née McConnell) (d. 1914). *Memories of Pioneer Days in Queensland*. London, Cranton, 1931.

Bartlett, Evelyn (1905–82). *The Emily Stories*. Perth, Infinite Publications, 1978.

[Barton, Charlotte] (1797–1862). *A Mother's Offering to her Children*. Sydney, printed at the *Gazette* Office, 1841.

Bauer, Margaret. *Ask Aunt Em*. Sydney, M. Bauer, n.d.

Bedford, Jean (1946–). *Country Girl Again*. Melbourne, Sisters, 1979; *Country Girl Again and Other Stories*. Fitzroy, Vic., McPhee Gribble, 1985; *Love Child*. Ringwood, Vic., Penguin, 1986; With Rosemary Creswell. *Colouring In: A Book of Ideologically Unsound Love Stories*. Fitzroy, Vic., Penguin/McPhee Gribble, 1986.

Bell, Betty (fl. 1957–86). *Mermaids Maybe. Flying Fish Never!* Bowen Hills, Qld, Boolarong Publications, 1986.

Bell, Georgina (1818–?). 'Diary'. Includes autobiographical narrative titled 'Family Traditions'. La Trobe Library. MS 11734. Box 1874/5.

Binns, Joan. 'Random Recollections of a Child Pioneer'. (Quoted in Jill Waterhouse's *A Light in the Bush. The Canberra Church of England Girls Grammar School and the Capital City of Australia, 1926–1977*. Deakin, CCEGGS, 1978. Unseen.)

Blake, Audrey (1916–). *A Proletarian Life*. Malmsbury, Vic., Kibble Books, 1984.

Blake, Katherine. *Are You Trying to Annoy Me?* London, Macmillan, 1969.

Blazeley, E. 'Mrs Blazeley Remembers for her Grand-daughter'. in Mary

Kinloch Whishaw. *Tasmanian Village. A Story of Carrick.* Hobart, M. K. Whishaw, 1963.

Bligh, Marjorie. *Life is for Living.* Devonport, C. L. Richmond & Sons, 1986.

'Boake, Capel' (Doris Boake Kerr) (1899–1945). *Painted Clay.* Melbourne, Australasian Authors' Agency, 1917.

Bonython, *Lady* Constance Jean (1891–1977). *I'm No Lady. The Reminiscences of Constance Jean, Lady Bonython, O.B.E. 1891–1977.* Ed. C. Warren Bonython. Adelaide, C. Warren Bonython, 1976–81.

Boswell, Annabella (1826–1916). *Early Recollections and Gleanings from an Old Journal.* London, 1908; *Further Recollections of My Early Days in Australia,* by A. A. C. D. Boswell. London, 1911; *Annabella Boswell's Journal.* Ed. Morton Herman. Sydney. Angus & Robertson, 1965.

Bottomley, Gill. 'The Luck of the Draw or the Fate of a Female Scholar'. *Against the Odds.* Ed. Heather Radi and Madge Dawson. Sydney, Hale & Iremonger, 1984. pp. 76–95.

Bowen, Stella (1895–1947). *Drawn from Life.* London, Collins, 1941. Subsequently published London, Virago, 1984.

Bradstock, Margaret and Wakeling, Louisa (eds). *Words from the Same Heart.* Sydney, Hale & Iremonger, 1987.

Brady, Mary Irene (1907–83). *There Were Five Creeks.* Melbourne, Kathleen Brady, 1984.

Brady, Veronica. '"We are Such Stuff..."'. *Sweet Mothers, Sweet Maids.* Ed. Kate Nelson and Dominica Nelson. Ringwood, Vic., Penguin, 1986.

Brennan, Mary (1889–). With Elaine McKenna. *Better Than Dancing.* Richmond, Vic., Greenhouse Publications, 1987.

Brinsmead, Pixie Hungerford. 'Hamlet on the Mountain's Brink (The Story of Bilpin)'. Royal Historical Society of Victoria. Box 78/4.

Brookes, May. *Wild Flowers and Wanderings: Under the North Star and the Southern Cross.* Paris, Imprimérie Francaise de l'Edition, 1925.

Brooks, Barbara. *Leaving Queensland.* (published with *The Train* by Anna Couani). Glebe, Seacruise Books, 1983.

Brotherton, Hilda (née Cleminson) (1891–). 'The Family Album: An Autobiography'. Fryer Library. F130.

Brouton, Pat (1943–). *The Cruel World of A Child.* Melbourne, Council of Adult Education, 1981.

Brown, Bud (1927–). *Coffee with Roses: Miss Brown's Story.* Kenthurst, NSW, Kangaroo Press, 1983.

Brown, Kathleen (1913–). *The First Born.* Kenthurst, NSW, Kangaroo Press, 1984.

Brown (Youngman), Margaret Emily. 'Memoirs of Margaret Emily Brown (Youngman). A Recording of 58 Years of Life Mainly in Port Fairy'. Written 1907. La Trobe Library. MS 11619. Box 1833/4.

Brown, Rose Barbara (1911–). *A Woman Who Tried.* Fremantle, Fremantle Arts Centre Press, 1982.

Brownell, Rhyllis Jean (1896–). *Recollections and Reflections.* Claremont, WA, R. J. Brownell, 1982.

Browning, Doris M. 'Memories of "Carinya" from 1911 to 1921'. (Perth, 1938). Battye Library. PR 11683.

Bruce, Mary Grant (1878–1958). *The Peculiar Honeymoon and Other Writings.* Ed. Prue McKay. Melbourne, McPhee Gribble, 1986.

'Budge, Price' (Annie Budge). *Dora West.* Melbourne, Gordon & Gotch, 1909.

Bundock, Mary. 'Notes on Early Recollections of Richmond River'. Mitchell Library. MSA 6939.

Burrell, Kath (1898–). *Happy Days.* Perth, Access Press, 1983.

Bushell, Alma E. (ed.). *Yesterday's Daughters: Stories of Our Past by Women over 70.* Melbourne, Nelson, 1976.

Butler, J. Marjorie (1896–). *Time Isn't Long Enough.* Melbourne, Hawthorn Press, 1971.

Buttrose, Ita (1942–). *Early Edition: My First Forty Years.* S. Melbourne, Macmillan, 1985.

Cain, Mary Jane (née Griffin). 'Reminiscences of Coonabarabran, NSW & district, 1844–1926'. Mitchell Library. MLDOC 2686.

Cameron, Elizabeth J. (1936–). *The Power from Within.* Melbourne, Spectrum, 1983.

Campbell, Adelaide Fanny Lyol (1897–). *Joy and Sorrow Interwoven.* Warradale, SA, E. J. Campbell, 1983.

Campbell, Clara Ellen (1845–1918). *The Memoirs of Clara Ellen Campbell 1861–1872.* Brisbane, Gordon & Gotch, 1919.

Campbell, Ellen. *An Australian Childhood.* London, Blackie, 1892; *Twin Pickles.* London, Blackie, 1898.

Campbell, Dame Kate (1899–). 'A Medical Life'. *The Half-Open Door.* Ed. Patricia Grimshaw and Lynne Strahan. Sydney, Hale & Iremonger, 1982. pp. 156–71.

Canavan, Beryl (1942–). *The Heart and Mind.* Adelaide, Author, 1981.

Cappiello, Rosa. *Paese Fortunato (Oh Lucky Country).* Transl. G. Rando. St Lucia, University of Queensland Press, 1984.

Carey, Gabrielle (1959–) and Lette, Kathy (1959–). *Puberty Blues.* Fitzroy, Vic., McPhee Gribble, 1979.

Carmichael, Grace ('Jennings Carmichael') (1868–1904). 'Early Station Memories'. *Australasian,* 9 November 1895, p. 894; 'My Old Station Home'. *Centennial Magazine,* February 1890.

Carter, Jan (ed). *Nothing to Spare.* Ringwood, Vic., Penguin, 1982.

Casey, Lady Maie (1892–1983). *An Australian Story 1837–1907.* London, Michael Joseph, 1962.

Casey-Congdon, Dorothy (1910–). *Casey's Wife.* Perth, Artlook, 1982.

Casely, Mary Ann. *Memoirs of Mrs R. S. Casely 1839–1916.* Norwood, Casely Family, 1975. Manuscript held La Trobe Library. MS 9762. Bay 18.

Cash, Deirdre. *See* 'Rohan, Criena'.

Caverhill, Jane (née Mack) (1841–94). 'Reminiscences 1840s–1850s'.

Written in 1881. La Trobe Library. H 15903 102/1.

Chapman, Anne Hale (1830–1908).'Reminiscences of Anne Hale Chapman (née Wilson) from 1835 to 1903'. Mitchell Library. MSS 2837.

Chettle-Goddard, Lilian Vera. *The Romance of History*. Sutherland, NSW, Author, 1987.

Chomley, Eliza (1842–1932). 'My Memoirs'. La Trobe Library. MS 9034. VSL Box 142/6(a).

Christesen, Nina. 'A Russian Migrant'. *The Half-Open Door*. Ed. Patricia Grimshaw and Lynne Strahan. Sydney, Hale & Iremonger, 1982. pp. 56–77.

Christie, Phoebe. With I. M. Spencer. 'The Memories of Mrs Phoebe Christie'. Perth, 1949. Battye Library. PR 12750.

Christina, Lucy (1913–). *Child of the Outback*. Fremantle, C. Lucy, 1982.

Churchward, Emily Emma (1853–1933). *In Paths Directed*. Ed. Stella Mary MacDonald. Hawthorndene, Investigator Press, 1984; *Emily Emma of Adelaide: reminiscences and autobiography…for the years 1853–1876*. Ed. Stella Mary Churchward MacDonald. Brighton, Vic., Mary MacDonald, 197?.

Cilento, *Lady* Phyllis (1894–1987). *My Life*. N. Ryde, NSW, Methuen Haynes, 1987.

Clare, Monica (1924–73). *Karobran. The Story of an Aboriginal Girl*. Chippendale, NSW, Alternative Publishing, 1978.

Clark, Caroline Emily (1825–?). 'Early Recollections'. Mortlock Library. PRG 331.

Clark, Mavis Thorpe (?1912–). 'Words About an Author'. *The Early Dreaming*. Comp. Michael Dugan. Milton, Qld. Jacaranda Press, 1980. pp. 9–21.

Clements, Theresa. *From Old Maloga: the Memoirs of an Aboriginal Woman*. Victoria, Fraser & Morphett, n.d.

Coaker, *Mrs* M. A. *Millie's Memoirs*. Perth, Lyn Glassford, 1984.

Coburn, Mary Kathleen. *A Pattern of Lives*. Melbourne, Author, 1983.

Coffey, Ida. *Look Up and Laugh*. Melbourne, National Press, 1945.

Cohn, Ola (1892–1964). 'Me in the Making'. Written 1950. La Trobe Library. MS 8506. Box 1023.

Colebrook, Joan. *A House of Trees*. London, Chatto & Windus, 1988.

Conigrave, Sarah. *My Reminiscences of Early Days: Personal Incidents on a Sheep and Cattle Run in South Australia*. Perth, 1914; Perth, Brokensha & Shaw, 1938.

Cooke, Deirdre. 'Straying from the Straight and Narrow'. *Sweet Mothers, Sweet Maids*. Ed. Kate Nelson and Dominica Nelson. Ringwood, Vic., Penguin, 1986. pp. 13–20.

Corbett, Barbara (1923–). *A Fistful of Buttercups*. Kenthurst, Kangaroo Press, 1983.

Cordner, Cherry. *A Mavis Singing: the Story of an Australian Family*. Kensington, University of NSW Press, 1986.

Costin, Evelyn R. (1901–). *Shadows on the Grass. An Autobiography from*

1901 to 1978 with its adjacent history. Apollo Bay, Vic., Edgewaters, 1981.

Cottrell, Dorothy (1902–57). *The Singing Gold.* London, Hodder & Stoughton, 1928; Boston, Houghton Mifflin, 1928.

Court, Margaret (1942–). With George McGann. *Court on Court.* London, W. H. Allen, 1976.

Couvreur, Jessie ('Tasma'). *Not Counting the Cost.* New York, D. Appleton, 1895.

Cowen, Rose Scott (1879–?). *Crossing Dry Creeks, 1879–1919.* Sydney, Wentworth Press, 1961.

Cowie, Bessie. *See* Lee, Bessie.

Cowle, Mary (1874–1964). 'Childhood Recollections of Mary Cowle (Nee Bird)'. Written 1932. *The Bird Family and Woodloes.* Canning District Historical Society, 1977.

Craig, Ailsa (1917–). *If Blood Should Stain the Wattle.* Sydney, Currawong, 1946.

Craney, Jan and Caldwell, Esther (eds.). *The True Life Story of-----.* St Lucia, University of Queensland Press, 1981.

Crawford, Eugénie, *see* McNeil, Eugénie.

Cree, Mary (1919–). *Edith May 1895–1974, Life in Early Tasmania.* Toorak, James Street Publications, 1983.

Cropley, Ruve (Calder). *Forty 'Odd' Years in a Manse.* Sydney, R. Cropley, 1962.

Crough, Nan. 'Autobiography'. La Trobe Library. MS 11767. Box 2014/8.

Crowle, Mary Beatrice (née Finucane) (1874–1972). 'Our Childhood in Australia'. National Library of Australia. MS 3154. Folder 5.

Crowley, Grace (1890–1979). 'A Personal View—the Student Years'. *Australian Women Artists: One Hundred Years 1840–1940.* Sel. Janine Burke. Melbourne, Melbourne University Union, 1976. pp. 10–13.

Cue, Kerry. *Crooks, Chooks and Bloody Ratbags.* Ringwood, Vic., Penguin, 1988.

Curmi, Kathleen. 'Not Unreasonably Angry'. *Sweet Mothers, Sweet Maids.* Ed. Kate Nelson and Dominica Nelson. Ringwood, Vic., Penguin, 1986. pp. 125–32.

Cusack, Dymphna (1902–81). 'Uncorrected Transcription of Notes done for an Autobiography'. National Library of Australia. MS 4621/91–248.

Dabbs, Jennifer (1938–). *Beyond Redemption.* Fitzroy, Vic., McPhee Gribble/Penguin, 1987.

Daly, *Mrs* Dominic D. (Harriet W.). *Digging, Squatting, and Pioneering Life in the Northern Territory of South Australia.* London, Sampson Low, 1887.

D'Aprano, Zelda (1928–). *Zelda: The Becoming of a Woman.* North Carlton, Vic., Z. D'Aprano, 1977.

Davidson, Robyn (1950–). 'The Mythological Crucible'. *Australia Beyond the Dreamtime.* Richmond, Vic., Heinemann, 1987. pp. 169–240.

Davies, Eliza (née Arbuckle). *The Story of an Earnest Life: A Woman's Adventures in Australia and in Two Voyages around the World.* Cincinnati, Central Book Concern, 1881.

Davis, Faye (1937–). *Paisley Print*. Fremantle, Fremantle Arts Centre Press, 1984.

Dawson, Madge. ' " When you marry never give up your work" ' *Against the Odds*. Ed. Heather Radi and Madge Dawson. Sydney, Hale &Iremonger, 1984. pp. 238–55.

Deacon, Vera. 'Making Do and Lasting Out'. *Depression Down Under*. Ed. Len Fox. Potts Point, NSW, Len Fox, 1977. pp. 80–104.

Deamer, Dulcie (1890–1972). 'The Golden Decade'. 1965. Mitchell Library. MSS 3173.

De Falbe, *Mrs* Emmeline (Leslie) (1828–1902). 'Letters and Recollections 1860–94'. Macarthur Family Papers. Mitchell Library. A 2977. Vol. 81; *My dear Miss Macarthur. The Recollections of Emmeline Macarthur 1828–1911*. Ed. Jane De Falbe. Kenthurst, Kangaroo Press, 1988. Extracts titled 'An Early-day Aristocrat', published *Bulletin* 10/3/54, pp. 24–5, 34 and 17/3/54, pp. 24–5, 31; Extract included in De Vries-Evans, Susanna. *Pioneer Women. Pioneer Land*. Sydney, Angus & Robertson, 1987. pp. 55–78.

De Gir, Paulette. *The Unbeatable Loser*. Glenroy, Vic., Le Paris Publications, 1980.

de Lepervanche, Marie. 'A Very Late Developer'. *Against the Odds*. Ed. Heather Radi and Madge Dawson. Sydney, Hale & Iremonger, 1984. pp. 134–55.

Deveson, Anne (1930–). Contrib. to *As the Twig is Bent*. Ed. Terry Lane. East Malvern, Dove Communications, 1979, pp. 81–93.

Dewar, *Mrs* E. W. 'Recollections of Wyuna'. Royal Historical Society of Victoria. Box 133/5.

Dohnt, Joan Marion (née Crook). *Memories of My Childhood at Purnong Landing*. Daw Park, J. M. Dohnt, 1987.

Donovan, Mavis (1924–). *The Stars Shine On*. Brisbane, M. Donovan, 1984.

Dorling, Irene. *Twentieth Century Family. An Autobiographical Trilogy*. Ed. Frank Campbell and Ian Fox. Waurn Ponds, Vic., Social History Museum, Deakin University, 1986.

Dorsch, Susan. 'As Opportunity Presents'. *Against the Odds*. Ed. Heather Radi and Madge Dawson. Sydney, Hale & Iremonger, 1984. pp. 96–113.

Drake, Mary (1912–). *The Trees Were Green*. Sydney, Hale & Iremonger, 1984.

Duffy, E. M. *Reminiscences of Whittlesea*. Kilmore, Lowden Publishing Co., n.d.

Duncan, Annie J. (1858–?). 'Reminiscences'. 6 vols. State Archives of South Australia. PRG 532/6.

Duncan, Pearl. 'A Teachers's Life'. *Fighters and Singers: the Lives of some Australian Aboriginal Women*. Ed. Isobel White, Diane Barwick and Betty Meehan. Sydney, George Allen & Unwin, 1985. pp. 40–54.

Duncan-Kemp, Alice. *Where Strange Gods Call*. Brisbane, Smith & Paterson, 1968; *Where Strange Paths Go Down*. Brisbane, Smith & Paterson, 1952.

Dyason, Diana (1919–). 'Preludes'. *The Half-Open Door*. Ed. Patricia Grimshaw and Lynne Strahan. Sydney, Hale & Iremonger, 1982. pp. 306–27.

Eakin, Robin. *Aunts Up the Cross*. London, Blond, 1965.

Eccles, Kerry. 'These Impossible Women'. *Sweet Mothers, Sweet Maids*. Ed. Kate Nelson and Dominica Nelson. Ringwood, Vic., Penguin, 1986. pp. 103–12.

Edgar, Lucy Anna. *Among the Black Boys: Being an Account of the History of an Attempt at Civilising some young Aborigines of Australia*. London, Emily Faithfull, 1865.

Edgeworth David, Mary (1888–1987). *Passages of Time: an Australian Woman 1890–1974*. St Lucia, University of Queensland Press, 1975.

Edmunds, Della (1917–). *Della, the Drover*. Julatten, Qld, Pinevale Publications and Della Edmunds, 1983.

Edwards, Florence. *The Joys and Sorrows of a Migrant Family*. Perth, Author, 1985.

Edwards, Marion (Bill). *Life and Adventures of Marion-Bill-Edwards, the Most Celebrated Man-Woman of Modern Times*. Melbourne, n.d.

Egerton Jones, Doris (1889–1973). *Peter Piper*. London and Melbourne, Cassell, 1913.

Ellement, Connie. With Ron Davidson. *The Divided Kingdom*. Fremantle, Fremantle Arts Centre Press, 1987.

Everton, Emily. 'Reminiscences of Waikerie' (1957); 'Reminiscences of Waikerie' (1944); 'Colourful Personalities' (n.d.); 'Reminiscences of Tea Tree Gully' (n.d.); 'More About Waikerie' (n.d.). Mortlock Library. D 4194/1–5(L).

Ey, Anna Victoria (1839–1917). *Early Lutheran Congregations in South Australia: Memoirs of a Pastor's Wife. . . .* Transl. Dorothea M. Freund. Payneham, SA, A. P. H. Freund, 1986.

Falk, Barbara (1910–) 'The Unpayable Debt'. *The Half-Open Door*. Ed. Patricia Grimshaw and Lynne Strahan. Sydney, Hale & Iremonger, 1982.

Falkiner, Suzanne (1952–). *Rain in the Distance*. Ringwood, Penguin, 1986.

Farmer, Beverley (1941–). *Alone*. Carlton, Vic., Sisters, 1980.

Farmers, Eileen Elizabeth. *See* 'Lane, Elizabeth'.

Faust, Beatrice (1939–). 'Eggshell Psyche'. *The Half-Open Door*. Ed. Patricia Grimshaw and Lynne Strahan. Sydney, Hale & Iremonger, 1982. pp. 220–43.

Fifield, Elaine. With Kevin Perkins. *In My Shoes*. London, W. H. Allen, 1967.

Fitton, Doris (1897–). *Not Without Dust & Heat*. Sydney, Harper & Row, 1981.

Fitzpatrick, Kathleen (1905–). *Solid Bluestone Foundations*. Melbourne, Macmillan, 1983. Also published Ringwood, Vic., Penguin 1986; 'A Cloistered Life'. *The Half-Open Door*. Ed. Patricia Grimshaw and Lynne Strahan. Sydney, Hale & Iremonger, 1982. pp. 120–33.

Flavel, Doreen E. With Donald S. McDonald. *The Promise and The*

Challenge. Adelaide, Doreen Flavel, 1986.

Ford, Effie M. *Princes Terrace*. Sydney, NSW, Bookstall Co., 1934.

Forshaw, Thelma (1923–). *An Affair of Clowns*. Sydney, Angus & Robertson, 1967.

Francis, Babette. 'The Distant Bells'. *Sweet Mothers, Sweet Maids*. Ed. Kate Nelson and Dominica Nelson. Ringwood, Vic., Penguin, 1986. pp. 185–214.

Franklin, Miles (1879–1954). *My Brilliant Career*. Edinburgh, William Blackwood, 1901; *Some Everyday Folk and Dawn*. Edinburgh, William Blackwood, 1909; *My Career Goes Bung*. Melbourne, Georgian House, 1946; *Cockatoos*. Sydney, Angus & Robertson, 1954; *Childhood at Brindabella*. Sydney, Angus & Robertson, 1963; unpublished short stories in Miles Franklin Papers. Mitchell Library. MSS 364.

Fraser, Catherine Jackson (*Mrs* Aleck, née Barbour) (1859–1954). 'The Memoirs of a Happy Favoured Australian Life'. Written 1944–7. Mitchell Library. MSS 3272.

Fraser, Dawn (1937–). With Harry Gordon. *Gold Medal Girl*. Melbourne, Lansdowne, 1965.

Freund, Dorothea (1903–). *I Will Uphold You*. Payneham, SA, A. P. H. Freund, 1985.

Fullerton, Mary (1868–1946). *Bark House Days*. Melbourne, S. J. Endacott, 1921; *The People of the Timber Belt*. London, A. M. Philpot, 1925; 'Memoirs'. Mitchell Library. MS 2342.

Gale, Dorothy (1903–). *Old Trangie History and Part of My Life*. Dubbo, Development and Advisory Publications of NSW, 1983.

Gantner, Neilma ('Neilma Sidney') (1922–). *Beyond the Bay*. Melbourne, Cheshire, 1966.

Gare, Nene (1919–). *A House with Verandahs*. Melbourne, Macmillan, 1980.

Garner, Helen (1942–). *Monkey Grip*. Fitzroy, Vic., McPhee Gribble, 1977; *Postcards from Surfers*. Fitzroy, Vic., Penguin/McPhee Gribble, 1985.

[Garrad, Gladys Eliza] (1905–). *Memoirs of Gladys Eliza Garrad*. Murgon, Qld, Herbert Garrad, 1981.

Gersch, Vera A. *Childhood Memories*. SA, V. Gersch, 1984.

Gerstad, Joan. *The Jungle Was Our Home*. London, Allen & Unwin, 1957.

Gifford, Helen (1935–). 'Raison d'Etre'. *The Half-Open Door*. Ed. Patricia Grimshaw and Lynne Strahan. Sydney, Hale & Iremonger, 1982. pp. 174–93.

Gifford, Margaret (1896–). *I Can Hear the Horses*. N. Ryde, NSW, Methuen-Haynes, 1983.

Gilbert, Dorothy (1885–1973). 'Country Life in the Later Nineteenth Century. Reminiscences by Dorothy Gilbert'. *South Australiana*. 12, 2 (1973) 57–70; [account of her childhood, written for S. Magarey] Adelaide, SA Archives. PRG 266/34.

Gilbert, Vivien (1929–). *Proud Butterfly*. N. Perth, V. J. Gilbert, 1982.

Giles, Zeny. 'April is the Cruellest Month'; 'But Your Ways are Strange to

Me'. *Displacements:Migrant Story-Tellers.* Comp. Sneja Gunew. Deakin University, 1982. pp. 52–4, 55–9; *Between Two Worlds.* Cammeray, NSW, The Saturday Centre, 1981.

Gilmore, Mary (1865–1962). *Old Days, Old Ways.* Sydney, Angus & Robertson, 1934, and N. Ryde, NSW, Angus & Robertson, 1986; *More Recollections.* Sydney, Angus & Robertson, 1935; *Hound of the Road.* Sydney, Angus & Robertson, 1922; 'My Childhood'. Mitchell Library. Dame Mary Gilmore collection. A 3293. Restricted indefinitely.

Glasson, Hannah Truscott (1845–) (née Hawke). 'Diary & Notes, 1916–1922, with a family tree of the Hawke family'. Mitchell Library. MSS 3523.

Goldstraw, Alice. *The Border of the Heytesbury.* Terang, *Terang Express* Office, 1937.

[Good, V. M. F.] (1887–1979). *Look to the Mountains. Viola's View 1887–1979: The Recollections of Viola Mary Frances Good.* Ed. by her daughter Catherine Good. Surrey Hills, Vic., D. Good, 1985.

Goode, Evelyn (d. 1927). *The Childhood of Helen.* London, Ward, Lock & Co., 1913; *Days That Speak.* London, Ward, Lock & Co., 1908.

Goolagong, Evonne (1951–). With Bud Collins. *Evonne! On the Move.* Sydney, Dutton, 1975; New York, E. P. Dutton, 1975.

Gorman, Anne. 'Letting Go'. *Sweet Mothers, Sweet Maids.* Ed. Kate Nelson and Dominica Nelson. Ringwood, Vic., Penguin, 1986. pp. 51–70.

Gow, Millicent (1885–1910). 'Papers' [Including reminiscences]. National Library of Australia. MS 2007.

[Graham, Eva Violet] (1890–). *The 'Recollections' of Eva Violet Graham.* Wauchope, NSW, H. R. Young, 1980.

Graham, *Mrs* K. (formerly *Mrs* G. Bormley) (1847–). 'Reminiscences of Mrs K. Graham'. Written 1920. Royal Historical Society of Victoria. Box 130/20.

Gray, Oriel (1920–). *Exit Left: Memoirs of a Scarlet Woman.* Ringwood, Vic., Penguin, 1985.

Green, Susan (1901–). *Ever a Fighter.* Melbourne, Spectrum, 1981.

Grieve, Norma (1925–). 'A Relatively Simple Affair'. *The Half-Open Door.* Ed. Patricia Grimshaw and Lynne Strahan. Sydney, Hale & Iremonger, 1982. pp. 246–59.

Grimston, Caroline Ann (1872–1957). 'The Days I Remember and the Years'. 2 vols. Mitchell Library. MSS 1967.

Hadow, Lyndall (1903–76). *Full Cycle and Other Stories.* Sydney, Collins, 1969.

Hale, Erica. *Catch the Sun.* Ringwood, Vic., Penguin, 1984.

Haley, Eileen and Rosser, Lillian. *Memories of an Australian Girlhood.* St Lucia, Hecate Press, 1982.

Halls, Geraldine ('Charlotte Jay') (1919–). *The Last Summer of the Men Shortage.* London, Constable, 1976.

Hammond, Joan (1912–). *A Voice, A Life.* London, Gollancz, 1970.

Hannan, Lorna. 'The Last Word'. *Sweet Mothers, Sweet Maids.* Ed. Kate Nelson and Dominica Nelson. Ringwood, Vic., Penguin, 1986, pp. 71–82.

Hanrahan, Barbara (1939–). *The Scent of Eucalyptus*. London, Chatto & Windus, 1973; *Sea-Green*. London, Chatto & Windus, 1974; *Kewpie Doll*. London, Chatto & Windus, 1984.

Harris, Daisy Vera. *'Every Life a Picture': The Autobiography of Daisy Vera Harris*. Perth, Author, 1986.

Harrison, Bessie. 'The Making of a Town'. Royal Historical Society of Victoria. MS 4814. Box 104/6.

Harrison, Bessie Lee. *See* Lee, Bessie.

Harrower, Elizabeth (1928–). *The Long Prospect*. London, Cassell, 1958; 'The Beautiful Climate'. *Modern Australian Writing*. Ed. Geoffrey Dutton. London, Collins, 1966. pp. 217–30.

Hasluck, *Dame* Alexandra (1908–). *Portrait in a Mirror*. Melbourne, Oxford University Press, 1981.

Hawker, Ruth. *An Emu in the Fowl Pen*. Adelaide, Rigby, 1967. Revised 1977, titled *Growing Up in the Outback*.

Hawkes, Val. 'Treaties and Bargains with God'. *Sweet Mothers, Sweet Maids*. Ed. Kate Nelson and Dominica Nelson. Ringwood, Vic., Penguin, 1986. pp. 1–12.

[Hay, Agnes Gosse] (1838–1909). 'Anglo-Australian'. *After-Glow Memories*. London, Methuen, 1905.

Hazzard, Shirley (1931–). [Beginning section of] *The Transit of Venus*. London, Macmillan, 1980.

Helpman, Mary. *The Helpman Family Story*. Adelaide, Rigby, 1967.

[Henry, Alice] (1857–1943). *Memoirs of Alice Henry*. Ed. Nettie Palmer. Melbourne, Alice Henry, 1944.

Henty (Pace), Jane. 'Old Memories of Mrs S. G. Henty'. La Trobe Library. MS 8511. Box 992/1.

Higgens, *Miss* H. R. *Cloud and Sunshine: an Autobiographical Sketch*. Ed. Rev. John Southey, with an introduction by Rev. Duncan S. McEachran. Melbourne, Religious Tract Society and Sunday School Union of Victoria, 1899.

Hiller, Christiane (née Petschel) (1840–?). 'Autobiography of Frau Pastor Christiane Hiller, whose family emigrated to Australia from Germany in 1848'. La Trobe Library. MS 10199. MSB 182.

Hoffmann, Pauline (1837–1917). 'Memoirs'. Transl. Elsa Hoffmann. Lutheran Archives. Adelaide.

Hogan, Eve. 'The Hessian Walls'. *Selected Lives: Personal Reminiscences*. Fremantle, Fremantle Arts Centre Press, 1983.

Holkner, Jean. *Taking the Chook and Other Traumas*. Ringwood, Vic., Penguin, 1987.

Holt, R. F. (ed.). *The Strength of Tradition: Stories of the Immigrant Presence in Australia 1970–81*. St Lucia, University of Queensland Press, 1983.

Holt, *Dame* Zara. *My Life and Harry*. Melbourne, Herald, 1968.

Hooper, Florence Earle (1870–1967). 'My Childhood Recollections'. Mitchell Library. MSS 1553.

Hughes, *Mrs* F. *My Childhood in Australia*. London, Digby, 1890?

Humphreys, Elizabeth Margaret J. (Gollan) (?1860–1938). *Recollections of a Literary Life*. By 'Rita'. London, Melrose, 1936.

Hunt, *Dame* Agnes. *Reminiscences*. Shrewsbury, 1935. Also published with title *This is My Life*. London, Blackie, 1938.

Hunt, Patsy. *Joy Cometh in the Morning*. Goulburn, Reme, 1985.

Hunter, Phoebe. *Phoebe Remembers*. Pemberton, Northcliffe Tourist Bureau, 1984.

Inglis, Amirah (1926–). *Amirah: An Un-Australian Childhood*. Richmond, Vic., Heinemann, 1983.

Jackamarra, Clara. In Kelly, Sheila M. *Proud Heritage*. Perth, Artlook, 1980.

James, Winifred Llewellin (1876–1941). *Patricia Baring*. London, Constable, 1908.

Jardine, F. M. *Part of the Way*. Esperance, Author, 1979.

Jarvis, Elsie. *All in a Day's Work*. Ilfracombe, Arthur H. Stockwell, 1980.

Jenner, Dorothy Gordon (c. 1900–71). *Darlings, I've Had a Ball*. Sydney, Ure Smith, 1975.

Jones, Suzanne Holly (1945–). *Harry's Child*. Brisbane, Jacaranda, 1964.

Jordan, *Pastor* Ellen C. *The Supreme Incentive*. East Burnswick, Vic., Author, 1969.

Jull, Roberta. (1896–). 'Personal Papers'. [Includes two autobiographical sketches] Battye Library.

Kannaluik, Emily Mitchell (1903–). 'Reminiscences and Sketches'. La Trobe Library. MS 11680. Box 1873/2.

Keesing, Nancy (1923–). *Garden Island People*. Sydney, Wentworth Books, 1975; *Riding the Elephant*. Sydney, Allen & Unwin, 1988.

Kelly, Gwen (1922–). *There is No Refuge*. London, Heinemann, 1961; *The Happy People And Others*. Ed. Anthony J. Bennett. Armidale, NSW, Kardoorair Press, 1988.

Kennedy, Marnie. *Born a Half-Caste*. Canberra, Australian Institute of Aboriginal Studies, 1985.

Kenny, Elizabeth (1886–1952). *And They Shall Walk*. New York, Dodd, Mead & Co., 1943.

Kent, Jacqueline. *In the Half Light. Life as a Child in Australia 1900–1970*. Sydney, Angus & Robertson, 1988.

Kent, Nancy. *The House That Jock Built*. Ed. Lorraine Nott. Beaudesert, Qld, Boolarong Publications, 1985.

Kerr, Anne. *Lanterns Over Pinchgut*. Melbourne, Macmillan, 1988.

Kerr, Doris Boake. *See* 'Boake, Capel'.

King, Georgina. 'The Autobiography of Georgina King'. 3 vols. Mitchell Library. MSS 273/3–5.

Kirwan, Valerie G. (1943–). *The Will to Fall*. Ringwood, Vic., Penguin, 1984.

Knowles, Marion Miller (1865–1949). *Barbara Halliday*. Melbourne, G. Robertson, 1896.

Knox, Dorothy (1902–). *Time Flies*. Adelaide, Rigby, 1982.

Kyne, Caty. 'The Sixties Saved Me'. *Sweet Mothers, Sweet Maids*. Ed. Kate Nelson and Dominica Nelson. Ringwood, Vic., Penguin, 1986. pp. 147–58.

Lambert, Kathleen ('Lyth'). *The Golden South. Memories of Australian Home Life from 1843 to 1888*. London, Ward and Downey, 1890.

Lanarch-Jones, Mary. 'AM + DG and After'. *Sweet Mothers, Sweet Maids*. Ed. Kate Nelson and Dominica Nelson. Ringwood, Vic., Penguin, 1986. pp. 93–102.

'Lane, Elizabeth'. *Mad as Rabbits*. Adelaide, Rigby, 1962; *Our Uncle Charlie*. Adelaide, Rigby, 1964.

Langford, Ruby (1934–). *Don't Take Your Love to Town*. Ringwood, Vic., Penguin, 1988.

Langley, Eve (1908–74). *The Pea Pickers*. Sydney, Angus & Robertson, 1942; *White Topee*. Sydney, Angus & Robertson, 1954.

Lansell-Smith, Dorothy. *Pioneering, Personalities and Places*. South Yarra, D. Lansell-Smith, 1981.

Layton, Aviva. *Nobody's Daughter*. Fitzroy, Vic., McPhee Gribble, 1982.

Lee, Bessie (1860–1950). *One of Australia's Daughters*. London, Ideal Publishing Union, 1900. New edn revised, London, James, 1924.

Lee, Nancy (1906–). *Being a Chum was Fun*. Melbourne, Listen and Learn Productions, 1979.

Lewis, Julie (1925–). 'Private Viewing'. *Memories of Childhood*. Ed. Lee White. Fremantle, Fremantle Arts Centre Press, 1978. pp. 87–92.

The Life, Adventures and Confessions of a Sydney Barmaid. Sydney, Panza Print, 1891.

Lindsay, Jane (1920–). *Portrait of Pa*. Sydney, Angus & Robertson, 1973.

Lindsay, Rose (1885–1978). *Ma and Pa*. Sydney, Ure Smith, 1963.

Lion, *Mme* Marie. 'Noel Aimir'. *Vers la Lumière*. Edinburgh, T. & A. Constable, 1910.

Liverani, Mary Rose (1939–). *The Winter Sparrows*. Melbourne, Nelson, 1975.

Lloyd, Jessie ('Silverleaf') (1843–85). *The Wheel of Life*. Sydney, G. Robertson, 1880.

Loch, Joice Nankivell (1893–). *A Fringe of Blue*. London, John Murray, 1968.

Lohrey, Amanda. 'Work-in-Progress or a Writer's Lament'. *Sweet Mothers, Sweet Maids*. Ed. Kate Nelson and Dominica Nelson. Ringwood, Vic., Penguin, 1986. pp. 215–35.

London, Joan (1948–). *Sister Ships*. Fremantle, Fremantle Arts Centre Press, 1986.

Lovell, Pat. Contrib. to *As the Twig is Bent*. Ed. Terry Lane. East Malvern, Dove Communications, 1979. pp. 43–54.

Lubbock, Adelaide (1906–). *People in Glass Houses: Growing Up at Government House*. Adelaide, Nelson, 1977.

Lutyens, Mary. *To Be Young*. London, Rupert Hart-Davis, 1959.

Lyons, *Dame* Enid (1897–1981). *My Life*. Melbourne, *Woman's Day*, 1949;

So We Take Comfort. London, Heinemann, 1965.

McArthur, Kathleen (1915–). *Bread and Dripping Days*. Kenthurst, NSW, Kangaroo Press, 1981.

McCrae, Frances Octavia Gordon (1847–1941). *The Piano Story*. Arthur's Seat, Vic., 1962.

McDonald, Anne (1961–). *Annie's Coming Out*. Ringwood, Vic., Penguin, 1980.

McDonald, Jessie Elaine (?1882–1948). 'Journalist's Child'. Written 1914. Royal Historical Society of Victoria. Box 53.

MacDonald, Mrs Josephine Antoinette (née Liardet) (1830–1928). 'Old Time Reminiscences of the Early Dawn of Melbourne, Victoria'. Royal Historical Society of Victoria. MS 000103. Box 40.

McDougall-Leitch, Myra. *Spindle Shanks*. Seaton, SA, M. McDougall-Leitch, 1984.

McEwin, Agnes (1858–1942). 'The Girlhood Reminiscences of Agnes McEwin'. La Trobe Library. MS 11690. Box 1868/3.

McFarlane, E. H. *Land of Contrasts*. Fortitude Valley, Qld, E. H. McFarlane, 1976.

McGregor, Mary Jane. 'Early Life of Mary Jane McGregor'. La Trobe Library. MS 8453. MSB 425. Extract published in Lucy Frost, *No Place for a Nervous Lady*. Fitzroy, Vic., McPhee Gribble/Penguin, 1984.

McGuire, Frances M. (1900–). *Bright Morning*. Adelaide, Rigby, 1975.

McIntosh, Magdalene. With Elaine Rothwell. 'Maddie'. *Aboriginal History*, 3 1–2 (1979) 3–24.

McK., K. (McKell, Katherine). *Old Days and Gold Days in Victoria (1851–1873) being Memories of a Pioneer Family*. Melbourne, Vidler, 1924.

McKenzie, Isobel. 'Consider the Years'. (1977) Battye Library. PR 8771.

McKenzie, Isobel Walker. 'Notes for an Autobiography'. Compiled c. 1968. Mitchell Library. MSS 2996/1.

McKenzie, Janet. *Ebenezer*. Blackwood, SA, New Creation Publications, 1983; *Fingal Tiger*. Blackwood, SA, New Creation Publications, 1982.

McKerron, Wilhelmina (1900–). *The Wheel of Destiny*. Ilfracombe, Devon, A. H. Stockwell, 1980.

Mackness, Constance (1882–?). 'Pioneering Gold-Diggers from Ballarat. My Childhood's Golden Mates'. Fryer Library; 'Facts about my Life 1882–1972; being reminiscences and including a note to her niece'. Mitchell Library. ML Doc 2563.

McLean, Linda (1917–). *Pumpkin Pie and Faded Sandshoes*. Sydney, Apcol, 1981.

McLean, Marjorie (née Hart) (1895–). 'Reminiscences of Kempsey c. 1897–c. 1907'. Written 1968. Mitchell Library. MSS 1916.

McManus, Mary A. (1844–?). *Reminiscences of the Early Settlement of the Maranoa District in the Late Fifties and Early Sixties*. Brisbane, E. A. Howard, 1913.

McNeil, Eugénie (1886–1983) and Crawford, Eugénie. *A Bunyip Close*

Behind Me. Ringwood, Vic., Penguin, 1972; *Ladies Didn't.* Ringwood, Vic., Penguin, 1984.

McQuinn, Phoebe (1912–). 'Sunshine of your Smile'. La Trobe Library.

McRobb, Millie (1908–). *The Lean Years.* Bunbury, WA, M. McRobb, 1985.

Main, Barbara. *Twice Trodden Ground.* Brisbane, Jacaranda, 1971.

Mangan, Kathleen (1906–). *Daisy Chains, War, then Jazz.* Melbourne, Hutchinson, 1984.

Marsden, Addie (1896–). *Child of the Footlights.* Balwyn, Vic., A. Marsden, 1984.

Maresch, Christine (1958–). *Hostage.* Melbourne, Nelson, 1983.

Masters, Muriel F. (1900–). *Seven Homes. Reminiscences.* Launceston, Muriel Masters, 1973.

Matthews, Enid Noel (1905–). *I'll be Better Tomorrow.* Melbourne, Spectrum, 1979.

Melba, *Dame* Nellie (1861–1931). *Melodies and Memories.* London, Butterworth, 1925.

Memoirs of Martha. An Autobiography. Edited by her Mistress. London, Barker, 1933.

Mickle, *Mrs* Margaret. 'Her Diary'. Written 1892. Royal Historical Society of Victoria. Box 40/1.

Miles, Bee. 'Prelude to Freedom' and 'For We are Young and Free'. Autobiographical papers in Frank Johnson Papers. Mitchell Library. MSS 1214/3 1214/22.

Miller, Connie. *After Summer Merrily: An Autobiographical Novel.* Fremantle, Fremantle Arts Centre Press, 1980; *Season of Learning.* Fremantle, Fremantle Arts Centre Press, 1983.

Milutinovic, Iris (1910–86). *I'm Still Here Aren't I?* Lenah Valley, Tas., Sheerwater Press, 1985.

Mitchell, Alice M. (1891–). Contrib. to *When We were Young.* Ed. Dorothy B. Watt. Stratford, Vic., Stratford Historical Society, 1979.

Mitchell, *Lady* Eliza (née Morrison). *Three Quarters of a Century.* London, Methuen, 1940.

Mitchell, Elyne (1913–). *Chauvel Country.* Melbourne, Macmillan, 1983.

Mitchell, Janet (1896–). *Spoils of Opportunity. An Autobiography.* London, Methuen, 1938.

Mitchell, Winifred. 'A Pilgrim's Progress'. *Against the Odds.* Ed. Heather Radi and Madge Dawson, Sydney, Hale & Iremonger, 1984. pp. 202–17.

Moncrieff, Gladys (1893–1976). *My Life of Song.* Adelaide, Rigby, 1971.

Moon, Enid (1900–). 'Myself When Young: Memoirs of a Galley Slave'. Mitchell Library. MSS 3885.

Moore, Frances Annie (1864–1961). 'Memoirs of Frances Annie Moore 1864–1961'. La Trobe Library. MS 9187. MSB 456.

Moore, Winsome, *Just to Myself, but...* Adelaide, Rigby, 1977.

Morgan, Gail (1953–). *Promise of Rain.* London, Virago, 1985.

Moppert, Fia. *Out of the Corner of One Eye*. Collingwood, Greenhouse Publications, 1981.

Morgan, Gail (1953–). *Promise of Rain*. London, Virago, 1985.

Morgan, Sally (1951–). *My Place*. Fremantle, Fremantle Arts Centre Press, 1987.

Morice, Lucy Spence. 'Reminiscences'. National Library of Australia. MS 1256.

Morris, Myra (1893–1966). *Dark Tumult*. London, Thornton Butterworth, 1939; *Us Five*. Melbourne, Melbourne Publishing Co., 1922.

Morrow, Dorothea T. (1900–86). *A Place by a River*. Perth, Author, 1986.

Motschall, Marjorie S. (1910–). *Wild Wood Days at Panton Hill*. Panton Hill, Braidwood Press, 1984.

[Mudge, Mary.]. 'Memoirs of the Late Mrs Mary Mudge'. La Trobe Library. MS 8504. MSB 426.

Murphy, Agnes G. *One Woman's Wisdom*. Manchester and New York, George Routledge & Sons, 1895.

Murray, Blanche ('Kathleen Collins'). *And So Say All of Us: Stories by Australian Women*. Ed. Pearlie Mc Neill and Marie McShea. Leura, NSW, Second Back Row Press, 1984. pp. 67–70.

Musgrave, Sarah (1830–1931). *The Wayback*. Parramatta, NSW, *Cumberland Argus*, 1926.

Nelson, Venetia. 'My Father's House'. *Sweet Mothers, Sweet Maids*. Ed. Kate Nelson and Dominica Nelson. Ringwood, Vic., Penguin, 1986. pp. 195–214.

Nicholson, Joyce (1919–). 'Destination Uncertain'. *The Half-Open Door*. Ed. Patricia Grimshaw and Lynne Strahan. Sydney, Hale & Iremonger, 1982. pp. 136–53.

Nihill, Sarah Jane (1826–1915). 'Reminiscences'. La Trobe Library.

No Regrets: An Anthology of Some Sydney Writers Edited by Themselves. Sydney, Sao Press, 1979.

Nolan, Cynthia ('Cynthia Reed') (?1913–76). *Daddy Sowed a Wind!* Sydney, Shakespeare Head, 1947.

Noonuccal, Oodgeroo. *See* Walker, Kath.

Norman, Lilith. 'The Realer World'. *The Early Dreaming*. Comp. Michael Dugan. Milton, Qld, Jacaranda Press, 1980. pp. 48–58.

Norrish, *Mrs* Thomas. 'Memories of Mrs Thomas Norrish née Christine Anne Wray' (1983). Battye Library. B/NOR.

O'Harris, Pixie (1903–). *Was It Yesterday?* Adelaide, Rigby, 1983; *Our Small Safe World*. Sydney, Boobook, 1986.

O'Leary, Zoe (1903–). *The Little Byron*. Chippendale, NSW, Alternative Publishing Co-operative, 1982.

Olive, Victoria (1883–1947). 'Reminiscences of Early Life and Teaching, 1883–1947'. Mitchell Library. MSS 2300.

Olson, Fanny (*Mrs* James Fletcher). *I Loved Teaching*. A. H. Massina, 1947.

Opie, Nan. With June Bosanquet. *The Other Woman that was Me*. Homebush West, NSW, Anzea, 1980.

O'Shane, Patricia. 'A Healthy Sense of Identity'. *Against the Odds*. Ed. Heather Radi and Madge Dawson. Sydney, Hale & Iremonger, 1984. pp. 28–37.

O'Sullivan, Margaret. 'Going Out to the World'. *Sweet Mothers, Sweet Maids*. Ed. Kate Nelson and Dominica Nelson. Ringwood, Vic., Penguin, 1986. pp. 165–174.

Palmer, Ruth. *'Wandoo': The Story of Charles E. Edwards*. Perth, Ruth Palmer, 1983.

Parker, *Mrs* Henry H. (née McIntyre) (1840–). 'Early Days at Lake Innes'. National Library of Australia. MS 3229.

Paterson, Alice F. *Life's Clouds, with Sunshine Intermingled: A True Australian Story by 'Solus'*. Adelaide, Scrymgour & Sons, 1897; *Mid Saltbush and Mallee: A True Australian Bush Story*. Adelaide, Scrymgour & Sons, 1897.

Patrick, Alison (1921–). 'Born Lucky'. *The Half-Open Door*. Ed. Patricia Grimshaw and Lynne Strahan. Sydney, Hale & Iremonger, 1982. pp. 196–217.

Payne, E. Lecky. *Beltana—Six Miles*. Adelaide, Rigby, 1974.

Pearce, *Mrs* (1833–?). 'Reminiscences of Mrs J. Pearce 1833–1917'. Mitchell Library. MLDoc 1708.

Pecket, Christine A. *Some Facets of My Life*. Hyde Park, SA, Peacock Publications, 1976.

Peet, Dorothy. 'Memories of the Old Gamble Farm at Nalkain in the Shire of Wyalkatchem'. Battye Library. QB/GAM.

Pepworth, Barbara (1955–). *Early Marks*. Sydney, Angus & Robertson, 1980.

Pfitzner, Laura. *Reflections at Eventide*. Glynde, SA, L. Pfitzner, 1981.

Phelan, Nancy (1913–). *A Kingdom by the Sea*. Sydney, Angus & Robertson, 1969.

Phillips, Joan. *Recollections at Robigana*. Brisbane, Boolarong Publications, 1982; republished in 1983 as *Those Days at Robigana*. Launceston, Regal Press.

Phipson, Joan (1912–). 'Reluctant Confessions'. *The Early Dreaming*. Comp. Michael Dugan. Milton, Qld, Jacaranda Press, 1980. pp. 48–58.

Pickup, Violet Emily (1914–). *Pages from the Past*. Canberra, V. E. Pickup, 1979.

Pope, Olive (1891–). *Olivia's Story*. Magill, Olive Pope, 1979; *Towards the Sunset*. Magill, Olive Pope, 1980; *Memories*. Magill, Olive Pope, 1978.

Poppleton, Daisy May. With Jean Michaelides. *Growing Up in Dugong*. Sydney, J. Michaelides & V. Packer, 1980.

Potter, Edith (1904–). *The Scone I Remember*. Scone, NSW, Scone & Upper Historical Society, 1981.

Power, Phyllis M. *From These Descended*. Kilmore, Homestead Books, 1977.

Praed, Rosa (*Mrs* Campbell Praed) (1851–1935). *My Australian Girlhood*. London, T. Fisher Unwin, 1902; *Australian Life: Black and White*.

London, Chapman & Hall, 1885; *An Australian Heroine*. London, Chapman & Hall, 1880.

Prichard, Katharine Susannah (1883–1969). *Child of the Hurricane*. Sydney, Angus & Robertson, 1963; *The Wild Oats of Han*. Melbourne, Lansdowne, 1928.

Prince, Agnes Melda. *Esther Mary, My Pioneer Mother*. Fremantle, Fremantle Arts Centre Press, 1981.

Purcell, Frances (née Lepherd) (1862–1935). *A Surry Hills Childhood, 1870*. Ed. Kenneth and Elaine Moon and Terry Kass. Armidale, UNE Publishing Unit, 1981.

Purnell, Kathryn (ed.). *Remember: An Anthology of the Wednesday Writers Adult Education Association Melbourne*. Newtown, Vic., Neptune Press, 1984.

Pusenjak, Honor. *As It Seemed to Me. Personal Recollections*. Nedlands, Apollo Press, 1982.

Quin, Tarella (1877–1934). *A Desert Rose*. London, Heinemann, 1912.

Quinn, Marjorie. 'Memoirs'. National Library of Australia. MS 2104.

Radi, Heather. 'Thanks Mum'. *Against the Odds*. Ed. Heather Radi and Madge Dawson. Sydney, Hale & Iremonger, 1984. pp. 168–85.

Radic, Thérèse (1935–). 'Still Life with Mirrors'. *The Half-Open Door*. Ed. Patricia Grimshaw and Lynne Strahan. Sydney, Hale & Iremonger, 1982; 'Extracts from a Half-Breed's Diary'. *Sweet Mothers, Sweet Maids*. Ed. Kate Nelson and Dominica Nelson. Ringwood, Vic., Penguin, 1986. pp. 113–24.

Rains, Fanny L. *By Land and Ocean or the Journal and Letters of a Young Girl who went To South Australia——*. London, Sampson Low, Marston Searle & Rivington, 1878.

Randall, Suze. *Suze*. Melbourne, Circus Books, 1977.

'Reed, Cynthia'. *See* Nolan, Cynthia.

Rees, Catherine E. *Recollections of the Early Days in Maleny*. Caloundra, Shire of Lansborough Historical Society, 1984.

Rennick, Joan (1903–). With Elizabeth Rennick. *Sketched from Memory*. Glen Iris, Vic., Elizabeth Rennick, 1982.

Reynolds, Broda. *Dawn Asper*. Sydney, NSW Bookstall Co., 1918.

'Richardson, Henry Handel' (Ethel Florence Lindesay Robertson) (1870–1946). *The Getting of Wisdom*. London, Heinemann, 1910; *Myself When Young*. Melbourne, Heinemann, 1948; *The Fortunes of Richard Mahony*. London, Heinemann, 1930; *The End of a Childhood and Other Stories*. London, Heinemann, 1934; reprinted as *The Adventures of Cuffy Mahony and Other Stories*. Sydney, Angus & Robertson, 1979.

Richmond, Faith. *Remembrance*. Sydney, Collins, 1988.

'Riley, Elizabeth' (Kerryn Higgs). *All That False Instruction*. Sydney, Angus & Robertson, 1975.

'Rivers, Georgia' (Marjorie Clark). *The Difficult Art*. London, Skeffington, 1930.

Roberts, Dulcie. *'When We Were Kids': Australiana.* Adelaide, D. Roberts, 1985.

Roberts, Ruby. With Rhoda Scott. *Each Sorrow Has its Meaning.* Algester, Queensland, Rodney A. Eivers, 1983.

Robertson, Jo. 'The Tender Bark'. *Memories of Childhood.* Ed. Lee White. Fremantle, Fremantle Arts Centre Press, 1978. pp. 7–17.

Robinson, Ruth (1917–). *Yabbies at Acton: a Story of Canberra. 1913–27.* Gordon, NSW, R. Robinson, 1984.

Rodd, Kate (1896–1984). 'Lisdillon: The Story of John Mitchell MHA, JP 1812–1880 & his Family'. Tasmaniana Library, Hobart.

Roe, Jill. 'First Matriculate...'. *Against the Odds.* Ed. Heather Radi and Madge Dawson. Sydney, Hale & Iremonger, 1984. pp. 56–75.

'Rohan, Criena' (Deidre Cash) (1928–62). *The Delinquents.* London, Gollancz, 1962; *Down by the Dockside.* London, Gollancz, 1963.

Rohan Kelly, Margaret. *'I am What I am'.* Port Lincoln, SA, Rivers of Life Publishing Co., 1985.

Rothberg, Yetta. *The Charwoman and the Child.* Richmond, Spectrum Publications, 1985.

Roughsey, Elsie. *An Aboriginal Mother tells of the Old and the New.* Edd. Paul Memmott and Robyn Horsman. Fitzroy, Vic., McPhee Gribble, 1984.

Rowe, Penelope (1946–). *Dance for the Ducks.* Sydney, Methuen, 1976.

Roysland, Dorothy A. *A Pioneer Family on the Murray River.* Adelaide, Rigby, 1977.

Rutherford, Anna. 'A Long Line of Maiden Aunts'. *Sweet Mothers, Sweet Maids.* Ed. Kate Nelson and Dominica Nelson. Ringwood, Vic., Penguin, 1986. pp. 133–46.

Rutledge, Helen. *My Grandfather's House: Recollections of an Australian Family.* Sydney, Doubleday, 1986.

Sabine, Margaret. 'Friends and Mentors'. *Against the Odds.* Ed. Heather Radi and Madge Dawson. Sydney, Hale & Iremonger, 1984. pp. 186–201.

Sansom, Ruth, *Through the Eyes of a Child: Sketches of a Tasmanian Childhood.* Hobart, Cat & Fiddle, 1977.

Sayer-Jones, Moya. *Little Sister.* Sydney, Allen & Unwin, 1988.

Seager, Joy D. (1899–). *Kangaroo Island Doctor.* Adelaide, Rigby, 1980.

Sealby, Winifred Kingsford. *Recollections, Personal and Scenic.* Gosford, Central Coast Printery, 1951.

Sharp, Donna. *Blue Days.* St Lucia, University of Queensland Press, 1986.

Shaw, Mary Turner (1906–). 'Education of a Squatter's Daughter'. *The Half-Open Door.* Ed. Patricia Grimshaw and Lynne Strahan. Sydney, Hale & Iremonger, 1982. pp. 280–303.

Sheiner, Robin. *Smile, the War is Over.* S. Melbourne, Macmillan, 1983.

Shelley, Noreen. 'Once Upon a Time'. *The Early Dreaming.* Comp. Michael Dugan. Milton, Qld, Jacaranda Press, 1980. pp. 73–81.

Shipley, V. M. *Hark, Hark My Soul*. Fremantle, Fremantle Arts Centre Press, 1981.

'Sidney, Neilma'. *See* Gantner, Neilma.

Simon, Ella. *Through My Eyes*. Adelaide, Rigby, 1978.

Sinclair, Fanny. 'Diary. Reminiscences of a Life', Mitchell Library. MSS 2222.

Skinner, Molly (1876–1955). *The Fifth Sparrow*. London, Angus & Robertson, 1973. MS versions Mollie Skinner Manuscripts and Correspondence. Battye Library. Acc/No 1396A.

Smith, Enga (1933–). *Saddle in the Kitchen*. East Perth, Nine Club, 1979.

Smith, Margaret (1943–). *The Margaret Smith Story*. London, S. Paul, 1965.

Smith, Shirley C. with Sykes, Bobbi. *Mum Shirl: An Autobiography*. Richmond, Heinemann, 1981.

Sneath, Beatrice (1897–). *Late Views of Life and Books*. Sydney, Wentworth Books, 1977.

Snowden, Mildred (1860–?). 'Reminiscences'. La Trobe Library. MS 10748. MSB 313.

Spence, Catherine (1825–1910). *An Autobiography*. Adelaide, W. K. Thomas, 1910; *Clara Morison*. London, John W. Parker, 1854.

Spence, Eleanor (1928–). *The October Child*. London, Oxford University Press, 1976; *Another October Child*. Blackburn, Vic., Collins Dove, 1988; 'A Special Sort of Dreaming'. *The Early Dreaming*. Comp. Michael Dugan. Milton, Qld, Jacaranda Press, 1980. pp. 93–101.

Sperling, Leone. *Mother's Day*. Glebe, Wild & Woolley, 1984.

'Stanley, Effie' (Charlotte Tilney) (c. 1834–94). *The Wilmots: A South Australian Story*. London, Elliot Stock, 1877.

Staniforth, Lilyan. 'Slipping the Knot'. *Sweet Mothers, Sweet Maids*. Ed. Kate Nelson and Dominica Nelson. Ringwood, Vic., Penguin, 1986. pp. 159–64.

Stawell, Mary Frances Elizabeth (Greene) (1830–1921). *My Recollections*. London, Private Print, 1911.

Stead, Christina (1902–83). *The Man Who Loved Children*. London, Peter Davies, 1940; *For Love Alone*. New York, Harcourt, Brace & Co., 1944; *Ocean of Story*. Ringwood, Vic., Penguin, 1986.

Stevenson, Sophia Judith. *Across the Vanished Years. Memories of a Pioneer Pastoral Family of Central Queensland*. Rannes, Qld, S. J. Stevenson, 1981.

Stewart, Julia Gertrude. 'Passages in the Life of a Finishing Governess' in Dallas, Stewart and Steele family papers. Mitchell Library. MSS 1218.

Stewart, Meg (1948–). *Autobiography of My Mother*. Ringwood, Vic., Penguin, 1985.

Stewart, Nellie (1858–1931). *My Life's Story*. Sydney, J. Sands, 1923.

Stigwood, Elizabeth (1887–). *Elizabeth Stigwood's Memoirs*. Collected and edited by Rhonda Brown and Marilyn Foster-Holmes of Writers' Workshops Inc., 1986.

Stirling, Amie Livingstone (1880–1945). *Memories of an Australian Child-*

hood 1880–1900. Melbourne, Schwartz Publishing, 1980.

Stirling, Elizabeth. *Memories of Aberfeldy*. Hamilton, Vic., Hamilton Education Centre, 1977.

Stokes, Agnes (b. 1867). *A Girl at Government House*. First published London, 1932, titled *The Autobiography of a Cook*. Ed. Helen Vellacott. Melbourne, John Currey O'Neil, 1982.

Strahan, Lynne (1938–). 'Novitiate of an Oyster'. *The Half-Open Door*. Ed. Patricia Grimshaw and Lynne Strahan. Sydney, Hale & Iremonger, 1982.

Street, *Lady* Jessie M. G. (1889–1970). *Truth or Repose*. Sydney, Australasian Book Society, 1966.

Summers, Vera Ada (1899–). *Personalities and Places*. Perth, V. Summers, 1978; *The Light of Other Days*. Perth, V. Summers, 1977.

Sutherland, Marjorie. 'Young Days in Music'. *Overland*, 40 (Summer 1968/69) 23–7.

Taylor, Barbara Turner. *The Life and Adventures of Barbara Turner Taylor*. n.p., n.d..

Taylor, Fairlie (1887–). *Schooldays with the Simpsons 1899–1906*. Tirav, NZ. S. Gordon Barnett, 1965; *Bid Time Return*. Sydney, Alpha Books, 1977; *Time Recalled*. Sydney, Alpha Books, 1978.

Taylor, Roslyn (1925–). *Your Hills Are Too High: An Australian Childhood*. Randwick, Redress Press, 1986.

Tennant, Kylie (1912–88). *The Missing Heir*. S. Melbourne, Macmillan, 1986.

Terry, Ethel Jennie (1895–). 'The Years 1900 to 1972. Memories from someone who has lived through this period'. Written 1972. Royal Historical Society of Victoria. Box 130/7.

Thompson, Patricia (1912–). *Accidental Chords*. Ringwood, Vic., Penguin, 1988.

Thonemann, H. E. *Tell the White Man*. Sydney, Collins, 1949.

Thorne, Elizabeth Ann (née Bisdee). 'Reminiscences 1818–1903'. Mitchell Library. ML Doc 1374.

Thorne, Jean. *Whistle at the Bridge*. Hobart, Cat & Fiddle, 1980.

Tilney, Charlotte. *See* 'Stanley, Effie'.

Tinning, Ruth E. *Backward Glances*. Montagu Bay, Ruth Tinning, 1977; *How Pippa Came to Australia*. Montagu Bay, Ruth Tinning, 1981.

Tisdall, Constance. *Forerunners*. Melbourne, Cheshire, 1961.

Todd, Laura. *A Place Like Home. Growing Up in the School of Industry 1915–22*. Ed. Amanda Midlam. Sydney, Hale & Iremonger, 1987.

Toner, Pauline. '"Martha, Martha, Thou Art Too Worldly"'. *Sweet Mothers, Sweet Maids*. Ed. Kate Nelson and Dominica Nelson. Ringwood, Vic., Penguin, 1986. pp. 33–44.

Triaca, Maria. *Amelia. A Long Journey*. Richmond, Greenhouse Publications, 1985.

Trist, Margaret (1914–86). *Morning in Queensland*. London, W. H. Allen, 1958; *In the Sun*. Sydney, Australasian Medical Publishing Co., 1943.

Tucker, Margaret. *If Everyone Cared*. Sydney, Ure Smith, 1977.

Turner, Ethel (1872–1958). *Three Little Maids*. Melbourne, Ward Lock, 1900.

Tyler, Mary Ann (née Brooksbank) (1840–1914). *The Adventurous Memoirs of a Gold Diggeress, 1841–1909*. Wellington, NSW, Kate Gibbs, 1985.

Uglow, Marion E. (1846–1926). 'Recollections of Marion E. Uglow'. Battye Library. 2957A.

Van Brakkel, Marie. *Nancy's Story*. Sydney, Beatty, Richardson & Co., n.d..

Van Langenberg, Carolyn. *Sibyl's Stories*. Fairfield, Pascoe Publishing, 1986.

Veal, Mary (comp.). *Every Year the Christmas Bush*. Geraldton, WA, Abrolhos Publications, 1985.

Vickery, Bessie. *See* Lee, Bessie

Vincent, Lizzie, *Broken Fetters*. Melbourne, Harrison Print, 1892.

Visontay, Czeizler Rose. *Boutique*. Transl. by Joseph Daniel. Sydney, C. R. Visontay, 1976.

Walker, Kath (1920–). *Stradbroke Dreamtime*. Sydney, Angus & Robertson, 1972; Contrib. to *As the Twig is Bent*. Ed. Terry Lane. Melbourne, Dove Communications, 1979.

Walker, Sarah Benson. *My Memories of Life in Hobart Town as recorded in 1884*. In Peter Benson Walker, *All that we Inherit*. Hobart, J. Walch & Sons, 1968.

Wallace, Judith (1932–). *Memories of a Country Childhood*. St Lucia, University of Queensland Press, 1977.

Ward, *Mrs* E. J. (1842–). *Out of Weakness Made Strong being a Record of the Life and Labours of Mrs E. J. Ward*. Sydney, 1903.

Ward, Glenyse (1949–). *Wandering Girl*. Broome, WA, Magabala Books, 1987.

Warren, Beatrice. *Emergency Nurse*. Waterloo, NSW, Federal Publishing Co., 1984.

Warren, Gerda. *My Childhood*. Wentworth Falls, Allen Warren, 1986.

Waterhouse, *Mrs* John. *The Medhursts of Mindale*. London, 1897; *For Marjory's Sake*. London, 1893.

Watson, Lilla (1940–). 'Sister, Black is the Colour of My Soul'. *Different Lives*. Ed. Jocelyne A. Scutt. Ringwood, Vic., Penguin, 1987. pp. 44–52.

Watson, Pauline (ed.). *The Crossing*. Sydney, Angus & Robertson, 1980.

Watts, *Mrs* Jane Isabella (1824–94). *Family Life in South Australia Fifty-Three Years Ago*. Adelaide, W. K. Thomas & Co., 1890; *Memories of Early Days in South Australia*. Adelaide *Advertiser*, 1882.

Weigall, A[nne] S. H. *My Little World*. Sydney, Angus & Robertson, 1934.

Welch, Faith. *My Life in Australia*. Ilfracombe, F. Welch, c. 1983; *More Reminiscences*. Ilfracombe, F. Welch, 1985.

West, Ida (1919–). *Pride Against Prejudice*. Canberra, Australian Institute of Aboriginal Studies, 1984.

Westgarth, Sophia. 'Reminiscences'. La Trobe Library. MS 9152. MSB 455.

Weston, Anne. 'Looking back: Childhood Reminiscences 1970'. Mitchell Library. MLDoc. 1641.

Whishaw, Mary Kinloch. *History of Richmond and Recollections from 1898 to 1920*. Launceston, M. K. Whishaw, 1973.

White, Isobel, et al. (ed.). *Fighters and Singers: the Lives of some Australian Aboriginal Women*. Sydney, Allen & Unwin, 1985.

Whitelaw, Eliza. 'Reminiscences'. Written 1900. La Trobe Library. MSB 22. MS 9195.

'Wickham, Anna' (Edith Hepburn) (1883–1947). 'Fragment of an Autobiography'. *The Writings of Anna Wickham*. Ed. R. D. Smith. London, Virago, 1984, pp. 51–157.

Williams, Justina (1916–). 'When the View is Clear'. *Memories of Childhood*. Ed. Lee White. Fremantle, Fremantle Arts Centre Press, 1978. pp. 19–30; *White River*. Fremantle, Fremantle Arts Centre Press, 1979.

Williams, May Rose (1890–). *Angels on Our Shoulders*. Ed. Susan Landfair. Sydney, Wentworth Books, 1973.

Willsmore, Mavis Jeane. *Beginnings*. Aldgate, SA, M. J. Willsmore, 1982.

Wilson, Rhonda (ed.). *Good Talk: The Extraordinary Lives of Ten Ordinary Australian Women*. Fitzroy, Vic., Penguin/McPhee Gribble, 1985.

Winter, Pamela. 'Reflections on a Piece of Knitting'. *Sweet Mothers, Sweet Maids*. Ed. Kate Nelson and Dominica Nelson. Ringwood, Vic., Penguin, 1986. pp. 175–84.

Woodley, Janice. *Not in This Way*. Adelaide, Rigby, 1965.

Wright, Charlotte May (1855–1929). *Memories of Far Off Days*. Ed. Peter A. Wright. Armidale, Peter Wright, 1985.

Wynford, *Lady* Edith Anne Best, (née Marsh). 'Memories of her Childhood, 1847–1860'. Mitchell Library. MLDoc 2597.

Yesterday's Youth: A Celebration of Times Past. Reminiscences of Carole Patterson, Dorothy Miller, Jean Arnold, Adrienne Cooper, Joyce Lazenby. Hobart, Authors, 1985.

Young, *Mrs* Charles Burney (1835–1925). *Glimpses of the Past*. Adelaide, reprinted from *The Advertiser* 8/6/1925.

Young, Ena *Mrs* [Autobiographical papers]. Mitchell Library. ML Doc 1922.

Young, *Mrs* Susan Bundarra. 'Reminiscences of Mrs Susan Bundarra Young [formerly Mrs James Buchanan] of Bundarra'. *Journal of the Royal Australian Historical Society*, 8 (1923), pp. 394–407.

Zurbo, Sandra (ed.). *Stories of her Life*. Collingwood, Outback Press, 1979.

Zwicky, Fay (1933–). *Hostages*. Fremantle, Fremantle Arts Centre Press, 1983; 'Teddy'. *Memories of Childhood*. Ed. Lee White. Fremantle, Fremantle Arts Centre Press, 1978. pp. 93–101.

Index